Professional XSL

Kurt Cagle
Michael Corning
Jason Diamond
Teun Duynstee
Oli Gauti Gudmundsson
Michael Mason
Jon Pinnock
Paul Spencer
Jeff Tang
Andrew Watt

Wrox Press Ltd. ®

Professional XSL

Published by Wrox Press Ltd,
Arden House, 1102 Warwick Road, Acocks Green,
Birmingham, B27 6BH, UK
Printed in the United States
ISBN 1-861003-57-9

Trademark Acknowledgements

Credits

Authors
Kurt Cagle
Michael Corning
Jason Diamond
Teun Duynstee
Oli Gauti Gudmundsson
Michael Mason
Jon Pinnock
Paul Spencer
Jeff Tang
Andrew Watt

Additional Material
Jirka Jirat
Paul Tchistopolskii
Jeni Tennison

Category Manager
Dave Galloway

Technical Architect
Dianne Parker

Technical Editors
Richard Deeson
Amanda Kay

Author Agent
Marsha Collins

Project Managers
Avril Corbin
Beckie Stones

Technical Reviewers
Danny Ayers
Martin Beaulieu
Maxime Bombardier
David Carlisle
Michael Corning
Sam Ferguson
Peggy Harp
Stephen Mohr
Dave Pawson
David Schultz
Andrew Watt
Warren Wiltsie

Production Coordinator
Tom Bartlett

Production Manager
Simon Hardware

Figures
Shabnam Hussain

Cover
Shelley Frazier

Proof Readers
Christopher Smith
Agnes Wiggers

Indexing
Bill Johncocks

About the Authors

Kurt Cagle

Kurt Cagle is a writer and developer specializing in XML and Internet-related issues. He has written eight books and more than one hundred articles on topics ranging from Visual Basic programming to the impact of the Internet on society, and has consulted for such companies as Microsoft, Nordstrom, AT&T and others. He also helped launch Fawcette's XML Magazine and has been the DevX DHTML and XML Pro for nearly two years.

Michael Corning

Michael Corning is a Memetic Engineer at Microsoft, busy building a software test infrastructure for Application Center based on the .NET Frameworks. At night he writes for Wrox Press, ASPToday.com, ActiveWeb Developer magazine, and has started a monthly column in XML Developer Magazine, called "Confessions of an XSLT Bigot". His first book was "Working with Active Server Pages", Que, 1997. Corning speaks at conferences around the world, preaching the good news of schema-based programming. When he's not working he's going out on dates with his wife (whom he adores), sailing his brand new West Wight Potter named "Finally", or reading. He is the proud father of three handsome sons, Christian, Seth, and Casey; and he's the property of three cats, Minnie, Dixie, and Nutmeg.

Acknowledgements: first, to my loving wife, Katy. She knows, only too well, the life of the writer's widow. To my bosses, Dan Casey and Tony Godfrey, for believing in me and letting me do so many things that scare the daylights out of me, like writing books. Finally, to my good friends and colleagues on the XML team, especially Jonathan Marsh, Derek Denny-Brown, and Chris Lovett; it has been an honor and the highlight of my career to work with you guys.

Jason Diamond

"Jason Diamond loves his mom."

Teun Duynstee

Teun Duynstee is lead developer at Macaw, a Dutch cutting edge Web-building and consulting firm, specializing in building complex enterprise web-applications on the Windows DNA platform. What he likes to do most are enthusing others with the great new possibilities of web technology and sleeping late.

You can reach him at: proxsl-feedback@duynstee.com

Oli Gauti Gudmundsson

Oli works for SALT, acting as one of two Chief System Architects of the SALT Systems, and Development Director in New York. He is currently working on incorporating XML and XSL into SALT's web authoring and content management systems. He has acted as an instructor in the Computer Science I course (Java) at the University of Iceland, and Java is one of his greatest strengths (and pleasures!). As a 'hobby' he's trying to finish his BS degree in Computer Engineering.

His nationality is Icelandic, but is currently situated in New York with his girlfriend Edda. He can be reached at: oli.gauti@salt.is

Michael Mason

Mike graduated from Oxford, UK, in 1999 with a BA in Computation, and began working for a local company called DecisionSoft. While there, Mike was involved in creating the XML Script language and related tools. He's now working for a London-based start-up called Digital Rum, developing mobile commerce applications using Java, XML, and XSLT.

Mike enjoys roller blading, karate, driving his car anywhere but London, and fiddling with Linux in his spare time. He's also a big fan of Buffy the Vampire Slayer, even though it might not be fashionable to mention it.

Mike can be reached at: mgm@eskimoman.net

Mike would like to thank all the folks at DecisionSoft, especially Philip and Ben for being great fun to work with when it all began, and Gareth for his help in getting v2 questions answered. He'd like to thank the gang, both in Oxford and London, for thinking being an author was cool and encouraging him with writing his chapters. The folks at Wrox have been very helpful, and he'd like to thank Marsha for answering all his newbie questions.

Jon Pinnock

Jonathan Pinnock started programming in Pal III assembler on his school's PDP 8/e, with a massive 4K of memory, back in the days before Moore's Law reached the statute books. These days he spends most of his time developing and extending the increasingly successful PlatformOne product set that his company, JPA, markets to the financial services community. He seems to spend the rest of his time writing for Wrox, although he occasionally surfaces to say hello to his long-suffering wife and two children.

JPA's home page is at: www.jpassoc.co.uk

My heartfelt thanks go to Gail, who first suggested getting into writing, and now suffers the consequences on a fairly regular basis, and to Mark and Rachel, who just suffer the consequences.

Paul Spencer

After three years of freelance XML consultancy, Paul decided at the end of 2000 that he had had enough of working 7-day weeks and founded alphaXML Ltd, of which he is CTO. Based in Henley-on-Thames in the UK, he leads an expanding team providing XML services throughout the world. Paul is XML adviser to the UK Inland Revenue, the Government Gateway and Office of the e-Envoy, so the workload never really dropped. However, he is determined to keep time free for sailing, where he tries to keep somewhere within sight of the top guys. His sailing claim to fame is that he once beat someone who had just returned from beating Dennis Connor.

Paul would like to thank all those who have given him the chance to do a job he loves, and Wrox for producing a writing schedule outside the sailing season.

Jeff Tang

Xiaofei, aka "Jeff", Tang is the principal software engineer at Tellngo, Inc, where he designs and develops voice-enabled enterprise applications using Nuance and Speechworks technologies and Java, C++, and VoiceXML. Previously, Jeff spent about six years working as a senior software engineer, technical lead, and consultant at companies Sprint, Informix, Cerner, and Perceptive Vision, Inc. He helped design and develop many enterprise systems, including clinical information systems, document imaging products, web-based computer telephony applications, Internet media applications, and enterprise order management systems. Prior to that, he worked for about five years in China as a software engineer developing a natural language processing/machine translation system, and database applications.

Andrew Watt

Andrew Watt is an independent consultant who enjoys few things more than exploring the technologies others have yet to sample. Since he wrote his first programs in 6502 Assembler and BBC Basic in the mid 1980's he has sampled Pascal, Prolog, and C++ among others. More recently he has focussed on the power of web-relevant technologies including Lotus Domino, Java, and HTML. His current interest is in the various applications of the Extensible Markup Meta Language, XMML, sometimes imprecisely and misleadingly called XML. The present glimpse he has of the future of SVG, XSL-FO, XSLT, CSS, XLink, Xpointer, etc. when they actually work properly together is an exciting, if daunting, prospect. He has just begun to dabble with XQuery. Such serial dabbling, so he is told, is called "life-long learning".

In his spare time he sometimes ponders the impact of web technologies on real people. What will be the impact of a Semantic Web? How will those other than the knowledge-privileged fare?

To the God of Heaven who gives human beings the capacity to see, think, and feel. To my father who taught me much about life.

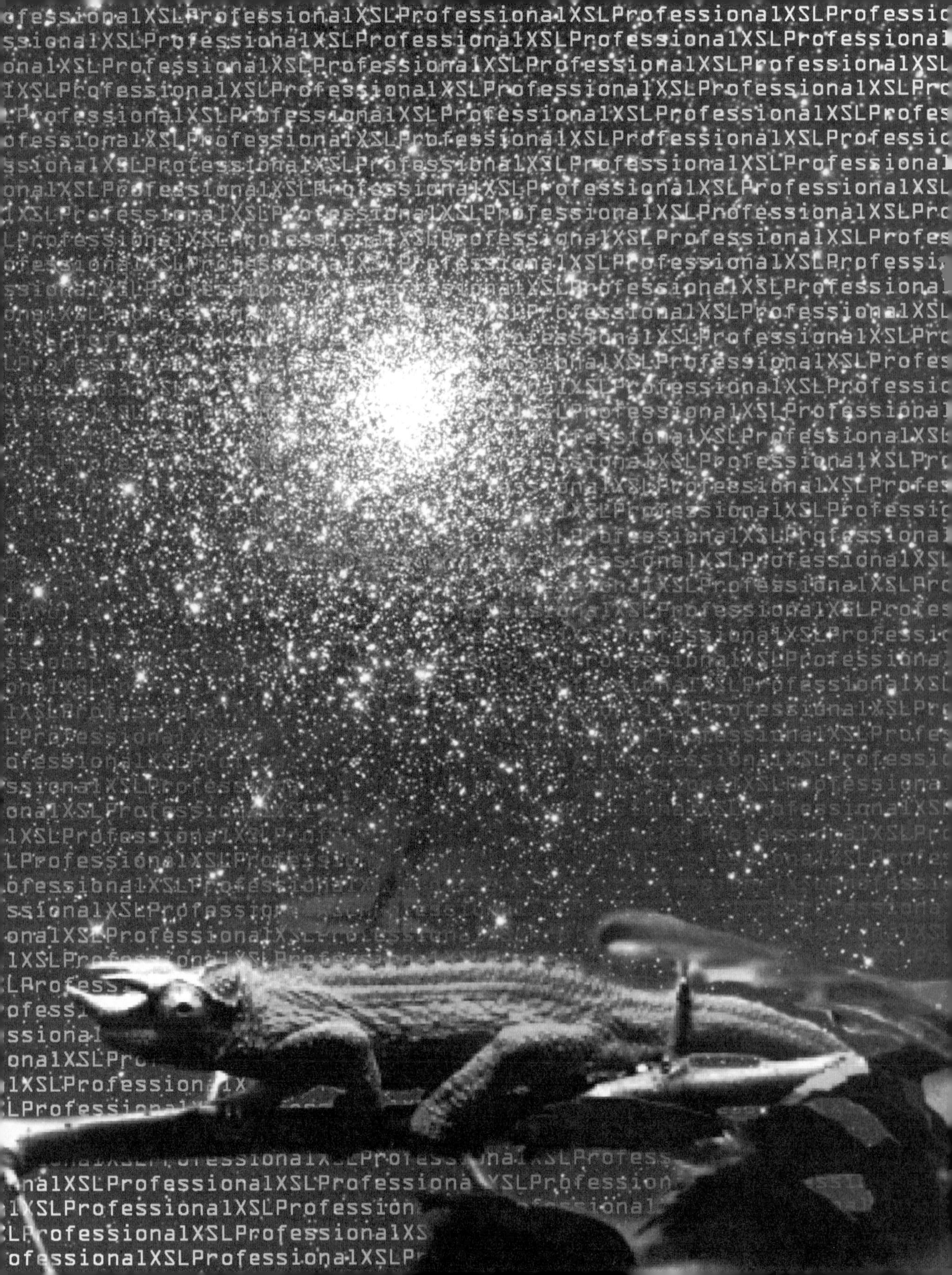

Table of Contents

Table of Contents

Table of Contents

Table of Contents

Table of Contents

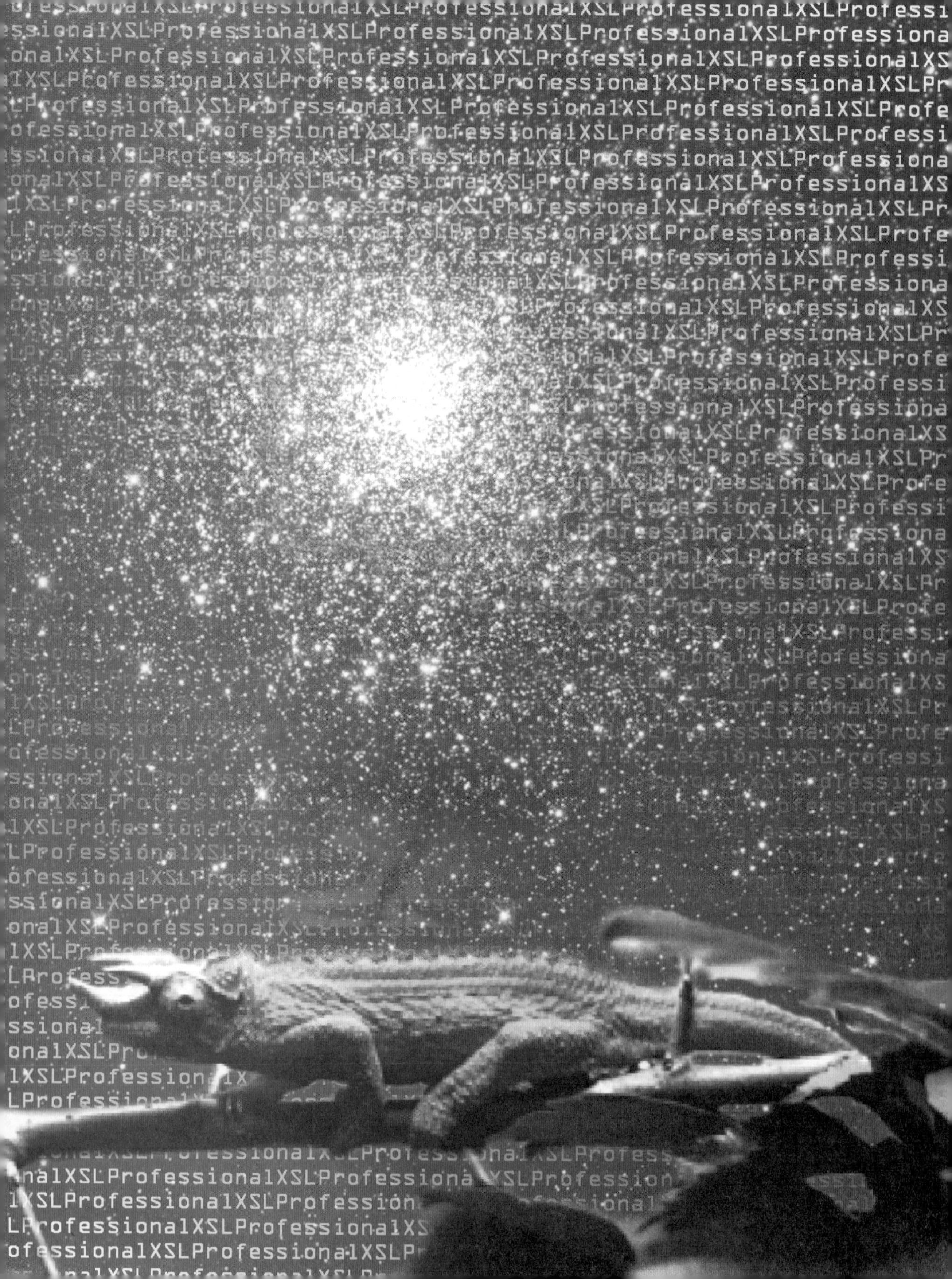

Introduction

The **Extensible Markup Language, XML**, has rapidly gained widespread acceptance as *the* language to use for structuring and describing data for web and, increasingly, enterprise-based applications. The beauty of XML is that it is text-based (therefore platform-independent) and extensible (allowing more meaningful descriptions of the underlying data). It's a way to describe the data regardless of how it will ultimately be used, separating content from presentation, and therefore lends itself well to situations where the data needs to be re-purposed for different end-uses. But when we want to do anything with the data, for example extract parts of it or present it in a non-XML format, we need something more than the XML specification alone.

The **Extensible Stylesheet Language, XSL**, was originally proposed to the World Wide Web Consortium (W3C) to provide a means for formatting XML data. The process of formatting XML requires several component parts:

- ❏ a method for specifying which parts of the source document to use

- ❏ a means of describing what operations should be carried out on those parts of the source data in order to produce the desired output document

- ❏ a way of incorporating instructions into the output document to indicate how it should be presented

The XSL specification soon branched into two: **XSL Transformations (XSLT)** and **XSL Formatting Objects (XSL-FO)**, each with a specific role to play in the overall transformation process.

A third, related, specification is **XPath**, which is a language for identifying parts of (and locations in) an XML document. XML data is represented as a hierarchical, tree-like structure of nodes, and XPath provides a syntax for defining expressions and including functions to drill down through the XML tree until specific nodes are reached.

XSLT is a language for stating what action should be taken when those specific nodes are found. It is used to write stylesheets that consist of templates to be applied when specified patterns are found in the source document – when a matching node is found the instructions in the template are followed, for example selecting and sorting the output. In this way an output document is produced. The XSLT language has a set of elements and functions for tasks such as copying an element, extracting text content or an attribute value into the output document, and outputting a sorted list of nodes. XSLT can be used in many applications, anywhere that XML data needs to be structurally modified, or where XML data needs to be transformed into a format suitable for presentation.

XSL-FO defines a set of formatting objects that can be included in the output document to indicate precisely how the data should be presented. At present, web browsers with the capability to understand and correctly render XSL-FO are scarce, although there are a few tools for rendering XSL-FO into other formats. It is more common for web applications not to use XSL-FO, but instead to incorporate HTML (or CSS, WML, VoiceXML, SVG, JavaScript, etc.) into the output for display in a suitable "browser".

There are numerous types of applications where the XML data does not need to be presented in a human-friendly format. For example, in business-to-business scenarios, applications run by different business partners need to communicate and share data, but each business invariably has its own preferred data format. XSLT can be used to perform the translations, enabling more efficient collaboration, with a wider range of business partners.

Even developers who don't need to present or exchange data, for example those working purely with data stores, can find uses for XSL. Data validation against schemas and generating XML documents from schemas are just two examples of where XSLT can help to automate and speed up the development process.

What this Book is About

This book teaches you the purpose and syntax of all three parts of the XSL "family" of technologies (XSLT, XSL-FO, and the related XPath). More importantly, it shows how to put XSL into practice, in a wide variety of applications, from transforming multiple suppliers' product information formats into a unified product catalog, to dynamically creating a WML web page for a mobile client, to generating graphical representations of XML content. By the time you've read the book you will have a clear understanding of what XSL is, what it can be used for, and how to go about incorporating it in your existing and future applications.

Who Should Use this Book?

This is a book for programmers who are already familiar with XML. If you do not have much knowledge of XML, it is advisable that you read a title like *Beginning XML* (ISBN 1-861003-41-2) or *Professional XML* (ISBN 1-861003-11-0) both published by Wrox Press.

There are really two groups of developers who may benefit from the information in this book:

❑ those who need to transform data to/from an XML format

❑ those who need to apply styling to their XML data for presentation purposes

The list of applications where XSL can be applied is almost endless, but covers many areas including business-to-business exchanges, web-based publication of content, and management of XML data stores.

Structure of the Book

The chapters are arranged to first teach you the fundamentals of XSL, before looking in more detail at typical real-world applications of XSL. Throughout the book there is a multitude of small examples to demonstrate the practical implementation of the concepts being presented. The arrangement of material is as follows:

- ❑ Chapter 1, **Introduction to XSL**, includes a refresher of the assumed XML knowledge, and explains in more detail the background to why a transformation language was developed for working with XML. It describes each of the parts that make up the XSL group of technologies. A basic introduction is given to the concept of XSLT stylesheets and how they are processed, and several real-world applications of XSL are described to indicate areas where XSL will be useful.

- ❑ Chapter 2, **Xpath – the XML Path Language**, contains a complete reference to the syntax of the XPath language, with examples to demonstrate its use. When using XSLT, XPath is essential for navigating and identifying specific parts of an XML document, and the judicious use of XPath can improve the performance of your XSLT stylesheets.

- ❑ Chapter 3, **XSLT Basics**, explains and demonstrates the core aspects of the XSLT language – everything you need to know to create stylesheets with sufficient functionality for many applications.

- ❑ Chapter 4, **Modular XSLT**, begins to look at more advanced techniques for working with XSLT and for improving the power and efficiency of the stylesheets. This includes the use of variables and parameters.

- ❑ Chapter 5, **External XSLT**, continues the coverage of advanced XSLT techniques by looking at how to incorporate external templates and documents. This chapter concludes with a look at improvements that are being considered for inclusion in future versions of the XSLT specification.

- ❑ Chapter 6, **Transformations Using DOM and SAX**, discusses both the XML Document Object Model and the Simple API for XML, from the point of view of transforming XML without the use of XSL. These programmatic interfaces can be used as an alternative to XSL or as a precursor to an XSL transformation, and the chapter includes a discussion of when each technique is most appropriate.

- ❑ Chapter 7, **Microsoft XSL Technologies**, contains information about the XSL-related features of Microsoft's MSXML3 and .Net framework products. Sample code includes using MSXML for data analysis and streaming, navigating, selecting, and transforming XML data using the .Net framework base classes.

- ❑ Chapter 8, **Optimizing Performance**, is based upon the real-world experiences of the author as he steps through a case study, highlighting some common problems you should be aware of when developing stylesheets, and giving advice on how to improve the performance of your XSLT stylesheets.

- ❑ Chapter 9, **CSS and XSL-FO**, discusses the XML styling technologies created by the W3C. Cascading Style Sheets is presented first, as it is widely supported by modern browsers. XSL-FO is based on similar principles but is intended for a wider range of output formats. Both are explained in sufficient detail to enable you to use them in your transformations.

- ❑ Chapter 10, **Common Structural Transformations**, looks at typical uses of XSLT that do not involve styling the output for display purposes, in other words those that structurally transform (for example, extract, modify, append, and merge) XML data. This includes transforming between business vocabularies, using stylesheets to generate new stylesheets, and working with data from a proprietary database.

❑ Chapter 11, **Adding Style with XSLT**, demonstrates the more usual way of adding presentation information to XML data (in other words using HTML and not XSL-FO). The sample application developed in this chapter shows how to use stylesheets to dynamically generate both HTML and WML-based representations of web pages, incorporating CSS, with the transformations taking place on the server or client as appropriate.

❑ Chapter 12, **Transforming to SVG**, explains the background to current graphical formats, in particular the Scaleable Vector Graphics (SVG) language. It then demonstrates writing stylesheets for generating SVG to produce a graph, format text, and draw shapes.

❑ Chapter 13, **Transforming to VoiceXML**, introduces the syntax of the VoiceXML language, a new XML-based method for voice-enabling web applications. The chapter covers how to get set up to use the currently available development tools. A sample application demonstrates how XSLT can be used to speed up the process of generating new VoiceXML output, particularly useful when the application is based on changing data sources.

❑ Chapter 14, **XSLT and XML Schemas**, demonstrates some of the useful ways in which XSLT and XML Schemas can be combined, for example using XSLT to generate an XML document instance from a Schema (and vice versa), creating stylesheets to validate XML documents against a Schema, and enforcing data integrity constraints using XSLT regular expressions.

❑ Chapter 15, **XSLT and the Future of XML**, presents a final example of XSLT transformations, this time as the basis of a Petri Net machine. Petri Nets are a tool for graphically and mathematically modeling systems, and in this chapter XSLT is used to transform Petri Net Markup Language (PNML) into SVG for graphical display. To round off the book, the chapter then presents a slightly different way to think about XSL programming, to inspire you for the future. XSL is a key part of Schema Based Programming (a term that encompasses XML-based application development) and this discussion will reinforce why XSL is crucial to developers working with XML.

❑ Case Study, **Online Content Publication**, demonstrates a typical real-world application of XSLT using many techniques presented elsewhere in the book. It shows how XSLT can be used at the heart of a web application, providing the end-user with a human-friendly view of the underlying content, along with the functionality to easily navigate to other parts of the document. The application uses both batch transformations to generate static HTML, and live transformations to generate some of the content on demand. It also serves to reinforce the message taught in earlier chapters that componentization and parameterization of stylesheets facilitates reuse and maintainability.

We have also provided relevant reference material in the appendices:

❑ Appendix A, **XPath Reference**, provides a complete reference to the XPath 1.0 specification.

❑ Appendix B, **XSLT Reference**, provides a complete reference to the XSLT 1.0 specification.

❑ Appendix C, **The XML Document Object Model**, covers all of the interfaces of the DOM Level 2 core, both the fundamental interfaces and the extended interfaces for working with XML documents.

❑ Appendix D, **SAX 2.0: The Simple API for XML**, lists and describes all of the interfaces and methods of SAX2.

❑ Appendix E, **XSLT Processors and Tools**, contains details of how to obtain and set up the (freely-available) commonly used XSL processors, many of which are required to run the examples in the book. It also covers examples of other useful tools that are available for free, such as tools to help you understand complex stylesheets.

- ❑ Appendix F, **Shorthand XSLT Tools**, looks at several approaches to speed up XSLT stylesheet development, with a detailed study of two such initiatives, XSLScript (a tool for rapidly generating XSLT) and XML Script (an alternative to XSLT).

- ❑ Appendix G, **Useful Resources**, suggests online resources and other books that may be of use for further reading.

Technologies Used in the Book

Because XML is a platform-neutral language (or, more precisely, a platform-neutral syntax), we have endeavored to keep the examples in the book as platform-neutral as possible. In some chapters HTML, Java, Visual Basic, Visual C++, C#, ASP, JSP, JavaScript, Windows Script Host, Oracle, and XSQL are used to illustrate specific programming techniques – however, the approaches used should be easily portable to other languages. Although we assume some general programming knowledge, all of the code is explained where necessary.

All of the examples provided in this book (unless otherwise stated) will work out-of-the-box with commonly-used, widely-available processors, as mentioned at the appropriate point in the book. Details of how to obtain and set them up are provided as an appendix.

Conventions

We have used a number of different styles of text and layout in this book to help differentiate between the different kinds of information. Here are examples of the styles we use and an explanation of what they mean:

Code has several styles. If it's a word that we're talking about in the text – for example, when discussing a For...Next loop, it's in this font. If it's a block of code that you can type as a program and run, then it's also in a gray box:

```
<?xml version 1.0?>
```

Sometimes you'll see code in a mixture of styles, like this:

```
<?xml version 1.0?>
<Invoice>
    <part>
        <name>Widget</name>
        <price>$10.00</price>
    </part>
</invoice>
```

In cases like this, the code with a white background is code we are already familiar with; the line highlighted in gray is a new addition to the code since we last looked at it.

Advice, hints, and background information come in this type of font.

Important pieces of information come in boxes like this.

Bullets appear indented, with each new bullet marked as follows:

- **Important Words** are in a bold type font
- Words that appear on the screen, in menus like File or Window, are in a similar font to that you would see on a Windows desktop
- Keys that you press on the keyboard, like *Ctrl* and *Enter*, are in italics

Customer Support

We've tried to make this book as accurate and enjoyable as possible, but what really matters is what the book actually does for you. Please let us know your views, either by returning the reply card in the back of the book, or by contacting us via e-mail at feedback@wrox.com.

Source Code and Updates

As you work through the examples in this book, you may decide that you prefer to type in all the code by hand. Many readers prefer this because it's a good way to get familiar with the coding techniques that are being used.

Whether you want to type the code in or not, we have made all the source code for this book available at our web site at the following address:

http://www.wrox.com/Books/Book_Down.asp?isbn=1861003579

If you're one of those readers who likes to type in the code, you can use our files to check the results you should be getting – they should be your first stop if you think you might have typed in an error. If you're one of those readers who doesn't like typing, then downloading the source code from our web site is a must!

Either way, it'll help you with updates and debugging.

Errata

We've made every effort to make sure that there are no errors in the text or the code. However, to err is human, and as such we recognize the need to keep you informed of any mistakes as they're spotted and corrected. Errata sheets are available for all our books, at http://www.wrox.com. If you find an error that hasn't already been reported, please let us know.

Our web site acts as a focus for other information and support, including the code from all our books, sample chapters, previews of forthcoming titles, and articles and opinion on related topics.

P2P

The online forums at p2p.wrox.com provides programmer to programmer™ support on a range of technologies. You can subscribe to the mailing lists and receive regular digests, or search the archives to find solutions to your programming queries.

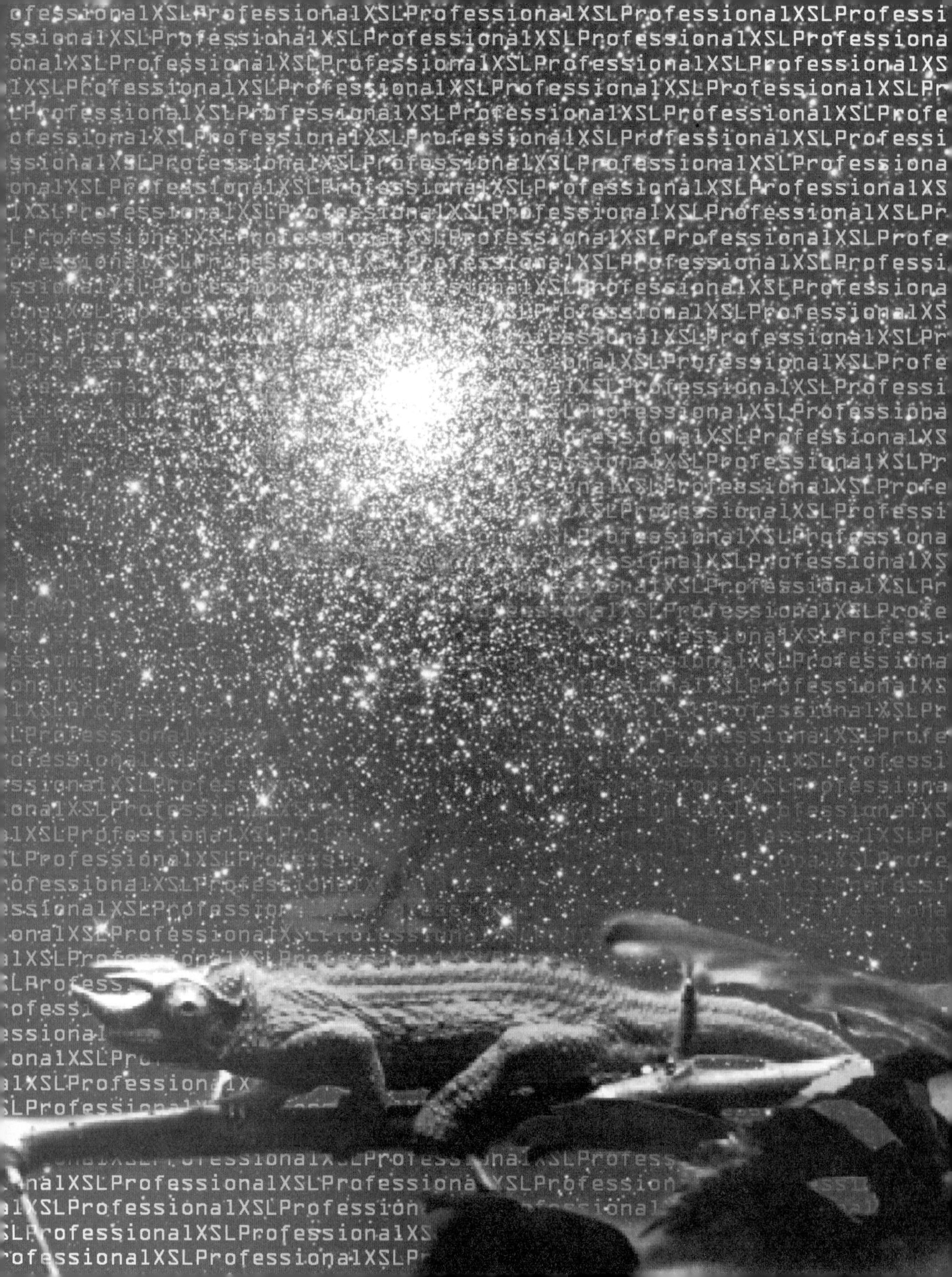

1

Introduction to XSL

Everyone who is familiar with the **Extensible Markup Language**, **XML**, should be aware of the fact that XML separates data from the presentation of that data. That is, after all, one of the features that makes XML so useful and versatile. The extensibility of the XML language allows developers to describe and structure data in their own custom formats, defining their own vocabularies – in other words, it allows them to create their own mark up languages. Also, as the XML data is text-based, it is platform-independent. The combination of these features offers huge potential in the field of web and information management applications – XML can be useful as a means of exchanging data between applications and organizations, and re-purposing data for different applications.

But XML alone is of limited use. Because the XML itself is not formatted for display, and because different businesses use custom formats that need translation, we need a way of *transforming* data from one format to another, selecting and restructuring relevant parts of an XML document, even adding new data, or formatting it for presentation purposes as required. This is the idea behind the **Extensible Stylesheet Language**, **XSL**.

XSL is an XML-based language for expressing **stylesheets** for manipulating XML data. Originally the XSL specification was intended purely for formatting XML, for example for display on the web, but it was soon realized that this process involves two distinct steps, each useful in its own right: transforming the data structure into other XML formats, and adding information about how the data should appear when displayed on a particular device. As a result, XSL in its current form contains two major components:

- ❑ **XSL Transformations** (**XSLT**), a language used for describing structural transformations of XML. XSLT is used for translating from an XML format into another format.

- ❑ **XSL Formatting Objects** (**XSL-FO**), a language used for describing formatting semantics. XSL-FO is used to describe how a document should look when displayed to a user, and is not about structured data at all. An XSL-FO processor applies the correct formatting.

Another specification connected to XSLT is:

❑   **XPath**, a selection syntax allowing us to select nodes within an XML document. XPath is used in XSLT to specify which nodes to use in a transformation, and for selecting XML content to include in an output document.

XSLT and XPath have been W3C Recommendations since late 1999, while XSL-FO is still in the drafting process. XSLT is by far the more mature of the two technologies, and currently has much more support in terms of tools and implementations.

In this book you'll learn the syntax of the XSLT and XPath languages, and how to program stylesheets to transform XML data, both structurally and into a range of formats suitable for various end uses. Although the XSL-FO specification has not progressed as rapidly as XSLT (to the extent that people are using XSLT to generate HTML for web presentation in the absence of XSL-FO processors), and implementations are limited (but appearing more frequently), we'll take a look at the XSL-FO formatting objects and learn how to use them to define how we want our documents to appear.

Occasionally XSLT is not the most effective tool to use for transformations, so we will also look at alternatives, such as using programmatic interfaces like the DOM and SAX, and how they can be integrated into an XSL solution.

Overview of XML

Throughout this book we assume that readers are familiar with XML and how it can be used. In this section we'll briefly recap that assumed knowledge with a quick tour of the XML features that are relevant to XSL.

Development of XML started in 1996, and version 1.0 became a W3C Recommendation in February 1998. The current version 1.0 (Second Edition) became a Recommendation in October 2000 and is available at http://www.w3.org/TR/REC-xml. XML is designed to be *the* data format for the web, and at the time of writing is being used by many thousands of web-based applications. It has, in fact, become a data transfer standard for almost all applications no matter whether they are web-based or not.

XML is a mechanism for storing structured data in text files. It stores the data in a hierarchical tree format, as we show below, and as such is well suited to storing tree-like structured information. XML is a bit like HTML, the format used for web documents, but it's focused on *representing* data, rather than describing the *presentation* of data. Presentation of the data comes later, using XSL. Because XML is a text format for storing data, it avoids many of the problems of using proprietary binary formats. All computer systems – PCs, Macintoshes, Unix servers, even expensive supercomputers – can read and write text files, making them automatically compatible with each other when they use XML.

An example XML document might look like this:

```
<?xml version="1.0" encoding="ISO-8859-1" ?>
<JobDescription>
  <Position>XSL Developer</Position>
  <Employer>Web Widgets, Inc.</Employer>
  <Location>
    <City>San Jose</City>
    <State>California</State>
  </Location>
```

```
    <Salary units="USD">40000</Salary>
    <Description>
        The successful candidate will have a wide range
        of web development skills, with proven XSL
        experience.
    </Description>
</JobDescription>
```

The first line of the document contains the **XML declaration**, which marks this document as being in XML version 1.0 format. The encoding attribute tells an XML processing tool which character set has been used to save the document. XML can support any **Unicode** character set (depending upon processor support) so is suitable for use in any language. (More information on the Unicode character set can be found at http://www.unicode.org.)

The rest of the document defines an **XML element** named JobDescription. Elements are the basic building blocks for XML documents, and because this element is the first one in the file, it is called the **document element**. Elements define the structure of an XML document – in the above example, the <JobDescription> element contains other elements: <Position>, <Employer>, <Location>, <Salary>, and <Description>. The <Location> element also contains the elements <City> and <State>. The <Salary> element has an attribute called units, which tells us extra information about that element. In this case, it tells us that the currency that the value contained in the <Salary> element is given in USD (US dollars).

It's easy to see how the text description of this document could be mapped into a tree structure, such as the following:

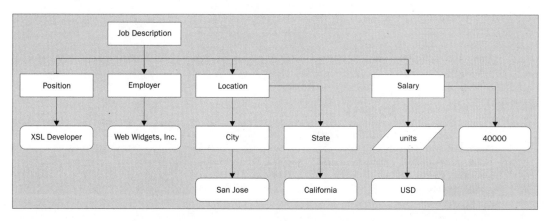

The XML document has been mapped into a tree, with each box in the diagram representing a **node**. Nodes are the basic building blocks of all trees, and our XML tree contains **element nodes** (such as Position), **attribute nodes** (such as units), and **text nodes** (such as "Web Widgets, Inc."). The root element of the tree is the JobDescription element node, which corresponds to the XML document element.

Note that the root *node* of the tree is not the same as the root *element*. The root node is "above" the root element, since XML allows a document to contain nodes such as comments and processing instructions before or after the root element. The tree structure used in XSL is explained in more detail in Chapter 2.

In order for this mapping into a tree structure to be easily and unambiguously performed, an XML document must follow a set of rules in order to be **well-formed**:

❑ All opening tags must be matched with the corresponding ending tag. Empty elements can use the empty tag format <empty />.

❑ Elements must be properly nested, so for example <bold>this <italic>is some</bold> text</italic> is not allowed.

❑ Attributes must be surrounded by quote characters; either " or ' will do.

❑ Elements cannot contain more than one attribute with the same name.

❑ Documents may contain only one root level element.

❑ XML is case sensitive, so jobdescription and JobDescription are different elements.

DTDs and Schemas

In addition to being well-formed, it's possible to specify that an XML document must be structured in a particular manner. For example, we might want to specify that when a document consists of a <JobDescription> root level element, it must contain a <Salary> element, with a units attribute. We can do this by specifying a **Document Type Definition** (**DTD**) or **Schema** to which the document must conform. An XML document that meets the requirements of a specified DTD or Schema is said to be **valid**.

For example, we can modify our example XML to include a reference to a DTD:

```
<?xml version="1.0" encoding="ISO-8859-1" ?>
<!DOCTYPE JobDescription SYSTEM "JobDescription.dtd" >
<JobDescription>
  <Position>XSL Developer</Position>
  <Employer>Web Widgets, Inc.</Employer>
  <Location>
    <City>San Jose</City>
    <State>California</State>
  </Location>
  <Salary units="USD">40000</Salary>
  <Description>
    The successful candidate will have a wide range
    of web development skills, with proven XSL
    experience.
  </Description>
</JobDescription>
```

We specified the DTD using the SYSTEM identifier syntax, which specifies a URI for locating the DTD. In this case the DTD is stored in the same location as the XML file – if on the local disk drive the DTD will be in the same directory, if via a web URL the DTD will use the same base URL as the XML document.

Inside the DTD, JobDescription.dtd, we specify which elements the document must contain, and how each of those elements must be structured. Note, for example, how we can specify that the units attribute of <Salary> must be one of three values (USD, GBP or JPY):

```
<?xml version="1.0" encoding="UTF-8"?>
<!ELEMENT JobDescription (Position, Employer, Location, Salary, Description)>
<!ELEMENT Position (#PCDATA)>
<!ELEMENT Employer (#PCDATA)>
<!ELEMENT Location (City, State)>
   <!ELEMENT City (#PCDATA)>
   <!ELEMENT State (#PCDATA)>
<!ELEMENT Salary (#PCDATA)>
<!ATTLIST Salary
   units (USD | GBP | JPY) #REQUIRED
>
<!ELEMENT Description (#PCDATA)>
```

Instead of using a DTD, we could use a W3C XML Schema to specify the document format, or another schema format supported by an XML parser. Because the W3C Schema specification was under development for a long period, other schema formats were used as an interim measure. The most popular of these is **XML-Data Reduced** (**XDR**), which is supported by, among others, the Microsoft XML processor.

Using a DTD has several drawbacks, all of which are addressed by Schemas:

❑   DTDs do not conform to XML syntax, while Schemas do. Thus an XML Schema can be read and manipulated using a standard XML processor.

❑   DTDs are based on basic text pattern matching, and as such do not permit complex validation such as "this is a date in DDMMYY format". Schemas allow definitions of custom datatypes, where we can declare, reuse, and inherit data definitions and structures.

More information on DTDs can be found at http://www.w3.org/XML/1998/06/xmlspec-report.htm and the XML Schemas specification is held (in three parts) at http://www.w3.org/TR/xmlschema-0 for the primer, http://www.w3.org/TR/xmlschema-1 for schemas themselves, and http://www.w3.org/TR/xmlschema-2 for a description of the datatypes used. XML-Data Reduced is described at http://www.w3.org/TR/1998/NOTE-XML-data-0105/.

Once we have designed an XML vocabulary for describing something, such as job openings, it would be nice to be able to reuse that vocabulary in other documents, rather than reinvent it. It's likely that XML documents will be required to contain elements from a wide range of such vocabularies, which is why **XML Namespaces** have been introduced.

XML Namespaces

Using a namespace, it is possible to combine different XML vocabularies without getting confused as to the meaning of element names. For example, suppose that we had a list of job vacancies, and we used a Position element to record the order those openings should be listed. We might come up with something like this:

```
<?xml version="1.0" encoding="UTF-8"?>
<JobList>
  <Item>
    <Position>0001</Position>
    <JobDescription>
      <Position>XSL Developer</Position>
```

```
      <Employer>Web Widgets, Inc.</Employer>
    </JobDescription>
  </Item>
  <Item>
    <Position>0002</Position>
    <JobDescription>
      <Position>Java Engineer</Position>
      <Employer>Web Widgets, Inc.</Employer>
    </JobDescription>
  </Item>
</JobList>
```

We now have four `<Position>` elements, which mean different things. Two mean the position of the job vacancy in the list, the other two contain a job title. XML namespaces allow us to place the `<JobDescription>` elements and all of their contained elements (`<Position>`, `<Employer>`, etc.) into a different namespace, so we don't get confused.

> *Note that using a `Position` element to denote list ordering in this way is bad design – here we're just using it as an example of how the meaning of elements can get confused and how namespaces help solve the problem. A better design would be to avoid this use of the `Position` element, and simply use the order of the `Item` elements in the XML document.*

A namespace can be introduced at the start of the document, and then used as a prefix to the elements in the document to distinguish them. XML elements use the syntax `<namespace:elementName>` to denote their membership of a particular namespace. A namespace is introduced using an `xmlns` attribute on the document element, which specifies a URI for the new namespace. For example, the following file declares a namespace "`jd`" into which `JobDescription` elements are placed:

```
<?xml version="1.0" encoding="UTF-8"?>
<JobList xmlns:jd="http://www.wrox.com/JobDescription">
  <Item>
    <Position>1</Position>
    <jd:JobDescription>
      <jd:Position>XSL Developer</jd:Position>
      <jd:Employer>Web Widgets, Inc.</jd:Employer>
    </jd:JobDescription>
  </Item>
  <Item>
    <Position>2</Position>
    <jd:JobDescription>
      <jd:Position>Java Engineer</jd:Position>
      <jd:Employer>Web Widgets, Inc.</jd:Employer>
    </jd:JobDescription>
  </Item>
</JobList>
```

XSLT relies heavily on namespaces to distinguish XSL processing instruction elements from the data elements that they manipulate and the output format elements into which they write, so it's important that you understand how they work. Further information is available at http://www.w3.org/TR/1999/REC-xml-names-19990114/.

The Need for Transformation/Formatting

While XML is great for representing data, it's difficult to describe the presentation of that data at the same time. In fact, this is one of the main reasons to use XML – separating data from its presentation allows us to focus on producing much more useful, reusable data. The tags we use in XML give an indication of the meaning and purpose of the data, whereas with a presentation format such as HTML we can only indicate how each piece of text should be displayed. Further, when creating a data format using XML we might not know how that data will eventually be used, indeed don't need to be concerned with it. When we wish to display our fantastically reusable data, however, we need to transform it into something that a human can read easily. While XML might look readable, it certainly doesn't look *nice*.

Separating data from its display also allows us to be more flexible. If a web site produces its main interface using XML, it can use a transformation layer to present itself to many different types of users. By including extra XSLT transformations, the site can, for example, support traditional web-browser based clients using HTML, mobile clients using WML (Wireless Markup Language), or even voice-based browsers using VoiceXML. When upgrading the site, only the underlying XML needs to change – web developers need to write and maintain just one version, rather than a version for each browser type that is supported. The XML content will contain all of the information a user could ever wish to see, and it can be trimmed and reduced according to client constraints, such as use of a mobile device with low bandwidth and limited screen size. The underlying data may be extracted from multiple data sources, both native XML and more traditional sources, such as databases. Transformations can be used to gather, restructure, filter, and redefine data into a format suitable for the application.

We also need to consider what happens when we wish to use our data in an application other than the one for which it was originally designed. The new application might work on the same underlying data, but not in the format we have it. It's also important that applications are free to use their own vocabularies internally, while being able to communicate with other applications, customers, and partners (such as in a B2B scenario) in the format they prefer. We might need to do some simple rearrangement of the data, some reduction in the data by removing certain parts, or some heavy-duty processing and calculation. Either way, the ability to translate between XML formats (and even non-XML formats) is critical, especially when we're talking about formats used by business-to-business (B2B) applications.

Introduction to XSL

XSL has been under development since 1997, but is based around two older technologies, **DSSSL** (**Document Style Semantics and Specification Language** – see http://www.w3.org/TR/1998/NOTE-spice-19980123.html) and **CSS** (**Cascading Style Sheets** – see http://www.w3.org/Style/CSS/draft). XSL (the standard originally containing both XSLT and XSL-FO) was first submitted to the W3C in 1997. Although they began as one, XSLT and XSL-FO were subsequently taken forward as separate specifications.

XSL-FO, as mentioned earlier, defines a set of formatting objects for specifying how XML data should be presented. An XSL-FO processor then uses these formatting objects when converting the data into its target format, for example PDF. (It is based on a similar concept to the Cascading Style Sheets standard often used with HTML, but is much more powerful.) At present, this part of the standard has only just begun to attract widespread interest, and tools that render XSL-FO into a usable format are scarce. Most applications where XML needs to be presented in a human readable format do not make use of XSL-FO. However, it is growing in popularity and in Chapter 9 of this book you'll learn how it works and how to use it.

The main focus of this book will be on XSLT. XSLT 1.0, along with the connected specification, XPath 1.0, became a Recommendation in November 1999. XSLT 1.1 currently (March 2001) has Working Draft status, as do the requirements for XSLT 2.0 and XPath 2.0 (available at http://www.w3.org/TR/xpath20req). Although these proposed improvements will be discussed in Chapter 5, the rest of the book uses XSLT 1.0 as later versions are not stable.

XPath allows the searching and navigation of XML documents and is a vital part of the transformation process, enabling us to specify which parts of a document we want to transform. The full XPath syntax, and its use in XSLT, is covered in Chapter 2.

XPath came from work on the **XPointer** specification (http://www.w3.org/TR/xptr), which was being developed as a fragment identifier for use when linking XML documents. It was realized that there were similarities in the requirements for a selection syntax for both XPointer and XSLT, and so XPath came to be.

As we stated earlier, XSLT is used to transform XML data from one structure to another. This transformation can be used to:

❑ create new content

❑ convert an XML data tree into another XML or non-XML format

❑ append/aggregate new content

❑ extract portions of the content

❑ carry out computational work, such as searching

❑ generate shell documents from schemas

XSLT is also extensively used for transforming data into a format suitable for presentation, such as:

❑ displaying in a web browser, by including in the output HTML, JavaScript, WML, XHTML, etc.

❑ customizing material for non-traditional 'browsers', for example rendering the data as VoiceXML

❑ incorporating graphics or transforming data into graphical representations, such as with SVG

Mastering the XSLT language and creating stylesheets to perform these kinds of transformation are the subject of the remainder of this book. For now we'll take a brief overview of how XSLT works.

XSLT Stylesheets

An XSLT **stylesheet** consists of a series of one or more **templates**, together with instructions based on XPath expressions that tell an XSLT processor how to match the templates against nodes in an XML **input document**. For each template, the processor looks through the input document until it finds a node matching the pattern specified in the template, and then applies the template to the data it finds. In this way it generates output from each matching template. The result of applying the templates to the input document is another XML document, called the **output** or **result document**. Note that the output could also be HTML, or even plain text, if the XSL processor supports it.

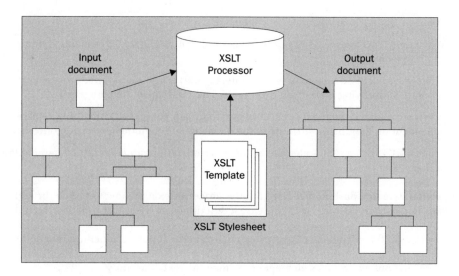

XSLT Processing Model

It is important to note that the XSLT processing model contains two approaches: a **declarative** (or **functional**) style in which the processor responds to XML elements as it encounters them, and an **imperative** style in which the processor is instructed to perform a series of operations explicitly. This is similar to the difference between functional programming and imperative programming. (Examples of functional languages include Lisp, ML, and Gofer, while examples of imperative languages include C, Java, and Pascal.)

For example, suppose we wished to transform a <JobDescription> element and its contents (left-hand side below) into an HTML fragment ready to display in a browser (right-hand side below):

```
<JobDescription>
     <Position>XSL Developer</Position>
     <Employer>Web Widgets, Inc.</Employer>
     <Location>
          <City>San Jose</City>
          <State>Calfornia</State>
     </Location>
     <Salary units="USD">40000</Salary>
     <Description>
          The successful candidate will have a
          wide range of web development skills,
          with proven XSL experience.
     </Description>
</JobDescription>
```

```
<h2>Vacancy</h2>
<h3>XSL Developer</h3>
<h3>Web Widgets, Inc</h3>
<p>San Jose, California</p>
<p>$40000</p>
<p>
The successful candidate will
have a wide range of web
development skills, with
proven XSL experience.
</p>
```

In a *declarative* style (also known as a "pull model" – more on this in Chapter 3), we tell the processor to react to certain XML elements when it encounters them in the input document. A description of the transformation between the two documents might be as follows:

❑   When a <JobDescription> element is encountered, first output an <h2> element containing the text "Vacancy", and then process any elements you find contained within <JobDescription>.

- ❑ When a `<Position>` element is encountered, output the text it contains inside an `<h3>` element.

- ❑ When an `<Employer>` element is encountered, output the text it contains inside an `<h3>` element.

- ❑ When a `<Location>` element is encountered, start a new paragraph, process any elements it contains by applying these rules over again, and then finish the paragraph.

- ❑ When a `<Salary>` element is encountered, output a paragraph containing a currency symbol dependent on the `units` attribute of the element, and then the text inside the element.

- ❑ When a `<Description>` element is encountered, output a paragraph containing the contents of the element.

In an *imperative* style (or "push model"), we tell the processor exactly how to search through and process the elements in the input document. In this case a description of the transformation might be as follows.

- ❑ For each of the `<JobDescription>` elements in the input document, do the following:

  - ❑ First output an `<h2>` element containing the text "`Vacancy`".

  - ❑ Output an `<h3>` element containing the text in the `<Position>` element underneath `<JobDescription>`.

  - ❑ Output an `<h3>` element containing the text in the `<Employer>` element underneath `<JobDescription>`.

  - ❑ Output a paragraph containing the text in the `<City>` element underneath the `<Location>` element underneath the `<JobDescription>` element and the text in the `<State>` element underneath the `<Location>` element underneath the `<JobDescription>` element.

  - ❑ Output a paragraph containing a currency symbol dependent on the `units` attribute of the `<Salary>` element underneath the `<JobDescription>` element, followed by the contents of the `<Salary>` element.

  - ❑ Output a paragraph containing the contents of the `<Description>` element underneath the `<JobDescription>` element.

A declarative approach is most useful when processing data that might be in many different formats, or contain any number of specialized elements, because it doesn't require us to know the document structure and specify precisely what will be encountered. Once we have decided that we need to format a particular chunk of XML, it's usually a good idea to run it through a declarative process that reacts to exactly how that data is formatted. However, for overall program logic, it's sometimes clearer to use an explicit imperative approach.

It's easy to see from the above example that the declarative approach is more reusable. If our job description XML format changes, say we include an address for the employer in the `<Location>` element, we simply add another template to deal with the new information. If part of the information is removed, say we no longer provide salary information for jobs, we don't actually need to change anything. The imperative method described above might break quite badly if part of the information it relies on is removed, because, instead of saying "*if* you encounter xxx, do this" we are saying "you *will* encounter xxx, so do this with it".

XSL tends to be written so that data is formatted for display using the declarative approach, with the data for display being chosen using an imperative approach. Sometimes, the two approaches will not be mixed at all. This happens most often when XSL is being used only for display purposes.

Tools

We've mentioned that XSL transformations are performed by an **XSL processor**. (XSLT processors for running XSLT stylesheets against an input document, and XSL-FO processors for taking XSL-FO documents and rendering them for display.) Throughout the book we'll be using many of these, and details of how to obtain them and set them up are given in Appendix E and Chapter 9 respectively.

XSLT processors are widely available. Later versions of Internet Explorer 5 have an XSLT processor (MSXML) built in, as does the newest Mozilla engine that powers Netscape 6 (the XSL processor is called TransforMiiX). The list of XSLT processors is impressive, including the MSXML parser from Microsoft, the Xalan-C++ and Xalan-Java processors from Apache, LotusXSL from IBM, Saxon from Michael Kay, and XT from James Clark. These processors can be written in any programming language, but the most popular ones tend to be C++ or Java based. The Microsoft MSXML3 parser, which includes an XSLT processor, can be used via the COM (also known as ActiveX) interface in Windows. Many of the XSLT processors are open source, and many implement the latest W3C standards.

XSLT is much more widely supported than XSL-FO, which is still in the process of being standardized. XSL-FO is certainly past its "bleeding edge" stage, however there are fewer processors supporting XSL-FO, and at present no web browsers support it. There are a few XSL-FO to PDF converters, though, and these make an excellent job of rendering formatting objects. PDF generators include FOP from Apache (http://xml.apache.org/fop/) and XEP from RenderX (http://www.renderx.com/FO2PDF.html). There is also the Antenna House XSL Formatter (http://www.antennahouse.com/xslformatter.html) that renders XSL-FO into a format suitable for the Windows GDI (Graphics Device Interface) to display.

How the Processors Work

An XSLT processor takes as input an XSLT stylesheet and an XML input document, and produces an XML output document. The approach used to achieve this varies from processor to processor. Some, such as Xalan from Apache and MSXML3 from Microsoft, allow the stylesheet to be compiled and stored in memory for better performance. There are processors available, such as XSLTC (www3.cybercities.com/x/xsltc), that take an XSLT stylesheet and produce (in the case of XSLTC) C++ code to perform the transformation described. Sun has released a technology preview of an XSLT-to-Java compiler, also called XSLTC. If the stylesheet is static, or changes infrequently, this can be a good way to achieve better performance in a heavy server application.

An XSL-FO processor takes as input an XSL-FO document containing formatting instructions. It then renders that document to the user by following the formatting instructions. Currently, most XSL-FO processors include an XSL-FO to PDF converter to produce PDF documents that can be viewed using a tool such as Adobe Acrobat Reader. In future XSL-FO processors will be integrated into web browsers such as Internet Explorer and Mozilla, and will be able to display documents directly to the user. The integration of XSL-FO processors into web browsers will be critical to the success of the formatting objects technology, and you should expect to see more support in the near future.

Further information on all of these processors can be found via http://www.w3.org/Style/XSL/.

Alternative Means of Transforming XML

XSLT is far from being the only mechanism for manipulating XML. Since XML is stored as plain text files, in principle it is simple to produce a program that will load the data into a tree structure and manipulate it. In fact, writing an XML parser is far from simple, and most programmers would rather let someone else do the hard work. In order to take advantage of an XML parser, there are two standard **application programming interfaces** (**APIs**) for accessing it:

❑ The **Document Object Model** (**DOM**) builds a tree representation of the document in memory, and allows retrieval and manipulation of the tree and its nodes. DOM implementations also provide a mechanism for serializing the in-memory tree back into a disk file, although the precise mechanism may depend on the processor.

❑ The **Simple API for XML parsing** (**SAX**) offers the programmer an event-driven view of an XML document as it is parsed. It notifies the programmer of events such as "document start" and "found a `<JobDescription>` element". It is the programmer's responsibility to keep track of any information that needs to be stored while processing. Because the whole XML document doesn't have to remain in memory at once, SAX can be used on much larger documents than a DOM parser can.

DOM and SAX transformations are generally more suited to being performed at the server level, since they are written in traditional programming languages such as C++ or Java. A handcrafted DOM or SAX transformation may perform better than an XSLT transform, which is why these methods are useful for server applications. There's no reason the output from a server-side transform shouldn't be used as the input for further XSL processing, however. In Chapter 6 we'll take a look at transformations using both the DOM and SAX approaches.

Uses of XSL

If you've been working with XML for any length of time you will probably already have realized that what we commonly term XML is really the core XML Recommendation plus quite a few supporting technologies, of which XSL is one. To take advantage of its capabilities and benefits we need to be able to manipulate the XML data, interrogate, merge, and transform it for sharing with programs and business partners, or add elements of style for presenting the data. The recommended way to do all these tasks is to use the XSL group of technologies covered in this book. Once you have mastered XSL, you will be able to:

❑ Convert between XML formats, and support applications such as Microsoft's BizTalk. While knowledge of XSL is not required for defining BizTalk mappings, it's a good example of where XSL can be useful.

❑ Style XML for presentation on browsers, creating web applications supporting multiple client types, from traditional web browsers through mobile phones and PDAs to telephones.

❑ Integrate server-side XML processing into an application, creating high performance XML-based systems.

❑ Use XSL-FO and CSS to produce high quality documents from XML data.

A solid understanding of XML and XSL transformations will give you a good grounding for mastering forthcoming XML-based technologies, such as:

❏   Automatic schema-based XML transformation tools for use with BizTalk.

❏   Microsoft's upcoming ASP.Net, the .Net framework, and its XML classes. These are important because XML is rapidly becoming the de facto standard for serializing object data in class frameworks.

❏   The Internet Information Services (IIS) XSL ISAPI plug in, which simplifies the use of XSL for performing transformations into HTML. It allows automatic execution of stylesheets on the server, picking different stylesheets based on client browser or content-type, caching of stylesheets for improved performance, and many other utility functions, such as support for WML.

❏   SQL-XML in SQL Server 2000, and Oracle's in-database XSLT processor. Since storage of XML in databases will become ever more important, database vendors are including direct support for XML functionality. Oracle, for example, offers indexing and searching of XML fields in database tables, and XSLT styling directly on the database server.

❏   ebXML, a forthcoming electronic business framework and a joint initiative of the United Nations and Oasis. The ebXML group advocates using XSLT to transform messages from external systems into their message format.

❏   Apache's Cocoon, an XML-based web-publishing framework. Cocoon aims to completely separate document content, style, and logic, and uses XSL to format documents into HTML, PDF, WML, and other formats.

❏   Sun Open Net Environment (ONE) – an XML-based smart web services platform. Sun ONE uses XML to allow web services to be "smart" and to configure themselves according to the access device used, such as traditional web browsers or the latest wireless devices.

Now that we have seen why XSL is so important, let's get down to the nitty-gritty of the languages. Before we start to learn the elements and functions that make up the XSLT language, we'll begin with a look at the XPath language for specifying which parts of the input document we want to transform.

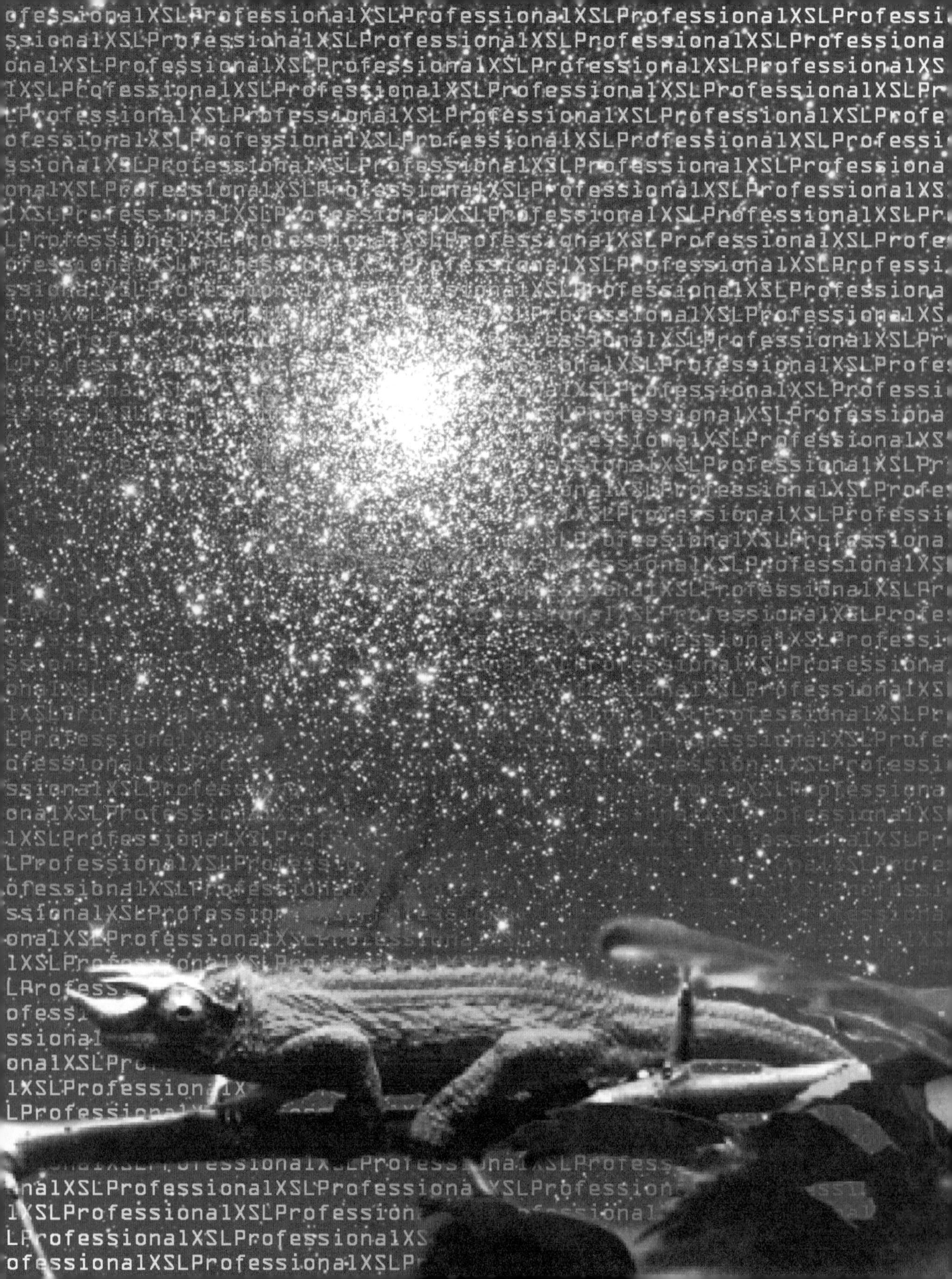

2

XPath – the XML Path Language

In Chapter 1 you learned that XSLT transformations are determined both by the logical structure of a source XML document and by the templates contained in an XSLT stylesheet. The XML Path Language, **XPath**, is the key to defining which template is or is not applied to any node in the source XML document. In other words, if you are to use XSLT to process the nodes in a source XML document in the way you want, then you need to understand XPath.

> *XPath and XSLT interact closely, so it isn't possible to teach you XPath without making some use of XSLT concepts and code that won't be thoroughly discussed until later chapters. You may find it helpful to come back and re-read this chapter, or parts of it, since once the XSLT material in later chapters is covered, the function of the XPath presented here will be clearer. Realizing that you may have little understanding of XSLT as yet, I have confined the XSLT code to the latter part of the chapter, and have written the XSLT material to show XPath working in some fairly straightforward yet practical examples.*

XPath was designed to be used by both XSLT and another specification, **XPointer**, where it is used to locate *tree fragments* within XML documents. In this chapter I will consider only those aspects of XPath which are relevant to XSLT, details of which are found in two W3C documents – the XML Path Language (XPath) Version 1.0 Recommendation of 16th November 1999 (http://www.w3.org/TR/1999/REC-xpath-19991116) and the XSL Transformations (XSLT) Version 1.0 Recommendation of the same date (http://www.w3.org/TR/1999/REC-xslt-19991116). If you wish to examine the use of XPath with XPointer, further information can be found at http://www.w3.org/TR/xptr.

Introduction to XPath

A concise definition of XPath would be "the notation that enables the targeted application of XSLT transformations". In other words, it enables a developer to choose which parts of a source XML document to process by the application of appropriate templates in order to produce the desired output tree.

What is XPath for?

As was indicated in Chapter 1, XSLT can be used for a multitude of purposes in an XML-based web site. Essentially all of those varied XSLT tasks depend on an appropriate and targeted use of XPath. To give you a flavor of XPath's capabilities, let's look at some real-world tasks and think about some of the choices we can make using XPath.

I would like to focus initially on the use of XSLT/XPath to produce web pages. For example, on an intranet we might be happy to display, using HTML or XHTML, *all* information in a particular database, whereas for a similar page destined to be displayed on an extranet or the Internet we may want to display only data items which are not considered confidential. XPath would allow us to make the necessary choices, either by letting us select for display only certain non-confidential elements in the source document or by filtering information on the basis of XML element attributes (such as a "security_level" attribute). On an e-commerce site we might want, for targeted web marketing purposes, to choose only to show items likely to be purchased by a person of a particular location, gender, or age group. Assuming that we had the necessary personal data of the user and that our product data is suitably classified, XPath can help us target the data we output. On a web site which has a "What's new?" page, we might filter or select the items to be displayed based on certain date criteria.

Similarly, when using XSLT/XPath as a key component in XML-based business-to-business (B2B) data interchange we have many similar tasks to perform, which require transformation of XML-based data using XSLT. Let's suppose that two businesses exchange purchase order information. It is essential that, despite differences in data structure between the business partners, the correct fragment of information is conveyed to the correct element or attribute in the other data store. XPath allows us to predictably select an element or attribute in the incoming data flow. XSLT is then used to process that selected XML fragment, building up a result tree corresponding to the recipient's data format. Imagine the chaos that might result if a date were inadvertently placed into the element meant to represent the number of items being ordered, or if the price for an expensive item were inadvertently replaced by the price for a cheap one. Efficient e-business demands correct and predictable interchange of information between business partners. XSLT and XPath are two of the keys to creating a quality assured process.

To sum up then, when used in XSLT, XPath **expressions** can have a variety of purposes including:

❏ Selecting nodes for processing

❏ Specifying conditions for different ways of processing a node

❏ Generating text to be inserted in the result tree

If you are used to handling source XML data, you will probably have already realized that selections such as those just mentioned will involve choices made on criteria such as the value of an XML element, the value of an XML attribute, or a range of other factors. XPath provides us with functionality to make such choices using a non-XML-based syntax.

XPath expressions will, in this context, enable us to focus our choices on the parts of the source XML documents that provide suitable data for creating our output or result tree. The most common and important type of XPath expression is the **location path**. In this chapter much of the detailed discussion of concepts and most of the examples will focus on these location paths.

How does XPath Work?

The purpose of XPath, when used with XSLT, is to direct an XSLT processor when navigating through the node tree of an XML source document (the **source tree**) in order to allow the desired selective processing of nodes in the XML source tree to produce the nodes in the **result tree**.

Many people seem to find XPath difficult to get to grips with. In part, this is due to the complexity and unfamiliarity of some of the syntax, and also due to a difficulty in grasping the overall picture, without being overwhelmed by the detail. So let's take a broad, non-technical look at how XPath works before delving deeper into the specifics of the XPath syntax and data model.

I have found that one of the most helpful ways to communicate the basic concept of how XPath works is to compare it to asking someone for street directions. Let's suppose you are looking for a particular building. Given your starting point, you are told to go in a specific direction (let's say North), to make a turning of a certain type when you reach a certain point (for example, "Turn right at the third intersection"), and are either told where your desired destination is located relative to those directions or are told some distinguishing characteristic of your desired destination (for example, "It is the fifth house on the right" or "It is the cafe next to the ice cream parlor").

Essentially, XPath works in the same way. It operates similarly to a set of street directions, guiding you through the tree of nodes in the XML source document.

The XPath jargon for the equivalent of a set of street directions is a **location path**. You will be seeing lots of examples of location paths throughout this chapter.

A key to getting to your desired street destination is to receive directions that correctly apply to your starting point. Similarly, in XPath, knowing your starting point – your **context** – is essential to predictably navigating the node tree of the XML source document. A particularly important part of the context is the **context node**. The context node is specified within the XSLT code that the XPath location path is being used with.

In street directions, for a North American city laid out in rectangular blocks, we can have movement in four axes: North, South, East and West. XPath also has **axes**, including the **parent** axis, the **ancestor** axis, the **child** axis and the **descendant** axis. In total XPath has 13 axes, some of which overlap – all of the axes will be explained in more detail later in this chapter.

Sticking with our street directions analogy, we can identify our destination building either by looking at the location relative to neighboring buildings (its 'context'), or by specifying some unique characteristic of the destination (its physical 'attributes'). XPath has both capabilities. An XPath statement in XSL that selects elements firstly specifies how to find the target element(s) by moving along one of the axes mentioned above. A **node-test** is then applied to check that the node is of the type specified, and an optional XPath **predicate** can then refine the nodes chosen, either on the basis of their position relative to other elements or on the basis of some characteristic that they possess, such as a certain attribute or value.

So, starting from a context node, in a simple XPath location path we have a **location step** consisting of:

❑ an axis

❑ a node-test

❑ a predicate (optional)

We will consider the details of the XPath axes, node-tests and predicates later in the chapter. For the moment, it is sufficient to grasp that these three entities form a location step, and location steps, in varying number, make up a location path, the equivalent of a set of street directions.

This is a simple example of a location path:

```
child::chapter[child::title]
```

Here, the axis is `child`. This is followed by a double colon as a separator, and then the node-test, which in this example is `chapter`. This tests that the child of the context node is an element node representing a `<chapter>` element. The final part of the location path is the predicate contained in square brackets, in this instance `[child::title]`. This predicate means that only `<chapter>` element nodes that have a `<title>` element node as a child are included in the returned **node-set**, that is the set of nodes reached by the location path.

The location path that I have just shown includes only one location step. However, a location path may contain more than one location step, separated by forward slash characters, `/`.

Location paths in XPath are of two types: **relative location paths** and **absolute location paths**. You can view these as roughly corresponding to street directions and coordinates on a map, respectively. We will look at several examples of each later in the chapter, but for now you just need to know that absolute location paths always have the **root node** (the top node in the document) as their context node, otherwise they are the same as relative location paths. This will become clear shortly when we look at nodes in more detail.

If multiple location steps are used in a relative location path, they are composed together from left to right, with respect to the context node. The initial location step selects a set of nodes relative to a context node. Each node in that set is used as a context node for the following step. The set(s) of nodes identified by that step are unioned together, and used as context nodes for the next step, and so on. A node-set is returned which may contain a single node, multiple nodes or may be empty.

To understand exactly how the XPath location steps work, we will first take a closer look at the XPath data model. Then we will take a closer look at the different parts of an XPath location step. We will be introducing a lot of new terms, but this will be followed by numerous examples, which should clarify what we have been looking at so far.

The XPath Data Model

XPath models an XML document as a tree. However, the XPath Recommendation leaves considerable latitude about how processors implement this, so you should view the tree as conceptual only. Any individual implementation is not obliged to implement the structure as a tree.

Note that any XML document to which XPath is applied must conform to the **Namespaces in XML Recommendation** (http://www.w3.org/TR/1999/REC-xml-names-19990114/).

If you have done any programming using the XML Document Object Model (DOM), you will know that an XML document can, conceptually, be viewed as a hierarchical tree of nodes. XPath similarly uses the concept of a tree of nodes to visualize the logical content of an XML document. However, there are differences in detail, some of which we will come across later in this chapter.

The XPath Recommendation describes seven node types:

- ❑ Root node (one and only one is present in each source document)
- ❑ Element node
- ❑ Attribute node
- ❑ Processing Instruction node
- ❑ Comment node
- ❑ Text node
- ❑ Namespace node

If you are familiar with both the XML 1.0 and Namespaces in XML Recommendations you will probably intuitively know which part of an XML source document each of those nodes refers to. Be sure to avoid confusing the root node and its child, an **element node** that represents the **element root** (the element in the XML document that contains all other elements).

The following simple XML document, when viewed conceptually in XPath, contains six of the seven types of node. The root node is present, although not visible, and is the parent of both a comment node and of the `<book>` element node. The `<book>` element node, in turn, has a child `<title>` element node. The `<title>` element node has a text node child, which has the value "XPath is here!" and also has a child attribute node whose name is "code" and whose value is "XPath". It also has a namespace node, whose value is inherited from the namespace node of its parent `<book>` element node. Although enclosed in the `<?  ?>` characters like processing instructions, the XML declaration at the top is not actually a processing instruction and thus has no corresponding processing instruction node.

```
<?xml version='1.0'?>
<!-- NodeTypes.xml -->

<book xmlns="http://www.xmml.com/">
  <title code="XPath">
    XPath is here!
  </title>
</book>
```

For each of the seven types of node there is a way of determining a **string-value**. For example, the string-value of the text node in the above code is `XPath is here!`. For some types of node, the string-value is part of the node. For other types of node, the string-value is computed from the string-value of its child nodes. We will see these in detail for the different types of node in the following sections.

The string-value of a node is one illustration of the subtle differences of approach between the DOM and XPath. For example, for element nodes and root nodes, the string-value of a node is not the same as the string returned by the DOM `nodeValue()` method.

In addition to having a string-value, some types of node also have an **expanded-name**, which consists of a local part and a namespace URI. The local part is a string. The namespace URI is either null or a string.

The namespace URI specified in an XML document can be a URI reference as defined in RFC2396 (http://www.ietf.org/rfc/rfc2396.txt). This means it can have a fragment identifier and can be relative. A relative URI should be resolved into an absolute URI during namespace processing. However, the namespace URIs of the expanded-names of nodes in the data model should be absolute. Two expanded-names are equal if they have the same local part, and either both have a null namespace URI or both have non-null namespace URIs that are equal.

XPath also includes a concept of **document order**. This is defined on all nodes in the document as the order in which the first character of each node appears in the XML representation of the document after general entities have been expanded. In practical terms, this means that the sequence of occurrence of element start tags is the same as the document order for a source document without external XML entities.

Root nodes and element nodes have an ordered list of child nodes. Nodes never share children – given two different nodes, none of the children of one node will be the same node as any of the children of the other node. Every node, other than the root node, has exactly one **parent**, which is either an element node or the root node. In other words, apart from the root node, only element nodes may be the parent of any other node. The **descendants** of a node are the children of the node and the descendants of the children of the node.

Now we have an understanding of how the tree is made up, let's have a look at the types of node in more detail.

Root Node

The root node is the root of the XPath tree. A root node may not occur in any other part of the tree. Each XPath tree may have one and only one root node. The string value of the root node is the concatenation of the string-values of all text node descendants of the root node in document order.

The root node does not have an expanded-name.

Element Nodes

There is an element node for each element in the XML source document. An element node has an expanded-name derived by expanding the **QName** (qualified name) in the element tag according to the W3C's Namespaces in XML Recommendation. The namespace URI of the element's expanded-name will be null if the QName has no prefix and there is no applicable default namespace.

The string value of an element node is the concatenation of the string-values of all text node descendants of the element node in document order.

The children of an element node are the element nodes, comment nodes, processing instruction nodes, and text nodes for its content. Entity references to both internal and external entities are expanded. Character references are first resolved.

Attribute Nodes

Each element node has an associated set of attribute nodes. The element node is the parent of each of these attribute nodes. However:

> **An attribute node is not a child of its parent element node.**

In other words, when a location path begins with `child::`, no attribute nodes are selected. Note that this is a further difference from the DOM, which does not treat the element bearing an attribute as the parent of the attribute.

Namespace Nodes

Each element has an associated set of namespace nodes, one for each distinct namespace prefix that is in scope for the element (including the xml prefix, which is implicitly declared by the Namespaces in XML Recommendation) and one for the default namespace if one is in scope for the element. The element is the parent of each of these namespace nodes. However:

> **A namespace node is not a child of its parent element.**

This means that a location path beginning child:: does not return any namespace nodes. Elements never share namespace nodes. For two different element nodes, none of the namespace nodes of one element node will be the same as the namespace nodes of the other element node.

In summary, this means that an element will have a namespace node:

❑ for every attribute of the element whose name starts with xmlns:

❑ for every attribute of an ancestor element whose name starts with xmlns: unless the element itself or a nearer ancestor re-declares the prefix

❑ for an xmlns attribute, if the element or some ancestor has an xmlns attribute, and the value of the xmlns attribute for the nearest such element is non-empty

Processing Instruction Nodes

There is a processing instruction node for every processing instruction, except for any processing instruction that occurs within the Document Type Declaration.

A processing instruction has an expanded-name – the local part is the processing instruction's target and the namespace URI is null. The string-value of a processing instruction node is the part of the processing instruction following the target (the application to which the processing instruction applies) and any whitespace. It does not include the "?>" characters which terminate the processing instruction. As mentioned previously, the XML declaration is not a processing instruction, and therefore there is no processing instruction node corresponding to the XML declaration.

Comment Nodes

There is a comment node for every comment in the source XML document, except for any comment that occurs within the Document Type Declaration. The string-value of a comment is the content of the comment not including the opening "<!--" characters or the closing "-->" characters. A comment node does not have an expanded-name.

Text Nodes

Character data in the source document is grouped into text nodes. As much character data as possible is grouped into each text node, thus a text node never has an immediately following or preceding sibling that is a text node.

The string-value of a text node is the character data. A text node always has at least one character of data. Each character within a CDATA section is treated as character data. Thus, <![CDATA[<]]> in the source document will be treated the same as <. Both will result in a single < character in a text node in the tree. Thus, a CDATA section is treated as if the <![CDATA[and]]> were removed and every occurrence of < and & were replaced by < and & respectively. A text node does not have an expanded-name.

Note that characters inside comments, processing instructions and attribute values do not produce text nodes. Line-endings in external entities are normalized to #xA as specified in the XML 1.0 Recommendation.

More XPath Concepts

The most general syntactical construction in XPath is the expression. The location path, mentioned earlier, is the most important type of XPath expression.

When an XPath expression is evaluated, it yields an object, which can be of one of four basic types:

- ❏ node-set
- ❏ Boolean (true or false)
- ❏ number (a floating-point number)
- ❏ string (a sequence of characters)

The node-set is a particularly important concept to grasp. An XPath node-set is an unordered set of nodes without duplicates.

In XSLT, when an XPath expression is evaluated, that evaluation is carried out in a **context**, which consists of five parts:

- ❏ a node (the **context node**)
- ❏ a pair of non-zero positive integers (the **context position** and the **context size**)
- ❏ a set of variable bindings
- ❏ a function library
- ❏ the set of namespace declarations in scope for the expression

XPath expressions typically occur within the attributes of XML elements, or specifically, in the case of XSLT, within the attributes of the XSLT elements.

Most of the XPath you are likely to use will depend on location paths. As mentioned earlier, there are two types of location path: absolute and relative. Both types of location path include the concept of a context node and location steps. As we said earlier, the essential difference is that for absolute location paths, the context node is consistently the root node.

As we saw earlier, a location path is made up of a number of location steps, and a location step is made up of an axis (which defines a set of nodes relative to the context node), a node-test (which selects a subset of this set of nodes) and an optional predicate (which further restricts the set of selected nodes). Let's look at these concepts in a little more detail.

XPath Axes

As mentioned earlier in the chapter, XPath has a total of 13 axes:

- ❑   child
- ❑   parent
- ❑   descendant
- ❑   ancestor
- ❑   descendant-or-self
- ❑   ancestor-or-self
- ❑   following-sibling
- ❑   preceding-sibling
- ❑   following
- ❑   preceding
- ❑   attribute
- ❑   namespace
- ❑   self

The **child axis** contains the children of a context node. Note that attribute nodes and namespace nodes are not children of the element nodes to which they relate. Thus the child axis never returns any attribute or namespace nodes in the returned node-set.

The **parent axis** consists of the node that is the parent of the context node, if such a parent node exists. Of course, when the root node of the document is the context node, it has no parent.

The **descendant axis** contains the descendants of the context node. A descendant is a child of the context node or a child of a child of the context node and so on, so while the child axis is part of the descendant axis, the reverse is not generally true. The descendant axis never contains attribute or namespace nodes.

The **ancestor axis** consists of the ancestors of the context node. The ancestors of the context node consist of the parent of the context node and the parent's parent and so on. The ancestor axis will always include the root node, unless the context node is the root node. As mentioned previously, the root node has no parent.

The **descendant-or-self axis** includes the nodes previously described as the descendant axis together with the context node itself.

The **ancestor-or-self axis** includes the nodes previously described as the ancestor axis together with the context node itself.

The **following-sibling axis** contains all the siblings (children of the context node's parent) that are after the context node in document order. If the context node is an attribute node or namespace node, the following-sibling axis is always empty. Even if an element node has multiple attributes, be careful to remember that for attribute nodes the following-sibling axis is empty.

The **preceding-sibling axis** contains all the siblings of the context node that come before the context node in document order. If the context node is an attribute node or namespace node then, as mentioned for the following-sibling axis, the preceding-sibling axis is empty.

The **following axis** contains all nodes in the same document as the context node that are after the context node in document order, excluding any descendants and excluding attribute nodes and namespace nodes. Be careful not to confuse the following-sibling axis with the following axis.

The **preceding axis** contains all nodes in the same document as the context node that are before the context node in document order, excluding any ancestors and excluding attribute nodes and namespace nodes. Be careful to distinguish the preceding-sibling axis from the preceding axis correctly.

The **attribute axis** contains the attributes of the context node. The attribute axis will be empty unless the context node is an element.

The **namespace axis** contains the namespace nodes of the context node. The namespace axis will be empty unless the context node is an element.

The **self axis** contains only the context node.

You may find it helpful (or at this stage totally confusing) to realize that the five axes ancestor, descendant, self, following and preceding do not overlap and together reference all element nodes in a document, in the same way that North, South, here, East and West are sufficient (in theory!) to direct a person to any given street address. This is illustrated in the following diagram, where node number 6 is the context node:

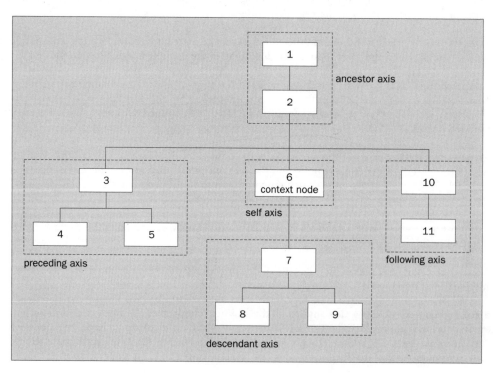

Node Tests

Each of the 13 axes has a **principal node type**. For the `attribute` axis and `namespace` axis the principal node types are, respectively, attribute node and namespace node. For all other axes the principal node type is the element node.

When a node test is carried out as part of a location step, the result of the node test is true if and only if the node type is of the principal node type for the axis in question, and in addition if the node test is a QName and "has an expanded-name equal to the expanded-name specified by the QName".

If you need to refresh your memory about the details of qualified names, they are described in the Namespaces in XML Recommendation located at http://www.w3.org/TR/1999/REC-xml-names-19990114.

Let's look at a few node tests in practice.

A node test `*` is true for any node of the principal node type for the axis it is being used with. For example, `child::*` will select all element children of the context node, since the `child` axis has the element principal node type.

It is possible to use a node test to select from the given axis all nodes of a particular type. For example, the node test `text()` is true for any text node, and `child::text()` will select any text node children of the context node.

Similarly, the node test `comment()` is true for any comment node.

Notice that things are a little more complex when we come to processing instruction nodes. The node test `processing-instruction()` is true for any processing instruction. In addition, the `processing-instruction()` test may have an argument that is a Literal. In that case, the node test is true for any processing instruction that has a name equal to the value of the Literal.

It is also possible to use a node test to select element nodes from the given axis for a particular element type, for example `<paragraph>`. Examples of this will be shown later.

Predicates

A predicate is an expression that filters a node-set with respect to an axis to produce a new node-set. (Those nodes that satisfy the expression in the predicate are included in the returned node-set. Conversely, those nodes that fail to satisfy the expression in the predicate are excluded from the returned node-set.) Therefore, to correctly use a predicate the axis must be taken into consideration.

The XPath Recommendation designates all of the axes listed earlier as either a **forward axis** or a **reverse axis**. When interpreting the meaning of some predicates it is important to be aware whether the axis to which the predicate is being applied is a forward axis or a reverse axis.

The XPath Recommendation states "an axis that only ever contains the context node or nodes that are after the context node in document order is a forward axis. An axis that only ever contains the context node or nodes that are before the context node in document order is a reverse axis". If you read those definitions from the Recommendation carefully you will see that the `self` axis is termed, by the Recommendation, both a forward axis and a reverse axis. In practice this makes little difference since the `self` axis can contain at most one node and therefore does not make use of predicates.

Being aware of whether an axis is a forward axis or a reverse axis becomes important when using the `position()` function in a predicate. This function is one of many supplied by XPath – we will look at a few more later in the chapter. This function determines the position of a node in a node-set with respect to an axis. It is defined to be the position of the node in the node-set ordered in **document order** if the axis is a forward axis, and ordered in **reverse document order** if the axis is a reverse axis.

Another frequent source of confusion is that the numbering of positions differs in XPath from that in some popular programming languages.

> **In XPath the first position is one (not zero).**

Let's look at some very simple examples of expressions that demonstrate this issue.

```
following-sibling::*[position()=1]
```

In the above example, the `*` node test selects all nodes in the `following-sibling` axis. The `following-sibling` axis is a forward axis, and so the sibling for which the `position()` function returns "1" is the sibling immediately following the context node in document order.

```
preceding-sibling::*[position()=1]
```

In contrast, when we look at the `preceding-sibling` location path, the sibling node for which the `position()` function returns 1 is the immediately preceding sibling, that is the first sibling encountered as one moves in reverse document order.

XPath Functions

The XPath Recommendation mentions a number of functions, which are included in the **core function library**.

There are several functions that operate on node-sets. You have already seen the `position()` function which returns a number equal to the context position from the expression evaluation context. We will later see the `last()` function, which returns a number equal to the context size from the expression evaluation context, and the `count()` function, which returns the number of nodes in the argument node-set.

The `id()` function returns a node-set selecting elements by means of their unique ID attribute. Here is a simple example using the `id()` function.

```
id("special")
```

This returns a node-set containing one element node which has the unique ID with value "special".

In addition to those functions, such as `position()`, which return a node-set, there are also functions within the core function library which return strings, Booleans or numbers.

The `string()` function returns a string. For example, it converts a node-set to a string by returning the string-value of the node in the node-set which is first in document order. If the node-set is empty, the `string()` function returns an empty string.

In addition, the core function library contains a number of functions for manipulating strings:

- ❑ `concat()`
- ❑ `starts-with()`
- ❑ `contains()`
- ❑ `substring()`
- ❑ `substring-before()`
- ❑ `substring-after()`
- ❑ `string-length()`
- ❑ `normalize-space()`
- ❑ `translate()`

In the core function library there are also a number of functions, which return a Boolean:

- ❑ `boolean()`
- ❑ `not()`
- ❑ `true()`
- ❑ `false()`
- ❑ `lang()`

Further functions in the core function library return a number:

- ❑ `number()`
- ❑ `sum()`
- ❑ `floor()`
- ❑ `ceiling()`
- ❑ `round()`

Details of the operation of all of these functions are to be found in Appendix A of this book, or in Section 4 of the XPath Recommendation at http://www.w3.org/TR/1999/REC-xpath-19991116.

XPath Syntax

XPath has two types of syntax in which XPath expressions can be expressed: **unabbreviated syntax** and **abbreviated syntax**. All XPath expressions can be expressed in unabbreviated syntax. Many, but not all, common XPath expressions or location paths can be expressed in abbreviated syntax.

Within both the unabbreviated syntax and the abbreviated syntax we can consider relative location paths and absolute location paths. We will look at examples of the available XPath syntax under the following four headings:

- ❑ Unabbreviated Relative Locations Paths
- ❑ Unabbreviated Absolute Location Paths
- ❑ Abbreviated Relative Location Paths
- ❑ Abbreviated Absolute Locations Paths

Both the unabbreviated syntax and the abbreviated syntax can be used with XSLT code. Since the abbreviated syntax is often much more succinct than the corresponding unabbreviated syntax, it is usual for developers to use only the abbreviated syntax within code rather than the more verbose unabbreviated syntax.

First, we will take a look at several examples of unabbreviated syntax in isolation, that is, without using any XSLT code. Later in the chapter we will look at the alternative, more succinct ways in which similar expressions can be expressed using the abbreviated XPath syntax. The final part of the chapter will demonstrate some XPath used in some simple examples of XSLT code.

Unabbreviated XPath Syntax

First let's look at a slightly more complex XML source document (`ForLocPaths.xml`) to explore the unabbreviated XPath syntax:

```xml
<?xml version='1.0'?>
<!-- This file is ForLocPaths.xml. Its purpose is to examine the
syntax of some simple XPath location paths. -->

<book>
  <title>Professional XSL</title>
  <chapters>
    <chapter number="1" title="Introduction to XSL"></chapter>
    <chapter number="2" title="XPath">
      <section number="1">
        <paragraph number="1">First paragraph.</paragraph>
        <paragraph number="2">Second paragraph.</paragraph>
        <paragraph number="3">Third paragraph.</paragraph>
        <paragraph number="4">Fourth paragraph.</paragraph>
      </section>
      <section number="2">
        <paragraph number="1">First paragraph.</paragraph>
        <paragraph number="2">Second paragraph.</paragraph>
      </section>
      <section number="3"></section>
    </chapter>
    <chapter number="3">XSLT Basics</chapter>
    <chapter number="4">Modular XSLT</chapter>
<!-- Many other chapters would in real life be listed here. -->
  </chapters>

  <appendices>
<!-- In this simple example we have not enumerated the appendices. -->
  </appendices>
</book>
```

We will use this example source document as we look successively at unabbreviated relative location paths and then, more briefly, at the unabbreviated absolute method.

Unabbreviated Relative Location Paths

In the remainder of this section I will illustrate, with a number of example XPath expressions, the unabbreviated syntax for relative location paths. For each I will give a general definition for the expression and then, using specific context nodes in the above example document, will describe the node-set that would result when the XPath expression is processed with such a context node.

The context node for the relative location paths will, when XPath is used with XSLT, be determined by the structure of the XSLT stylesheet.

```
child::paragraph
```

This expression selects the <paragraph> child element nodes of the context node. In our example file, if the context node were the <book> element node then an empty node-set would be returned, because the <book> element has no child <paragraph> elements. If, however, the context node were the <section> element in Chapter 2 with attribute number="1", then a node-set containing four paragraph nodes would be returned.

```
child::*
```

The expression child::* selects all element node children of the context node. If the context node has children other than element nodes then those are not included within the node-set. For example, if the context node represented the <book> element, the node-set would contain the element nodes which represent the <title>, <chapters> and <appendices> elements. Remember that only children, not descendants in general, are included in the node-set.

```
child::text()
```

The above expression will select all text node children of the context node. In our example document, if the context node were the node representing the <book> element an empty node-set would be returned. If the context node was the node representing the <paragraph> number 1 in <section> number 2 of the <chapter> number 2, then a node-set consisting of one text node with the value "First Paragraph" would be returned.

```
child::node()
```

Now the expression will select *all* node children of the context node. Note that this differs from child::* which selects only *element* nodes within the node-set, whereas child::node() will also include namespace and attribute nodes too.

```
attribute::number
```

The attribute::number expression returns the attribute nodes with name number under the context node. Be careful to distinguish this type of location path (which selects an attribute node) from examples that you will see later which select an element node on the basis of attributes that it may have. In our sample XML source document, if the context node were the node representing a <paragraph>, <section> or <chapter> element node, then the number attribute node would be returned in the node-set. Otherwise, in our example source document, an empty node-set would be returned.

```
attribute::*
```

Here, the expression returns all attribute nodes of the context node. If the context node were the element node representing the `<chapter>` element for Chapter 1, then a node-set would be returned which would contain two attribute nodes: those representing the `number` and `title` attributes related to Chapter 1.

```
descendant::paragraph
```

This location path will select all `<paragraph>` elements that are descendants of the context node. In our sample document, if the context node were the node representing either the `<book>` element or the `<chapters>` element, we would retrieve a node-set containing a total of six nodes, one for each of the `<paragraph>` elements in our document. If, however, our context node were the node representing the first `<section>` element for Chapter 2, a node-set containing four nodes representing `<paragraph>` elements would be returned.

```
ancestor-or-self::chapter
```

The `ancestor-or-self::chapter` location path selects the `<chapter>` element node(s) representing ancestors of the context node and, if the context node is a `<chapter>` element, it will also be returned. In our example document, if the context node were the node representing the `<chapters>` element, this would equate to an empty node-set (since the context node is neither a `<chapter>` element nor does it have any `<chapter>` element nodes as ancestors). If, however, our context node were a node representing a `<section>` element, then it would return a node-set containing one node, which would represent the `<chapter>` element within which the `<section>` element is contained.

```
descendant-or-self::section
```

Now our location path selects the node representing the `<section>` element descendants of the context node and, if the context node represents a `<section>` element, includes the context node as well. In our sample document, if the context node represented the `<chapter>` element for Chapter 2, a node-set would be returned containing three nodes representing the three `<section>` elements which are children of the `<chapter>` element for Chapter 2. If the context node were the node representing the `<chapters>` element, we would have the same returned node-set including all `<section>` element nodes, but note that these are now grandchildren of the context node. If, however, the context node represented the `<chapter>` element for Chapter 3, it would return an empty node-set, since our source document contains no `<section>` elements within Chapter 3.

```
self::paragraph
```

The `self::paragraph` location path selects the context node if it represents a `<paragraph>` element. That is, it returns a node-set containing one node representing a `<paragraph>` element or otherwise selects nothing (returns an empty node-set).

Using More Complex Paths

So far, the examples shown have been simple ones containing just a single location step. However, XPath location paths may include more than one location step. In the examples that follow I will illustrate some examples using multiple location steps, describing in abstract terms the meaning of those paths and, by reference to our example source document, illustrating the node-sets which are produced.

```
child::chapter/descendant::paragraph
```

Here, the location path includes two location steps. It selects the <paragraph> element descendants of the <chapter> element children of the context node. For example, if the context node represented the <chapters> element in our sample document, it would return a node-set containing six element nodes representing the <paragraph> elements contained within Chapter 2.

Looking at location paths with multiple location steps, you can read the location path left-to-right or right-to-left. Use whichever of these approaches you find most helpful to visualize which nodes are produced.

Taking the `child::chapter/descendant::paragraph` location path from left-to-right, we can thus read it as "Look for all the <chapter> element nodes which are children of the context node, and for each of these, return any <paragraph> element nodes which are their descendants".

If we adopt the right-to-left approach, the location path could be translated as, "Include all <paragraph> elements that are descendants of any <chapter> element children of the context node".

> *Note that these approaches do not necessarily represent the approach that an XSLT processor might use. They are offered simply as an aid for you to visualize which nodes will be included in the returned node-set.*

```
child::*/child::paragraph
```

Here again we have a multiple location step path. It selects all <paragraph> grandchildren of the context node. In our example document, if the context node represented the <chapters> element it would return an empty node-set, because the <chapters> element node has no children element nodes which themselves have <paragraph> element children. However, if the context node were the <chapter> element node for Chapter 2 it would return a node-set containing six paragraph nodes, namely the <paragraph> element children of the three <section> element node children of the context node. Of course, as the third <section> element node has no <paragraph> children, it doesn't add any elements to the result set.

Predicates

I mentioned earlier in the chapter that location paths consist of an axis, a node test, and an optional predicate. Up to now, I have shown you examples of location paths that had an axis and node test, but no predicate. So let's take a look at a few examples of unabbreviated relative location paths using predicates.

```
child::paragraph[position()=1]
```

The predicate is the code contained in square brackets, and allows us to select the first <paragraph> element child of the context node by use of the `position()` function. In our sample document, if the context node represented the first <section> element node in Chapter 2, then the returned node-set would contain just the first <paragraph> element node child of that <section> element.

In XPath the `position()` function returns the position of a node within a node-set. Note that position 1 denotes the first position in a group of siblings. This is in contrast to, for example, the Java language, which uses index zero to represent the first element in an array. If you are used to programming in a language that uses a zero index, take particular care when using predicates like this that you have chosen the element node intended.

```
child::paragraph[position()=last()]
```

This usage selects the last <paragraph> element child of the context node. The predicate uses the function position() in combination with last() to return the position of the last <paragraph> element node child of the context node. The following location path is similar, but will return the last but one <paragraph> element child of the context node:

```
child::paragraph[position()=last()-1]
```

Predicates Returning Multiple Nodes

The predicates you have seen so far in this section have all chosen a single node for inclusion in the returned node-set. However, XPath functions also allow the returned node-set defined by a predicate to contain more than one node.

```
child::paragraph[position()>1]
```

Here a node-set is implied which may contain more than one <paragraph> element node, depending on the number of matching <paragraph> element nodes. In essence, all but the first <paragraph> element node children of the context node are selected. Thus if there are more than two matching <paragraph> element nodes, the returned node-set will have more than one contained node. Looking again at our sample document, with the context node as the first <section> element node in Chapter 2, then there are four child <paragraph> element nodes which match the child::paragraph axis and node test. The predicate [position()>1] excludes the <paragraph> element node at position 1, meaning that the remaining three <paragraph> element nodes make up the returned node-set.

```
following-sibling::chapter[position()=1]
```

Here our location path selects the next <chapter> sibling of the context node. Thus, in our example document, if the context node were the <chapter> element for Chapter 1, then the element node which is returned in the node-set would be the <chapter> element node whose number attribute has the value of "2". Similarly, if the second <chapter> element node were the context node, the returned node-set would contain one <chapter> element node whose number attribute would have the value of "3". Remember that it is document order that determines the following-sibling, rather than any attribute that an element may have.

```
preceding-sibling::chapter[position()=1]
```

The preceding-sibling::chapter[position()=1] location path returns the previous <chapter> element node sibling of the context node. Thus in our example document, if the context node represented the <chapter> element whose number attribute had the value of "3", the returned node-set would contain the element node representing the <chapter> element whose number attribute has the value of "2". Again, note that it is document order (in this example, reverse document order) that determines whether or not a node is in the node-set, not just the value of any attributes. Remember, too, that the preceding-sibling axis is a reverse axis and that the sibling node returned is the first one encountered when moving in reverse document order.

Note that preceding-sibling is a different axis. As the position() function's meaning is relative to the axis involved, it will have a different effect here to, say, the following-sibling or child axes. When the preceding-sibling axis is applicable, then position() returns element nodes met when going *backwards* through the sibling nodes. It may help you to return to the notion of street directions and think of how the instruction "turn right" ends with you heading East if you were originally on the North "axis" but if you were originally on a South "axis" that same instruction of "turn right" would result in you heading West.

```
child::chapters/child::chapter[position()=2]/child::section[position()=2]
```

The above location path involves three location steps and contains two predicates. And as you can see, such unabbreviated relative location paths can become fairly long. The location path selects the second <section> element child of the second <chapter> element node that is a child of the <chapters> element node that is a child of the context node. In our example document, if the context node represented the <book> element, then the location path would return a node-set containing the second <section> element of Chapter 2. If the context node were anything other than the node representing the <book> element then an empty node-set would be returned.

Predicates Using Attributes

As well as selecting element nodes based on their position, we can also select them based on the type or value of their attributes. First, let's look at selecting an element on the basis of the presence of a particular type of attribute.

```
child::chapter[attribute::number]
```

This location path will select all element nodes that represent <chapter> elements which are children of the context node and which also possess a number attribute. In our example document, if the context node represented the <chapters> element, there are four element nodes that represent <chapter> elements that are children of the context node. All four of those children happen to possess a number attribute; therefore all four element nodes are included in the node-set. If there were an element node representing a <chapter> element that did not possess a number attribute, then it would be excluded from the node-set.

```
child::chapter[attribute::number][position()=3]
```

Here we see a combination of two predicates being used to make a more precise selection of element nodes than the preceding example, with the additional predicate [position()=3] refining the selection further. Now, when applied to our example document, our returned node-set is reduced from four <chapter> element nodes to just the <chapter> element node in the third position in document order.

```
child::chapter[attribute::title="XPath"]
```

This location path demonstrates the use of a predicate to choose elements on the basis of the presence of an attribute of a particular *value* for the element. In our example document, if the context node were the node representing the <chapters> element then there are a total of four child nodes representing <chapter> elements. Each of those <chapter> elements has an attribute called title, therefore all four <chapter> element nodes are included within the node-set selected by the location step child::chapter[attribute::title], but only one of those has a title attribute with a value as specified. Therefore, only one <chapter> element node is present after the full predicate is applied. Remember, this location path selects an element node on the basis of the value of one of its attributes. It does not select the attribute itself. The location path for selecting an attribute node was illustrated earlier in this section.

Predicate Order

We can combine predicates in different orders. Typically, that will mean selecting different nodes to be returned in the node-set. For example, if we reverse the order of the predicates used in the penultimate example in the previous section, we have:

```
child::chapter[position()=3][attribute::number]
```

The new location path selects the `<chapter>` element child of the context node which is in position 3 and if that third `<chapter>` element has an attribute node called number then the node will be included in the returned node-set. However, if that third `<chapter>` element node had no number attribute, then an empty node-set would be returned. In our example, if the context node were the element node representing the `<chapters>` element, then the third element node representing a `<chapter>` element would be selected. Since it does have a number attribute, it would be included in the returned node-set.

Let's take a look at another usage of relative locations paths that, quite possibly, will at first glance look similar to the example we have just been looking at.

```
child::chapter[child::title="Introduction to XSL"]
```

So what will this path give us in the returned node-set? Let's suppose our context node is the node representing the `<chapters>` element. There are four `<chapter>` element nodes as children. When we come to evaluate the predicate we need to be careful not to walk into a trap. One of the `<chapter>` elements has a `title` attribute with the value "Introduction to XSL" but there is no `<title>` element node that is a child of that or any of the other of the `<chapter>` element nodes. Remember that, in this case, the predicate refers to an element node called `title` whose string-value is equal to "Introduction to XSL". So, an empty node-set is returned.

If we did want to choose the element node representing Chapter 1, we would need to modify the predicate from `[child::title="Introduction to XSL"]` to `[attribute::title="Introduction to XSL"]`.

Predicates Using "and" and "or"

The two keywords and and or can be used in a predicate to combine the predicate choices we have seen so far.

```
child::*[self::chapter or self::appendix][position()=last()]
```

This location path introduces a choice within the first predicate to select either the `<chapter>` or `<appendix>` children of the context node, whichever appears last in document order.

The and keyword can be used in a similar way, to return nodes that match more than one node-test.

Having looked at a representative selection of examples using unabbreviated relative location paths, I'd now like to move on to look at some examples that use unabbreviated absolute location paths.

Unabbreviated Absolute Location Paths

In this section I will explain and illustrate the usage of unabbreviated syntax for absolute location paths. Remember that, like relative location paths, absolute location paths have a context and location steps. Absolute location paths can be viewed as a special case of relative location paths – a special case where the context node is consistently the root node.

> **All absolute location paths start with the forward slash character to indicate that they are absolute.**

A forward slash by itself selects the root node of the document containing the context node. If followed by a relative location path, such as those we have seen in the previous section, the node-set returned is that which the relative location path would select assuming that the root node of the document is the context node. Let's look at some examples.

```
/child::*
```

This location path selects all element nodes that are children of the root node. In a well-formed XML document there can be only one child element of the root node – the document element. In our sample XML document the returned node-set would hence only contain the <book> element node. The node representing the comment would not be included in the node-set since it is not an XPath element node. If, however, the location path had read /child::node() then the comment node would have been included in the returned node-set.

```
/descendant::paragraph
```

This unabbreviated absolute location path selects all the <paragraph> elements in the same document as the context node. In other words, it selects all the <paragraph> element nodes that are descendants of the root node. In our sample document the returned node-set would contain six nodes representing <paragraph> element nodes.

```
/descendant::section/child::paragraph
```

Now our location path selects all the <paragraph> elements that have a <section> element parent. In our sample document there are three <section> element nodes, which together have a total of six child <paragraph> element nodes. So the returned node-set would contain those six <paragraph> element nodes. For our example document, coincidentally, this example and the previous one return the same node-set, but that occurs solely because all the element nodes which represent <paragraph> elements are children of element nodes which represent <section> elements. If we also had <paragraph> elements within, for example, appendices, which were not children of nodes representing <section> elements, then the location path /descendant::paragraph would have included those, whereas the location path /descendant::section/child::paragraph would not.

```
/descendant::chapter[position()=3]
```

Here, the returned node-set contains the third <chapter> element node in the document. In our sample document, this will be the third <chapter> element node in document order, which in this case has a number attribute with the value "3".

Abbreviated Syntax

As you will have seen with more complex XPath location path examples in preceding sections, unabbreviated location paths can become quite lengthy. Since those same location paths may need to be included within the values of attributes of XSLT elements, it makes a lot of sense, in terms of readability and debugging, to have a more concise syntax to express the more commonly used location paths or expressions.

To the best of my knowledge, there is no discernible performance benefit obtained by using abbreviated syntax. The benefit is simply in being able to use a less verbose means of expressing an XPath location path. At times you may find that the available abbreviated syntax does not allow you to express the selection needs of your program, in which case you will need to use the unabbreviated syntax described earlier.

Abbreviated Relative Location Paths

One of the most commonly used axes in location paths is the `child` axis. In the abbreviated syntax the `child` keyword and double colon separator can be omitted: in effect, the default axis is the `child` axis. This gives us very succinct location paths when using the `child` axis, as shown in the following examples.

```
paragraph
```

The location path `paragraph` selects those element nodes that are children of the context node and also represent `<paragraph>` elements. The unabbreviated equivalent location path is `child::paragraph`. In general, any named child elements of the context node can be selected by using the element name on its own as the location path. The `*` location step can be used also:

```
*
```

Now, *all* element nodes that are children of the context node are selected. The unabbreviated equivalent location path is `child::*`.

```
text()
```

The above location path selects all text node children of the context node. The unabbreviated equivalent location path is `child::text()`.

```
.
```

The `.` location path selects the context node itself. The unabbreviated equivalent location path is `self::node()`.

```
..
```

The `..` location path selects the parent of the context node. The equivalent unabbreviated location path is `parent::node()`.

Just as the `child` axis can be markedly abbreviated, so too can the `attribute` axis by use of the 'at' @ symbol, as shown in a number of the following examples.

```
@number
```

`@number` selects the number attribute of the context node. The unabbreviated equivalent location path is `attribute::number`.

```
@*
```

The location path `@*` selects all the attributes of the context node. The unabbreviated equivalent location path is `attribute::*`.

```
..@number
```

Here, we are selecting the number attribute of the parent of the context node. The equivalent unabbreviated location path is `parent::node()/attribute::number`.

When it comes to the predicate, the `position()` function is the default function. So in:

```
paragraph[1]
```

the predicate `[1]` implies the default `position()` function to select the first `<paragraph>` child node of the context node. The unabbreviated equivalent location path is `child::paragraph[position()=1]`.

```
paragraph[last()]
```

Now we see a similar form to select the last `<paragraph>` child element node of the context node. The unabbreviated equivalent location path is `child::paragraph[position()=last()]`.

```
paragraph[@number="2"]
```

The above location path selects all the `<paragraph>` element children of the context node having a number attribute with value "2". The equivalent unabbreviated location path is `child::paragraph[attribute::number='2']`.

```
paragraph[@type="confidential"][3]
```

The location path now selects the third `<paragraph>` child of the context node having a type attribute of value "confidential". The equivalent unabbreviated location path is `child::paragraph[attribute::type="confidential"][position()=3]`.

```
paragraph[4][@security="confidential"]
```

This time we are selecting the fourth `<paragraph>` child of the context node if it has a security attribute with value of "confidential". The equivalent unabbreviated location path is `child::paragraph[position()=4][attribute::security="confidential"]`.

```
*/paragraph
```

This path selects all grandchildren element nodes of the context node that are also `<paragraph>` elements. The unabbreviated equivalent location path is `child::*/child::paragraph`.

```
chapter[title="XPath"]
```

The location path here selects the `<chapter>` element children of the context node having one or more `<title>` element children with string-value equal to "XPath". The equivalent unabbreviated location path is `child::chapter[child::title="XPath"]`.

```
chapter/section[1]/paragraph[3]
```

The location path above selects the third child <paragraph> element node of the first <section> element node that is a child of the <chapter> nodes that are children of the context node. The unabbreviated equivalent location path is `child::chapter/child::section[position()=1]/child::paragraph[position()=3]`.

```
.//paragraph
```

The double slash notation is another shortcut and indicates the use of `descendant::` rather than `child::`. The above line thus selects all the <paragraph> element nodes that are descendants of the context node. The equivalent unabbreviated location path is `self::node()/descendant-or-self::node()/child::paragraph`.

```
chapter//paragraph
```

This location path selects the nodes that represent the <paragraph> element descendants of the <chapter> element children of the context node. The equivalent unabbreviated location path is `child::chapter/descendant::paragraph`.

```
chapter[@number and @title]
```

The predicate `[@number and @title]` only allows <chapter> children of the context node that have both a `number` attribute and a `title` attribute into the result-set. The equivalent unabbreviated location path is `child::chapter[attribute::number and attribute::title]`.

Having looked at relative location paths that use the abbreviated XPath syntax, we're ready to move on to some examples of absolute location paths that use the abbreviated syntax.

Abbreviated Absolute Location Paths

```
/
```

The unabbreviated absolute location path syntax for the root node, the forward slash character, can hardly be abbreviated further and is the same in the abbreviated syntax.

```
//paragraph
```

The `//paragraph` location path selects all <paragraph> nodes which are descendants of the root node. Thus the location path selects all <paragraph> element nodes in the document. The unabbreviated equivalent location path is `/descendant::paragraph`.

```
/book/chapter[2]/section[1]/paragraph[3]
```

The above abbreviated absolute location path selects the third paragraph of the first section of the second chapter of the <book> element, the <book> element being a child of the root node. The unabbreviated equivalent location path is `/child::book/child::chapter[position()=2]/child::section[position()=1]/child::paragraph[position()=3]`. As you can see, the abbreviated syntax is substantially shorter than the unabbreviated for location paths such as this.

```
//chapter/section
```

Looking at this location path, we see it selects all `<section>` nodes that have `<chapter>` nodes as a parent element (and are descendants of the root node). In other words, it selects all `<section>` elements in the same document as the context node that have a `<chapter>` element parent. The unabbreviated equivalent location path is `/descendant::chapter/child::section`.

```
//chapter[@number="2"]
```

Here, we are selecting all `chapter` descendants of the root node with an attribute `number` with value "2". The equivalent unabbreviated location path is `/descendant::chapter[attribute::number='2']`.

Common Pitfalls

XPath syntax, partly because of the duplication of unabbreviated syntax in an abbreviated form and partly because of subtleties of the details of how an XSLT processor operates, has some location paths which must be constructed with great care to ensure that you make the selection(s) that you intended. In this section I will demonstrate a couple of examples where you need to be particularly careful.

❑   The location path `//paragraph[1]` does not mean the same as the location path `/descendant::paragraph[1]`. The former selects all descendant `<paragraph>` elements that are the first `<paragraph>` children of their parents. The latter selects the first descendant `<paragraph>` element in the source document. The unabbreviated syntax equivalent for the former location path is `/descendant-or-self::node()/child::paragraph[position()=1]`.

❑   Similarly, be careful to remember that certain axes work in document order, whereas other axes work in reverse document order.

❑   When using the `position()` function, remember that the first selected node returns 1 as the result of the `position()` function, not zero.

❑   Be careful to distinguish code that selects element nodes based on the value of their attributes such as `child::chapter[attribute::number]` from location paths which choose the attribute itself, such as `child::chapter/attribute::number`.

Worked Examples

So far in this chapter we have looked at XPath expressions or location paths in isolation. From this point on we will look at some very simple practical examples using XPath location paths within very simple XSLT transformations. Later chapters in this book will demonstrate more complex usage of XPath. Depending on how quickly you like to "get your hands dirty" you may prefer to try these examples straight away or return to this section after you have read some of the chapters covering the key points of XSLT.

I won't attempt in any of these examples to explain the full details of how XSLT works, but simply give you enough information to follow what is happening. The following chapters will explain the fundamentals of XSLT to you in greater detail.

Downloading and Installing Instant Saxon

If you are going to try out these examples you need a working XSLT processor. I have chosen Michael Kay's Instant Saxon XSLT processor since it, in accordance with its name, can be downloaded and installed on a 32-bit Windows machine almost "instantly". Installation details are given in Appendix E.

At the time of writing, Instant Saxon 6.0.2 is the most up to date *stable* version available for download. It was written to support the XSLT 1.0 Recommendation. None of the examples in this chapter require the use of the newer features suggested in XSLT 1.1, therefore you should be able to run this code with virtually any version of the available XSLT processors.

> *A full discussion of XSLT processors and similar tools is given in Appendix E. If you do not have access to a Windows machine or prefer to use another XSLT processor, refer to this appendix for relevant information.*

In the following examples I assume you have installed Instant Saxon into c:\InstantSaxon and that all XML source files and XSL stylesheets are also present in that directory.

All the examples that follow have been tested and work on Instant Saxon 6.0.2 on Windows 98 SE and Windows 2000. The examples used do not make use of any proprietary extensions to XSLT or XPath so should work unchanged using any XSLT/XPath compliant processor on any particular platform.

The XML Source

In order to show you how you can navigate around an XML source document, I shall pick a fairly simple example, yet one that has enough levels in the tree hierarchy to give us something to get our teeth into and try out some examples of what XPath can do.

The XML source document that I will use for the rest of this chapter follows: I have called the file Source.xml. If you are using Instant Saxon, be sure to save or copy this file to whichever directory contains your Instant Saxon installation in order to use the command lines as shown later in the chapter.

```xml
<?xml version='1.0'?>
<book>
  <title>Professional XSL</title>
  <chapters>

    <chapter>
      <chapterNo>2</chapterNo>
      <chapterTopic>XPath</chapterTopic>
      <chapterAuthor>Andrew Watt</chapterAuthor>
      <chapterSections>
        <chapterSection>Section 1</chapterSection>
        <chapterSection>Section 2</chapterSection>
        <chapterSection>Section 3</chapterSection>
        <chapterSection>Section 4</chapterSection>
        <chapterSection>Section 5</chapterSection>
        <chapterSection>Section 6</chapterSection>
      </chapterSections>
    </chapter>
```

```
      <chapter>
        <chapterNo>3</chapterNo>
        <chapterTopic>XSLT Basics</chapterTopic>
        <chapterAuthor>Paul Spencer</chapterAuthor>
        <chapterSections>
           <chapterSection>Section 1</chapterSection>
           <chapterSection>Section 2</chapterSection>
           <chapterSection>Section 3</chapterSection>
           <chapterSection>Section 4</chapterSection>
           <chapterSection>Section 5</chapterSection>
           <chapterSection>Section 6</chapterSection>
        </chapterSections>
      </chapter>

      <chapter>
        <chapterNo>4</chapterNo>
        <chapterTopic>Modular XSLT</chapterTopic>
        <chapterAuthor>Kurt Cagle</chapterAuthor>
        <chapterSections>
           <chapterSection>Section 1</chapterSection>
           <chapterSection>Section 2</chapterSection>
           <chapterSection>Section 3</chapterSection>
           <chapterSection>Section 4</chapterSection>
           <chapterSection>Section 5</chapterSection>
           <chapterSection>Section 6</chapterSection>
        </chapterSections>
      </chapter>

   </chapters>
</book>
```

So, let's use a very simple XSLT stylesheet to take a simple, non-selective look at the data contained in our XML source file. To do that we will use a stylesheet named `Root.xsl`. Again that file should be saved in the `c:\InstantSaxon` directory, or whichever directory you chose for the installation of Instant Saxon.

```
<?xml version='1.0'?>
<xsl:stylesheet version="1.0"
                xmlns:xsl="http://www.w3.org/1999/XSL/Transform">

<xsl:template match="/">
  <xsl:apply-templates/>
</xsl:template>

</xsl:stylesheet>
```

When applied to the XML source document, the stylesheet should display the content of each element in the whole XML document in turn due to the application of default templates to each element of the XML source document (see the next chapter for a more detailed review of default templates).

To create this output using Instant Saxon, open an MS DOS window, change to the directory in which you installed Instant Saxon and then issue the following command on the command line:

saxon Source.xml Root.xsl > Root.txt

It is important that both the `Source.xml` source file and the `Root.xsl` stylesheet are present in the Instant Saxon directory. If they are not, the full document paths will need to be specified to avoid Instant Saxon generating an error.

The following file, `Root.txt`, should be produced (although the appearance may vary a little between text editors):

```
<?xml version="1.0" encoding="utf-8"?>
Professional XSL

2
XPath
Andrew Watt

Section 1
Section 2
Section 3
Section 4
Section 5
Section 6




3
XSLT Basics
Paul Spencer

Section 1
Section 2
Section 3
Section 4
Section 5
Section 6




4
Modular XSLT
Kurt Cagle

Section 1
Section 2
Section 3
Section 4
Section 5
Section 6
```

You will notice that the output file is hardly a thing of beauty and that there is a lot of extraneous whitespace. But don't worry about that. Handling of whitespace in XSLT has some non-obvious subtleties that will be explained to you in later chapters. Our only purpose at the moment is to make sure that your installation of Instant Saxon is working properly. If you are using any other XSLT processor the output may look slightly different.

Notice that the content of every element in the XML source document is reproduced. Perhaps surprisingly, you will see an XML declaration at the beginning of the output file (XML is the default output method of Instant Saxon), despite the file suffix being .txt.

So how does this work? In the XSLT stylesheet the line:

```
<xsl:template match="/">
```

does much of the work. What does it mean? The <xsl:template> element's match attribute has a value which is an XPath location path. It selects the root node in the source document. The <xsl:apply-templates/> element which follows causes the list of content of the elements in the source document to be output, by invoking the default templates which the XSLT processor applies when no other template is specified.

Typically, we would want to be able to filter/select which source elements are used and/or process these in ways that may differ for each element in the source document. XSLT provides ways to do that, as you will see in later chapters. Ironically, to be able to show you in real code how to use XSLT/XPath to select elements to display, I first need to show you how to avoid elements in the source document being displayed due to the default behavior of the XSLT processor.

If you wondered why there are so few real code examples in the XPath and XSLT Recommendations now you know. It isn't the most natural thing to teach you first how to suppress the default output. But that's what we need to do now.

Creating a Default Template

So, if we are going to be able to use XPath selectively, how are we going to get rid of all those unwanted elements? Well, the default behavior of the XSLT processor only operates in the absence of a more specific template to match a node. So let's write a template for every node in the source document. The following XSLT stylesheet, MatchAll.xsl, includes just such a template:

```
<?xml version='1.0'?>
<xsl:stylesheet version="1.0"
                xmlns:xsl="http://www.w3.org/1999/XSL/Transform">

<xsl:template match="/">
  <xsl:apply-templates/>
</xsl:template>

<xsl:template match="*">
<!-- This template matches all elements other than the root which is
explicitly matched by the first template above
As it is empty nothing is output for elements other than the root. -->
</xsl:template>

</xsl:stylesheet>
```

To apply this stylesheet to the Source.xml document enter the following at the command prompt:

saxon Source.xml MatchAll.xsl > Matched.txt

So what happens? How does it work? Broadly what happens is this. The root node is matched by the first template which tells the XSLT processor to recursively apply any other templates to children of the root node. Since this is done recursively, the children of the children are also examined to see if they match any template. All the element nodes will match the template `<xsl:template match="*">` (since it contains the XPath location path `*`) so it is applied to each element node in the source document. The XSLT processor recognizes that for each element node the `<xsl:template match="*">` provides a higher priority match than the default template. So, for each descendant of the root node, the template in effect says "do nothing" thus suppressing the default behavior of the XSLT processor.

If you want to see if it works try it: your output file, `Matched.xml`, should look like this:

```
<?xml version="1.0" encoding="utf-8"?>
```

So it works!

Now that we know how to use XPath and XSLT to produce an empty output document we are ready to use more specific XPath expressions to demonstrate how XPath is used.

Using Context

As I explained earlier in the chapter, all XPath expressions are evaluated according to the applicable context. So in our XSLT code we need to create a specific context. Let's choose the `<chapterTopic>` element as our intended context. To create our selected context we have to select the node representing the `<chapterTopic>` element. We can achieve this with the absolute abbreviated location path `/book/chapters/chapter/chapterTopic`. The location path can be used in an XSLT `<xsl:template>` element to extract the chapter topics from our `Source.xml` file. In the following stylesheet, `Topic.xsl`, the complete location path is not used at once but is split over four templates.

```
<?xml version='1.0'?>
<!-- Topic.xsl -->

<xsl:stylesheet version="1.0"
                xmlns:xsl="http://www.w3.org/1999/XSL/Transform">

<xsl:template match="/">
  <xsl:apply-templates/>
</xsl:template>

<xsl:template match="*">
<!-- This template matches all elements other than the root which is
explicitly matched by the first template above
As it is empty nothing is output for elements other than the root unless any of
the following templates match -->
</xsl:template>

<xsl:template match="book">
  <xsl:apply-templates/>
</xsl:template>

<xsl:template match="chapters">
  <xsl:apply-templates/>
</xsl:template>
```

```
<xsl:template match="chapter">
  <xsl:apply-templates/>
</xsl:template>

<xsl:template match="chapterTopic">
  <xsl:value-of select="."/>
</xsl:template>

</xsl:stylesheet>
```

At the command prompt we type:

Saxon Source.xml Topic.xsl > Topic.txt

And the output XML file we get looks like this:

```
<?xml version="1.0" encoding="utf-8"?>




XPath




XSLT Basics




Modular XSLT
```

Visually it's horrible isn't it? But it has reproduced the content of each of the `<chapterTopic>` elements of our source XML document, which is what we wanted. Yes, there is a lot of unwanted whitespace too. You will learn about how to control whitespace later in the book.

The stylesheet (very crude though it is) moved the context from the `<book>` element node to the `<chapters>` element node, then to the `<chapter>` element node, and finally to the `<chapterTopic>` node. Once the context is the `<chapterTopic>` element then we can use the `<xsl:value-of>` element to display the value of each `chapterTopic` in turn, as shown above.

Adding Content

Let's adapt the `Topic.xsl` stylesheet to display the chapter numbers and authors as well. We add the code snippets indicated by the highlighted sections below to our stylesheet, and save it as `NoAut.xsl`:

```xml
<?xml version='1.0'?>
<!-- NoAut.xsl -->
<xsl:stylesheet version="1.0"
                xmlns:xsl="http://www.w3.org/1999/XSL/Transform">

<xsl:template match="/">
  <xsl:apply-templates/>
</xsl:template>

<xsl:template match="*">
<!-- This template matches all elements other than the root which is
explicitly matched by the first template above
As it is empty nothing is output for elements other than the root unless any of
the following templates match -->
</xsl:template>

<xsl:template match="book">
  <xsl:apply-templates/>
</xsl:template>

<xsl:template match="chapters">
  <xsl:apply-templates/>
</xsl:template>

<xsl:template match="chapter">
  <xsl:apply-templates/>
</xsl:template>

<xsl:template match="/book/chapters/chapter/chapterNo">
  <xsl:value-of select="."/>
</xsl:template>

<xsl:template match="/book/chapters/chapter/chapterTopic">
  <xsl:value-of select="."/>
</xsl:template>

<xsl:template match="/book/chapters/chapter/chapterAuthor">
  <xsl:value-of select="."/>
</xsl:template>

</xsl:stylesheet>
```

Note that templates 3, 4 and 5 are still required here, because no `select` attribute is given for the `apply-templates` elements so only child nodes are searched for each time. These templates are thus needed to progress down the document. Also note that the `match` attributes in templates 6, 7 and 8 use absolute location paths in this case.

Issue the following Instant Saxon command on the command line:

saxon Source.xml NoAut.xsl > NoAut.txt

The output file, `NoAut.xml` should look like the following:

```
<?xml version="1.0" encoding="utf-8"?>




2
XPath
Andrew Watt




3
XSLT Basics
Paul Spencer




4
Modular XSLT
Kurt Cagle
```

Again our output is not beautiful, but the simple XPath location paths we used allowed us to selectively display element content in our document. Remember we first had to suppress the default behavior of the XSLT processor and then create templates to display the chapter number, chapter topic and chapter authors for each of the three chapters.

Note that the example file I chose, `Source.xml`, only contains elements: there are no attributes. In addition you have yet to learn the basics of XSLT. I hope, however, that these examples have illustrated to you some simple uses of XPath location paths.

If, after you read later chapters, you feel you have grasped how to move the context node using successive `<xsl:template>` elements containing only `<xsl:apply-template>` elements, you may feel it appropriate to experiment further with a variety of location paths.

However, if these examples, simple though they are, have seemed a little too much at this stage then move on to Chapter 3 and return later to experiment with XPath when you feel more comfortable with XSLT itself.

XPointer, XLink & XQuery

The primary focus of this chapter has been on the relevance of XPath as an adjunct technology to XSLT. However, XPath also has relevance, indeed increasing importance, with respect to other emerging XML technologies: XPointer, XLink and XQuery.

XPointer

The XML Pointer Language, XPointer, is currently a "Last Call" Working Draft at the W3C. The January 2001 XPointer draft can be viewed at http://www.w3.org/TR/2001/WD-xptr-20010108. Any future updates to that draft may be viewed at http://www.w3.org/TR/xptr.

XPointer is built on a foundation of XPath expressions, but has extensions to the data model and in the functions supported. For example, XPointer broadens the XPath notion of a **node** to include points and ranges. The extended concept is called, in XPointer, a **location**.

XPointer's extensions to XPath allow it to:

❑   Address points and ranges as well as whole nodes

❑   Locate information by string matching

❑   Use addressing expressions in URI references as fragment identifiers (after suitable escaping)

Currently, since XPointer is still at Working Draft, implementations are few and some implement only part of the draft specification. A list of the available full or partial XPointer implementations may be viewed at http://www.w3.org/XML/Linking.

Scalable Vector Graphics, SVG, implements a small subset of XPointer, in conjunction with simple XLinks (see next section).

XLink

The XML Linking Language, XLink, is also worth a brief mention since XPointer makes use of XLink functionality in locating XML document fragments. XLink is intended to provide linking functionality similar to that provided by the HTML/XHTML <a> element, but also provides a range of more complex linking structures. Detailed consideration of those is beyond the scope of this chapter.

Further information on XLink, currently at Proposed Recommendation stage, is located at http://www.w3.org/TR/2000/PR-xlink-20001220/. When the final Recommendation is released, it will be located at http://www.w3.org/TR/xlink.

Within SVG, XLink is used with the limited subset of XPointer that is implemented in SVG to make selections. For example, SVG uses XLink and XPointer to make available pre-defined elements, as in the following example:

```
<?xml version="1.0" standalone="no"?>
<!DOCTYPE svg PUBLIC "-//W3C//DTD SVG 20001102//EN"
"http://www.w3.org/TR/2000/CR-SVG-20001102/DTD/svg-20001102.dtd">
<svg width="500" height="300">
  <desc>Example showing simple use of XLink and XPointer within SVG.</desc>
  <defs>
    <g id="MyGraphic">
      <desc>MyGraphic - a simple graphic consisting of four rectangles.</desc>
      <rect x="20" y="20" width="16" height="16"/>
      <rect x="40" y="20" width="16" height="16"/>
      <rect x="20" y="40" width="16" height="16"/>
      <rect x="40" y="40" width="16" height="16"/>
    </g>
  </defs>
  <use x="45" y="10" xlink:href="#MyGraphic" />
</svg>
```

The code:

```
xlink:href="#MyGraphic"
```

is the so-called "bare names" form of XPointer and can also be written as:

```
xlink:href="#xpointer(id('MyGraphic'))"
```

At present the former works well with the Adobe SVG Viewer version 2 Beta 4, but the latter does not. It is likely that such problems will be resolved by the time you read this. However, full availability of complete XPointer implementations may well take a little longer.

Further information on XLink implementations is located at http://www.w3.org/XML/Linking.

XQuery

It may well be that XQuery will be the most important implementation of, or development from, XPath. Given that increasing volumes of information are being held as XML, it is of enormous importance that efficient means to query that information are developed. Just as XPath was extended to support XSLT and XPointer, so XPath can be expected to be further extended within the XQuery functionality.

The first public Working Draft of the Requirements for XPath 2.0 has recently been released, and it is clear that improvements in functionality within XPath to use XML Schema and XQuery are important items on the agenda for XPath's development.

The XML Query Language, XQuery, is currently at first public Working Draft stage, so its details are particularly subject to change, but XQuery is highlighted here because of its likely long-term importance.

The XQuery drafts (there are five inter-related documents) are:

- ❑ XQuery – A Query Language for XML at http://www.w3.org/TR/2001/WD-xquery-20010215
- ❑ XML Query Data Model at http://www.w3.org/TR/query-datamodel
- ❑ XML Query Algebra at http://www.w3.org/TR/query-algebra
- ❑ XML Query Requirements at http://www.w3.org/TR/xmlquery-req
- ❑ XML Query Use Cases at http://www.w3.org/TR/xmlquery-use-cases

A joint task force between the XSL Working Group (responsible for XPath and XSLT) and the XQuery Working Group has been asked to ensure, as far as is possible, compatible data models, syntax etc. between XPath 2.0, XSLT 2.0 and XQuery 1.0.

Thus, while today (and particularly within the context of this book) the primary importance of XPath is as a foundation to XSLT, I hope you can see that the importance of XPath is likely to grow considerably as the XPointer, XLink and XQuery technologies reach full implementation.

Summary

In this chapter you were introduced to many of the aspects of the XML Path Language, XPath, which you are likely to use with Extensible Stylesheet Language Transformations, XSLT. We looked at:

❑ The purpose of XPath

❑ XPath Syntax in its various forms (abbreviated and unabbreviated, relative and absolute)

❑ The XPath Data Model

❑ XPath Functions

We also created a simple skeleton XSLT stylesheet, which will allow you to try out your understanding of XPath. In the next chapter we'll look at the core aspects of the XSLT language, and will further see the role that XPath plays.

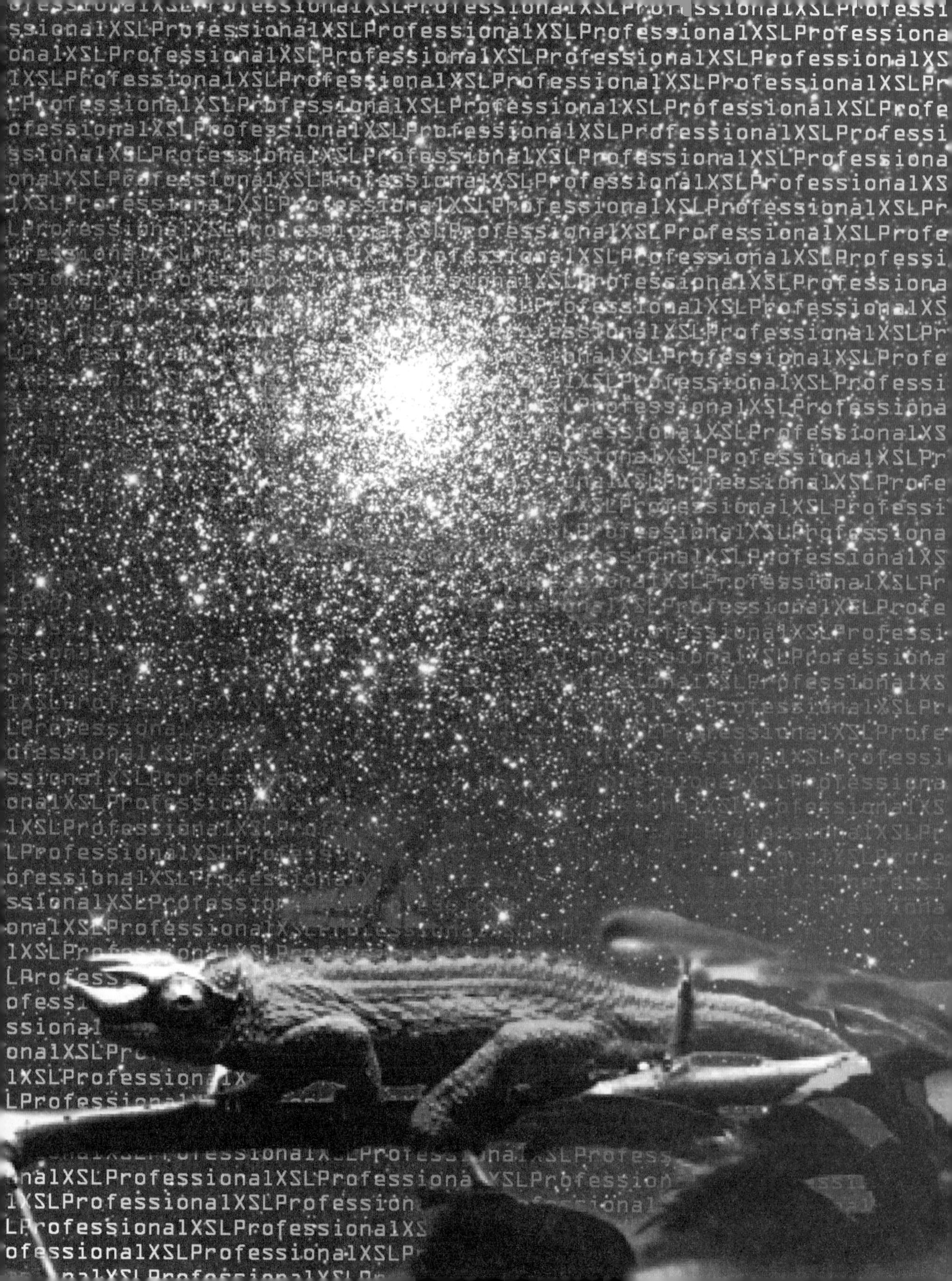

3

XSLT Basics

In this chapter, we will build on Chapters 1 and 2 to provide you with enough information to start building useful XSLT stylesheets. I will introduce a number of the elements that make up the language, providing examples of their use. We will also look at a few of the functions built into the language and see how XSLT manages namespaces, whitespace and some other important issues.

To illustrate the concepts I introduce, we will work mainly with two documents, one that is textual in content, and one that is more data oriented. The former is a Shakespeare play (Hamlet), and the latter is a book catalog that could, for example, have been extracted from a relational database. Both documents are given in the code download for the chapter.

By the end of the chapter, you will:

- ❑ have a clearer picture of the processing model of XSLT
- ❑ know the difference between push and pull model stylesheets, and when to use each
- ❑ understand the use of the most important XSLT elements
- ❑ understand the use of a few of the built-in functions
- ❑ understand the basic rules of how XSLT copes when there are conflicts in the stylesheet
- ❑ know more about the built-in template rules and how to over ride them

XSLT Processing

Before delving into the detail of XSLT elements and functions, let's start by looking in detail at how an XSLT processor, such as XT, Saxon or MSXML3, processes a document. We will look at the model from an abstract view – becoming an XSLT processor ourselves and working our way through a document and stylesheet. We'll then look at the two fundamental ways in which this model can be used.

More information on these processors can be found in Appendix E. Later in this chapter I will be mainly using XT to process XSLT stylesheets, but any of these processors can be used. XT is similar in use to Instant Saxon, which was introduced in Chapter 2.

The XSLT Processing Model

Although we often talk of an XSLT processor as something that turns one XML document into another (or into an HTML or text document), this is not strictly true. The specification actually talks in terms of a **source tree** (or **input** tree) and a **result tree**. There is therefore an assumption that, for example, if we are starting from a text document rather than an existing DOM tree, it has been turned into some sort of tree structure before the XSLT processor starts its work, and that the result tree will be used for further processing or serialized in some way to create another text document.

The model, including formatting, therefore looks like this:

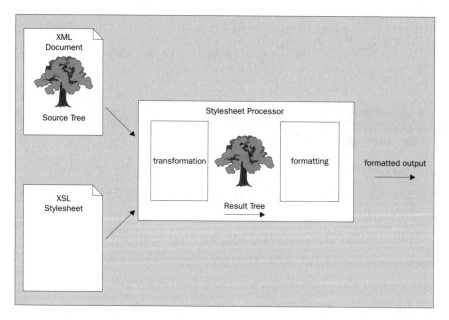

This concept is simple enough. But you will have read in Chapter 1 that XSLT is a declarative language and uses templates. How does this work in practice? Let's have a look at a simple XML document and stylesheet, and walk through the processing.

Processing a Document

Here is my XML document – it is the book catalog that you will be familiar with if you have read *Professional XML* (Wrox Press, ISBN 1-861003-11-0), although I have cut it down to just two books, removed some elements and renamed it `shortcatalog.xml`:

```xml
<?xml version="1.0" encoding="utf-8" standalone="yes"?>
<Catalog>
  <Book>
    <Title>Designing Distributed Applications</Title>
    <Authors>
      <Author>Stephen Mohr</Author>
    </Authors>
    <PubDate>May 1999</PubDate>
    <ISBN>1-861002-27-0</ISBN>
    <Price>$49.99</Price>
  </Book>
  <Book>
    <Title>Professional ASP 3.0</Title>
    <Authors>
      <Author>Alex Homer</Author>
      <Author>Brian Francis</Author>
      <Author>David Sussman</Author>
    </Authors>
    <PubDate>October 1999</PubDate>
    <ISBN>1-861002-61-0</ISBN>
    <Price>$59.99</Price>
  </Book>
</Catalog>
```

We'll look at the XSLT stylesheet we use to transform this document shortly, but let's now become an XSLT processor and see what happens. We already know that, as an XSLT processor, we cannot use the source XML, but need a tree representation based on the structure and content of the document. So here it is:

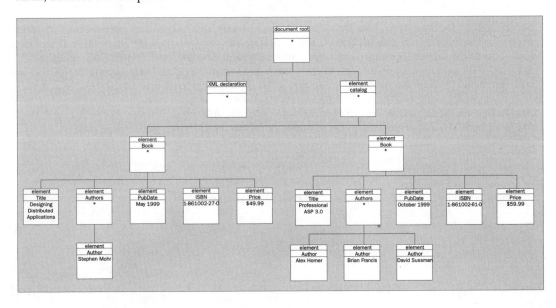

Each node is described by a block of three rectangles. In the top rectangle is the node type, with the node name in the rectangle below it. The bottom rectangle contains an asterisk if the node has element content, and the text if it has text content.

At the top of the tree is the **root node** or **document root**. Don't confuse this with the **root element** (or **document element**) familiar from XML. The document root is the base of the document, and has the document element (<Catalog>) as a child. It also has the XML declaration and any other top-level nodes (which might be comments or processing instructions) as children. The document element contains two child <Book> elements, and these hold the information about the books.

So now we have the tree structure, we can start to populate and process it. This is the processing model we will use:

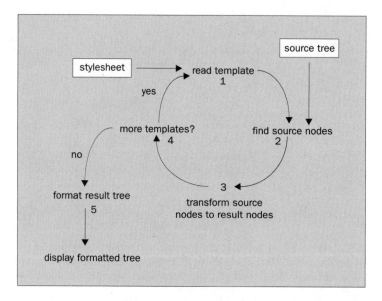

Before XSL processing starts, both the source document and XSLT stylesheet must be loaded into the processor's memory. How this happens is dependent on the implementation. One option is that both are loaded as DOM documents under the control of a program. Another option is that the stylesheet is referenced by a processing instruction in the source XML document. IE5 can operate in this way, and will automatically load the stylesheet when the XML document is loaded.

And here is the XSLT stylesheet (TitleAndDate.xsl) we will use to process the shortcatalog.xml to get a new XML document listing just the titles of the books and their publication dates:

```
<?xml version="1.0" encoding="utf-8" standalone="yes"?>
<xsl:stylesheet
   version="1.0"
   xmlns:xsl="http://www.w3.org/1999/XSL/Transform">

<xsl:template match="/">
   <xsl:apply-templates/>
</xsl:template>
```

```
<xsl:template match="Catalog">
  <Books>
    <xsl:apply-templates/>
  </Books>
</xsl:template>

<xsl:template match="Book">
  <Book>
    <xsl:value-of select="Title"/>, <xsl:value-of select="PubDate"/>
  </Book>
</xsl:template>

</xsl:stylesheet>
```

Once the documents are in memory, we can start our processing. The XSL processor starts by reading the template for the document root from the stylesheet (step 1). Here is that template:

```
<xsl:template match="/">
  <xsl:apply-templates/>
</xsl:template>
```

The first line indicates that it is a template, with a `match` attribute to indicate the node or nodes it is matching. The attribute value is an XPath expression, in this case just being the / to indicate the document root.

Working round the diagram, at step 2 we find the source node (strictly, the node-set, but here it will comprise a single node) in the source tree that the template matches. This will be the document root. The second line of the template moves us on to step 3 and indicates that we will execute whatever templates apply to the children of this node. The document root has two children – the XML declaration and the <Catalog> element.

Looking through the stylesheet, there is no template for the XML declaration (XSLT does not give us access to this node), but there is one for the <Catalog> element. Processing a document using XSL is a recursive process, and we are now back to step 1 with a new template. Here is the template:

```
<xsl:template match="Catalog">
  <Books>
    <xsl:apply-templates/>
  </Books>
</xsl:template>
```

This contains some text, which looks like another element called <Books>. As our diagram indicates, we will transform this into a result node at step 3. It also contains an <xsl:apply-templates/> instruction, so we will again look for templates to execute matching the child nodes.

The only children of the <Catalog> element are the two <Book> elements, so we will read the template for these elements and go round the circle again. Here is the template:

```
<xsl:template match="Book">
  <Book>
    <xsl:value-of select="Title"/>, <xsl:value-of select="PubDate"/>
  </Book>
</xsl:template>
```

This time, for each <Book> element we are creating a <Book> element in the result tree. Into this, we are placing the value of the <Title> element, then some literal text comprising a comma and a space, then the value of the <PubDate> element.

> *Note that the value of an element in XSLT is not the same as with the Document Object Model (DOM). With the DOM, the value of an element is always null, while in XSLT it is the text between the start and end tags.*

At this point we stop since we have no more <xsl:apply-templates/> elements. This means that no other elements in the source document will get processed, but then that's what we wanted.

So how are we constructing the result tree? Let's work this one from the bottom up. When we execute the template for <Book>, we create the new <Book> element, and then replace the line:

```
<xsl:value-of select="Title"/>, <xsl:value-of select="PubDate"/>
```

with the result of evaluating the statements. For the first book, that will be:

```
Designing Distributed Applications, May 1999
```

So overall, our result node will look like:

```
<Book>Designing Distributed Applications, May 1999</Book>
```

Since we have two <Book> elements in the source tree, we will get two <Book> elements in the result tree:

```
<Book>Designing Distributed Applications, May 1999</Book>
<Book>Professional ASP 3.0, October 1999</Book>
```

Similarly, in the template for <Catalog>, we will replace the line:

```
<xsl:apply-templates/>
```

with the results generated by executing the instruction. This will put the two <Book> elements we have created inside a <Books> element. The result tree now looks like this:

```
<Books>
   <Book>Designing Distributed Applications, May 1999</Book>
   <Book>Professional ASP 3.0, October 1999</Book>
</Books>
```

I have added the line breaks and formatting to make the output look better.

Moving back to the first template we came across, the one for the document root, we can see that this adds no further content, so our output is exactly as I have just shown.

In our processing model, we now break out of our cycle and format the output (step 5). In this case, we have no formatting, so there is no further processing. Later in this book, we will see how we can format using a standard web-browser and HTML, or using the Formatting Objects part of the XSL specification (XSL-FO).

Note that the XSLT specification says that "… XSLT is not intended as a completely general-purpose XML transformation language. Rather it is designed primarily for the kinds of transformations that are needed when XSLT is used as part of XSL." However, in the majority of cases, XSLT is used independently of XSL-FO, just as we are doing here and will do again when we produce HTML using XSLT. The specification acknowledges this with the statement "… XSLT is also designed to be used independently of XSL."

Using any of the processors described in Appendix E we can run the XSLT stylesheet with the XML. For example, if we now invoke XT with the command line:

xt shortcatalog.xml TitleAndDate.xsl TitleAndDate.xml

we produce a file `TitleAndDate.xml` with the content:

```
<?xml version="1.0" encoding="utf-8"?>
<Books>
  <Book>Designing Distributed Applications, May 1999</Book>
  <Book>Professional ASP 3.0, October 1999</Book>
</Books>
```

XT has put an XML declaration at the top, but otherwise it is exactly as we generated ourselves.

Push and Pull Models

In HTML, there is only one way of applying styles with an external stylesheet, and that is by using **Cascading Style Sheets (CSS)**. In this case, the structure of the output is usually determined by the source HTML, while the CSS stylesheet determines the appearance of each item within that structure. There are exceptions to this – some aspects of CSS2, such as tables and the use of absolute positioning, allow the stylesheet to control the structure of the output. Unfortunately, CSS2 is not well supported by browsers, and absolute positioning can give a display that is very dependent on the size of the browser window.

The CSS model can be referred to as a **push model**. The source document controls the format, while the stylesheet controls the appearance within that structure. An alternative model is a **pull model**, where the stylesheet provides the structure, and the XML document acts as a data source. As we will see in a moment, XSLT can support both push and pull models, each being appropriate in different circumstances.

The Push Model with CSS

This extract from a Shakespearean play (`HamletExtract.xml`) will be used in the following samples to illustrate the push model of stylesheet design:

```
<?xml version="1.0"?>
<EXTRACT>
<ACT><TITLE>ACT I</TITLE>

<SCENE><TITLE>SCENE I.  Elsinore. A platform before the castle.</TITLE>
<STAGEDIR>FRANCISCO at his post. Enter to him BERNARDO</STAGEDIR>

<SPEECH>
<SPEAKER>BERNARDO</SPEAKER>
<LINE>Who's there?</LINE>
</SPEECH>
```

```
<SPEECH>
<SPEAKER>FRANCISCO</SPEAKER>
<LINE>Nay, answer me: stand, and unfold yourself.</LINE>
</SPEECH>

<SPEECH>
<SPEAKER>BERNARDO</SPEAKER>
<LINE>Long live the king!</LINE>
</SPEECH>

<SPEECH>
<SPEAKER>FRANCISCO</SPEAKER>
<LINE>Bernardo?</LINE>
</SPEECH>

<SPEECH>
<SPEAKER>BERNARDO</SPEAKER>
<LINE>He.</LINE>
</SPEECH>

<SPEECH>
<SPEAKER>FRANCISCO</SPEAKER>
<LINE>You come most carefully upon your hour.</LINE>
</SPEECH>

<SPEECH>
<SPEAKER>BERNARDO</SPEAKER>
<LINE>'Tis now struck twelve; get thee to bed, Francisco.</LINE>
</SPEECH>

<SPEECH>
<SPEAKER>FRANCISCO</SPEAKER>
<LINE>For this relief much thanks: 'tis bitter cold,</LINE>
<LINE>And I am sick at heart.</LINE>
</SPEECH>

<SPEECH>
<SPEAKER>BERNARDO</SPEAKER>
<LINE>Have you had quiet guard?</LINE>
</SPEECH>

<SPEECH>
<SPEAKER>FRANCISCO</SPEAKER>
<LINE>Not a mouse stirring.</LINE>
</SPEECH>

<SPEECH>
<SPEAKER>BERNARDO</SPEAKER>
<LINE>Well, good night.</LINE>
<LINE>If you do meet Horatio and Marcellus,</LINE>
<LINE>The rivals of my watch, bid them make haste.</LINE>
</SPEECH>

<SPEECH>
<SPEAKER>FRANCISCO</SPEAKER>
<LINE>I think I hear them. Stand, ho! Who's there?</LINE>
</SPEECH>
</SCENE>
</ACT>
</EXTRACT>
```

Jon Bosak has marked up all of Shakespeare's plays in XML. An index to them can be found at http://www.andrew.cmu.edu/user/akj/shakespeare and a zip file to download them all at http://metalab.unc.edu/bosak/xml/eg/shaks200.zip.

With a play such as this, we will generally want our display to follow the structure of the source. We can style the XML with CSS in just the same way as we would with HTML. All we have to do is associate styles with element names as we have here in `Hamlet.css`:

```css
ACT TITLE {
   display:block;
   font-size:24pt;
   font-weight:bold;
   margin-bottom:12pt;
}

SCENE TITLE {
   display:block;
   font-size:16pt;
   margin-bottom:6pt;
}

STAGEDIR {
   display:block;
   font-style:italic;
   margin-top:6pt;
   margin-bottom:6pt;
}

SPEAKER {
   display:block;
}

LINE {
   display:block;
   margin-left:2em;
}
```

If we add a line to reference the CSS stylesheet near the top of the file `HamletExtract.xml` to create `HamletCss.xml`:

```xml
<?xml version="1.0"?>
<?xml-stylesheet type="text/css" href="Hamlet.css"?>
<EXTRACT>
<ACT><TITLE>ACT I</TITLE>
```

then we can view the file in IE5 or Netscape 6. This is the result in IE5:

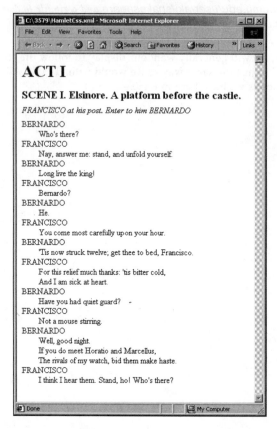

As you can see, the order of the text in the display is the same as that in the XML source, which is what we mean by a push model.

If you are used to using CSS with HTML, you might have noticed in particular the statement:

```
display:block;
```

within each style rule. This is used here to ensure that each of the elements starts on a new line. The alternatives are display:inline and display:none. You probably don't use these in HTML, as HTML contains elements such as <DIV> and <P> that are implicitly block elements, while others, such as <I> and <B>, are implicitly inline elements. However, with XML, elements do not contain implicit display features like this, so the line is essential. I will not discuss the rest of the CSS here, since it is covered in more detail in Chapter 9.

The Push Model with XSLT

So how do we achieve the same sort of effect with XSLT? It is not difficult to create an identical display to that above by using XSLT to transform the XML into a document that combines HTML and CSS. We will be seeing that later in the book, but for now we will create a simple HTML page.

We can do this easily since both HTML, as an application of SGML, and XML, as a subset of SGML, use similar formats. The important thing is that our XSLT stylesheet is well-formed XML. My file, Hamlet.xsl, is one such example:

```
<xsl:stylesheet
  version="1.0"
  xmlns:xsl="http://www.w3.org/1999/XSL/Transform">

<xsl:template match="*|/"><xsl:apply-templates/></xsl:template>

<xsl:template match="EXTRACT">
  <HTML>
    <HEAD>
      <TITLE>Hamlet</TITLE>
    </HEAD>
    <BODY>
      <xsl:apply-templates/>
    </BODY>
  </HTML>
</xsl:template>

<xsl:template match="ACT/TITLE">
  <H1><xsl:value-of select="."/></H1>
</xsl:template>

<xsl:template match="SCENE/TITLE">
  <H2><xsl:value-of select="."/></H2>
</xsl:template>

<xsl:template match="STAGEDIR">
  <P><I><xsl:value-of select="."/></I></P>
</xsl:template>

<xsl:template match="SPEAKER">
  <DIV><xsl:value-of select="."/></DIV>
</xsl:template>

<xsl:template match="LINE">
  <DIV><xsl:value-of select="."/></DIV>
</xsl:template>

</xsl:stylesheet>
```

If we change the top of our XML document HamletExtract.xml to use the above transformation like this:

```
<?xml version="1.0"?>
<?xml-stylesheet type="text/xsl" href="Hamlet.xsl"?>
<EXTRACT>
<ACT><TITLE>ACT I</TITLE>
```

and save it as HamletXsl.xml, we can view the result in IE5.

Note that to view this directly, you will need to have MSXML3 installed in replace mode (see Appendix E). Otherwise, you can just carry out the transformation using XT or Saxon, and view the resulting HTML.

This is the result in IE5 (this time, you cannot use Netscape since the processing instruction we have used is specific to IE):

and this is the HTML that is generated by XT – that is, using the command:

xt HamletExtract.xml Hamlet.xsl Hamlet.html

```
<HTML>
<HEAD>
<TITLE>Hamlet</TITLE>
</HEAD>
<BODY>
<H1>ACT I</H1>
```

```
<H2>SCENE I.  Elsinore. A platform before the castle.</H2>
<P>
<I>FRANCISCO at his post. Enter to him BERNARDO</I>
</P>
<DIV>BERNARDO</DIV>
<DIV>Who's there?</DIV>

<DIV>FRANCISCO</DIV>
<DIV>Nay, answer me: stand, and unfold yourself.</DIV>

<DIV>BERNARDO</DIV>
<DIV>Long live the king!</DIV>

<DIV>FRANCISCO</DIV>
<DIV>Bernardo?</DIV>

<DIV>BERNARDO</DIV>
<DIV>He.</DIV>

<DIV>FRANCISCO</DIV>
<DIV>You come most carefully upon your hour.</DIV>

<DIV>BERNARDO</DIV>
<DIV>'Tis now struck twelve; get thee to bed, Francisco.</DIV>

<DIV>FRANCISCO</DIV>
<DIV>For this relief much thanks: 'tis bitter cold,</DIV>
<DIV>And I am sick at heart.</DIV>

<DIV>BERNARDO</DIV>
<DIV>Have you had quiet guard?</DIV>

<DIV>FRANCISCO</DIV>
<DIV>Not a mouse stirring.</DIV>

<DIV>BERNARDO</DIV>
<DIV>Well, good night.</DIV>
<DIV>If you do meet Horatio and Marcellus,</DIV>
<DIV>The rivals of my watch, bid them make haste.</DIV>

<DIV>FRANCISCO</DIV>
<DIV>I think I hear them. Stand, ho! Who's there?</DIV>

</BODY>
</HTML>
```

I have used <DIV> elements rather than, say, <P> elements, as they do not add vertical space. However, it is easy to change this in the XSLT stylesheet if you prefer a different appearance. In later chapters, we will use CSS to provide more control over the display format.

So how did this work? Let's work through again from the root node. As before, the template for the root node causes all templates for its children to be executed. In this case, we will execute the template for the <EXTRACT> element next. This simply builds the structure of our HTML page, then executes any templates matching its children such that results are inserted inside an HTML <BODY> element.

Most of the other templates are self-explanatory and build up the HTML page. But what happens when we look for a template that matches the <SPEECH> element? In fact, we have no template for this element, but we do have a template with match="*|/". In XPath, the pipestem symbol (|) acts as an "or" and the asterisk means match any element. We will therefore execute this template for the SPEECH element. Our template reaches the children of this element (<SPEAKER> and <LINE>) because of the <xsl:apply-templates/> in the template. How do we know not to apply this template for other elements, such as <LINE>, which have their own templates? This is a matter for which templates have priority or precedence, topics we will cover later in the chapter.

As with the CSS example, this is clearly a push model of a stylesheet. As we come across an element in the source document, we execute its template. This type of stylesheet is typified by the presence of several short templates and the use of <xsl:apply-templates/>. Now we will look at a stylesheet that uses the pull model – something that is next to impossible with CSS.

The Pull Model with XSLT

In a pull model stylesheet, the XML source document acts purely as a data source and its structure is largely irrelevant. The stylesheet itself provides the structure of the output document.

Let's look at a simple example based on the full source of the play, Hamlet.xml, which is provided in the code download for the book. Here is our stylesheet, count.xsl:

```
<xsl:stylesheet
  version="1.0"
  xmlns:xsl="http://www.w3.org/1999/XSL/Transform">

<xsl:template match="PLAY">
<HTML>
  <HEAD>
    <TITLE>Counting</TITLE>
  </HEAD>
  <BODY>
    <P>There are <xsl:value-of select="count(//PERSONA)"/> individual
      characters in Hamlet.</P>
    <P>
      <xsl:for-each select="ACT">
        <xsl:value-of select="TITLE"/> has <xsl:value-of
          select="count(SCENE)"/> scenes,
      </xsl:for-each>
      making a total of <xsl:value-of select="count(//SCENE)"/>.
    </P>
  </BODY>
</HTML>
</xsl:template>

</xsl:stylesheet>
```

This is the result of applying the stylesheet to the play (for example, by using XT to apply the stylesheet to Hamlet.xml and produce the HTML result):

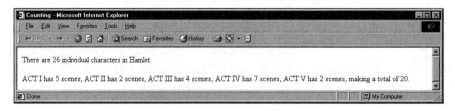

This bears little resemblance to anything in the play. Instead, the stylesheet has provided the structure of the output, pulling in data as it is needed. You will also notice the use of the built-in `count()` function in this example. We will meet this later when we look at the elements and functions in detail.

The pull model is characterized by a few large templates and use of the `<xsl:value-of>` element so that the stylesheet controls the order of items in the output. Compare this to the push model, where we had more and smaller templates with the output largely following the structure of the XML source document.

I mentioned earlier that XSLT is often thought of as a declarative language. However, it also contains the flow control and looping instructions typical of a procedural language. Typically, a push model stylesheet emphasizes the declarative aspects of the language, while the pull model emphasizes the procedural aspects.

Of course, these definitions are not absolute. Most stylesheets will contain elements of the push and elements of the pull models. However, it is useful to keep the two models in mind as it can make your stylesheet development simpler.

We have now looked at how XSLT stylesheets are created and seen examples of both push and pull models. In doing this, we have come across several of the XSLT elements and their attributes, and the built-in `count()` function. We will look at these and other elements in more detail, shortly.

A Word About Namespaces

You can get a long way with XML without any knowledge of **namespaces**, but you won't get far with XSL! For a start, an XSL processor uses namespaces to indicate which elements to process itself and which to put directly into the result tree. Let's start with a quick review of namespaces in general, and then look at the three main uses of namespaces in XSL.

Because we can define our own element and attribute names in XML, there is always the chance that we will want to use the same name with different meanings in a document. If I am processing XML that is describing metalworking, I might want to create an element in my output called `<template>`. As we have seen, XSLT has an element with the same name, so I might try something like this:

```
<template match="pattern">
  <template><value-of select="."/></template>
</template>
```

The purpose of XML namespaces is to make our element names unique. In this case, it would disambiguate my two `<template>` elements, so that the XSL processor knows that it must process the first, but that the second should be copied directly to the output tree.

XML namespaces use a **Uniform Resource Identifier** (**URI**) to ensure uniqueness of names. Why a URI? Simply that a key aspect of a URI is that it is unique. When we use the URI such as `http://www.wrox.com/namespaces`, a registration authority allocates the domain name `wrox.com` to Wrox Press and to nobody else. It is then up to Wrox to ensure that any URIs within this domain are unique.

So we can make our `template` elements unique by associating them with a namespace. One way to do this is with a **namespace prefix**, and that is what we have been doing with the XSLT namespace in our examples so far. We have associated the prefix `xsl` with the URI `http://www.w3.org/1999/XSL/Transform` using the reserved `xmlns` attribute within our `stylesheet` element:

```
<xsl:stylesheet
  version="1.0"
  xmlns:xsl="http://www.w3.org/1999/XSL/Transform">
```

Since the `stylesheet` element itself is part of the XSLT namespace, this also uses the prefix. As you can see, the prefix is separated from the element name by a colon.

In the terminology of the W3C recommendation (http://www.w3.org/TR/REC-xml-names), `xsl:stylesheet` is a **qualified name** (or **QName**), `xsl` is a **prefix** and `stylesheet` is a **local part**.

So we could modify our stylesheet to look like this:

```
<xsl:stylesheet
  version="1.0"
  xmlns:xsl="http://www.w3.org/1999/XSL/Transform">

  <xsl:template match="pattern">
    <template><value-of select="."/></template>
  </xsl:template>
</xsl:stylesheet>
```

Now the XSL processor knows to process the elements starting `xsl:` and to place other elements directly into the result tree.

Let's also declare a namespace for our `<pattern>` and `<template>` elements:

```
<xsl:stylesheet
  version="1.0"
  xmlns:xsl="http://www.w3.org/1999/XSL/Transform"
  xmlns:wrox="http://www.wrox.com/namespaces">

  <xsl:template match="wrox:pattern">
    <wrox:template><value-of select="."/></wrox:template>
  </xsl:template>
</xsl:stylesheet>
```

Now that we have done this, we can make either of these namespaces the default namespace for the document by removing the colon and prefix in the namespace declaration and the prefix and colon in element and attribute names that use that namespace. Note that we can do this with either namespace, so the following two documents are equivalent.

Here is the document with the Wrox namespace as default:

```
<xsl:stylesheet
  version="1.0"
  xmlns:xsl="http://www.w3.org/1999/XSL/Transform"
  xmlns="http://www.wrox.com/namespaces">

  <xsl:template match="pattern">
    <template><value-of select="."/></template>
  </xsl:template>
</xsl:stylesheet>
```

This is the document with the XSLT namespace as default:

```
<stylesheet
   version="1.0"
   xmlns="http://www.w3.org/1999/XSL/Transform"
   xmlns:wrox="http://www.wrox.com/namespaces">

   <template match="wrox:pattern">
     <wrox:template><value-of select="."/></wrox:template>
   </template>
</stylesheet>
```

In the example above, we have used namespaces for three distinct purposes, although we used the Wrox namespace for two of these:

❑ to indicate which elements were part of the XSLT namespace and so should be processed by the XSL processor

❑ to match elements, such as the `<pattern>` element, in the source tree only if they belong to a certain namespace

❑ to ensure that elements in the result tree, such as `<template>`, belong to the namespace we want

Let's just look a little more at matching namespace-qualified nodes in the source tree. Take the case where we have a stylesheet that is operating on an XML Schema document. We might have a line in our stylesheet such as:

```
<xsl:apply-templates select="xsd:complexType"/>
```

If we have not specified the namespace we are using for the `xsd` prefix in our stylesheet, our XSLT processor will match on the complete name `xsd:complexType` (since the colon is a valid part of an XML element name). If we then have another schema using `xs` as a qualifier rather than `xsd`, or using the XML Schema namespace as the default, we will no longer get matches in our stylesheet. This is unlikely to be what we want. By specifying the XML Schema namespace in our stylesheet, we can be certain that we will match XML Schema elements whatever prefix they are using, or even if they have no prefix because they belong in the default namespace of our source document.

In general in this book, we will use the `xsl` prefix for XSLT elements and suitable qualifiers for other namespaces.

XSLT Elements

In this section, we will recap all the elements we have used so far, and meet several others. With these you will be able to create the vast majority of the XSLT stylesheets you might want. In the next chapter, we will meet more elements; some of these you will require less often, while others provide more advanced functionality.

We will be looking at the most frequently used aspects of these elements. For fuller descriptions refer either to the XSLT recommendation or to a source such as the *XSLT Programmer's Reference 2nd Edition* (ISBN 1-861005-06-7 from Wrox Press).

<xsl:stylesheet>

This is simply the container element for all other elements within an XSL stylesheet. In most cases, this means it will be the document element of a stylesheet document.

A stylesheet can be embedded within another document, in which case an id attribute of this element can be used to allow a reference to the stylesheet.

The <xsl:stylesheet> element must contain a version attribute, indicating the version of XSLT that is being used. Currently, this is always 1.0 or 1.1.

The most important change between version 1.0 and version 1.1 of XSLT is that the latter allows multiple output documents to be created from a single XML source document and stylesheet. The full list of changes is documented as an appendix to the XSLT 1.1 specification (http://www.w3.org/TR/xslt11), which is at working draft stage at the time of writing.

The element is also likely to contain several namespaces, as we saw above. Firstly, there will be the XSLT namespace itself to tell the XSL processor which elements to process and which to pass unchanged to the output tree. Then there might be a namespace for XSL formatting objects (which we will look at in Chapter 9), namespaces for elements and attributes we will be matching in the source document, and namespaces for elements we might be creating in the output document. For example, if we wanted to use a stylesheet to document an XML Schema document, producing HTML output, our xsl:stylesheet start tag might look like this:

```
<xsl:stylesheet
  version="1.0"
  xmlns:xsl="http://www.w3.org/1999/XSL/Transform"
  xmlns:xsd="http://www.w3.org/1999/XMLSchema"
  xmlns="http://www.w3.org/TR/REC-html40">
```

In this case, we have defined HTML as our default namespace, and used explicit qualifiers for the XSLT and XML Schema namespaces.

Other optional attributes of the <xsl:stylesheet> element relate to namespace prefixes in the result tree and extension elements (which we will meet later in the book).

This element is used to inform the XSL processor of the format of the result tree. Earlier we used the following example (count.xsl) without using <xsl:output>:

```
<xsl:stylesheet
  version="1.0"
  xmlns:xsl="http://www.w3.org/1999/XSL/Transform">

<xsl:template match="PLAY">
<HTML>
  <HEAD>
    <TITLE>Counting</TITLE>
  </HEAD>
  <BODY>
```

```
    ...
  </BODY>
</HTML>
</xsl:template>

</xsl:stylesheet>
```

We used various HTML elements directly in our stylesheet, and these were copied directly to the result tree. Since the stylesheet is an XML document, the HTML included in it must itself be well-formed XML, and hence the HTML copied to the result tree will also be well-formed XML. This well-formed XML could meet the rules of the Extensible Hypertext Markup language, XHTML (see *Beginning XHTML*, ISBN 1-861003-43-9), but this is not essential to the operation of the stylesheet.

If the transformed result tree is being saved as a file, the last stage of XSLT processing will be to serialize the result tree. It seems reasonable to assume that this will also be well-formed XML. In most cases, this would not cause problems, but some HTML browsers (particularly older ones) have difficulty with constructs such as <HR/>, preferring just the opening tag <HR> without a closing tag for a horizontal rule. HTML also allows attributes without values (as in <OPTION selected>). Again, this is not well-formed XML, but some browsers will object to the alternative form of <OPTION selected="selected">. For this reason, alternative forms of serialization are supported through the <xsl:output> element. When, as in the example above, the element is omitted, the serialized output will obey rules we will look at later. In this case, it would be XML.

This element has an optional method attribute that specifies the form that the serialization should take. The three possible values are xml, html and text. The xml option is simple enough – the serialized output will be well-formed XML. The html option handles the cases shown above by converting the tags to the more normal HTML styles of <HR> and <OPTION selected>, and the text method provides a pure text output, removing all tags and converting entity and character references to their text equivalents.

Let's take a simple stylesheet, output.xsl, that creates some HTML, and try the different forms of <xsl:output>. Since we now know more about the use of namespaces in XSL, we will also declare the unqualified names copied to the output to be in the HTML namespace.

```
<xsl:stylesheet
  version="1.0"
  xmlns:xsl="http://www.w3.org/1999/XSL/Transform"
  xmlns="http://www.w3.org/TR/REC-html40">

<xsl:output method="html" indent="yes"/>

<xsl:template match="/">
  <HTML>
  <HEAD><TITLE>Testing the xsl:output element</TITLE></HEAD>
  <BODY>
    <P>
      This is a simple stylesheet to show the effect of the xsl:output element.
      There is an &lt;HR/> element after this line.
    </P>
    <HR/>
    <SELECT>
      <OPTION value="1">First option</OPTION>
```

```
         <OPTION selected="selected" value="2">Second (selected) option</OPTION>
         <OPTION value="3">Third option</OPTION>
      </SELECT>
   </BODY>
   </HTML>
</xsl:template>

</xsl:stylesheet>
```

In general in this chapter, we will leave out the HTML namespace declaration for simplicity.

We have specified our output method as html. We have also specified that we want the result indented, by putting in the attribute indent="yes". Although the XSLT recommendation does not specify what action the XSL processor should take as a result of this, with some processors it can make the result more readable.

What source XML shall we apply this to? The answer is any! This is the ultimate pull model stylesheet – it totally ignores the input XML, creating its result tree based only on the content of the stylesheet. Since we have some XML we used earlier, we can run the stylesheet using:

xt hamlet.xml output.xsl output.htm

We are not really interested in what the resulting HTML looks like when rendered. What we want to see is the HTML code produced (output.htm):

```
<HTML xmlns="http://www.w3.org/TR/REC-html40">
<HEAD>
<TITLE>Testing the xsl:output element</TITLE>
</HEAD>
<BODY>
<P>
      This is a simple stylesheet to show the effect of the xsl:output element.
      There is an &lt;HR/&gt; element after this line.
   </P>
<HR>
<SELECT><OPTION value="1">First option</OPTION><OPTION selected value="2">Second
(selected) option</OPTION><OPTION value="3">Third option</OPTION></SELECT>
</BODY>
</HTML>
```

Note that this is "traditional" HTML. If we want to create XHTML, which is well-formed XML, we should use an output method of xml since the changes made by the html method do not create a well-formed XML document. We would also have to make other changes to the stylesheet, such as changing all element names to lower case.

Now, changing just one line of output.xsl will switch the output method to xml:

```
<xsl:output method="xml" indent="yes"/>
```

Save the file as `output2.xsl`. The result of using this stylesheet is that the `<HR>` element is changed to the empty tag syntax and the `selected` attribute of the `<OPTION>` element is given its attribute value:

```
<?xml version="1.0" encoding="utf-8"?>
<HTML xmlns="http://www.w3.org/TR/REC-html40">
<HEAD>
<TITLE>Testing the xsl:output element</TITLE>
</HEAD>
<BODY>
<P>
      This is a simple stylesheet to show the effect of the xsl:output element.
      There is an &lt;HR/&gt; element after this line.
    </P>
<HR/>
<SELECT>
<OPTION value="1">First option</OPTION>
<OPTION selected="selected" value="2">Second (selected) option</OPTION>
<OPTION value="3">Third option</OPTION>
</SELECT>
</BODY>
</HTML>
```

Note that, although I have specified my output as XML, this does not mean I am producing XHTML. That is up to me to control, by obeying XHTML rules such as using lower case for all tag names.

With XT, the `indent` attribute did not affect the HTML output, but it improved the layout of the XML version. With any XSL processor, it is best to experiment to see the difference this attribute makes.

Finally, let's make one more change to our `output.xsl`:

```
<xsl:output method="text" indent="yes"/>
```

Save the file as `output3.xsl`. Our result when using XT now looks like this:

```
Testing the xsl:output element
      This is a simple stylesheet to show the effect of the xsl:output element.
      There is an <HR/> element after this line.
    First optionSecond (selected) optionThird option
```

All the tags have now been removed, and the entity references `&lt;` and `&gt;` have now been replaced by their corresponding characters. This is clearly important if we are, for example, using our stylesheet to create a comma-separated file from an XML input document. Another attribute of `<xsl:output>` that helps under these circumstances is the `encoding` attribute. This allows us to specify a character set such as `iso-8859-1` for our output. Any character outside this set will cause an error to be reported.

Earlier, we were using XSLT without the `<xsl:output>` element and creating well-formed XML. This is normally the default, but if the result tree meets all of the following three criteria, the serialized output will be HTML by default:

❑ the root node has at least one element child

❑ the expanded-name of the first element child of the root node of the result tree has local part `html` (in any combination of upper and lower case) and a null namespace URI

❑ any text nodes preceding the first element child of the root node of the result tree contain only whitespace characters

Other attributes of `<xsl:output>` provide much more control over the output. They can:

❑ define the version of XML or HTML being created

❑ control aspects of the XML declaration

❑ indicate the SYSTEM and PUBLIC identifiers of the DOCTYPE

❑ control the MIME type of the output

❑ control how CDATA sections are handled

These are described in detail in the XSLT recommendation and in reference books such as the *XSLT Programmer's Reference.*

<xsl:template>

We have just looked at `<xsl:output>`, which is known as a **top-level** element as it can only occur as a child of the `<xsl:stylesheet>` element. We'll now look at `<xsl:template>`, which is another top-level element.

The `<xsl:template>` element contains the information required to produce a node in the result tree. We have seen several examples in the stylesheets we have been producing.

In the examples we have used so far, we have employed a `match` attribute, for example:

```
<xsl:template match="EXTRACT">
```

The attribute value is an XPath expression that will tell us which nodes in the source tree will cause this template to execute.

When using XPath expressions, there is always the possibility that several templates will match a single element. For example, if you look back to the listing of `HamletExtract.xml`, you will see that both acts and scenes have titles. In our previous stylesheet `Hamlet.xsl`, we had the templates:

```
<xsl:template match="ACT/TITLE">
  <H1><xsl:value-of select="."/></H1>
</xsl:template>

<xsl:template match="SCENE/TITLE">
  <H2><xsl:value-of select="."/></H2>
</xsl:template>
```

What if we had another template:

```
<xsl:template match="TITLE">
  <P><xsl:value-of select="."/></P>
</xsl:template>
```

Which template would be executed when our `<xsl:apply-templates>` finds a scene's title?

One thing we can do is add a `priority` attribute to the `<template>` element:

```
<xsl:template match="TITLE" priority="1">
  <P><xsl:value-of select="."/></P>
</xsl:template>
```

This will allow the stylesheet to select the highest priority template, and only execute that. The value of the `priority` attribute can be any positive or negative integer or real number: the higher the number, the higher the priority. The default priority is between -0.5 and 0.5, so this new template will always be matched for any `<TITLE>` element, and the more specific `ACT/TITLE` and `SCENE/TITLE` templates will never be matched.

This is just one method of resolving conflicts when there are multiple templates matching a pattern. Later, in the section *Template Match Conflicts*, we will look at the others and the rules that determine in general which template is instantiated.

The `<xsl:template>` element has two further optional attributes. One is `name`, which is used with the `<xsl:call-template>` element, and the other is `mode`, which provides additional flexibility in the use of templates. We will meet both these attributes in Chapters 4 and 5.

<xsl:apply-templates>

Along with the `<xsl:template>` and `<xsl:value-of>` elements, this is the workhorse of the XSLT world. It is the element that controls which templates are used at any point while building the result tree.

It can have two attributes, of which we have already met the `select` attribute. This simply takes as its value an XPath expression that controls which elements in the source tree will be processed. This pattern can be simple, like most of those we have been using, or much more complicated, using any of the rules of XPath. Note that the `select` attribute is optional. If it is missing, all child nodes will be processed.

The second attribute is the `mode` attribute. Since this relates to the `mode` attribute in `<xsl:template>`, we will again be leaving this to Chapter 4.

As well as its attributes, `<xsl:apply-templates>` can have two sub-elements. The first is `<xsl:sort>`, which alters the order in which selected nodes are processed, and the second is `<xsl:with-param>`, which provides a method of passing parameters to templates. We will look at `<xsl:sort>` shortly, but leave `<xsl:with-param>` to Chapter 4.

<xsl:value-of>

This element is always contained within a template and simply writes the text node (or nodes) of the element pointed to by the XPath expression identified in its `select` attribute to the result tree.

The `select` attribute works in much the same way as it does in `<xsl:apply-templates>`, taking an XPath expression as its value. However, with `<xsl:apply-templates>`, if there are several matches, the relevant templates are instantiated multiple times. With `<xsl:value-of>`, only the first instance is used. Also, unlike with `<xsl:apply-templates>`, in this case the attribute is mandatory.

The value of this expression is always written to the result tree as a string, so some conversion might need to take place first. A number is converted to the string representation of that number. If a node contains sub-nodes, the value is the concatenation of the values of all the sub-nodes. So, for example, for our document `HamletExtract.xml`, we could include within the `<SCENE>` template a line:

```
<xsl:value-of select="SPEECH[3]"/>
```

This will return a value that is the concatenation of the values of the `<SPEAKER>` and `<LINE>` elements of the third `<SPEECH>`. This is the speech that will be selected:

```
<SPEECH>
<SPEAKER>BERNARDO</SPEAKER>
<LINE>Long live the king!</LINE>
</SPEECH>
```

So the text returned will be BERNARDOLong Live the king!.

Finally, if the result is a Boolean, it will be converted to one of the strings `true` or `false`.

<xsl:copy> and <xsl:copy-of>

These two elements copy information from a source node directly to the result tree. `<xsl:copy>` performs what is known as a **shallow** copy. This means that it copies only the node and any namespace – not its descendants or attributes. `<xsl:copy-of>` performs a **deep** copy, copying not only the node and any namespace, but all its attributes and descendants.

`<xsl:copy-of>` is useful for copying sections of the XML source tree unchanged to the result tree, while `<xsl:copy>` gives more control of what will be copied. For example, we might want to list some key data from `Hamlet.xml`. We could do this with the following simple stylesheet (`Playkey.xsl`):

```
<xsl:stylesheet
  version="1.0"
  xmlns:xsl="http://www.w3.org/1999/XSL/Transform">

<xsl:output method="xml" indent="yes"/>

<xsl:template match="text()"/>

<xsl:template match="PLAY">
  <xsl:copy>
```

```
      <xsl:apply-templates/>
    </xsl:copy>
  </xsl:template>

  <xsl:template match="TITLE | PERSONAE">
    <xsl:copy-of select="."/>
  </xsl:template>

</xsl:stylesheet>
```

The result of this is to copy the element `<PLAY>` (but not its descendants) to the result tree as the document element, then list the title of the play, the Dramatis Personae, and the title of each Act and Scene. Note that we have used the line:

```
<xsl:template match="text()" />
```

to ensure that the built-in templates do not cause extraneous text to be output. The result when this is applied to `Hamlet.xml` looks like this:

```
<?xml version="1.0" encoding="utf-8"?>
<PLAY>
<TITLE>The Tragedy of Hamlet, Prince of Denmark</TITLE>
<PERSONAE>
<TITLE>Dramatis Personae</TITLE>

<PERSONA>CLAUDIUS, king of Denmark. </PERSONA>
<PERSONA>HAMLET, son to the late, and nephew to the present king.</PERSONA>
<PERSONA>POLONIUS, lord chamberlain. </PERSONA>
<PERSONA>HORATIO, friend to Hamlet.</PERSONA>
<PERSONA>LAERTES, son to Polonius.</PERSONA>
<PERSONA>LUCIANUS, nephew to the king.</PERSONA>

<PGROUP>
<PERSONA>VOLTIMAND</PERSONA>
<PERSONA>CORNELIUS</PERSONA>
<PERSONA>ROSENCRANTZ</PERSONA>
<PERSONA>GUILDENSTERN</PERSONA>
<PERSONA>OSRIC</PERSONA>
<GRPDESCR>courtiers.</GRPDESCR>
</PGROUP>

<PERSONA>A Gentleman</PERSONA>
<PERSONA>A Priest. </PERSONA>

<PGROUP>
<PERSONA>MARCELLUS</PERSONA>
<PERSONA>BERNARDO</PERSONA>
<GRPDESCR>officers.</GRPDESCR>
</PGROUP>

<PERSONA>FRANCISCO, a soldier.</PERSONA>
<PERSONA>REYNALDO, servant to Polonius.</PERSONA>
<PERSONA>Players.</PERSONA>
```

```
<PERSONA>Two Clowns, grave-diggers.</PERSONA>
<PERSONA>FORTINBRAS, prince of Norway. </PERSONA>
<PERSONA>A Captain.</PERSONA>
<PERSONA>English Ambassadors. </PERSONA>
<PERSONA>GERTRUDE, queen of Denmark, and mother to Hamlet. </PERSONA>
<PERSONA>OPHELIA, daughter to Polonius.</PERSONA>
<PERSONA>Lords, Ladies, Officers, Soldiers, Sailors, Messengers, and other
Attendants.</PERSONA>
<PERSONA>Ghost of Hamlet's Father. </PERSONA>
</PERSONAE>
<TITLE>ACT I</TITLE>
<TITLE>SCENE I.  Elsinore. A platform before the castle.</TITLE>
<TITLE>SCENE II.  A room of state in the castle.</TITLE>
<TITLE>SCENE III.  A room in Polonius' house.</TITLE>
<TITLE>SCENE IV.  The platform.</TITLE>
<TITLE>SCENE V.  Another part of the platform.</TITLE>
<TITLE>ACT II</TITLE>
<TITLE>SCENE I.  A room in POLONIUS' house.</TITLE>
<TITLE>SCENE II.  A room in the castle.</TITLE>
<TITLE>ACT III</TITLE>
<TITLE>SCENE I.  A room in the castle.</TITLE>
<TITLE>SCENE II.  A hall in the castle.</TITLE>
<TITLE>SCENE III.  A room in the castle.</TITLE>
<TITLE>SCENE IV.  The Queen's closet.</TITLE>
<TITLE>ACT IV</TITLE>
<TITLE>SCENE I.  A room in the castle.</TITLE>
<TITLE>SCENE II.  Another room in the castle.</TITLE>
<TITLE>SCENE III.  Another room in the castle.</TITLE>
<TITLE>SCENE IV.  A plain in Denmark.</TITLE>
<TITLE>SCENE V.  Elsinore. A room in the castle.</TITLE>
<TITLE>SCENE VI.  Another room in the castle.</TITLE>
<TITLE>SCENE VII.  Another room in the castle.</TITLE>
<TITLE>ACT V</TITLE>
<TITLE>SCENE I.  A churchyard.</TITLE>
<TITLE>SCENE II.  A hall in the castle.</TITLE>
</PLAY>
```

Of course, we could equally well use the same stylesheet for other plays marked up in the same format.

This example shows a common use of `<xsl:copy-of>`, but perhaps a rather contrived example for `<xsl:copy>`, since we could equally well have used a different template for the `<PLAY>` element:

```
<xsl:template match="PLAY">
   <PLAY>
      <xsl:apply-templates/>
   </PLAY>
</xsl:template>
```

This would also have allowed us to use a different element name in the result tree from that in the source tree. So let's look at another use of `<xsl:copy>`.

We said earlier that `<xsl:copy>` gives us more control over the copying operation than `<xsl:copy-of>`. We used this just now to control which descendants of the `<PLAY>` element we would copy. Another use is if we have a source tree that is mainly XHTML, but with some additional elements from a different namespace. Much of the web site at http://www.alphaxml.com is written in XHTML. However, there is a glossary application that is used to explain technical terms. An example of the source code that might be used on this site is:

```
<p>The <em>Extensible Markup Language</em> provides a universal mechanism for
marking up data on the web. Unlike <g:term>HTML</g:term>, which is a language
based around displaying data in a web browser, <g:term>XML</g:term> puts no
constraints on the purpose for which the data will be used, but merely describes
the structure of the data. XML can therefore be used (and is used) for any
application that involves the transfer of data across the web for either display
or computation purposes.</p>
```

Here, the `<p>` and `<em>` elements are from the XHTML namespace, which is used as the default for the document. The `<term>` element is from a different namespace for the glossary, using the prefix g.

When we process this, we want to copy the XHTML elements unchanged, but carry out some additional processing on the `<g:term>` elements. `<xsl:copy>` lets us do this. This is an extract from the template used on that site (reformatted for display):

```
<xsl:template match="*|@*|text()">
  <xsl:copy>
    <xsl:apply-templates select="*|@*|text()" />
  </xsl:copy>
</xsl:template>

<xsl:template match="g:term">
  <a target="_blank" class="glossary">
    <xsl:attribute name="href">
      glossary/glossary.asp?glossary=AlphaGlossary.xml&amp;term=
      <xsl:value-of select="."/>
    </xsl:attribute>
    <xsl:value-of select="."/>
  </a>
</xsl:template>
```

In this example, the first template will be run for all elements, attributes and text nodes apart from the `<g:term>` element (for which the second template takes priority). This will copy the node to the result tree and apply templates for its children. If one of those children is a `<g:term>` element, the second template will be run. This simply creates an anchor (`<a>`) element in the result tree with an href attribute whose value depends on the enclosed text. For the term "HTML", the result will be:

```
<a
  target="_blank"
  class="glossary
  href="glossary/glossary.asp?glossary=AlphaGlossary.xml&amp;term=HTML">
  HTML
</a>
```

Control Flow Elements

The following five elements allow us to control execution within a template in a manner analogous to procedural languages. These are `<xsl:if>`, `<xsl:choose>`, `<xsl:when>`, `<xsl:otherwise>`, and `<xsl:for-each>`. The first of these gives a simple if... then... construct. The next three provide the equivalent of if... then... else... and the switch statement in many languages, and the last provides looping.

<xsl:if>

This element is used within a template purely to make execution of the enclosed statements conditional on the result of a test. It has a mandatory `test` attribute, which contains an expression that will return a Boolean result. The enclosed statements will be executed if the result of the test is `true`.

The test expression may involve the use of XSLT functions. We shall cover a couple of the functions included in XSLT at the end of this chapter, but their use in the following code is self-explanatory.

Common uses for `<xsl:if>` are testing for error conditions, or treating the first or last elements of a collection differently from the others. For example, the following template (`ListCharacters.xsl`) lists all the characters in Hamlet, placing a comma and space after all but the last:

```xsl
<xsl:stylesheet
  version="1.0"
  xmlns:xsl="http://www.w3.org/1999/XSL/Transform">

<xsl:output method="html" indent="yes"/>

<xsl:template match="PLAY">
<HTML xmlns="http://www.w3.org/TR/REC-html40">
  <HEAD>
    <TITLE>Listing Characters</TITLE>
  </HEAD>
  <BODY>
    <P>
      The characters in Hamlet are:
      <xsl:for-each select="//PERSONA">
        <xsl:value-of select="."/>
        <xsl:if test = "position() != last()">, </xsl:if>
      </xsl:for-each>
    </P>
  </BODY>
</HTML>
</xsl:template>

</xsl:stylesheet>
```

And this is the result after being applied to `Hamlet.xml`:

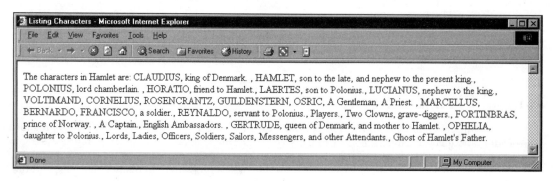

Note that this element only allows an `if... then...`; if we want an `else...`, we must use `<xsl:choose>`, which we will look at next.

<xsl:choose>, <xsl:when>, and <xsl:otherwise>

These elements provide the equivalent of a switch statement, and can therefore also be used to provide an if... then... else... construct.

Here is an example of them in use in HamletWithLines.xsl, which is modified from a previous stylesheet (Hamlet.xsl):

```
<xsl:stylesheet version="1.0"
  xmlns:xsl="http://www.w3.org/1999/XSL/Transform">

<xsl:output method="html" indent="yes"/>

<xsl:template match="*|/"><xsl:apply-templates/></xsl:template>

<xsl:template match="text()|@*"><xsl:value-of select="."/></xsl:template>

<xsl:template match="EXTRACT">
<HTML xmlns="http://www.w3.org/TR/REC-html40">
    <HEAD>
      <TITLE>Hamlet</TITLE>
    </HEAD>
    <BODY>
      <xsl:apply-templates/>
    </BODY>
  </HTML>
</xsl:template>

<xsl:template match="ACT/TITLE"><H1><xsl:value-of select="."/></H1></xsl:template>

<xsl:template match="SCENE/TITLE"><H2><xsl:value-of
select="."/></H2></xsl:template>

<xsl:template match="STAGEDIR"><P><I><xsl:value-of
select="."/></I></P></xsl:template>

<xsl:template match="SPEAKER"><DIV><xsl:value-of select="."/></DIV></xsl:template>

<xsl:template match="LINE[position()=last()]">
  <DIV>
    <xsl:value-of select="."/>
    <xsl:choose>
      <xsl:when test="../SPEAKER='BERNARDO'">
        <HR style="color:silver"/>
      </xsl:when>
      <xsl:when test="../SPEAKER='FRANCISCO'">
        <HR style="color:black"/>
      </xsl:when>
      <xsl:otherwise> <!-- this is the trap for unrecognized speakers -->
        <DIV style="color:silver">
          !! oops, I don't know this speaker !!
        </DIV>
      </xsl:otherwise>
    </xsl:choose>
  </DIV>
</xsl:template>

<xsl:template match="LINE"><xsl:value-of select="."/></xsl:template>

</xsl:stylesheet>
```

I have added the `<xsl:output>` element and HTML namespace that we did not know about earlier. But the important part is the new template, which simply puts a different shade of horizontal rule under the last line of each speech, depending on the speaker. This is how it looks when applied to `HamletExtract.xml`:

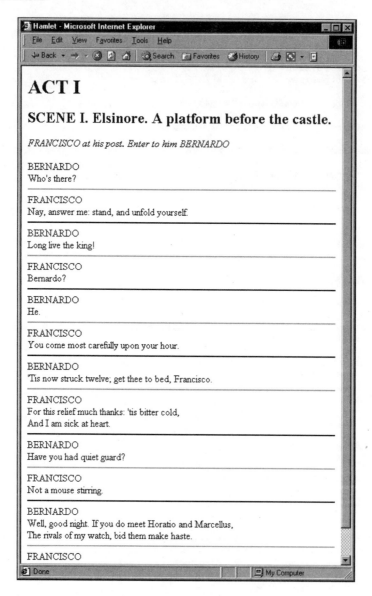

In my first attempt at this stylesheet, I misspelled the name "FRANCISCO" as "FRANSISCO" in the new template. This was the result:

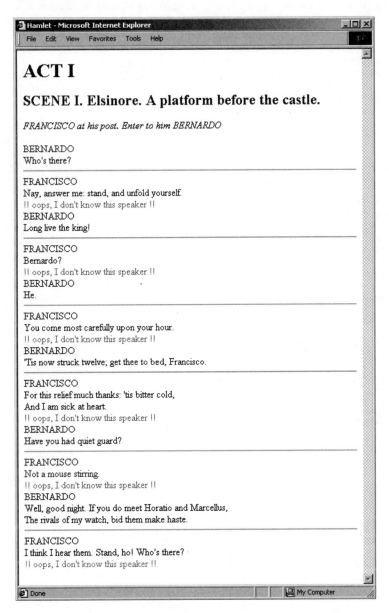

As you can see, the `<xsl:otherwise>` can be used to trap errors, as it has done here.

<xsl:for-each>

The last of the control flow elements, `<xsl:for-each>`, has already been seen in action when we were counting the number of scenes in each act. Here is the stylesheet (`count.xsl`) that we used:

```
<xsl:stylesheet
  version="1.0"
  xmlns:xsl="http://www.w3.org/1999/XSL/Transform">

<xsl:template match="PLAY">
<HTML>
  <HEAD>
    <TITLE>Counting</TITLE>
  </HEAD>
  <BODY>
    <P>There are <xsl:value-of select="count(//PERSONA)"/> individual
      characters in Hamlet.</P>
    <P>
      <xsl:for-each select="ACT">
        <xsl:value-of select="TITLE"/> has
        <xsl:value-of select="count(SCENE)"/> scenes,
      </xsl:for-each>
      making a total of <xsl:value-of select="count(//SCENE)"/>.
    </P>
  </BODY>
</HTML>
</xsl:template>

</xsl:stylesheet>
```

The `<xsl:for-each>` statement effectively allows us to embed a template inside another. Instead of the `<xsl:for-each>` statement, we could have used `<xsl:apply-templates>`, and made the contents of the `<xsl:for-each>` a separate template:

```
<xsl:stylesheet
  version="1.0"
  xmlns:xsl="http://www.w3.org/1999/XSL/Transform">

<xsl:template match="PLAY">
<HTML>
  <HEAD>
    <TITLE>Counting</TITLE>
  </HEAD>
  <BODY>
    <P>There are <xsl:value-of select="count(//PERSONA)"/> individual
      characters in Hamlet.</P>
    <P>
      <xsl:apply-templates select="ACT"/>
      making a total of <xsl:value-of select="count(//SCENE)"/>.
    </P>
  </BODY>
</HTML>
</xsl:template>

<xsl:template match="ACT">
  <xsl:value-of select="TITLE"/> has
  <xsl:value-of select="count(SCENE)"/> scenes,
</xsl:template>

</xsl:stylesheet>
```

So when should you use `<xsl:for-each>` and when should you use `<xsl:apply-templates>`? Often, the same template will be executed as a result of several XPath expression matches. In this case, using `<xsl:apply-templates>` provides re-usability in the same way that a function call does in a procedural language. On other occasions, it is largely a matter of style, and you should use whichever makes your stylesheet easier to understand. As we saw earlier, a push model stylesheet tends to use `<xsl:apply-templates>` most of the time to execute specific template rules as elements are found in the source tree, while a pull model is more likely to have a single large template with `<xsl:for-each>` statements to execute the embedded rule at a specific point in the stylesheet.

XSLT has the concept of a **context** node, which is important when using relative XPath expressions. In the stylesheet above, the line:

```
<xsl:template match="ACT">
```

sets the context node to the `<ACT>` element. In the following line:

```
<xsl:value-of select="TITLE"/> has
```

the expression is relative to this context node. There are two ways of changing the context node in XSLT: `<xsl:template>` is one, and `<xsl:for-each>` is the other. These are the only ways of changing the context node. Using an XPath expression in a `test` attribute, for example, does not do this.

`<xsl:sort>`

This seems to be a good point to introduce `<xsl:sort>`. This element can be used inside `<xsl:apply-templates>` or `<xsl:for-each>` to alter the order in which nodes are processed. In most cases, when either of these statements selects these nodes, they will be processed in **document order** – that is, the order in which they were encountered when processing the document from top to bottom. This order can be altered using `<xsl:sort>`.

At the start of this chapter, we introduced a book catalog with just two books in it and a simplified structure. Now is a good time to use the full catalog, `catalog.xml`, which is available in the code download. Here are the first two books from this version:

```xml
<?xml version="1.0" encoding="utf-8" standalone="yes"?>
<!--======= The Wrox Press Book Catalog Application ========-->

<Catalog>
<Book id="1861003323">
    <Title>Professional VB6 XML</Title>
    <Authors>
        <Author>James Britt</Author>
        <Author>Teun Duynstee</Author>
    </Authors>
    <Publisher>Wrox Press, Ltd.</Publisher>
    <PubDate>March 2000</PubDate>
    <Abstract>Shows the VB community how to take advantage of XML
     technology and the available implementations</Abstract>
    <Pages>725</Pages>
    <ISBN>1-861003-32-3</ISBN>
    <RecSubjCategories>
        <Category>Programming</Category>
        <Category>Visual Basic</Category>
        <Category>XML</Category>
```

```
    </RecSubjCategories>
    <Price>$49.99</Price>
    <CoverImage>3323.gif</CoverImage>
</Book>
<Book id="1861003129">
    <Title>XSLT Programmer's Reference</Title>
    <Authors>
        <Author>Michael Kay</Author>
    </Authors>
    <Publisher>Wrox Press, Ltd.</Publisher>
    <PubDate>April 2000</PubDate>
    <Abstract>Learn how to use the XSLT language to develop
    web applications</Abstract>
    <Pages>800</Pages>
    <ISBN>1-861003-12-9</ISBN>
    <RecSubjCategories>
        <Category>Internet</Category>
        <Category>XML</Category>
        <Category>XSL</Category>
    </RecSubjCategories>
    <Price>$34.99</Price>
    <CoverImage>3129.gif</CoverImage>
</Book>
...
</Catalog>
```

We will be using this quite a bit later in the chapter, but for now we will use it to see the effect of `<xsl:sort>`. Firstly, let's get a list of the book titles using `ShowTitles.xsl`:

```
<xsl:stylesheet
  version="1.0"
  xmlns:xsl="http://www.w3.org/1999/XSL/Transform">

<xsl:template match="/"><xsl:apply-templates/></xsl:template>

<xsl:template match="Catalog">
  <xsl:for-each select="Book">
    <DIV><xsl:value-of select="Title"/></DIV>
  </xsl:for-each>
</xsl:template>

</xsl:stylesheet>
```

When applied to `catalog.xml`, this gives the result:

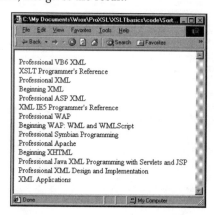

If you look through the catalog, you will see that this is the order in which the books are listed. Now let's add an `<xsl:sort>` statement to the stylesheet (and re-save it as `CatalogSort.xsl`):

```
<xsl:stylesheet
  version="1.0"
  xmlns:xsl="http://www.w3.org/1999/XSL/Transform">

<xsl:template match="/"><xsl:apply-templates/></xsl:template>

<xsl:template match="Catalog">
  <xsl:for-each select="Book">
    <xsl:sort select="@id"/>
    <DIV><xsl:value-of select="Title"/></DIV>
  </xsl:for-each>
</xsl:template>

</xsl:stylesheet>
```

The books are now listed in the order of their `id` attributes. These are their ISBN numbers without the hyphens. We could have just used the ISBN numbers, but the sort would then get confused if the style of hyphenation was not consistent. This is the result of using the stylesheet above on `catalog.xml`:

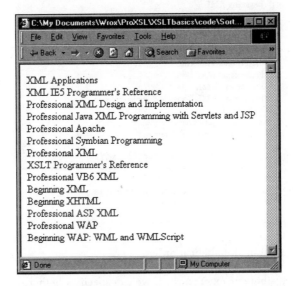

Inspection of the catalog will show that the titles are now listed in ISBN order.

There are various optional attributes of `<xsl:sort>` that control the sorting. We have already used `select`. Had we omitted this, the string value of the current node would have been used, rather than the `id` attribute. In this case, since the node has element content, this is not really a safe option (the string value would be the concatenation of the string values of the descendant nodes), but had we instead created a template for the `<Title>` element, we could have sorted on this by using the default value for the `select` attribute. The stylesheet might then have looked like this (`CatalogSort2.xsl`):

```xml
<xsl:stylesheet
  version="1.0"
  xmlns:xsl="http://www.w3.org/1999/XSL/Transform">

<xsl:template match="/">
  <xsl:for-each select="Catalog/Book/Title">
    <xsl:sort/>
    <DIV><xsl:value-of select="."/></DIV>
  </xsl:for-each>
</xsl:template>

</xsl:stylesheet>
```

And the result on transforming `catalog.xml` would have looked like this:

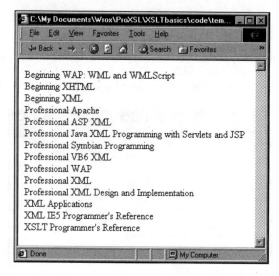

Because it is now applied to the `<Title>` elements, the line:

```xml
<xsl:sort/>
```

causes the titles to be output in alphabetical order.

Using the `data-type` attribute of `<xsl:sort>`, we can specify whether the data on which we are sorting is `text` (the default) or `number`. We sorted our ISBN values as text, which works in this case of fixed length strings, but in other cases, there would be a difference. The sequence of numbers from 1 to 20 sorted as text would be:

1,10,11,12,13,14,15,16,17,18,19,2,20,3,4,5,6,7,8,9

The `order` attribute has two possible values: `ascending` (the default) and `descending`, which are self-explanatory.

The `lang` attribute controls language-specific sorting orders. For example, in German, it is conventional to include the letter ä after the letter a, while in Swedish it would come after z. The possible values are the same as those of the `xml:lang` attribute and are specified in IETF RFC 1766 (http://www.cis.ohio-state.edu/htbin/rfc/rfc1766.html), "Tags for the Identification of Languages".

When sorting textual information, we can choose whether upper-case or lower-case values come first using the `case-order` attribute. This has values of `upper-first` and `lower-first`. If the former is used, when values start with the same letter, values starting with upper-case letters will occur in the output before any starting with lower-case letters. The default for this is language-dependent, and not specified in the recommendation. With no language specified, both XT and SAXON ignore case when sorting.

Sorting can be achieved on multiple criteria by using `<xsl:sort>` elements sequentially. In this case, sorting will occur first using the criteria defined by the first element, then sorted within these results using the later elements in order. If, for some strange reason, we wanted to sort all the speeches of Hamlet first in order of speaker, then by number of lines in the speech, then in alphabetical order of the text, we could use the following stylesheet, `HamletSort.xsl`:

```
<xsl:stylesheet
  version="1.0"
  xmlns:xsl="http://www.w3.org/1999/XSL/Transform">

<xsl:template match="/">
  <xsl:apply-templates select="//SCENE"/>
</xsl:template>

<xsl:template match="SCENE"><xsl:for-each select="SPEECH">
  <xsl:sort select="SPEAKER"/>
  <xsl:sort select="count(LINE)"/>
  <xsl:sort select="LINE"/>
  <DIV><xsl:value-of select="SPEAKER"/></DIV>
  <xsl:for-each select="LINE">
    <DIV><xsl:value-of select="."/></DIV>
  </xsl:for-each>
</xsl:for-each></xsl:template>

</xsl:stylesheet>
```

Using this just on our extract of the first scene (`HamletExtract.xml`), all Bernardo's speeches come before Francisco's, then for each speaker, all the one line speeches come before the two line speeches and within these criteria, the speeches are listed in alphabetical order. Notice that the apostrophe comes before any letters, as it does in English-language dictionaries:

<xsl:number>

The <xsl:number> element is used to determine the position of a node in the source tree. As such, it is useful for tasks such as numbering sections of a document and providing a table of contents. Various attributes allow control and formatting of the number produced.

The main control over the number produced is the `level` attribute. This can have one of three values, `single`, `any`, or `multiple`. The first of these is used to produce a number based on a node's position in relation to its siblings, for example, to number bullet points. The second is used to number nodes regardless of their level in the document hierarchy and can be used, for example, to number footnotes. And the last provides a number based on the level of a node in the hierarchy, such as you might use for numbering sections and sub-sections in a report.

Other attributes are available to say which nodes will be included in the numbering scheme and where in the source tree the numbering should start. As well as providing these controls over the number associated with a node, the <xsl:number> element provides formatting of the numbers. For example, when we use `value="multiple"`, we can specify that a section is to be numbered as 1.1.3 or A.1.3, or even 1.A.iii if we so desire. In fact, <xsl:number> provides all the flexibility in numbering and formatting of the number that we might expect from a word processor.

When we look at the `position()` function later in this chapter, we will look again at <xsl:number> to provide a comparison of the possible effects.

<xsl:text>

The <xsl:text> element is used to put a text string into the result tree. Isn't that what we have been doing by including the text in the stylesheet? Well yes, but there are two circumstances where we might need more control.

The first is when we are using entity references. If we include the text < in our stylesheet, what do we want written to the result tree? It could be the same text string, < or it could be the single character <. The disable-output-escaping attribute lets us control this. If the value of this attribute is no, or the attribute is omitted, the result tree will contain the entity reference (<), but if the value is yes, the result will be the < character. This is useful if we are, for example, outputting a text string or code in some scripting language.

The second use of <xsl:text> is to control whitespace handling. Careful choice of examples has avoided this issue so far, but now is the time to see how XSLT controls the use of whitespace in its output. In general, a text node in the stylesheet is copied to the result tree, as we have seen in many of our examples. For example, we created a comma-separated list of book titles using:

```
<xsl:value-of select="Title"/>, <xsl:value-of select="PubDate"/>
```

Here we had a text node consisting of a comma followed by a space, and this was copied directly to the result tree.

Frequently, we will use whitespace in our stylesheets for formatting. For example, the code above could have been written as:

```
<xsl:value-of select="Title"/>,
<xsl:value-of select="PubDate"/>
```

In this case, the comma, any space characters that there might be after the comma, the newline character, and the several spaces used to indent the next line would all be output. However, since we were creating HTML and not embedding this within a <PRE> element, the HTML processor (in other words the browser) will convert these to a single space.

However, what about where we do not have a character such as a comma? The default behavior is that all text nodes that consist *only* of whitespace are ignored and not copied to the result tree. This allows us to use whitespace to format our stylesheet without worrying about it reaching our output.

There are two ways to vary this behavior. The first is in the XML source itself. If an ancestor element of the text node that contains only whitespace has an xml:space attribute with a value of preserve (and no intervening element has an xml:space attribute with a value of default), then whitespace will be preserved. This can give an equivalent result to the <PRE> element in HTML. If we want to control whitespace through the stylesheet itself, we use <xsl:text>. Within this element, all whitespace is preserved, even if a text node comprises only whitespace.

While on the subject of whitespace, if you are creating an HTML output you might be tempted to put in a non-breaking space character like this:

```
<xsl:value-of select="elem1"/> <xsl:value-of select="elem2"/>
```

Unfortunately, this is not well-formed XML since   is not one of the built-in entity references in XML 1.0. (I put the version in here, in the hope that it will be included in a later version!)

Here are three ways around that problem. The first is to use a character reference instead:

```
<xsl:value-of select="elem1"/> <xsl:value-of select="elem2"/>
```

This is fine if you know you will remember what that reference is the next time you look at the stylesheet (and you are not expecting others to have to understand it easily).

The second is to use <xsl:text>:

```
<xsl:value-of select="elem1"/>
  <xsl:text> </xsl:text>
<xsl:value-of select="elem2"/>
```

Again, this works, but is a bit long-winded. The third is to put a DTD internal subset into your stylesheet to define the entity:

```
<!DOCTYPE xsl:stylesheet [
  <!ENTITY nbsp " ">
]>
```

Now you can use   to your heart's content!

<xsl:element>

Up to now, when we have wanted to include an element in the result tree, we have just gone ahead and typed the start and end tags into the stylesheet. In most cases, that works. However, it will not work if the element name depends on data in the source XML document.

In this case we use <xsl:element> to create the element for us. This is used most frequently when creating an element-rich result tree from an attribute-rich source tree. However, we don't have an attribute-rich document to play with, so we will simply create element names based on the id attributes of the books in our catalog. We cannot use the id values themselves as element names. (Why not? Think back to your XML specification or wait to see at the end of this section.) So we will use the following code (id.xsl):

```
<xsl:stylesheet
  version="1.0"
  xmlns:xsl="http://www.w3.org/1999/XSL/Transform">

<xsl:template match="/">
  <xsl:apply-templates select="Catalog/Book"/>
</xsl:template>

<xsl:template match="Book">
  <xsl:element name="id{@id}"/>
<xsl:text>
</xsl:text>
</xsl:template>

</xsl:stylesheet>
```

Notice the line:

```
<xsl:element name="id{@id}"/>
```

The part in braces is an **attribute value template,** a feature of XSLT we will be meeting in the next chapter. This is the required format for the value of the name attribute.

Notice also the use of <xsl:text>:

```
<xsl:text>
</xsl:text>
```

The purpose of this was to put a line break between each element of the output. This is only there to make the resulting serialized document more readable. And here it is (when applied to catalog.xml):

```
<?xml version="1.0" encoding="utf-8"?>
<id1861003323/>
<id1861003129/>
<id1861003110/>
<id1861003412/>
<id1861004028/>
<id1861001576/>
<id1861004044/>
<id1861004583/>
<id186100303X/>
<id1861003021/>
<id1861003439/>
<id1861002858/>
<id1861002289/>
<id1861001525/>
```

There is another occasion you might want to use <xsl:element>. Because the element allows a namespace attribute, it provides more control over the namespace than we have when including the element as literal text in the stylesheet. Just as we have made the element name in the result tree dependent on the content of the input tree, we can do the same with a namespace. Like the name attribute, the value of this attribute is an attribute value template.

The final, optional, attribute of <xsl:element>, called use-attribute-sets, allows us to specify an attribute set to use with the defined element. Such sets of attributes can be defined using the <xsl:attribute-set> element.

Why couldn't we use the id values themselves as element names earlier? Our id values start with a digit – remember from the XML specification that an element name must start with an alphabetic character or an underscore or colon. Of course, we would never use a colon as this is used as a separator between a namespace prefix and local name.

<xsl:attribute>

You will probably find that you use <xsl:attribute> more often than <xsl:element>, particularly if you are creating HTML output.

This element allows us to create an attribute name and/or value in the result tree based on data in the source tree. For example, in our book catalog we have references to images of the book covers, such as:

```
<CoverImage>3323.gif</CoverImage>
```

If we were to display information from the catalog by creating an HTML page, we would want to create an <IMG> element referring to this image. Something like:

```
<IMG src="covers/3323.gif">
```

We can do this using an attribute value template. The following stylesheet, covers.xsl, creates a table of book titles and images:

```
<xsl:stylesheet
  version="1.0"
  xmlns:xsl="http://www.w3.org/1999/XSL/Transform">

<xsl:output method="html"/>

<xsl:template match="/">
  <xsl:apply-templates select="Catalog"/>
</xsl:template>

<xsl:template match="Catalog">
  <TABLE><xsl:apply-templates select="Book"/></TABLE>
</xsl:template>

<xsl:template match="Book">
  <TR>
    <TD><xsl:value-of select="Title"/></TD>
    <TD>
      <IMG>
        <xsl:attribute name="src">
          covers/<xsl:value-of select="CoverImage"/>
        </xsl:attribute>
      </IMG>
    </TD>
  </TR>
</xsl:template>

</xsl:stylesheet>
```

Note that we have used the line:

```
<xsl:output method="html"/>
```

This ensures that the resulting `<IMG>` element does not use the empty element syntax. The serialized output will have an element of the form:

```
<IMG src="covers/4583.gif">
```

rather than:

```
<IMG src="covers/4583.gif"/>
```

This ensures compatibility with a greater range of older browsers.

The part we are most interested in is:

```
<IMG>
  <xsl:attribute name="src">
    covers/<xsl:value-of select="CoverImage"/>
  </xsl:attribute>
</IMG>
```

Note that normally I would put the `<xsl:attribute>` element and all its content on a single line. This is because this element contains a text node (`covers/`), and so the additional whitespace will be included in the output. I have only reformatted this line to make it fit within the constraints of the printed page.

All the code above is doing is creating the `<IMG>` element in the output with a `src` attribute using the value of the text node of the `<CoverImage>` element in the source tree. In this case, we have included some additional text to provide the correct relative URL for the images.

This screenshot shows the first four books:

Note that you would not use both an `<xsl:attribute>` and an `<xsl:element>` element. Instead you would use an attribute value template.

We have now covered the main elements of XSLT. With these, you can write many useful stylesheets. We will next look at two important aspects of XSLT – default templates and what happens when several templates match the same pattern.

Default Templates

Have you ever accidentally (or deliberately) applied an empty stylesheet to a document? For example, if we apply `empty.xsl`:

```
<xsl:stylesheet
  version="1.0"
  xmlns:xsl="http://www.w3.org/1999/XSL/Transform"/>
```

to `shortcatalog.xml`, the result is:

```
<?xml version="1.0" encoding="utf-8"?>


    Designing Distributed Applications

        Stephen Mohr

    May 1999
    1-861002-27-0
    $49.99


    Professional ASP 3.0

        Alex Homer
        Brian Francis
        David Sussman

    October 1999
    1-861002-61-0
    $59.99
```

Although the stylesheet was empty, the output is not. The reason for this is that XSLT, as we saw briefly in Chapter 2, contains some default templates to match elements, attributes, and text nodes that are not matched elsewhere.

The main templates in this category are:

```
<xsl:template match="*|/">
  <xsl:apply-templates/>
</xsl:template>

<xsl:template match="text()|@*">
  <xsl:value-of select="."/>
</xsl:template>
```

The first of these matches the document root and all elements. In both cases, it causes processing to continue by applying an `<xsl:apply-templates>` instruction to all child nodes. This means that, if you have a template matching an element buried deep in your source tree, but no template for one or more of its ancestors, the default template will cause processing to continue until that element is reached.

The second template matches text nodes and all attributes, causing the values of these to be output.

The combination of the first template, ensuring that the document root and all elements are processed, and the second, ensuring that all the text is copied to the result tree, is what generated our output.

There are also default templates for comments, processing instructions and namespace nodes, each saying "do nothing". Finally, in Chapter 4, we will meet another default template covering the mode attribute, which we have not met in detail yet.

Remember that these are only defaults. If you define your own templates, they will over-ride these. It could be that you are only processing a few elements in a document and don't want others processed. In this case, including the following line in your stylesheet will ensure that this happens:

```
<xsl:template match="*"/>
```

Template Match Conflicts

When several templates match the same source node, the XSLT processor needs rules for choosing which template to use. In fact, because of the existence of the default templates, every stylesheet will contain multiple rules matching any node. Luckily, XSLT provides a clear set of rules for deciding which template to use.

We will see in Chapter 5 that one stylesheet can import another. If there is a conflict over which rule to apply when one belongs to the importing stylesheet and one to an imported stylesheet, the rule in the importing stylesheet is said to have to higher **precedence**, and will be the rule applied. If the conflict is between rules in imported stylesheets, then stylesheets imported later have higher precedence than those imported earlier. Of course, imported stylesheets can import other stylesheets. If you get into this situation, the recommendation handles all cases using the concept of an **import tree**. Refer to the XSLT Recommendation itself to understand this.

The default rules are treated as though they were imported before the stylesheet itself, and so have the lowest possible import precedence.

Template rules can also have a **priority** assigned. We saw how to do this earlier, when discussing the `<xsl:template>` element. Where a priority is not assigned, a default priority value is used. These default priorities are in the range -0.5 to 0.5. In general, the more specific the match expression, the higher the priority.

If there is still a conflict after applying the precedence rules, the rule with the highest priority is applied.

It is possible that there will still be a conflict after the priority rules have been applied. This is treated as an error. The stylesheet processor will either indicate this error in some way or choose the last rule in the stylesheet that matches the pattern.

XSLT Functions

After that little aside to understand a couple of important areas of XSLT, we can get back to what XSLT can do for us. Now that we have covered the most important elements, we can cover the most important functions.

In Chapter 2, XPath core functions were introduced. In addition, XSLT has some functions of its own. While the core XPath functions are available to XSLT, the XSLT defined functions are not available to XPath when it is used beyond the confines of XSLT. The functions that we take a closer look at now are actually core XPath functions, but exist in the XSLT namespace.

The names of these functions usually give away what they do. Those we will cover here are:

- ❏   position()
- ❏   last()
- ❏   name()
- ❏   count()

We will also look at accessing nodes in a node-set by index.

position() and last()

In many cases, we will want to select nodes based on their position in a node-set. This is what we did in ListCharacters.xsl when we made the list of characters in Hamlet, to ensure that the last character did not have a comma after his name:

```
<xsl:if test="position()!=last()">, </xsl:if>
```

As well as checking against last(), we can check against any index into the node-set. It is this that means we do not need a first() function to match the last() function. Instead, we just look for a position() of 1. To apply a template only if there is only one matching elem node, we would use:

```
<xsl:template match="elem[position()='1' and position()=last()]">
```

Note that the first matching node has an index of 1, and not 0.

As well as using the position within a test, we can use the value of the position() function to number our nodes. Earlier, we looked at <xsl:number>, which provides us with a number relating to a node's position in the source tree. In contrast, position() provides a number relating to the position in a node-set, which might be after a sort operation. It can therefore be used to provide a number relating to a node's position in the result tree.

We can very easily demonstrate this difference by using both methods to number the books in our catalog. We will produce a table of book titles with the results of numbering using <xsl:number> and position().

This is our stylesheet, `position.xsl`:

```
<xsl:stylesheet version="1.0"
  xmlns:xsl="http://www.w3.org/1999/XSL/Transform"
  xmlns="http://www.w3.org/TR/REC-html40">

<xsl:template match="/">
  <TABLE BORDER="1">
    <TR>
      <TD>Title</TD>
      <TD>position()</TD>
      <TD>xsl:number</TD>
    </TR>
    <xsl:apply-templates select="Catalog/Book"/>
  </TABLE>
</xsl:template>

<xsl:template match="Book">
  <TR>
    <TD><xsl:value-of select="Title"/></TD>
    <TD align="center"><xsl:value-of select="position()"/></TD>
    <TD align="center"><xsl:number/></TD>
  </TR>
</xsl:template>

</xsl:stylesheet>
```

This is extremely simple. The template for the document root creates the table and applies the template for the `<Book>` elements. Each time the `<Book>` template executes, it adds a row to the table and puts in the book title with the result of applying `<xsl:number>` and `position()` to the current `<Book>` element.

The result of applying this stylesheet to `catalog.xml` looks like this:

Title	position()	xsl:number
Professional VB6 XML	1	1
XSLT Programmer's Reference	2	2
Professional XML	3	3
Beginning XML	4	4
Professional ASP XML	5	5
XML IE5 Programmer's Reference	6	6
Professional WAP	7	7
Beginning WAP: WML and WMLScript	8	8
Professional Symbian Programming	9	9
Professional Apache	10	10
Beginning XHTML	11	11
Professional Java XML Programming with Servlets and JSP	12	12
Professional XML Design and Implementation	13	13
XML Applications	14	14

In this case, the results are the same since the node-set produced by the select attribute in the <xsl:apply-templates> element will be in document order. However, we can sort the catalog alphabetically by changing the template for the document root (number.xsl):

```
<xsl:template match="/">
  <TABLE BORDER="1">
    <TR>
      <TD>Title</TD>
      <TD>position()</TD>
      <TD>xsl:number</TD>
    </TR>
    <xsl:apply-templates select="Catalog/Book">
      <xsl:sort select="Title"/>
    </xsl:apply-templates>
  </TABLE>
</xsl:template>
```

Now the results will be somewhat different:

Title	position()	xsl:number
Beginning WAP: WML and WMLScript	1	8
Beginning XHTML	2	11
Beginning XML	3	4
Professional Apache	4	10
Professional ASP XML	5	5
Professional Java XML Programming with Servlets and JSP	6	12
Professional Symbian Programming	7	9
Professional VB6 XML	8	1
Professional WAP	9	7
Professional XML	10	3
Professional XML Design and Implementation	11	13
XML Applications	12	14
XML IE5 Programmer's Reference	13	6
XSLT Programmer's Reference	14	2

The position() function has produced numbering in the order of the node-set provided to the <Book> template (which is also the order in the result tree), while the <xsl:number> element has kept the numbering as it was in the source tree (so each title is numbered as it was in the previous example).

name()

The name() function merely returns the name of the node. If applied to a node-set rather than a node, the optional node parameter can identify the node required. Where there is more than one match, the function returns the first.

There are often occasions when you want to display a node name. For example, I often use XSLT stylesheets to document XML Schemas. In one of these, I want to display the facets of an element. Don't worry if you are not familiar with XML Schema, the important thing is that each facet is defined by its element name and the value of its value attribute. An extract of the stylesheet I use is:

```
<table>
  <xsl:for-each select="*">
    <tr>
      <td><xsl:value-of select="name()"/>:</td>
      <td><xsl:value-of select="@value"/></td>
    </tr>
  </xsl:for-each>
</table>
```

We therefore list each facet name and value attribute value in two columns in a table.

count()

The final function we will consider here is the count() function, which returns the number of nodes in a node-set.

In the book catalog, catalog.xml, we could provide a template to list the titles of all the books with more than one author:

```
<xsl:template match="Book[count(//Authors)>1]">
  <xsl:value-of select="Title"/>
</xsl:template>
```

Or, we might want to sort the books by the number of authors (CountAuthors.xsl):

```
<xsl:stylesheet
  version="1.0"
  xmlns:xsl="http://www.w3.org/1999/XSL/Transform">

<xsl:template match="/">
  <xsl:apply-templates select="Catalog"/>
</xsl:template>

<xsl:template match="Catalog">
  <xsl:for-each select="Book">
    <xsl:sort select="count(Authors/Author)" data-type="number"/>
    <P>
      <xsl:value-of select="Title"/> has
      <xsl:value-of select="count(Authors/Author)"/> author(s)
    </P>
  </xsl:for-each>
</xsl:template>

</xsl:stylesheet>
```

The result will be a list of books sorted in increasing number of authors order, and saying how many authors there are in each.

Summary

In this chapter, we have learnt the basics of XSLT through discussion and examples. In particular, we have seen:

❑ How XSLT is a declarative language with procedural elements, matching XPath expressions to apply templates to nodes in the source tree, while including control flow elements to provide the procedural aspects.

❑ The push and pull models, and where each is most suitable. We have also seen that most stylesheets will use some combination of these.

❑ A number of the elements used in XSLT, and how we can write useful stylesheets with just this subset of the language.

❑ A few of the functions built into the language, and how we can use these to give more control over our processing.

❑ How the built-in template rules ensure that all nodes are processed (unless we over ride them) and how XSLT knows which rule to apply when there is a conflict.

Before we move on to more advanced XSLT processing, why not try a few stylesheets of your own, perhaps gathering more statistics about Hamlet or displaying the book catalog in different ways?

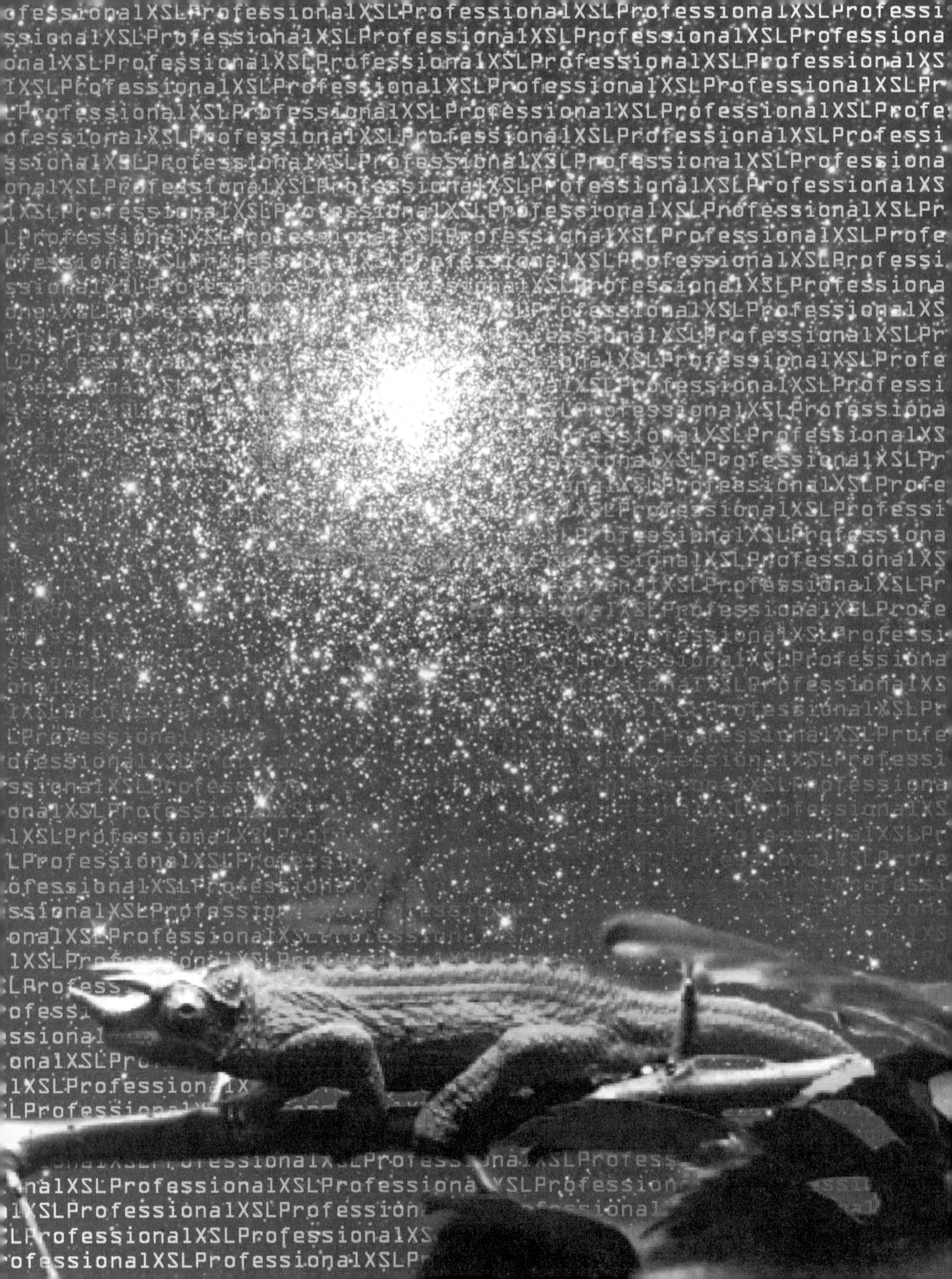
ProfessionalXSL

4

Modular XSLT

XSLT seems to be one of those languages with a large "Ah, ha!" factor – most people who work with XSLT struggle over it for several weeks (or in some cases, months) trying to prize out of the sometimes cryptic syntax and convoluted restrictions some semblance of similarity with the languages that they are used to. Then, one day, usually after too many hours grappling with a recalcitrant script, it suddenly clicks into perspective with a flash of insight.

The closest analogy that I can think of was the advent of Object Oriented Programming (OOP) techniques back in the late 1980s. OOP was certainly a powerful paradigm, but for those of us used to working with structural programs that marked the thinking of the time, it was also a remarkably slippery and subtle concept, until one night (at least for me), it all made sense at once.

However, in both the cases of OOP and XSLT declarative programming, that "Ah, ha!" factor meant only that I stood upon one plateau, unaware that the level of understanding I had so painfully acquired was largely illusory, for the mountain started up again after only a short ledge of respite.

The divide between basic XSLT and the advanced XSLT that we will be covering in the next two chapters marks this same kind of plateau and cliff-face dilemma. Once you have mastered the basics of XPath and axes, matching templates and applied calls, you have enough to build many reasonably powerful XSLT applications. However, just as the differences between structural and OOP programming are both surprisingly minimal and just as surprisingly profound (think of the differences between C and C++, for instance), these foundation pieces for XSLT get you only halfway up the mountain even though the knowledge yet to be acquired seems fairly trivial at first glance.

This chapter is going to look at those pieces that can turn single XSLT documents into foundation pieces for powerful XSLT-based frameworks of components. In most cases, the changes have to do with the addition of four conceptually simple ideas:

❑   **Intermediate State**. The use of *variables* and *parameters* makes it possible to create temporary XML structures that can be used for everything from simplifying code to creating data structures that are independent of the "cascading" order of matching templates.

❑   **Functional Modularity**. With the use of *named templates* and *modal matched templates*, you can effectively wrap your frequently used routines in library functions that can be applied from any number of templates. In conjunction with `<xsl:import>` and `<xsl:include>` XSLT elements, functional modularity makes it possible to build framework applications, significantly extending the reach of XSLT beyond the local transformation.

❑   **External Resources**. The `document()` function (especially in conjunction with most XSLT parsers' `node-set()` function) gives a mechanism for working with documents outside of the primary one being parsed, and in conjunction with HTTP can also pass web service type requests to other servers.

❑   **Programmatic Extensions**. While not yet completely standardized between different XSLT processors, most processors support a mechanism for adding additional XPath functions that can let developers access components for business rule processing, and work with system resources (such as database or LDAP stores); most processors also provide enhanced processing capabilities such as regular expressions or the invoking of system commands.

The effects of working with these "advanced" features of XSLT can be quite dramatic – at the very least a move away from large, ungainly XSLT documents to a distributed framework of component "library" transformations that significantly simplify coding. At the other end of the spectrum, these features can lead to a radical change in the type of coding that you perform, using XSLT for everything from handling business logic for applications to calling XSLT as a routing mechanism for invoking device transactions.

The code covered in this chapter focuses primarily on generic XSLT code, though it uses the MSXML3 parser and IIS 5.0 to illustrate the use of these resources on the server. Setup instructions for this parser can be found in Chapter 7. For more information about the specific uses of the different XSLT processors, see Appendix E.

In this chapter I shall also concentrate on the first two aspects of "advanced XSLT" listed above – creating intermediate state and functional modularity. In the next chapter these ideas will be enhanced by the use of external resources (through the `document()` function, `<xsl:import>` and `<xsl:include>` elements, and the proposed `<xsl:document>` interface of XSLT 1.1), and the extension of XSLT via Java classes or COM objects.

The Value of Variables

When you are writing a transformation, one of the walls that you may come up against will be the need to repeat a great deal of code, sometimes for the most trivial of applications. As one of the simplest examples, suppose that you had an HTML output file in which you have multiple references to an e-mail address that you want to make into a live anchor link. Such linked messages can get remarkably lengthy, and it would make sense to create a shortcut to contain the full text. For example, the following will both launch an e-mail program and (at least in the case of Outlook) will include a Subject: field in the mail:

```
<a href="mailto:cagle@olywa.net?subject=Wrox+Professional+XSL:">Kurt Cagle</a>
```

In general, it would be nice to have a much simpler reference instead of having to constantly type this out. This is where **variables** come in handy. A variable lets you associate a name with either a block of XML, an XPath string or numeric expression, or a set of nodes. In the above instance, for example, you could use a variable `mailLink`:

```
<xsl:variable name="mailLink">
   <a href="mailto:cagle@olywa.net?subject=Wrox+Professional+XSL:">Kurt Cagle</a>
</xsl:variable>
```

Once defined, you can then reference the variable in an XPath expression by using the syntax $*varname*. For instance, the following will place the contents of the expression into the output stream of the XSLT document:

```
<!-- mailtotest.xsl -->
<xsl:stylesheet xmlns:xsl="http://www.w3.org/1999/XSL/Transform" version="1.0">

<xsl:variable name="mailLink">
   <a href="mailto:cagle@olywa.net?subject=Wrox Professional XSL:">Kurt Cagle</a>
</xsl:variable>

<xsl:template match="/">
  <html>
    <body>
      <div>For additional information, please contact
      <xsl:copy-of select="$mailLink"/>.</div>
    </body>
  </html>
</xsl:template>

</xsl:stylesheet>
```

Note here that the command `<xsl:copy-of>` rather than `<xsl:value-of>` is used – the contents of a variable are given as an XML tree fragment, which puts them in something of a gray zone between ordinary text and node sets. Unlike a CDATA section, the content will be output as XML, and yet as a tree fragment it cannot be searched directly, although this limitation can be overcome with the (semi-)proprietary XPath function `node-set()`, discussed later in this section. If you do use `<xsl:value-of>`, the contents of the XML tree fragment will be reduced as with ordinary XML to just the text nodes – the tags themselves are discarded.

You can build variables that employ the contents of other variables. For instance, it might be more advantageous to keep the specific e-mail information – name, e-mail address, message – in their own variables, so they can be referenced independently by more than just the link. You can then build up the complete expression in another variable (here `mailLink`):

```
<!-- mailtotest2.xsl -->
<xsl:stylesheet xmlns:xsl="http://www.w3.org/1999/XSL/Transform" version="1.0">

<xsl:variable name="address">cagle@olywa.net</xsl:variable>
<xsl:variable name="subject">Wrox Professional XSLT</xsl:variable>
<xsl:variable name="addressee">Kurt Cagle</xsl:variable>

<xsl:variable name="mailLink">
  <a href="mailto:{$address}?subject={$subject}:"><xsl:value-of
    select="$addressee"/></a>
</xsl:variable>
```

```
<xsl:template match="/">
  <html>
    <body>
      <div>For additional information, please contact
      <xsl:copy-of select="$mailLink"/>.</div>
    </body>
  </html>
</xsl:template>

</xsl:stylesheet>
```

The curly braces in the `href` attribute are employed to get around a restriction in the XML specification – you cannot technically include angle-bracketed markup code in an attribute, which means that you could not use an expression such as:

```
<!--Warning!!! This is NOT valid -->
<a href="mailto:<xsl:value-of select="$address"/>?subject=<xsl:value-of
select="$subject"/>:"><xsl:value-of select="$addressor"/></a>
</xsl:variable>
```

Because of that limitation, the brace notation "`{}`" has been introduced instead. With this notation, the contents of the braces are evaluated as if they were XPath expressions. Thus, `href="mailto:{$address}"` would evaluate the `$address` variable as an XPath expression and put the result into the output (`href="mailto:`**cagle@olywa.net**`"`).

The brace notation can be mixed with text, as it is in the above example. In this case, the attribute's value is known as an **attribute value template**.

There are three noteworthy restrictions on attribute value templates. Firstly, they can be used with attributes of any literal result element, but only certain attributes of XSLT elements. See Appendix B for details of which attributes allow the use of attribute value templates.

Secondly, because the contents of the braces must fit into attributes, they cannot evaluate to an XML tree fragment. As a consequence, there is an implicit conversion to string performed by the braces – internal elements and attributes are stripped, leaving only the composite result of all of the text nodes in the input.

A third limitation with attribute value templates is that they cannot be nested – handy as that capability might seem. For instance, it is NOT possible to use braces to dereference a variable based upon the name created by another variable:

```
<a href="mailto:{${concat('ad','dress')}}"/>
```

This will simply generate a parse error. Another, subtle, implication from this is that the "`$`" character that delimits variables should not be taken as a dereference operator (analogous to the `*` operator in C or C++), or the "`$`" operator in Perl). An XSLT processor works by creating a simple table of variables in memory, and doesn't really have the notion of a pointer to other resources. Thus, `$$myPtr`, where the variable `$myPtr` contained the expression "`address`", will likewise generate a parse error.

Note: this is not to say that such a capability wouldn't be very, very useful. Especially in conjunction with parameterization, the ability to dereference variables at multiple levels could make XSLT far more suitable for work in general processing applications, and would be a critical feature of any real XML-based programming language.

The select Attribute of <xsl:variable>

There are actually two ways of setting the contents of variables. While you can place XML fragments into the body of variables, you can also use the select attribute to place the content of an XPath expression – strings, numeric results, or node sets – directly into the variable. This has two advantages over working with XML tree fragments: the amount of typing you need to do drops considerably, and you can directly work with the results of any XPath expression as if you were working with a node set.

For example, the variables $colorType and $borderType in the following code (boxedContext.xsl) put together a switch that determines what CSS class is used for displaying a block of HTML code:

```
<!-- boxedContext.xsl -->
<xsl:stylesheet xmlns:xsl="http://www.w3.org/1999/XSL/Transform" version="1.0">
<xsl:variable name="colorType" select=" 'boxedRed' "/>
<xsl:variable name="borderType" select=" 'thick' "/>

<xsl:template match="/">
  <xsl:apply-templates select="*"/>
</xsl:template>

<xsl:template match="document">
  <html>
    <head>
      <style>
        .boxedRed_thick {width:300px;height:360px;
          background-color:maroon;color:white;border:inset 4px maroon;
          overflow-x:hidden;overflow-y:auto; padding:5px;}
        .boxedRed_thin {width:300px;height:360px;
          background-color:maroon;color:white;border:solid 1px black;
          overflow-x:hidden;overflow-y:auto; padding:5px;}
        .boxedBlue_thick {width:300px;height:360px;
          background-color:navy;color:white;border:inset 4px navy;
          overflow-x:hidden;overflow-y:auto; padding:5px;}
        .boxedBlue_thin {width:300px;height:360px;
          background-color:navy;color:white;border:solid 1px navy;
          overflow-x:hidden;overflow-y:auto; padding:5px;}
      </style>
    </head>
    <body>
      <xsl:apply-templates select="head"/>
      <xsl:apply-templates select="body"/>
    </body>
  </html>
</xsl:template>

<xsl:template match="head">
  <div class="{$colorType}_{$borderType}" style="height:180px;
    overflow-y:hidden;">
    <h1><xsl:value-of select="title"/><br/>
    <h2><xsl:value-of select="author"/><br/>
    <h3>Chapter <xsl:value-of select="chapter/@number"/>: <xsl:value-of
        select="chapter"/><br/>
    <h6>Copyright <xsl:value-of select="copyright"/>
    </h6></h3></h2></h1>
  </div>
</xsl:template>
```

```
<xsl:template match="body">
  <div class="{$colorType}_{$borderType}">
  <xsl:copy-of select="*|text()"/>
  </div>
</xsl:template>
</xsl:stylesheet>
```

The variables `colorType` and `borderType` together determine the overall look of the output, with `colorType` having the possible values `'boxedRed'` or `'boxedBlue'`, while `borderType` can have the possible values `'thick'` or `'thin'`. This method of selecting a style for a block of text is clearly useful when many documents draw on a standard, comprehensive stylesheet that defines rules for displaying a block according to its function. Should a new 'house style' be chosen, it is then only necessary to update the styles defined in this common stylesheet, and reapply the transform to render your documents according to the updated aesthetic. For example, if the stylesheet is applied to the document `midnightRain.xml` (supplied with the code download), it will produce the output shown:

It's worth taking a closer look at the variable definitions shown in bold at the beginning of `boxedContext.xsl`. Within the `select` attribute, the content is actually enclosed in two sets of quotes. The first set of quotes marks the attribute boundaries, so in this case the content of the attribute is what's in between the double quotes (" "). The interior single quotes (' '), on the other hand, denote the variable as a string type rather than an XPath expression. If the content was not additionally quoted, then XSLT would treat the expression as an XPath expression and attempt to find child nodes with the names of `boxedRed` or `boxedBlue`, which isn't what was intended here. It doesn't matter whether the inner quotes are single quotes and the outer ones are double or vice versa, but it does matter that the two types of quotes are different.

Finally, the values of the two variables are concatenated within the `class` attribute of the literal `<div>` tag, using an attribute value template.

Variable Selections and Node-Sets

Above we saw the `select` attribute of `<xsl:variable>` used to give the variable a set textual value. However, you can also use the `select` attribute to retrieve sets of nodes from an XPath query and store them into a variable. For example, one common task in XSLT that's very nearly impossible to implement using matched templates can be solved fairly simply using variables – namely eliminating redundant information from a list of items.

For an example, let's look at a list of authors of Wrox books. It is not atypical for a single author to contribute to several books, or for a book to have several authors, so that trying to generate a list of all of the authors in a given catalog of Wrox books (a partial version of which is shown below) is likely to reveal a great deal of redundant information.

```xml
<?xml version="1.0" encoding="utf-8" standalone="yes"?>
<!--======= The Wrox Press Book Catalog Application =======-->

<Catalog>
<Book>
  <Title>Professional VB6 XML</Title>
  <Authors>
    <Author>James Britt</Author>
    <Author>Teun Duynstee</Author>
  </Authors>
  <Publisher>Wrox Press, Ltd.</Publisher>
  <PubDate>2000-03-01</PubDate>
  <Abstract>Shows the VB community how to take advantage of XML technology and the
available implementations</Abstract>
  <Pages>725</Pages>
  <ISBN>1-861003-32-3</ISBN>
  <RecSubjCategories>
    <Category>Programming</Category>
    <Category>Visual Basic</Category>
    <Category>XML</Category>
  </RecSubjCategories>
  <Price>$49.99</Price>
  <CoverImage>3323.gif</CoverImage>
</Book>
<Book>
  <Title>XSLT Programmer's Reference</Title>
  <Authors>
    <Author>Michael Kay</Author>
  </Authors>
  <Publisher>Wrox Press, Ltd.</Publisher>
  <PubDate>2000-04-01</PubDate>
  <Abstract>Learn how to use the XSLT language to develop web
applications</Abstract>
  <Pages>800</Pages>
  <ISBN>1-861003-12-9</ISBN>
  <RecSubjCategories>
    <Category>Internet</Category>
    <Category>XML</Category>
    <Category>XSL</Category>
  </RecSubjCategories>
  <Price>$34.99</Price>
  <CoverImage>3129.gif</CoverImage>
</Book>
<!-- Additional Books -->
</Catalog>
```

119

The exact script to reduce redundant XML information is fairly involved, but can essentially be broken down into two steps. The first involves creating a temporary, alphabetically sorted list of authors, potentially including redundant information where authors are listed more than once. When this list has been generated, a second list gets created from it by ignoring any entry in the first list that is the same as the previous entry. Because the data is sorted alphabetically, this ensures that only one of each item found makes its way to the second list.

Here is the `listAuthors.xsl` stylesheet:

```xsl
<xsl:stylesheet xmlns:xsl="http://www.w3.org/1999/XSL/Transform"
  xmlns:msxml="urn:schemas-microsoft-com:xslt" version="1.0">

<xsl:output method="html" media-type="text/html"/>

<!-- root match -->
<xsl:template match="/">
  <!-- create initial set of authors as tree fragment, sorted by LAST name  -->
  <xsl:variable name="redundant.authors.tf">
    <xsl:for-each select="//Author">
      <xsl:sort select="substring-after(.,' ')"/>
      <!-- this selects the text immediately following the first significant
      space in the author's name - the assumption here being that author's may
      have only one first name but may have a last name with two or more
      parts. -->
      <xsl:copy-of select="."/>
    </xsl:for-each>
  </xsl:variable>

  <!-- convert the redundant author list from tree fragment to a node-set-->
  <xsl:variable name="redundant.authors"
    select="msxml:node-set($redundant.authors.tf)"/>

  <!-- filter out redundant information -->
  <xsl:variable name="reduced.authors.tf">
    <!-- For each author in the $redundant.authors nodeset -->
    <xsl:for-each select="$redundant.authors/*">
      <!-- save the current position and author-->
      <xsl:variable name="pos" select="position()"/>
      <xsl:variable name="current.author" select="."/>
      <!-- if the author is the first one given, or doesn't duplicate
      the previous (sorted) author in the list, copy the author node.
      This will remove redundant authors from the list. -->
      <xsl:if
        test="$pos=1 or not($current.author = $redundant.authors/*[$pos - 1]) ">
        <xsl:copy-of select="."/>
      </xsl:if>
    </xsl:for-each>
  </xsl:variable>

  <!-- convert the reduced author list from a tree fragment to a node-set -->
  <xsl:variable name="reduced.authors"
    select="msxml:node-set($reduced.authors.tf)"/>
```

```
<!-- output the result -->
<table border="3">
  <caption style="font-family:Verdana;font-size:14pt;">
    Wrox Author Book Count
  </caption>
  <tr style="background-color:navy;color:white;">
    <th>Wrox Authors</th>
    <th>Number Published</th>
  </tr>
  <xsl:for-each select="$reduced.authors/*">
    <xsl:variable name="current.author" select="."/>
    <tr>
      <!-- output the name of the current author -->
      <td><xsl:value-of select="."/></td>
      <!-- output the number of books the author has written for Wrox -->
      <td align="right">
      <xsl:value-of
        select="count($redundant.authors/Author[.= $current.author])"/>
      </td>
    </tr>
  </xsl:for-each>
</table>
</xsl:template>

</xsl:stylesheet>
```

And here is the resulting HTML page displayed in a browser:

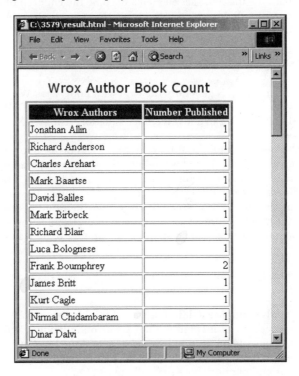

There are a number of aspects to working with variables that this example highlights. One of the first is the use of the `node-set()` function. This particular function is a somewhat uncomfortable legacy of some last minute wrangling in the W3C specification. There were basically two schools of thought about the usage of XSLT in the committee, one of which felt that the primary purpose of the language should be to produce markup output (such as HTML). The second group, however, saw it as a more multi-purpose language that could be used to produce any XML. As a consequence, they needed to maintain XML stores that could be created and manipulated outside of the scope of the initial XML data.

The result was a compromise called an **XML Tree Fragment**, which could be output as XML but which was supposed to be treated only as text internally. However, the ability to create XML dynamically, that can then be manipulated, makes XSLT far more powerful. The language can now handle a host of programming/processing tasks that would otherwise be quite beyond it – creating internal look up tables, storing the intermediate results of computations, sorts, or filtering (as shown in the code listing), and generating interim code that can be further manipulated based upon later conditions.

As a consequence, most producers of XSLT processors have included a special extension function called `node-set()`, which converts tree fragments into valid XML code that can be manipulated within XSLT. Because this is an extension, it requires its own namespace to work properly (in the case of the MSXML3 parser, `xmlns:msxml="urn:schemas-microsoft-com:xslt"`) and the usage varies (slightly) from one parser to the next. A note to the W3C concerning XSLT 1.1 changes recommends that the `node-set()` function be deprecated and that the node-set functionality rather than XML Tree Fragments become the standard for working with variable content, but this has not yet been adopted by the W3C.

Unfortunately, until then, this means that XSLT code that generates tree-fragment content will need to be processed through `node-set()` to be useful. The variable that holds the contents of such a node-set becomes a sort of 'node' itself – the node-set elements become the children of the variable. Thus, for instance, you would enumerate all of the author nodes in the reduced data set from the above example with the statement:

```
<xsl:for-each select="$reduced.authors/*">
```

This variable is kept in memory (as is generally the case with node-sets). While this won't usually get you into trouble when your XSLT transformation is working on an XML DOM, it can be more problematic if your XSLT is working in a low memory situation, using SAX.

One of the more useful aspects of such variables is that they can be used to cut down on processing. For instance, the XPath expression "`//Author`" is a relatively expensive operation – it requires that every node in the tree be searched to find any with the name `Author`, which for a tree with several thousand nodes could be a significant time hit. While there are ways of reducing the time to do this, the simplest way to reduce processing time for multiple searches is to save the result of the first `//Author` search into a variable and then just call the processed list instead of performing the search (or sort) again. This is how the `count()` routine in the example displayed the number of books that a writer actually wrote:

```
<td align="right">
  <xsl:value-of select="count($redundant.authors/Author[.=$current.author])"/>
</td>
```

Variable-centric XSLT tends to impose a different way of thinking about programming. In essence, you become focused on the processing of lists rather than acting on individual items. Traditional programming tends to concentrate on each individual item and the links that item has, not the abstract list that contains the item. In other words, you sort a list by rearranging the items, and you filter a list by re-linking individual items and purging those that fall out.

Contrast this with XSLT where, given an unsorted, unfiltered author list, the first pass sorts the list and returns a second list. This list in turn is filtered to remove redundant information, resulting in a third list. This list in turn may be transformed again to generate a table (which is primarily a list of row elements). You use one list to create a second, which creates a third, and so forth. It is potentially less efficient than individual item generation (and certainly so with use of tree-fragments, since XML needs to be converted back into node-sets after every operation) but because these are common operations in XSLT they can be heavily optimized in the compiler itself, simplifying the operation dramatically for the writer of the transformation. Once the tree-fragment limitation is dropped, however, working with lists in this manner is actually somewhat more efficient, as individual nodes that don't need to be processed can be copied directly to the output stream.

One key issue that may emerge, however, is size. Each time you generate a node-set within a variable, such a node-set becomes a surrogate DOM. For relatively high memory situations where the XML source is also a DOM this isn't likely to prove that problematic, but for low memory situations where the XML source is provided through a SAX interface, this could be tricky, as the benefits of XSLT processing via SAX (high performance, low memory usage) disappear in the face of these large DOM-based entities. In that case, it may be preferable to break up your transformations into a series of stepped transformations, where each XSLT script handles one pass in the process (`sort.xsl`, `filter.xsl`, `makeTable.xsl`, etc.). For more details on DOM and SAX, see Chapter 6.

Variables by themselves are useful for creating temporary state in an otherwise stateless environment, but they fail to address a related problem – how to modify that state from the outside. If there was some way to pass information into a template (or a stylesheet) that could change its behavior, give it a manufactured data set to work with, or keep track of the number of times an operation has taken place, it would significantly expand what XSLT could do. This is where parameters come into their own – and leads us into the next section.

Parameter Power

A **parameter** is a special type of variable that can be set by an outside call. In the XML world, it serves precisely the same function as a parameter in a function call in the procedural realm – it passes information into a template or stylesheet for processing.

Parameterized stylesheets essentially let you pass information into an XSLT document, and provide one of the most significant ways of turning XSLT from a simple style language to a remarkably sophisticated programming language. The parameters discussed here are global parameters that work within the scope of the XSLT document itself – they are universally accessible from anywhere within the stylesheet. Parameters that are local to individual templates will be discussed later in this section.

The formal definition of a parameter is nearly identical to that of a variable, and comes in one of three basic flavors:

```
<xsl:param name="paramName"/>
<xsl:param name="paramName" select="XPathExpr"/>
<xsl:param name="paramName">XML Tree Fragment Content</xsl:param>
```

In the first case, the parameter is declared, but assumed to have no contents – the parameter would evaluate as being false in a test, or as being equivalent to the empty string (""). This form generally assumes that some external DOM code will fill the contents of this field before processing the XSLT.

The second form is the most typical, and gives a default value to the parameter if no external value is defined. As with a variable, this can be a string, a number, or an XPath expression specifying a node-set with zero or more members. Note that this value is overwritten if the parameter is set from the outside.

The final form is rarer for parameters than it is for variables, principally because of the limitations introduced by XML Tree Fragments and node-set(). At any given scope (such as the global scope of the document) parameters must precede both variables and most other code – at the template level, in fact, a parameter declaration can only be placed at the beginning of the template definition. Because of this, it is difficult to put generated code directly into parameters.

Parameters can be used to turn XSLT documents into mini-programs. For example, consider again the table generated in the previous example by the stylesheet listAuthors.xsl. The display criterion on the filtering was based upon sorting by the last name in ascending alphabetical order. However, people often want to change the sort order if the list is long (such as file names in a directory listing). By adding a parameter that sets the sort order to ascending or descending, the same stylesheet can be used to output both forms. The file is re-saved as paramListAuthors.xsl.

```
<xsl:stylesheet xmlns:xsl="http://www.w3.org/1999/XSL/Transform"
    xmlns:msxml="urn:schemas-microsoft-com:xslt" version="1.0">

<xsl:output method="html" media-type="text/html"/>

<!-- Note default value for parameter -->
<xsl:param name="order" select=" 'ascending' "/>

<!-- root match -->
<xsl:template match="/">

  <!-- create initial set of authors as tree fragment, sorted by LAST name   -->
  <xsl:variable name="redundant.authors.tf">
    <xsl:for-each select="//Author">
      <xsl:sort select="substring-after(.,' ')" order="{$order}"/>
      <xsl:copy-of select="."/>
    </xsl:for-each>
  </xsl:variable>
  ...
```

In this particular case, the parameter order is used to set the order attribute of the <xsl:sort> command that sorts the list prior to culling redundant names.

Parameters and the Outside World

While the use of these global parameters can obviously serve to simplify XSLT code, what may be far from obvious is how you go about calling these parameters or setting them outside the stylesheet. In an ASP application, for instance, it would be useful to pass the arguments of a query string or form request to an XSLT document as a parameter. Additionally useful would be the capability to take an XML message (such as a SOAP enveloped procedure call) and transform that into a request to parametrically process an XSLT document. Fortunately, both these things can be done quite simply, and the advantages that can be gained from parameter-enabling your XSLT can greatly influence the flexibility of your transformations.

XSLT presents an interesting paradox. The XSLT language itself has become remarkably uniform across the industry, but the techniques for manipulating the XSLT change dramatically from one server environment to the next, to such an extent that it is difficult to create a consistent "one size fits all" solution for Microsoft IIS, Apache, Solaris, etc. The examples given here are specific to IIS 4 and above, but the principles involved should be easy to emulate in JSP or other server scripting languages.

In both ASP and JSP, the principal avenue to access the server input stream is the Request object. This interface lets you reference by name an argument from a query string or a form post, as well as query server variables and (at least in the case of IIS) server side cookies. With access to these elements, you can create a very robust XSLT-based architecture that relies simply on the URL mechanism and doesn't require complex SOAP structures (also known as XML Protocol) or RPCs (Remote Procedure Calls) – though in the next section a SOAP interface is also explored.

A request-based architecture can be implemented in one of four different ways:

❑ In the DOM, the script assigns a specific (known) request property to a variable, retrieves a corresponding parameter from the XSLT document and sets the parameter to the variable. This is the way that most ASP-XSLT code is currently written, but this ties the ASP page to one and only one XSLT document. I call this the **explicit mapping architecture**.

❑ The specific stylesheet contains its own parameter set, and the names of these parameters can be used to query the Request object directly. One advantage to this is that you can substitute different stylesheets to handle different situations and the underlying ASP code doesn't need to change to meet the needs of each stylesheet. I call this the **implicit architecture**.

❑ Taking this one step further, the URL of the source to be processed, the URL of the stylesheet to process the source XML, or both could be passed in as parameters, and the script could then instantiate these, apply the appropriate transform, pass other parameters as needed, then send the resulting output back to the client. I call this the **dynamic mapping architecture**.

❑ SOAP messages can be used for remote procedure calls and for invoking web services (though URLs can as well). By passing a SOAP message with the name of the method being invoked as a reference to a stylesheet, the first argument being a reference to (or a container of) an XML data source, and subsequent arguments being parameters, you can use the dynamic mapping architecture to process the information. Because SOAP methods can also be data typed, this methodology works well with web services. I call this an **XSLT services architecture** and it is covered in much more detail in the next chapter.

We'll look at an example now, in particular an ASP page XServ.asp that illustrates a dynamic mapping architecture in action. Written in JScript, XServ.asp calls a JavaScript class called XServ.js, which provides methods for loading both a data source and a stylesheet from parameters passed via a URL query string or form post, and then queries the stylesheet to ascertain which parameters should be read from the query properties.

The code for XServ.js is as follows:

```
// XServ.js written in JScript
function XServ()
{
  this.request=requestFn;
  this.loadSource=loadSource;
  this.loadFile=loadFile;
  this.loadStylesheet=loadStylesheet;
```

```
  this.loadRequestParameters=loadRequestParameters;
  this.transform=transform;
  this.source=null;
  this.stylesheet=null;
  this.output=new ActiveXObject("MSXML2.FreeThreadedDOMDocument");
  this.getContentType=getContentType;
  this.setParameter=setParameter;
  this.setTransform=setTransform;
  this.error=null;
}

function loadFile(requestName,filePath,extension)
{
  var xmlDoc=new ActiveXObject("MSXML2.FreeThreadedDOMDocument");
  if (requestName==null){requestName="";}
  var requestPath=requestFn(requestName);
  if (""+requestPath != "undefined")
  {
    try{
      if (requestPath.indexOf(".")== requestPath.length - 4){}
    }
    catch(e){
      requestPath=requestPath + extension;
    }
  }
  else
  {
    requestPath=filePath;
  }
  xmlDoc.async=true;
  xmlDoc.load(Server.mapPath(requestPath))
  return xmlDoc;
}

function loadSource(requestName,sourcePath)
{
  this.source=loadFile(requestName,sourcePath,".xml");
}

function requestFn(requestName)
{
  // This should be overridden for custom request objects
  requestValue=Request(requestName);
  return requestValue;
}

function loadStylesheet(requestName,xformPath)
{
  this.stylesheet=loadFile(requestName,xformPath,".xsl");
}

function loadRequestParameters()
{
  var params=this.stylesheet.selectNodes("xsl:stylesheet/xsl:param");
  for (var i=0;i<params.length;i++)
```

```
    {
      param=params[i];
      paramName=param.getAttribute("name");
      paramValue="" + this.request(paramName);
      if (!(""+paramValue == "undefined")){
        if (paramValue.substr(1,1)=="@"){
          param.setAttribute("select",paramValue.substr(2));
        }
        else {
          var re=new RegExp("'","gi")
          param.setAttribute("select","'" + paramValue.replace(re,"&#8217;") +"'")
        }
      }
    }
  }
}

function setParameter(paramName,paramValue)
{
  var param=this.stylesheet.selectSingleNode("xsl:stylesheet/xsl:param[@name='"
    + paramName + "']");
  if (param){
    if (!(""+paramValue == "undefined")){
      if (paramValue.substr(1,1)=="@"){
        param.setAttribute("select",paramValue.substr(2));
      }
      else {
        param.setAttribute("select","'" + paramValue +"'")
      }
    }
  }
}

function getContentType(defaultContentType)
{
  if (defaultContentType==null){defaultContentType="text/xml";}
  var outputNode=this.stylesheet.selectSingleNode("xsl:stylesheet/xsl:output");
  if (""+this.request("contentType")!="undefined"){
    defaultContentType=this.request("contentType");
    outputNode=false;
  };
  if (outputNode){
    contentType=outputNode.getAttribute("media-type");
    if (contentType==""){
      contentType=defaultContentType;
    }
  }
  else {
    contentType=defaultContentType;
  }
  return contentType;
}

function setTransform(stylesheet)
{
  this.stylesheet=stylesheet;
}
```

```
function transform()
{
    this.source.transformNodeToObject(this.stylesheet,this.output);
    return this.output;
}
```

Next we list `XServ.asp`, which includes `XServ.js`:

```
<%@language="JavaScript"%>
<#include file="XServ.js" >
<%
// ***************** Start main()
function main()
{
    Response.expires=-1;
    var xserv=new XServ();
    xserv.loadSource("source","index.xml");
    xserv.loadStylesheet("xform","identity.xsl");
    Response.ContentType=xserv.getContentType("text/html");
    xserv.loadRequestParameters();

    xserv.transform();
    if (xserv.output.parseError.reason == ""){
        Response.write(xserv.output.xml);
    }
    else {
        Response.write(xserv.output.parseError.reason);
    }
}

main();

%>
```

The `main()` function will likely not change substantially from application to application, except for defining default files and content type.

The `requestName` parameter that both `LoadSource()` and `LoadStylesheet()` use in `XServ.js` translates to `source` and `xform` in `XServ.asp`. These parameters will then be queried from the command string. If either or both of the parameters are not passed from that string, then the code also specifies filenames that will be used instead. For instance, the declaration:

```
xserv.loadSource("source","index.xml");
xserv.loadStylesheet("xform","identity.xsl");
```

tells ASP to look in the query string parameter "`source`" for the name of the source XML file. If the parameter is not given, then the file `index.xml` will be used instead. Similarly, `identity.xsl` is used if no stylesheet is given in the parameter `xform` (the identity transform, `identity.xsl`, outputs exactly what was passed into it: note that it is an important transformation in creating XHTML services as well).

Thus, if these files were contained within a web-shared folder 3579 on your own computer, and the page was called with the URL:

http://localhost/3579/xserv.asp?source=catalog&xform=paramListAuthors

then the source document used for the transformation would be "catalog.xml" and the stylesheet transformation would be "paramListAuthors.xsl". Similarly:

http://localhost/3579/xserv.asp?source=catalog&xform=paramListAuthors&order=descending

would not only request these files, but because the file paramListAuthors.xsl has a global parameter called order, this parameter would be set to "descending", changing the order of the table from A first to z first. You should note that there is no explicit order parameter requested in the ASP code – it is determined solely from the default order parameter value within the XSLT document.

On the other hand, what happens when the URL is just:

http://localhost/3579/xserv.asp

In this particular case, the specified default files of index.xml and identity.xsl are used instead. This makes it possible to assign a central access point on your web site that can even be set up in the application's IIS folder as the default page. Especially when combined with the use of form posts, this can make the web site appear to revolve around a single URL.

One key point in the XServ.asp script is the method xserv.getContentType(). The purpose of getContentType() is to ascertain the "intent" of the XSL stylesheet – whether the XSL transformation produces plain text, XHTML, XML, or some other MIME-type output such as SVG. The assumption that the XServ.asp script makes is that the content produced by the transformation is itself XML based (in other words, you couldn't use XServ.asp to generate plain text or HTML that's not itself well-formed XML). Put another way, the <xsl:output> element of the stylesheet is always assumed to have a method attribute of "xml":

```
<xsl:output method="xml">
```

However, another <xsl:output> attribute, media-type, can be set to the MIME type of the desired output. For example:

```
<xsl:output method="xml" media-type="text/html">
```

would tell the XServ.asp application (through the function getContentType()) that the MIME type of the output should be set to "text/html". In turn, this will tell the browser to display the result as an HTML document, rather than as XML (text/xml would display as the latter). In XServ.asp, we pass a default MIME type into getContentType() as a string ("text/html"), which will set the MIME type if no media-type attribute of the <xsl:output> element is included.

There is another point in the architecture that deserves special mention. The example given here assumes that the parametric information comes exclusively from the IIS Request object, but it does so in a rather oblique fashion. Rather than calling Request() directly, the code wraps this call in a JavaScript function called requestFn(). One consequence of this is that a calling ASP function could implement a different version of requestFn() that overrides the current one and pulls from a different source. Allowing for this sort of overloading makes it easy for this code to be called on the client-side rather than on the server (where the parameters could be defined conceivably by the contents of <form> elements), or for the request parameters to come from an XML message (such as a SOAP object).

Finally, you can also pass a `contentType` parameter through a query string or form post – this will override the content type output of the transformation, letting you see an XHTML document as XML, or switch between a WML and an XHTML view, etc. Thus:

```
http://localhost/3579/xserv.asp?source=catalog&xform=paramListAuthors&
order=descending&contentType=text/xml
```

will convert the default content type of the document (which in this case is `text/html`) into `text/xml`.

Parameters and Web Services

We'll take a brief diversion here, before moving on to the realm of named templates. A great deal of time and energy has been spent by companies pushing the notion of web services. A **web service** basically sends either a URL data string, a form post, or an XML message (such as a SOAP document) to a server, which takes the parameters being passed and uses them to evaluate system functions, call complex business rules, or handle other activities. Typically, the web service in turn sends back a response that contains the "result" of the service – the canonical example seems to be querying the current price of Microsoft stock, which at the moment would appear a rather depressing proposition.

One way of thinking about a web service is to see it as a method call against a specific object (typically represented by a URL path), with parameters specifying details of the interaction. For example, suppose (jumping back to the book publishing application here) that you had an application that needed a list of books in a given category as a SOAP message. The `catalog.xml` file is updated periodically to reflect the most recent published work, but that process is independent of any queries against it. A web service could retrieve the information through a simple URL call:

```
http://localhost/3579/wroxcatalog?method=getBooksByCategory&category=XSL
&sortby=Title
```

The result may in turn come back as a SOAP message (I'm dropping `<SOAP-ENV:Head>` information for simplicity):

```xml
<SOAP-ENV:Envelope xmlns:SOAP-ENV="http://schemas.xmlsoap.org/soap/envelope"
   SOAP-ENV:encodingStyle="http://schemas.xmlsoap.org/soap/encoding/">
  <SOAP-ENV:Head>
  ...
  </SOAP-ENV:Head>
  <SOAP-ENV:Body>
      <Book>
          <Title>XSLT Programmer's Reference</Title>
          <Authors>
             <Author>Michael Kay</Author>
          </Authors>
          <Publisher>Wrox Press, Ltd.</Publisher>
          <PubDate>2000-04</PubDate>
          <Abstract>Learn how to use the XSLT language to develop web
          applications</Abstract>
          <Pages>800</Pages>
          <ISBN>1-861003-12-9</ISBN>
          <RecSubjCategories>
             <Category>Internet</Category>
             <Category>XML</Category>
             <Category>XSL</Category>
          </RecSubjCategories>
          <Price>$34.99</Price>
          <CoverImage>3129.gif</CoverImage>
      </Book>
  </SOAP-ENV:Body>
</SOAP-ENV:Envelope>
```

However, this information could in fact be set up to work just with an XSLT stylesheet and query string or form parameters. The name of the transformation (getBooksByCategory.xsl) is the same as the name of the method being invoked, and in this case, the catalog.xml file is called implicitly by the XServ2.asp file below (located by the document path 3579/wroxcatalog and set to be the default file):

```
<%@language="JavaScript"%>
<!--#include file="XServ.js" -->
<%
// ***************** Start main()
function main()
{
  Response.expires=-1;
  var xserv=new XServ();
  xserv.loadSource("","catalog.xml");
  xserv.loadStylesheet("method","identity.xsl");
  Response.ContentType=xserv.getContentType("text/xml");
  xserv.loadRequestParameters();

  xserv.transform();
  if (xserv.output.parseError.reason == ""){
    Response.write(xserv.output.xml);
  }
  else {
    Response.write(xserv.output.parseError.reason);
  }
}

main();

%>
```

XServ2.asp is nearly identical to XServ.asp, with the exception of the default settings. It could host any number of methods (XSLT transformations) against the default catalog.xml.

It's instructive to note that the LoadSource() function has had its requestName parameter set to "" – in essence indicating that the only query string parameter that can match the source would be one with a blank name, something that can't be passed through either a query string or a form post. The practical consequence of this is to "lock" the source so that nothing can change it – the XServ function will always use catalog.xml (as given).

So, our "method" getBooksByCategory now becomes the following XSLT transformation, getBooksByCategory.xsl:

```
<xsl:stylesheet xmlns:xsl="http://www.w3.org/1999/XSL/Transform"
  xmlns:msxml="urn:schemas-microsoft-com:xslt"
  version="1.0">
  <xsl:param name="category" select="''"/>
  <xsl:param name="sortby" select="'Title'"/>
  <xsl:output method="xml" media-type="text/xml" omit-xml-declaration="yes"/>

  <xsl:template match="/">
    <SOAP-ENV:Envelope xmlns:SOAP-ENV="http://schemas.xmlsoap.org/soap/envelope"
      SOAP-ENV:encodingStyle="http://schemas.xmlsoap.org/soap/encoding/">
```

```
      <SOAP-ENV:Body>
        <xsl:choose>
          <xsl:when test="$category=''">
            <xsl:apply-templates select="//Book">
              <xsl:sort select=".//*[name(.)=$sortby]"/>
            </xsl:apply-templates>
          </xsl:when>
          <xsl:otherwise>
            <xsl:apply-templates
              select="//Book[RecSubjCategories/Category=$category]">
              <xsl:sort select=".//*[name(.)=$sortby]"/>
            </xsl:apply-templates>
          </xsl:otherwise>
        </xsl:choose>
      </SOAP-ENV:Body>
    </SOAP-ENV:Envelope>
  </xsl:template>

  <xsl:template match="Book">
    <xsl:copy-of select="."/>
  </xsl:template>
</xsl:stylesheet>
```

This new XSLT transformation has two parameters – category, which filters the output to just the required category, and sortby, which determines the order of the resulting books based upon the given property name.

As a side note, if you want to sort content without knowing ahead of time which element will be the sort key, think about using the following XPath query:

```
<xsl:sort select=".//*[name(.)=$sortby]"/>
```

XSLT-based web services can get considerably more complex (and such complexity will be explored in greater detail throughout this and the next chapter), but the underlying message that I want to get across here is that web classes do not require extensive amounts of procedural code, but can in fact be handled quite readily using XSLT alone. Especially in cases involving the generation of XML, XSLT-based transformations in conjunction with the dynamic mapping architecture can often give you more flexible, robust code than pure object-oriented procedural languages, such as Java, C#, or VB, alone. Of course, the combination of the two can prove devastatingly powerful.

Building with Named Templates

Named templates entered into the XSLT specification fairly late in the game, but they are absolutely essential when it comes to moving beyond all but the simplest of applications. A named template can be thought of as a localized stylesheet – it has parameters and can be invoked by name rather than as the result of a match. The syntax of named templates is straightforward:

```
<xsl:template name="templateName">

  <!-- A parameter with no default -->
  <xsl:param name="param0"/>
  <!-- A parameter with a default value of "value1" -->
  <xsl:param name="param1" select="value1"/>
```

```
<!-- A parameter with the parameter content given as a tree fragment (XSLT
1.0) or a node-set (XSLT 1.1) -->
<xsl:param name="param2">
  <!-- parameter content -->
</xsl:param>

<!-- template content -->
</xsl:template>
```

Calling a template is about as straightforward. The <xsl:call-template> command calls a named template and passes parameters to the template using the <xsl:with-param> element:

```
<xsl:call-template name="templateName">

  <xsl:with-param name="param0" select="new_value0"/>
  <xsl:with-param name="param1" select="new_value1"/>
  <xsl:with-param name="param2">
    <!-- other parameter content-->
  </xsl:with-param>

</xsl:call-template>
```

There are a few subtle differences between <xsl:apply-templates> and <xsl:call-template>. <xsl:apply-templates> attempts to find a match pattern from any template in the stylesheet (or in any includes or imports), while <xsl:call-template> calls one specific template: hence the change from plural (templates) to singular (template).

A second distinction between the two is that <xsl:apply-templates> supports the mode attribute, which limits the match to only those templates that have mode attributes with the same value. Note that if no mode attribute is specified, the match is limited to only those templates that also have no mode attribute. A named template does not support the mode attribute (unless the named template is also a match template, which occurs *very* seldom).

Before we go on with our tour of named templates, there is another point to note about the mode attribute. In Chapter 3 we looked at all the default templates of a stylesheet except one – the default template for mode templates:

```
<xsl:template match="*|/" mode="m">
  <xsl:apply-templates mode="m"/>
</xsl:template>
```

Such a default template exists for each value m of the mode attribute of <xsl:apply-templates> elements within the stylesheet. For examples of the mode attribute in use, see the Case Study.

Now back to named templates. In the XSLT world, these are analogous to functions in the procedural world, with the parameters corresponding directly to functional parameters. Consider a simple example – a named template that converts a string of text to upper or lower case:

```
<xsl:template name="changeCase">
  <xsl:param name="sourceStr"/>
  <xsl:param name="case" select="'lower'"/>
  <xsl:choose>
```

```
      <xsl:when test="$case='upper'">
        <xsl:value-of select="translate($sourceStr,
         'abcdefghijklmnopqrstuvwxyz',
         'ABCDEFGHIJKLMNOPQRSTUVWXYZ')"/>
      </xsl:when>
      <xsl:when test="$case='lower'">
        <xsl:value-of select="translate($sourceStr,
         'ABCDEFGHIJKLMNOPQRSTUVWXYZ',
         'abcdefghijklmnopqrstuvwxyz')"/>
      </xsl:when>
      <xsl:otherwise>
        <xsl:value-of select="$sourceStr"/>
      </xsl:otherwise>
    </xsl:choose>
  </xsl:template>
```

The `changeCase` template takes two arguments – a source string (`sourceStr`) and an optional case identifier (`case`), which defaults to "`lower`". The template uses the XPath `translate()` function to translate all (English) uppercase characters to lowercase or vice versa depending upon the value of `case` – if neither of these matches, by the way, the function returns the source string untransformed thanks to the `<xsl:otherwise>` element.

The named template would then be called using the `<xsl:call-template>` element, analogous to the VB `call` keyword (which is typically implied rather than invoked explicitly):

```
<xsl:call-template name="changeCase">
  <xsl:with-param name="sourceStr" select="'This is a test.'"/>
  <xsl:with-param name="case" select="'upper'"/>
</xsl:call-template>
```

This would place:

THIS IS A TEST

into the output stream. Additionally, you could pass the same information into a variable. For example, the following (working against the `catalog.xml` file discussed earlier in this chapter), would convert each title to uppercase and place it in a table):

```
<xsl:template match="Book">
  <xsl:variable name="titleStr" select="Title"/>

  <xsl:variable name="ucTitle">
    <xsl:call-template name="changeCase">
      <xsl:with-param name="sourceStr" select="$titleStr"/>
      <xsl:with-param name="case" select="'upper'"/>
    </xsl:call-template>
  </xsl:variable>

  <tr><td><xsl:value-of select="$ucTitle"/></td></tr>
</xsl:template>
```

That weakness in the current W3C specification previously mentioned shows up most obviously here. The same issue that forces variable content to be tree fragments means that if you use a named template to generate XML (one of its more common uses) from variables, you will need to make sure that you use the `node-set()` function to convert the variables' contents *back* to a node-set.

Example: Paging Results

Consider the problem of paging. When you have a large database of items, sending a lengthy query result back to the client all at once is often neither practical nor desirable. Instead, it's far more common for web designers to create paged output in which only 20, 30, or some other item count is displayed at a time. Typically, the process for generating such a page can be broken into four distinct steps:

1. Order the initial dataset. This stage could be omitted if the dataset comes from a source already ordered appropriately.

2. Pass the dataset to a named template along with the current page and the page size. This will generate a paged XML structure that includes just the items that were filtered.

3. Transform the filtered list into some appropriate display output structure. This is done with modal matched templates, which occur frequently in conjunction with named templates.

4. Finally, create a navigational bar – this lets you jump from one page to the next of the data either sequentially or randomly. Navigational bars can either be form or query-string driven – the example below illustrates both techniques.

The stylesheet we will look at, `page.display.xsl`, performs all four of these operations, and demonstrates how sophisticated such XSLT applications can get. Designed to work with `XServ.asp`, the `page.display` transformation demonstrates how all four of these pieces can be tied together to create a single stand alone application. Such a transformation would then be called as:

http://localhost/3579/xserv.asp?source=catalog&xform=page.display&sortBy=Title&page=2&pageSize=10

which would retrieve the second page of ten records from the catalog, sorted by title and displayed in a table.

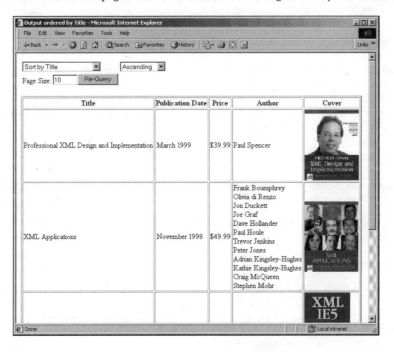

Let's now turn to the stylesheet. One of the principle tricks in turning your XSLT into an application, at least through a mechanism such as `XServ.asp`, is to declare global parameters that you'll want to be able to access using a form or query string. In the case of the `page.display` transform, the user can set four parameters: `sortBy` to determine what field in the recordset to sort by, `sortOrder` to determine whether the sorting is ascending or descending, `pageSize` to indicate how many records to display per page, and `page` to indicate which page to show. Additionally, `source` and `xform` are also declared in order to pass the source XML and transforming XSLT into any form or query string requests in the resulting page output.

```
<xsl:stylesheet xmlns:xsl="http://www.w3.org/1999/XSL/Transform"
    xmlns:msxml="urn:schemas-microsoft-com:xslt" version="1.0">

<xsl:output method="xml" media-type="text/html" omit-xml-declaration="yes"/>

<xsl:param name="sortBy" select="'Title'"/>
<xsl:param name="sortOrder" select="'ascending'"/>
<xsl:param name="page" select="1"/>
<xsl:param name="pageSize" select="5"/>
<xsl:param name="source"/>
<xsl:param name="xform"/>
```

The first template is a root node match and exists solely to get things started. In this case it simply moves the context to the first element of the source document (named `<Catalog>`).

```
<xsl:template match="/">
  <xsl:apply-templates select="*"/>
</xsl:template>
```

The next template element is generic; it defines and filters the dataset, as well as laying out the page by specifying the HTML output framework. Notice that at this level the amount of implementation code is very minimal – most of the XSLT calls other named templates, in a manner analogous to the way that, almost invariably, a `main()` function in VB or C++ will primarily consist of subroutine calls.

First, the variables `sortedItems.tf` and `pagedItems.tf` are defined, to process the original data into the sorted and paginated forms, and these routines are deliberately kept very generic. They could easily be turned into external named templates themselves. The `msxml:node-set()` function is used to convert the resultant tree fragments (indicated by ".tf") from the `<xsl:call-template>` calls into the node sets, `sortedItems` and `pagedItems`.

```
<xsl:template match="/*">

  <!-- sort the items by the $sortBy parameter -->
  <xsl:variable name="sortedItems.tf">
    <xsl:for-each select="*">
      <xsl:sort select="*[name(.)=$sortBy]" order="{$sortOrder}"/>
      <xsl:copy-of select="."/>
    </xsl:for-each>
  </xsl:variable>

  <xsl:variable name="sortedItems" select="msxml:node-set($sortedItems.tf)"/>

  <!-- extract the given page of records from the sorted set -->
  <xsl:variable name="pagedItems.tf">
    <xsl:call-template name="page.filter">
```

```
        <xsl:with-param name="dataset" select="$sortedItems"/>
        <xsl:with-param name="page" select="$page"/>
        <xsl:with-param name="pageSize" select="$pageSize"/>
     </xsl:call-template>
  </xsl:variable>

  <xsl:variable name="pagedItems" select="msxml:node-set($pagedItems.tf)"/>
```

It should be noted that if you are working with a database through an interface such as ADO, you might be better off using the database to extract the sorted and filtered data, passing the query string parameters into the SQL call from the DOM. However, where the data involved isn't so large as to justify the creation of an explicit relational database for it, or where the data is generated from a larger database located remotely to the server, or where the data comes from some other XML/XSLT process, performing these transformations directly make a lot more sense.

Most of the rest of the code in the stylesheet is devoted to generating the display output from the pagedItems node set. This dramatically illustrates one of the real benefits of variables – using them to store intermediate node-sets. Thus, the amount of generated output code can be cut down to a small subset of what would be needed without variables, making processing faster and easier to decouple.

Again notice that the actual drawing of the output here is handled by "subroutines" of named templates (in particular a template with the name page.filter is called). An additional advantage to this approach is that it is possible to override the default behavior of named or matched templates using <xsl:import> statements – the more encapsulated the code is, the easier it is to override parts of the code without having to rewrite the entire routine. This is discussed further in the next chapter.

This next part of the template draws a navigation bar that lets users select what they want to use as their sort criteria, which direction they want to sort in, and how many records they wish to display per page. Because sort criteria and column display are very much tied into the specific schemas being employed, this code is not generic, though it is easily adapted. Note how other named templates are called here.

```
    <html>
      <head>
        <title>Output ordered by <xsl:value-of select="$sortBy"/></title>
      </head>
      <body>
        <!-- draw the form navbar to set $sortBy, $sortOrder, and $pageSize -->
        <xsl:call-template name="page.navbar.form.draw"/>

        <!-- display the table of items -->
        <xsl:call-template name="items.display">
          <xsl:with-param name="pagedItems" select="$pagedItems"/>
        </xsl:call-template>

        <!-- draw the navbar of pages, along with previous and next buttons -->
        <xsl:call-template name="page.navbar.draw">
          <xsl:with-param name="datasetLength" select="count($sortedItems/*)"/>
          <xsl:with-param name="page" select="$page"/>
        </xsl:call-template>

      </body>
    </html>
  </xsl:template>
```

page.filter

The actual named `page.filter` template, called from within the definition of the `pagedItems.tf` variable, is quite simple – it uses an `<xsl:for-each>` loop to retrieve only those records that fall within a given range of positions (calculated using the `position()` function). Note that in such a loop, you do still need to explicitly copy each node that satisfies the condition into the output stream (this is a common source of errors in XSLT code, by the way).

```
<xsl:template name="page.filter">
  <xsl:param name="dataset"/>
  <xsl:param name="page"/>
  <xsl:param name="pageSize"/>

  <xsl:for-each select="$dataset/*[(position()&gt;($page - 1) * $pageSize) and
    (position() &lt;= $page * $pageSize)]">
    <xsl:copy-of select="."/>
  </xsl:for-each>

</xsl:template>
```

items.display

The next named template, `items.display`, creates the table for display based upon the `pagedItems` node-set. Obviously, this template is very specific to the data being displayed. There was a deliberate effort here to separate the display of the table from the navigational or form elements on the page – this gives you the flexibility of rearranging or omitting specific elements without having to significantly rewrite code. This modularization, as mentioned previously, also makes it much simpler to override specific behaviors without having to get into the messy innards of the code.

```
<xsl:template name="items.display">
  <xsl:param name="pagedItems"/>
  <table border="2">
    <tr>
      <th>Title</th>
      <th>Publication Date</th>
      <th>Price</th>
      <th>Author</th>
      <th>Cover</th>
    </tr>
    <xsl:for-each select="$pagedItems/*">
      <tr>
        <td><xsl:value-of select="Title"/></td>
        <td>
          <xsl:call-template name="datetime.expand">
            <xsl:with-param name="date" select="PubDate"/>
          </xsl:call-template>
        </td>
        <td><xsl:value-of select="Price"/></td>
        <td>
          <xsl:for-each select="Authors/Author">
            <xsl:value-of select="."/>
            <xsl:if test="position()!=last()">
              <br/><xsl:text> </xsl:text>
            </xsl:if>
          </xsl:for-each>
```

```
          </td>
          <td>
            <img src="images/{CoverImage}" height="150"/>
          </td>
        </tr>
      </xsl:for-each>
    </table>
  </xsl:template>
```

Note that this template calls yet another named template, `datetime.expand`.

datetime.expand

The accepted format for rendering dates in XML is the format YYYY-MM-DDTHH:MM:SS.FF. For example, January 14, 2001 at 3:57.35PM would be rendered as 2001-01-14T15:57.35. One of the primary advantages of expressing dates in this fashion is that such dates can be sorted alphabetically as text, rather than requiring complex internal date conversions. However, this particular format is hardly readable, so a named template, `datetime.expand`, is used to convert a numeric month to its name and abbreviation by bringing node-sets into duty as a lookup table.

By storing information as look up tables within the XSLT stylesheet, it is much easier to handle conversions than if the routine was written as a series of `<xsl:if>` statements. In addition to using this technique for converting dates, it can be used to store critical trigonometric values for graphical output (as shown in Chapter 12), potential array values for a select box, lists of states, and so forth.

```
<xsl:variable name="month_names.tf">
  <month name="January" abbreviation="JAN"/>
  <month name="February" abbreviation="FEB"/>
  <month name="March" abbreviation="MAR"/>
  <month name="April" abbreviation="APR"/>
  <month name="May" abbreviation="MAY"/>
  <month name="June" abbreviation="JUN"/>
  <month name="July" abbreviation="JUL"/>
  <month name="August" abbreviation="AUG"/>
  <month name="September" abbreviation="SEP"/>
  <month name="October" abbreviation="OCT"/>
  <month name="November" abbreviation="NOV"/>
  <month name="December" abbreviation="DEC"/>
</xsl:variable>
<xsl:variable name="month_names" select="msxml:node-set($month_names.tf)"/>

<!-- datetime.expand converts dates of the form YYYY-MM-DD to dates of the form
Month YYYY or DD Month YYYY. It uses $month_names as if it was an array. -->
<xsl:template name="datetime.expand">
  <xsl:param name="date"/>

  <xsl:variable name="year" select="substring($date,1,4)"/>
  <xsl:variable name="month" select="number(substring($date,6,2))"/>
  <xsl:variable name="day" select="substring($date,9,2)"/>
  <xsl:value-of select="$day"/><xsl:text> </xsl:text>
  <xsl:value-of select="$month_names/*[$month]/@name"/><xsl:text> </xsl:text>
  <xsl:value-of select="$year"/>
</xsl:template>
```

page.navbar.draw

We saw above that to draw the navigation bar for different pages, the `page.navbar.draw` named template is called. This template actually calls two distinct subtemplates – `page.navbar.cell.draw` to handle the display of individual page numbers and `page.navbar.cell.pn.draw` to draw the "previous" and "next" buttons. In both cases the output of these routines is created from the query string. Note that you could also use form fields and a form submission to pass the parameters from an HTML page, a technique that is displayed with the template `page.navbar.form.draw`. This template is called to produce the navigation bar that sets the sorting parameters, and we will look at it shortly.

```
<xsl:template name="page.navbar.draw">
  <xsl:param name="datasetLength"/>
  <xsl:param name="page"/>
  <table>
    <tr>
      <xsl:call-template name="page.navbar.cell.pn.draw">
        <xsl:with-param name="datasetLength" select="$datasetLength"/>
        <xsl:with-param name="page" select="$page"/>
        <xsl:with-param name="state" select="'previous'"/>
      </xsl:call-template>

      <xsl:call-template name="page.navbar.cell.draw">
        <xsl:with-param name="datasetLength" select="$datasetLength"/>
        <xsl:with-param name="page" select="$page"/>
        <xsl:with-param name="currentPage" select="1"/>
      </xsl:call-template>

      <xsl:call-template name="page.navbar.cell.pn.draw">
        <xsl:with-param name="datasetLength" select="$datasetLength"/>
        <xsl:with-param name="page" select="$page"/>
        <xsl:with-param name="state" select="'next'"/>
      </xsl:call-template>
    </tr>
  </table>
</xsl:template>
```

page.navbar.cell.draw

The `page.navbar.cell.draw` named template demonstrates a number of useful XSLT techniques. One of the most powerful (albeit more complicated) capabilities of templates is **recursion** – they can call themselves with slightly different parameters. XSLT does not include a construct that corresponds to the procedural `for` token, an omission that can seem strange. The primary reason for this has to do with the nature of variables in XSLT – once a variable is defined, it cannot be redefined in the same scope. This can prove problematic in trying to enumerate over an index (such as trying to display a list of all of the page numbers that are available in a given dataset), since you can't define something like:

```
<xsl:for index="i" start="0" while= "$i &lt; 10" increment="1"/>
```

as the index variable `i` would then be redefined each time within the same scope. (It would be useful if you could, as it would radically simplify some of the recursive hoops that have to be jumped through to get all but the simplest operations done, but at the current time there is no plan for such a construct – though the use of XML Query Language in XSLT 2.0 may change that.)

In the case of this particular named template, the routine is initially called with the `currentPage` parameter set to 1. The routine generates HTML output to create one linked `<td>` element if `currentPage` doesn't have the same value as `page`, or a highlighted but dead element if `currentPage` is the same as `page`. The routine then checks to see if the current page is the last page to be displayed. If not, `page.navbar.cell.draw` is called again, but this time with `currentPage` incremented by one.

The other noteworthy aspect of this particular routine relates to the way that query strings are constructed. URLs use ampersand characters (&) to separate parameters, but XML sees the ampersand as an escape character. As a consequence, to separate the query string values you need to use `"&amp;"` to generate the ampersand, not just `"&"`.

```
<xsl:template name="page.navbar.cell.draw">
  <xsl:param name="datasetLength"/>
  <xsl:param name="page"/>
  <xsl:param name="currentPage"/>

  <xsl:choose>
    <xsl:when test="$page=$currentPage">
      <td>
        <b><xsl:value-of select="$currentPage"/></b>
      </td>
    </xsl:when>
    <xsl:otherwise>
      <td>
        <a href="xserv.asp?source={$source}&amp;xform={$xform}
           &amp;contentType={$contentType}&amp;sortBy={$sortBy}
           &amp;sortOrder={$sortOrder}&amp;page={$currentPage}
           &amp;pageSize={$pageSize}"><xsl:value-of select="$currentPage"/>
        </a>
      </td>
    </xsl:otherwise>
  </xsl:choose>

  <xsl:if test="$currentPage &lt; ceiling($datasetLength div $pageSize)">
    <xsl:call-template name="page.navbar.cell.draw">
      <xsl:with-param name="datasetLength" select="$datasetLength"/>
      <xsl:with-param name="page" select="$page"/>
      <xsl:with-param name="currentPage" select="$currentPage + 1"/>
    </xsl:call-template>
  </xsl:if>
</xsl:template>
```

page.navbar.cell.pn.draw

`page.navbar.cell.pn.draw` generates a very similar output to `page.navbar.cell.draw`, except that instead of displaying the possible page numbers in the set, it generates arrows for moving to the previous or next set of records. The same routine is used for generating both previous and next elements, determined by setting the `state` parameter to either `"previous"` or `"next"`.

```
<xsl:template name="page.navbar.cell.pn.draw">
  <xsl:param name="datasetLength"/>
  <xsl:param name="page"/>
  <xsl:param name="state"/>
```

```
    <xsl:if test="$state='previous'">
      <xsl:choose>
        <xsl:when test="$page = 1">
          <td>&lt;&lt;&lt;&lt;</td>
        </xsl:when>
        <xsl:otherwise>
          <td>
            <a href="xserv.asp?source={$source}&amp;xform={$xform}
              &amp;contentType={$contentType}&amp;sortBy={$sortBy}
              &amp;sortOrder={$sortOrder}&amp;page={$page - 1}
              &amp;pageSize={$pageSize}">&lt;&lt;&lt;&lt;
            </a>
          </td>
        </xsl:otherwise>
      </xsl:choose>
    </xsl:if>
    <xsl:if test="$state='next'">
      <xsl:choose>
        <xsl:when test="$page = ceiling($datasetLength div $pageSize)">
          <td>&gt;&gt;&gt;&gt;</td>
        </xsl:when>
        <xsl:otherwise>
          <td>
            <a href="xserv.asp?source={$source}&amp;xform={$xform}
              &amp;contentType={$contentType}&amp;sortBy={$sortBy}
              &amp;sortOrder={$sortOrder}&amp;page={$page + 1}
              &amp;pageSize={$pageSize}">&gt;&gt;&gt;&gt;
            </a>
          </td>
        </xsl:otherwise>
      </xsl:choose>
    </xsl:if>
  </xsl:template>
```

page.navbar.form.draw

`page.navbar.form.draw` provides an alternative mechanism for passing information, utilizing form fields rather than query string properties to pass information. The name of each form element corresponds to the XSLT parameter being processed. Because it is conceivable that there may be more than one form on a page, the name of the form is partially generated using the XSLT `generate-id()` function, which creates a unique identifier.

Form elements can work more effectively in creating interfaces that keep the inner workings of the parameter-passing off the browser's navigation bar. You can pass parameters that are not specifically set by the user through the use of the `<input type="hidden" ?/>` XHTML element (for example, passing `source` and `xform` to the server).

```
  <xsl:template name="page.navbar.form.draw">
    <form name="form{generate-id()}" method="post" action="xserv.asp">
      <table>
        <tr>
          <td>
            <select name="sortBy" value="{$sortBy}">
              <option value="Title">
                <xsl:if test="$sortBy='Title'">
```

```
                        <xsl:attribute name="selected" value="'yes'"/>
                      </xsl:if>
                      Sort by Title
                    </option>
                    <option value="PubDate">
                      <xsl:if test="$sortBy='PubDate'">
                        <xsl:attribute name="selected">yes</xsl:attribute>
                      </xsl:if>
                      Sort by Publication Date
                    </option>
                    <option value="Price">
                      <xsl:if test="$sortBy='Price'">
                        <xsl:attribute name="selected">yes</xsl:attribute>
                      </xsl:if>
                    . Sort by Price
                    </option>
                  </select>
              </td>
              <td>
                <select name="sortOrder" value="{$sortOrder}">
                  <option value="ascending">
                    <xsl:if test="$sortOrder='ascending'">
                      <xsl:attribute name="selected">yes</xsl:attribute>
                    </xsl:if>
                    Ascending
                  </option>
                  <option value="descending">
                    <xsl:if test="$sortOrder='descending'">
                      <xsl:attribute name="selected">yes</xsl:attribute>
                    </xsl:if>
                    Descending
                  </option>
                </select>
              </td>
            </tr>
            <tr>
              <td>Page Size:
                <input type="text" name="pageSize" value="{$pageSize}" size="5"/>
                <input type="submit" value="Re-Query"/>
              </td>
            </tr>
          </table>
          <input type="hidden" name="source" value="{$source}"/>
          <input type="hidden" name="xform" value="{$xform}"/>
          <input type="hidden" name="page" value="1"/>
        </form>
  </xsl:template>

</xsl:stylesheet>
```

One brief thought about the data source – an XSLT transformation can be very efficient, but if the initial data source is large, even the smallest transformation can be brought to its knees. One of the aims of the above XSLT stylesheet is to reduce the amount of processing to the absolute minimum before applying the visualization style to the data by sorting and filtering the contents first. Something to note as well – it may be more efficacious to separate the sorting, filtering, and displaying into three separate transformations that could then query the current state (something best achieved through the extension mechanism discussed in the next chapter) to determine whether a cached resource is available. An already sorted list shouldn't need to be repeatedly sorted, cached pages don't need to be filtered again, and (for that matter) already generated output for a given sorted, filtered list shouldn't have to be recreated from scratch.

When you are designing your transformations, you should thus be prepared to explore issues such as caching of resources (keeping both XML and XSLT structures in memory, for instance) and providing some additional way of caching database queries that generate XML data to minimize this particular bottleneck. A further example of caching data on the client is given in Chapter 8.

Summary

While this chapter pushes the boundary of complexity, it also demonstrates how output can be generated easily via a server-side interface. The key to developing such an application is to recognize where functionality can be effectively modularized and to move away from the monolithic transformations that can't be reused for other applications.

Modularity is a critical first step in building applications in any programming language, but XSLT applications have reuse features other than cutting and pasting templates into other documents. To move beyond this, you will need to start working with external resources – XML data coming from sources other than the document to be transformed, XSLT components imported from external files, extensions written using Java or COM that give XSLT access to system resources, and so forth. In the next chapter, you can explore some of these alternative mechanisms, and gain an insight into XSLT's potential as an integral part of sophisticated distributed applications drawing on resources from all over the Internet.

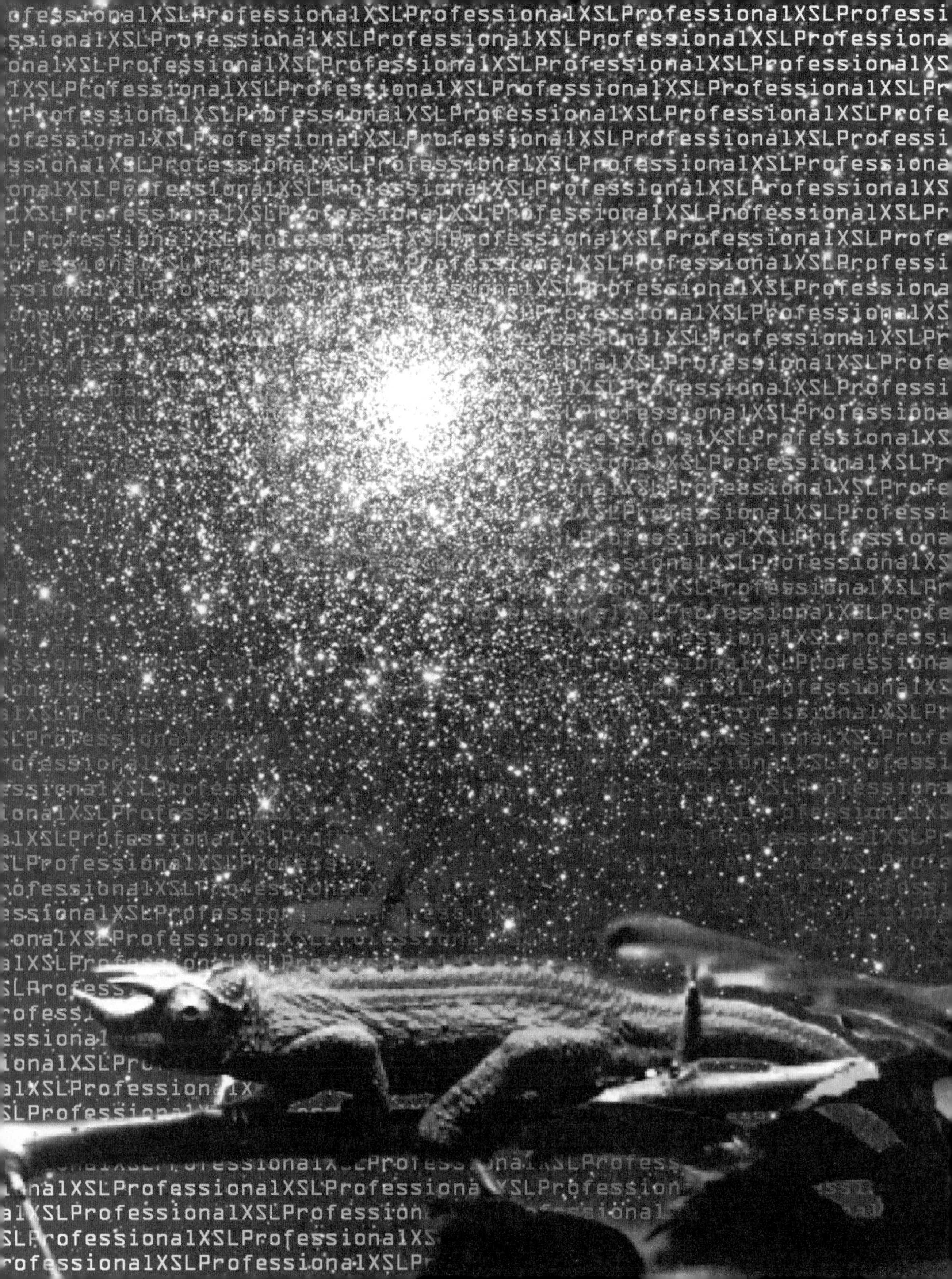
XSLProfessional

5

External XSLT

XML is often hyped as a distributed language, and this claim certainly has an antecedent in SGML. There is a compelling argument that in an SGML view of the world, you don't have discrete "files" per se – documents may be rich and deep, extending (through the use of entities) into other documents that occupy the whole space of information. However, due in large part to the current emphasis on data-centric XML, the distributed aspects of the language are sometimes lost.

The concept of a distributed application means many different things to different people, so it's worth exploring what exactly is being discussed here. A good working definition is that in a distributed application the data resources and/or the operant code exist in more than one process. By that definition, most COM-based programming can actually be considered distributed programming, so there is usually an implication that the processes exist on different machines.

> *This however is a fairly artificial distinction arising from the architectures of COM and CORBA, which tend to regard brokered objects existing within a given machine's boundaries quite differently from objects that exist outside of that machine's boundaries.*

XML, of course, offers no such distinction. In an XML-based world, it is useful to think of XML as the mediator of information between two or more devices. A useful analogy can be found in the realm of physics. Simplistically, when the state of an electron in orbit around an atomic nucleus changes, it emits a photon. This photon will then be absorbed by other atoms in the vicinity. In many cases, the photon is simply retransmitted and the atom returns to its previous state. However, there will be times when an atom on receiving a photon enters a new state and transmits a different type of photon. In fact, there are times when an atom will hold on to a photon until it has absorbed a second or even third. A new photon will then be emitted, and the atom will be left in a new state, depending on the nature of the multiple photons absorbed.

We can think of devices on the Internet (or within an intranet) as being atoms, and the XML information they communicate with as equivalent to the photons in the above analogy. XML is a "daton", a mediating element that contains information that can potentially change the state of the device that intercepts it. This 'intercepting device' resembles the atom in the analogy above when absorbing a photon – it receives information in the form of XML from some other online device, processes the information, and sends new XML information back out without knowing intimate details about the state of the device that sent the XML in the first place.

So what does this have to do with XSLT? As it turns out, quite a bit. XSLT consumes XML and (usually) produces XML as output. In many cases, XSLT has single input and output sources, but through the use of parameters, the document() function, and extensions, XSLT can in fact consume multiple sources of XML. It's also possible to generate multiple output streams through the use of extensions (which are to be available internally with the <xsl:document> element should the current XSLT 1.1 working draft become a formal recommendation).

Moreover, XSLT is, like the web, stateless – it manipulates the state of an application through the characteristics of the XML that it consumes and produces. In other words, an XSLT transformation can be thought of as the XML-based idealization of a pure device, close to being completely independent of the platform on which it runs. This is a critical aspect of developing peer-to-peer based systems that are dynamic, flexible, inexpensive, and scalable, and as a consequence has implications for everything from document management to gaming, shared environments to B2B and B2C networks, and instant messaging to e-mail.

One of the defining characteristics of such a "device-and-mediator" network is its simplicity – the HTML-based Internet works because it employs a simple language for the manipulation of a specific type of device, namely a browser. XML has similarly caught on because it provides a simple, universal way of encoding information, although in all likelihood the vast majority of XML schemas for the next few years will probably end up as XHTML, because the browser paradigm still so strongly informs our interaction with the Internet. XSLT is perfectly well designed for generating XHTML from XML resources (or even from well-formed XHTML-like languages such as the Wireless Markup Language or VoiceXML, that employ intermediate namespaces for specialized functions), for both interpreting and generating enveloping schemas such as SOAP or MIME-XML, and for the retrieval of XML resources according to other XML resources, regardless of where those resources are located or what they ultimately represent.

This chapter, as the second covering advanced XSLT topics, looks at the distributed characteristics of XSLT, shows how XSLT can be used to build a distributed XSLT application, and explores the potential of XSLT in the distributed arena as well as pointing out some of the pitfalls.

Documents and the Hyperspace World

One of the more critical concepts for the ancestors of XML was that of the **entity**. In SGML an entity is a reference to a block of text somewhere beyond the immediate boundaries of a document. Such entities could include not just SGML or XML, but also pure text and character encodings. However, entities also had some serious limitations, not least of which being that they could only really be created as part of the initial DTD of the document – to use a document within another, the specific document inclusion became very much a part of the definition of the document.

XML has another problem with entities. An entity is not something that can be easily manipulated within an XML document through a typical DOM parser, because such entities are effectively defined outside the primary XML document, and XSLT in particular has very little in the way of explicit "entity control". This is a deliberate design decision, based primarily upon a basic principle of well-formed XML. As much as possible, the XSLT processor should treat external documents as simply XML structures, but entities can represent anything from a single character to an entire network of interrelated documents. Restricting the domain of external resources to pure XML structures both simplifies the processor and reduces the possible permutations that the XSLT processor must be able to handle. This is the reason why when working with XSLT, stylesheets may only access files that are themselves XML documents – an XHTML page, a WML deck, an SVG document, and so on.

This is not as onerous a burden as it appears on the surface, by the way, although it can complicate life in the short term. Nearly any document type can be wrapped in an XML envelope (the underlying principle of SOAP) and manipulated through XSLT. Thus, if you have code to perform the initial wrapping, you could run such things as delimited text files, INI files, SQL Server Scripts, JavaScript code, and just about anything else through your XSLT code. Clearly, however, processing these types of files with XSLT would require some pretty extensive work, making it less of a practical proposition.

One of the most powerful functions of XSLT is the document() function, and I'd now like to move on to look at some XSLT techniques involving this function. At its simplest, the function loads an XML document and converts it into a node-set (though since the document must be an XML document, that node-set consists of the single root node of the document – it could conceivably have child nodes, by the way, it's just that these child nodes are not an enumerable part of the initial node-set list).

document() and XInclude

Perhaps the simplest application of the document() function is to provide a mechanism for creating an "XInclude Processor". **XInclude** is a tacit recognition on the part of the W3C that the proposed XLink mechanism was too complicated for the task of including simple portions of one XML document within another.

The W3C's current working draft XInclude specification (http://www.w3.org/TR/xinclude) defines the solitary element of the xinclude namespace, <xinclude:include>, as having two attributes:

❑ href specifies the location of the XML file to be included.

❑ parse indicates how the file is to be parsed. When this attribute is not specified, a value of "xml" is implied, indicating that the included XML should be parsed as XML. If parse is set to the value "text", the included XML is parsed as escaped text characters (replacing "<" with "<" and so forth in the included document).

The file xincludeTest.xml below illustrates a sample file that uses the <xinclude:include> syntax:

```
<?xml-stylesheet type="text/xsl" href="xinclude.xsl"?>
<html xmlns:xinclude="http://www.w3.org/1999/XML/xinclude">
<head>
  <title>HTML Document with the xinclude element.</title>
</head>
<body>
<h1>Test</h1>
<pre style="font-family:Arial;font-size:10pt;color:maroon;">
<xinclude:include href="sample_copy.xml" parse="xml"/>
</pre>
</body>
</html>
```

Note the use of the `<xmlns:xinclude>` namespace to define the `<xinclude:include>` element. This namespace declaration is essential if you are following strict W3C conventions.

The above file references the following brief XML file `sample_copy.xml`:

```
<div>
<h1>Loaded Document</h1>
<p>This is an external document.</p>
</div>
```

The output would be produced as shown. (Note, we haven't seen the stylesheet `xinclude.xsl` yet, but will look at this shortly. In this instance, it simply passes the HTML, as well as that included with `<xinclude:include>`, to the output document.)

You can use the following XSLT snippet to embed the XML content of any `<xinclude:include>` element's URI in the source document. The code is simple enough when the `parse` attribute equals "xml", because in that case, the XSLT processor copies the node-set referenced by `document(@href)` directly to the output stream:

```
<xsl:template match="xinclude:include">
  <xsl:choose>
    <xsl:when test="@parse='xml'">
      <xsl:copy-of select="document(@href)"/>
    </xsl:when>
    ...
```

Things however are much more complicated when you consider the attribute `parse='text'` for loading an XML document as escaped text. This is one area where XML itself isn't really an option, because you are attempting to convert a node-set into its escaped notation, something that is not currently covered by the XSLT Recommendation. To get around this, an extension namespace was created using Microsoft's MSXML3 parser's extension capability covered in greater detail in the section headed *Extensibility* later in this chapter. The function `xutils:NodesetToString()` converts an XML node-set into an escaped version of the same node-set.

The full `xinclude.xsl` file is a filter file implementing the XInclude functionality – it can be used to filter an XHTML document to expand all `<xinclude:include>` references. Note that this may also be a useful file to reference as an imported file, discussed later under the heading *The Importance of Imports.*

```
<!-- xinclude.xsl -->
<xsl:stylesheet xmlns:xsl="http://www.w3.org/1999/XSL/Transform"
                xmlns:msxml="urn:schemas-microsoft-com:xslt"
                xmlns:xinclude="http://www.w3.org/1999/XML/xinclude"
                xmlns:xutils="http://www.vbxml.com/cagle/schemas/xutils"
                version="1.0">
  <xsl:output method="xml" media-type="text/xml"/>

  <xsl:template match="/">
    <xsl:apply-templates select="*"/>
  </xsl:template>

  <!-- an identity template, useful for sending all input other than
  the xinclude:include node to the output stream -->

  <xsl:template match="*|@*|text()">
    <xsl:copy><xsl:apply-templates select="*|@*|text()"/></xsl:copy>
  </xsl:template>

  <!-- Match all xinclude:include nodes in the source -->

  <xsl:template match="xinclude:include">
    <xsl:choose>
      <xsl:when test="@parse='xml'">
        <xsl:copy-of select="document(@href)"/>
      </xsl:when>
      <xsl:when test="@parse='text'">
        <xsl:variable name="textNodes" select="document(@href)"/>
        <xsl:value-of select="xutils:NodesetToString($textNodes)"/>
      </xsl:when>
      <!-- default case (equivalent to parse='xml') -->
      <xsl:otherwise>
        <xsl:copy-of select="document(@href)"/>
      </xsl:otherwise>
    </xsl:choose>
  </xsl:template>

  <!-- This implements the xutils namespace function NodesetToString(),
  which converts a node-set to an XML string representation -->

  <msxml:script language="JavaScript" implements-prefix="xutils">
    function NodesetToString(nodeset){
      var buf="";
      //for each node in the nodeset
      for (i=0;i&lt;nodeset.length;i++){
        var node=nodeset[i];
        // convert the node into text and add it to the buffer
        buf+=node.xml;
      }
      // return the buffer
      return buf
    }
  </msxml:script>

</xsl:stylesheet>
```

If in the `xincludeTest.xml` file you change the `parse` attribute to `"text"` the output will not be live XML, but rather escaped XML as shown:

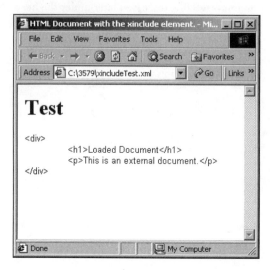

This illustrates one way that `<xinclude:include>` can prove useful – it essentially allows you to display sample XML and XSLT files directly without having to manually escape the output.

Loading Resource Files with document()

In the previous chapter, one of the more useful design patterns reliant on the use of variables was that of constructing lookup tables. While you can create sets of nodes using template construction methods within variables, you are probably just as likely to want to load resources from external files so that they are available for further manipulation. The `document()` function provides a very effective solution in such cases.

For instance, consider a common problem when producing forms – how do you handle items in a drop-down list box with a large number of potentially dynamic entries? For illustration, take a look at a form in which a user can choose a country, to be then shown a list of the states or provinces in that country.

From an XSLT standpoint this is something of a challenge. While it is possible to store the country/state information within the XSLT document itself, the amount of information involved suggests this would be a good candidate for remote storage within its own XML structure, to be brought into the XSLT stylesheet at run time. In addition to keeping the XSLT code cleaner, this has the added advantage of letting you switch from one language to another, simply by importing a different XML document – distinctly useful when dealing with localization issues.

The following code, `regions.xml`, has the regions (states or provinces) for both the United States and Canada. Note that this could easily be extended to other countries as well, though the regions may be counties or other municipal subdivisions.

```xml
<countries>
  <country id="USA" title="United States">
    <region id="AK">Alaska</region>
    <region id="AL">Alabama</region>
    <region id="AZ">Arizona</region>
```

```
    <region id="AR">Arkansas</region>
    <region id="CA">California</region>
    <region id="CO">Colorado</region>
    <region id="CT">Connecticut</region>
    <region id="DE">Delaware</region>
    <region id="DC">District of Columbia</region>
    <region id="FL">Florida</region>
    <region id="GA">Georgia</region>
    <region id="HI">Hawaii</region>
    <region id="ID">Idaho</region>
    <region id="IL">Illinois</region>
    <region id="IN">Indiana</region>
    <region id="IA">Iowa</region>
    <region id="KS">Kansas</region>
    <region id="KY">Kentucky</region>
    <region id="LA">Louisiana</region>
    <region id="MA">Massachusetts</region>
    <region id="MD">Maryland</region>
    <region id="ME">Maine</region>
    <region id="MI">Michigan</region>
    <region id="MN">Minnesota</region>
    <region id="MO">Missouri</region>
    <region id="MS">Mississippi</region>
    <region id="MT">Montana</region>
    <region id="NE">Nebraska</region>
    <region id="NV">Nevada</region>
    <region id="NH">New Hampshire</region>
    <region id="NJ">New Jersey</region>
    <region id="NM">New Mexico</region>
    <region id="NY">New York</region>
    <region id="NC">North Carolina</region>
    <region id="ND">North Dakota</region>
    <region id="OH">Ohio</region>
    <region id="OK">Oklahoma</region>
    <region id="OR">Oregon</region>
    <region id="PA">Pennsylvania</region>
    <region id="RI">Rhode Island</region>
    <region id="SC">South Carolina</region>
    <region id="SD">South Dakota</region>
    <region id="TN">Tennessee</region>
    <region id="TX">Texas</region>
    <region id="UT">Utah</region>
    <region id="VA">Virginia</region>
    <region id="VT">Vermont</region>
    <region id="WA">Washington</region>
    <region id="WV">West Virginia</region>
    <region id="WI">Wisconsin</region>
    <region id="WY">Wyoming</region>
</country>
<country id="CAN" title="Canada">
    <region id="AL">Alberta</region>
    <region id="BC">British Columbia</region>
    <region id="MA">Manitoba</region>
    <region id="NB">New Brunswick</region>
    <region id="NW">Northwest Territories</region>
    <region id="NS">Nova Scotia</region>
```

```
      <region id="ON">Ontario</region>
      <region id="QB">Quebec</region>
      <region id="SA">Saskatchewan</region>
      <region id="YU">Yukon</region>
   </country>
</countries>
```

A routine to create a drop-down box is probably not something that you will want to make as a full
transformation. Instead, it'd be much more common for the routine to be implemented as an extended
tag that you use to process XHTML. With that in mind, you may end up defining a tag called
<regions> with two attributes, code (for country code) and region indicating the region to use as a
default if none is otherwise specified. The file RegionsDisplay.xml shows how this may be called:

```
<?xml-stylesheet type="text/xsl" href="regions.select.xsl"?>
<html>
  <head>
    <title>Sample Form</title>
  </head>
  <body>
    <h1>Provinces List</h1>
    Province: <regions code="CAN" region="BC"/>
    <h1>States List</h1>
    State: <regions code="USA" region="WA"/>
  </body>
</html>
```

The transformation regions.select.xsl consists of a standard identity template coupled with a
template to catch any <regions> element. It recasts attributes as parameters before passing the result
to the named template regions.show. This latter template in turn does most of the actual work of
formatting the output:

```
<xsl:stylesheet xmlns:xsl="http://www.w3.org/1999/XSL/Transform"
    xmlns:msxml="urn:schemas-microsoft-com:xslt"
    version="1.0">
  <xsl:output method="xml" media-type="text/html"/>

  <xsl:template match="/">
    <xsl:apply-templates select="*"/>
  </xsl:template>

  <xsl:template match="*|@*|text()">
    <xsl:copy><xsl:apply-templates select="*|@*|text()"/></xsl:copy>
  </xsl:template>

  <xsl:template match="regions">
    <xsl:variable name="countryCode">
      <xsl:choose>
        <xsl:when test="@code"><xsl:value-of select="@code"/></xsl:when>
        <xsl:otherwise>USA</xsl:otherwise>
      </xsl:choose>
    </xsl:variable>
    <xsl:call-template name="regions.show">
      <xsl:with-param name="countryCode" select="$countryCode"/>
      <xsl:with-param name="region" select="@region"/>
```

```
      <xsl:with-param name="document" select="."/>
    </xsl:call-template>
  </xsl:template>

  <xsl:template name="regions.show">
    <xsl:param name="countryCode"/>
    <xsl:param name="document"/>
    <xsl:param name="region"/>
    <xsl:variable name="regions" select="document('regions.xml',$document)/
     countries/country[@id=$countryCode]/region"/>
    <select id="regions" name="regions">
      <xsl:for-each select="$regions">
        <xsl:sort select="."/>
        <option value="{@id}"><xsl:if test="@id=$region">
          <xsl:attribute name="selected">selected
          </xsl:attribute></xsl:if>
        <xsl:value-of select="."/></option>
      </xsl:for-each>
    </select>
  </xsl:template>
</xsl:stylesheet>
```

Of particular interest in this stylesheet is the element:

```
<xsl:variable name="regions" select="document('regions.xml',$document)/
  countries/country[@id=$countryCode]/region"/>
```

This variable makes a call to the document() function to retrieve the file regions.xml. However, a problem arises here in that a named template has no file context – the named template has no preconception of where to look for the indicated file. The second argument to the document() function provides this. So, you pass the function a node (technically a node-set, though only the first node is used), and the URL for the XML document associated with that node to serve as the path for the document() function to use.

Confused? Don't worry, with practice the concept will become comfortable – if the file regions.xml is in the same directory as the source file (in this case RegionsDisplay.xml), then:

```
document('regions.xml',.)
```

will retrieve the file. On the other hand, if regions.xml is in a child directory called resources relative to RegionsDisplay.xml, then the file path (the first argument) would remain the same, but the relative path would change to reflect this:

```
document('regions.xml', 'resources/'.)
```

Note that if the URL referenced in the first argument is absolute, then this will always override anything implied by the second argument.

Once the document() element retrieves XML data, this data is returned as a node-set that can be searched using XPath expressions. Thus the select statement in the regions variable definition retrieves the regions associated with a given country code:

```
select="document('regions.xml',$document)/countries/country[@id=
  $countryCode]/region"/>
```

155

document() and Node-Set Arguments

The first argument of the document() function can be a node-set instead of a single string. If this is the case, then the function evaluates a text value for each node of the node-set and uses that value as a URL to retrieve the respective documents. This can be especially useful when you need to search across a set of documents. As a practical example, suppose that you had a collection of catalogs – a catalog of catalogs if you will – and you wanted to search across them all to retrieve a list of books by a given author. The 'catalog catalog', catalogs.xml, appears below:

```
<catalogs>
  <catalog href="general_lit.xml">General Literature</catalog>
  <catalog href="science_fiction.xml">Science Fiction/Fantasy</catalog>
  <catalog href="horror.xml">Horror</catalog>
  <catalog href="romance.xml">Romance</catalog>
  <catalog href="computer.xml">Computer/Technical</catalog>
  <catalog href="art.xml">Art/Photography/Graphic Design</catalog>
</catalogs>
```

We can now use a single document() function to access the contents of each document in turn acting a bit like some kind of index facility. Creating a list of the aforementioned books by an author given by the variable $author would then be achieved as follows:

```
<xsl:variable name="BooksByGivenAuthor"
  select="document(document('catalogs.xml',.)//catalog/@href),.)
    //Book [Authors/Author=$author]"/>
```

This can be deconstructed as:

❑ document('catalogs.xml',.) – the inner document() function reads the contents of catalogs.xml from the source file path into a node-set.

❑ ~//catalog/@href – this XPath reduces the above node-set to include only those <catalog> elements with href attributes. Note that if you use //catalog without the qualifying @href, you'll end up with a set of nodes the values of which are the text of each catalog, rather than the value being the href attribute. In other words, the document() function does an implicit <xsl:value-of> on each node in the node-set, and it is the resulting text that is used as the file reference.

❑ document(~,.) – the outer document() function creates a node-set containing each catalog referenced in the reduced node set, such as general_lit.xml, science_fiction.xml, etc.

❑ ~//Book[Authors/Author=$author] – this expression applies to the node-set of all catalogs created by the outer document() function, and retrieves any <Book> elements for which <Author> children of the <Authors> element match the value given in the variable author.

document() and Empty Arguments

There is one final useful feature of the document() function. If you pass an empty string (" ") as the first parameter to a document() function in a stylesheet, the result will be a handle to the root node of that stylesheet itself. Be alert to the following caveat, however – the document so referenced is the stylesheet as stored in the file that the stylesheet originally came from, not the current instance of the stylesheet. Thus, if you have a parameter myParam with a default value in your stylesheet and an external agent overrides the default, then calling:

```
document()/xsl:stylesheet/xsl:param[@name='myParam']/@select
```

will retrieve the default value for the parameter, not the current, overridden value in the "live" stylesheet. However, it turns out that in spite of this restriction, the capability of a stylesheet to reference itself can be used to good effect for many tasks such as producing documentation.

Overstuffed Stylesheets

The document() function effectively extends the "reach" of the dataset being manipulated, making it possible to work with multiple input documents in a distributed fashion. However, XSLT stylesheets can become hideously complex as you try to get a burgeoning variety of matched templates, named templates, parameters, and variables all working together to create anything but the very simplest of pages. For instance, in the *regions* example earlier in this chapter, it is very likely that you will wish to employ other transformations in addition to creating a region list in an XHTML file.

Back in the early days, a program was typically confined to a single document, which sorely limited the extent to which you could build programs with common functionality. By introducing the concept of modular programming and the ability to include external files, procedural programming made the transition from creating functions to building frameworks. This same approach can be applied to XSLT, taking XSLT programming into a considerably more powerful realm.

The Importance of Imports

There are in fact two distinct mechanisms that XSLT uses to pull external XSLT resources into a stylesheet – <xsl:include> and <xsl:import>. The distinctions between the two are subtle but important.

The command <xsl:include> works by retrieving a stylesheet and in effect 'pasting' the contents of the stylesheet directly into the calling XSLT document at the point that the <xsl:include> occurs. Note that the requested stylesheet (referenced by the href attribute) must be a valid stylesheet itself, though it doesn't necessarily need to have a root node match, as the importing document will probably have one.

Essentially, <xsl:include> inserts the referenced file into the primary document as if it had been read directly from the stream, which means that if the calling XSLT contains a template identical to a template in the included file, an error will occur. This is because a stylesheet may not have more than one template with the same "signature" – that is, the same match pattern and the same name, mode, and priority attributes.

The other element, <xsl:import>, works in a similar fashion, but is somewhat more subtle in effect. Whereas <xsl:include> referenced files are added in when the loading document is first compiled, <xsl:import> files are loaded in afterwards (though these elements have to be declared as top-level elements in an XSLT document, even before the <xsl:output> and <xsl:param> elements). Once loaded, the <xsl:import> file is only used if the calling document does not already have an identically named parameter or template, or if the **priority** of the matched template that is imported is *higher* than the priority of the importing document's template.

Priority requires a word of explanation here, though it was mentioned in Chapter 3. When an <xsl:apply-templates> call is made, there may be more than one template in the stylesheet matching the pattern requested. As an example, if you were attempting to match a <Book> element in a catalog, both of the following templates will match:

```
<xsl:template match="Book">
  <!-- process Book -->
</xsl:template>
```

```
<xsl:template match="*">
  <!-- process generic element-->
</xsl:template>
```

However, only one template can be evaluated for any given context, even if more than one match is made. How does the XSLT processor determine which template to apply? What happens in practice is that match expressions are prioritized on the basis of their generality, with more general expressions being of lower priority. The template with the most specific match criteria will be the one selected, though if there are two templates that have the same priority, then the one that appears *last* is chosen. The following table contains a more complete set of rules (as set forth by the XSLT Recommendation) determining priority:

Condition	How Priority is Calculated
If the pattern consists of a qualified name (a QName) with or without an axis specifier, such as `match="Book"` or `"parent::Book"`	The priority is 0
If the pattern consists of a wildcard character, with or without an axis specifier (for example, `ancestor::`)	The priority is -0.25
If the pattern is just a node test with or without an axis specifier, such as `ancestor::node()`	The priority is -0.5
Any other case (for example, `Book[Title='myTitle'])`	The priority is 0.5
If the pattern contains multiple alternatives, each alternative is considered as a separate template for purposes of computation	`Book|*` has two priorities, with values 0 and -0.25 respectively

From this table then, the Book template above has a priority of 0, while the "*" template's priority works out at -0.25. Thus, the Book template will be applied to all <Book> elements, while the other, generic template will be selected for any other node at this level in the XML tree.

Imported templates automatically have a priority lower than any matches in the importing document. This means that if you define a root node match in an imported template and also have a root node match in the importing document, then the template in the importing document will typically override the template in the imported one.

The only way to overcome the built-in precedence for equivalent templates when using <xsl:import> is through use of the priority attribute, which allows a template to be assigned any number as its priority. Thus, we are able to give imported templates a higher priority than the default, so preventing templates in the importing document overriding them. The template with the higher priority will always prevail, regardless of place of origin. Thus, modifying the examples given earlier:

```
<xsl:template match="Book" priority="0">
  <!-- process Book -->
</xsl:template>

<xsl:template match="*" priority="2">
  <!-- process generic element-->
</xsl:template>
```

the generic template matching "*" will be evaluated over the specific Book one.

In cases where two templates *in the same document* have the same priority for a given match, the last one given in the document will always have precedence. This is what makes it possible to "override" a predicated template (that is, one with the square brackets [] containing predicate conditions) with a different predicated template, since in general all predicated templates have equal priority.

The one case to watch out for, however, is duplicate templates. A template match has much the same characteristics in XSLT as signatures or mangling of parameters have for C++ or Java expressions – if the parser can't resolve the difference between two templates, then they are considered equal, which in turn will generate an error.

Finally, the referenced document in the <xsl:include> statement automatically has equal priority to the calling document – this means that duplicate templates (which are easy to avoid in single documents) can become much more problematic. It is for this reason that the <xsl:import> statement was included – by having a stylesheet with implicitly lower priorities than any templates in the calling stylesheet, it becomes possible to "subclass" one template with another, and even (to a certain extent), to inherit the characteristics of the called template within an identical calling one. Put another way, this opens up the possibility of creating object-oriented XSLT code.

The Beginnings of OO XML

Those of you with an eye toward object-oriented programming might be observing a few familiar patterns here that I definitely want to expand upon. What exactly is a stylesheet? Forgetting for a moment the semantics of "styling" an XML document, what you have is an object that contains specific routines, called templates, which when applied to a data source perform some action, along with a set of properties, called parameters, that can be used to affect global behavior.

Viewed from this angle, a stylesheet bears a distinct similarity to a class, as you might find in C++ or Java. You may have already drawn this parallel as you've read previous chapters, but now the characteristics of OOP-like structure become quite glaring. An external stylesheet, if imported, can be thought of as a parent class that the loading stylesheet inherits from. If the importing stylesheet contains a template with the same match signature, then it is overloading the method initially defined in the imported stylesheet with its own specific implementation.

For example, consider a stylesheet (table.xsl) that generates a table in a completely generic fashion as shown:

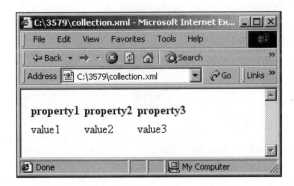

The code for the stylesheet is as follows:

```
<xsl:stylesheet xmlns:xsl="http://www.w3.org/1999/XSL/Transform"
    xmlns:msxml="urn:schemas-microsoft-com:xslt"
    version="1.0">
<xsl:output method="xml" media-type="text/html"/>
<xsl:param name="sortElement" select="name(/*/*[1]/*[1])"/>
<xsl:param name="sortOrder" select=" 'ascending' "/>

<xsl:param name="columns">
  <xsl:for-each select="/*/*[1]/*">
    <column id="{name(.)}" title="{name(.)}"/>
  </xsl:for-each>
</xsl:param>

<!-- The root template calls the generic template with mode="Table" -->
<xsl:template match="/">
  <xsl:apply-templates select="*" mode="Table"/>
</xsl:template>
```

The `columns` parameter above uses the names of the properties of the first record to generate the column headings, and could easily be overridden with a structure of the form:

```
<xsl:param name="columns">
  <column id="property1" title="property1_label"/>
  <column id="property2" title="property2_label"/>
</xsl:param>
```

The generic `mode="Table"` template called by the root template converts the XML tree fragment into a node-set, then builds the primary table structure, consisting of a header row that displays the columns listed in the column section, then iterates through each row in the table, outputting columns in the indicated order. The template also automatically orders the output by the column named in the `sortElement` parameter, or the first element if none are explicitly given:

```
<xsl:template match="/*" mode="Table">
  <xsl:variable name="columns.ns" select="msxml:node-set($columns)"/>
  <table class="Table" cellpadding="3" cellspacing="0">
    <tr class="Table_Head_Row">
      <xsl:for-each select="$columns.ns/*">
        <th class="Table_Head_Cell">
          <xsl:choose>
            <xsl:when test="@title">
              <xsl:apply-templates select="@title" mode="Table_Head"/>
            </xsl:when>
            <xsl:otherwise>
              <xsl:apply-templates select="@id" mode="Table_Head"/>
            </xsl:otherwise>
          </xsl:choose>
        </th>
      </xsl:for-each>
    </tr>
    <xsl:apply-templates select="*" mode="Table_Row">
      <xsl:sort select="*[name(.)=$sortElement]" order="{$sortOrder}"/>
      <xsl:with-param name="columns.ns" select="$columns.ns"/>
    </xsl:apply-templates>
  </table>
</xsl:template>
```

The mode="Table_Row" template called in the above template draws each record's row. Note the use of classes here – the row classes are given as Table_Row0 or Table_Row1 depending upon whether the row is even or odd. This makes it possible to create ledger effects with alternating styles on alternating lines. Set the stylesheet reference for Table_Row1 to that of Table_Row0 to present all rows in a single style.

Also, take a look at the way that the columns "array" parameter interacts with the properties of each record:

```
<xsl:template match="*" mode="Table_Row">
  <xsl:param name="columns.ns"/>
  <xsl:variable name="properties" select="*"/>
  <tr class="Table_Row{position() mod 2}">
    <xsl:for-each select="$columns.ns/*">
      <xsl:variable name="column" select="@id"/>
      <xsl:variable name="property" select="$properties[name(.)=$column]"/>
      <td class="Table_Cell{position() mod 2}">
        <xsl:apply-templates select="$property" mode="Table_Cell"/>
      </td>
    </xsl:for-each>
  </tr>
</xsl:template>

<xsl:template match="*|@*" mode="Table_Head">
  <xsl:value-of select="."/>
</xsl:template>

<xsl:template match="*" mode="Table_Cell">
  <xsl:value-of select="."/>
</xsl:template>

</xsl:stylesheet>
```

The mode="Table_Head" template enables you to "subclass" the output for any table column head to apply additional formatting or integrate scripted event code. Similarly, the mode="Table_Cell" template allows you to subclass the output for any table cell by specifying the property you want to match along with any filtering required. For example, if you have a dollar price given as 32229.95 (it's a big book...) and you want to format it as currency, the following template would override the generic case for any columns with a property of Price:

```
<xsl:template match="Price" mode="Table_Cell">
  $<xsl:value-of select="format-number(.,'###,###.00')"/>
</xsl:template>
```

The columns are determined by a variable called, appropriately enough, columns, and default to all of the columns contained in the first record. Note that there is no reference to any of the elements contained in the book catalog – so as long as the data source has a structure of the form:

```
<collection>
  <item>
    <property1>value1</property1>
    <property2>value2</property2>
    <property3>value3</property3>
  </item>
</collection>
```

the transformation will generate a table.

This fairly hairy code may seem overkill just to create a table. However, the advantage to code like this becomes apparent when you start importing it into other stylesheets. You can inherit this stylesheet in another stylesheet, "overloading" templates and parameters to handle the exceptions that require special treatment. For example, suppose that you want to create a table from the catalog.xml file, used in the previous chapter, that has just one column showing the cover, with the abstract and authors underneath. This stylesheet, ImageAndAbstract.xsl, subclasses the table.xsl file to output only one column and contains a template to format it to display a book's picture, abstract, and authors:

```xsl
<xsl:stylesheet xmlns:xsl="http://www.w3.org/1999/XSL/Transform"
    xmlns:msxml="urn:schemas-microsoft-com:xslt"
    version="1.0">
  <xsl:import href="table.xsl"/>
  <xsl:output method="xml" media-type="text/html"/>

  <xsl:param name="columns">
    <column id="Abstract" title="Wrox Titles"/>
  </xsl:param>

  <xsl:template match="Abstract" mode="Table_Cell">
    <!--Note that mode="Table_Cell" covers the contents within an already
    defined TD element. That's why you can have what appears to be non-contained
    XML in the template output, since there is an implicit TD already wrapping
    the contents. -->
    <img src="images/{../CoverImage}"/><br/>
    <div>
      <!-- Insert the abstract itself -->
      <xsl:copy-of select="."/><br/>
      by <xsl:for-each select="../Authors/Author">
        <xsl:value-of select="."/>
        <!-- Follow an author's name with...-->
        <xsl:choose>
          <!-- ...'and' for the penultimate writer -->
          <xsl:when test="position()=last() - 1 and last()&gt; 1"> and
          </xsl:when>
          <!-- ...a comma for other writers except the last -->
          <xsl:when test="position()&lt;last()">, </xsl:when>
          <!-- ...nothing for the last or only author -->
          <xsl:otherwise/>
        </xsl:choose>
      </xsl:for-each>
    </div>
    <hr/>
  </xsl:template>
</xsl:stylesheet>
```

Because most of the heavy duty structural lifting is accomplished by the table.xsl stylesheet, the ImageAndAbstract.xsl file needs only to "subclass" one particular element to handle it. As it still has the Abstract context for that particular record, it can find additional information using axis functions (the "../" part of the various select attributes that takes a step back along the location path).

The Super Apply-Imports

It should be pointed out that importing files can work at several levels. For example, the
`ImageAndAbstract.xsl` stylesheet could itself be inherited by a stylesheet that puts more of an HTML
wrapper around the contents (`AbstractHTMLPage.xsl`):

```
<xsl:stylesheet xmlns:xsl="http://www.w3.org/1999/XSL/Transform"
    xmlns:msxml="urn:schemas-microsoft-com:xslt"
    version="1.0">
  <xsl:import href="ImageAndAbstract.xsl"/>

  <xsl:template match="/">
    <html>
    <head>
      <title>Wrox Books</title>
    </head>
    <body>
      <h1>The Wrox Book Catalog</h1>
      <p>The following is a selection of the many titles that Wrox offers
      the professional programmer:</p>
      <div style="width:300px">
        <xsl:apply-imports/>
      </div>
    </body>
    </html>
  </xsl:template>
</xsl:stylesheet>
```

This stylesheet inherits `ImageAndAbstracts.xsl`, which in turn inherits `table.xsl`. The inheritance is made stronger by using the element `<xsl:apply-imports/>`. I would now like to go into this particular element in greater detail.

Take a look at the original `table.xsl` file – you'll notice that there is in fact a template that already matches the root node:

```
<xsl:template match="/">
  <xsl:apply-templates select="*" mode="Table"/>
</xsl:template>
```

Since this also invokes the match for table, by overriding this all-important node in `AbstractHTMLPage.xsl`, you would think it would cause the whole process to break down. This is the problem that `<xsl:apply-imports/>` overcomes.

Looking back at the use of classes in OOP languages, there is again a parallel for this XSLT element in C++ and Java's `super()` method. This method effectively tells the C++/Java parser to apply the methods for a class contained in the parent class. In XSLT, `<xsl:apply-imports>` has similar, although not identical, operation, instructing the XSLT processor to restrict the set of matches to those templates contained in imported documents not in the calling document. The match being called is the current context node – in a way, it is as if `<apply-templates>` was called, with the condition that its domain be restricted to imported stylesheets.

When used with `catalog.xml`, the `AbstractHTMLPage.xsl` stylesheet produces:

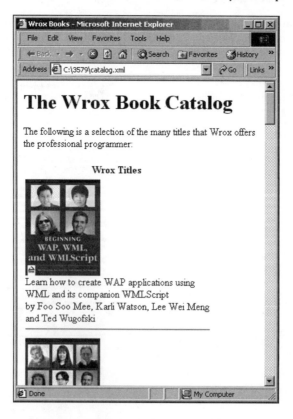

Which is Better: Import or Include?

So is it better to import or include a file? As with so much of XSLT, the answer depends upon what you are attempting to do. The following criteria should help decide:

<xsl:include/> is Best

- ❑ If you want to bring in only templates that will not be explicitly overridden (as this will generate errors if such a template is redefined after the include)

- ❑ If you wish to draw on external `<msxml:script>` code – see *Extensibility* later in the chapter

- ❑ If you wish to define variables or parameters so that they may not be over-written

- ❑ If you wish to achieve the fastest compilation for your XSLT

<xsl:import/> is Best

- ❑ If you want to make it possible to subclass templates, parameters, or global variables

- ❑ If you want to be able to apply imported stylesheets while redefining certain match templates

- ❑ If you want to create a more extensive framework of inherited stylesheets

In general, then, the primary advantage that includes have over imports is in preventing a template, variable, or parameter from being redefined (or at least causing an error when parsed). Personally, I find imports to be preferable to includes, even though they incur slightly larger memory overheads. However, `<xsl:import>` is in many ways like creating an inherited class in Java – unless you are very clear about exactly what the purpose of an imported template is, you can seriously wrap yourself around an axle trying to figure out why perfectly good code no longer works.

Extensibility

While XSLT is powerful, it has some fairly obvious limitations. Indeed, the XSLT specification explicitly states that XSLT is not a complete language, even for XML processing:

> *"XSLT is not intended as a completely general-purpose XML transformation language. Rather it is designed primarily for the kinds of transformations that are needed when XSLT is used as part of XSL."*

Be that as it may, XSLT is being pressed into service to do a great deal more than it was ever designed to achieve, and this in turn has led many XSLT processor manufacturers to incorporate extension mechanisms. Unfortunately, there is not yet a uniform standard for implementing such extensions, although the XSLT 1.1 Working Draft does include provision for standardizing these implementations. This will be a welcome move that will undoubtedly make it much easier to create a consistent interface for XSLT users.

In the meantime however, we are forced to choose proprietary extension mechanisms. The one that I shall be using is that adopted by Microsoft, although Java-based extension mechanisms are similar in scope and implementation. The underlying concept is simple – an extension is implemented as a *namespace* that can be invoked from within XPath expressions. In essence, the namespace functions as a class. For example, if you had a set of math functions that did things like return the minimum (`min()`) or maximum (`max()`) value in a node-set, then once the `Math` namespace is declared, the XSLT processor recognizes elements of this namespace as methods to be called accordingly:

```
<xsl:template match="Data">
  The minimum value = <xsl:value-of select="Math:min(Values)"/>.
</xsl:template>
```

The first (and generally most useful) extension mechanism requires the use of the `<msxml:script>` element. The `msxml:` namespace has been used in previous chapters as the namespace for handling `node-set()` conversions, but the `<msxml:script>` element it supports is equally useful.

For instance, one of the principal problems many people face when dealing with XSLT is a need to work with dates. The standard for formatting dates "YYYY-MM-DD" makes it easy to sort on date information, but it is much more difficult to do things that should seem simple – determining the day of the week, finding the interval between two dates, adding an interval to a date to get another date. While it is possible to use XSLT to generate this information, the routines can become hideously complex. However, JavaScript actually contains a number of routines that make scripting dates somewhat more feasible. It is a relatively simple step to convert these routines into a class that can be used with XSLT thanks to the `<msxml:script>` element.

To define the namespace extension, in the `<xsl:stylesheet>` header you need both to specifically declare the `msxml:` namespace and to set up a namespace that uniquely identifies your own code. For instance, the following declares the `date:` namespace:

```
<xsl:stylesheet xmlns:xsl="http://www.w3.org/1999/XSL/Transform"
                xmlns:msxml="urn:schemas-microsoft-com:xslt"
                xmlns:date="urn:schemas-cagle-com:date"
                exclude-result-prefixes="msxml"
                version="1.0">
```

Typically, when a namespace is manipulated within an XSLT document, the processor automatically assumes that the namespace should be passed into the output XML. Unfortunately, this isn't always the case, and there are a number of instances where completely spurious namespace definitions end up in the final results. The `exclude-result-prefixes` attribute instructs the processor which output elements to not pass namespace declarations for, although if the output *does* contain an element with that prefix, the command will be ignored.

Once the namespace is declared, it needs to be defined. This is where the `<msxml:script>` element comes in. This element lets you specify the language to use within the block. Note that this extension talks to the Windows Scripting Runtime, which implies that you can only use languages that you have on your server in the script block. If you have IE 5 installed, then you have as a default JavaScript and VBScript, but you can choose to add languages such as Perlscript (for which information can be found at http://www.activestate.com/Products/ActivePerl/Download.html). Use the `language` attribute to specify which language you wish the contained text to be interpreted as, and don't forget to use the correct escape sequences (&amp, &gt, and so on) when required. Note that different XSLT parsers handle the extension issue differently (see Michael Kay's book *XSLT Programmer's Reference* published by Wrox for more information on using Java to handle similar extensions).

The `<mxsml:script>` node is also controlled by the `implements-prefix` attribute, associating the functions with the specific namespace prefix previously declared in the stylesheet. For example, the following header describes part of the `date:` namespace, the `convertToJSDate()` function. Note that like XSLT, JavaScript is case sensitive:

```
<msxml:script language="JavaScript" implements-prefix="date">
  function convertToJSDate(date){
      year=parseInt(date.substr(0,4));
      month=parseInt(date.substr(5,2));
      day=parseInt(date.substr(8,2));
      newDate=month + "/" +day +"/" + year;
      if (date.length &gt; 11){
          newDate +=' '+ date.substr(11,8);
      }
      var dt=new Date(newDate);
      return dt;
  }
```

The parameters that can be passed into or out of such scripted namespaces are strictly limited to data types that are explicitly supported by XSLT – strings, numbers, node-sets and XML tree fragments. Note that there is no limitation on return value types if they are used only by other functions (such as the `convertToJSDate()` function, which returns a JavaScript `Date` object to be consumed by other routines), but if the result ends up in the output stream then any other data type will generate an error.

There is a certain amount of overhead associated with loading in the scripting engine during a transformation, but the cost involved in adding additional functions is considerably smaller than the initialization. Put another way, it is probably more efficient to build an entire library of functions than to just associate one function per namespace and have a number of namespaces. In addition to this, you can also tie in named and matched templates to turn your stylesheet into a function library. This is illustrated in the `date.xsl` file given below (interspaced with explanations), which provides a number of useful routines for adding date capabilities to XSLT:

```
<xsl:stylesheet xmlns:xsl="http://www.w3.org/1999/XSL/Transform"
                xmlns:msxml="urn:schemas-microsoft-com:xslt"
                xmlns:date="urn:schemas-cagle-com:date"
                xmlns:doc="urn:schemas-cagle-com:document"
                exclude-result-prefixes="msxml doc date"
                version="1.0">
  <xsl:output method="xml" media-type="text/xml"/>
```

The `doc:` namespace is this author's space for defining documentation within XSLT files. This namespace provides a useful way to document the functionality of a stylesheet, and also illustrates how you can even treat an XSLT document as the input for an XSLT transformation. The `doc:` namespace stylesheet (Documentation Maker) is available without charge from my own web site at http://www.kurtcagle.com.

```
<doc:summary>
   <doc:title>Kurt's Date Routines</doc:title>
   <doc:filename>date.xsl</doc:filename>
     <doc:version>1.0</doc:version>
     <doc:dateCreated>2001-01-05</doc:dateCreated>
     <doc:lastModified>2001-01-24</doc:lastModified>
   <doc:description><b>Kurt's Date Routines</b> add a number of
   functions and named templates that can be used as utilities
   in your XSLT to add date function capabilities. Kurt's Date
   Routines are copyright 2001 by
   <a href="mailto:cagle@olywa.net">Kurt Cagle</a>. For use in
   commercial products, please contact the author for permissions.
```

```
     To use in your code, make sure that the date: namespace is
     declared in your xsl:stylesheet node:
<pre>
<![CDATA[
<xsl:stylesheet xmlns:xsl="http://www.w3.org/1999/XSL/Transform"
                xmlns:msxml="urn:schemas-microsoft-com:xslt"
                xmlns:date="urn:schemas-cagle-com:date"
                version="1.0">
]]>
</pre>
     and that you import the date.xsl stylesheet:
<pre>
<![CDATA[<xsl:import href="date.xsl"/>]]>
</pre>
    </doc:description>
  </doc:summary>
```

The date:Today() function returns the current date in "YYYY-MM-DDTHH:NN:SS" notation. This is especially useful for generating time stamps, and for updating files.

```
<doc:function>
  <doc:language>JavaScript</doc:language>
  <doc:signature>date:Today()</doc:signature>
  <doc:description>date:Today() returns the current date and time
   in  YYYY-MM-DDTHH:NN:SS notation.</doc:description>
</doc:function>
```

The date:DayOfWeekName() function returns the day of the week as a name in the current OS language (that is, "Friday" in English, "Freitag" in German, etc.). While it is possible to write a DayOfWeek function in XSLT directly, it is hideously complex and slow, and it is generally better to take advantage of system resources to do it.

```
<doc:function>
  <doc:language>JavaScript</doc:language>
  <doc:signature>date:DayOfWeekName(date)</doc:signature>
  <doc:param name="date" description="The date in YYYY-MM-DD or
   YYYY-MM-DDTHH:NN:SS notation"/>
  <doc:description>date:DayOfWeekName() returns the name of the
   current day of the week. </doc:description>
</doc:function>
```

The date:DayOfWeekNumber() function returns the day of the week as a number, with Sunday being 1 and Saturday being 7. While the JavaScript function typically handles the conversion as 0 to 6, XSLT uses 1 as its base array index. This is useful for generating special labels for given dates as node-sets, then referencing those labels using the position() function.

```
<doc:function>
  <doc:language>JavaScript</doc:language>
  <doc:signature>date:DayOfWeek(date)</doc:signature>
  <doc:param name="date" description="The date in YYYY-MM-DD or
   YYYY-MM-DDTHH:NN:SS notation"/>
  <doc:description>date:DayOfWeek() returns the number of the
   current day of the week, with Sunday=1 and Saturday=7.
  </doc:description>
</doc:function>
```

The `date:AddInterval()` function lets you add a specific interval of time to a given date, specifying both the amount and units of time. Note that the dates given here (and throughout this section) assume the same YYYY-MM-DD format. Thus, `date:AddInterval("2001-03-15",25, "days")` will return the value "2001-04-09", 25 days after the 15th of March.

```
    <doc:function>
      <doc:language>JavaScript</doc:language>
      <doc:signature>date:AddInterval(date,interval,units)</doc:signature>
      <doc:param name="date" description="The date in YYYY-MM-DD or
        YYYY-MM-DDTHH:NN:SS notation"/>
      <doc:param name="interval" description="The interval is an
        integer or floating point number the tells how many units
        should be added to the given date. Note that interval can be
        negative (interval prior to a given date and time)."/>
      <doc:param name="units" default="days" description="The unit of
        time that the interval indicates. Values include {'years',
        'months', 'days', 'hours', 'minutes', 'seconds'}."/>
      <doc:description>AddInterval will add to the date an amount as
        given by interval , scaled to the appropriate units, and returns
        the date in YYYY-MM-DDTHH:NN:SS notation. For example,
<pre>
<![CDATA[<xsl:value-of select="date:AddInterval('2001-01-
02T23:10:05',3,'months')"/>]]>
</pre>
        will place the date '2001-04-02T23:10:05' into the output stream.
      </doc:description>
    </doc:function>
```

The `date:DateDiff()` function provides a way of comparing two dates, returning a value in the specified units. This is useful for determining if a given process has expired yet.

```
    <doc:function>
      <doc:language>JavaScript</doc:language>
      <doc:signature>date:DateDiff(date1,date2,units)</doc:signature>
      <doc:param name="date1" description="The starting date in
        YYYY-MM-DD or YYYY-MM-DDTHH:NN:SS notation"/>
      <doc:param name="date2" description="The ending date in
        YYYY-MM-DD or YYYY-MM-DDTHH:NN:SS notation"/>
      <doc:param name="units" default="days" description="The unit
        of time that the interval indicates. Values include {'years',
        'months', 'days', 'hours', 'minutes', 'seconds'}."/>
      <doc:description>DateDiff takes two dates in YYYY-MM-DDTHH:NN:SS
        notation and returns the difference between them in the units
        specified. For example,
<pre>
<![CDATA[<xsl:value-of select="date:DateDiff('2001-01-02T23:10:05','2001-04-
02T23:10:06','months')"/>]]>
</pre>
        will place the value 3 (for three months) into the output stream. Note that
        all values are rounded down, so date:DateDiff('2001-01-02T23:10:05','2001-
        04-02T23:10:04','months')will return two months, because it is one second
        shy of three months.
      </doc:description>
    </doc:function>
```

The two functions convertToJSDate() and convertFromJSDate() are private functions that the routines use to handle the internal JavaScript date representation (which isn't in the "YYYY-MM-DD" format). In general, there is no reason why you should need to call these functions directly, although they are called by the other routines.

This block defines the date: prefix implementation for all the functions given above. Because XSLT 1.0 can only handle XSLT datatypes, you have to work with a little indirection to get date values passed back and forth (hence convertToJSDate() and convertFromJSDate() being private – they are only called within functions).

```
<msxml:script language="JavaScript" implements-prefix="date">
  function convertToJSDate(date){
    year=parseInt(date.substr(0,4));
    month=parseInt(date.substr(5,2));
    day=parseInt(date.substr(8,2));
    newDate=month + "/" +day +"/" + year;
    if (date.length &gt; 11){
      newDate +=' '+ date.substr(11,8);
    }
    var dt=new Date(newDate);
    return dt;
  }

  function convertFromJSDate(dt){
    year=dt.getYear();
    month=dt.getMonth();
    day=dt.getDate();
    hours=dt.getHours();
    minutes=dt.getMinutes();
    seconds=dt.getSeconds();
    newDate=year+"-"+leftFill(month+1)+"-"+leftFill(day);
    newDate+="T"+leftFill(hours)+":"+leftFill(minutes)+":"+
      leftFill(seconds);
    return newDate;
  }

  function AddInterval(date,interval,units){
    var dt=convertToJSDate(date);
    switch(units){
      case "year":
      case "years":{
        dt.setFullYear(dt.getFullYear()+interval);
        break;
      }
      case "month":
      case "months":{
        dt.setMonth(dt.getMonth()+interval);
        break;
      }
      case "day":
      case "days":{
        dt.setDate(dt.getDate()+interval);
        break;
      }
```

```
      case "hour":
      case "hours":{
        dt.setHours(dt.getHours()+interval);
        break;
      }
      case "minute":
      case "minutes":{
        dt.setMinutes(dt.getMinutes()+interval);
        break;
      }
      case "second":
      case "seconds":{
        dt.setSeconds(dt.getSeconds()+interval);
        break;
      }
    }
    return convertFromJSDate(dt);
}

function leftFill(num,digits,char){
  num=num.toString();
  if (""+digits=="undefined"){
    digits=2;
  }
  if (num.length &gt; digits){
    return num;
  }
  else {
    buf="";
    if (""+ char=="undefined"){
      char="0";
    }
    for (var index=0;index&lt;digits;index++){
      buf+=char;
    }
    return (buf+num).substr((buf+num).length-digits);
  }
}

function DateDiff(date1,date2,units){
  if (""+units=="undefined"){
    units="days";
  }
  var dt1=convertToJSDate(date1);
  var dt2=convertToJSDate(date2);
  var diff=dt2-dt1;
  switch(units){
    case "year":
    case "years":{
      unit_diff=parseInt(diff/(1000*24*3600*365));
      break;
    }
    case "month":
    case "months":{
      yearMonths=parseInt((dt2.getFullYear()-dt1.getFullYear()))*12;
      unit_diff=yearMonths+(dt2.getMonth()-dt1.getMonth());
```

```
          break;
        }
      case "day":
      case "days":{
          unit_diff=parseInt(diff/(1000*24*3600));
          break;
        }
      case "hour":
      case "hours":{
          unit_diff=parseInt(diff/(1000*3600));
          break;
        }
      case "minute":
      case "minutes":{
          unit_diff=parseInt(diff/(1000*60));
          break;
        }
      case "second":
      case "seconds":{
          unit_diff=diff/1000;
          break;
        }
      }
    return unit_diff;
  }

  function DayOfWeekName(date){
    var dt=convertToJSDate(date);
    var weekdayNames = new Array("Sunday", "Monday",
      "Tuesday","Wednesday","Thursday","Friday","Saturday");
    weekday = dt.getDay();
    return(weekdayNames[weekday]);
  }

  function DayOfWeekNumber(date){
    var dt=convertToJSDate(date);
    return dt.getDay()+1;
  }

  function Today(){
    var dt=new Date();
    return(convertFromJSDate(dt));
  }
</msxml:script>
```

The root node match here will almost certainly be overridden (the date.xsl file is specifically designed to be imported) and only exists to demonstrate output if it isn't called indirectly.

```
<xsl:template match="/">
<div>
  <xsl:call-template name="date.display">
    <xsl:with-param name="date" select="'2001-02-15T23:01:02'"/>
    <xsl:with-param name="showTime" select="'yes'"/>
    <xsl:with-param name="timeMode" select="'AM-PM'"/>
  </xsl:call-template>
  <br/>
  <xsl:call-template name="date.display">
    <xsl:with-param name="date" select="date:AddInterval('
    2001-02-15T23:01:02',-7,'days')"/>
  </xsl:call-template>
  <br/>
```

```
        <xsl:value-of select="date:DateDiff('2001-02-15T23:01:02',
        '2002-02-15T23:01:02')"/>
        <br/>
        <xsl:value-of select="concat(date:Today(),':',date:DayOfWeekName
        (date:Today()))"/>
    </div>
</xsl:template>
```

Below, `months.tf` is a variable that contains the names of the months in a node-set, for formatting purposes. Note that while it would be easy enough to write a `getMonthName()` function in JavaScript, the intent of `date.xsl` is to provide only those routines in JavaScript which can't be easily generated from XSLT – this limits the amount of cross platform conversion work taking it to a different implementation of the parser. Additionally, in XSLT 2.0, it won't be necessary to create a tree fragment and then convert that into a node-set, as child XML content is automatically converted into a node-set if at all possible in 2.0.

```
<xsl:variable name="months.tf">
  <month>January</month>
  <month>February</month>
  <month>March</month>
  <month>April</month>
  <month>May</month>
  <month>June</month>
  <month>July</month>
  <month>August</month>
  <month>September</month>
  <month>October</month>
  <month>November</month>
  <month>December</month>
</xsl:variable>
<xsl:variable name="months" select="msxml:node-set($months.tf)"/>
```

The named template `date.display` actually formats the YYYY-MM-DD dates into more human readable forms. By keeping the mechanism for formatting as an XSLT block, it makes it possible to subclass the output of this for differing formats without having to write a lot of script code. It also calls the subordinate template `time.display` (which can also act independently on the time portion of a date) in order to better handle the presentation of time in a web page.

```
<xsl:template name="date.display" doc:description="This converts a
    date in the form YYYY-MM-DD or YYYY-MM-DDTHH:MM:SS into a string
    of the form 'month-name day, year' or 'month-name day, year
    @ HH:MM:SS AM' respectively">
<xsl:param name="date" doc:description="The date in YYYY-MM-DD
    or YYYY-MM-DDTHH:MM:SS notation."/>
<xsl:param name="showTime" select="'yes'" doc:description="Flag
    that indicates whether the time part is shown or not (only if
    time in date is specified)"/>
<xsl:param name="timeMode" select="'AM-PM'" doc:description="This
    flag indicates the mode to display the
    time. With 'AM-PM' the output is a twelve hour clock with
    AM/PM appended, while with '24hr' the output is given using
    the 24 hour military clock."/>
<xsl:value-of select="concat($months/*[number(substring($date,6,2))],
    ' ',number(substring($date,9,2)),',    ',substring($date,1,4))"/>
<xsl:if test="($showTime='yes') and string-length($date)&gt; 11">
    <xsl:text> @ </xsl:text>
    <xsl:call-template name="time.display">
```

```
          <xsl:with-param name="time" select="substring($date,12)"/>
          <xsl:with-param name="timeMode" select="$timeMode"/>
      </xsl:call-template>
    </xsl:if>
</xsl:template>
```

The functions work on the fact that the date portion of a date/Time object has 10 characters for the date, one character ("T") dividing date and time, and 8 characters for the 24 hour time. Knowing this, you can extract specific units of time (months for instance) just by knowing the position and length of the relevant characters (substring($date,6,2) for months).

```
<xsl:template name="time.display" doc:description="This converts a
   time in the form HH:NN:SS into AM/PM time.">
   <xsl:param name="time" doc:description="The time in HH:NN:SS
     notation with a 24 hour clock"/>
   <xsl:param name="timeMode" select="'AM-PM'"
     doc:description="This flag indicates the mode to display the
     time. With 'AM-PM' the output is a twelve hour clock with
     AM/PM appended, while with '24hr' the output is given using
     the 24 hour military clock."/>
   <xsl:choose>
     <xsl:when test="$timeMode='AM-PM'">
       <xsl:variable name="hours" select="number(substring($time,1,2))"/>
       <xsl:variable name="minutes" select="substring($time,4,2)"/>
       <xsl:variable name="seconds" select="substring($time,7,2)"/>
       <xsl:variable name="newHours">
         <xsl:if test="$hours=0">12</xsl:if>
         <xsl:if test="$hours &gt; 0 and $hours &lt;12">
           <xsl:value-of select="$hours"/>
         </xsl:if>
         <xsl:if test="$hours=12">12</xsl:if>
         <xsl:if test="$hours &gt; 12">
           <xsl:value-of select="$hours - 12"/>
         </xsl:if>
       </xsl:variable>
       <xsl:variable name="meridian">
         <xsl:choose>
           <xsl:when test="$hours &lt; 12">AM</xsl:when>
           <xsl:otherwise>PM</xsl:otherwise>
         </xsl:choose>
       </xsl:variable>
       <xsl:value-of select="concat($newHours,':',$minutes,':',$seconds,' ',
         $meridian)"/>
     </xsl:when>
     <xsl:otherwise>
       <xsl:value-of select="$time"/>
     </xsl:otherwise>
   </xsl:choose>
</xsl:template>
</xsl:stylesheet>
```

As you may have noticed, providing working code for something even as simple as a set of date routines can open up a can of worms.

The Future of Stylesheets: XSLT 1.1

XSLT is very much a work in progress. When the specification was first proposed, its role was seen very much as a mechanism for transforming XML into HTML or preferably into a new style language, such as XSL-FO, capable of telling browsers far more precisely how different output requirements should be handled. While the language has adapted surprisingly well to the whole issue of data transformation using XML, making it more a programming language than a styling language, a few somewhat glaring deficiencies are desperately in need of attention.

To that end, James Clark, the author of the initial specification and the developer of one of the first XSLT processors, has proposed an upgrade to the XSLT 1.0 specification to W3C. As of this writing, the Saxon XSLT 6.2 parser has implemented the XSLT 1.1 working draft code. The new proposal exists in part to rectify a number of major issues that have arisen in the use of the parser, and to recognize that there needs to be a more coherent mechanism for handling external resources.

There are five primary changes to the XSLT specification addressed in XSLT 1.1:

❑   The abolition of the ResultTree Fragment type and the removal of the need for `node-set()`-type extensions

❑   The addition of `<xsl:document>` to handle multiple output streams

❑   Specification for blocks of script language

❑   Parameterization of imported templates

❑   A formal mechanism to standardize the inclusion of extensions

It should be pointed out that the XSLT 1.1 document is currently a working draft, and is very much subject to change. As a consequence, always check that your code complies with the current formal XSLT Recommendation document before using any new features (you can see the latest version of the XSLT 1.1 working draft at http://www.w3.org/TR/xslt11).

The Abolition of node-set()

In late fall of 1999, the XSLT specification had been through any number of modifications since its introduction nearly two years before, and there was a need to get it into play as quickly as possible to support the rapidly burgeoning XML market. One issue that had proved contentious was the role of XML Tree Fragments and the balance of responsibilities between the XSLT processor company and the end user.

The thinking at the time held that there were real dangers in letting people build XSLT code within a variable or parameter, because of the very real possibility that the contents of the variable become ill-formed XML in use, as well as the somewhat more remote prospect of the generated code introducing infinite loops. Both *are* possible, of course, yet they are just as possible within procedural programming, but people don't limit the functionality of C++ or Java because of that possibility.

Hence the introduction of the Result Tree Fragment (see the previous chapter), which was more than text but not quite a full node-set. As it turned out, the advantages of being able to generate XML in an intermediate state proved very useful, and most parser manufacturers chose to implement such a concept by building a namespace extension defining a couple of functions, such as the `node-set()` function.

The XSLT 1.1 specification eliminates the XML Tree Fragment data-type altogether from XSLT, and makes official what had been semi-official for some time – you can now generate XML within a variable and have that XML be a "live" node-set if it is so structured. In practice, this eliminates the need for the `node-set()` function and makes it easier to write compact code, as well as eliminating some XPath referencing problems that implementations such as `node-set()` bring to the party.

Multiple Output Streams

An XSLT transformation is curiously one sided. As this chapter has demonstrated, there are several mechanisms available for the creation of XSLT documents working with multiple input streams, in addition to the primary stream. However this multiplicity of streams on the input is not matched on the output side, where there is effectively only a single path out – the output stream.

Yet the ability to work with multiple output streams could transform XSLT from a reasonably powerful engine for modifying XML into an integral part of the modern web. Consider, for instance, an XSLT transformation that accepts a SOAP message containing a purchasing request. A question arises about what you do with the output stream. Should the message be formatted into an XML stream and sent on to another XSLT processor (or something else in the queue)? Should the output be an HTML document that gets sent back to the browser? Should the output be a status message? And what happens if an error occurs with the incoming stream, or if caching of preprocessed HTML is incorporated into the transformation?

With multiple output streams, on the other hand, all of these things can take place within one XSLT transformation. One stream could send a receipt message back to the client indicating the message was received and was (at first blush) valid. A second stream could create a new internal record from the SOAP data and pass that information to a database or a message queue. A third output path could send a status message to a log mechanism to record the transaction. A fourth might send the XML to another vendor to facilitate the purchase of the order, while two more messages could be created to send to the credit card company to debit the client's account and to the manufacturer to fulfill the purchase.

Ironically, what this will end up doing is eliminating the need for a lot of server-side scripting code. The XSLT in this case becomes more like a router mechanism, deciding based upon multiple input streams the kinds of processing that need be done, then either handling the messages or sending them on to other XSLT processes to be resolved there. As more databases, embedded devices, transactions, and computer systems become either XML or HTTP-enabled, this ability to process and route will likely make XSLT extraordinarily pervasive throughout programming for many years to come, especially as the traditional HTML browser becomes only a minority player in the vast cloud of Internet-enabled devices.

The `<xsl:document>` element strongly resembles the `<xsl:output>` element, which makes sense as its primary function is to output XML to a given URL. Specifically, the structure given in the current Working Draft is as follows:

```
<xsl:document
    href = { uri-reference }
    method = { "xml" | "html" | "text" | qname-but-not-ncname }
    version = { nmtoken }
    encoding = { string }
    omit-xml-declaration = { "yes" | "no" }
    standalone = { "yes" | "no" }
    doctype-public = { string }
    doctype-system = { string }
    cdata-section-elements = { qnames }
    indent = { "yes" | "no" }
    media-type = { string }>
    <!-- Content: template -->
</xsl:document>
```

Note that there are several intriguing consequences of this structure. First of all, the output does not have to be XML. As a consequence of this, an XML SOAP message may arrive that, through XSLT, creates a complex SQL stored procedure script, which is then used by a database engine to perform complex updating. Other possibilities include XML in the form of WML (Wireless Markup Language) being sent remotely to thousands of wireless hand-held devices, or information being converted into an audio server format so that a system could actually dial a person to replay an appropriate message. Files can be processed that read in a log, update it in code, then write the log back out to the corresponding file, all within one XSLT script.

Generalized Script Blocks and Extensions

One of the earliest experimental precursors to XSLT, the Microsoft XSL Tech Preview proposal of December 1998, included the idea of an `<xsl:script>` block defining functions that could be referenced by `<xsl:eval>` elements. While a good idea in theory, it had the tendency to create code that was more JavaScript or VBScript than XSL. The command did not feature in the XSLT 1.0 specification, but by then most XSLT processors implemented some form of scripting extension that relied either on Microsoft's COM or Java. The current proposal for XSLT 1.1 basically adopts Microsoft's `<msxml:script>` command wholesale, though adding a couple of additional attributes strengthens the idea considerably:

```
<!-- Category: top-level-element -->
<xsl:script
  implements-prefix = ncname
  language = "ecmascript" | "javascript" | "java" | other language designators
  src = uri-referencereference to an external script block
  archive = uri-references to other libraries>
  <!--Script Contents-->
</xsl:script>
```

Note that this `<xsl:script>` declaration is not the same as Microsoft's defunct namespace from their XSL Technology preview with the same prefix; rather it is a feature of XSLT 1.1 and seems to be closer in spirit to the current `msxml` implementation, where it is possible to define namespace functions that work within the context of XPath.

The `src` attribute makes it possible to reference an external source file, which can both simplify XSLT scripts and make sophisticated XSLT frameworks possible. It allows an entire library of external routines to be defined to load when required. Such libraries would be independent of the XSLT processor in terms of script language. The code could be anything from Java to C# to Visual Basic and – so long as the system supports that language – precompiled, making it much faster in implementation than non-compiled code. Again, this concept works well in conjunction with the notion of XSLT as a router language.

The `archive` attribute similarly supports this interpretation of XSLT. The URI points to a whitespace-delimited list of a set of URIs, each referencing an archive. Each archive is a set of classes or libraries to be preloaded before the function being defined is implemented, making it possible to load external objects and resources and reference them from within a script.

The other aspect of the extension functionality in the XSLT 1.1 specification is that the language now allows objects other than primary XSLT data types to be passed into XSLT (this is actually the behavior that the MSXML parser uses now, but most other XSLT processors don't yet allow this). Thus such things as the server-side `Request` and `Response` objects can be passed into an XSLT document to be queried directly, rather than using complex ASP to query the incoming header object then passing that into the XSLT core. This would look something along the lines of:

```
<xsl:script language="Java" implements-prefix="request"
  src="javax.servlet.servletRequest"/>
```

```
<xsl:variable name="data" select="request:getParameter('data')"/>.
```

You should be aware of the fact that this particular aspect of the 1.1 specification is still very much in contention, as different languages tend to have very different ways of referencing objects. While standardization of this particular aspect of XSLT would go a long way towards its universal adoption, it will undoubtedly go through many iterations before an acceptable one is found.

The Parameterization of Import Templates

Earlier in this chapter an example was given of using `<xsl:apply-imports/>` to create a type of super function that can call an inherited template. However, one thing that I deliberately glossed over was that such imports are not currently parameterized – `<xsl:apply-imports/>` cannot call a named template that has parameters. This was a major lapse in the design of XSLT 1.0, because it meant that the object-oriented characteristics of the language could only go so far.

The XSLT 1.1 specification rectifies this omission by letting you send parametric information as children of the `<xsl:apply-imports/>` node. This effectively means that you could create an XSLT named template that acted as a virtual class, then pass parameters that would extend this template in much the same way that a child class might add or omit parameters before calling the base class with its set of required parameters.

As an example, consider a base template within a stylesheet `myBanner.xsl` that creates specific output according to the particular user agent that initiated the request:

```
<xsl:template name="createDisplayBanner">
  <xsl:param name="user_agent"/>
  <xsl:param name="title"/>
  <xsl:choose>
    <xsl:when test="$user_agent='Mozilla 4'">
      <!-- output a display banner for Netscape 4 -->
    </xsl:when>
    <xsl:when test="$user_agent='IE5'">
      <!-- output a display banner for IE 5 -->
    </xsl:when>
    <xsl:otherwise>
      <!-- output generic display banner.-->
    </xsl:otherwise>
  </xsl:choose>
</xsl:template>
```

Later, your requirements change, and you wish to output a WML banner for WAP clients. Rather than rewriting this whole routine, in XSLT 1.1 you could simply inherit the template in another stylesheet:

```
<xsl:import href="myBanner.xsl"/>
<xsl:template name="createDisplayBanner">
  <xsl:param name="user_agent"/>
  <xsl:param name="title"/>
  <xsl:choose>
    <xsl:when test="$user_agent='WAP'">
```

```
      <!-- output a display banner for WAP Device -->
    </xsl:when>
    <!-- If not the new case, apply the imported original template -->
    <xsl:otherwise>
      <xsl:apply-imports>
        <xsl:with-param name="user_agent" select="$user_agent"/>
        <xsl:with-param name="title" select="$title"/>
      </xsl:apply-imports>
    </xsl:otherwise>
  </xsl:choose>
</xsl:template>
```

This would also apply to matched templates by the way, as they also support the use of attributes.

As with `<xsl:document>`, expect this to have a profound impact upon the ability to create XSLT framework systems that begin to rival the sophistication of the Java foundation classes or the various implementations of Microsoft's foundation class systems.

XSLT 2.0 and Beyond

In Appendix G of the XSLT 1.0 specification, there is a "wish-list" of features to be added to the XSLT specification. It is instructive to consider that the document is now over eighteen months old, and many of the features seem to have been rendered moot by more immediate concerns; for example:

❑ The rendering of result tree fragments and the inclusion of document content in tree fragments go away because tree fragments themselves are obsolete

❑ Support for style rules will likely never happen as XSLT moves farther from its styling roots

❑ Support for entity references have been largely made moot by the changes in XMLBase and XMLInclude, not to mention the more extensive XLink and XPointer specs

Even though the language has not changed dramatically in the last year, the uses and methodologies involved with the language certainly have. Such standards as XML Query Language and the final version of the XML Schema raise the issues of data type support to a whole new level, and the next generation of XSL will need to address the notion of *datatype* in a much more sophisticated manner. The growing rise of peer-to-peer networks is also challenging the scope of the language, and far from pushing back to a closer version of the parent SGML specification, XSLT is being called upon to handle ever increasing complexity.

The questions that are raised in the new context form the basis for the XSLT 2.0 requirements document (http://www.w3.org/TR/xslt20req). While the document is fairly extensive, many of the issues revolve around the nature of working within a distributed environment:

❑ Permitting a document to contain a local stylesheet that applies only to it, even in the context of being processed by an including stylesheet.

❑ Generating and manipulating namespaces directly (currently a major problem with XSLT 1.1).

❑ Handling the difficulties inherent in namespace collisions (as you can tell, namespaces aren't as clean a solution as they were initially envisioned to be).

❑ Handling the formatting of data types. This focuses primarily on dates, but in fact the integration of schema and stylesheets will likely raise issues about the formatting of any type of data.

❑ Extending documents to handle non-XML text.

❑ The ability to author extensions to XSLT in XSLT. This would have a significant impact upon the ability to create XSLT libraries and frameworks.

❑ The handling of transformations on large XML documents. This requirement has spawned the creation of entire classes of software products called XML servers, but the need to be able to transform and process large documents is still largely unfulfilled.

❑ Providing support for lexical and typed comparisons. Again this is where data type and formatting intersect, as it would be useful to create a data type of tokens (such as days of the week) and then determine whether #Sunday < #Tuesday.

❑ Simplifying the process of eliminating redundant information in XPath queries (see Chapter 4 for some idea of how complex this can be). Ideally, it should be possible to do a simple XPath query like select=" //item[unique(@name)]" to only select the first instance of any redundant name set.

Additionally, the XPath specification (which is intimately tied to XSLT) has also garnered a wish list of its own (at http://www.w3.org/TR/xpath20req). This list includes:

❑ Extend the core function set to include things such as min() and max()

❑ Better quantify node-set Boolean operations

❑ Permit unions and intersections of node-sets within XPath expressions

❑ Provide a conditional statement within XPath. It should be possible to say:

```
<xsl:value-of select="if(@filename,@filename,'default.xml')"/>
```

for instance, which would check to see if a filename is defined, and return the filename if it is or return the name of a default filename if not. This would radically simplify XSLT as well.

❑ Provide string functions to do general-purpose replacements (possible using regular expressions), padding, and case conversion.

❑ Provide support for primitive schema data types, such as dates, numeric type, and scientific notation.

❑ Make it possible to rectify an enumerated attribute list into a series of tokens, and access them accordingly.

❑ Retrieve an element or attribute based upon its data type.

XPath is likely to prove a critical part of another technology, XML Query. Consider the problem: how do you locate information? This is the fundamental question that has consumed the XML Query Language group for more than a year, and their observations (see http://www.w3.org/TR/query-algebra/) are likely to form the basis of a new W3C recommendation. The XPath language approaches the problem from the viewpoint of XML's explicit pyramid structure, and while it is a good start for manipulating the various elements and attributes of XML, there are several areas where it is a little weak. XPath has only primitive knowledge of data types, includes only basic string searching capabilities, and is not terribly well suited to handling queries on polymorphic structures.

On the other hand, the XML Schema Definition Language, or part two of the specification to be more precise (found at http://www.w3.org/TR/xmlschema-2/) introduces a very robust – some might say too robust – solution for specifying both simple data types, such as date-time or enumerated sets, and complex data types (structures of elements and attributes). One consequence of the richness of this description is that queries also become considerably more sophisticated. For instance, if you have the ability to specify an enumeration of values in an element, you can also define the concept of "less-than" and "greater-than" as an element's position relative to another in the same list. A query that then asks "Find all colors less than yellow in the rainbow" would return a set of colors such as {green, blue, indigo, violet}.

XSLT has a very strong dependence upon XPath, and it only makes sense that the dependency with XML Query will be stronger. XML Query almost certainly will include more robust text pattern matching (regular expressions) that challenge the traditional boundaries of text nodes. XSLT has provisions for sorting and filtering based upon ordering criteria other than numbers or strings, but the provisions currently are little more than "*To Be Done*" segments of the specification and must yet be completely fleshed out. The functional manipulation available to XML Query will likewise impact on XSLT 2.0, as queries will undoubtedly become more complex and verbose to accommodate data types and polymorphism.

Another, perhaps simpler, change that may take place is the loosening of restrictions on variable reassignments. While such a language may become a little less "pure", it will likely be considerably more accessible for developers. This will be of paramount importance when variables are used in conjunction with data types, since more complex data types will in turn demand more complex operations on those variables (envision matrix operations or regular expression support as just two examples).

However, the most likely evolution of the language will be the development of core frameworks that extend functionality in the same way that Java or C++ class frameworks have expanded their language usage. Any language is only as valuable in practice as the set of libraries supporting it, but with the revisions likely in the XSLT 1.1 specification, those libraries should quickly proliferate.

Summary

The document() function is perhaps the most important capability in XSLT, especially once the corresponding <xsl:document> function comes on line with XSLT 1.1. These two capabilities make it possible to work with XML from anywhere and send it anywhere. This is the antithesis of the file system approach to operating systems – there really are no files in the XML world, only sources and sinks for streams. One consequence of this is that XSLT will likely end up proving pivotal in the development of large scale peer-to-peer networks, because it sees the world in universal terms – universal locations, universal formats, universal processing instructions.

Moreover, the advent of the ability to import XSLT code makes it possible to develop a truly global programming language capable of working as easily on documents spanning countless servers as documents in the same directory. Because XSLT is also XML, the extensible nature of the language blurs the boundaries between data and procedure and shifts the focus of programming away from an orientation on objects and towards an orientation on pure relationships.

The XLST language itself is evolving, both in terms of the core functionality and in the increasing realization that XML/XSLT has its own, somewhat unique, object-oriented structure. The authors of the specification have seen it grow in scope from being a language for "styling" XML for formatted output into a primary mechanism for providing transformations of XML data through the current extensive web infrastructure (note that a translation – moving something – is also a transformation). The ability to create multiple output streams will only enhance that, putting XSLT increasingly in the role of mediating and routing XML.

The scripting extension mechanisms similarly have a major effect upon XSLT, since via scripting it becomes possible for an XSLT transformation to communicate with the outside world, to take advantage of an operating system's capabilities, to talk to non XML data, and to physically control devices. Because it is also possible to bundle other languages within XML, this will mean that you can combine the extensibility and malleability of XML with the rapid processing capabilities necessary to control the increasing plethora of micro-servers and clients that populate the web, from cell phones to production robots.

XSLT is protean – more than most languages out there, it has the ability to change and reshape itself in response to changes in its environment. Of course, this can be said to be true of viruses as well, and therein lies both the power and the challenge of XSLT. Up until now, the Web has had a certain insulating factor by dint of the extreme variety of systems out there. XSLT has the potential to render many of these differences moot; this means that it becomes easier to communicate between computers (and hence between people using those computers) but it also makes it that much easier to create "viral" systems that have a dynamic very different from those in use today, for good or ill.

Finally, XSLT, like XML itself, will likely disappear into the substrate of programming. While XSLT by itself can be something of a bear to write, it is actually a very simple language that could lend itself well to programming through intention. As with XML, it is the simplicity of the language that will ultimately lead to its adoption at the heart of most computer systems. The next few years should be fun.

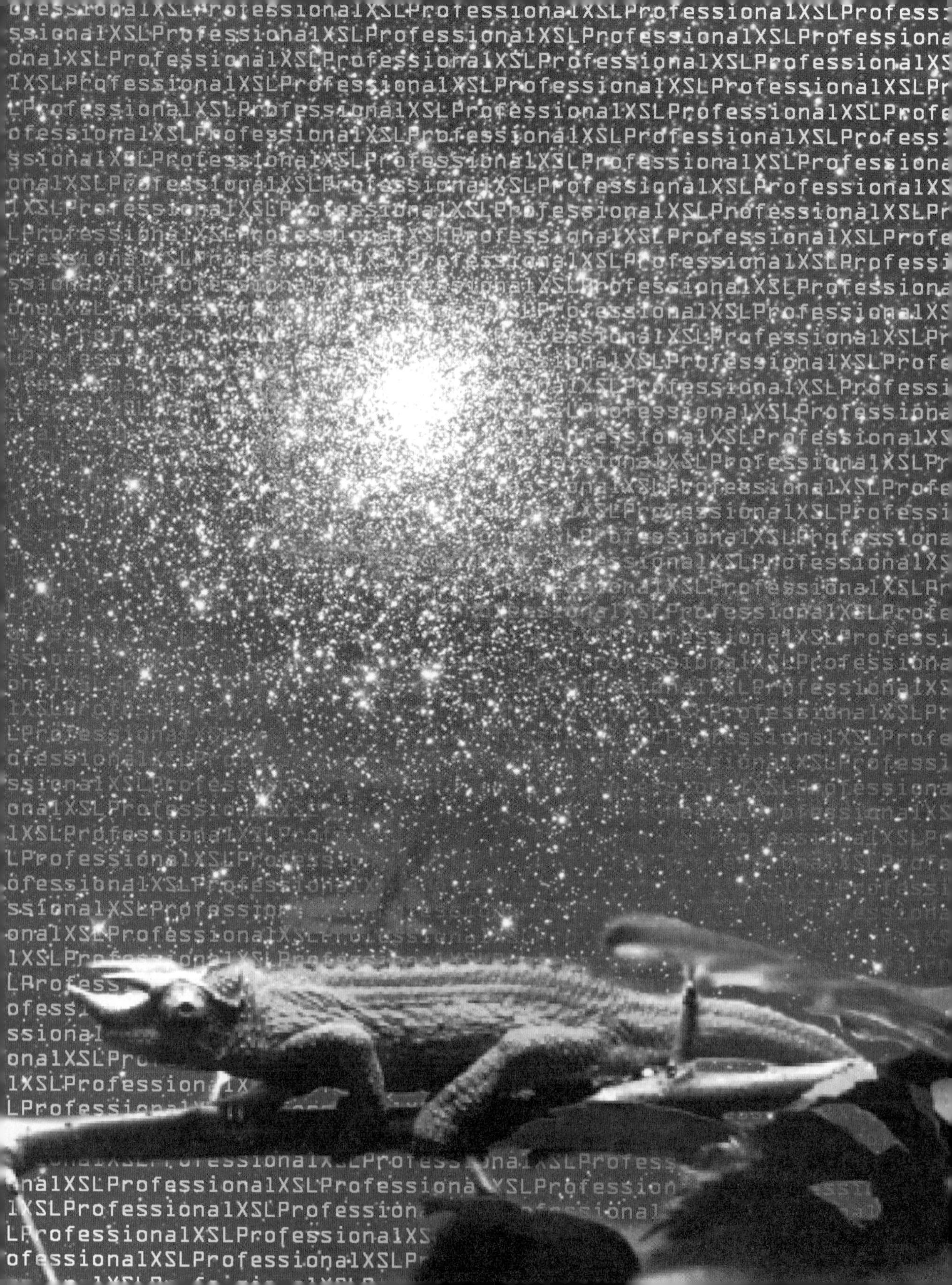

6

Transformations Using DOM and SAX

By this point in the book, you may well be feeling somewhat in awe of the amazing power of XSL. In fact, you may even be beginning to think that you won't be needing that old-fashioned procedural programming stuff quite so much in future, so this makes a good time for a cynical old-timer to throw a wrench in the works. After all, this isn't the first time that traditional programming has been given a premature burial.

The thing is that XSL is, as we described in Chapter 1, a declarative language. This is pretty cool if your primary interest in life is *data*, rather than *programming*. As it is, declarative languages usually limit you to solving only a subset of the full set of problems: there'll always be something that evades capture and must be dealt with procedurally. Don't get me wrong: if it's a good declarative language (like XSL), the subset of solvable problems will fill a significant part of the whole picture. In many cases, you will indeed be able to develop excellent transformations without a need to resort to old-fashioned, procedural code. However, we won't be looking at any of these rosy pictures here. This chapter is about the weird stuff, where the XSL approach breaks down and we have to try something else. Speaking personally, I actually prefer the weird stuff, but I guess that's because I'm a dyed-in-the-wool programmer.

In fact, this chapter represents considerable value for money, in that it describes not one, but *two* alternative, yet standard, approaches, both of which use old-style APIs. The first of these uses the **Document Object Model**, or **DOM**, while the second will employ **SAX**, the **Simple API for XML**. We can sum up the difference between the two approaches by saying that with DOM, a program is in charge, whereas in SAX, an event-driven API, the XML is in charge. We'll see what this actually implies later.

In this chapter, you will learn when and how to use each of these tools for carrying out XML transformations. This will inevitably involve some programming, but I'll try to keep things as straightforward as possible, and explain any unusual concepts along the way. We'll mostly be using Java and VBScript, and almost all of the samples can be followed using tools available as free downloads. The only exception is right at the end, where I've been unable to resist the temptation to use a bit of Microsoft Visual Basic; you'll see why when we get there.

When to Use DOM or SAX Instead of XSLT

Before we look at the technicalities (the "how"), let's briefly talk about the type of transformation engine that might be appropriate for a given traditional programming approach (the "when").

The kind of situation I'm thinking about is one where good, old-fashioned procedural code can make short work of something that may only be handled with great difficulty, if at all, in a declarative language.

The key place where XSL scores badly is in the manipulation of textual data. XSL is strongly geared towards operations on an entire text string, whether you're searching for a match against it, or performing some kind of substitution. However, if you're looking to do something that acts on sub-strings of a text element, XSL starts to struggle – the example we'll be using for this chapter concerns precisely this type of problem.

I should point out, as an aside, that the Microsoft XSLT implementation does in fact include a proprietary extension that allows you to execute script code in the body of a stylesheet. In some ways, this would seem to offer us the best of both worlds. However, the bad news is that the current W3C XSLT Recommendation has no provision for this, so we really do have to abandon XSLT entirely if we wish to incorporate procedural code. A remedy for this has been proposed in the Working Draft of the XSLT 1.1 Specification, but this is far from stable at the time of writing.

Another area where XSL isn't appropriate is where the transformation references a third party system. For example, consider the task of translating an XML document from US English into UK English, say. Somewhere along the line, you're going to need a database containing the translations ("color" into "colour", "sidewalk" might be "pavement" and so on). Now, although you could just about code this up in XSL, it would be a pretty horrendous and inefficient process, and you'd be much better off using a traditional database application.

For our sample, let's imagine that we have an XML document that contains information on a collection of books. The kind of information we might need is simple stuff like title, author, publisher and ISBN. We might also like to throw in an attribute like "category", indicating what type of book it is. Here's what it might look like (`library.xml`):

```xml
<?xml version="1.0"?>
<library>
  <book category="fiction">
    <author>J.K.Rowling</author>
    <title>Harry Potter and the Philosopher's Stone</title>
    <publisher>Bloomsbury</publisher>
    <ISBN>0747532745</ISBN>
  </book>
  <book category="non-fiction">
    <author>Julian Cope</author>
    <title>The Modern Antiquarian</title>
    <publisher>Thorsons</publisher>
    <ISBN>0722535996</ISBN>
  </book>
  <book category="humor">
    <author>Peter Blegvad</author>
    <title>The Book of Leviathan</title>
    <publisher>Sort Of</publisher>
```

```
       <ISBN>0953522725</ISBN>
    </book>
    <book category="fiction">
      <author>O'Brien, Flann</author>
      <title>The Third Policeman</title>
      <publisher>Flamingo</publisher>
      <ISBN>0586087494</ISBN>
    </book>
    <book category="fiction">
      <author>Flann O'Brien</author>
      <title>At Swim-Two-Birds</title>
      <publisher>Penguin</publisher>
      <ISBN>0141182687</ISBN>
    </book>
    <book category="fantasy">
      <author>Pinnock, Jonathan</author>
      <title>Professional DCOM Application Development</title>
      <publisher>Wrox</publisher>
      <ISBN>1861001312</ISBN>
    </book>
  </library>
```

Clearly there are a lot of useful tricks that standard XSL transformation techniques can do with this, ranging from simple data shuffling to filtering out books within a particular category. However, have you noticed the one small problem lurking in there? It's that <author> element. As you can see, we weren't particularly rigorous with the format of the name here, and it's quite possible that a search for everything by Flann O'Brien might miss "The Third Policeman" (a pity, because I think it's quite possibly the greatest book ever written by anyone). Frankly, XSL is not really up to the job of sorting it all out. It's bad enough having to reorganize the ordering of first and last names, without having to deal with forms such as the abbreviated Ms Rowling. At least I resisted the temptation to include "Mr Bunny's Guide to ActiveX", by Carlton Egremont III.

So what are we to do? Well, I think it looks like time to dust off our programming hats again ...

XML DOM

The XML Document Object Model is a platform- and language-neutral API for working with XML and HTML documents. It defines objects representing the various parts of these documents, and interfaces for dynamically accessing and manipulating them. The progress of the XML DOM specification is controlled by the World Wide Web Consortium, and the main resource for information is on their web site, at http://www.w3.org/DOM.

The definition of such a standard normally takes a considerable amount of time and effort. In recognition of this, the W3C have taken a highly pragmatic approach, and are building up the DOM specification level by level. Each level firms up as much of the specification as is practical, leaving out anything requiring more debate until later levels. For this reason, the Level 1 specification assumes the document is already in memory, whilst the Level 2 specification defines an interface, DOMImplementation, that includes the method createDocument() to load in a document from a specified URL.

At the time of writing, the present state of affairs is that the Level 1 specification was endorsed by the W3C as a Recommendation on October 1, 1998, and the Level 2 specification was endorsed as a Recommendation on November 13, 2000 but has yet to filter through into commercially available implementations. The Level 3 specification is still a Working Draft.

187

Objects and Interfaces in Five Minutes Flat

We're not going to get very far into our discussion without raising the subject of **objects**, so we should probably tackle that one head-on before we start. If you're not familiar with object-orientated programming, don't worry – it's one of those big programming concepts that are actually relatively straightforward underneath all the jargon. Here's the big idea:

> **An object is a lump of data that includes an integral set of instructions for manipulating that data.**

These instructions are called **methods**. The actual data in an object is contained in **properties**. Some of these methods and properties (the **public** ones) are available to the outside world, whilst others are **private** to that object. Objects have a pre-set structure, defining which methods they support, and which properties they have, referred to as a **class definition**. One class may derive from another, in which case it **inherits** the other's methods and properties, and adds a few more of its own which override any duplicated, inherited methods.

An **interface** is similar to a class, in that it's a specification of an object's behavior in terms of methods and properties. The difference is that an object can implement more than one interface. This is referred to as **multiple inheritance**. This isn't really a particularly unusual concept. I think we are all familiar with the idea of presenting a different face to the world depending on whether or not we are dealing with our boss or our dearly beloved, or even someone who does not speak our language – we have 'multiple interfaces' for use in different situations.

Finally, an object can choose either to **implement** an interface, or **extend** it. In the former case, it must supply code for every single method in that interface. In the latter case, however, it can just select which methods it wants to override with its own versions and accept the default implementation for the other ones. It can also add a few more of its own methods and properties.

To illustrate, let's consider a somewhat light-hearted object representing myself, the author of this chapter. To encapsulate my behavior, the object implements a number of interfaces, among them will need to be included the interfaces WriteBooks and SlobInFrontOfTV. The interface WriteBooks could contain (amongst others) the following methods:

```
ComposeExample()
ExplainSomething()
MissDeadline()
```

and properties like:

```
bankBalance
tiredness
desperation
```

The basic SlobInFrontOfTV interface has no properties, except maybe a value for consciousnessLevel, but will certainly contain the following core set of methods:

```
watchSomething()
drinkBeer()
belch()
```

For this particular author, the interface would be modified to have its own implementation of `watchSomething()` to represent my individual tastes, and to extend the interface to include the method `pressRemoteControlAtRandom()`, to the chagrin of all others in the room. Now I think we're ready to move on to the really funny stuff.

The Document Object Model

The principle behind programming with the XML Document Object Model is pretty straightforward. The first stage involves using a parser to translate your XML document into an in-memory tree of objects representing every element and attribute. Having done that, you can use the methods in those objects' interfaces to navigate around the document, extracting information, and changing it to your heart's content. When you have finished, you can, if you want, convert the in-memory object hierarchy back into XML.

If we take a look at the start of our example XML document, this is what the DOM representation looks like:

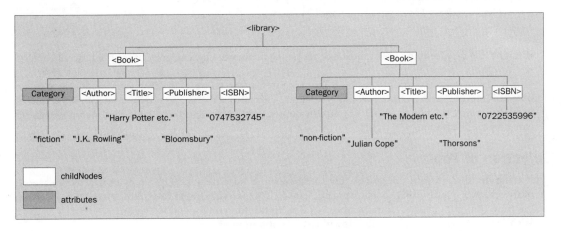

The key classes in the DOM are `Node`, `Document`, `Element` and `NodeList`.

❑ `Node` represents a single node in the hierarchy. A node, in this context, is any part of the document.

❑ `Document`, not unnaturally, represents the entire document. The fact that the entire document can also be regarded as a single node is reflected in the fact that the `Document` class is derived from `Node`.

❑ `Element` represents any XML element; again, this class is derived from `Node`.

❑ The `Node` class contains a property called `childNodes`, which is of type `NodeList`. As the name suggests, this is simply a list of nodes, at the next stage down in the hierarchy. It's also possible to construct a `NodeList` artificially using specific selection criteria, as we'll see in the example coming up.

There are a number of other classes in the DOM, but these four are sufficient to get started, and I think the first programming example is well overdue.

DOM Programming Using Java

The first thing we're going to do is write a Java application, and then we're going to do pretty much the same thing in VBScript. The reason for doing VBScript is that there are an awful lot of VBScript programmers around, whilst the reason for doing Java is just to show that I'm not completely biased towards Microsoft. The Java implementation is also a much better illustration of the Document Object Model, which is why we're going to do it first. If you can't wait for VBScript, feel free to skip a few pages, although I'd rather you stuck around, because I think you'll find it useful, even if Java isn't your language of choice.

Outline of the Problem

Remember our XML document, `library.xml`? What I'd like to do is remove those nasty unstructured `<author>` elements, and replace them with something a little more useful, like this, for example:

```
<author>
    <firstname>J.K.</firstname>
    <lastname>Rowling</lastname>
</author>
```

It might also be nice to be able to just extract books in a particular category or, optionally, all categories.

Our program will take three command line arguments: the name of the input XML file, the name of the output XML file, and an optional category filter. The output file is essentially a rewritten version of the input file, using the above format for author names, and only including books that match the search category if specified.

Selection of Tools

Having decided on Java, we've now got to cast around for a parser. With an eye towards the second half of the chapter, we're going to use Apache Xerces. This is available at http://xml.apache.org/xerces-j. At the time of writing, the version number is 1.2.3, so the file you'll need is `Xerces-J-bin.1.2.3.zip`. We'll find out what to do with the download in just a moment.

You'll also need a Java Development Kit, release 1.1 or later. If you don't happen to have one lying around, your best bet is to download the Sun Java 2 Platform, Standard Edition from http://java.sun.com/j2se/1.3. However, this is a pretty massive download (30 Mbytes or so), and if you're pushed for bandwidth, JDK 1.1 is quite acceptable. This is still available from http://java.sun.com/products/jdk/1.1, although even this is a good 8 Mbytes, so you might want to get this ready well in advance.

We'll use `Notepad` for our editor, or – if you're running Unix – `vi`, or whatever else you've got lying around. So we've got a completely free development environment. Let's go.

Setting Up the Environment

We'll do this in a few stages.

Step 1: Install JDK

This is the easy bit! JDK pretty much installs itself. Under Windows, for example, it comes as a self-extracting executable, and all you have to do is follow the instructions.

Step 2: Install Xerces

We should create a self-contained area for our experiments, so I suggest creating a new directory somewhere convenient, called something like "XML". Xerces comes as an all-platform zip file. What this means in practice is that, whatever the platform you're using, you should move the file to the new directory, and issue the command line (from within the XML directory):

```
jar xf Xerces-J-bin.1.2.3.zip
```

I prefer this method to using WinZip or similar, although that approach should also work fine. You will find that you now have the following directory structure within your new directory:

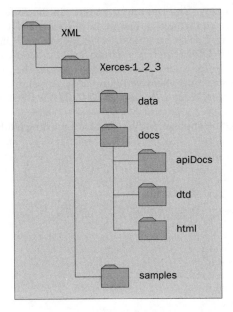

You should find a set of .html files in apiDocs – this is the official documentation. The business end of the package is the xerces.jar file in the top-level directory. This Java archive (indicated by the .jar extension) contains the classes that let us interface with the Xerces parser.

Step 3: Modifying the Class Path

The big question that we need to resolve now is how to tell our Java compiler where to find these classes. We do this by amending the value of our trusty environment variable CLASSPATH. Under Windows NT and 2000, you can do this via the System icon on the control panel, either selecting the tab labeled Environment, or choosing Advanced and then Environment variables in Windows 2000. You'll need to amend it so that it includes the full pathname of the xerces.jar archive. You should also check that the path contains the current directory, ".".

So, for example, if your XML tree is on your c: drive, you'll need to add the following:

```
.;c:\XML\xerces-1_2_3\xerces.jar
```

If you'd rather not amend your class path for every application on your system, you can instead pass it as a parameter when you eventually compile your Java classes. Instead of the command:

```
javac sourcecode.java
```

you should issue the command:

```
javac sourcecode.java -classpath c:\XML\xerces-1_2_3\xerces.jar
```

The Code

I think we're ready to start coding. You can find the source in the code download, as DOMTransform.java. As we go through, I'll point out the various DOM objects we're using, and also which methods we're invoking. I don't propose to cover the entire DOM here, by the way – this chapter isn't intended to be a complete DOM reference. However, in practice, you should find that once you're familiar with a few of the methods, it's not too taxing to work out the rest. If you do need more information on DOM, there's a comprehensive reference in Appendix D of this book, and also a chapter devoted to the subject in Wrox's *Professional XML* (ISBN 1-861003-11-0).

OK – let's get on with writing the application. We start by importing all the Java classes that we will need:

```
import java.io.FileReader;
import java.io.FileWriter;

import javax.xml.parsers.DocumentBuilderFactory;
import javax.xml.parsers.DocumentBuilder;

import org.w3c.dom.Document;
import org.w3c.dom.NodeList;
import org.w3c.dom.Node;
import org.w3c.dom.Element;
import org.w3c.dom.Text;

import org.xml.sax.InputSource;

import org.apache.xml.serialize.XMLSerializer;
```

We'll see how these get used as the program goes on. The only slightly peculiar thing is the org.xml.sax.InputSource reference. Surely SAX is in the second half of the chapter? Well, it turns out that InputSource is a useful helper class for providing input to both forms of the Apache parser (there's a SAX one as well, in case you hadn't guessed), and we will be using it in our DOM-based code.

The standard Java main() method declaration appears next: it contains the initial code that will be executed when we start the class up. The method transform() reads in the command line arguments:

```
public class DOMTransform
{
    public static void main(String[] args) throws Exception
    {
        DOMTransform transformObj = new DOMTransform();
        transformObj.transform(args);
    }
```

```
public void transform (String[] args) throws Exception
{
    if (args.length == 0)
        throw new Exception ("No input file specified");

    String inFile = args[0];

    if (args.length == 1)
        throw new Exception ("No output file specified");

    String outFile = args[1];

    String catFilter = "all";

    if (args.length >= 3)
        catFilter = args[2];

    boolean fAll = false;

    if (catFilter.compareTo ("all") == 0)
        fAll = true;
```

Notice that if the category filter is left out as a parameter on the command line, all items are included in the transformation.

OK, this is where the fun starts. We need to access our DOM parser, and we do this by means of some code that is entirely proprietary to Xerces (we'll see that the Microsoft version is completely different later on). The parser is implemented as a `DocumentBuilder` object. This is because what it actually does is build a document object model from the incoming data source, by the method `parse()`, which returns a `Document` object, one of the DOM objects that we talked about earlier. Now we have an entry point into the rich functionality of the DOM.

At this point, you might be wondering why there is all this proprietary stuff to deal with before reaching into the standard DOM API. The reason is that, at Level 1 at any rate, the DOM specification assumes that the document has already been loaded into memory. Level 2 of the DOM specification includes a new interface, `DOMImplementation`, which has a method called `createDocument()` that standardizes this. However, at the time of writing, most parsers have yet to adopt Level 2 functionality and, like Xerces, they tend to merrily do their own thing instead.

```
System.out.println("Commencing transformation ...");

DocumentBuilderFactory factoryObj = DocumentBuilderFactory.newInstance();
DocumentBuilder domBuilderObj = factoryObj.newDocumentBuilder();

FileReader inFileObj = new FileReader(args[0]);
Document domObj = domBuilderObj.parse (new InputSource(inFileObj));
```

The next few lines set up a `NodeList` for us containing all the book nodes. We do this in three stages:

1. Locate all the instances of `<library>` elements, and put them into a `NodeList`. There should actually only be one `<library>` element and, strictly speaking, we should check that this is really the case. Alternatively, we could specify a DTD that requires only one such element be present, and let the parser check the document for validity. (You can, incidentally, check whether or not the parser is performing validation by the `isValidating()` method of the `DocumentBuilder` object.)

2. Assuming that we indeed have only one `<library>` element, we extract the object representing it using the `item()` method of the `NodeList` object mentioned in the preceding stage 1. This returns a `Node` object, which we need to cast to `Element` for the next step, allowing us access to the methods in the `Element` interface.

3. Finally, we use the `getElementsByTagName()` method of the `<library>` element object to set up our `NodeList` containing all instances of `<book>` nodes:

```
NodeList libraryListObj = domObj.getElementsByTagName ("library");
Element libraryObj = (Element) libraryListObj.item(0);
NodeList booksObj = libraryObj.getElementsByTagName ("book");
```

Next, we find the number of book nodes in the `NodeList` set up in the above code, and initiate a large loop to process each book node within the `NodeList` in turn.

The first thing to do in this loop is to extract the `Node` object representing a single book, by using the `item` method of the `NodeList` object, casting it into an `Element` object. Then we extract the value of the book's `category` attribute using the `getAttribute()` method:

```
int numBook = booksObj.getLength();

for (int intBook = 0; intBook < numBook; intBook++)
{
    Element bookObj = (Element) booksObj.item(intBook);
    String category = bookObj.getAttribute("category");
```

If either all categories are being selected, or the current book belongs to the selected category, we need to process the book object accordingly. Here, the first thing we do is separate the `<author>` element in a similar manner to the way we extracted the `<library>` element above. We create a `NodeList` containing all `<author>` elements in the current book, by using the `getElementsByTagName()` method of the book object. Then, assuming that there is one and only one `<author>` element, we extract its `Node` object using the `item()` method of the author `NodeList`, again casting to `Element`:

```
if (fAll || (category.compareTo (catFilter) == 0))
{
    NodeList authorsObj = bookObj.getElementsByTagName ("author");
    Element authorObj = (Element) authorsObj.item(0);
```

Now we've got our hands on the `<author>` element, we can get its associated text (remember, this is what we're intending to fix!). Again, we're making assumptions about the structure of the document, so in real life we would either impose a DTD, or carry out a run-time check. However, if the document is structured as we expect, the author text will be located in the first child element. We can extract the `Node` representing this by using the `getFirstChild()` method of the author `Element`. We cast it into a type of object that we haven't encountered before, `Text`. This is another class derived from `Node` (via `CharacterData`), and it represents a purely textual element. By extracting the actual text into a string using the `Text` object's `getData()` method, we get a string containing the author's name. As we will be using this string to construct two new child elements, `<firstname>` and `<lastname>`, we can now safely destroy the original `Text` object, by means of the `removeChild()` method of the author `Element`:

```
Text textObj = (Text) authorObj.getFirstChild ();
String authorString = textObj.getData ();
authorObj.removeChild (textObj);
```

At this point, we're ready to separate out the first and last names of the author. This is implemented with procedural code, so I won't go into too much detail as my aim is to explain the DOM interface. The rather simplistic rules that I'll use are:

- ❏ If there's a comma in the name, assume that the form is 'surname, first name', for example 'Doe, John'. The first name will be John and the last name Doe.

- ❏ Otherwise, if there's a period in the name, assume that it includes initials, for example J.K.Doe. The first name shall be J.K. and the last name Doe.

- ❏ Otherwise, assume that it's plain John Doe. The first name is John and the last name is Doe.

As you can see, it's not particularly rigorous, but this isn't really the place for devoting vast reams of space to intricate name parsing routines.

```
String firstName = "";
String lastName = authorString;

int comma = authorString.indexOf (',');

if (comma == -1)
{
    int period = authorString.lastIndexOf ('.');

    // The name includes a period
    if (period != -1)
    {
        firstName = authorString.substring (0, period + 1);
        lastName = authorString.substring (period + 1);
    }
    else
    {
        int space = authorString.indexOf (' ');

        // The name is regular John Doe format
        if (space != -1)
        {
            firstName = authorString.substring (0, space);
            lastName = authorString.substring (space + 1);
        }
    }
}

// The name includes a comma
else
{
    lastName = authorString.substring (0, comma);
    firstName = authorString.substring (comma + 2);
}
```

OK, we're nearly there. We still have to create the new child elements to hold the first and last names that we've extracted. For each name, we use the `createElement()` method of the all-encompassing `Document` object to create an unattached `Element` object with the appropriate tag name. We then give it a pure text node as a child, with the `Document` object's `createTextNode()` method, where the parameter gives the contents for the node. We attach this to the newly created element by means of the `appendChild()` method. Finally, we attach the new node to the author element, again by means of the `appendChild()` method:

```
            Element firstNameObj = domObj.createElement ("firstname");
            textObj = domObj.createTextNode (firstName);
            firstNameObj.appendChild (textObj);
            authorObj.appendChild (firstNameObj);

            Element lastNameObj = domObj.createElement ("lastname");
            textObj = domObj.createTextNode (lastName);
            lastNameObj.appendChild (textObj);
            authorObj.appendChild (lastNameObj);
        }
```

But what if our book category doesn't match the selected filter? Well, we're going to have to remove it from the document, I'm afraid. We do this by means of our old friend, removeChild(), this time on the element representing the library. The next couple of lines are required because this particular parser keeps the NodeList in sync with its parent node, so we have to decrement our counters for our loop to remain in step.

```
        else
        {
            libraryObj.removeChild (bookObj);

            numBook--;
            intBook--;
        }
    }    // End for
```

> Note that this doesn't happen with every parser: as we'll see shortly, the Microsoft behavior is quite different. You should make sure you're clear on how the particular parser that you're using works.

Finally, we need to write our new document out to file. We do this via a class unique to Xerces called XMLSerializer. All we do is instantiate this, point its output stream to a standard Java FileWriter object representing our output file, by means of the setOutputCharStream() method, and hit the serialize button:

```
        FileWriter outFileObj = new FileWriter (outFile);
        XMLSerializer serializerObj = new XMLSerializer ();
        serializerObj.setOutputCharStream (outFileObj);
        serializerObj.serialize (domObj);

        System.out.println ("Transformation complete");
    }
}
```

Compiling and Running

This is purely a command line application, so on Windows we'll need to open up a DOS box, and navigate to the directory containing the source. Under Unix we'll need to use an xterm. This is how we compile it:

```
javac DOMTransform.java
```

Before running it, make sure that our `library.xml` file is in the same directory, unless you want to type out the full path for it. This is how we would run our application to extract all the fiction books:

```
java DOMTransform library.xml javalibrary.xml fiction
```

and this is what we have in the newly-created `javalibrary.xml`:

```xml
<?xml version="1.0"?>
<library>
    <book category="fiction">
        <author>
            <firstname>J.K.</firstname>
            <lastname>Rowling</lastname>
        </author>
        <title>Harry Potter and the Philosopher's Stone</title>
        <publisher>Bloomsbury</publisher>
        <ISBN>0747532745</ISBN>
    </book>
    <book category="fiction">
        <author>
            <firstname>Flann</firstname>
            <lastname>O'Brien</lastname>
        </author>
        <title>The Third Policeman</title>
        <publisher>Flamingo</publisher>
        <ISBN>0586087494</ISBN>
    </book>
    <book category="fiction">
        <author>
            <firstname>Flann</firstname>
            <lastname>O'Brien</lastname></author>
        <title>At Swim-Two-Birds</title>
        <publisher>Penguin</publisher>
        <ISBN>0141182687</ISBN>
    </book>
</library>
```

This should give a taste of how we can use the DOM from within a traditional procedural application.

DOM Programming Using VBScript

The Apache implementation of the DOM conforms well to the standard. However, as you might expect, Microsoft has added one or two extra tricks of its own. Let's take a look at how the same application looks if we program it in VBScript. As before, we wish to do this in a stand-alone program that can be run without the likes of Internet Explorer, so we're going to use the Windows Script Host. This is a neat little package that enables you to simply run VBScript or JScript code as if it were a compiled program. In case you haven't got it on your system, you can download it from http://www.microsoft.com/msdownload/vbscript/scripting.asp. This is very straightforward to install; all you need do is run the self-installing executable, and follow the instructions.

The Code

Again, the source of our example is available from Wrox as part of the download, and it's called `DOMTransform.vbs`. We'll take a look at it, piece by piece, below. The first difference is that there are no `import` statements, and no direct references to DOM concepts such as `Document`, `Node` or `Element`. This is because VBScript, like all scripting languages, is a very **weakly-typed** language, as opposed to Java, which is **strongly-typed**. In a weakly-typed language the association of a variable with its type (`Document`, `Node`, `Element` or whatever) occurs at run-time, rather than at compile-time (after all, there is no compile-time with a scripting language).

The net result is that you could be forgiven for thinking that the DOM isn't referenced at all. But the objects are all there lurking in the background, hidden away from sight. This is the reason why we looked at the Java version first, where they are out in the open, unashamed.

The first section of code extracts the file names and category filter from the input command line. This is similar to the equivalent section in the Java program, except that it uses the `WScript` object to extract the arguments. This object comes as part of the Windows Script Host run-time package, and contains a number of useful methods for developing WSH applications. It's described in more detail in the standard MSDN documentation.

```
If (WScript.Arguments.Count = 0) Then
   WScript.Echo ("No input file specified")
   WScript.Quit (1)
End If

inFile = WScript.Arguments(0)

If (WScript.Arguments.Count = 1) Then
   WScript.Echo ("No output file specified")
   WScript.Quit (2)
End If

outFile = WScript.Arguments(1)

catFilter = "all"
If (WScript.Arguments.Count > 2) Then catFilter = WScript.Arguments(2)

fAll = false
If (catFilter = "all") Then fAll = true

WScript.Echo ("Commencing transformation ...")
```

The code to read in and parse the document is radically different, however. Here, all we need to do is instantiate a `Document` object using the VBScript function `CreateObject()`, specifying the `XMLDOM` class identifier, and invoke its `load()` method.

Hold on a moment! What `load()` method? The DOM specification for `Document` doesn't mention a `load()` method! Well, it's one of those Microsoft extras I warned you about, I'm afraid. Admittedly, this is one of those cases that is not covered by the DOM specification. However, whereas the Xerces implementation got round the problem by defining some altogether new classes, Microsoft have simply extended the `Document` interface. It's neat, though, isn't it?

> *Incidentally, Appendix B of Professional XML lists the entire Microsoft DOM implementation, identifying all proprietary extensions.*

```
Set xmldoc = CreateObject ("Microsoft.XMLDOM")
xmldoc.load (inFile)
```

The code up to the point where we get hold of the author element, again follows a similar path to the Java version:

```
Set oLibraryList = xmldoc.getElementsByTagName ("library")
Set oLibrary = oLibraryList.item(0)
Set oBookList = oLibrary.getElementsByTagName ("book")

For i = 0 To (oBookList.length - 1)
   Set oBook = oBookList.item(i)
   category = oBook.getAttribute ("category")

   If ((fAll = true) Or (category = catFilter)) Then
       Set oAuthors = oBook.getElementsByTagName ("author")
       Set oAuthor = oAuthors.item(0)
```

Now we once again veer off into Microsoft extension territory. Instead of having to extract the textual data from the first child of the author element, we simply require the text() method of the author Element object. Not only that, but it works both ways:

```
author = oAuthor.text
oAuthor.text = ""
```

I think that's pretty neat, too. If, however, you want to stick to the standard, you should use this instead:

```
Set oChild = oAuthor.firstChild
author = oChild.data
oAuthor.removeChild (oChild)
```

which isn't that much more awkward, I suppose.

The next segment performs the data transformation, and is very similar to the Java version. First, we check for the presence of a comma. If we find one, then we take the first name as whatever is after the comma, and the last name as whatever comes before it:

```
Dim firstName
Dim lastName

index = InStr (1, author, ",")

If (index > 0) Then
    lastName = Left (author, index - 1)
    firstName = Right (author, Len (author) - (index + 1))
Else
```

If there's no comma, we search for the last period, using the variable start to indicate the beginning of the last name:

```
index = 0
Do
    start = index + 1
    index = InStr (start, author, ".")
Loop Until index = 0
```

If there are any, we extract the initials to use as the first name, and the remainder to use as the last name:

```
If (start > 1) Then
    firstName = Left (author, start - 1)
    lastName = Right (author, Len (author) - (start - 1))
```

Otherwise, we need to find the space between the first and last names:

```
Else
    index = InStr (1, author, " ")

    firstName = Left (author, index - 1)
    lastName = Right (author, Len (author) - index)
End If
End If
```

Now we're setting up the new child elements to hold the first and last names. Again, I've streamlined the code slightly by using the Microsoft text() extension:

```
Set oFirst = xmldoc.createElement ("firstname")
oFirst.text = firstName
oAuthor.appendChild (oFirst)

Set oLast = xmldoc.createElement ("lastname")
oLast.text = lastName
oAuthor.appendChild (oLast)
```

Now we come to what happens if the book is not in the current category. Notice that this time around we don't need to decrement our loop counter. This is because in the Microsoft implementation of the DOM, the NodeList is set up once statically, and is not updated to reflect changes to its parent node. This is another area where Level 1 of the DOM skimps over details rather than laying down strict rules, leaving it up to the implementers to resolve the nitty-gritty for a working interface.

```
Else
    oLibrary.removeChild (oBook)
End If
Next
```

Finally, we save the amended document in our output file, using a further Microsoft extension to the Document class, save():

```
xmldoc.save (outFile)

WScript.Echo ("Transformation complete")
```

Again, this is something that isn't covered by the DOM. However, as with the load() method, Microsoft have decided to extend the existing interface rather than provide a new one altogether.

Running

Again, this is purely a command line application, so we'll need to open up a DOS box and navigate to the folder containing the source file. This time around there's no compilation step, and we go straight to running. Again, we must first ensure that our `library.xml` file is in the same directory or has the full path given on the command line.

The installation of the Windows Scripting Host should have associated all files with extension `.vbs` with itself, so all we need to do to execute a script is type its name. This is how we would now run our application to extract all the fiction books:

```
DOMTransform.vbs library.xml VBlibrary.xml fiction
```

And with any luck, you'll see the same result as `javalibrary.xml` last time.

SAX

Straightforward and logical as it is, the DOM is, frankly, a somewhat blunt instrument for analyzing XML documents. Every time you use it, it has to read in and parse the entire document before any processing can start. This isn't a problem with small documents like the miniature library in our example, but once you're dealing with anything of reasonable size, you're liable to be making serious use of that ol' egg-timer. This may well be quite acceptable if your transformation truly affects the entire document, but if all you're doing is some kind of search or filter operation, it's hard to justify. We need something a little subtler, and this is where SAX comes in.

The Basics

The Simple API for XML uses an event-driven approach. A SAX parser doesn't wait until the document is completely loaded before we can do anything with it. Instead, as it traverses the document, it reports back to us on whatever it finds. It's kind of "Hey, look at this, I've found the start of a grandchild element!" and "Oh look! A processing instruction!". At first, this seems a little peculiar. The most common use of event-driven processing is to handle user interfaces of course (because the last thing we want is to be looping around all the time asking if the user's clicked that button yet), but for dealing with data? Trust me, though: this is a cool and funky approach. What's more, from the point of view of this book especially, it reflects the logical model of XSLT transformations.

If we were to show the two approaches diagrammatically, DOM would look something like this:

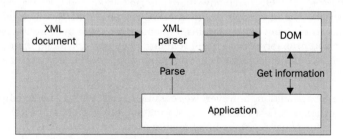

Whereas the SAX approach is more like this:

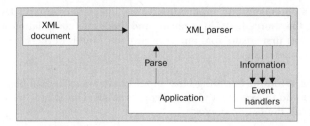

A Brief History of SAX

SAX is remarkable in that it isn't owned by anyone. It doesn't belong to any consortium, standards body, company or individual. So it doesn't survive because so-and-so says that you must use it in order to comply with standard X or because company Y is dominant in the marketplace. It survives because it's simple and it works.

SAX arose out of discussions on the XML-DEV mailing list (now hosted by OASIS at http://www.oasis-open.org/) aimed at resolving incompatibilities between different XML parsers (this was back in the infancy of XML in late 1997). David Megginson took on the job of coordinating the process of specifying a new API, and then declared the SAX 1.0 specification frozen on 11 May 1998. A whole series of SAX 1.0-compliant parsers then began to emerge, both from vast corporations (IBM and Sun, for example) and from enterprising individuals (such as James Clark). All of these parsers were freely available for public download.

Eventually, a number of shortcomings in the specification became apparent, and David Megginson and his merry men got back to work, finally producing the SAX 2.0 specification on 5 May 2000. David Megginson's site (http://www.megginson.com) is, incidentally, well worth a visit for up-to-date information.

At the time of writing, not all the SAX 1.0 parser writers have taken up the challenge of upgrading to SAX 2.0. This is probably because there are already several big contenders in the fray: Sun Java API for XML Parsing (JAXP), the Apache project's Xerces parser, which we've already encountered earlier in the chapter, and another new pretender, that we'll meet in a minute or two. The Apache software actually originates from IBM, who donated the source from their xml4j project. For the purposes of this chapter, we will continue to use the Apache Xerces parser.

SAX is actually specified as a set of Java classes which, up until recently, meant that if you wanted to do any serious work with it, you had to do some Java programming, using JDK 1.1 or later. There are parsers emerging for other languages (Perl and Python, for example), but until late in 2000, there was no agreed standard for C++ or COM. Actually, there still isn't an agreed C++ standard, but on October 27 of that year, Microsoft released version 3 of their XML Parser and SDK, which includes full COM support for SAX 2.0. It is highly likely that this implementation will become the de facto COM (and hence Visual Basic and probably Visual C++) standard. You can download the parser and the SDK from http://msdn.microsoft.com/xml/general/xmlparser.asp; you'll need both in order to use the Microsoft SAX implementation.

In deference to the SAX tradition, however, we're going to start with a Java example. I'll take you through the construction of a Java SAX 2.0 transformation application, and I'll then show you a Visual Basic application that provides the same functionality using the Microsoft COM classes. This time around, we can't use VBScript, because VBScript does not support events, and events are crucial to SAX. Instead, we'll use straight Visual Basic. I appreciate that, unlike the other tools that I've used in this chapter, this is not a free download, but it's so important that I think it's worth a brief look anyway.

When to Use SAX

If SAX is so much better than DOM, why don't we use it all the time? The answer is that, yes, SAX is a lot leaner and quicker than DOM, but there are a few downsides:

❑   It's a less intuitive API to master (despite the fact that the S in SAX stands for "Simple").

❑   It doesn't give you any control over the order in which the data is supplied to your application. You could use it to build up your own in-memory image of the data, but you'd then be introducing all of the inefficiencies of DOM.

❑   Because there's no complete in-memory image, there's no easy way of serializing the document back into XML. If you're converting from XML to XML, you have to do the formatting yourself.

SAX is best suited for applications where you're extracting and transforming a subset of the data, perhaps into a non-XML form. So that's what we're going to do for our next example. We're going to do pretty much the same filtering and transformation as we did with the DOM, but the output is going to be to a comma-separated variable (CSV) file.

Developing a SAX 2.0 Transformation Application in Java

I think we're ready to try some SAX 2.0 development. We'll use the same Xerces parser that we used for the DOM version, as this is fully SAX 2.0 compliant. The approach I'd like to take is to build up the application step by step, introducing a new SAX concept at each stage, so that by the time we complete the application, we've covered most of what you need to know. Before we start, there are a few bits of preparatory work to undertake that I'd like to lead you through.

How to Receive SAX Events

One final thing before we get started. As I said above, SAX is an event-driven interface; but how do we actually catch these events? Well, what we're going to do is write a Java class that **implements** one of the SAX interfaces. If we pass the reference of an instance of that interface class to our parser, the parser can then use that interface to talk back to us. So, in effect, we're actually becoming part of the parser ourselves!

We specify that a class implements an interface by declaring it like so:

```
public class MyClass implements ContentHandler
```

MyClass is the name of my new class, and ContentHandler is the name of the interface it draws on. In fact, ContentHandler is the most important interface in SAX, as it's used to communicate to us any events encountered. So, what we're doing here is creating a class that contains methods that a SAX-aware parser knows about and can interact with.

The ContentHandler interface contains a whole series of methods, most of which as a rule we don't really want to be bothering with. Fortunately, SAX provides us with a standard default implementation for most of them called – no prizes for guessing – DefaultHandler. Actually, DefaultHandler is a busy little bee providing default implementations for one or two other interfaces as well. So rather than *implement* ContentHandler, we can instead *extend* DefaultHandler, like this:

```
public class MyClass extends DefaultHandler
```

We can then pick and choose which methods we want to provide our own implementations of, in order to trap specific events. (Remember, overriding inherited methods is known as overloading.) As things are, the base class (DefaultHandler in this case) provides its own implementation of the core methods for use by MyClass. So if the ContentHandler interface declares the method doSomethingorOther(), whenever the doSomethingorOther() method of MyClass's implementation of ContentHandler is invoked, the method called is actually DefaultHandler.doSomethingorOther(). This is because DefaultHandler provides the default implementation of doSomethingorOther().

However, if we provide our own implementations for methods, then they are used instead. In our example above, if we implemented our own version of doSomethingorOther(), the method invoked would now be MyClass.doSomethingorOther(). This might do something totally different from DefaultHandler's implementation.

A Basic SAX Application

In our first example, all we're going to do is instantiate the parser, and trap the events that signal the start and end of the document. You can find the source for this example in the download, and it's called SAXTransform1.Java.

The code starts by importing all the Java classes that it needs:

```
import java.io.FileReader;

import javax.xml.parsers.SAXParserFactory;
import javax.xml.parsers.SAXParser;

import org.xml.sax.XMLReader;
import org.xml.sax.InputSource;
import org.xml.sax.SAXException;
import org.xml.sax.Attributes;
import org.xml.sax.helpers.DefaultHandler;
```

Now comes our class declaration and main method:

```
public class SAXTransform1 extends DefaultHandler
{
    public static void main(String[] args) throws Exception
    {
        SAXTransform1 transformObj = new SAXTransform1();
        transformObj.read(args);
    }
```

The main() method declaration is required by Java to denote the piece of code that will be executed when we start up the class. It prints out a message, creates a new instance of itself and invokes a method called read(), passing it any command line arguments that it has received. The void part of the main() declaration, incidentally, means that the program doesn't return a value back to its caller, and the throws Exception part means that if anything happens that it can't cope with, it throws the exception back to the caller to handle. We'll see more on exceptions later.

Let's look at the `read()` method:

```
public void read (String[] args) throws Exception
{
    if (args.length == 0)
        throw new SAXException ("No input file specified");

    String inFile = args[0];

    SAXParserFactory factoryObj = SAXParserFactory.newInstance();
    SAXParser saxParserObj = factoryObj.newSAXParser();

    XMLReader readerObj = saxParserObj.getXMLReader();
    readerObj.setContentHandler (this);

    FileReader fileObj = new FileReader(inFile);
    readerObj.parse(new InputSource(fileObj));
}
```

The `SAXParserFactory` and `SAXParser` interfaces are entirely specific to the Apache implementation. SAX is similar to DOM in this respect, in that there is no standard way defined to instantiate an XML reader object (`XMLReader`). Once we've got one, however, we are safely in SAX territory. The first thing we do is call its `setContentHandler()` method, passing a reference to the current object, `this`. This tells SAX that the current object is the active content handler for the parsing process, so it will know to invoke this object's methods to handle SAX events. To do the parsing, we need to invoke the `parse` method for the `XMLReader` object. This takes as its argument an object of the SAX class `InputSource`, which we must first construct from a `FileReader` object created from the filename in the command line argument list.

Moving on, we come to the methods that we're overloading in our extension of `DefaultHandler`:

```
public void startDocument() throws SAXException
{
    System.out.println("Starting ...");
}

public void endDocument() throws SAXException
{
    System.out.println("... Finished");
}

public void startElement(String uri, String localName, String qName,
 Attributes atts) throws SAXException
{
    System.out.println("Element is " + qName);
}
}
```

The first of these, `startDocument()`, traps the start of document event, and the second, `endDocument()`, traps the end of document event. The third one, `startElement()`, traps the start of element event, and simply prints out the qualified name of each XML element that it encounters. And that's our first SAX application complete.

This is purely a command line application, so in Windows we'll need to open up a DOS console, and move to wherever the source is. Before we compile anything, we should check that we have the class path set up correctly. If you haven't done this yet, refer back to the DOM setup section, otherwise proceed to compile the application as follows:

```
javac SaxTransform1.java
```

Before running, again make sure that our library.xml file is in the same directory, and execute with the command line below:

```
java SaxTransform1 library.xml
```

This is what you should see:

```
Starting ...
Element is library
Element is book
Element is author
Element is title
Element is publisher
Element is ISBN
Element is book
Element is author
Element is title
Element is publisher
Element is ISBN
Element is book
Element is author
Element is title
Element is publisher
Element is ISBN
Element is book
Element is author
Element is title
Element is publisher
Element is ISBN
Element is book
Element is author
Element is title
Element is publisher
Element is ISBN
Element is book
Element is author
Element is title
Element is publisher
Element is ISBN
... Finished
```

Well, it's a start. However, by this point – believe it or not – you've actually covered most of the main principles of SAX. The remaining parts of an XML document are handled in a similar fashion: write an event handler for the event that we wish to process and let the XML reader call our implementation of the ContentHandler interface when it detects the event.

Extracting Data

If we're going to do anything with the document, we're going to need to extract textual content. To do this, we'll need to override a further method in the `DefaultHandler` interface: `characters()`. The declaration of this method looks like this:

```
public void characters(char[] chars, int start, int len) throws SAXException
```

This method gets fired whenever the parser encounters a chunk of character data. Note my use of the word 'chunk': there is no obligation on the parser writer to deliver all the character data between two tags as a single block. (If you think about it, this is actually quite reasonable – after all, the string might turn out to be extremely long, and it could make for a very clumsy parser implementation.) All that this means from an application point of view is that you may need to build up your string from a number of `characters()` events.

The other thing we're going to do in this example is impose some filtering. This will involve incorporating a similar category filter to that in our DOM example, plus adding some code to extract the `category` attribute from each `<book>` element. Let's take another look at our `startElement()` declaration:

```
public void startElement(String uri, String localName, String qName,
  Attributes atts) throws SAXException
```

In particular, let's turn our attention to the last parameter, `Attributes`. There are four methods available with this object:

❑ `getLength()` returns an integer giving the number of attributes found.

❑ `getName()` returns the name of the attribute at a specified position in the list (starting from 0).

❑ `getValue()` returns the value of an attribute; we can either specify which attribute by giving it a string containing the attribute name, or by specifying its position in the list (starting from 0).

❑ `getType()` returns the type of an attribute; again we can either specify which attribute by name or by position. The various types are described in Appendix E.

Let's put all this into practice. Copy the code from `SAXTransform1.java` to `SAXTransform2.java`, and change all references from `SAXTransform1` to `SAXTransform2`.

The code will draw on the same library classes as the first example:

```
import java.io.FileReader;

import javax.xml.parsers.SAXParserFactory;
import javax.xml.parsers.SAXParser;

import org.xml.sax.XMLReader;
import org.xml.sax.InputSource;
import org.xml.sax.SAXException;
import org.xml.sax.Attributes;
import org.xml.sax.helpers.DefaultHandler;
```

We need to add some private properties to the class:

```
public class SAXTransform2 extends DefaultHandler
{
    private String catFilter;
    private boolean fAll = false;
    private boolean fInclude = false;
    private StringBuffer elemValue = new StringBuffer();

    public static void main(String[] args) throws Exception
    {
        SAXTransform2 transformObj = new SAXTransform2();
        transformObj.read(args);
    }
}
```

The first of these is the category filter that we're going to obtain from the second, optional, command line argument. The two flags will indicate whether or not all books are to be included, and whether or not the book currently being processed is to be included, respectively. The final variable will hold the value of the data for the current element.

We're also going to make some changes to the read() method:

```
public void read (String[] args) throws Exception
{
    if (args.length == 0)
        throw new SAXException ("No input file specified");

    String inFile = args[0];

    catFilter = "all";

    if (args.length >= 2)
        catFilter = args[1];

    if (catFilter.compareTo ("all") == 0)
        fAll = true;

    SAXParserFactory factoryObj = SAXParserFactory.newInstance();
    SAXParser saxParserObj = factoryObj.newSAXParser();

    XMLReader readerObj = saxParserObj.getXMLReader();
    readerObj.setContentHandler (this);

    FileReader fileObj = new FileReader(inFile);
    readerObj.parse(new InputSource(fileObj));
}
```

The startDocument() and endDocument() methods remain unchanged:

```
public void startDocument() throws SAXException
{
    System.out.println("Starting ...");
}

public void endDocument() throws SAXException
{
    System.out.println("... Finished");
}
```

The code to extract the category filter should be familiar from the DOM transformation example. Here's the new version of `startElement()`:

```java
public void startElement(String uri, String localName, String qName,
  Attributes atts) throws SAXException
{
    if (qName.equals("book"))
    {
        String category = atts.getValue("category");

        if (category == null)
            throw new SAXException("Book category not specified");

        if (fAll || (category.compareTo (catFilter) == 0))
            fInclude = true;
        else
            fInclude = false;
    }

    else
    {
        if (fInclude)
            elemValue.setLength(0);
    }
}
```

Here, the choice of what to do depends on whether or not the element we're dealing with is a <book> or not. If the element is <book>, we shall determine whether or not to include it in the output by making use of the incoming `atts` argument for the first time. We use its `getValue()` method to – well – get its value, and then check to see if it matches the filter, setting the `fInclude` flag accordingly. If, on the other hand, we're dealing with something other than a <book> element, we check to see if we're currently including stuff, in which case we reset the element value buffer to zero length. We won't have any data just yet – that's coming up with the next event.

The next event is `characters()`, which gets fired when the parser has come across some character data within the element:

```java
public void characters(char[] chars, int start, int len) throws SAXException
{
    if (fInclude)
        elemValue.append(chars, start, len);
}
```

As you can see, all we do with it is append it to our character buffer – remember that there's no guarantee that it'll all arrive in one big chunk.

Finally, we're going to override `DefaultHandler`'s `endElement()` method, which is invoked whenever the parser comes across the end of an element:

```java
public void endElement(String uri, String localName, String qName)
  throws SAXException
{
    if (qName.equals("book"))
        fInclude = false;

    if (fInclude)
        System.out.println("Element " + qName + " is " + elemValue.toString());
}
```

If we've reached the end of a book element, we simply reset the fInclude flag to be ready for the next <book>, without including the <book> element itself in the output. Otherwise, if the element is to be included, we output the value of the element from our string buffer.

And that's it for the second example.

OK, let's compile it, run it and see what happens. Let's extract the text for the elements in all the fiction books. The commands will be:

```
javac SaxTransform2.java
java SAXTransform2 library.xml fiction
```

and this is what we should see:

```
Starting ...
Element author is J.K.Rowling
Element title is Harry Potter and the Philosopher's Stone
Element publisher is Bloomsbury
Element ISBN is 0747532745
Element author is O'Brien, Flann
Element title is The Third Policeman
Element publisher is Flamingo
Element ISBN is 0586087494
Element author is Flann O'Brien
Element title is At Swim-Two-Birds
Element publisher is Penguin
Element ISBN is 0141182687
... Finished
```

Transformation

This is all well and good, but we're not actually doing any transformations yet. It's time for version 3. Once again, copy SAXTransform2.java to SAXTransform3.java, and change all occurrences of SAXTransform2 to SAXTransform3. Remember our aim is to transform the incoming XML into a CSV file.

We need to import one more standard Java class, FileWriter, for handling output:

```
import java.io.FileReader;
import java.io.FileWriter;

import javax.xml.parsers.SAXParserFactory;
import javax.xml.parsers.SAXParser;

import org.xml.sax.XMLReader;
import org.xml.sax.InputSource;
import org.xml.sax.SAXException;
import org.xml.sax.Attributes;
import org.xml.sax.helpers.DefaultHandler;
```

There are also a couple of new private data members for our class:

```
public class SAXTransform3 extends DefaultHandler
{
    private String catFilter;
    private boolean fAll = false;
    private boolean fInclude = false;
    private StringBuffer elemValue = new StringBuffer();
    private String outFile;
    private FileWriter outWriter;
```

The first of these holds the name of the output CSV file, and the second holds the object we'll use for actually writing to it. The main() method remains effectively the same as before:

```
public static void main(String[] args) throws Exception
{
    SAXTransform3 transformObj = new SAXTransform3();
    transformObj.read(args);
}
```

Moving on, we need to extract the output file name from the command line. It's between the input file name and the optional category filter:

```
public void read (String[] args) throws Exception
{
    if (args.length == 0)
        throw new SAXException ("No input file specified");

    String inFile = args[0];

    if (args.length == 1)
        throw new SAXException ("No output file specified");

    outFile = args[1];

    catFilter = "all";

    if (args.length >= 3)
        catFilter = args[2];

    boolean fAll = false;

    if (catFilter.compareTo ("all") == 0)
        fAll = true;

    SAXParserFactory factoryObj = SAXParserFactory.newInstance();
    SAXParser saxParserObj = factoryObj.newSAXParser();

    XMLReader readerObj = saxParserObj.getXMLReader();
    readerObj.setContentHandler (this);

    FileReader fileObj = new FileReader(inFile);
    readerObj.parse(new InputSource(fileObj));
}
```

There's a small change to `startDocument()`, to open our output file:

```
public void startDocument() throws SAXException
{
    System.out.println("Commencing transformation ...");

    try
    {
        outWriter = new FileWriter (outFile);
    }

    catch (java.io.IOException e)
    {
        throw new SAXException ("Failed to open output file, reason " +
                                e.toString ());
    }
}
```

and a similar one to `endDocument()` to close it:

```
public void endDocument() throws SAXException
{
    try
    {
        outWriter.close ();
    }

    catch (java.io.IOException e)
    {
        throw new SAXException ("Failed to close output file, reason " +
                                e.toString ());
    }

    System.out.println ("Transformation complete");
}
```

`startElement()` and `characters()` remain unchanged:

```
public void startElement(String uri, String localName, String qName,
  Attributes atts) throws SAXException
{
    if (qName.equals("book"))
    {
        String category = atts.getValue("category");

        if (category == null)
            throw new SAXException("Book category not specified");

        if (fAll || (category.compareTo (catFilter) == 0))
            fInclude = true;
        else
            fInclude = false;
    }

    else
    {
        if (fInclude)
            elemValue.setLength(0);
    }
}
```

```
    public void characters(char[] chars, int start, int len) throws SAXException
    {
        if (fInclude)
            elemValue.append(chars, start, len);
    }
```

However, the real fun and joy comes in endElement(). We start off by checking to see if we're at the end of a <book> element, and whether it has been included in the transformed output. If it has, we write a terminating line feed to our output file:

```
    public void endElement(String uri, String localName, String qName)
        throws SAXException
    {
        if (qName.equals("book"))
        {
            if (fInclude)
            {
                try
                {
                    outWriter.write ('\n');
                }

                catch (java.io.IOException e)
                {
                    throw new SAXException ("Failed to write to file, reason " +
                                           e.toString ());
                }

                fInclude = false;
            }
        }
```

The next segment should look reasonably familiar from the DOMTransform code. The only difference is that we're transforming data into a form suitable for a CSV file.

```
        if (fInclude)
        {
            String elemString = elemValue.toString ();

            if (qName.equals("author"))
            {
                int comma = elemString.indexOf (',');

                if (comma == -1)
                {
                    String firstName = "";
                    String lastName = elemString;

                    int period = elemString.lastIndexOf ('.');

                    if (period != -1)
                    {
                        firstName = elemString.substring (0, period + 1);
                        lastName = elemString.substring (period + 1);
                    }
```

```
        else
        {
            int space = elemString.indexOf (' ');

            if (space != -1)
            {
                firstName = elemString.substring (0, space);
                lastName = elemString.substring (space + 1);
            }
        }

        elemString = lastName + ", " + firstName;
    }
}

try
{
    outWriter.write (elemString + ", ");
}

catch (java.io.IOException e)
{
    throw new SAXException ("Failed to write to file, reason " +
                            e.toString ());
}
}
```

Let's try it out. We compile it in the usual manner. Here's our new command line invocation:

```
javac SaxTransform3.java
java SAXTransform3 library.xml fiction.csv fiction
```

and here's our resulting `fiction.csv` file:

```
Rowling, J.K., Harry Potter and the Philosopher's Stone, Bloomsbury, 0747532745,
O'Brien, Flann, The Third Policeman, Flamingo, 0586087494,
O'Brien, Flann, At Swim-Two-Birds, Penguin, 0141182687,
```

although it looks much prettier in Microsoft Excel, which will take a CSV file as its input, treating commas as cell delimiters and carriage returns as row delimiters:

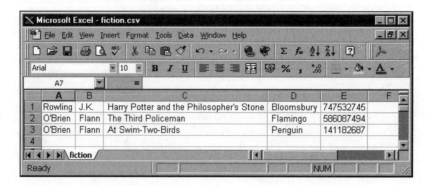

Exception Handling

If there's a problem with the well-formedness or validity of our XML when we're using the DOM, there's only one place where it can go wrong: in the initial `parse()` call. However, under SAX, the parsing is going on all the time, and it can throw out a problem at any point.

Just as an example, let's create new version of `library.xml`, with a corrupt entry at the end of the document. Change the existing file as below:

```
<book category="fantasy">
    <author>Pinnock, Jonathan
    <title>Professional DCOM Application Development</title>
    <publisher>Wrox</publisher>
    <ISBN>1861001312</ISBN>
</book>
```

and save this as `badlibrary.xml`. Issue the following command:

```
java SAXTransform3 badlibrary.xml badfiction.csv fiction
```

You should see something like this:

```
Commencing transformation ...
org.xml.sax.SAXParseException: The element type "author" must be terminated by the
matching end-tag "</author>".
        at org.apache.xerces.framework.XMLParser.reportError(XMLParser.java:1056)
        at
org.apache.xerces.framework.XMLDocumentScanner.reportFatalXMLError(XMLDocumentScan
ner.java:635)
        at
org.apache.xerces.framework.XMLDocumentScanner.abortMarkup(XMLDocumentScanner.java
:684)
        at
org.apache.xerces.framework.XMLDocumentScanner$ContentDispatcher.dispatch(Compiled
Code)
        at org.apache.xerces.framework.XMLDocumentScanner.parseSome(Compiled Code)
        at org.apache.xerces.framework.XMLParser.parse(XMLParser.java:948)
        at SAXTransform3.read(SAXTransform3.java:57)
        at SAXTransform3.main(SAXTransform3.java:25)
```

So what happened? Well, the parser has thrown an error during the parsing process, and there's nothing there to catch it, so it works its way all the way to the top, and the program bombs out. Reasonable in the circumstances, but there are two problems with this. First of all, we have no idea where in the document the problem occurred. More seriously, if we take a look at our CSV file, it turns out that we've got a complete blank, despite the fact that the fault is located almost right at the end of the document. Now, depending on how much of a purist you are, there are two positions we can adopt on catching such errors, both of which require some extra work. On the one hand, we can say that by containing ill-formed XML, the whole document is invalid, and we should therefore discard the empty CSV file out of hand. Or we could take a more pragmatic approach, and say that, well, hey, we were *nearly* there, and we might as well give our user *something*. (Taking this a little further, you could almost envisage a *recovery* transformation, to restore corrupted partial XML documents to a useable state!) But either way, we are going to have to do something.

Well, I'm a pragmatist at heart, so I'm going to add some code to close the CSV file cleanly in the case of a parser error. But before we go ahead and make the change, there's one other thing I'd like to take a look at. You may have noticed that there's a point in the code where we throw a SAXException if the category attribute is null. It would be nice if we could signal to the user the place where this occurred. Given that we have no idea where we currently are in the document, is there a way of finding out? Fortunately, there is, and it's called a Locator **object**.

All we need to do to get hold of a Locator object is overload another of DefaultHandler's methods, called setDocumentLocator(). This takes an object of type Locator, which we can have as a private data member of our class, and can then be used to find out whereabouts we are in the parsing process at any time. Watch for the caveat here: it's not actually mandatory for the parser to provide a Locator, so we need to check that the object is non-null. Experience has also shown that different parsers can produce different interpretations of where we are. However, Xerces is sensible, and provides a useful Locator object, which we can make good use of in the final version of our application.

Speaking of which ...

Let's start off in the usual way by copying SAXTransform3.java to SAXTransform4.java. Change all references to SAXTransform3 to SAXTransform4.

We need to import a couple more SAX classes:

```
import java.io.FileReader;
import java.io.FileWriter;

import javax.xml.parsers.SAXParserFactory;
import javax.xml.parsers.SAXParser;

import org.xml.sax.XMLReader;
import org.xml.sax.InputSource;
import org.xml.sax.SAXException;
import org.xml.sax.Attributes;
import org.xml.sax.helpers.DefaultHandler;
import org.xml.sax.SAXParseException;
import org.xml.sax.Locator;
```

Then we need to add a new private data member to our class, to hold our Locator object:

```
public class SAXTransform4 extends DefaultHandler
{
    private String catFilter;
    private boolean fAll = false;
    private boolean fInclude = false;
    private StringBuffer elemValue = new StringBuffer();
    private String outFile;
    private FileWriter outWriter;
    private Locator locatorObj;
```

Next, because we're going to be closing the output file in a number of different places now, we'll put this code into a separate private method:

```
private void closeOutFile () throws SAXException
{
    try
    {
        outWriter.close ();
    }

    catch (java.io.IOException e)
    {
        throw new SAXException ("Failed to close output file, reason " +
                                e.toString ());
    }
}
```

Our `main()` method remains pretty much the same:

```
public static void main(String[] args) throws Exception
{
    SAXTransform4 transformObj = new SAXTransform4();
    transformObj.read(args);
}
```

There's a small but significant change to our `read()` method:

```
public void read (String[] args) throws Exception
{
    if (args.length == 0)
        throw new SAXException ("No input file specified");

    String inFile = args[0];

    if (args.length == 1)
        throw new SAXException ("No output file specified");

    outFile = args[1];

    catFilter = "all";

    if (args.length >= 3)
        catFilter = args[2];

    boolean fAll = false;

    if (catFilter.compareTo ("all") == 0)
        fAll = true;

    SAXParserFactory factoryObj = SAXParserFactory.newInstance();
    SAXParser saxParserObj = factoryObj.newSAXParser();

    XMLReader readerObj = saxParserObj.getXMLReader();
    readerObj.setContentHandler (this);
    readerObj.setErrorHandler (this);

    FileReader fileObj = new FileReader(args[0]);
    readerObj.parse(new InputSource(fileObj));
}
```

This tells the parser to refer all errors back to our main object, in the same way as the content events that we're already handling.

startDocument remains the same as before, as do characters() and endElement(), but there's a small change to endDocument() to make use of our new closeOutFile() method:

```
public void endDocument() throws SAXException
{
    closeOutFile ();
    System.out.println ("Transformation complete");
}
```

Here's the overridden setDocumentLocator() method:

```
public void setDocumentLocator(Locator loc)
{
    locatorObj = loc;
}
```

There wasn't much to that one, was there?

And this is where we use it, in the code for startElement():

```
public void startElement(String uri, String localName, String qName,
  Attributes atts) throws SAXException
{
    if (qName.equals("book"))
    {
        String category = atts.getValue("category");

        if (category == null)
        {
            closeOutFile ();

            String error = "Book category not specified";

            if (locatorObj != null)
                error += (" at line " + locatorObj.getLineNumber()
                            + ", column " + locatorObj.getColumnNumber());

            throw new SAXException(error);
        }
```

There are two changes here. First of all, we close the file to save what we've parsed already. Secondly, we use our Locator object to get the place in the document where the error has occurred, before throwing an exception back to SAX.

All we've got left to write are the overloaded methods to catch SAXParseExceptions. There are three of them, one for warnings, one for errors and one for fatal errors. In all cases, we do the same thing: report the location of the problem, and close the output CSV file. Here they are:

```
    public void warning(SAXParseException exception) throws SAXException
    {
        System.err.println("Warning at line " + exception.getLineNumber() +
                            ", column " + exception.getColumnNumber());
        closeOutFile ();

        throw exception;
    }

    public void error(SAXParseException exception) throws SAXException
    {
        System.err.println("Error at line " + exception.getLineNumber() +
                            ", column " + exception.getColumnNumber());
        closeOutFile ();

        throw exception;
    }

    public void fatalError(SAXParseException exception) throws SAXException
    {
        System.err.println("Fatal error at line " + exception.getLineNumber() +
                            ", column " + exception.getColumnNumber());
        closeOutFile ();

        throw exception;
    }
```

Notice that the SAXParseException object conveniently gives us the location of the problem, in its getLineNumber() and getColumnNumber() methods.

So we now have an implementation that deals appropriately with errors. I like to call this "Safe SAX". (You don't know how long I've been waiting to write that...)

Let's finish off by compiling it and trying it out on a couple of rather shady documents. First of all, the ill-formed document that scuppered SAXTransform3 earlier:

```
java SAXTransform4 badlibrary.xml badfiction.csv fiction
```

Here's what we see:

```
Commencing transformation ...
Fatal error at line 38, column 11
org.xml.sax.SAXParseException: The element type "author" must be terminated by the
matching end-tag "</author>".
        at org.apache.xerces.framework.XMLParser.reportError(XMLParser.java:1056)
        at
org.apache.xerces.framework.XMLDocumentScanner.reportFatalXMLError(XMLDocumentScan
ner.java:635)
        at
org.apache.xerces.framework.XMLDocumentScanner.abortMarkup(XMLDocumentScanner.java
:684)
        at
org.apache.xerces.framework.XMLDocumentScanner$ContentDispatcher.dispatch(Compiled
Code)
        at org.apache.xerces.framework.XMLDocumentScanner.parseSome(Compiled Code)
        at org.apache.xerces.framework.XMLParser.parse(XMLParser.java:948)
        at SAXTransform4.read(SAXTransform4.java:74)
        at SAXTransform4.main(SAXTransform4.java:41)
```

Well, there's the line and column number, so I'm feeling better already. And, oh joy, oh joy, we have a fully populated `badfiction.csv` file.

Let's try something else, and create a new document, `nocatlibrary.xml` by again modifying the bottom of `library.xml` like so:

```
    </book>
    <book>
        <author>Pinnock, Jonathan</author>
        <title>Professional DCOM Application Development</title>
        <publisher>Wrox</publisher>
        <ISBN>1861001312</ISBN>
    </book>
```

This is well-formed XML, but one book is missing that vital `category` attribute. So how does our program react? Here goes:

```
java SAXTransform4 nocatlibrary.xml nocatfiction.csv fiction
```

This is what we see:

```
Commencing transformation ...
org.xml.sax.SAXException: Book category not specified at line 33, column 11
        at SAXTransform4.startElement(SAXTransform4.java:113)
        at org.apache.xerces.parsers.SAXParser.startElement(Compiled Code)
        at
org.apache.xerces.validators.common.XMLValidator.callStartElement(Compiled Code)
        at
org.apache.xerces.framework.XMLDocumentScanner$ContentDispatcher.dispatch(Compiled
Code)
        at org.apache.xerces.framework.XMLDocumentScanner.parseSome(Compiled Code)
        at org.apache.xerces.framework.XMLParser.parse(XMLParser.java:948)
        at SAXTransform4.read(SAXTransform4.java:74)
        at SAXTransform4.main(SAXTransform4.java:41)
```

Again, there's our line and column number. And, if we take a look, we can see that `nocatfiction.csv` is populated as well.

Playing SAX the Microsoft Way

Version 3 of the MSXML SDK contains Microsoft's first official implementation of SAX 2.0. It packages up SAX as a set of COM components. There isn't space here to go into COM in any great detail; for the purposes of this example, you can think of a COM component as just another type of object with interfaces, like the ones we've encountered already. The crucial difference is that the interfaces are defined in a language-neutral form. There's more information on COM in the Wrox book *Beginning ATL 3.0 COM Programming*, (ISBN 1-861001-20-7).

In order to try out this SDK, we are however going to have to use a Microsoft language and development environment, and I've settled on Microsoft Visual Basic 6. Microsoft Visual C++ would be equally valid, as it supports COM just as well as VB.

Setting up the Project

We'll start by creating a new Visual Basic project. Next, we need to make sure that the MSXML SDK type library is available to us; we can do this via Project | References:

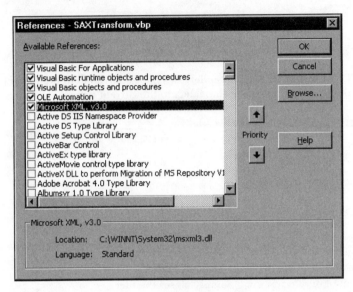

Save the project as SAXTransform1.vbp, with main form SAXTransform1.frm. This will be the only form that our project is going to contain. It will, however, need to include a couple of class modules: one to handle content events, and one to handle error events.

The Content Handler Class

VB6 doesn't have a concept of extending an interface, although it has been introduced in later releases. So, rather than extending a default implementation of the content handler interface as with DefaultHandler, we're going to have to implement the whole of ContentHandler itself. All this really means is that we have to include a number of tiresome empty methods in our class. We do this by creating a new class module, calling the class ContentHandlerImpl and its file ContentHandlerImpl.cls. The magic line comes at the start of the code:

```
Implements IVBSAXContentHandler
```

This tells VB that we're implementing the SAX content handler interface. Let's look at the rest of the code for the class. First of all, we declare a few variables. The list should look familiar from the Java example, with one exception, m_oReader – I'll come back to this in a little while.

```
Option Explicit

Implements IVBSAXContentHandler

Public m_oReader As IMXReaderControl
Public m_strOutFile As String
Public m_strCatFilter As String
Private m_strEntry As String
Private m_strValue As String
```

```
Private m_fAll As Boolean
Private m_fInclude As Boolean
Private m_oLocator As IVBSAXLocator

Private Sub Class_Initialize()
    m_fAll = False
    m_fInclude = False
End Sub
```

Here's the first of our overridden event handlers, which is equivalent to the Java characters(). As before, all we're doing is appending the characters to the current string:

```
Private Sub IVBSAXContentHandler_characters(strChars As String)
    If (m_fInclude) Then m_strValue = m_strValue + strChars
End Sub
```

And here's our documentLocator():

```
Private Property Set IVBSAXContentHandler_documentLocator(ByVal RHS
        As MSXML2.IVBSAXLocator)
    Set m_oLocator = RHS
End Property
```

The VB equivalent of endDocument() simply closes the file:

```
Private Sub IVBSAXContentHandler_endDocument()
    Close #1
End Sub
```

There's a minor point to note in endElement(), in that we build up a whole line before writing it out to file. This is because the VB Print # statement always appends a newline character to a line, so we can't simply output each element as we come across it. We output the whole entry on encountering the next <book> element to be included in the result-set:

```
Private Sub IVBSAXContentHandler_endElement(strNamespaceURI As String,
                                            strLocalName As String,
                                            strQName As String)

    Dim strFirstName As String
    Dim strLastName As String
    Dim intIndex As Integer
    Dim intStart As Integer

    If (strQName = "book") Then
        If (m_fInclude) Then
            Print #1, m_strEntry
            m_fInclude = False
        End If
    Else
```

Here's all the code to transform the author's name. The algorithm used should be getting familiar by now:

```
        If (m_fInclude) Then
            If (strQName = "author") Then
                strFirstName = ""
                strLastName = m_strValue

                intIndex = InStr(1, m_strValue, ",")

                If (intIndex = 0) Then
                    intIndex = 0

                    Do
                        intStart = intIndex + 1
                        intIndex = InStr(intStart, m_strValue, ".")
                    Loop Until intIndex = 0

                    If (intStart > 1) Then
                        strFirstName = Left(m_strValue, intStart - 1)
                        strLastName = Right(m_strValue, Len(m_strValue) -
                          (intStart - 1))
                    Else
                        intIndex = InStr(1, m_strValue, " ")

                        strFirstName = Left(m_strValue, intIndex - 1)
                        strLastName = Right(m_strValue, Len(m_strValue) -
                          intIndex)
                    End If

                    m_strValue = strLastName + ", " + strFirstName
                End If
            End If
```

Here's the point where we build up our line for the output file. Strictly speaking, we should strip out the trailing comma at the end of a line before printing; but Excel won't mind:

```
            m_strEntry = m_strEntry + m_strValue + ", "
        End If
    End If
End Sub
```

These events that follow won't be needed, but still require blank definitions:

```
Private Sub IVBSAXContentHandler_endPrefixMapping(strPrefix As String)

End Sub

Private Sub IVBSAXContentHandler_ignorableWhitespace(strChars As String)

End Sub

Private Sub IVBSAXContentHandler_processingInstruction(strTarget As String,
                                                       strData As String)

End Sub

Private Sub IVBSAXContentHandler_skippedEntity(strName As String)

End Sub
```

In `startDocument()` all we do is open the file, and check to see if we're including everything in the transformation:

```
Private Sub IVBSAXContentHandler_startDocument()
    Open m_strOutFile For Output As 1

    If (m_strCatFilter = "all") Then
        m_fAll = True
    Else
        m_fAll = False
    End If
End Sub
```

In `startElement()` we come across the second, more significant, difference between Microsoft and Java in the area of error handling. This is one of the places where Microsoft has deviated significantly from the SAX specification in order to dodge the problem of throwing errors in a language-neutral environment. Microsoft's solution is quite neat, in that they've provided a whole new interface, `MXReaderControl`, which we can use for controlling the XML reader. We'll come to how we actually access that interface in a little while, but first let's see what it does for us.

There are three methods in `MXReaderControl`: `abort()`, `resume()` and `suspend()`. Each of these methods does pretty much what is says on the box. So Microsoft has gone a little further than just providing an exception raising mechanism, and has given us a considerable degree of control over the progress of the SAX parser. This would prove extremely useful if, for example, we needed to temporarily suspend parsing whilst some asynchronous processing (maybe involving a third party system) took place. At a stroke, the range of viable applications has been increased quite significantly.

However, the only method we're using here is `abort()`. We'll see it in action as we look at our `startElement()` equivalent. Firstly, we disable the built-in VB error handling by the line `On Error Resume Next`. This allows us more scope for handling problems as we encounter them. Then, we attempt to get the category for the book:

```
Private Sub IVBSAXContentHandler_startElement(strNamespaceURI As String,
                                              strLocalName As String,
                                              strQName As String,
                                              ByVal oAttributes
                                              As MSXML2.IVBSAXAttributes)

    Dim strCategory As String
    Dim strError As String

On Error Resume Next

    If (strQName = "book") Then
        strCategory = oAttributes.getValueFromName("", "category")
```

If it isn't there, SAX will set an error number for us. For the purposes of this example, we'll interpret anything non-zero as indicating the absence of a `category` attribute. If this happens, we construct a message using the `Locator`, as in Java:

```
        If (Err.Number <> 0) Then
            Close #1

            strError = "Book category not specified"

            If (IsObject(oLocator)) Then strError = strError + " at line " +
                Str(oLocator.lineNumber) + ", column " +
                Str(oLocator.columnNumber)
            MsgBox (strError)
```

Having reported the error, we cease parsing, by invoking the `abort()` method of our `MXReaderControl` interface:

```
            m_oReader.abort
        End If
```

The rest of the code is simply a matter of determining whether the current element is to be included in the transformed file, and clearing the strings representing the current CSV entry and element:

```
        If (m_fAll Or (strCategory = m_strCatFilter)) Then
            m_fInclude = True
        Else
            m_fInclude = False
        End If

        m_strEntry = ""
    Else
        If (m_fInclude) Then m_strValue = ""
    End If
End Sub
```

And, finally, here's one more event that we're not really bothered with:

```
Private Sub IVBSAXContentHandler_startPrefixMapping(strPrefix As String,
                                                    strURI As String)

End Sub
```

Error Handling

Now we've seen the content handler class, let's take a look at our error handler class. We create this in very much the same way, except that this one's called `ErrorHandlerImpl`. This is what it looks like:

```
Option Explicit

Implements IVBSAXErrorHandler

Private Sub IVBSAXErrorHandler_error(ByVal oLocator As MSXML2.IVBSAXLocator,
                                     strErrorMessage As String,
                                     ByVal nErrorCode As Long)
    MsgBox ("Error: " + strErrorMessage + " at line " +
            Str(oLocator.lineNumber) + ", column " +
            Str(oLocator.columnNumber))
    Close #1
End Sub
```

```
     Private Sub IVBSAXErrorHandler_fatalError(ByVal oLocator As
                                     MSXML2.IVBSAXLocator,
                                     strErrorMessage As String,
                                     ByVal nErrorCode As Long)
         MsgBox ("Fatal error: " + strErrorMessage + " at line " +
                 Str(oLocator.lineNumber) + ", column " +
                 Str(oLocator.columnNumber))
         Close #1
     End Sub

     Private Sub IVBSAXErrorHandler_ignorableWarning(ByVal oLocator As
                                     MSXML2.IVBSAXLocator,
                                     strErrorMessage As String,
                                     ByVal nErrorCode As Long)
         MsgBox ("Warning: " + strErrorMessage + " at line " +
                 Str(oLocator.lineNumber) + ", column " +
                 Str(oLocator.columnNumber))
         Close #1
     End Sub
```

This looks very similar to the `error()`, `fatalError()` and `warning()` methods in our previous Java code, so we won't spend any more time on it – instead we'll move straight on to our main form.

The Form

This is what the form looks like:

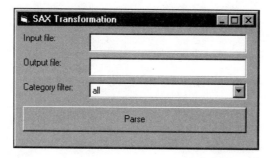

The text fields are called `txtInFile` and `txtOutFile` respectively. The combo box, `cmbCatFilter`, is of the dropdown list style, and the command button is called `cmdParse`. Let's see the code behind it.

All the `Form_Load()` code does is load up the category filter combo box:

```
Private Sub Form_Load()
    cmbCatFilter.AddItem ("all")
    cmbCatFilter.AddItem ("fiction")
    cmbCatFilter.AddItem ("humor")
    cmbCatFilter.AddItem ("non-fiction")
    cmbCatFilter.AddItem ("self-improvement")

    cmbCatFilter.ListIndex = 0
End Sub
```

But the code invoked when we press the magic **Parse** button, cmdParse_Click(), is more interesting: we start off by creating an instance of our ContentHandlerImpl class, and assign the names of the output file and category filter to the appropriate properties:

```
Option Explicit

Private Sub cmdParse_Click()

    Dim oContentHandler As ContentHandlerImpl
    Dim oErrorHandler As ErrorHandlerImpl
    Dim oReader As SAXXMLReader

On Error Resume Next

    Set oContentHandler = New ContentHandlerImpl
    oContentHandler.m_strOutFile = txtOutFile.Text
    oContentHandler.m_strCatFilter = cmbCatFilter.Text
```

Next, we create an instance of our ErrorHandlerImpl class:

```
    Set oErrorHandler = New ErrorHandlerImpl
```

Now we create the XML Reader object, and set up its content and error handlers:

```
    Set oReader = New SAXXMLReader
    Set oReader.contentHandler = oContentHandler
    Set oReader.errorHandler = oErrorHandler
```

The next line is deceptively simple. We're basically telling the content handler object how to access the reader control interface. We do this by setting the oReader object in ContentHandlerImpl (which you may recall is of type IMXReaderControl) equal to the oReader object in the main form (which is of type SAXXMLReader). How on earth does this work? Well, Visual Basic knows that, under the hood, the SAXXMLReader object also implements the IMXReaderControl interface, and so it very decently returns a reference to that interface *on the very same XML reader object*.

```
    Set oContentHandler.m_oReader = oReader
```

Finally, we set the whole parsing process off:

```
    oReader.parseURL (txtInFile.Text)
```

And let's tell the user when we're finished:

```
    MsgBox ("Transformation complete")
End Sub
```

Trying Out the Example

Let's try a few experiments, starting off with one we know should work:

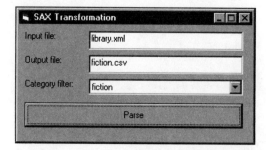

This produces exactly the same CSV file (`fiction.csv`) as before. OK, let's try something a little trickier:

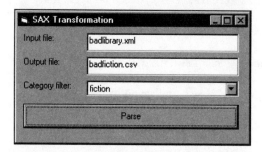

Now when we click **Parse**, we see this:

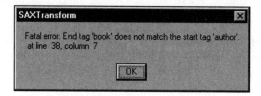

However, as before, we still have a useable CSV file (`badfiction.csv`).

Here's something else for you to try, while we're here. Comment out the line that sets up the error handler in the main form (using an apostrophe character):

```
Set oReader = New SAXXMLReader
Set oReader.contentHandler = oContentHandler
'     Set oReader.errorHandler = oErrorHandler
```

If you attempt to parse `badlibrary.xml` now, you will still get the correct CSV file, but there will be no error notification. The parser has *no* intrinsic default error reporting!

Finally, let's uncomment the error handler set-up line, and try another test:

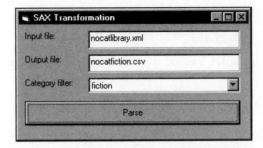

This is what happens:

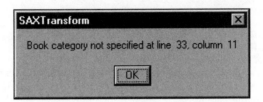

But the CSV file will still have been created, as before.

I think we can safely say that we have successfully duplicated our Java functionality in Visual Basic.

Filtering and Writing XML

The next question is: can we go any further with the Microsoft implementation? CSV files may be great for legacy applications, but what if we want to output some real XML? Well, the SAX 2.0 specification has nothing about output, but if we take a look at the Microsoft implementation, we see a promising-looking interface called MXXMLWriter. It turns out that this, combined with a standard SAX interface called XMLFilter, offers the functionality we require.

An XML filter is similar to an XML reader, except that it takes its input from another XML reader, rather than an input XML file. What's so good about that, I hear you ask? Well, what it means in practice is that the filter intercepts all events before the XML reader proper gets hold of them, and it can then either handle these events itself or just pass them up to the primary XML reader to deal with. Typically, an XML filter implements its own XMLReader interface as well as XMLFilter.

The Microsoft XML writer is, in fact, just an implementation of all our favorite interfaces, such as ContentHandler and so on, that happens to write out everything that it receives, in well-formed XML. I'm getting the feeling that if we couple this with an XML filter, something magical could happen. So let's try it out.

Setting Up the Project

We'll start off by creating another VB project as we did for our first VB SAX example, and saving it as SAXTransform2.vbp, with main form SAXTransform2.frm. This will be the only form that our project is going to contain. As well as this, our project is going to contain a couple of class modules, one to implement the filter class, and the other to handle content events. We'll leave error handling out this time, to avoid cluttering up the code too much.

The Main Form

This time around, I'd like to start with the main form, as this will give us an idea of where we are going. We might as well copy the one from the first example, as the input requirements are identical. The Form_load() method is identical, too.

However, the cmdParse_Click() method is radically different. We start off by creating a Reader object *and* a Writer:

```
Private Sub cmdParse_Click()
    Dim oWriter As MXXMLWriter
    Dim oReader As SAXXMLReader
    Dim oFilter As FilterImpl
    Dim saxFilter As IVBSAXXMLFilter
    Dim saxReader As IVBSAXXMLReader

On Error Resume Next

    Set oReader = New SAXXMLReader
    Set oWriter = New MXXMLWriter
```

Next, we create a Filter object, and pass our category filter into it. This is done via a public method this time around, because we'll need to pass it on one further step inside the filter. We'll see what the filter looks like in a little while.

```
    Set oFilter = New FilterImpl
    oFilter.putCatFilter (cmbCatFilter.Text)
```

The next thing we have to do is set up the filter's parent: in other words the XML Reader object that is going to provide the filter's content events and so on. To do this, we need to get hold of the IVBSAXXMLFilter interface to our Filter object:

```
    Set saxFilter = oFilter
    Set saxFilter.Parent = oReader
```

Having done that, we need another interface to our filter, IVBSAXXMLReader, to set up its content and error handlers: but what do we set them to? We set them to the same as our XML writer's handler interfaces:

```
    Set saxReader = oFilter
    Set saxReader.contentHandler = oWriter
    Set saxReader.errorHandler = oWriter
```

OK, we're ready to go now, so let's kick off the parsing process:

```
    saxReader.parseURL (txtInFile.Text)
```

Finally, we take the output from our XML writer and send it to the designated output file:

```
    Open txtOutFile.Text For Output As 1
    Print #1, oWriter.output
    Close #1

    MsgBox ("Transformation complete")
End Sub
```

The Filter

We create our filter class by writing a new class module, calling the class `FilterImpl` and its file
`FilterImpl.cls`. Here's how it starts. The first method in the class, the class initialization method,
creates an instance of our content handler implementation class. We haven't looked at this yet, but there
are no prizes for guessing that it's going to look quite similar to the one from our last example.

```
Option Explicit

Implements IVBSAXXMLFilter
Implements IVBSAXXMLReader

Dim m_oParent As IVBSAXXMLReader
Dim m_oContentHandler As ContentHandlerImpl
Dim m_strBaseURL As String
Dim m_strSecureBaseURL As String

Private Sub Class_Initialize()
    Set m_oContentHandler = New ContentHandlerImpl
End Sub
```

Next, here are the two methods in `IVBSAXXMLFilter` that we need to implement. The first one sets up
a reference to the parent XML reader, and sets up its content handler to match our implementation.
The second one simply returns a reference to the parent:

```
Private Property Set IVBSAXXMLFilter_parent(ByVal RHS As MSXML2.IVBSAXXMLReader)
    Set m_oParent = RHS
    Set m_oParent.contentHandler = m_oContentHandler
End Property

Private Property Get IVBSAXXMLFilter_parent() As MSXML2.IVBSAXXMLReader
    Set IVBSAXXMLFilter_parent = m_oParent
End Property
```

Next, a couple of methods for reading and writing the base URL. All we need to do is save it in a
property so that we can retrieve it later:

```
Private Property Let IVBSAXXMLReader_baseURL(ByVal url As String)
    m_strBaseURL = url
End Property

Private Property Get IVBSAXXMLReader_baseURL() As String
    IVBSAXXMLReader_baseURL = m_strBaseURL
End Property
```

The next pair of methods exchange their setup information and return a reference to the filter's content
handler. We save this reference as the child of the content handler implementation object; don't be too
concerned about the significance of this yet – it will become clearer when we see the content handler
implementation class itself.

```
Private Property Set IVBSAXXMLReader_contentHandler(ByVal RHS As
                                        MSXML2.IVBSAXContentHandler)
    Set m_oContentHandler.m_oChild = RHS
End Property

Private Property Get IVBSAXXMLReader_contentHandler() As
                                        MSXML2.IVBSAXContentHandler
    Set IVBSAXXMLReader_contentHandler = m_oContentHandler.m_oChild
End Property
```

We bounce the DTD handler, entity resolver and error handler back to our parent:

```
Private Property Set IVBSAXXMLReader_dtdHandler(ByVal RHS As
                                        MSXML2.IVBSAXDTDHandler)
End Property

Private Property Get IVBSAXXMLReader_dtdHandler() As MSXML2.IVBSAXDTDHandler
    Set IVBSAXXMLReader_dtdHandler = m_oParent.dtdHandler
End Property

Private Property Set IVBSAXXMLReader_entityResolver(ByVal RHS As
                                        MSXML2.IVBSAXEntityResolver)
End Property

Private Property Get IVBSAXXMLReader_entityResolver() As
                                        MSXML2.IVBSAXEntityResolver
    Set IVBSAXXMLReader_entityResolver = m_oParent.entityResolver
End Property

Private Property Set IVBSAXXMLReader_errorHandler(ByVal RHS As
                                        MSXML2.IVBSAXErrorHandler)

End Property

Private Property Get IVBSAXXMLReader_errorHandler() As MSXML2.IVBSAXErrorHandler
    Set IVBSAXXMLReader_errorHandler = m_oParent.errorHandler
End Property
```

Similarly, any features and properties are to be handled by our parent:

```
Private Function IVBSAXXMLReader_getFeature(ByVal strName As String) As Boolean
    IVBSAXXMLReader_getFeature = m_oParent.getFeature(strName)
End Function

Private Function IVBSAXXMLReader_getProperty(ByVal strName As String) As Variant
    IVBSAXXMLReader_getProperty = m_oParent.getProperty(strName)
End Function
```

All parsing is passed up to our parent as well:

```
Private Sub IVBSAXXMLReader_parse(ByVal varInput As Variant)
    m_oParent.parse varInput
End Sub

Private Sub IVBSAXXMLReader_parseURL(ByVal strURL As String)
    m_oParent.parseURL strURL
End Sub

Private Sub IVBSAXXMLReader_putFeature(ByVal strName As String,
                                       ByVal fValue As Boolean)
    m_oParent.putFeature strName, fValue
End Sub

Private Sub IVBSAXXMLReader_putProperty(ByVal strName As String,
                                        ByVal varValue As Variant)

End Sub
```

Next, a couple of methods to read and write the secure base URL. As with the base URL, all we need do is save it so that we can give it back later:

```
Private Property Let IVBSAXXMLReader_secureBaseURL(ByVal url As String)
    m_strSecureBaseURL = url
End Property

Private Property Get IVBSAXXMLReader_secureBaseURL() As String
    IVBSAXXMLReader_secureBaseURL = m_strSecureBaseURL
End Property
```

Finally, a method of our own, to pass the category filter on to our content handler implementation:

```
Public Sub putCatFilter(ByVal strCatFilter As String)
    m_oContentHandler.m_strCatFilter = strCatFilter
End Sub
```

The Content Handler

We've seen one of these already. However, this one, while retaining some similar features, is a little different in places. The class initialization method is similar to the previous one, although there are now one or two more flags to initialize. Note that this time we initialize the inclusion flag to True, because we need to include all the XML before the first <book> tag in the output.

```
Option Explicit

Implements IVBSAXContentHandler

Public m_oChild As IVBSAXContentHandler
Public m_strCatFilter As String
Dim m_fAll As Boolean
Dim m_fInclude As Boolean
```

```
Dim m_fIncluding As Boolean
Dim m_fAuthor As Boolean
Dim m_strValue As String

Private Sub Class_Initialize()
    m_fAll = False
    m_fInclude = True
    m_fIncluding = False
    m_fAuthor = False
End Sub
```

The startDocument() method sets up the category filter like last time. However, we also have to pass the event on to our child reader. By the way, whilst we're discussing this class, you should always bear in mind that the child reader that we're referring to is connected directly to the XML writer. So all we're really doing is selecting what to pass on to the XML writer.

```
Private Sub IVBSAXContentHandler_startDocument()
    If (m_strCatFilter = "all") Then
        m_fAll = True
    Else
        m_fAll = False
    End If

    m_oChild.startDocument
End Sub
```

Let's see what our startElement() method looks like. There's a slightly tricky bit of code at the start, using a pair of flags to decide whether or not the current part of the input document is to be included in the output. We need both flags because determining inclusion or otherwise is done on a book by book basis. The end of a book is trapped by the endElement() event for a <book> element; however, we don't want to include any carriage returns (treated as "ignorable whitespace", of which more below) until we get to the start of the next <book> element.

```
Private Sub IVBSAXContentHandler_startElement(strNamespaceURI As String, _
                                              strLocalName As String, _
                                              strQName As String, _
                                              ByVal oAttributes As _
                                              MSXML2.IVBSAXAttributes)
    If (m_fIncluding) Then
        m_fInclude = True
        m_fIncluding = False
    End If
```

Next, we find out if this new element is a book, and if so, set the inclusion flag as appropriate:

```
    If (strQName = "book") Then
        Dim strCategory As String
        strCategory = oAttributes.getValueFromName("", "category")

        If (m_fAll Or (strCategory = m_strCatFilter)) Then
            m_fInclude = True
        Else
            m_fInclude = False
        End If
    End If
```

If this element is to be included, we pass the event on to our child, and then check to see if this is the start of an author element. If it is, we set the flag accordingly, and initialize the author name string:

```
    If m_fInclude Then
        m_oChild.startElement strNamespaceURI, strLocalName, strQName,
                              oAttributes

        If (strQName = "author") Then
            m_fAuthor = True
            m_strValue = ""
        End If
    End If
End Sub
```

The characters() method only does anything when the current element is being included. If it's an author, it simply appends the characters received on to the end of its running string. If not, it passes the characters() event to the child:

```
Private Sub IVBSAXContentHandler_characters(strChars As String)
    If (m_fInclude) Then
        If (m_fAuthor) Then
            m_strValue = m_strValue + strChars
        Else
            m_oChild.characters strChars
        End If
    End If
End Sub
```

The endElement() method is, as before, the business end of the application. This is where the author name normalization is carried out. This is slightly different to the previous version, as names of the form "Doe, John" now have to be processed, rather than being passed unchanged to the CSV file:

```
Private Sub IVBSAXContentHandler_endElement(strNamespaceURI As String,
                                            strLocalName As String,
                                            strQName As String)

    Dim strFirstName As String
    Dim strLastName As String
    Dim intIndex As Integer
    Dim intStart As Integer

    If (m_fAuthor) Then
        strFirstName = ""
        strLastName = m_strValue

        intIndex = InStr(1, m_strValue, ",")

        If (intIndex = 0) Then
            intIndex = 0

            Do
                intStart = intIndex + 1
                intIndex = InStr(intStart, m_strValue, ".")
            Loop Until intIndex = 0
```

```
                If (intStart > 1) Then
                    strFirstName = Left(m_strValue, intStart - 1)
                    strLastName = Right(m_strValue, Len(m_strValue) - (intStart
                     - 1))
                Else
                    intIndex = InStr(1, m_strValue, " ")

                    strFirstName = Left(m_strValue, intIndex - 1)
                    strLastName = Right(m_strValue, Len(m_strValue) - intIndex)
                End If
            Else
                strLastName = Left(m_strValue, intIndex - 1)
                strFirstName = Right(m_strValue, Len(m_strValue) - (intIndex + 1))
            End If
```

Once we've sorted out the first and last names, we need to create XML elements for them. This can be achieved by simply replicating the events that occur when parsing the XML and passing the parsed elements on to the child:

```
            m_oChild.startElement "", "", "firstname", Nothing
            m_oChild.characters strFirstName
            m_oChild.endElement "", "", "firstname"

            m_oChild.startElement "", "", "lastname", Nothing
            m_oChild.characters strLastName
            m_oChild.endElement "", "", "lastname"


            m_fAuthor = False
        End If
```

Below, we check to see if we need to set the inclusion flag:

```
        If (m_fIncluding) Then
            m_fInclude = True
            m_fIncluding = False
        End If
```

If this element is to be included, we must end it correctly by passing the endElement event on to the child:

```
        If (m_fInclude) Then m_oChild.endElement strNamespaceURI, strLocalName,
            strQName
```

Finally, we check to see if we have just completed a <book> element. If so, we need to signal that we are now ready to include elements again:

```
    If (strQName = "book") Then m_fIncluding = True
End Sub
```

The remaining methods simply pass the events unchanged to the child, checking if the inclusion flag is currently set when appropriate:

```
Private Property Set IVBSAXContentHandler_documentLocator(ByVal loc As
                                                MSXML2.IVBSAXLocator)
    Set m_oChild.documentLocator = loc
End Property

Private Sub IVBSAXContentHandler_endDocument()
    m_oChild.endDocument
End Sub

Private Sub IVBSAXContentHandler_endPrefixMapping(strPrefix As String)
    m_oChild.endPrefixMapping strPrefix
End Sub

Private Sub IVBSAXContentHandler_ignorableWhitespace(strChars As String)
    If (m_fInclude) Then m_oChild.ignorableWhitespace strChars
End Sub

Private Sub IVBSAXContentHandler_processingInstruction(strTarget As String,
                                                strData As String)
    If (m_fInclude) Then m_oChild.processingInstruction strTarget, strData
End Sub

Private Sub IVBSAXContentHandler_skippedEntity(strName As String)
    If (m_fInclude) Then m_oChild.skippedEntity strName
End Sub


Private Sub IVBSAXContentHandler_startPrefixMapping(strPrefix As String,
                                                strURI As String)
    m_oChild.startPrefixMapping strPrefix, strURI
End Sub
```

Transforming XML to XML with SAX

Let's try running it, with our favorite XML:

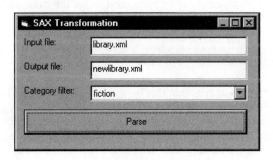

This is the content of the generated file, `newlibrary.xml`:

```
<?xml version="1.0" encoding="UTF-16" standalone="no"?>
<library>
    <book category="fiction">
     <author><firstname>J.K.</firstname><lastname>Rowling</lastname></author>
        <title>Harry Potter and the Philosopher's Stone</title>
        <publisher>Bloomsbury</publisher>
        <ISBN>0747532745</ISBN>
    </book>
    <book category="fiction">
        <author><firstname>Flann</firstname><lastname>O'Brien</lastname></author>
        <title>The Third Policeman</title>
        <publisher>Flamingo</publisher>
        <ISBN>0586087494</ISBN>
    </book>
    <book category="fiction">
        <author><firstname>Flann</firstname><lastname>O'Brien</lastname></author>
        <title>At Swim-Two-Birds</title>
        <publisher>Penguin</publisher>
        <ISBN>0141182687</ISBN>
    </book>
    </library>
```

Well, it's a little ragged in places, but nonetheless it's a perfectly serviceable, well-formed XML file.

The Rest of SAX

We've now covered the essentials of SAX, or at least the lion's share of what we might need for carrying out transformations. However, there are one or two remaining aspects of SAX that might turn out to be useful and I'd now like to take you by the hand for a little walk through of these. In particular, we'll be looking at the remaining features of the `ContentHandler` and `XMLReader` interfaces.

Other Methods of ContentHandler

First of all, there are some methods in this interface that we haven't yet covered. Here are the most useful.

ignorableWhitespace

The first is `ignorableWhitespace()`, and the method is, for the most part, ignorable whitespace itself. In Java, it has the following definition:

```
public void ignorableWhitespace(char[] chars, int start, int len)
    throws SAXException
```

The sharper-eyed amongst you will spot that this is very similar to our old friend `characters()`. However, this will only be called if we've got a validating parser, and a document containing a DTD or schema. Although a DTD can state that an element may only contain children and not PCDATA, it can still contain whitespace (spaces, tabs and newlines) for readability. If it does, a validating parser will report these characters by triggering an `ignorableWhiteSpace()` event rather than a `characters()` type one. A non-validating parser, on the other hand, won't be able to tell whether the characters are ignorable whitespace or PCDATA, so it will report all characters by means of `characters()` events.

The upshot is that, unless you are particularly interested in reproducing the structure of the document exactly, you can safely ignore `ignorableWhiteSpace()` events.

processingInstruction

The next event method in `ContentHandler` is `processingInstruction()`. Unsurprisingly, this method is used to catch processing instructions, such as:

```
<?someApplication someParam?>
```

which provide instructions for some application processing the XML. The Java declaration of `processingInstruction()` is as follows:

```
public void processingInstruction(String target, String data)
  throws SAXException
```

In this case, `target` would be "someApplication", and `data` would be "someParam".

I'm sure I don't need to remind you at this point that the XML declaration at the start of an XML document is *not* a processing instruction, and as such it won't cause you to receive a `processingInstruction()` event. Or at least, if it does, then switch to another parser, quick.

skippedEntity

This is another DTD-related event, which gets called whenever a DTD entity is skipped. Non-validating parsers can skip entities if the item in question hasn't been encountered in the declarations, which can happen if the entity is declared in an external subset of the DTD. Any parser is also permitted to skip entities, depending on the values of a couple of parser features, as explained in the next section.

Other Methods of XMLReader

There are also a few methods in this interface that we have so far skipped over but that deserve a mention.:

getFeature and setFeature

One of the neat features of SAX introduced with version 2.0 is the concept of **features**. The idea behind this is that there are a number of optional features that may be switched on or off at any time. An example of such a feature is `http://xml.org.sax/features/external-general-entities`, which in fact is one of the features referred to in the preceding section. If this feature is turned on, all external general entities (in other words, text) are included in the parsing process; otherwise, they are not. Notice the fully qualified name; parser implementers are encouraged to include their own features.

To determine the status of a feature, the method to use is `getFeature()`:

```
public boolean getFeature(String name) throws
  SAXNotRecognizedException, SAXNotSupportedException
```

To set the value of a feature, the method to use is `setFeature()`:

```
public void setFeature(String name, boolean value) throws
  SAXNotRecognizedException, SAXNotSupportedException
```

(although Microsoft has, slightly perversely, renamed this as `putFeature()` to fit in with Microsoft naming conventions).

getProperty and setProperty

These are similar to getFeature() and setFeature(), except that the item referenced by the string name is an Object, rather than a Boolean value. As an example, there's an optional SAX 2.0 interface called LexicalHandler (which we won't be looking at in detail here). The interface provides a way to extract lexical information from a parsed XML document, such as comments and CDATA section boundaries. If a parser supports this, an application can obtain a reference to the object by invoking getProperty() with a name of http://xml.org.sax/properties/lexical-handler. Both Apache and Microsoft support LexicalHandler, incidentally.

Here are the two method declarations:

```
public Object getProperty(String name) throws
    SAXNotRecognizedException, SAXNotSupportedException
```

```
public void setProperty(String name, Object value) throws
    SAXNotRecognizedException, SAXNotSupportedException
```

Again, Microsoft uses the name putProperty().

Summary

Despite the unquestionable power of XSL, there are still many cases where traditional programming solutions, assisted by the DOM and SAX APIs, have an important role to play. Briefly, the DOM offers a straightforward, no-nonsense way to enable you to find your way around the document, tweaking it as you see fit. SAX is a more subtle approach that will pay dividends where speed or system resource consumption is an issue.

SAX is becoming increasingly important, especially now that Microsoft has moved in and extended it, and it may yet prove to be *the* tool of choice for complex transformations. The SAX XML filter and Microsoft XML writer together form a particularly powerful combination, and if you find XSLT straining under the load, you might be well advised to put the work SAX's way.

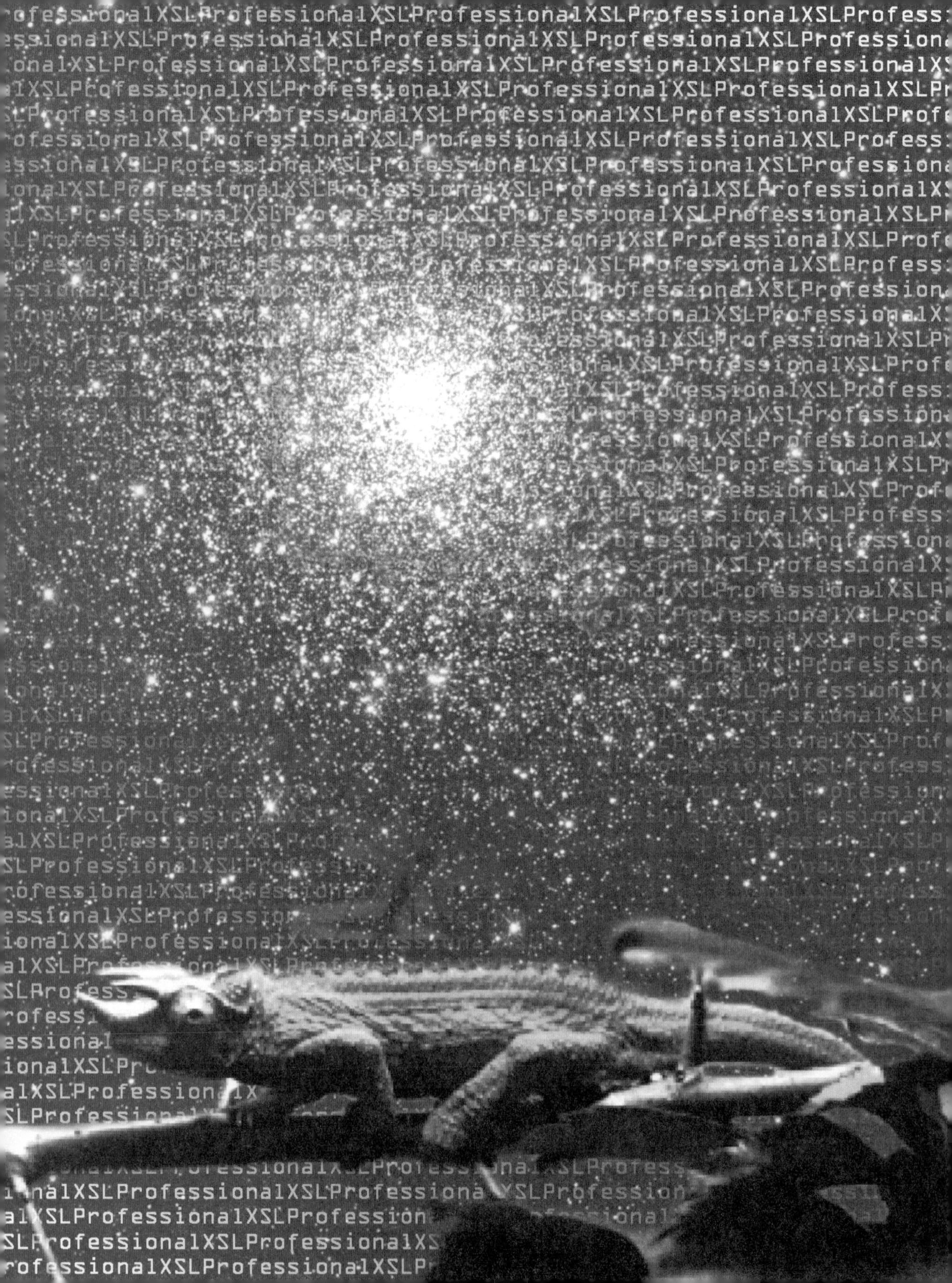

7

Microsoft XSL Technologies

When it comes to supporting industry-wide standards, Microsoft does not have the best of reputations. Their much-touted "embrace and extend" philosophy is commonly, if a little cynically, regarded as an insidious ploy, used to win the confidence of well-intentioned developers who then find themselves locked into Microsoft's stranglehold by the proprietary enhancements unavailable from any other vendor.

However, such allegations of deviousness do not bear close scrutiny and appear to be largely irrelevant to Microsoft's XML strategy as it stands today. It has demonstrated a surprising level of dedication to the recommendations that define XML and its applications. When it comes to XML, interoperability is key, and Microsoft seem to be taking this very much to heart.

This chapter covers today's state-of-the-art XML and XSLT implementations as currently realized in Microsoft's XML Parser release 3.0 (**MSXML3**). It also introduces tomorrow's leading-edge technologies, as exemplified by the classes found in the System.Xml namespace of Microsoft's up and coming **.NET framework**.

The Microsoft XML Parser is much more than its name implies. The version 3.0 release not only includes implementations of the W3C's Document Object Model (DOM) and the Simple API for XML version 2 (SAX2) but also boasts APIs for efficiently transforming XML documents using the W3C's XSLT 1.0 Recommendation. Add to this support for a proprietary but functional XML-based schema language (XDR), and top it all off with classes for simplifying the sending and receiving of XML documents over HTTP, and you have a package that enables the rapid development of distributed, cross-platform applications.

Given the wide variety of functionality offered by MSXML, this chapter focuses on its XPath/XSLT-related features and so only scratches the surface of its full range of functionality. We'll take a brief tour of the traditional DOM implementation, examine its XPath extension functions to see how they ease navigation, and learn how to transform documents using both the convenience methods added to the DOM itself and the more advanced XSLT-specific interfaces.

Because MSXML is a COM component, it's usable from a plethora of languages. Since for the majority of Windows developers Visual Basic is the language of choice, the larger examples in this chapter will be presented in VB. However, little snippets are presented in VBScript, JScript, C#, and Visual C++ throughout the text. Despite the slight variations in syntax, the semantics and logic of each example should be readily apparent even to those of you not accustomed to these languages.

MSXML3

MSXML has had a rich and colorful history. Since its initial debut with Internet Explorer 4.0, each release has come closer to what could be reasonably considered full W3C conformance. The version 3.0 release is the first version that most consider a usable, conformant implementation.

The version 2.0 releases of MSXML implemented a pre-Recommendation draft of the XSL specification with a syntax best forgotten for the reasons covered briefly in Chapter 8. Since the version 3.0 release has yet to be widely deployed, however, the old syntax (identified by the http://www.w3.org/TR/WD-xsl namespace URI) is the only practical means of performing client-side transformations. The release of Internet Explorer 6 should rectify this, but until then, to use the new features of version 3.0 requires that your customers perform the separate MSXML installation step.

Since it's not entirely obvious which version of the XML component may or may not be installed on a given machine, the following table identifies each release's file names and version numbers. Products that might have installed a particular version of MSXML as part of their installation process are listed on the right-hand side. Throughout this chapter we'll assume that you want to use and have installed the version 3.0 release, as detailed shortly.

MSXML release	File name	File version	Products
1.0	msxml.dll	4.71.1712.5	Internet Explorer 4.0
1.0a	msxml.dll	4.72.2106.4	Windows 95, OEM Service Release 2.5 and Internet Explorer 4.0a
1.0 Service Pack 1 (SP1)	msxml.dll	4.72.3110.0	
2.0	msxml.dll	5.0.2014.0206	Internet Explorer 4.01, Service Pack 1 (SP1), and Internet Explorer 5.0
2.0a	msxml.dll	5.0.2314.1000	Office 2000 and Internet Explorer 5.0a
2.0b	msxml.dll	5.0.2614.3500	Windows 98, Second Edition and Internet Explorer 5.0b
2.5 Beta 2	msxml.dll	5.0.2919.38	-
2.5a	msxml.dll	5.0.2919.6303	Internet Explorer 5.01
2.5	msxml.dll	5.0.2920.0	Windows 2000

MSXML release	File name	File version	Products
2.5 Service Pack 1 (SP1)	`msxml.dll`	8.0.5226	Internet Explorer 5.01, Service Pack 1 (SP1) or Internet Explorer 5.5
2.6 January 2000 Web Release	`msxml2.dll`	7.50.4920.0	-
2.6 Beta 2	`msxml2.dll`	8.0.5207.3	SQL Server 2000 Beta 2
2.6	`msxml2.dll`	8.0.6518.1	SQL Server 2000 or BizTalk
3.0 March 2000 Web Release	`msxml3.dll`	7.50.5108.0	-
3.0 May 2000 Web Release	`msxml3.dll`	8.0.7309.3	-
3.0 July 2000 Web Release	`msxml3.dll`	8.0.7520.1	-
3.0 September 2000 Web Release	`msxml3.dll`	8.0.7722.0	-
3.0 Release	`msxml3.dll`	8.0.7820.0	-

Note that certain versions are hosted in different DLLs, and it is therefore possible to have multiple releases installed at the same time.

To determine what versions are currently installed on your machine, navigate to your `System32` directory (usually located under `C:\WINDOWS\` or `C:\WINNT\`) and right click on the DLL(s) in question. Click on the **Property** option. As in the following figure, the **Version** tab shows the file version, which you can then use with the above table to ascertain which release is installed.

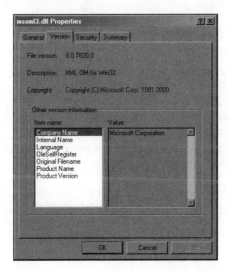

When browsing through your system directory, you might also notice the `msxml2a.dll`, `msxml2r.dll`, `msxml3a.dll`, or `msxml3r.dll` files. These are resource DLLs containing localized error messages to display when parsing malformed documents. These don't need to be registered (nor can they be) but they are required for MSXML to function.

Installation

The Microsoft XML Parser version 3.0 release can be downloaded from http://msdn.microsoft.com/xml/. Invoking the executable will install and register the components in **side-by-side mode**. This means that any previous installation of MSXML will not be replaced by the version 3.0 release and will be used by default, ensuring that applications built and tested using older components will continue to work as expected.

If you wish to install MSXML3 in **replace** mode, you must also download and invoke the `xmlinst.exe` utility from the same site. This modifies your registry so that the ProgIDs and CLSIDs used to create class instances for previous versions of MSXML will instead create instances of the updated classes included with MSXML3. According to Microsoft, this places your machine in a potentially unstable and unsupported state, but it's the only way to "trick" legacy applications (like Internet Explorer) into using the new components without needing to be recompiled.

While the `xmlinst.exe` utility comes with a detailed `ReadMe.txt` file, installing MSXML3 in replace mode is as easy as running the utility from the command prompt or even just double clicking on it from within Explorer.

Invoking `xmlinst.exe` with the `-u` command line option will remove the registry entries for any and all versions of MSXML installed on your machine. This effectively makes them unusable. In order to restore the default registry entries for a particular release, use the `regsvr32.exe` utility. For example, to restore the entries for MSXML 2.6 open a command prompt window and type:

regsvr32.exe msxml2.dll

and to restore those entries for MSXML 3.0, placing your machine back in side-by-side mode, type:

regsvr32.exe msxml3.dll

Also available from the same site is the **MSXML SDK**. This contains MSXML documentation in the form of a compiled HTML Help file and is highly recommended. Included in the documentation are helpful XPath and XSLT references that are so useful that you might consider adding them as shortcuts to your Desktop or QuickLaunch toolbar – they are relevant to general standards-compliant XSL development as well as MSXML usage.

The SDK also comes with the headers and libraries required by some development environments. Visual Basic and Visual C++ developers don't necessarily need these files since the type library is embedded in the DLL and it's relatively painless to add a reference from your Visual Basic project or "`#import`" the DLL when using Visual C++.

XML Documents

The centerpiece of the MSXML framework is the **document**. Both the upcoming XML Information Set specification (http://www.w3.org/TR/xml-infoset/) and the existing XSLT Recommendation refer to XML documents as nothing more than abstractions. Source trees are transformed into result trees. There is absolutely no requirement that either of these trees be serialized using XML 1.0 syntax, though most people tend to think of it that way – as if the transformation involved files and not trees. With MSXML, these trees are manipulated using the MSXML2.DOMDocument class.

MSXML's document is an implementation of the W3C's Document Object Model (DOM) document with several Microsoft-specific extensions. The properties and methods available to applications are defined in the MSXML2.IXMLDOMDocument and MSXML2.IXMLDOMDocument2 interfaces. The IXMLDOMDocument2 interface is an extension of IXMLDOMDocument and includes several new methods in the version 3.0 release.

> *Those new to MSXML3 might be wondering why the identifiers used throughout this chapter are prefixed with MSXML2 instead of MSXML3. Usually, version-dependent ProgIDs are suffixed with a version identifier – not prefixed with one. Version independent ProgIDs on the other hand typically don't encode any version information in the identifier so, as newer versions are installed, the ProgIDs instantiate the most recent version of the component. When MSXML 2.6 was released, however, both the version-dependent and version-independent ProgIDs were explicitly prefixed with MSXML2. This makes it possible for applications previously compiled using the "old" MSXML prefix to continue using the legacy components without introducing any compatibility problems that might have been introduced by the substantially improved 2.6 release. This is how installing MSXML in side-by-side mode was made possible. By continuing to use the MSXML2 prefix, older applications using the version-independent MSXML ProgIDs are shielded from the more radically updated version 3.0 components, but at the same time such features are available to newer applications that explicitly request MSXML 2.6 and above.*

Instantiating Documents

It's possible to instantiate either **rental-threaded** or **free-threaded** documents using the appropriate ProgID or CLSID. As the rental-threaded model includes intrinsic mechanisms to protect documents from concurrent access and the consequent possible corruption, it can offer improved performance over free-threaded documents.

To instantiate a rental-threaded document, use the ProgID:

```
MSXML2.DOMDocument
```

or the CLSID:

```
CLSID_DOMDocument
```

These are the version-independent identifiers, but unless you've installed MSXML3 in replace mode, you'll consistently create a 2.6 release document. The version-*dependent* identifiers are:

```
MSXML2.DOMDocument.3.0
```

```
CLSID_DOMDocument30.
```

In a similar way, free-threaded documents are created using either one of the ProgIDs:

    MSXML2.FreeThreadedDOMDocument

    MSXML2.FreeThreadedDOMDocument.3.0

or one of the CLSIDs:

    CLSID_FreeThreadedDOMDocument

    CLSID_FreeThreadedDOMDocument30

For example, to create a rental-threaded document in VBScript, use the following:

```
' VBScript
Dim objDocument
Set objDocument = CreateObject("MSXML2.DOMDocument")
```

Explicitly creating a version 3.0 document using JScript is achieved like so:

```
// JScript
var objDocument = new ActiveXDocument("MSXML2.DOMDocument.3.0");
```

If you're using Visual Basic 6.0, you'll want to add a reference to your project before instantiating a document in order to take advantage of the support for early binding. Select the Project | References menu item and check the Microsoft XML, v3.0 reference:

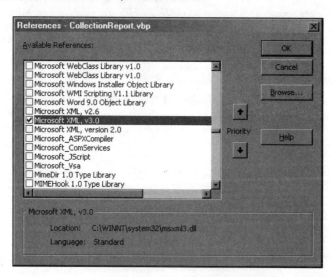

Once a reference is added, declaring and instantiating a free-threaded document in Visual Basic requires the following:

```
' Visual Basic
Dim objDocument As MSXML2.IXMLDOMDocument2
Set objDocument = New MSXML2.FreeThreadedDOMDocument
```

By explicitly declaring the type of the variable in this manner, it's possible to take advantage of the handy IntelliSense features provided by the Visual Basic IDE. Declaring the type of the variable as an interface rather than a class allows it to refer to both rental-threaded and free-threaded documents.

The simplest way for Visual C++ developers to access MSXML is to #import the DLL before use:

```
// Visual C++
#import "C:\WINNT\System32\msxml3.dll" named_guids
using namespace MSXML2;

// …

IXMLDOMDocument2Ptr pDocument(CLSID_FreeThreadedDOMDocument30);
```

While it's not strictly necessary to import the type library in order to use MSXML in Visual C++ (since the headers and libraries are available in the SDK), the wrapper classes that are generated make coding with these interfaces much more convenient and less error-prone.

Loading and Saving XML

Before we can perform any sort of transformation using XSLT, we'll need to load both a source document and a stylesheet into memory. In many cases, we'll also want the result document to persist in memory. IXMLDOMDocument includes several methods for populating an XML document and preserving it in this form. These are Microsoft-specific methods, since the W3C's DOM (prior to Level 3) doesn't specify any methods for loading or saving documents.

To load a document use the load() method. Its parameter can be a string containing a filename or URL, an IIS Request object, a SafeArray of bytes, another DOMDocument, or any object that implements IStream, ISequentialStream, or IPersistStream. It returns a Boolean indicating whether the load operation was successful or not.

By default, loading occurs asynchronously so it's entirely possible that, before the document actually finishes populating itself, the statement following the load() call will start to be executed. When loading asynchronously, the readyState property or the onreadystatechange event can be used to determine when loading has completed. However, you may want to turn off the async property of the document before loading any XML so that this issue doesn't create a problem.

The following sample loads an XML document, collection.xml, and displays a message box if it should fail for any reason:

```
' Visual Basic
objDocument.async = False

Dim boolResult As Boolean
boolResult = objDocument.load("C:\MyXML\collection.xml")

If boolResult = False Then
  Dim objParseError As MSXML2.IXMLDOMParseError
  Set objParseError = objDocument.parseError
  MsgBox objParseError.reason
End If
```

It's also possible to create an XML data tree by parsing any arbitrary string. To do this, use the `loadXML()` method, which returns a Boolean, in the same manner as `load()`.

```
// JScript
objDocument.async = false;
var boolResult = objDocument.loadXML("<hi>Hello, XML.</hi>");
// Don't forget to check for parse errors.
```

Conversely, to save a document use the `save()` method. The `save()` method's parameter is a Variant indicating the destination. As with the `load()` method this can be a string containing a local filename. It cannot, however, contain a URL. It can also be an IIS `Response` object, another `DOMDocument`, or any object that implements `IStream`, `IPersistStream`, or `IPersistStreamInit`.

```
// Visual C++
HRESULT hr = pDocument->save(_variant_t(L"C:\\MyXML\\collection.xml"));
```

Navigating the DOM using XPath

In order to best demonstrate the functionality of MSXML, we'll use it to gather some simple statistics from a rather contrived XML document describing somebody's music collection. From this file we will report the total number of albums and tracks along with the total playing time for the collection as a whole.

The samples used throughout the rest of this chapter will assume that the following XML (`collection.xml`) has been successfully loaded. You will notice that the file contains many international characters, so it must be saved as UTF-8, as indicated by the `encoding` attribute of the top level element:

```
<?xml version="1.0" encoding="UTF-8"?>
<collection>
  <owner>jason@injektilo.org</owner>
  <album>
    <artist>Radiohead</artist>
    <title>OK Computer</title>
    <track m="4" s="44">Airbag</track>
    <track m="6" s="23">Paranoid Android</track>
    <track m="4" s="27">Subterranean Homesick Alien</track>
    <track m="4" s="24">Exit Music (For a Film)</track>
    <track m="4" s="59">Let Down</track>
    <track m="4" s="21">Karma Police</track>
    <track m="1" s="57">Fitter Happier</track>
    <track m="3" s="50">Electioneering</track>
    <track m="4" s="45">Climbing up the Walls</track>
    <track m="3" s="48">No Surprises</track>
    <track m="4" s="19">Lucky</track>
    <track m="5" s="24">Tourist</track>
  </album>
  <album>
    <artist>Sigur Rós</artist>
    <title>Ágætis Byrjun</title>
    <track m="1" s="36">Intro</track>
    <track m="10" s="4">Svefn-G-Englar</track>
    <track m="6" s="47">Starálfur</track>
    <track m="7" s="47">Flugufrelsarinn</track>
    <track m="8" s="11">Ný Batterí</track>
```

```
        <track m="7" s="10">Hjartað Hamast (Bamm Bamm Bamm)</track>
        <track m="10" s="18">Viðar Vel Til Loftárasa</track>
        <track m="8" s="3">Olsen Olsen</track>
        <track m="7" s="56">Ágætis Byrjun</track>
        <track m="4">Avalon</track>
    </album>
    <album>
        <artist>Sunny Day Real Estate</artist>
        <title>LP2</title>
        <track m="2" s="29">Friday</track>
        <track m="3" s="5">Theo B</track>
        <track m="3" s="19">Red Elephant</track>
        <track m="3" s="33">5/4</track>
        <track m="4" s="25">Waffle</track>
        <track m="5" s="28">8</track>
        <track m="4" s="47">Iscarabald</track>
        <track m="4" s="52">J'Nuh</track>
        <track m="5" s="9">Rodeo Jones</track>
    </album>
</collection>
```

As you can see, this document has a relatively simple structure. The names of the collection's owner, the artists, album titles, and tracks are not relevant for our purposes. We will just be counting the occurrences of album and track elements and totaling the playing time for each track (represented by the h, m, and s attributes for hours, minutes, and seconds).

Iterating across node lists (or node-sets as they're called in XPath) and testing each node against the specific criteria you're interested in constitutes the traditional approach to navigating the DOM. It results, however, in an abundance of tedious and error-prone code, all of which is firmly coupled to the structure of your XML document. For example, the following subroutine (in Visual Basic) gathers the statistics necessary for our simple report:

```vb
Private Sub GetStatistics()
    ' Reset the totals to 0.
    ClearTotals

    ' The child nodes of a collection element could include
    ' an owner element.
    Dim objMaybeAlbum As MSXML2.IXMLDOMNode
    Set objMaybeAlbum = m_objCollection.documentElement.firstChild

    Do Until objMaybeAlbum Is Nothing
        If objMaybeAlbum.nodeName = "album" Then
            m_intTotalAlbums = m_intTotalAlbums + 1

            ' The child nodes of album elements could include
            ' artist and title elements.
            Dim objMaybeTrack As MSXML2.IXMLDOMNode
            Set objMaybeTrack = objMaybeAlbum.firstChild

            Do Until objMaybeTrack Is Nothing
                If objMaybeTrack.nodeName = "track" Then
                    m_intTotalTracks = m_intTotalTracks + 1
```

```
                        ' QueryInterface for IXMLDOMElement so
                        ' that we can use the getAttribute method.
                        Dim objTrack As MSXML2.IXMLDOMElement
                        Set objTrack = objMaybeTrack

                        ' AddTime checks for missing attributes
                        ' and handles the overflow from seconds to
                        ' minutes and from minutes to hours.
                        AddTime _
                            objTrack.getAttribute("h"), _
                            objTrack.getAttribute("m"), _
                            objTrack.getAttribute("s")

                        Set objTrack = Nothing
                    End If

                    ' Get the next possible track.
                    Set objMaybeTrack = objMaybeTrack.nextSibling
                Loop

                Set objMaybeTrack = Nothing
            End If

            ' Get the next possible album.
            Set objMaybeAlbum = objMaybeAlbum.nextSibling
        Loop

        Set objMaybeAlbum = Nothing

        ' DisplayReport simply displays a message box with the
        ' results now stored in the form-level variables.
        DisplayReport
    End Sub
```

Note that this is just one subroutine to use within a larger application. The form-level variables and the `ClearTotals`, `AddTime`, and `DisplayReport` helper subroutines are not included here, for simplicity. However, the source code is available in its entirety in the code download for this chapter.

The report we've generated is ridiculously simple and consists of only three lines in a message box:

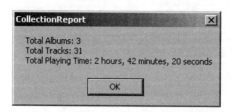

In order to gather these statistics, we've used the `firstChild` and `nextSibling` properties to walk along the document. These properties are part of the standard W3C DOM interfaces, so should be familiar to those who've used the DOM from other languages. MSXML, though, has extended the DOM to include two methods that greatly reduce the amount of code necessary to traverse documents, namely `selectNodes()` and `selectSingleNode()`.

The `selectNodes()` method accepts an XPath expression as its only parameter and returns a standard DOM node list. The `selectSingleNode()` method, as its name implies, returns only a single node – the first node in the tree that matches the evaluation of the specified XPath expression.

The following example demonstrates how `selectNodes()` can be used to gather the statistics for our report:

```
Private Sub GetStatistics2()
    ClearTotals

    Dim objNodeList As MSXML2.IXMLDOMNodeList

    ' This XPath expression only returns album elements.
    Set objNodeList = m_objCollection.selectNodes("/collection/album")
    m_intTotalAlbums = objNodeList.length

    ' Get all the track elements that are children of album elements.
    Set objNodeList = m_objCollection.selectNodes("/collection/album/track")
    m_intTotalTracks = objNodeList.length

    Dim objTrack As MSXML2.IXMLDOMElement

    ' Get the first track in the list.
    Set objTrack = objNodeList.nextNode

    Do While Not objTrack Is Nothing
        AddTime _
            objTrack.getAttribute("h"), _
            objTrack.getAttribute("m"), _
            objTrack.getAttribute("s")

        ' Get the next track.
        Set objTrack = objNodeList.nextNode
    Loop

    DisplayReport
End Sub
```

This version not only contains less code than the previous example, which means it's easier to initially develop and maintain, but it's also more efficient. The XPath engine is not only highly optimized, it's also internal to the component and so avoids the overhead of calling via the COM layer.

It's still necessary, though, to iterate over the track elements in order to total the playing time. MSXML only supports XPath expressions that result in what the XPath Recommendation calls a node-set, and the DOM calls a NodeList. In the coverage of the XSL support provided by the .NET framework later in this chapter, we'll see how this final loop can be avoided using the `Evaluate` method.

MSXML3 supports the entire range of XPath expressions as described in Chapter 2 – including the use of axis specifiers and predicates. Due to the massive deployment of MSXML before the final Recommendation from the W3C, though, the default syntax for these expressions is *not* XPath – they're actually "XSL Patterns". While similar, the two languages certainly aren't compatible. The simple examples we've looked at so far are conformant to both the Working Draft and Recommendation XPath syntaxes, but attempting to do much more would likely result in an error. In order to use these more sophisticated features, the document needs to be informed of what syntax it should use, by setting a special property, `SelectionLanguage`.

The `IXMLDOMDocument2` interface includes a `setProperty()` method to allow Microsoft to add features to its implementation without affecting the external interface. At the moment there are only two widely used properties: `SelectionLanguage` and `SelectionNamespaces`. The `setProperty()` method requires two parameters. The first is a string indicating the property being set, and the second is the value for that property as a Variant.

So, the default value for the `SelectionLanguage` property is `XSLPattern`, and in order to use the full XPath syntax, we must set this property to `XPath`.

Since XPath allows the node test part of each location step to contain an optional prefix indicating what namespace the URI is declared in, MSXML provides the `SelectionNamespaces` property, allowing developers to provide the necessary namespace declarations required to properly perform such node tests. If an expression includes a prefixed node test without this property having been set by an appropriate declaration, `selectNodes()` will not be able to return a match.

The format for the `SelectionNamespaces` property value is identical to what would appear in the namespace declaration of a serialized XML document. For example:

```
objDocument.setProperty("SelectionNamespaces", &_
                  "xmlns:foo='http://foo' xmlns:bar='http://bar'")
```

This binds the prefixes `foo` and `bar` to their namespace URIs. After this call, `selectNodes` will match nodes against documents with similar declarations (although it's not required that the prefix be identical – just the namespace URI).

Transforming Documents

Microsoft's DOM includes two more important extension methods that can be invoked, not only on documents but on any node in a document: `transformNode()` and `transformNodeToObject()`. Both of these methods accept a stylesheet as a parameter in the form of a second loaded document. `transformNode()` returns a string containing the result of the transformation. `transformNodeToObject()` accepts a second Variant parameter, which can be another `DOMDocument` or any object that implements `IStream`. The result tree is either constructed or serialized using this second parameter.

We can rewrite our report generator using the `transformNode()` method and XSLT:

```
Private Sub GetStatistics3()
    ' Create and load the stylesheet.
    Dim objTransform As MSXML2.IXMLDOMDocument2
    Set objTransform = New MSXML2.DOMDocument30
    objTransform.load "collection.xslt"

    ' Generate the report.
    Dim strReport As String
    strReport = m_objCollection.transformNode(objTransform)

    Set objTransform = Nothing

    ' Show the user the results of the transform.
    MsgBox strReport
End Sub
```

If `collection.xslt` denotes the following transform, our report will be identical to the previous two versions:

```xml
<?xml version="1.0" encoding="UTF-8"?>
<xsl:transform version="1.0"
  xmlns:xsl="http://www.w3.org/1999/XSL/Transform">
  <xsl:output method="text" encoding="UTF-8"/>

  <xsl:template match="/">

    <xsl:text>Total Albums: </xsl:text>
    <xsl:value-of select="count(/collection/album)"/>
    <xsl:text>&#xD;&#xA;</xsl:text>

    <xsl:text>Total Tracks: </xsl:text>
    <xsl:value-of select="count(/collection/album/track)"/>
    <xsl:text>&#xD;&#xA;</xsl:text>

    <xsl:variable name="total-seconds" select="
      sum(/collection/album/track/@h) * 3600 +
      sum(/collection/album/track/@m) * 60 +
      sum(/collection/album/track/@s)"/>

    <xsl:text>Total Playing Time: </xsl:text>
    <xsl:value-of select="floor($total-seconds div 3600)"/>
    <xsl:text> hours, </xsl:text>
    <xsl:value-of select="floor($total-seconds div 60) mod 60"/>
    <xsl:text> minutes, </xsl:text>
    <xsl:value-of select="$total-seconds mod 60"/>
    <xsl:text> seconds</xsl:text>

  </xsl:template>

</xsl:transform>
```

Besides requiring even less application code than the previous examples, XSLT makes it possible to drastically alter the format of the final report. Our demonstration application displays the report in a message box, which limits the results to simple strings, but a real product could easily generate HTML and display it in an embedded web browser control.

Advanced Transformations

Performing simple transformations on documents using MSXML's `transformNode()` and `transformNodeToObject()` methods turned out to be refreshingly straightforward. The amount of processing carried out behind the scenes is not insignificant, however. With each call to either of the methods, the stylesheet parameter is "compiled" into some internal data structure more suitable for transformations than the generic DOM. This is in addition to the effort required to actually build the DOM containing the stylesheet in the first place. If the same stylesheet is used to transform multiple source documents (as is often the case) the repeated compilations can have a drastic impact on performance.

In order to avoid the overhead of compiling identical stylesheets, MSXML3 supports the `IXSLTemplate` and `IXSLProcessor` interfaces. Applications load and compile their stylesheets once only, using an XSL "template" interface. Don't confuse the term template here with the individual templates elements contained within XSL transforms. Individual transformations are then performed using processors created by this interface.

The template/processor model is designed so that multiple processors created from the same template can use the same, cached transform. As a result, the DOM containing the stylesheet is required to be free-threaded. Transforms are compiled by pointing the `stylesheet` property of a template to a loaded document containing the XSLT. Once that's done, the `createProcessor()` method can create as many processors as might be needed by your application.

Setting the `input` property of the processor specifies the source tree for the transformation. Invoking the `transform()` method applies it. The result tree is output to the object specified in the `output` property of the processor. This can be a document or any of the custom streams supported by `transformNodeToObject()`.

If the `output` property is not set, the processor buffers output until the `output` property is read, clearing the processor's buffer.

The following example shows how we would generate our report using such a pre-compiled template:

```
Private Sub GetStatistics4()
    ' Create and load the stylesheet.
    Dim objTransform As MSXML2.IXMLDOMDocument2
    Set objTransform = New MSXML2.FreeThreadedDOMDocument30
    objTransform.load "collection.xslt"

    ' Compile the stylesheet.
    Dim objTemplate As MSXML2.IXSLTemplate
    Set objTemplate = New MSXML2.XSLTemplate30
    Set objTemplate.stylesheet = objTransform

    ' Create a processor and set the source document.
    Dim objProcessor As MSXML2.IXSLProcessor
    Set objProcessor = objTemplate.createProcessor
    objProcessor.input = m_objCollection

    ' Perform the actual transformation.
    objProcessor.transform

    ' Get the result as a string so that we can display it.
    Dim strReport As String
    strReport = objProcessor.output

    Set objTransform = Nothing
    Set objTemplate = Nothing
    Set objProcessor = Nothing

    ' Show the user the report.
    MsgBox strReport
End Sub
```

The above, contrived example isn't very useful. A more realistic situation might include a high-traffic web site where multiple XML documents throughout the site are styled using a common transform. The sample does show, however, that using a template and processor isn't that much more difficult than the `transformNode()` methods. In fact, in order to take advantage of some relatively common XSLT features such as those we'll be covering next, it's necessary to use processor objects, because only they expose the functionality required to realize these tasks.

Parameters

XSLT allows top-level parameters, which act much in the same way as command-line arguments for applications. Parameters make it possible to influence the transformation without modifying the source tree or the stylesheet. It's expected that the process initiating the transform provide some means of supplying values for these parameters. In MSXML, this is achieved through IXSLProcessor and its addParameter() method.

The first parameter required by addParameter() is the local parameter name specified by the top-level <xsl:param> element's name attribute within the stylesheet. This is a simple string and should not include any prefix. The second parameter to the method is the actual value to assign to the parameter. This is a Variant and can be either a Boolean, number, string, or node-set (IXMLDOMNodeList). A shortcut is also available allowing you to pass in a single node, in which case it gets wrapped in a node-list. The third parameter to the method is optional and specifies the namespace URI, if any, that the parameter name is qualified with.

For example, we could parameterize our report so that it won't include the playing time if the application indicates not to:

```
Private Sub GetStatistics5()
    ' Create and load the stylesheet.
    Dim objTransform As MSXML2.IXMLDOMDocument2
    Set objTransform = New MSXML2.FreeThreadedDOMDocument30
    objTransform.Load "collection-param.xslt"


    ' Compile the stylesheet.
    Dim objTemplate As MSXML2.IXSLTemplate
    Set objTemplate = New MSXML2.XSLTemplate30
    Set objTemplate.stylesheet = objTransform


    ' Create a processor and set the source document.
    Dim objProcessor As MSXML2.IXSLProcessor
    Set objProcessor = objTemplate.createProcessor
    objProcessor.input = m_objCollection


    ' Add parameter to exclude the playing time.
    objProcessor.addParameter "include-playing-time", False


    ' Perform the actual transformation.
    objProcessor.Transform


    ' Get the result as a string so that we can display it.
    Dim strReport As String
    strReport = objProcessor.output


    ' Release our objects
    Set objTransform = Nothing
    Set objTemplate = Nothing
    Set objProcessor = Nothing


    ' Show the user the report.
    MsgBox strReport
End Sub
```

Before applying the above transform, the addParameter() method was invoked on the processor. Notice that it's invoked on the processor and not the template – it's possible to specify separate parameter values for different processors created from the same template. The parameterized stylesheet, collection-param.xslt, is shown below:

```xml
<?xml version="1.0" encoding="UTF-16"?>
<xsl:transform version="1.0" xmlns:xsl="http://www.w3.org/1999/XSL/Transform" >
  <xsl:output method="text" encoding="UTF-8"/>

  <xsl:param name="include-playing-time" select="true()"/>

  <xsl:template match="/">

    <xsl:text>Total Albums: </xsl:text>
    <xsl:value-of select="count(/collection/album)"/>
    <xsl:text>&#xD;&#xA;</xsl:text>

    <xsl:text>Total Tracks: </xsl:text>
    <xsl:value-of select="count(/collection/album/track)"/>
    <xsl:text>&#xD;&#xA;</xsl:text>

    <xsl:variable name="total-seconds" select="
      sum(/collection/album/track/@h) * 3600 +
      sum(/collection/album/track/@m) * 60 +
      sum(/collection/album/track/@s)"/>

    <xsl:if test="$include-playing-time">
      <xsl:text>Total Playing Time: </xsl:text>
      <xsl:value-of select="floor($total-seconds div 3600)"/>
      <xsl:text> hours, </xsl:text>
      <xsl:value-of select="floor($total-seconds div 60) mod 60"/>
      <xsl:text> minutes, </xsl:text>
      <xsl:value-of select="$total-seconds mod 60"/>
      <xsl:text> seconds</xsl:text>
    </xsl:if>

  </xsl:template>

</xsl:transform>
```

The <xsl:param> element specifies the name and default value (using the select attribute). The section that outputs the total playing time is simply wrapped in an <xsl:if> element testing this parameter. More complex stylesheets could include many more parameters, conferring on the transforming application as much control as the stylesheet author desires.

User-Defined Extension Functions

Besides parameters, IXSLProcessor allows you to add extension functions to the transformation context. Unlike many other Microsoft extensions, these extension functions are explicitly accounted for and permitted by the XSLT specification. The specifics on how such functions should be realized are left up to the implementation, however.

XSLT includes the function-available() function that accepts a QName (a string in the form of "prefix:local" for user-defined extension functions or just "local" for built-in functions) and returns a Boolean indicating whether the "function library" for that particular processor includes an implementation for that function.

Extension functions are added to a processor's library using the `addObject()` method, which requires two parameters. The first parameter can be any object that implements `IDispatch`, and the processor adds each method implemented by the object to its function library. The second parameter is the namespace URI used to identify functions implemented by the first parameter.

The following JScript sample, `addObject.js`, demonstrates how to add an object to a processor:

```
// JScript
// create and load the transform
var transform = new ActiveXObject("MSXML2.FreeThreadedDOMDocument.3.0");
transform.load("c2f.xslt");

// create a template and compile the transform.
var template = new ActiveXObject("MSXML2.XSLTemplate.3.0");
template.stylesheet = transform;

// create and load our source document
var source = new ActiveXObject("MSXML2.DOMDocument.3.0");
source.load("celsius.xml");

// create an empty result document so that we can save it.
var result = new ActiveXObject("MSXML2.DOMDocument.3.0");

// create a processor and set the source and result
var processor = template.createProcessor();
processor.input = source;
processor.output = result;

// add our extension function
processor.addObject(new converter(), "http://injektilo.org/c2f");

// do the transformation
processor.transform();

// save the result so that we can view it
result.save("fahrenheit.xml");

// our constructor
function converter() {
  this.c2f = celsius2fahrenheit;
}

// our lone method
function celsius2fahrenheit(celsius) {
  return celsius * 9 / 5 + 32;
}
```

Note that the `converter` constructor builds an instance with a single member named `c2f`. Using this instance, `c2f` can be thought of an alias for the `celsisus2fahrenheit()` function. (Isn't JScript fun?)

The `celsius2fahrenheit()` function is declared as accepting a single, un-typed parameter. In our example, the actual type of the parameter ends up being a string, but JScript is kindly coercing it into a number for us. In XPath and XSLT there are four types of values: node-sets, Booleans, numbers, and strings. To discover what type of value was passed into a function, it's possible to use JScript's `typeof` operator. Note that node-set values will have a type of `object` (actually an `IXMLDOMNodeList` object).

The file `c2f.xslt` uses the extension function:

```xml
<?xml version="1.0" encoding="UTF-16"?>
<xsl:transform
  version="1.0"
  exclude-result-prefixes="io"
  xmlns:xsl="http://www.w3.org/1999/XSL/Transform"
  xmlns:io="http://injektilo.org/c2f">
  <xsl:output method="xml" indent="yes"/>

  <xsl:template match="temperatures">
    <temperatures>
      <xsl:apply-templates/>
    </temperatures>
  </xsl:template>

  <xsl:template match="c">
    <f><xsl:value-of select="io:c2f(string(.))"/></f>
  </xsl:template>

</xsl:transform>
```

Notice the second namespace declaration on the document element to bind the `io` prefix to the namespace URI that we specified when adding the object to the processor. The `exclude-result-prefixes` attribute is used to prevent a similar namespace declaration from appearing in the output stream.

The extension function is actually invoked in the template that matches `<c>` elements. Unlike built-in XPath/XSLT functions, the name is a QName consisting of the prefix and the function name. In this example, we explicitly "converted" the current node into a string that, as prescribed in the XPath specification, implies the concatenation of all descendant text nodes. It would have been possible to pass in the current node itself (as a node-set containing a single node) but we would have needed to retrieve the first node in the list, using the `item()` method, and then access that node's `text` property before we could use it. JScript can only automatically coerce between built-in data types and not user-defined ones such as this.

Microsoft XSLT Extensions

MSXSL

The command line **MSXSL utility** is a simple but useful wrapper around `IXSLTemplate` and `IXSLProcessor`. Using this executable it's possible to execute transformations from the command prompt or even from a batch file as part of an automated build process. Some may believe that the abundance of today's rich graphical user interfaces makes command-line processing obsolete, but there are many situations in which there's no GUI available to perform a specific task that you require and so the "inconvenience" of having to type in a command is greatly overshadowed by the flexibility that the command-line approach provides.

For example, the current dearth of XSLT "debuggers" can make developing transforms rather difficult. One technique that you can use is to place an `xml-stylesheet` processing instruction into your source document and let Internet Explorer perform the transformation for you. This approach won't work, though, when the transform requires parameters. Additionally, since IE's File | Save As feature only allows you to save the source document (as opposed to the result), using IE proves rather difficult when the result of the transform needs to be processed by another application in order to check its validity.

By virtue of the executable's simple command-line application, I find myself invoking MSXSL on a regular basis in order to help not only with these debugging tasks, but also with more general-purpose application processing. It has also proven invaluable for building web sites where the content for static pages is authored in XML and transformed into HTML before being uploaded to the server.

MSXSL requires MSXML3 to be installed on your computer, in either side-by-side or replace mode. You can currently download MSXSL from http://msdn.microsoft.com/downloads/ (look under Web Development I XML I XSL) in both source and compiled incarnations.

Once you've placed `MSXSL.exe` in your `PATH` – simply placing it in your `Windows` directory should achieve this – invoking MSXSL couldn't be easier. For example, simply issuing the command:

msxsl.exe collection.xml collection.xslt

from a command prompt would output our report to the console, as shown here:

The list of options supported by MSXSL can be viewed by the `-?` command-line option or by reading the Word document that comes with the download. Any options need to be specified in front of the source and stylesheet filenames. Parameters to the stylesheet are specified after the stylesheet filename, where each parameter is immediately followed by an equal sign and its value. The command:

msxsl collection.xml collection.xslt foo=bar baz=quux

would initialize the stylesheet parameters `foo` and `baz` with the string values "bar" and "quux".

MSXSL's output can be persisted to a file in two different ways. MSXSL outputs its result to the `stdout` stream, so it can be redirected using the > operator. For example:

msxsl collection.xml collection.xslt > report.txt

will save our report in `report.txt`. The other method uses MSXSL's `-o` option to inform MSXSL to what file it should send the results. So:

msxsl -o report.txt collection.xml collection.xslt

effectively produces the same result as the shell's redirection operator.

Using the command prompt's built-in piping mechanism, it's also possible to put a document through several successive transformations without writing a single line of code. Let's assume that you have an XML document marked up using Schema A and that you also have an XSLT document (`a2b.xslt`) that can transform instances of Schema A into instances of Schema B. Given another XSLT document (`b2c.xslt`) that can transform instances of Schema B into instances of Schema C, it's possible to transform any instance of Schema A indirectly into an instance of Schema C, even though the authors of `a2b.xslt` knew nothing about Schema C and, likewise, the authors of `b2c.xslt` knew nothing about Schema A.

The command that makes this transformation possible is:

msxsl a.xml a2b.xslt | msxsl – b2c.xslt > c.xml

The first part of the command transforms a.xml using a2b.xslt and directs the result to the standard output stream stdout. Instead of appearing on the console, it is then piped (using the | operator) to form the input for the second part of the command that transforms it with b2c.xslt. The result of the transformation is now redirected to the file c.xml using the > operator. The dash (-) in the middle command informs MSXSL that the source document should be read in from the standard input stream stdin (by default, your keyboard) instead of a named file. The pipe operator basically takes whatever is output to stdout during the execution of the command to its left and pours it into stdin to be read during execution of the command to its right. It's also possible for MSXSL to read stylesheets from stdin as well, by using a dash in place of the stylesheet filename.

This is definitely not the most efficient way to perform this transformation, since the result of the first transform is serialized and then loaded into a whole new DOM for the second transformation, but it's quick enough for one-offs and certainly a much more efficient use of your time than developing a2c.xslt or even an application that uses the two existing transforms in a more efficient manner. Old school UNIX hackers, as well as the new Linux breed, should feel right at home using these techniques.

XSL ISAPI Filter

The **XSL ISAPI filter** is another wrapper for MSXML3 candy, but one geared more towards webmasters than developers. Similar in concept to the Apache Project's **Cocoon**, the XSL ISAPI filter is a configurable, server-side transformation tool that makes it possible to serve XML-based content as HTML, WML, XSL-FO, or any number of other XML-based formats. The filter basically intercepts all requests for files ending with a .xml extension and transforms them according to the stylesheets appropriate to that document.

ISAPI can be downloaded from http://msdn.microsoft.com/downloads/ (look under Web Development | XML | XSL again). It comes in a self-extracting archive that contains the actual filter, its source code, documentation, and a number of samples.

The server-side stylesheets are configured using an XML configuration document stored on the server. These configuration files are indicated by including an extra attribute on the <?xml-stylesheet?> processing instruction located inside each XML document:

```
<?xml-stylesheet type="text/xsl" href="client.xslt"
    server-config="server.xml"?>
```

The server.xml file indicated in the above snippet could look like this:

```
<server-styles-config>
  <device target-markup="WML1.1">
    <stylesheet href="wml11.xslt"/>
  </device>
  <device browser="IE" version="5.0">
    <stylesheet href="ie50.xslt"/>
  </device>
  <device browser="Netscape" version="6.0">
    <stylesheet href="moz60.xslt"/>
  </device>
</server-styles-config>
```

The user agent making the request is used to determine the actual stylesheet to apply to the document. There are a number of attributes that can be used to determine a device match. The one that matches first wins. If none of the devices match, the document is sent untouched to the client (where it's possible that the client's browser could perform a client-side transformation indicated by the `href` attribute of the `xml-stylesheet` processing instruction above).

By including multiple stylesheet elements inside a single device element, it's possible to chain transformations, much like the piping we did earlier with the MSXSL utility:

```
<device>
   <stylesheet href="a2b.xslt"/>
   <stylesheet href="b2c.xslt"/>
</device>
```

One of the more exciting features of the XSL ISAPI filter is the ability to dynamically generate XML content using ASP and then have ISAPI intercept and transform it for the client. To indicate which ASP scripts generate XML and should then be filtered, the page should include an `xml-stylesheet` processing instruction and be saved with a `.pasp` extension.

Detailed installation instructions on how to install and configure the filter are included in the download. As you can see, using XSLT on the server is a simple and yet extremely powerful tool that can facilitate the separation of content and presentation, often so hard to achieve in the real world.

.NET

For the benefit of those of you who have spent the last couple of years marooned on a desert island, and have therefore missed all the hype, the .NET Framework is Microsoft's latest component technology offering. Like COM, it allows multiple languages to interoperate, albeit in a much more unified and consistent manner. The framework includes a host of classes providing the functionality required to create not just your typical graphical user interface applications, but also scalable web-based applications and services. Each of these is a founded on a pervasive XML substrate in the form of the `System.Xml` namespace that contains all the XML classes. There are many other core .NET technologies that rely on the XML classes in this namespace.

The .NET Framework XML classes were heavily influenced by the development and application of Microsoft's "legacy" MSXML components. For this reason, experienced MSXML users will instantly recognize the `XmlDocument` and `XslTransform` classes.

There are several significant enhancements introduced in the .NET XML classes. The first and most profound change is the paradigm shift from the "push" model espoused by the Simple API for XML (SAX) to the "pull" model introduced by .NET's `XmlReader` class. While not specifically related to XSL per se, it's so fundamental to the functioning of XML classes that it warrants some exploratory coverage at least.

This chapter does not provide an introduction to .NET or the new language designed to take advantage of it, C#. I assume a certain amount of familiarity with both the framework and the language. Despite this, the material should be readily digestible by those experienced in just about any object-oriented language – especially Java. For a more formal introduction to these topics, pick up a copy of *Introducing .NET* (ISBN 1-861004-89-3) or *C# Programming with the Public Beta* (ISBN 1-861004-87-7), both from Wrox Press.

The classes within the `System.Xml` namespace are hosted in the `System.Xml.dll` assembly. Since this assembly is not referenced by default, it's necessary to add a reference to your project (if you're using Visual Studio.NET 7.0 Beta 1) or specify the assembly using the /r option when compiling from a command prompt.

When using Visual Studio.NET, take the conspicuous lack of IntelliSense for any of the XML classes as a hint that you need to add `System.Xml.dll` as a reference for your project. Select Project | Add Reference from the menu bar and select the assembly, as in the following figure:

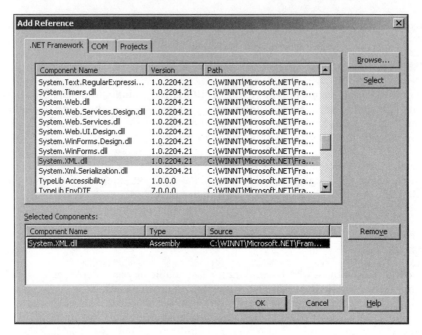

Compiling the examples from a command prompt is performed like so:

csc /r:System.Xml.dll ReportCollection.cs

In the following sections, we'll be exploring the four core XML abstractions provided by the .NET Framework: `XmlReader`, `XmlDocument`, `XmlNavigator`, and `XslTransform`. Using these classes, we'll be able to efficiently stream, randomly navigate, perform XPath selections against, and transform our XML documents. As in the previous section discussing MSXML3, we'll work our way towards performing full XSLT transformations by briefly exploring the classes that make up the namespace. This time, though, the examples comparing the different approaches to processing and transforming documents will be written entirely in C#.

Please note that this information is based on the Beta 1 release of the Visual Studio .NET and its SDK. It's known that changes will occur between this version and the Beta 2, and probably again before the final release. The classes and methods discussed herein should remain relatively stable, though. Consult the MSDN Library at http://msdn.microsoft.com/library/ for the latest documentation.

XmlReader

The extensive support for XML in the .NET Framework begins with `System.Xml.XmlReader`. This abstract class is used to iterate over the nodes in an XML document. Similar to fire-hose database cursors, `XmlReader` moves forward only. This "restriction" results in a significant boost in performance – it's no longer necessary for the entire document to be loaded into memory before processing can be done, something which isn't feasible with large, multi-megabyte sized documents.

Both versions of the Simple API for XML (SAX), the Java API developed by users of the XML-DEV mailing list (as covered in Chapter 6), offer similar functionality – providing fast, forward-only, streaming access to XML data. The major difference with SAX, though, is how clients access that data; SAX employs a "push" model. As the XML document is parsed, events are fired informing the listener (the client who initiated the read) of the type of node currently being parsed, and any other information pertaining to that type. SAX clients must minimally implement the `org.xml.sax.ContentHandler` interface in order to receive the notifications for these types of events. The SAX parser (which, interestingly, implements the unrelated `org.xml.sax.XMLReader` interface) invokes the methods defined in `ContentHandler`.

While MSXML3 introduced support for SAX2, the .NET Framework has abandoned it altogether. The problem with SAX is that the client has to distribute the logic necessary for interpreting the SAX events across the various methods defined in the `ContentHandler` interface. This division has proved counter-intuitive for many developers.

Microsoft's solution is to implement a "pull" model. Using this technique, the minimum amount of code to parse an XML document is a `while` loop and a `switch` statement. An `XmlReader` object is advanced to the next node in the stream by invoking the `Read()` method, which returns `false` if there are no more nodes left to read.

```
while (xmlReader.Read())
{
    // examine and process node here with a switch statement
}
```

When positioned at a node, `XmlReader` provides numerous properties and methods that allow clients to query the current node type and its information items. The `NodeType` property, for example, returns an `XmlNodeType` enumeration, which can be any of `Document`, `Element`, `Attribute`, `Text`, `Whitespace`, `ProcessingInstruction`, etc. Many node types have names, which can be queried using the `Name` property. This returns the raw qualified name as it appears in the XML document. There also exist `NamespaceURI`, `LocalName`, and `Prefix` properties. The `Value` property retrieves the text value of the current node allowing access to the content of attribute and text nodes.

The important thing to note here is that it's the client that initiates every operation. The information isn't pushed onto the client, in the way that it is with a SAX parser. This makes it possible for clients to control exactly what work should be done. For example, whether or not external parsed entities are resolved can be decided on an individual basis. This is possible as .NET reports node types of `EntityReference` to the client, who can then make the decision whether or not to invoke the `ResolveEntity()` method.

The XmlReader abstraction makes it possible to represent disparate data sources as XML and this is its real advantage. The .NET Framework ships with two concrete XmlReader derivatives: XmlTextReader and XmlNodeReader. XmlTextReader parses an XML document. Its constructor can accept a URI (string), a System.IO.TextReader, or a System.IO.Stream. The XmlNodeReader's constructor takes an XmlNavigator (which we'll learn about later in this chapter – think of it as a lightweight DOM cursor). It's entirely possible to develop your own custom XmlReader implementations.

The following example, in C#, shows how to iterate over the collection.xml document from the previous section:

```csharp
// C#
using System;
using System.Xml;

// gather statistics using XmlReader

public class ReportCollection
{
    public static void Main()
    {
        int totalAlbums = 0;
        int totalTracks = 0;
        int totalHours = 0;
        int totalMinutes = 0;
        int totalSeconds = 0;

        // create our XmlReader on the collection
        XmlReader xmlReader = new XmlTextReader("collection.xml");

        while (xmlReader.Read())
        {
            if (xmlReader.NodeType == XmlNodeType.Element)
            {
                switch (xmlReader.Name)
                {
                case "album":

                    ++totalAlbums;
                    break;

                case "track":

                    ++totalTracks;

                    if (xmlReader.MoveToAttribute("h"))
                    {
                        totalHours +=
                            Int32.FromString(xmlReader.Value);
                    }

                    if (xmlReader.MoveToAttribute("m"))
                    {
                        totalMinutes +=
                            Int32.FromString(xmlReader.Value);
                    }
```

```
                    if (xmlReader.MoveToAttribute("s"))
                    {
                        totalSeconds +=
                            Int32.FromString(xmlReader.Value);
                    }

                    break;
            }
        }
    }

    xmlReader.Close();

    // normalize the minutes and seconds

    totalMinutes += totalSeconds / 60;
    totalSeconds %= 60;

    totalHours += totalMinutes / 60;
    totalMinutes %= 60;

    // output our report

    Console.WriteLine("Total Albums: {0}", totalAlbums);
    Console.WriteLine("Total Tracks: {0}", totalTracks);
    Console.WriteLine(
        "Total Playing Time: {0} hours, {1} minutes, {2} seconds",
        totalHours,
        totalMinutes,
        totalSeconds);
    }
}
```

Since we are using an XmlTextReader, the document will not be loaded into memory in its entirety. This is the preferred way to process large XML documents. Of course, for a document as small as our sample, we didn't gain much – if anything. Streaming is typically used for documents that are too big to fit into available memory, resulting in excessive paging, and thus degrading performance significantly.

One thing to note from the above example is the manner in which attributes are accessed. Successive calls to Read() will never position the reader on an attribute node. This is because attributes are not regarded as children of the elements they're attached to, but rather as metadata in which "real" content generally should not appear. XmlReader provides several methods that allow clients to iterate over the attributes of an element. In the example above we used the MoveToAttribute() method, which positions us on a specific named attribute. That method is also overloaded – creating another version of the method for other types of parameters – so it can accept an integer index as opposed to a string. To iterate over the attributes without regard to their name or position, use the MoveToFirstAttribute(), MoveToNextAttribute(), and MoveToElement() methods.

XmlDocument

The .NET analog of the W3C DOM is System.Xml.XmlDocument, a concrete class that implements most of the methods of DOM Level 2. It has its roots in the DOMDocument of MSXML, so developers used to that should feel right at home with this new improved version. The API has not only been streamlined, but augmented with many handy overloads (something COM won't allow) to make developers' lives that much easier.

Like MSXML's DOMDocument, but unlike all Java DOM implementations, where official language-level bindings do actually exist, XmlDocument does not implement an officially sanctioned abstract interface along the lines of org.w3c.dom.Document. It doesn't even implement a Microsoft-specific interface like IXMLDOMDocument. This means that DOM implementations cannot be interchanged as they can in Java space. In practice, this shouldn't be a problem since it's possible to implement custom XmlReader and XmlNavigator objects that can each be used to populate an XmlDocument.

In the new example, ReportCollection2.cs, loading and navigating documents occurs almost identically to our previous examples using MSXML:

```csharp
// C#
using System;
using System.Xml;

// gather statistics using XmlDocument navigation methods

public class ReportCollection2
{
    public static void Main()
    {
        int totalAlbums = 0;
        int totalTracks = 0;
        int totalHours = 0;
        int totalMinutes = 0;
        int totalSeconds = 0;

        // create and load the collection document
        XmlDocument xmlDocument = new XmlDocument();
        xmlDocument.Load("collection.xml");

        XmlNode maybeAlbum = xmlDocument.DocumentElement.FirstChild;

        while (maybeAlbum != null)
        {
            if (maybeAlbum.NodeType == XmlNodeType.Element &&
                maybeAlbum.Name == "album")
            {
                ++totalAlbums;

                XmlNode maybeTrack = maybeAlbum.FirstChild;

                while (maybeTrack != null)
                {
                    if (maybeTrack.NodeType == XmlNodeType.Element &&
                        maybeTrack.Name == "track")
                    {
                        ++totalTracks;

                        // cast the node down to an XmlElement so we can use the
                        // HasAttribute and GetAttribute helper methods
                        XmlElement trackElement = (XmlElement)maybeTrack;

                        if (trackElement.HasAttribute("h"))
                        {
                            totalHours += Int32.FromString(
                                trackElement.GetAttribute("h"));
                        }
```

```
                              if (trackElement.HasAttribute("m"))
                              {
                                  totalMinutes += Int32.FromString(
                                      trackElement.GetAttribute("m"));
                              }

                              if (trackElement.HasAttribute("s"))
                              {
                                  totalSeconds += Int32.FromString(
                                      trackElement.GetAttribute("s"));
                              }
                          }

                          // get the next track
                          maybeTrack = maybeTrack.NextSibling;
                      }
                  }

                  // get the next album
                  maybeAlbum = maybeAlbum.NextSibling;
              }

              // normalize the minutes and seconds

              totalMinutes += totalSeconds / 60;
              totalSeconds %= 60;

              totalHours += totalMinutes / 60;
              totalMinutes %= 60;

              // output our report

              Console.WriteLine("Total Albums: {0}", totalAlbums);
              Console.WriteLine("Total Tracks: {0}", totalTracks);
              Console.WriteLine(
                  "Total Playing Time: {0} hours, {1} minutes, {2} seconds",
                  totalHours,
                  totalMinutes,
                  totalSeconds);
          }
      }
```

There shouldn't be any surprises in the above example. Navigating an XmlDocument is similar to navigating the W3C or MSXML DOM. What is interesting, though, is what you *can't* do with an XmlDocument that you *can* with an MSXML DOMDocument: the extremely helpful selectNode() and transformNode() family of methods are not present in XmlDocument objects.

XmlNavigator

The System.Xml.XmlNavigator abstract class provides a random-access "cursor" over an in-memory document. It provides much of the same functionality as XmlReader without the restriction that it must be forward only. It can also be used to modify a document. Multiple navigators can be positioned on various nodes in a document (or even the same node) at the same time, and modifications made through a navigator are seen immediately by other navigators as they traverse the tree. Additionally, XmlNavigator provides the XPath node selection functionality that is conspicuously absent from XmlDocument.

XmlNavigator is an abstract class. The concrete implementation that you'll most likely use is System.Xml.DocumentNavigator, which navigates over XmlDocument instances, although it's always possible to create your own custom XmlNavigator implementation.

`XmlNavigator` includes a multitude of methods to alter its location in a document. Like `XmlReader`, it includes the methods:

- ❑ `MoveToAttribute()`
- ❑ `MoveToFirstAttribute()`
- ❑ `MoveToNextAttribute()`
- ❑ `MoveToElement()`

Unlike `XmlReader`, though, it provides:

- ❑ `MoveToParent()` (similar to `XmlNode.ParentNode` property)
- ❑ `MoveToFirstChild()` (similar to `XmlNode.FirstChild` property)
- ❑ `MoveToLastChild()` (similar to `XmlNode.LastChild` property)
- ❑ `MoveToNext()` (which moves to the next sibling, much like the `XmlNode.NextSibling` property)
- ❑ `MoveToPrevious()` (which moves to the previous sibling, much like the `XmlNode.PreviousSibling` property)

There are also navigational methods provided with no simple equivalents in `XmlDocument`, such as:

- ❑ `MoveToFirst()`, which positions the navigator on the first child of the current node's parent
- ❑ `MoveToLast()`, which positions the navigator on the current node's last child.

Finally, `XmlNavigator` includes the methods:

- ❑ `MoveToFirstSelected()`
- ❑ `MoveToLastSelected()`
- ❑ `MoveToNextSelected()`
- ❑ `MoveToPreviousSelected()`

Each `XmlNavigator` instance is capable of selecting nodes in a document based on some specified XPath expression, in a similar fashion to how the `select` attribute works for `<xsl:apply-templates>` and `<xsl:for-each>` elements. The context node for the selection is the node that the navigator is currently positioned on, and selection is performed using the `Select()` method. Once this is done, the methods given above can be used to walk along the node list.

The following example, `ReportCollection3.cs`, shows how we can use `XmlNavigator` and its `Select()` method to gather the statistics for our report:

```
using System;
using System.Xml;

public class ReportCollection3
{
    public static void Main()
    {
        int totalAlbums = 0;
        int totalTracks = 0;
        int totalHours = 0;
        int totalMinutes = 0;
        int totalSeconds = 0;
```

```
XmlDocument xmlDocument = new XmlDocument();
xmlDocument.Load("collection.xml");

XmlNavigator xmlNavigator = new DocumentNavigator(xmlDocument);

// the navigator's context is initially the document (root) node.
xmlNavigator.Select("collection/album");

while (xmlNavigator.MoveToNextSelected())
{
    ++totalAlbums;

    XmlNavigator xmlNavigator2 = xmlNavigator.Clone();

    // the cloned navigator's context is the currently selected
    // album. so this expression selects only the track children
    // of the current album.
    xmlNavigator2.Select("track");

    while (xmlNavigator2.MoveToNextSelected())
    {
        ++totalTracks;

        if (xmlNavigator2.HasAttribute("h"))
        {
            totalHours += Int32.FromString(
                xmlNavigator2.GetAttribute("h"));
        }

        if (xmlNavigator2.HasAttribute("m"))
        {
            totalMinutes += Int32.FromString(
                xmlNavigator2.GetAttribute("m"));
        }

        if (xmlNavigator2.HasAttribute("s"))
        {
            totalSeconds += Int32.FromString(
                xmlNavigator2.GetAttribute("s"));
        }
    }
}

// normalize the minutes and seconds.

totalMinutes += totalSeconds / 60;
totalSeconds %= 60;

totalHours += totalMinutes / 60;
totalMinutes %= 60;

// output our report.

Console.WriteLine("Total Albums: {0}", totalAlbums);
Console.WriteLine("Total Tracks: {0}", totalTracks);
Console.WriteLine(
    "Total Playing Time: {0} hours, {1} minutes, {2} seconds",
    totalHours,
    totalMinutes,
    totalSeconds);
    }
}
```

Invoking `Select()` discards any previous selection that may have been made on the navigator. This is why it was necessary to clone the navigator in our example above, using the `Clone()` method. Since the navigator is really only a pointer to the document, this is a lightweight operation.

`XmlNavigator` also includes the `SelectSingle()` method. Despite its name, it does not affect the current selection, but positions the navigator at the first node of the resulting node-set.

Like MSXML's `selectNodes()` and `selectSingleNode()` methods, `Select()` and `SelectSingle()` only allow XPath expressions that result in node-sets. To evaluate an expression that results in a Boolean, number, or string, rather than a node-set, `XmlNavigator` provides the `Evaluate()` method. The expression that you pass to it doesn't even need to access the nodes in the document. Look at the following line of code, which outputs bar to the console:

```
Console.WriteLine(xmlNavigator.Evaluate("substring('foobarbaz', 4, 3)"));
```

`Evaluate()` is declared as returning an `object`, and will need to be cast to a `bool`, `double`, or `string` as appropriate, or converted using `System.Convert()`. It's important to watch out for the types of "shortcut" expressions that we all make when developing transforms. For example, in XSLT, node-sets are implicitly converted to their string value when needed. The `Evaluate()` method isn't as helpful – given the following XML document:

```
<foo bar='baz'>quux</foo>
```

the following line of code will throw a `System.Xml.XPath.XPathException`:

```
Console.WriteLine(xmlNavigator.Evaluate("/foo/@bar"));
```

The result of this XPath expression is actually a node-set containing a single attribute node. In order to use the `Evaluate()` method to retrieve the string value of that attribute ("baz"), we would need to rewrite the expression like this:

```
Console.WriteLine(xmlNavigator.Evaluate("string(/foo/@bar)"));
```

Our next `XmlNavigator` sample, `ReportCollection4.cs`, demonstrates how to use the `Evaluate()` method to compile our statistics:

```
using System;
using System.Xml;

public class ReportCollection4
{
    public static void Main()
    {
        int totalAlbums = 0;
        int totalTracks = 0;
        int totalHours = 0;
        int totalMinutes = 0;
        int totalSeconds = 0;

        XmlDocument xmlDocument = new XmlDocument();
        xmlDocument.Load("collection.xml");
```

```
            XmlNavigator xmlNavigator = new DocumentNavigator(xmlDocument);

            // gather our statistics.

            totalAlbums = (int)xmlNavigator.Evaluate(
                "count(collection/album)");
            totalTracks = (int)xmlNavigator.Evaluate(
                "count(collection/album/track)");

            // xpath numbers are returned as doubles so casting
            // to int doesn't work unless we cast to a double first.
            // Or, we could use the System.Convert utility class.

            totalHours = Convert.ToInt32(
                xmlNavigator.Evaluate("sum(collection/album/track/@h)"));
            totalMinutes = Convert.ToInt32(
                xmlNavigator.Evaluate("sum(collection/album/track/@m)"));
            totalSeconds = Convert.ToInt32(
                xmlNavigator.Evaluate("sum(collection/album/track/@s)"));

            // normalize the minutes and seconds.

            totalMinutes += totalSeconds / 60;
            totalSeconds %= 60;

            totalHours += totalMinutes / 60;
            totalMinutes %= 60;

            // output our report.

            Console.WriteLine("Total Albums: {0}", totalAlbums);
            Console.WriteLine("Total Tracks: {0}", totalTracks);
            Console.WriteLine(
                "Total Playing Time: {0} hours, {1} minutes, {2} seconds",
                totalHours,
                totalMinutes,
                totalSeconds);
        }
    }
```

If we were gathering statistics for a large number of collections, we could gain a slight performance enhancement by compiling our XPath expressions. XmlNavigator provides a Compile() method that accepts an XPath expression as a string and returns the compiled version of that expression as an object. The Select(), SelectSingle(), and Evaluate() methods can each accept either an XPath expression as a string or the compiled expression object equivalent.

```
object expression = xmlNavigator.Compile("count(collection/album)");
Console.WriteLine(xmlNavigator.Evaluate(expression));
```

The advantages of pre-compiling our XPath expressions are similar to those obtained by pre-compiling our stylesheets using MSXML's XSLTemplate object, and are also available for .NET's XslTransform object as we'll now see.

XslTransform

Transforming documents with the .NET Framework couldn't be easier. The `System.Xml.Xsl.XslTransform` class is the equivalent of MSXML's `XSLTemplate` object. Unlike the other XML classes, `XslTransform` lives in the `System.Xml.Xsl` namespace even though it's hosted in the same `System.Xml.dll`.

After instantiating and loading a new stylesheet, invoking any of the `Transform` overloads applies the transformation. Each of the methods requires an `XmlNavigator` and a currently undocumented and unusable `NSParamList` parameter that must be set to `null`. One of the overloads returns an `XmlReader`, while the remaining methods have a third parameter of type `XmlWriter`, `TextWriter`, or `Stream` indicating to where the result document should be sent.

> *If you use the ILDASM tool, you will see that all of the NSParamList methods in the Beta 1 release are marked "private" so it's impossible to invoke any of them without reflection. This indicates that it's highly unlikely that they would function correctly even if we were to go to the trouble of trying to dynamically invoke them.*

In the next example, `ReportCollection5.cs`, we generate a report by applying a transformation similar to `collection.xslt` used previously and writing the result document to the console:

```
using System;
using System.Xml;
using System.Xml.Xsl;

// generate a report using XslTransform.

public class ReportCollection5
{
    public static void Main()
    {
        // create and load the transform.
        XslTransform xslTransform = new XslTransform();
        xslTransform.Load("collection2.xslt");

        // create and load our source document.
        XmlDocument xmlDocument = new XmlDocument();
        xmlDocument.Load("collection.xml");

        XmlNavigator xmlNavigator = new DocumentNavigator(xmlDocument);

        // apply the transformation, writing the result document
        // out to the console.
        xslTransform.Transform(xmlNavigator, null, Console.Out);
    }
}
```

Unfortunately, the `XslTransform` class in the Beta 1 release doesn't implement the entire XSLT 1.0 Recommendation. `<xsl:variable>` and `<xsl:param>` are two notable omissions. Named templates and certain axis specifiers like `parent`, `ancestor`, `preceding-sibling`, and `following-sibling` are also unsupported. Sadly, anything but the most trivial stylesheets are next to impossible without this support, so the next section looks at how to leverage MSXML3 from C#. For the purposes of the sample then, the original transform will have to be modified to remove the `<xsl:variable>` element as follows (`collection2.xslt`):

```
<?xml version="1.0" encoding="UTF-16"?>
<xsl:transform version="1.0"
    xmlns:xsl="http://www.w3.org/1999/XSL/Transform">
    <xsl:output method="text" encoding="UTF-8"/>

    <xsl:template match="/">

        <xsl:text>&#xD;&#xA;</xsl:text>

        <xsl:text>Total Albums: </xsl:text>
        <xsl:value-of select="count(/collection/album)"/>
        <xsl:text>&#xD;&#xA;</xsl:text>

        <xsl:text>Total Tracks: </xsl:text>
        <xsl:value-of select="count(/collection/album/track)"/>
        <xsl:text>&#xD;&#xA;</xsl:text>

        <xsl:text>Total Playing Time: </xsl:text>
        <xsl:value-of select="floor((
                sum(/collection/album/track/@h) * 3600 +
                sum(/collection/album/track/@m) * 60 +
                sum(/collection/album/track/@s))
            div 3600)"/>
        <xsl:text> hours, </xsl:text>
        <xsl:value-of select="floor((
                sum(/collection/album/track/@h) * 3600 +
                sum(/collection/album/track/@m) * 60 +
                sum(/collection/album/track/@s))
            div 60) mod 60"/>
        <xsl:text> minutes, </xsl:text>
        <xsl:value-of select="(
                sum(/collection/album/track/@h) * 3600 +
                sum(/collection/album/track/@m) * 60 +
                sum(/collection/album/track/@s))
            mod 60"/>
        <xsl:text> seconds</xsl:text>

    </xsl:template>

</xsl:transform>
```

Additionally, a bug in the current product consistently outputs the XML declaration – even when the output method is specified as `"text"` or when an `omit-xml-declaration` attribute with a value of `"yes"` is included. Hopefully, these deficiencies will be remedied in the next release. Until then, it's always possible to use MSXML3 via the COM interoperability facilities offered by Visual Studio and .NET.

MSXML in .NET

MSXML3 is currently the only way to take advantage of a complete XSLT 1.0 implementation using Microsoft technologies. It also provides some of the advanced features, such as parameters and extension functions, that aren't currently possible with the Beta 1 release.

Fortunately, using MSXML3 from C# is even easier than using it from Visual Basic or Visual C++. Since C# is a type-safe, garbage-collected language, we can say goodbye to `QueryInterface`, Variants, safe arrays, smart pointers, reference cycles, and many of the other issues that beset today's COM developers. Compare the following example with those shown in the MSXML3 section or even your own code.

If you're using Visual Studio.NET, the only thing required to use MSXML from a C# application is to add it as a reference in your project. Select Project | Add Reference, switch to the COM tab, and choose Microsoft XML, v3.0:

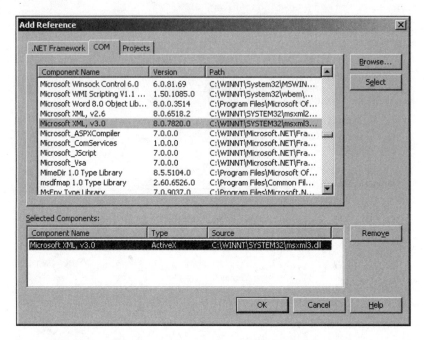

Once the reference has been added to the project, the MSXML interfaces and classes are available for use as if they were regular .NET types.

The following example shows how we could use our original transform to generate the report by using MSXML from C#:

```csharp
using System;
using MSXML2;

// generate a report using MSXML3.

public class ReportCollection6
{
    public static void Main()
    {
        // create and load the source document.
        IXMLDOMDocument2 collection = new DOMDocument30();
        collection.load("collection.xml");

        // create and load the transform.
        IXMLDOMDocument2 transform = new FreeThreadedDOMDocument30();
        transform.load("collection.xslt");

        // compile the transform.
        IXSLTemplate template = new XSLTemplate30();
        template.stylesheet = transform;
```

```
        // create the processor and apply the transformation.
        IXSLProcessor processor = template.createProcessor();
        processor.input = collection;
        processor.transform();

        // output the report.
        Console.WriteLine(processor.output);
    }
}
```

The .NET Framework includes the `tlbimp.exe` utility which, can be invoked from a command prompt to generate a .NET assembly to act as a proxy for legacy COM components. Executing:

tlbimp C:\WINNT\SYSTEM32\msxml3.dll

will create a file named `MSXML2.dll` in the current directory. This new DLL is a .NET assembly and can be referenced when compiling applications that use classes found in the MSXML2 namespace. For example, to compile the previous example from a command prompt, enter the following command from the same directory that the generated `MSXML2.dll` and `ReportCollection6.cs` files live in:

csc /r:MSXML2.dll ReportCollection6.cs

It's possible to include the /out option to specify a different filename for the generated assembly. This might be a good idea since the MSXML 2.6 component is also hosted in a file named `msxml2.dll`.

Summary

In this chapter we have taken a brief tour of both of Microsoft's core XSLT technologies. We learned how to load, transform, and save XML documents using MSXML's `DOMDocument`. We also learned how easy it is to navigate a document using Microsoft's XPath extensions. The `XSLTemplate` and `XSLProcessor` objects allowed us to compile stylesheets for maximum efficiency, and apply transformations with parameters and our own custom extension functions.

Microsoft's new .NET Framework provides several key advantages over MSXML and other XML APIs. It introduces a fundamentally improved model for processing XML documents with its `XmlReader` abstraction. Its `XmlNavigator` class greatly simplifies navigating documents, both with and without the use of XPath. While support for XSLT is not yet fully implemented, we can expect full conformance by the final release. Until then, MSXML is a pleasure to develop with from the new C# language.

In the next chapter we'll be seeing Microsoft implementations again, as we step through a case study in improving stylesheet performance and efficiency.

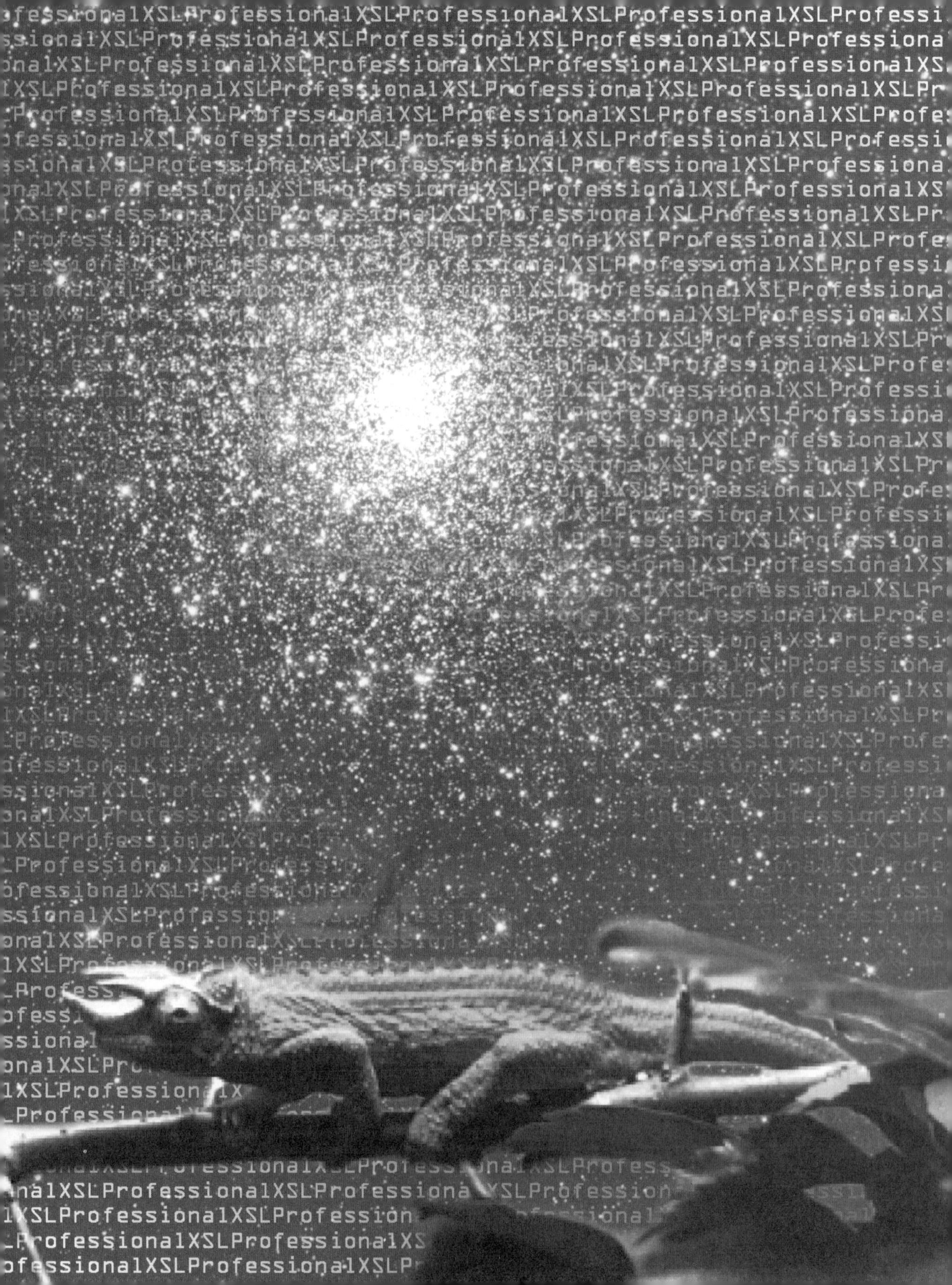
XSLProfessional

8

Optimizing Performance

This chapter will help you write XSL Transformations that are fast and scalable and, to illustrate how proper design can impact performance and scalability, I begin this chapter with a personal story.

A few months ago I created my most ambitious XSLT transform to date. This new transform was designed to do some pretty heavy lifting on XML files containing thousands of nodes. Once I had the basic design working with test data I threw industrial strength XML files at it. The transform "worked", so I knew there was no patently erroneous logic in it, but after about six minutes of processing it had gobbled up all available 480 MB of virtual memory. I was sad.

The month before I had encountered a performance issue with a transform that occurred when the node count exceeded a certain threshold. To solve the problem I had modified the script so that when this threshold was reached, I warned the user to reduce the filtered set of data with more restrictive queries. At the time, this was the most expedient solution to my scalability problem. As usual, expedience was the enemy of justice; I deferred further research into the cause of the bottleneck.

I was on the point of taking the same approach with my latest invention, but before I did, I ran the transform past our XSLT high priest (aka Program Manager) at Microsoft, Jonathan Marsh. A few minutes later Jonathan wrote back suggesting I replace the multiple `msxsl:node-set()` method calls (which used complex predicates) with a set of cascading tree variables (each subsequent variable was created from a variable created earlier in the code).

By the end of the day I had retooled my transform, and when I ran the same real-world data that had choked earlier, the transform completed processing in twelve to thirteen seconds and used almost no virtual memory.

I was as delighted as I had been despondent only hours before, and from this purple haze of joy emerged an object lesson: the performance and scalability of commercial software is more often brought down by pilot error than by intrinsic technical deficiency. We ask a lot from our systems. The least we can do is give those systems instructions of the greatest possible efficiency. With XSLT, when you write your transforms properly, its performance rocks.

Later in this chapter I'll show you the details of the fixes that I implemented for both these errant transforms and you, too, will have a chance to marvel at the power of XSLT.

But first, I'm going to discuss a couple of traps you can fall into when beginning your XSLT programming career and which will sap your transforms' performance drastically. Beware that, if you don't come to terms with these issues you will be plagued by them regardless of how long you code in XSLT. I taught myself to play tennis, and on the way I also taught myself many bad tennis habits. My serve was embarrassing then; it's embarrassing now. Don't let this happen to your programming career. Let's clear out the easy to make mistakes now so you will write ever better and more powerful transforms in the future.

Performance Traps

Generally, there are three inter-related errors (more specifically, three stages of performance issues) that if not caught will cut your transforms off at the knees:

- ❏ Calling a script engine (such as JavaScript) inside XSLT transforms through `<xsl:script>` or `<msxsl:script>`
- ❏ Poor XSLT design
- ❏ Poor architectural design

There are cases where script is used in place of a more appropriate XSLT domain-specific solution, and this sort of lazy XSLT design can be a very easy sin to fall into. However, bad architectural decisions are the most pernicious and most often overlooked cause of disappointing XSLT performance. All three of these problems are related, and the following sections will treat each one in turn. This chapter will suggest ways you can evaluate and optimize your programming and architectural contribution to system design to maximize performance.

Stage I: Script in Transforms

XSLT may be powerful, but it isn't omnipotent, so its designers provided XSLT with a way to "farm out" functionality to scripting engines such JScript, VBScript, or Perl. XSLT uses the `<script>` tag that can be bound to a namespace and used to invoke a scripting language. Examples of typical syntax are given below. While there are times when this feature is very useful (for example, to make use of regular expressions in XSLT), script is often counter-productive.

There are three broad reasons for the use of script in XSLT. First, sometimes even expert XSLT programmers must employ script to overcome the in-built constraints of the XSLT language. Second, programmers will resort to script in transforms because they just can't get used to thinking in terms of trees or to solving programming problems without tools such as the assignment operator. The third, and perhaps most common, justification for using script in transforms is that the programmer simply couldn't see any other way to get the job done.

Before I go on, perhaps I should explain why script can hobble a transform's performance. Script code in a transform falls under the "late-bound" category of executable code. The other category is the so-called "early-bound" application compiled from source code, such that all addresses for all functions that may be used are known and compiled into the executable. Late-bound applications, however, do not have this optimization; before calling a function a late-bound program must first "look up" the address in a lookup table. Think of early-bound applications as having a "speed dial" feature.

When a transform calls a user-defined function in a language such as ECMAScript, several things happen, and they happen every time a scripted function is called. Here's the low-down: there is overhead *each time* an Active Scripting Engine is invoked and more overhead while the scripting engine interprets the script, executes it, and passes or returns arguments. The bottom line is that your application is working its tail off in a scripting environment. Script can be very easy to implement, but the cost of this simplicity is wasted CPU cycles, which is of course detrimental to efficiency.

Surmounting XSLT Language Constraints

As you read in the introductory chapter, for most people who program the Web, XSLT offers a very different kind of programming. Encapsulating a fresh design methodology was a chief objective for the designers of the XSLT language. There are two major alternatives for XSLT programmers on coming up against missing functionality in XSLT. Firstly, they can extend the language itself, as supported by the XSLT Specification (see http://www.w3.org/TR/xslt11/#extension). Secondly, as I explain below, a transform can be extended by adding programmable components to the stylesheet within <script> elements.

Actually, XSLT programmers don't necessarily need to design the extensions themselves. Instead, they can use an XSLT parser that includes extensions missing from other XSLT parser vendors' products. For example, the SAXON parser has a whole host of extensions (see Michael Kay's *XSLT Programmer's Reference 2nd edition*, ISBN 1-861005-06-7, for details) that make it an excellent choice under certain circumstances.

Microsoft's msxml3.dll, on the other hand, limits most of its proprietary extensions to the realm of the XML processor and follows the XSLT specification pretty closely. However, Microsoft has included a feature in msxml3.dll that has tremendous potential for XSLT programmers – namely its XSLTemplate and XSLProcessor objects plus the ability for XSLT programmers working on the Windows platform to access any Component Object Model method that returns text from an XSLT transform (see *Enhancing XSL* by Kurt Cagle on http://msdn.microsoft.com/xml/articles/enhancingxsl.asp).

Both of these topics are beyond the scope of this chapter, but if you need the performance that comes by avoiding script, and if the only way to avoid script is to extend the language (either directly as with SAXON or indirectly as with Microsoft's approach), then I recommend you look further into these two alternatives before resorting to your own binary augmentation.

The Case of the Missing Operator

Another point stressed in Chapter 1, and even more strongly in Chapter 15, is that XSLT is a *declarative* programming language by nature, and so lacks an assignment operator. Ironically, an almost unconscious reliance on the assignment operator is the mark of a traditional programmer, while freedom from that same operator is the mark of a declarative programmer newly liberated by XSLT.

Declarative languages aim to specify what the computer should do, rather than the detailed procedures required to do it. The best way to keep the programmer out of processes that the computer is better qualified to manage is to withhold two of the most fundamental constructs exploited by traditional languages where the programmer calls all the shots.

The other of these missing constructs is the program variable, an address in memory that can hold dynamic data. While variables enable programmers to write powerful and flexible programs, there are side effects that programmers need to be aware of. These occur when using the same variable in two different parts of a program, and can mean that if the value is changed for the benefit of one part of the program, there may be unexpected side effects for the other part of the program.

This has been an acceptable cost for programmers to pay given the richness of code that variables allow. But in the world of XSLT, programming tasks occupy a much smaller domain. XSLT programs are interested primarily in the transformation of text, indeed, of data. Within this constrained problem, domain program variables are no longer indispensable.

Perhaps to soften the culture shock a little, the XSLT creators decided to keep the term "variable" (and the related term, "parameter"). Strictly speaking, there is an extremely limited implementation of the assignment operator; it's the one that gives an <xsl:variable> element its original value. The difference, of course, is that once set within a template, the variable cannot be reset. In this respect, variables are more like program constants.

Also, the scope of an <xsl:variable> is much more limited in XSLT than in traditional programming languages. Local scope in JScript, for example, is defined by the function. In XSLT, an <xsl:variable> declared inside a an <xsl:if> element is local only to that element. These two factors can provide some of the most vexing of the early challenges that face beginner XSLT programmers.

Most of the time, XSLT can achieve the same result through *recursion* that procedural code achieves through *assignment*. And so, where a more constrained problem domain makes program variables moot, recursion provides the way for declarative programmers to still solve a great deal of what procedural programmers are able to through the assignment operator without detracting in the slightest from the expressive power of XSLT.

By eliminating the assignment operator and its side effects, XSLT potentially offers more robust applications. In traditional programming, for example, global variables are generally discouraged because they tend to make for closely-coupled interdependent code – by changing one part of the program you can introduce unexpected changes elsewhere. Interdependent code is harder to follow and consequently more prone to errors and harder to debug. Since XSLT doesn't let you get into this mess in the first place, an entire species of bug is neatly eliminated from the XSLT programmer's world.

XSLT programs also tend to be far easier to maintain and extend, because there's less for the programmer to have to keep track of. Fixing one thing tends not to break something else. Similarly, if a new feature is added, the new feature is less likely to interfere with extant code. Pay close attention to the evolution of the Petri Net simulator in Chapter 15 and you will see all these advantages in action.

So, how does the well-informed XSLT programmer go about eliminating unnecessary script from their transform? Let's now look at one programmer's progression from a procedural to a declarative approach in programming.

From Scripted to Scriptless Transforms

When creating the MSXML plugin, an explicit goal of the Microsoft XML team was to build a parser that could take advantage of as much W3C work (from Recommendations to Notes) as possible. For this reason, the team decided to include an implementation of an Extensible Stylesheet Language in the parser. Although this work began in Internet Explorer 4.0, Microsoft's XSL wasn't really in place until Internet Explorer 5.0. Knowing how critical XSL would be for the XML parser, they felt the risks involved in shipping an implementation before the standards process was complete would be outweighed by the benefits of introducing this technology early to the programming community.

To make matters even more confusing, while Microsoft was shipping the XSL version in Internet Explorer 5.0 the W3C decided to split the development of the formatting objects of XSL (XSL-FO) into a specification separate from the transformation one that was then nearing completion. The W3C felt it was more important that the XML community start using XSLT rather than wait until both XSLT and XSL-FO were ready for release. The result was that "XSL" came to be an inclusive moniker for both these technologies, but by then Microsoft's proprietary transform engine was christened "XSL" not "XSLT" and was already shipping with Internet Explorer 5.0.

Microsoft created the Component Object Model, or COM, some years before so that (among other reasons) application developers could extend their application's functionality by the use of late-bound script. Active Server Pages is perhaps the preeminent example of the power of this extensibility. Microsoft's XML team wanted to empower users of their XML parser in the same way, especially as the XSL implementation that shipped with Internet Explorer 5.0 wouldn't be nearly as powerful as the official W3C-sanctioned version of XSLT.

Since there are many early adopters of XML who relied on XSL, let's take a look at some old XSL (in other words, scripted) stylesheets and compare them to the latest (that is, scriptless) XSLT equivalent transforms.

> *By the way, being an "old XSL" programmer myself with a collection of dozens of old XSL stylesheets representing over two year's worth of development, I need to follow a convention to keep old code separate from new: I refer to XSL files as "stylesheets" and XSLT files as "transforms", and use the .xsl and .xslt extensions to differentiate source code on the file system. Even if you yourself do not face a similar situation, closely following these examples will illustrate many of the pervasive pitfalls programmers must avoid in order to create powerful, fast, and reliable XSLT applications.*

These stylesheets and transforms are designed to render attribute-normal form XML into an HTML grid that can be filtered and sorted. You may have realized by now, especially if you have been working with XML for a while, that you could describe data using XML elements alone with no attributes, or "element-normal form XML". Active Data Objects (ADO), however, uses the opposite approach, "attribute-normal form XML", where attributes are the primary unit for conveying the data of an XML document. Early versions of the stylesheets we shall be looking at were based on Internet Explorer 5.0's XSL, so you will find these early versions necessarily rely more on script than later versions.

Although intermediate versions of the transform use far less script and enhance performance by a general policy of eliminating it, script remains in these intermediate transforms because of an assumption that a documented limitation on the XPath sum() function would necessitate reliance on script. The assumed limitation was that sum() wouldn't work if the node-list contains values that cannot be rendered as a number. As you will see shortly, a little additional application of XPath gives a predicate, or "data signature", that can deal with anomalous data. As a result, the first XSLT transform finally succeeds in being script-free and claims the distinction of being a pure XSLT solution.

Other versions of the script-free transforms go one more step and highlight a performance issue based on system architecture. These transforms employ XSLTemplate/XSLProcessor objects, and though these MS XSLT interfaces were designed for the server, simpler code allows them to reside on the client. The key to avoiding stage three performance issues, in other words bad architectural design, is to spread the processing across all tiers of an n-tier architecture, fully optimizing the performance advantages of each tier. Migrating the sample spreadsheet HTML files to ASP would be very easy since the hard part, wiring the parameters to the transform, is now already done.

In the Beginning...

In the beginning (circa early 1999) Bill (Gates) created XSL as implemented in Internet Explorer 5.0. This was probably the first time script-programmers encountered a declarative language aside from SQL. Most programmers had their hands full coming to terms with this exotic new form of programming so, in a way, it was almost a blessing that XSL wasn't as powerful as XSLT. And, since XSL supported script, XSLT-weary programmers always had something familiar to fall back on. However, this combination of a steep learning curve and provision of support for the familiar has resulted in a relatively high proportion of less efficiently written stylesheets knocking around out there.

In the following example I have included the actual comments made by the XSL programmer at design time. This makes for interesting reading, especially as with the benefit of hindsight we are all faultless programmers! First, let's see what the programmer was thinking when trying to build the stylesheet, to try to identify some common issues and misconceptions that other programmers might face. Each of these issues has a preferred solution in XSLT, and this section will conclude by mapping these several issues to their proper XSLT renditions.

The following screenshot shows the application in action – it is founded on a central XSL stylesheet that converts data fetched from a SQL database using ADO into HTML for display as a sortable/filterable table, providing totals for all numeric columns.

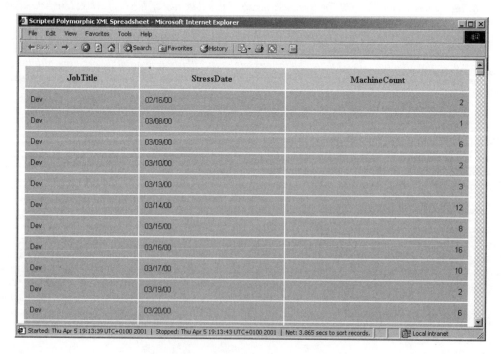

I recommend you download the entire sample code for this chapter from the Wrox web site – you will find it is organized into four sections. Of particular interest are the three folders named "scripted", "scriptfree", and "templatized" containing different versions of this XML spreadsheet. Each version evolves from its predecessor, so they all have essentially the same functionality, but later ones are more efficient. In the following paragraphs I will try to indicate the correct version of the transform and its corresponding folder.

OK, let's start with the header for this HTML table. For readers unfamiliar with ADO 2.5, an inline schema (bold text below) precedes the actual data to define the type of data in the recordset. `getADO.xml` is a typical example, abbreviated for clarity:

```xml
<xml xmlns:s='uuid:BDC6E3F0-6DA3-11d1-A2A3-00AA00C14882'
  xmlns:dt='uuid:C2F41010-65B3-11d1-A29F-00AA00C14882'
  xmlns:rs='urn:schemas-microsoft-com:rowset'
  xmlns:z='#RowsetSchema'>
  <s:Schema id='RowsetSchema'>
    <s:ElementType name='row' content='eltOnly' rs:CommandTimeout='30'>
      <s:AttributeType name='title_id' rs:number='1' rs:writeunknown='true'>
        <s:datatype
          dt:type='string'
          rs:dbtype='str'
          dt:maxLength='6'
          rs:maybenull='false'
        />
      </s:AttributeType>
      ...
    </s:ElementType>
  </s:Schema>
  <rs:data>
    <z:row title_id='PS1372'
      title='Computer Phobic AND Non-Phobic Individuals: Behavior Variations'
      type='psychology    '
      pubdate='10/21/91'
      advance='7000.0000'
      royalty='10'
      price='21.5900'
      ytd_sales='375'
      net='6190.3750'
    />
    ...
  </rs:data>
</xml>
```

The HTML table corresponding to the above XML is deceptively simple. The table's headings came from the `name` attribute of each `AttributeType` in the schema. However, the data comes from the `<rs:data>` element's children, creating the problem of binding a `<z:row>` tag to its corresponding `<s:AttributeType>` (see bold text in the XML above) so that data appears under the correct column in the HTML table. The following stylesheet's novice XSLT programmer couldn't figure out how to do this without resorting to the 'old school' technique of the associative array.

His strategy, then, was to add an element to an array for each `AttributeType` encountered in the ADO schema, as shown below in bold text in code taken from `ado3.xsl`:

```
<xsl:for-each select="xml/s:Schema/s:ElementType/s:AttributeType" >
  <!-- to enable sorting, set the ONCLICK attribute for each TH tag
       and note that the CSS style for TH is set to
       text-transform:capitalize so that the first character in the
       field names is capitalized -->
  <TH>
    <xsl:attribute name="title">Click(alt) to sort(reverse)</xsl:attribute>
    <xsl:apply-templates select="s:datatype"/>
      <xsl:value-of select="@name"/>
  </TH>

  <!-- since we can't use an XSL pattern to link the datatype element
       with the corresponding data element, make an associative array
       so that when the data element is rendered it can look to the
       array for the element with the name of the data attribute to
       get the data type -->
  <xsl:eval>copySchema()</xsl:eval>
</xsl:for-each>
```

All the script functions in this stylesheet are defined inside the `<xsl:script>` element near the end of the code, so when a function is given separately, as below, remember that in actuality it appears with all the others in a single `<xsl:script>` element.

With the exception of scripted functions, I will work through this stylesheet from top to bottom, so I really do recommend you download the source code if you can, as having it available while reading will make things clearer. The script of `copySchema()` to add an item to the array is simple:

```
<xsl:script><![CDATA[
  var index=1;
  var pageSize=4;
  var firstRow=1;
  var lastRow=3;
  var totals=new Array();
  // schema[] is used by style(), displayTotal(), and render()
  var schema=new Array();

  function copySchema()
  {
    var thisFld=this.getAttribute("name");

    schema[thisFld]=this.firstChild.getAttribute("dt:type");
  }

  ...

]]></xsl:script>
```

There's another poignant feature of this strategy in that not only is the XSL supplemented by JScript, but the JScript itself uses DOM programming techniques. As you will see later in this chapter, mixing XSLT and DOM APIs within `<script>` elements is a common and unnecessary mistake.

In the TBODY tag, appearing next in the stylesheet, the programmer uses the schema array to find the datatype of each element appearing in the table body and footer. This datatype value dictates the alignment for the text and whether or not the value is to be summed. Here is that TBODY element now:

```
<TBODY>
  <!-- this order-by argument will be captured by the grid.htm script and
       modified as the user selects fields to sort on -->
  <xsl:for-each select="xml/rs:data/z:row" order-by="nothing">

    <!-- this test argument will be captured by the grid.htm script and
         modified as the user moves forward and backward through the
         recordset n records per pass -->
    <xsl:if test="context()">

      <TR class="data">

        <!-- get each data attribute in each data row selected by the
             for-each context above -->
        <xsl:for-each select="@*">
          <TD>
          <!-- text alignment is a function of datatype, and datatype is
               now in an associative array by data attribute name (note the
               difference in technique between the following assignment of
               an new HTML attribute value and the technique used above in
               the THEAD section)-->
          <xsl:attribute name="align"><xsl:eval>style()</xsl:eval></xsl:attribute>

          <!-- the render() function converts ISO 8601 dates to formatted
               JScript dates and it formats numbers, too -->
          <xsl:eval>render()</xsl:eval>
          </TD>
        </xsl:for-each>
      </TR>
    </xsl:if>
  </xsl:for-each>
</TBODY>
```

The style() function returns the text "right" or "left" as appropriate, to use as the value of the align attribute in the stylesheet output, and is the first time the schema array is put into service.

```
function style()
{
  var thisFld=this.nodeName;
  var dt=schema[thisFld];
  if("dateTime"==dt || "int"==dt || "i8"==dt || "number"==dt)
    return "right";
  else
    return "left";
}
```

The render() function does a bit more work. Its job is to format numbers (and pass through all other data), including enclosing negative numbers in parentheses, using a built-in XSL function.

By the way, if you really insist on using script in `msxml3.dll` you will have to produce your own JScript code to replace the XSL function `formatNumber()` used here. Indeed, the XSLT transform that Microsoft provides to convert your XSL to XSLT does just this: it dumps all the `XTLRuntime`-based functions into bare JScript. All the more reason to do whatever is necessary to avoid scripting in your transforms.

```
function render()
{
  var thisFld=this.nodeName;
  var val=this.nodeValue;
  var dt=schema[thisFld];
  if("int"== dt)
    return formatNumber(val,"###,###");
  else if("i8" == dt || "number"==dt)
    if (val<0)
      return "("+formatNumber(Math.abs(val),"$###,###.00")+")";
    else
      return formatNumber(val,"$###,###.00");
  else
    return val;
}
```

Let's continue our stroll down memory lane with a brief look at the footer code for the output table:

```
<TFOOT id="gridTotals">
  <!-- sum() function rolls up the totals for each number field into an
       associative array that's used by the displayTotal() function to
       render the totals in the TFOOT section of the table -->
  <xsl:for-each select="xml/rs:data/z:row/@*">
    <xsl:eval>sum()</xsl:eval>
  </xsl:for-each>
  <TR>
    <!-- go back over the data attribute meta data and properly display
         the totals stored by the sum() function -->
    <xsl:for-each select="xml/s:Schema/s:ElementType/s:AttributeType" >
      <!-- only number values will be returned by displayTotal() so all
           cells in TFOOT can be right justified -->
      <TD align='right'>
        <!-- display formatted numbers fetched from the associative array
             created with the sum() function -->
        <xsl:eval>displayTotal()</xsl:eval>
      </TD>
    </xsl:for-each>
  </TR>
</TFOOT>
```

The first `xsl:for-each` construct sends each attribute through the `sum()` function; a waste of CPU cycles in itself. A more efficient algorithm would catch the numeric values as the `for-each` loop does its work. But since the programmer didn't know how to bind data to schema, this was the best technique he knew.

At any rate, the sum() function's purpose is to add the values of each row of numeric attributes:

```
function sum()
{
  var thisFld=this.nodeName;
  if (!isNaN(this.nodeValue))
  {
    if (isNaN(totals[thisFld]))
      totals[thisFld]=0;
    else
      totals[thisFld]+=parseFloat(this.nodeValue);
  }
}
```

and the displayTotal() function takes from the array the total computed for each addable column and displays it at the bottom of the table in the appropriate column:

```
function displayTotal()
{
  var thisFld=this.getAttribute("name");
  var val=totals[thisFld];
  if (isNaN(val)) return;
  switch (schema[thisFld])
  {
    case "int":
      mask="###,###";
      break;
    case "i8":
      mask="$###,###.00";
      break;
    case "number":
      mask="$###,###.00";
      break;
    default:
      mask="#,###.00%"
  }
  if (val<0)
    return "("+formatNumber(Math.abs(val), mask)+")";
  else
    return formatNumber(val, mask)
}
```

Recapping the Scripting Issues

So, what were the central issues for this programmer? Most important was his ignorance. Since he didn't know how to bind data to a schema he had to resort to creating an associative array, and he had to create three script functions to manage and use that array. Secondly, he had to deal with a fundamental weakness in XSL, that is the absence of XPath functions such as sum(). Also, recursion in XSL, for the purpose of summing a node-list, was not possible. With those two options offered by XSLT foreclosed to our hapless programmer, he had to resort to another array and more script to compute and display arithmetic calculations.

There is another issue worth noting about the sum() function. All numeric fields are summed, even those whose total is meaningless (for example, the Royalty column). Fixing this with script is probably not possible because the solution rests in merging incoming data with rendering decisions previously specified by the user and captured in an XML file. Subsequent views of this data would fetch these viewing preferences and display the data to the user accordingly.

A Final Warning

There's one more warning when using script in XSLT: the script is virtually impossible to debug in real time. You can't step through the code; you can't even use an alert box to display debug messages, nor the status line to assert values for variables. All script processing is performed inside the XSL processor and is completely opaque to the programmer. You're flying blind – it's not advised.

To see how hard debugging can be in XSL, explore the reason for including the following in the sum() function:

```
if (isNaN(totals[thisFld]))
   totals[thisFld]=0;
```

The Debrief

In this section our apprentice XSLT programmer ate the fruit of the Schema subtree by adding each AttributeType name attribute to an associative array called schema in the copySchema() function. This schema array is subsequently used by all other functions to look up a name attribute value and thereby determine that attribute's data type. A second associative array holds the total values for each column of the table. XML DOM API calls are made from script to navigate the DOM for attribute names and node values. This design is unnecessarily complicated (and hard to follow).

Intermediate XSLT

Now we shall move away from the early XSL implementation of Internet Explorer 5.0 and into XSLT proper. This is a good reflection of how relief comes to struggling XSLT programmers as the language matures. XSLT doesn't do a lot of things differently from XSL, but those things it does improve upon have dramatic consequences for design, implementation, and performance. This section will deal the problems of binding sub-trees and dealing with node values that cannot be converted to numbers using XSLT.

The implicit point throughout this chapter is that the more work an optimized component such as the XSLT processor can do (as opposed to the late-bound scripting engine), the faster the transform. The goal, remember, is to learn to employ sound XSLT techniques to deal with common programming problems that usually cause programmers to resort to sub-optimal script implementations unnecessarily.

Binding Subtrees

In this next intermediate version of the transform, you'll see what a difference XSLT coupled with a little understanding can make. All but the sum() function are coded without script in this version of the transform. The transform is included in this chapter, in part, because it shows how to set up an XSLT file for scripting (a technique that's different in XSL). The last transform in this section does away with the scripted sum() function altogether.

The key technique to extricate ourselves from the performance pits of the XSL version will be to connect two subtrees together with an XPath expression. We need a data signature that permits the transform to know that the `price` attribute in the data represents a number data type. Let's firstly revisit the `getADO.xml` file to remind ourselves how the `price` attribute is associated with a defined data type:

```
<xml>
  <s:Schema id='RowsetSchema'>
    <s:ElementType name='row' content='eltOnly' rs:CommandTimeout='30'>
      <s:AttributeType name='price' rs:number='7'
      rs:nullable='true' rs:writeunknown='true'>
        <s:datatype
          dt:type='number'
          rs:dbtype='currency'
          dt:maxLength='8'
          rs:precision='19'
        />
      </s:AttributeType>
    </s:Schema id='RowsetSchema'>
  <rs:data>
    <z:row title_id='PS1372'
      title='Computer Phobic AND Non-Phobic Individuals: Behavior Variations'
      type='psychology    '
      pubdate='10/21/91'
      advance='7000.0000'
      royalty='10'
      price='21.5900'
      ytd_sales='375'
      net='6190.3750'
    />
  </rs:data>
</xml>
```

This XPath expression can be used in a stylesheet to bind data to its inline ADO schema:

```
/xml/s:Schema/s:ElementType/s:AttributeType [@name=name(current())]
```

Our programmer could have achieved this with the equivalent predicate [@name = **context()!nodeName()**] using the old **XSL Patterns** notation. The key difference is in the way XSL Patterns isolates the name of the current attribute, shown in bold. It is far from intuitive, so we can forgive the programmer for overlooking this approach. Besides, since there was no equivalent function for `format-number()` in XSL, he'd have had to use script to render the formatting anyway.

Here's how this XSLT data signature works. The context iterates through each row's attribute collection so that the data signature references the name of each attribute with `name(current())`. The left side of the predicate traces a path from the root element all the way to the `AttributeType` node in the Schema sub-tree. If that node's `name` attribute equals the name of the `data` attribute, the two subtrees are bound. Now the transform can interrogate either subtree. For example, when displaying the data the transform needs to know the data type it is working on. This data signature, when appended to the predicate above, will return the data type from the inline ADO 2.5+ schema:

```
/xml/s:Schema/s:ElementType/s:AttributeType[@name=name(current())]/s:datatype
```

So this XSLT code (note the additional bold predicate) will set the `align` attribute to `"right"` for all numbers that should be displayed as currency:

```
<xsl:when
   test="/xml/s:Schema/s:ElementType/s:AttributeType
   [@name=name(current())]/s:datatype
   [@dt:type='i8' or @dt:type='number']">
   <xsl:attribute name="align">right</xsl:attribute>
   $<xsl:value-of select="format-number(.,'#,##0.00')" />
</xsl:when>
```

There now, isn't that better than all that script? This is the power of XSLT. Seventy-eight lines of procedural code vanish. Along with its disappearance go all manner of maintenance and extension issues. The resulting (self-describing) data becomes its own program processed by a blazingly fast XSLT processor.

Now we need to resolve the summing problem.

A Robust sum() Function Call

Earlier in this chapter our misguided, if well-intentioned, XSLT programmer used an associative array to store the sum of all instances of each attribute in the data section of the XML file. The sum was computed using XML DOM API calls. This is not very efficient and is probably not a strategy that would scale well.

In the previous section you learned how to bind data instances to the appropriate metadata for that instance in the schema. But how does XSLT handle empty data? That is, what happens if a given attribute is not in some row? Can XSLT still total the node-list for the given attribute? And what happens if the attribute is present, but it has no data; it's an empty string (not the same thing as a null value – a concept that's foreign to XML)? Finally, how does XSLT handle "corrupt" data (data that's not what its metadata claims it to be – for example, an alphabetic character instead of a numerical digit)?

Left to its own devices, for the most part XSLT dodges the issue. If it finds data that it cannot coerce to a numeric type, it effectively stops processing the node-list because adding any character to a subtotal returns "NaN" (standing for "not a number") and any number then added to "NaN" will also return "NaN".

One thing to do is to be more precise in your instructions. Even though you can't manually preprocess a node-list before you try to sum it, you can provide the `sum()` function with a data signature that filters out troublesome values for you.

In the spreadsheet the totaling process iterates the schema, not the data. This is because sums are only computed on numeric data types. Recall from the scripted spreadsheet that all data attributes (note the "@*" employed in the data signature below) are "summed", but only sums with actual values (sums computed on numeric, not string values) would be displayed.

```
<xsl:for-each select="xml/rs:data/z:row/@*">
   <xsl:eval>sum()</xsl:eval>
</xsl:for-each>
```

The efficiency of this strategy is inversely proportional to the number of string values in the data, itself directly affected by the number of rows of data.

However, now that we've bound our data to a schema we can reverse the strategy and iterate through a much smaller data space (the schema) to identify those attribute names whose data type is numeric. For each of these, the transform calls a template that computes the sum of the data for attributes with that name, in other words those matching the XPath expression `current()/@name`.

```
<xsl:when test="@dt:type='number'">
  <xsl:value-of select="sum(/root/row/@*[name()=current()/@name])" />
</xsl:when>
```

But we also need to limit this node-list to include only those values that can be cast to a numeric value, so we add another filter to this step. The XPath expression to do this attempts to convert the node value first to a number, then to a string. The expression then admits only those nodes that do not return "NaN". Here's a modified version of the expression incorporating this change in bold:

```
<xsl:when test="@dt:type='number'">
  $<xsl:value-of select= sum(/root/row/@*[name()=current()/@name]
    [string(number(.))!='NaN'] )" />
</xsl:when>
```

Finally, we wrap the whole operation in the `format-number()` XPath function to format these totals:

```
<xsl:when test="@dt:type='number'">
  $<xsl:value-of select= "format-number( sum(/root/row/@*[name()=
    current()/@name] [string(number(.))!='NaN'] ), '#,##0.00' )" />
</xsl:when>
```

To see three design strategies in action on the same data, type the following line into Internet Explorer: http://<your server/your vroot>/scriptfree/spreadsheet.htm, ensuing you have first placed the relevant files from the download in your local host's root folder. The sample can process either SQLXML or ADO data; note also how non-numeric values appear in the table, and how the different strategies handle them (or not, as the case may be). I shall leave modifying the behavior of the template in spreadsheet1.xslt to bypass the non-numeric data as an exercise for the reader, though here's a tip: you won't actually have to modify the total template itself to get it to properly sum the Advance column.

Again, the task of the human programmer is to accurately tell the computer what to compute and how to format it. As a declarative language, XSLT takes it from there and does the tricky stuff itself. This verges on actual magic.

Minimize the Performance Impact of Script

As you have now seen, the XML application that forms the subject of this chapter can be written without a single user-defined function in script. Other applications may not be so accommodating, and you may find that sometimes there is absolutely no alternative but to extend your transform with script. If you find yourself in this situation there is one thing you can do to minimize the overhead imposed by invoking a scripting engine to marshal parameters and interpret the script.

Have a look at this particularly naïve implementation of script:

```
<xsl:value-of select="user:doSomething(.)"/>
<xsl:for-each
  select="someNodeList[@someAttrib = user:doSomething (.)]">
  ...
</xsl:for-each>
```

This code block would be *n*-1 times more inefficient (where n was the number of nodes in someNodeList) than the following alternative:

```
<xsl:variable name="somethingDone" select="user:doSomething (.)"/>
<xsl:value-of select="$ somethingDone "/>
<xsl:for-each select="a[@b = $ somethingDone]">...</xsl:for-each>
```

Now the scripted function, user:doSomething(.), is called once only, and the results are stored in the XSLT variable somethingDone. The rest of the transform uses that optimized data structure instead of making repeated calls to the scripting engine.

> **Note: this technique can't be used with the old Microsoft XSL in Internet Explorer 5.0 because it lacks support for variables.**

Recap of Stage I Performance Issues

That just about wraps it up for my advice on avoiding or at least minimizing the performance hit scripting engines exact upon your transforms. Before I continue on to Stage II performance issues that highlight problems arising from bad XSLT design, I shall summarize the main points of this first section.

Best practices for avoiding Stage I performance issues:

❑ Script hurts performance because there's a great deal of extra processing when an XSLT processor has to delegate to one or more scripting engines. **Avoid script at all costs if your XSLT performance is more important than ease of programming**.

❑ **Avoid script by using XPath expressions** (data signatures). XPath is a tricky language to learn, similar in difficulty and power to Regular Expressions. If you are relentless in your pursuit of XPath enlightenment you will be able to use data signatures in place of scripted functions that apply the XML DOM. XPath can be extremely powerful and highly reusable, so be an avid collector of useful data signatures. Treat those data signatures as a corporate asset; they're every bit as powerful as business rules are for the middle tier.

❑ **Don't believe everything you read in the XSLT literature**. The best example of this trap is the sum() function. If you try to use sum() on a node-list that may contain string data (or any data that cannot be coerced to numeric) you will get the useless result "NaN". But use of this predicate in the sum() method's argument , [string(number(.))!='NaN'], means you can sidestep this to always return a numeric result.

❑ When all else fails, **call a script once and put its result in an XSLT variable** whenever possible, then use that XSLT variable later in your transform rather than repeating the script call. This minimizes the performance penalty incurred by calling a scripting engine.

This first main section has focused on why script hurts and how to avoid or minimize the pain. The next main section takes up Stage II performance issues that arise from bad XSLT design. By the end of the next section this chapter's underlying sample application, the XML spreadsheet, will not only have some extra features, but it will outperform the scriptless version of the spreadsheet we have just seen.

You will also see how easy it can be to get into trouble when you start working on XSLT designs that are a little out of your depth. As you read the next section I want you to keep the following thought near the front of your mind: if one of your XSLT transforms doesn't perform, assume pilot error before concluding that XSLT doesn't scale. If you do this then, like me, I am sure you will often be pleasantly surprised and will avoid wasting a lot of work by throwing code away that would work well with just a few tweaks in the right places.

Stage II: Bad Design, Feature Creep, and Ambition

Bad design is, sadly, all too easy. Two things conspire with the dark side of the programmer's nature to create programs that, for all their good intentions, fail to perform. They are **feature creep** and **ambition**, both close relatives and drinking buddies. The XML spreadsheet you've seen so far is a foster child of this troublesome pair. Flushed with the success and almost universal acclaim this simple piece of programming produced, our intrepid programmer felt empowered and glowed with hubris. Then a new customer came along with an intriguing requirement: render the spreadsheet as a **sparse matrix**. That is, display cell values only when they are different from preceding cells, thus making the spreadsheet easier to use, for there would be less for the eye to take in. "Less is more", argued our customer persuasively. Even more persuasive was the large sack of cash he carried. "Hey, I can do that, no problem!" retorted our immodest programmer like a shot.

I think you can see now how ambition sires feature creep. Well, after a few days' work, sure enough, the sparse matrix spreadsheet was finished and working ... as long as you didn't throw too much data at it that is. When it comes to memory, bad design is insatiable; and memory is a real, very *limited*, commodity. Bad designs can dispatch more RAM in a few minutes than was even available to developers five years ago.

So let's look at the new spreadsheet code to see what went so wrong, and how our contrite programmer made it right.

How to Do Less with More

All the spreadsheets in this chapter do pretty much the same thing: they display hierarchical XML data in the rectangular format of an HTML table. It's just that some of the transforms (those in the "templatized" folder of the code download for this chapter) provide this service faster than others. So now we shall continue our journey and study the next phase in the application's evolution.

The first of this batch of transforms is the sparseSlow.xslt file (note the .xslt file extension indicating that this is a true XSLT transform, not an IE 5.0 XSL stylesheet). As its name suggests, the transform is the slowest of the fully XSLT code examples. In fact, if you use the hugeData.xml file included in the code download as the data source you will bring the spreadsheet practically to its knees. Even with a data file like advance2.xml, the sparseSlow.xslt code remains two orders of magnitude slower than transforms like sparseOptimized.xslt. Let's take a closer look at how sparseSlow.xslt works, or doesn't, as the case may be.

Before we look at the sickly XSLT itself, let's consider the symptoms. On a laptop with 196MB of RAM using an x86 Family 6 Model 6 Stepping 10 processor, running sparseSlow.xslt on 1,229 nodes of XML data in bigData.xml takes 10 seconds (the later versions, sparseFaster.xslt and sparseOptimized.xslt, provide the same functionality yet require a mere 0.10 seconds or less). Oh, and each time you page through the 1,229 rows of the spreadsheet you incur this 10 second delay, regardless of the page size you have specified. If you're really daring, try sparseSlow.xslt with hugeData.xml just to stretch its weak algorithm even further.

> The sample code for this section is in the "templatized" folder along with the
> `spreadsheet.htm` file to let you choose from five different XSLT transforms and
> three different data files. But beware! As the purpose of this section is to highlight the
> impact of performance on large files, `hugeData.xml` contains over 7,000 nodes.

Much of the `sparseSlow` transform remains the same as its scripted predecessors. The difference is in
how the body of the spreadsheet is rendered – all the transforms in this section render data in the table
only when the data is different from data that has already appeared. For example, only the first row of
the `JobTitle` column has any data (all other rows share the value "Dev").

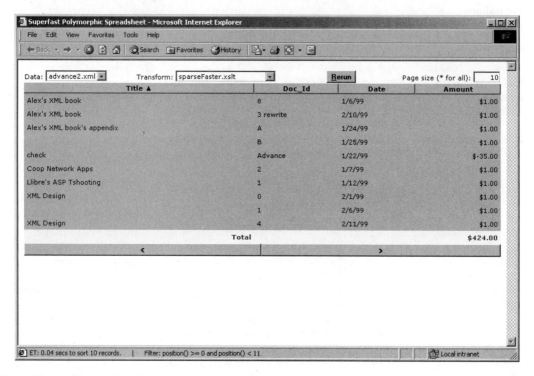

Now follows the template that is called first from `sparseSlow.xslt`, using bold text to indicate the
main differences from previous versions. The bold code appearing in the body determines whether or
not current data has previously appeared.

```
<xsl:template match="xml">
  <xsl:for-each select="rs:data/z:row">
    <xsl:sort select="@*[name()=$field]" order="{$order}"
              data-type="{$dataType}"/>
    <xsl:variable name="fsAttribs" select="following-sibling::z:row[1]/@*"/>
    <xsl:variable name="psAttribs" select="preceding-sibling::z:row[1]/@*"/>
    <xsl:variable name="rPos" select="position()"/>
    <xsl:variable name="rowClass" select="position() mod 2"/>
    <xsl:if
      test="position() &gt;= $lowerBound and position() &lt; $upperBound">
      <tr class="data{$rowClass}" title="data{$rowClass}">
      <xsl:for-each select="@*">
```

```
            <td>
            <xsl:choose>
              <xsl:when
                test="/xml/s:Schema/s:ElementType/s:AttributeType
                [@name=name(current())][s:datatype/@dt:type='int' or
                s:datatype/@dt:type='i2' or s:datatype/@dt:type='r4']">
                <xsl:attribute name="align">right</xsl:attribute>
                <xsl:value-of select="format-number(.,'#,##0')" />
              </xsl:when>
              <xsl:when
                test="/xml/s:Schema/s:ElementType/s:AttributeType
                [@name=name(current())][s:datatype/@dt:type='i8'
                or s:datatype/@dt:type='number']">
                <xsl:attribute name="align">right</xsl:attribute>
                $<xsl:value-of select="format-number(.,'#,##0.00')" />
              </xsl:when>
              <xsl:otherwise>
                <xsl:variable name="pos" select="position()"/>
                <xsl:variable name="preAttribs" select="parent::z:row[1]/@*"/>
                <xsl:choose>
                <xsl:when test="$rPos=1" >
                  <xsl:value-of select="current()" />
                </xsl:when>
                <xsl:otherwise>
                  <xsl:call-template name="display">
                    <xsl:with-param name="pos" select="$pos"/>
                    <xsl:with-param name="psAttribs" select="$psAttribs"/>
                    <xsl:with-param name="preAttribs" select="$preAttribs"/>
                  </xsl:call-template>
                </xsl:otherwise>
                </xsl:choose>
              </xsl:otherwise>
            </xsl:choose>
            </td>
          </xsl:for-each>
          </tr>
        </xsl:if>
      </xsl:for-each>
    </xsl:template>
```

The code in the inner otherwise clause calls the named template display that's causing all the trouble and slowing everything down. This template is a wholly new approach to that in previous spreadsheet transforms. It appears next in sparseSlow.xslt:

```
<xsl:template name="display">
  <xsl:param name="pos"/>
  <xsl:param name="psAttribs"/>
  <xsl:param name="preAttribs"/>

  <xsl:variable name="lastSib" select="$preAttribs[$pos - 1]"/>
  <xsl:variable name="lastCous" select="$psAttribs[$pos - 1]"/>
  <xsl:variable name="lastSibs" select="$preAttribs[position() &lt; $pos]"/>
  <xsl:variable name="lastCousins" select="$psAttribs[position() &lt; $pos]"/>
```

```
<xsl:choose>
  <xsl:when test="$psAttribs[$pos]=$preAttribs[$pos]">
    <xsl:call-template name="display">
      <xsl:with-param name="pos" select="$pos - 1"/>
      <xsl:with-param name="psAttribs" select="$lastCousins"/>
      <xsl:with-param name="preAttribs" select="$lastSibs"/>
    </xsl:call-template>
  </xsl:when>
  <xsl:otherwise>
    <xsl:if test="$pos &gt; 0">
      <xsl:value-of select="."/>
    </xsl:if>
  </xsl:otherwise>
</xsl:choose>
</xsl:template>
```

Static Code Analysis

Static code analysis is an important technique in the software tester's repertoire. It comes in a variety of flavors from the rigorous code reviews of cleanroom software engineering and other design-based disciplines, to the informal self reviews conducted by the programmer, to the automated analysis of source code by test programs.

The sparseSlow.xslt transform is the central design for this section of the chapter. I made several improvements to sparseSlow.xslt in order for it to process large XML trees more efficiently. The first performance enhancement comes simply from searching for multiple occurrences of each of the XSL variables defined in the transform. Very often, to determine a node set for a variable, all data in the tree will be scanned, so eliminating any wasted scans is vital to good performance, therefore always think carefully about any variable you define. In traditional programming, unused variables are extremely common because they are generally harmless, but in XSLT, variables can contain whole XML files. They can be far from trivial.

Think of it this way: what's worse than closing a business that's losing money? Closing one you only *think* is losing money, when in reality it transpires that the 'lost' money is in fact due to incompetent accounting. So what's worse than throwing away a sophisticated transform that consumes too much memory or time? Throwing away one that's wasting that memory or time without adding any value to the transform, and so could be salvaged.

So what did I find while searching for all uses of each variable? Here it is, the first variable declared during the template that builds the body of the spreadsheet:

```
<xsl:variable name="fsAttribs" select="following-sibling::z:row[1]/@*"/>
```

Early designs of this transform experimented with the following-sibling axis instead of the preceding-sibling axis. When the latter was settled on as the preferred axis, evidently not all traces of the previous experiments were excised. This oversight was adding an additional 10% to the processing time.

Variables can be extremely powerful, as you will see throughout the rest of this chapter, so use them aggressively, but, as in life, temper your good intentions with wisdom.

In the `sparseSlow` transform the `fsAttribs` variable stores the first `following-sibling` of each attribute in each row of XML data. The cost on a simple XML tree like `bidData.xml` is fairly low but at 3,687 "cells" of XML data, clearly measurable.

One final point emphasizing the importance of static code analysis: the orphan variable noted above was found in `sparseOptimized.xslt` because that transform was copied from an early version of `sparseFaster.xslt`. This kind of "notepad inheritance" is dangerous because defective code, like defective genes, can be inherited.

The Second Performance Improvement

The second performance improvement comes a few lines later (and we haven't even reached the display template yet), and it's a big one. After you're sure all your variables are being used (and you're also sure there isn't a design that could avoid them altogether), your final check during static code analysis should be to confirm that the variables are created "just in time".

For example, a common way to improve the performance of an application is to improve its perceived performance. The spreadsheet does this by only processing a subset of the data at one time. The `bigData.xml` file has over 1,000 nodes (and `hugeData.xml` has over 7,000), but the reader can only fit around twenty-five on the screen at once. Instead of rendering all the data and making the user scroll vertically through it, the spreadsheet uses "horizontal" scrolling through successive pages of data, as if reading a book.

If you look carefully in `sparseSlow.xslt` at the template matching all XML tags, you will see that variables are all being created *before* the data is filtered into the pages. This is the main reason performance on `sparseSlow.xslt` is so ... well, slow. We scan all the data each time the transform is called; and remember, it's called every time the user moves the data page forward or back.

Merely moving the `<if>` tag before the variables significantly reduces the amount of data scanned, yielding performance gains inversely proportional to chosen page size and of up to 100 times. The benefits are even greater for `hugeData.xml`, cutting 254 seconds down to 0.45 seconds – over 500 times faster. Here's the optimized spreadsheet transform `sparseOptimized.xslt`, followed by a detailed discussion of the emboldened text:

```
<xsl:template name = "displayBody">
  <xsl:variable name = "pk" select="msxsl:node-set($distinctTree)/distinct/*"/>
  <xsl:variable name = "rowRange"
    select = "$rows[position() &gt;= $lowerBound and
    position() &lt; $upperBound]"
  />
  <xsl:for-each select = "$pk">
    <xsl:variable name = "pkVal" select = "."/>
    <xsl:for-each select = "$attribs">
      <xsl:variable name = "fieldIndex" select = "position()"/>
      <xsl:variable name = "fieldName" select = "@name"/>
      <xsl:if test = "name($pkVal) = $fieldName">
        <xsl:variable name = "curRows"
          select = "$rowRange[@*[$fieldIndex]=$pkVal]"
        />
        <tr style = "background-color:lightsteelblue">
          <td><xsl:number value = "position() + $rowMultiplier"/></td>
          <td><xsl:value-of select = "$pkVal"/></td>
          <xsl:for-each select = "$curRows[1]/@*[name()!=$fieldName]">
```

```
            <xsl:call-template name = "displayValue">
              <xsl:with-param name = "val" select="."/>
              <xsl:with-param
                name = "dt"
                select = "$attribs[@name=name(current())]/s:datatype/@dt:type"
              />
            </xsl:call-template>
          </xsl:for-each>
        </tr>
        <xsl:for-each select = "$curRows[position()>1]">
        <tr>
          <td><xsl:number value = "position() + $rowMultiplier + 1"/></td>
          <td></td>
          <xsl:for-each select = "@*[name()!=$fieldName]">
            <xsl:call-template name = "displayValue">
              <xsl:with-param name = "val" select = "."/>
              <xsl:with-param
                name = "dt"
                select = "$attribs[@name=name(current())]/s:datatype/@dt:type"
              />
            </xsl:call-template>
          </xsl:for-each>
        </tr>
        </xsl:for-each>
      </xsl:if>
    </xsl:for-each>
  </xsl:for-each>
</xsl:template>
```

You may have noticed that I reinvested some of the performance savings from the data page into creating a line-numbering column in the spreadsheet, with the final bold line of code above.

The lesson here is to use XSLT the way you would use a big database server: keep most of the data hidden until it's needed. Before I discuss the third performance improvement made to sparseOptimized.xslt I want to make a secondary point about the similarity I'm drawing here between XSLT and RDBMS. Many XSLT developers get this trick of just-in-time data management back to front. That is, they continue to use the database server to feed chunks of data to the client, instead of caching a large data set on the client itself and using a client process to chunk data to the screen. The combination of the power of XML as self-describing data and the efficiency of filtering XML data with XSLT makes over-reliance on database servers a thing of the past.

I will now complete this discussion of XSLT technique by focusing on improving the performance of your XSLT applications by taking a group-based approach to building the sparse matrix output sketched out in the displayBody template of sparseOptimized.xslt above.

The Third Performance Improvement

Now I'll take a closer look at the actual algorithm used by sparseOptimized.xslt to generate the sparse matrix. As you will see a little later, clarity should be considered a highly prized feature of your software (clean is simple, and simple is good). The "cousins" and "siblings" used in sparseSlow.xslt worked, for the most part, but looking at the template now makes me wonder how the algorithm was ever conceived in the first place. Surely there must be a simpler technique?

The "grouping problem" in XSLT is one of the trickiest to solve. Given my success in improving the project with which I opened this chapter, I was optimistic that an application of cascading tree variables could provide the same sparse matrix output but with more lucid code.

The first step in using the cascading tree variable technique is to generate a node-list of distinct values. Here's what sparseOptimized.xslt uses. The distinctTree variable below is used by the displayBody template, and consists of a call to the distinct template printed next.

```
<xsl:variable name="distinctTree">
  <xsl:call-template name="distinct">
    <xsl:with-param name="field" select="$field"/>
  </xsl:call-template>
</xsl:variable>
```

```
<xsl:template name="distinct">
  <xsl:param name="field"/>
  <xsl:variable
      name="filteredRows"
      select="$rows[position() &gt;= $lowerBound and
              position() &lt; $upperBound]"
  />
  <xsl:variable name="sorted">
    <sorted>
      <xsl:for-each select="$filteredRows">
        <xsl:sort select="@*[name()=$field]"/>
        <xsl:copy>
          <xsl:value-of select="@*[name()=$field]"/>
        </xsl:copy>
      </xsl:for-each>
    </sorted>
  </xsl:variable>
  <xsl:for-each select="msxsl:node-set($sorted)/sorted">
    <distinct>
      <xsl:for-each select="z:row">
        <xsl:if test="position()=1 or preceding-sibling::z:row[1] != .">
          <xsl:element name="{$field}"><xsl:value-of select="."/></xsl:element>
        </xsl:if>
      </xsl:for-each>
    </distinct>
  </xsl:for-each>
</xsl:template>
```

The distinct template accepts the name of a field then sorts that field and filters out redundant data. Voilà, a distinct list.

Did you notice a little trick? Computing a distinct list for a large file (even one as small as bigData.xml) will take a noticeable amount of time. The same logic that suggests we determine data for display just-in-time suggests we create a distinct clause in a similar fashion. So the distinct list is taken from the number of nodes within the pre-filtered range of position() values. This trick, of course, is not always required, so should you use this technique yourself you can leave out the filteredRows variable, replacing it with the data signature of your XML file. The rest of the distinct template is reusable just as it is.

The displayBody template of sparseOptimized.xslt uses this distinct list by creating a variable named pk (for "primary key"). The template iterates through this list of names comparing the names to those held in the second variable created by the displayBody template, rowRange. The rowRange variable contains the subtree of data currently on the logical page of data visible to the user.

To make this easier to follow, I've copied the gist of the underlying XML file below:

```
<s:Schema id="RowsetSchema">
  <s:ElementType name="row" content="eltOnly" rs:CommandTimeout="30">
    <s:AttributeType
      name="JobTitle"
      rs:number="1"
      rs:writeunknown="true">
      <s:datatype
        dt:type="string"
        rs:dbtype="str"
        dt:maxLength="15"
        rs:maybenull="false"
      />
    </s:AttributeType>
    <s:AttributeType
      name="Alias"
      rs:number="2"
      rs:writeunknown="true">
      <s:datatype
        dt:type="string"
        rs:dbtype="str"
        dt:maxLength="10"
        rs:maybenull="false"
      />
    </s:AttributeType>
    <s:AttributeType
      name="Machines"
      rs:number="3" rs:nullable="true"
      rs:writeunknown="true">
      <s:datatype
        dt:type="int"
        dt:maxLength="4"
        rs:precision="10"
        rs:fixedlength="true"
      />
    </s:AttributeType>
    <s:extends type="rs:rowbase"/>
  </s:ElementType>
</s:Schema>
<rs:data>
```

```
    <z:row JobTitle="Dev" Alias="a-willip" Machines="2"/>
    <z:row JobTitle="Dev" Alias="ABEYER" Machines="1"/>
    <z:row JobTitle="Dev" Alias="ABEYER" Machines="1"/>
    <z:row JobTitle="Lab" Alias="vladr" Machines="2"/>
    <z:row JobTitle="Lab" Alias="vladr" Machines="2"/>
    <z:row JobTitle="Other" Alias="administra" Machines="1"/>
    <z:row JobTitle="Other" Alias="administra" Machines="1"/>
    <z:row JobTitle="UE" Alias="miclariv" Machines="1"/>
  </rs:data>
```

From this <data> element occurring at the end, the transform would create the following list of values in the pk variable: Dev, Lab, Other, UE. It would also have the eight rows of data in the rowRange variable. It would then iterate through the pk list of values and the three attributes in the attribs variable. When it finds an attribute with a name matching a pk value's name (for example, the JobTitles attribute name matches the name of the "Dev" node in the pk variable) the template creates another variable of rows. These new rows are included in the variable only when the attribute of interest has the pk's value. For example, with the "Dev" pk value, this would be the first attribute. Out of the eight rows of data, this operation thus fetches the first three rows.

The rest of the template has two jobs that are easy by comparison. First, display all the attributes for the first row of this subset of data, then skip the pk attribute and print all the values of the remaining attributes. If you notice, the pk value is printed separately; in one case the first line of a group is printed and in the other the rest of the group's rows are printed. In both instances, it uses the same data signature; one that excludes the pk value from the selection. This is the basic principle of the grouping mechanism.

The call to the displayValue template exists primarily to abstract the rendering of numeric data from string data. The displayValue template has parameters consisting of the value of the attribute to print and a data signature pointing into the inline data type schema.

Recap of Stage II Performance Issues

I hope this section was fairly straightforward. The guidelines for building efficient designs are at least easy to articulate, even though they are endlessly challenging to implement. Before I close the chapter with a brief discussion of the impact of architectural decisions on XSLT performance, I will restate the three guidelines now:

Best practices for avoiding stage II performance issues:

❏ **Be sure not to create redundant variables**. Use static code analysis to confirm that every declared XSLT variable is used at least once in the transform.

❏ **Create a variable just before it's required**, especially important as the node count of your XML data increases. A corollary is to ship as much data to the client from the server as possible; hide most of that data, and display just a subset at a time.

❏ **Create variables from a minimal number of nodes**. This guideline is a complement of the one just given and covers the classic case of a distinct list of values: when the node-list is large, break it up into smaller chunks and create a distinct list from the smaller subset.

Stage III: Bad Architecture

OK, so far we've covered performance hits resulting from script in transforms and other bad XSLT design issues. In the sparseOptimized transform you saw the use of a very straightforward technique for generating a distinct list replacing the more convoluted preceding-sibling navigation. Both techniques produced the same outcome, a sparse matrix spreadsheet, but the tree variable-based sparseOptimized transform was twice as efficient as sparseSlow.xslt.

If it wasn't for msxsl:node-set() and tree variables you'd have to work a whole lot harder to produce a distinct list. Traditionally, generating a distinct list required two chained transformations in script on the server or the client. Each of those separate transforms is implemented in one transform and without any script in the optimized transform. The following file, ChainedTransformations.htm, demonstrates a typical example of producing a distinct list of node values using this other method.

```
<HTML>
<HEAD>
<META NAME="GENERATOR" Content="Microsoft Visual Studio 6.0">
<TITLE>Chained Transformations Demo</TITLE>
<SCRIPT LANGUAGE="javascript">
<!--
window.onload=init;
function init()
{
  data2=data.cloneNode(false);
  data2.async=false;
  data.transformNodeToObject(sort.documentElement, data2);
  alert(data2.transformNode(distinct.documentElement));
  output.innerText=data2.xml
}
//-->
</SCRIPT>

</HEAD>
<BODY>

<P id="output"></P>
<xml src="../templatized/bigData.xml" id="data"></xml>
<xml src="sort.xslt" id="sort"></xml>
<xml src="distinct.xslt" id="distinct"></xml>
</BODY>
</HTML>
```

And now see the two transforms referred to in the last two <xml> elements, sort.xslt:

```
<xsl:stylesheet
   version="1.0"
   xmlns:xsl="http://www.w3.org/1999/XSL/Transform"
   xmlns:rs='urn:schemas-microsoft-com:rowset'
   xmlns:z='#RowsetSchema'
   exclude-result-prefixes="xsl rs z"


>
<xsl:output method="xml" indent="yes"/>
```

```
<xsl:template match="/">
  <sorted>
  <xsl:for-each select="xml/rs:data/z:row">
    <xsl:sort select="@JobTitle"/>
    <item>
      <xsl:value-of select="@JobTitle"/>
    </item>
  </xsl:for-each>
  </sorted>
</xsl:template>

</xsl:stylesheet>
```

and `distinct.xslt`:

```
<xsl:stylesheet version="1.0"
                xmlns:xsl="http://www.w3.org/1999/XSL/Transform" >
<xsl:output method="xml" indent="yes"/>

<xsl:template match="/">
  <distinct>
    <xsl:for-each select="sorted/item">
      <xsl:if test="position()=1 or preceding-sibling::item[1] != .">
        <item><xsl:value-of select="."/></item>
      </xsl:if>
    </xsl:for-each>
  </distinct>
</xsl:template>

</xsl:stylesheet>
```

So, the tree variable approach is clearer, easier to implement, and more flexible and reusable than this approach that hard wires the file dependencies.

Recap of Stage III Performance Issues

You have already seen the trade-off between overhead in setting up variables and the subsequent efficiency they can yield when properly implemented. A similar trade-off generally applies for client server architectures.

Here are the basic rules:

❑ **Squeeze as much work into as few transforms as possible**.

❑ As noted at the end of the previous section, **cache large data sets on the client, but keep most of it hidden from the user** until it's absolutely necessary to dispense it. Pages of viewed data are similar to cursors of fetched data on the server.

❑ **Find the sweet spot between reducing requests to the database server and overloading the client**.

❑ **Use OLAP data** (SQL queries persisted as XML files) whenever possible to minimize impact on the database server. And when you query a database server for XML, be sure you sort it coming off the server. This way you may be able to skip the sort variable in the template that produced a distinct list of node values earlier in the chapter.

Also, when using Microsoft's `msxml3.dll`:

❑ Cache compiled transforms if they are to be used repeatedly (as with the spreadsheet when they are invoked every time the user requests a page of data).

❑ Maximize the power of the server by caching ASP transforms with the use of application scope for `XSLTemplate` and `XSLProcessor` objects. `XSLProcessor` has the added advantage of efficiently passing parameters to the transform. All the transforms in the "templatized" folder of sample code for this chapter uses these XSLT interfaces. By moving them to an ASP page the spreadsheet would be available to less capable browsers.

❑ Use the Microsoft XSL ISAPI 2 (for native code) or the new .NET Mobile Controls (for managed code) to get even more power from the XSLT interfaces and the new .NET classes. Both technologies are available on the http://msdn.microsoft.com web site although be warned that they are beta code and therefore subject to change.

The After Dinner Anecdote

Returning to our little story at the beginning of this chapter, and again, keeping the private details private, let's take a look at how a single strategic change in design saved an XSLT application from an ignoble end.

When programmers teach themselves a new technique they often don't fully understand it and can easily find themselves in trouble. In this chapter and elsewhere in the book, you've seen how powerful tree variables can be, as long as your XSLT processor supports them, as `msxml3.dll` does. As I mentioned early in the chapter, when I first encountered tree variables, they revolutionized my thinking of transforms, but initially I misused them out of ignorance and lack of imagination and was actually on the verge of abandoning the design.

Here's what I did wrong. My XML schema was fairly hierarchical and I visualized the XML data much like a tree view control in a file system. However, the visualization of data was only half the overhead. My transform needed to do some pretty tricky updating of old XML data with new, and in my first attempt at using the tree variable I essentially used the same data signature each time I created a variable. For example, here's the data signature for the first variable:

```
<xsl:variable name="fileGroup" select="msxsl:node-set($root)/root/
  problem[path=$pathName]/file" />
```

and here's the next one:

```
<xsl:variable name="problemGroup" select="msxsl:node-set($root)/root/
  problem[path=$pathName] [file=$fileName]/probId" />
```

and here's another (there were others, but you get the picture):

```
<xsl:variable name="lineGroup" select="msxsl:node-set($root)/root/
  problem[path=$pathName] [file=$fileName][probId=$probId] [context=
  $contextName]/line" />
```

This is a variation on the "notepad inheritance" I talked about earlier. Again, I just copied and pasted each data signature as I progressed down the XML schema. This worked fine on test data, but died a slow and embarrassing death, consuming 480MB of virtual memory over a six minute interval.

The following replacements resurrected the transform allowing it to complete the entire processing of 5,000 nodes in about 15 seconds without the use of any virtual memory.

Here are the first two lines of the main part of the transform:

```
<xsl:variable
  name="problems"
  select="msxsl:node-set($root)/root/problem[path=$pathName]"
/>
<xsl:variable
  name="fileGroup"
  select="$problems/file"
/>
```

I followed this same pattern of creating new data signatures by extending rather than simply copying preceding data signatures for all such expressions in the transform, earning myself a very happy boss into the bargain. I was happy too.

Some Surprises

Among the more rewarding things about working in the world of transforms are the surprises along the way. While writing this chapter there were several in store for me. For a start, scripted transforms didn't hurt performance as much as expected: the difference between baseline (setting aside the perverse versions) and optimized versions was less than expected. However, it was far easier to get orders of magnitude performance gains than I had expected, and certainly easier than squeezing performance out of more traditional procedural code. Moving an <xsl:if> element up three lines gave two to three orders of magnitude performance gains or better, depending on XML data size.

Another big surprise I found was that using a filtered <xsl:for-each> was slower than using an <xsl:if> tag to implement the filter. Here's how sparseFaster.xslt, supposedly the better technique for invoking a template, calls the template that displays its spreadsheet body:

```
<xsl:apply-templates select="xml/rs:data/z:row[position() &gt;= $lowerBound and
  position() &lt; $upperBound]" >
  <xsl:sort select="@*[name()=$field]" order="{$order}" data-type=
    "{$dataType}" />
</xsl:apply-templates>
```

And this is how sparseSlowImproved.xslt performs the same task:

```
<xsl:apply-templates select="xml"/>

<xsl:template match="xml">
  <xsl:for-each select="rs:data/z:row">
    <xsl:sort select="@*[name()=$field]" order="{$order}" data-type=
      "{$dataType}" />
    <xsl:if test="position() &gt;= $lowerBound and position() &lt; $upperBound">
      ...
    </xsl:if>
```

Try it yourself. Run `sparseFaster.xslt` (on my test machine this took a hair over 11 seconds), and then run `sparseSlowImproved.xslt` (the same machine ran this 20% faster).

This was surprising because it seems to conflict with the conventional wisdom, not to mention other Wrox authors ... this might be accounted for by the fact that `sparseFaster.xslt` repeatedly calls another template and `sparseSlowImproved.xslt` makes one call to its template with all filtering taking place there. On the other hand if `sparseSlowImproved.xslt` is changed to use the complex predicate in the `<xsl:for-each>` element as used in `sparseFaster.xslt`, `sparseSlowImproved.xslt` lost all advantage, coming in at a shade over 11 seconds.

Oh, and I found it disarmingly easy to get into serious trouble. In one case failing to remove one line of code did no harm to the transform; it still worked as designed, but the orphan XSLT element exacted a 10% performance penalty. Placement of elements was also crucial. In both the case of the misplaced `<xsl:if>` element and the orphan `<xsl:value-of>` tag, the cause was not ignorance but plain carelessness.

So the good news is that XSLT does not require a huge investment of intellectual capital to make the most of its power. XSLT does require you to think clearly but it rewards you handsomely for wording its instructions carefully and it helps if you can think like a tree.

Overview

Software has value in three dimensions. The first, and most important, is performance, but the second dimension is all too often overlooked. Could the average programmer follow the code – for that matter, could the code's author follow it a year later, or would they quickly become bogged down trying to decipher intractable logic? Value in this dimension also pays dividends in lower maintenance costs. The third dimension of value in software is how easily the design can be extended, both to take advantage of emerging technology and to add features that customers want.

In all cases a determining factor of this value is the lucidity of the implementation. The samples in this chapter cover the whole spectrum, from the early verbose versions that sometimes even become opaque, to the more finely honed logic of later versions. These later versions are faster and are prime candidates for extensions like pivot table functionality.

Be that as it may, the topic of this chapter is performance and here I think we have covered quite a range of factors. Here's a summary according to the three stages that have defined the structure of this discussion.

Stage I: Script makes extending any application that supports a scripting engine easy, but there's no free lunch to be had here: ease of coding and performance work against each other. When you need high performance you must spend time purging script from your transforms. With XSLT there's a catch though: to obviate the need for script, you must be a master of XPath – a single good data signature can be substituted for pages of code – but XPath is not the easiest language to master. Don't make excuses though, just make learning it a top priority. Also, when you stumble across effective, well-crafted data signatures, hoard them up for use later. In those cases where script is the only available means to achieve a stated task, be it due to your lack of skill or the lack of power in XSLT itself, then whenever possible make just one call to the function and store the result in an XSLT variable for use in the transform.

Stage II: Good design is good. There's no design that can be too good and this is particularly true for XSLT – strive for excellence. Always assume there's a better way, never stop looking for it. Pay attention to the fundamentals and the detail. Be paranoid about loops. Watch where your XSLT variable declarations are placed. Variables can be your best friends in XSLT (see an especially satisfying example of this in the Petri Net simulator of Chapter 15), they help you abstract the data processed by your transform, and in the process make your programming problem clearer, more tractable. So:

❑ Be sure to use every variable that you create

❑ Create the variable just before it's required (in other words, send large sets of data to the client, but hide all data until it's requested by the user)

❑ Create variables (whose data is not for display) from a minimal number of nodes (the classic case is a distinct list of values: when the node-list is large, break it up into smaller chunks to create a distinct list from the smaller subset)

Stage III: Architecture. Question authority, don't let yourself get locked into a cell of conventional wisdom. Remember that both clients and servers are doubling in power every eighteen months, and bandwidth is increasing even faster than that. Thin clients have their place, but it's a smaller place every day. Spread the wealth around. Push your clients to the limit. Use technologies like Microsoft's ISAPI 2 and .NET Mobile Controls that help you determine how strong those clients are, then load 'em up. On the server, take the opposite tack: if you can cache a compiled transform (as you can with Microsoft's XSLTemplate and XSLProcessor objects) then do it. On the server you want to be frugal – every cycle you save is a cycle you can use to support another client. Use your SQL Server in ways that have only recently become a practical proposition: use SQL2000's SQLXML ISAPI (instead of ActiveX Data Objects) to fetch richly hierarchical XML trees. If you do, you won't need most of the code described in this chapter (because that code was designed to process flat ADO-generated XML). But the most important lesson from Stage III: learn to play well with everybody; make friends with network guys and database administrators, with web masters who are jumping into clustered servers and with that brave pioneer, the .NET programmer. *You* can't do it all, but a well-architected system can.

Bonus Special Move: I closed this chapter with what turned out to be the simplest and by far the most powerful performance technique I've yet found in XSLT: exploit your hierarchy. First create variables that contain the most data. Then, as you proceed into deeper sub-trees of this "global" data, create XSLT variables from preceding XSLT variables. You will see me return to this technique in Chapter 15, but there I'm using the technique principally to create elegant and compact code. Either way, you win.

And the last lesson I've learned and want to share with you is this: keep the faith – XSLT rocks. Even when you think it sucks, when you feel it literally suck away millions of bytes of virtual memory, keep the faith. If you get into trouble, ask for help.

Summary

In this chapter we've used a real-life experience to highlight areas where your XSLT stylesheet performance can be improved. These can be grouped into three broad pieces of advice:

❑ Avoid using script wherever possible

❑ Use variables carefully

❑ Make appropriate use of the capabilities of both the client and server

Having read this, along with the XSLT you've learned in previous chapters, you should be well on the way to writing ever more advanced and efficient stylesheets. We're now going to take a side step away from XSLT, and look at the other side of XSL – the formatting objects part of the specification. The next chapter begins with a look at the "pre-cursor" to XSL-FO, that is Cascading Style Sheets.

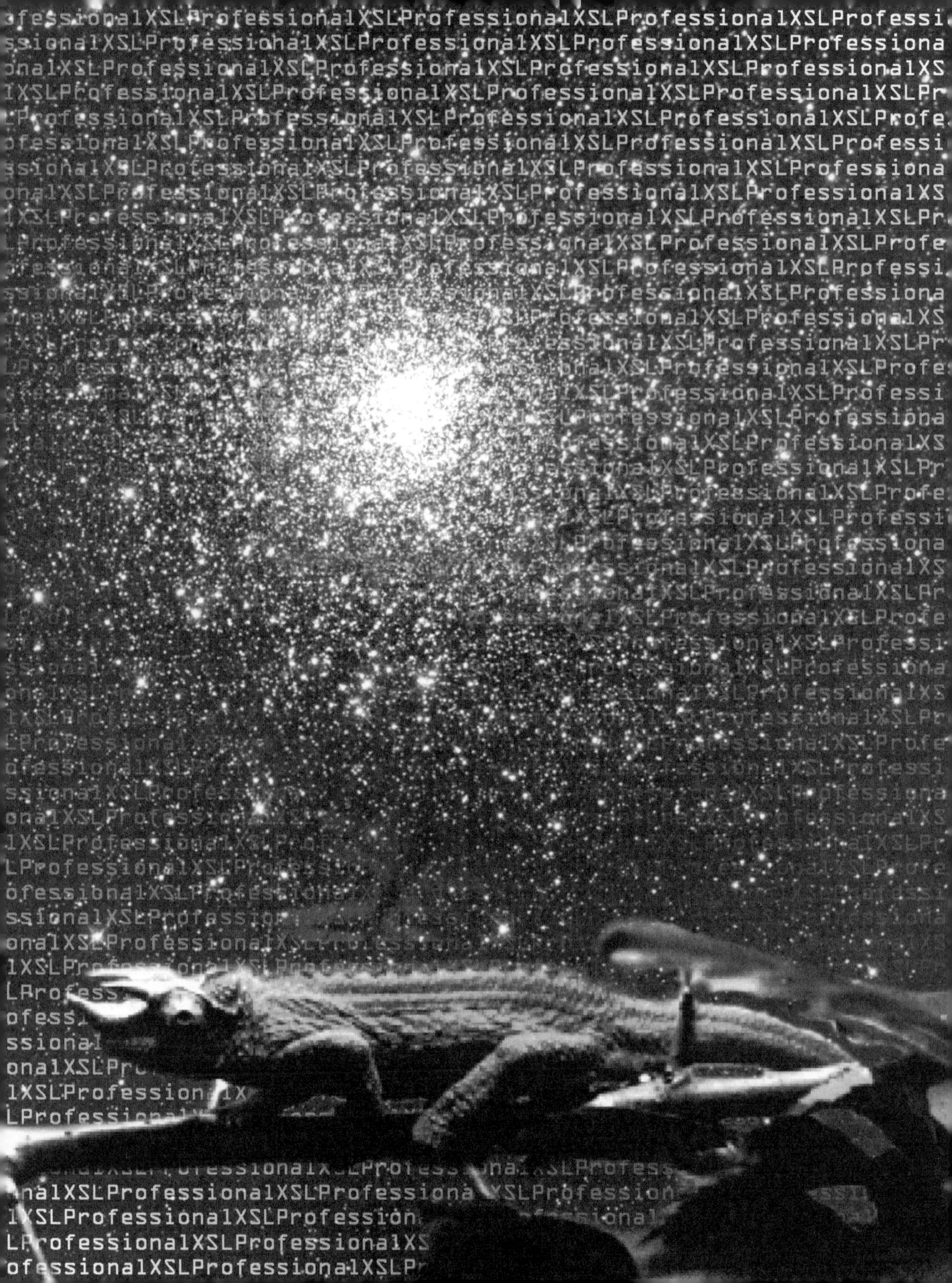

9

CSS and XSL-FO

In order to effectively communicate the meaning of XML documents and data to human beings, rather than machines, it is essential that the data be presented in a way that can be easily assimilated. For most users of the Web or readers of printed documents, a file containing multiple XML elements is far from legible as it stands – we need a way of providing attractive presentation of our XML data and documents. **Cascading Style Sheets, CSS**, and **Extensible Stylesheet Language Formatting Objects, XSL-FO**, provide two alternative ways of styling or presenting XML data for human readers. CSS is a W3C technology based on a non-XML syntax, and is intended to separate content and display in HTML and XML. XSL-FO, on the other hand, is a part of the W3C Extensible Stylesheet Language, XSL, and together with XSLT provides an XML-based syntax for the display of XML data.

CSS can be applied to markup generated by XSLT transformations, as seen previously in this book, or can be applied directly to raw XML data. XSL-FO is designed to produce display for screen or paper that can be expressed with a high degree of precision. Both technologies offer exciting possibilities but each is in a transitional stage, and some important aspects are as yet only partially implemented.

The CSS2 and XSL-FO specifications total over 700 pages, and in this chapter I shall attempt to provide an insight into how these technologies work and the potential they have.

By the time you have completed the chapter you should know a little about:

- ❑ basic principles of using CSS with HTML and XML
- ❑ what a CSS stylesheet looks like
- ❑ how to link an XML document to a CSS stylesheet
- ❑ the importance of the CSS `display` property for achieving layout of XML
- ❑ how to use CSS with XSLT transformations
- ❑ some basic principles of XSL-FO
- ❑ how to create a simple XSL-FO document using XSLT
- ❑ how to create a simple PDF document using XSLT and XSL-FO

Techniques for Applying Style to XML

So far in this book we have said very little, other than in passing, about applying style to XML or to the HTML/XHTML output of XSLT transformations. The emphasis on transformations is understandable – XSLT technology is relatively stable, and although it may change a little in future versions, many tools to exploit it are currently available, as detailed in Appendix E. The XSLT aspect of XSL became a Recommendation in November 1999 and is widely accepted as a standard. We can carry out real-world XSL transformations with acceptable performance in many situations and, if we know what we are doing, can reliably expect to produce appropriate and consistent output trees and documents.

In contrast, when we look at the available methods for applying style directly to XML, or to XML that has been transformed into HTML/XHTML, we find a much less satisfactory situation.

Of the two technologies available for styling XML (CSS and XSL-FO), CSS is primarily web-focused, whereas XSL-FO is designed with many more facilities to accurately control layout for paper output. However, in practice, both CSS and XSL-FO have a significant distance to go to realize their full potential. The problems or limitations arise partly from a lack of suitable tools, which itself is a consequence of, in the case of XSL-FO and at the time of writing, the lack of a final XSL-FO Recommendation.

CSS has had two full W3C Recommendations in existence for some time. The initial version of CSS, CSS Level 1, was produced in December 1996 (updated in January 1999), and the CSS Level 2 Recommendation was finalized in May 1998. However, problems have arisen because of patchy implementation of CSS functionality in successive versions of the more popular browsers. Internet Explorer 3 and Netscape Navigator 4.x nominally implemented some parts of CSS1, but the functionality achieved was minimal. It is not my intention for this chapter to examine in detail which versions of which browser do or do not implement particular parts of the CSS Recommendations. Suffice it to say that, at the time of writing (January 2001), there are still significant questions about the implementation of CSS2 in the latest versions of perhaps the two most widely used web browsers, Internet Explorer 5.5 and Netscape 6. Ideally, one would want to assume that web users have the latest available versions of their favored browser, but it is poor business practice to exclude potential customers who may not have upgraded to the latest version. So for the time being it is necessary when using CSS to write web pages in a way that allows the use of older browsers with their more limited, even non-standard, CSS implementations.

However, despite these limitations in browser implementation of CSS, it would be unfair to imply that all is doom and gloom. It is possible to use a significant part of CSS functionality with reasonable confidence in Internet Explorer 5 and Netscape 6, particularly those CSS Level 1 capabilities that style HTML and XHTML. However, Internet Explorer and Netscape 6 have different strengths and weaknesses, making cross-browser solutions far from straightforward right now. As users progressively upgrade to Netscape 6 and Internet Explorer 5.x, more extensive use of parts of CSS becomes realistic for commercial web sites, taking us closer to the ideal of separating content and presentation.

Screenshots in this chapter are shown mostly using Internet Explorer 5.5. Netscape 6 rendered some CSS correctly but with gaps, and on occasion seemed completely unable to find the style information for certain files. Yet Netscape 6 implements the powerful attribute selectors from CSS2, which IE 5.5 does not. Disappointingly, the W3C Amaya browser also seemed to have a decidedly incomplete implementation of CSS2 and failed to display XML with CSS at all in some examples.

Thus we are in the patchy, if a little encouraging, situation that we can make use of a significant proportion of CSS by sticking to the most modern browsers although, as you will see in the examples, problems persist even then. In addition, tools available to produce and display XSL-FO are still pretty rudimentary. As we progress through the chapter though, I will describe some of the very promising XSL-FO tools that are beginning to arrive.

The situation is moving rapidly. The output from examples presented here is a snapshot in time – as browsers and FO viewers mature, I expect to see significantly greater scope for use of both CSS and XSL-FO.

At the time of writing, XSL-FO has reached the Candidate Recommendation stage (to be found at http://www.w3.org/TR/2000/CR-xsl-20001121/). The Candidate Recommendation is entitled "*Extensible Stylesheet Language (XSL) Version 1*" but is essentially concerned with XSL Formatting Objects only. The draft specification is of a substantial length and of significant complexity. Much of the complexity not found in CSS arises from the desire to add functionality to allow precise and consistent output, along with the need to support multiple languages, which requires that languages with right-to-left or top-to-bottom orientation, as opposed to the familiar left-to-right of English, be accommodated. It is unlikely that full implementations of the XSL-FO specification will be available immediately once the Recommendation is finalized, but there are encouraging signs that high quality XSL-FO formatters and viewers are not too distant.

In theory, a pure XSL stylesheet processor would prepare XML-based data for presentation on a variety of media, according to stylesheets for each medium. Broadly, a two-step process is followed. The first step is the data transformation and filtering using XSLT, similar to the many examples you have seen so far in this book, but in this instance producing XSL-FO. The second step is "formatting", which takes the result tree from this XSLT transformation and prepares it for display. Details of formatting will be discussed later in this chapter.

To the best of my knowledge there is no "web browser" compatible with XSL-FO (or even a significant subset of XSL-FO). Therefore to display XSL-FO it has been necessary, until recently, to take the process one step further and convert the XSL-FO to another format such as the **Portable Document Format** (**PDF**). Later in this chapter I will show you an example of how that is done using XSLT and Apache's FOP (Formatting Objects Processor), the latter of which supports a subset of XSL-FO elements. I also briefly look at the preview release of an XSL Formatter that displays XSL-FO natively. This will give you a hint of what future browsers may be capable of.

Write Once, Display Anywhere

One of the fundamental principles underpinning XML is the separation of content and presentation. Thus, unlike successive versions of HTML that progressively incorporated presentational elements led by the competition between the browsers from Netscape and Microsoft, XML has no presentation elements built in.

The absence of presentation-orientated elements in XML allows, in theory, a complete separation of styling and content. In practice, though, styling often depends directly on content. Take for example the case of styling a lengthy XML document: its length may well preclude the use of styling options that would available for shorter documents – if the output had to be contained in a leaflet of particular dimensions, say.

In principle, XML data originating from large XML files or from a proprietary RDBMS format that provides XML functionality can be used for display in a variety of browsers (be they desktop or mobile browsers). It may also be output via other media, including paper and potentially non-visual media such as voice browsers and Braille, and methods of using XSLT to format XML for display on a number of such devices are described elsewhere in the book. Viewed from a data integrity point of view, XML, coupled with appropriate styling through XSLT, takes significant steps towards the goal of "Write once, display anywhere".

The display of data on mobile browsers or, more generally, on browsers of varying capabilities is attracting much attention and investment at present. However, many such browsers have a small display and color is limited to 1-bit (black and white), meaning that the degree of styling that may be applied is quite restricted. For this reason, I shall restrict the discussion of styling issues to desktop browsers or browsers with similarly sophisticated display capabilities. The likelihood of mobile browsers being able to process CSS stylesheets or carry out XSL-FO formatting in the near future is pretty remote. To be realistic, it will be a significant task to fully implement XSL-FO functionality on desktop browsers, never mind mobile browsers, even assuming it is a desirable or relevant prospect.

CSS Principles

In this section, and those that follow, I will illustrate the principles of CSS using HTML elements. Note that style applied to HTML elements may also be applied to similarly or arbitrarily named XML elements. Thus, apart from the different mechanism required for linking to a stylesheet, much of the following can be directly applied to XML elements as well.

One of the basic principles of CSS is to, at least partially, achieve the separation of content from the styling of that content. When an external stylesheet is linked to an HTML document (using the `<LINK>` element or `@import` notation, which are described shortly), the separation of content and style in a document is essentially close to complete. When using styling attributes directly embedded within individual HTML or XHTML elements, while having "closer control", we mix up content and presentation – creating for ourselves or colleagues a potential maintenance nightmare.

Let's briefly consider the maintenance benefits of using external CSS stylesheets exclusively for a web site with 250 static pages. If we confine our style information to external stylesheets only, then we can change the appearance of the whole site in a consistent manner by editing one document, namely the external CSS stylesheet concerned. Contrast that with the maintenance work involved in changing CSS properties in perhaps dozens of elements on each of the 250 pages. The benefit of using external stylesheets is evident for such a site with static pages, but it also applies to sites that dynamically generate their content, for example using servlets. It is far more efficient to keep styling information in a single CSS file (or small set of CSS files) and keep graphic designers' tampering fingers away from most of the code.

> *Note that, typically, CSS refers to "style sheets" (two words) and XSL refers to "stylesheets" (one word). Within this chapter the two styles are used interchangeably.*

Introduction to Cascading Style Sheets

One of the principle aims of applying CSS in external CSS stylesheets is to allow you to create a class of XML or HTML document to be displayed in a consistent manner throughout a web site by simply applying the same CSS stylesheet.

CSS Techniques

So, let's move on to see how CSS is actually used. Initially, I will demonstrate the use of CSS with HTML/XHTML and later describe techniques for using CSS and XML together. But as far as CSS is concerned a `<P>` element in HTML is just the same as a `<P>` element in XML, although the meaning in a particular XML dialect could be entirely different.

CSS style may be applied using the four principle mechanisms below, all illustrated in the code sample further on in this section.

- ❑ Linking an external CSS stylesheet

- ❑ Importing an external stylesheet

- ❑ A "style sheet" nested in a `<STYLE>` element

- ❑ Inline style information

Whichever technique we use to incorporate CSS styling, we must inform the user agent, traditionally a web browser, of the location of any external CSS code. Within the head of a simple HTML 4.0 document we can link to external stylesheets using either the HTML `<LINK>` element or using the `@import` notation. If we do not wish to use external CSS stylesheets, then we can inform the user agent of the CSS to apply by the `<STYLE>` element within the HTML head tags, or by using a `style` attribute for individual HTML elements. Imported stylesheets are automatically merged with any other CSS rules contained within the `<STYLE>` element, with local rules taking precedence over imports. Note that CSS code contained within a `<STYLE>` element is referred to as a "stylesheet" even though it is included within an HTML document.

The code that follows, `SimpleCSS.html`, illustrates all four techniques. However, it is not intended to be run, as you would not usually include both a `<LINK>` element and the equivalent `@import` notation to reference the same external CSS stylesheet.

```
<!DOCTYPE HTML PUBLIC "-//W3C//DTD HTML 4.0 Transitional//EN"
"http://www.w3.org/TR/REC-html40/loose.dtd">
<!-- SimpleCSS.html -->
<HTML>
<HEAD>
<TITLE>Simple CSS Example</TITLE>
<LINK REL=STYLESHEET TYPE="text/css"
      HREF="http://www.xmml.com/prettyHTML.css">
<STYLE TYPE="text/css">
   @import url(http://www.xmml.com/prettyHTML.css);
/* There now follows two CSS rules which select individual HTML elements. */
/* This next rule will make all text contained in <H1> elements throughout
   the document blue and underlined */
   H1 { color: blue; text-decoration:underline; }

/* The next rule will make all text in <H2> elements in the document red but
   the text won't be underlined or otherwise decorated. */
   H2 { color: red; text-decoration:none; }
</STYLE>
</HEAD>

<BODY>
<H1>Using Cascading Stylesheets is easy! This headline is blue and
underlined.</H1>
<BR>
<H2>This sub-heading is red and is not underlined.</H2>
<BR>
<P STYLE="color: green; text-decoration:underline;">This paragraph, however, is in
green underlined text.</P>

</BODY>
</HTML>
```

Remember that HTML is not case-sensitive, whereas XHTML is. To use the above code in XHTML 1.0 it would be necessary to use lower case throughout for element names and attributes.

Before moving on to examine the *how* of this inclusion more closely, let's take a moment to consider the various options in a little more detail. We know that it is possible to import external stylesheets using either @import notation or the <LINK> element. For practical purposes the two techniques are functionally the same, and each is also capable of importing more than one stylesheet at a time. I suggest that you choose whichever you prefer and stick with it. Using the <STYLE> element or inline styling is really only appropriate for small web sites, or very rare special cases in larger sites, because of the increased maintenance requirements mentioned earlier.

If you use more than one technique the "most local" applicable style rule will prevail. In other words, if you apply a particular inline style to an individual element then that will take precedence over any rule given in a <STYLE> element or external stylesheet. Similarly CSS rules in the <STYLE> element will take priority over those in imported or linked stylesheets.

Let's examine the two methods of linking to an external CSS stylesheet. If you use XSLT to produce HTML/XHTML formatted with CSS, then you will use one of these methods of linking, as well as the XML syntax described later in the chapter. The <LINK> element:

```
<LINK REL=STYLESHEET TYPE="text/css"
      HREF="http://www.xmml.com/prettyHTML.css">
```

associates the HTML file with a (fictional) CSS external stylesheet situated at the URI http://www.xmml.com/prettyHTML.css.

If prettyHTML.css provides the same rules as those given by the <STYLE> element in the code above, it consists of the following code. For clarity, I tend to place each property-value pair on a separate line to make it easier for me to spot simple mistakes like omitting a semicolon, particularly in longer stylesheets.

```
H1 {
   color: blue;
   text-decoration:underline;
   }

H2 {
   color: red;
   text-decoration:none;
   }
```

Similarly, the notation:

```
<STYLE TYPE="text/css">
   @import url(http://www.xmml.com/prettyHTML.css);
   <!-- The other CSS rules go here -->
</STYLE>
```

would cause that same (fictional) external CSS stylesheet file to be imported from the URI http://www.xmml.com/prettyHTML.css.

Note that in practice we would not use both the `<LINK>` element and `@import` notation to import the same external CSS stylesheet into one HTML document. The presence of both linking techniques in one HTML document is for illustrative purposes only. However, if you do use both `<LINK>` and `@import` in the same HTML document, you will find that whichever one comes later in the document takes priority. Thus in our code above, since `@import` is placed later in the `<HEAD>` element than the `<LINK>` element, the rules from `@import` take precedence where there is overlap.

CSS Rules

CSS works primarily on the basis of **rules**. Looking at our sample HTML document, `SimpleCSS.html`, the following two rules are specified within the `<STYLE>` element in the head of the document:

```
H1 { color: blue; text-decoration:underline; }
H2 { color: red; text-decoration:none; }
```

The same two rules were given in the illustrative `prettyHTML.css` stylesheet, and a single CSS rule is expressed in the `style` attribute of the `<P>` element towards the end of the `SimpleCSS.html` document:

```
<P STYLE="color: green; text-decoration:underline;">This paragraph, however, is in
green underlined text.</P>
```

Notice that there are differences between the syntax of CSS rules contained within stylesheets and those contained inline within individual HTML/XHTML elements.

How do CSS rules work? A CSS rule simply creates an association between the **name of an element** in a HTML or XML document and a **CSS property**.

The simplest form of CSS rule applies one CSS property to one element. For example, the following CSS rule, which uses the syntax applicable within the `<STYLE>` element or within an external CSS stylesheet, would apply a red color to any text contained in an HTML `<H2>` tag:

```
H2 {color: red;}
```

The above rule is made up of two parts; the first, which in this example consists of the text "H2", is called the **selector** and consists of the element (or tag) name without its opening and closing angled brackets. For obvious reasons, it is termed an **element selector**. The remainder of the rule within the curly braces is the **declaration**.

Our simple example declaration is itself formed of two parts: the name of a CSS **property**, followed by a **value** for that CSS property, separated by a colon and terminated by a semi-colon. In our example, the CSS property is "color" and the value is "red". Within the declaration it is possible to list more than one property, as in each of the rules in the `<STYLE>` element of our sample HTML document. When there is more than one property defined within a declaration, the semi-colon serves as separator between properties.

In our HTML example, the external stylesheets contain the same rules as given within the HTML document, and so all the applicable style rules are visible in the sample. The HTML output is displayed in the following figure. In the screenshot here, you may not be able to see any difference in color between the <H1>, <H2>, and <P> tags, but the underlining of the text contained within <H1> and <P> tags should be apparent.

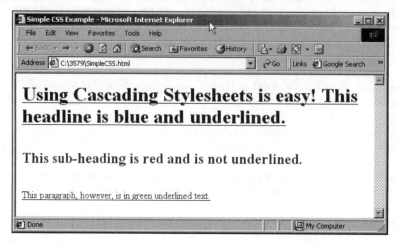

There are three types of selector reliably available to us when using CSS:

❑ Element type

❑ class

❑ ID

In addition, CSS2 also provides **attribute selectors**, which are potentially very powerful but are not yet implemented in Internet Explorer.

In our previous example we used three CSS rules for selecting element types (<H1>, <H2>, and <P> elements) in the source HTML document to apply styles to. We'll now look at the other two widely implemented selectors.

When we want to apply style on the basis of the class attribute of an HTML element, we again use CSS rules, but the syntax of the selector is slightly different.

If we have HTML such as the <P> element below, which has a CLASS attribute with value "plain":

```
<P CLASS="plain">This text should be blue and undecorated and is chosen by using a
<b>class</b> selector.</P>
```

then we can use the following CSS **class selector** rule to apply a particular style selectively to <P> elements which have a CLASS attribute of value "plain":

```
P.plain {color: blue; text-decoration: none;}
```

The syntax for a class selector is the element name without angle brackets, followed by a period and the value of the CLASS attribute to match. Thus we have P.plain as the selector for the <P> element with CLASS attribute of value "plain".

The syntax for using **ID selectors** is again slightly different. To selectively apply a style to <P> elements with ID attributes of value `"fancy"`, such as:

```
<P ID="fancy">This paragraph should be red and italicized and is chosen by means
of the ID attribute as selector for the CSS rule.</P>
```

we could use the rule:

```
P#fancy {color: red; font-style: italic;}
```

or this more general one, which would have the same effect on <P> elements:

```
*#fancy {color: red; font-style: italic;}
```

The latter `*#fancy` syntax would apply to *any* element with an ID attribute of value `"fancy"`. As you might expect, the asterisk is a wildcard matching any element, and the hash character indicates that an ID attribute value follows. The P#fancy syntax would apply to only a <P> element that had an ID attribute of value `"fancy"`.

However, note the important fact that if we want to make use of the CLASS attribute or the ID attribute as a selector, then we have to alter the content of our data source, by incorporating CLASS or ID attributes, in order to achieve the desired output for given elements. Thus the distinction between content and presentation becomes a little blurred.

To demonstrate the use of the CLASS attribute and ID attribute selectors, let's add two additional paragraphs to our HTML source code, and save it as `SimpleCSS2.html`. Next, save a copy of `prettyHTML.css` as `classyHTML.css` and we will add two additional rules, one to select a style to apply by a CLASS selector and the other to apply a style by an ID selector. For ease of comparison, I have also moved the <P> element type selector into the `classyHTML.css` file, so the syntax may be directly compared.

```
<!DOCTYPE HTML PUBLIC "-//W3C//DTD HTML 4.0 Transitional//EN"
"http://www.w3.org/TR/REC-html40/loose.dtd">
<!-- SimpleCSS2.html -->
<HTML>
<HEAD>
<TITLE> Example of CSS Class and ID selectors</TITLE>
<LINK REL=STYLESHEET TYPE="text/css"
      HREF="http://www.xmml.com/classyHTML.css">
</HEAD>

<BODY>
<H1>Using Cascading Stylesheets is easy! This headline is blue and
 underlined.</H1>
<BR>
<H2>This sub-heading is red and is not underlined.</H2>
<BR>

<P>This paragraph, however, is in green underlined text.</P>
<BR>
<P CLASS="plain">This text should be blue and undecorated and is chosen by using
 a <b>class</b> selector.</P>
<BR>
<P ID="fancy">This paragraph should be red and italicized and is chosen by means
 of the ID attribute as selector for the CSS rule.</P>

</BODY>
</HTML>
```

In the `classyHTML.css` file we define the following rules:

```
H1 {
    color: blue;
    text-decoration:underline;
    }

H2 {
    color: red;
    text-decoration:none;
    }

P   {
    color: green;
    text-decoration:underline;
    }

P.plain {
    color: blue;
    text-decoration: none;
    }

P#fancy {
    color: red;
    font-style: italic;
    }
```

Viewed in Internet Explorer 5.5, our document looks like this:

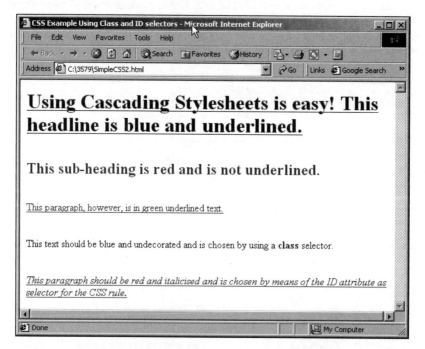

So, let's look more closely at the CSS rules in `classyHTML.css` that control the appearance of our five items (two headers and three paragraphs):

```
H1 { color: blue; text-decoration:underline; }
H2 { color: red; text-decoration:none; }
P {color: green; text-decoration:underline;}
P.plain {color: blue; text-decoration: none;}
P#fancy {color: red; font-style: italic;}
```

The appearance of the two headers is unchanged and is determined, as before, by element type selectors for the <H1> and <H2> elements. The first paragraph is unchanged in appearance, using the same rule given inline in `SimpleCSS.html`, although moving the rule to the `classyHTML.css` external stylesheet requires we now use the curly braces.

The fourth rule is new. It is applied only to <P> elements that have a CLASS attribute of "plain". Because it is a more specific rule than the third rule specified for <P> elements, it takes precedence when a <P> element has a "plain" value for the CLASS attribute. Note that both the color property and the text-decoration property are over-ridden in the rule to which the P.plain selector applies, although declarations in the lower priority rule not covered in the applied rule will persist.

The final rule specifies an ID attribute selector to match <P> elements having ID attributes of value "fancy", such as the last <P> element in our HTML file. It is fairly straightforward to see why it has red colored, italic text – both these properties are explicitly declared in this last rule. If you're surprised that it is also underlined, we need to go back to the generic rule for the <P> element, which stated:

```
P {color: green; text-decoration:underline;}
```

When the P#fancy selector applies to a particular element with the "fancy" ID attribute value, the green color property of the generic rule is over-ridden and the text becomes red. Similarly, the implicit value "normal" of the font-style property is over-ridden by the explicitly declared property value of "italic". But notice that the generic text-decoration property for a <P> element is "underline" and that is *not* mentioned in the rule declaration. Therefore the underline is applied to paragraphs with the "fancy" ID, despite (actually because of) the absence of an explicit declaration for the text-decoration property. Note that within a document only one element may have a particular ID attribute, that is it uniquely identifies that element within the document.

Grouping Selectors

In a commercial web site, the number of style rules can be considerable, particularly if we make heavy use of CLASS and ID attributes in our web pages. It makes sense to structure our elements with the aim of minimizing maintenance. (Don't forget how much less onerous a task maintenance is if external CSS stylesheets alone are used, avoiding internal rules within HTML documents.) One relevant feature offered by CSS allows us to create groups of elements with shared rules, each selector separated from the next by a comma.

To illustrate, let's take a simple example grouping elements that follow a common formatting rule, and thus letting us ensure consistency of font and color between <H1>, <H2>, and <H3> elements on our web site:

```
H1, H2, H3 {font-family:arial, sans-serif; color:red;}
```

In addition we might want to control the relative font size of our three heading elements with a set of rules something like this:

```
H1 {font-size: 28pt;}
H2 {font-size: 24pt;}
H3 {font-size: 18pt;}
```

If our stylesheet contains both these rules, then <H1> elements will use (as first choice) an Arial font of 28pt size and be colored red. The actual appearance of an <H1> element depends on the combination of CSS properties specified in the rules that apply to a particular element.

Now, should we want to use a serif font, say Times New Roman, in all HTML header elements, we only need change a single CSS rule (because of the grouping) rather than all three. Of course, in such a simple stylesheet the benefit is fairly trivial, but it can be very useful for rapidly achieving a consistent new look by altering CSS rules of more complex applications.

Inheritance of Properties

What happens if we have, as would inevitably occur in all but the most trivial HTML pages, elements nested within each other? Essentially, any CSS properties of the ancestor elements that have not been specifically overridden by a new rule are applied – this in fact being the origin of the name: styles 'cascade' down to all descendants of an element until explicitly overruled.

This process is called **inheritance** and can be seen, for example, in the behavior of <B> or similar elements set within a <P> element in an HTML page, such as here:

```
<P>Extensible Markup Language, XML, should really have been called <B>XMML</B>
because "XML" is actually a markup <I>meta<I> language.</P>
```

The bits of text contained within both the <B> and <I> element pairs inherit the properties (apart from their explicit bold and italic properties respectively) from their parent <P> element.

Let's produce this example with the file XMML.html:

```
<!DOCTYPE HTML PUBLIC "-//W3C//DTD HTML 4.0 Transitional//EN"
"http://www.w3.org/TR/REC-html40/loose.dtd">
<HTML>
<HEAD>
<LINK REL=STYLESHEET TYPE="text/css" HREF="Test.css">
<TITLE>XML or XMML?</TITLE>

</HEAD>

<BODY>
<P>Extensible Markup Language, XML should really have been called
<B>XMML</B> because "XML" is actually a markup <I>meta</I> language.</P>
</BODY>
</HTML>
```

and the `Test.css` external stylesheet:

```
P {
   background-color: #CCCCCC;
   color: green;
   text-decoration:underline;}
B, I  {
   color: red;
   }
```

Now we can selectively change the color of the inline elements `<B>` and `<I>` to give an altered color display, as shown in the following screenshot:

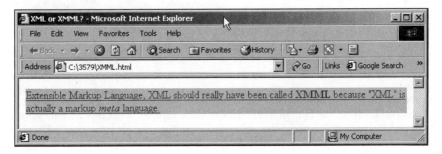

The words "XMML" and "meta" both appear in red – but keep the more standard properties of `<B>` and `<I>` elements – since the color of each is over-ridden by the rule:

```
B, I {color: red;}
```

Let's return to our original example code. In some settings where particular attention is being called to bolded text we might include a similar rule that would explicitly override the text color properties of the containing paragraph. We could use a rule like this:

```
B {color: red;}
```

Let's create a new HTML file, `SimpleCSS3.html`, by changing the `<LINK>` element of `SimpleCSS2.html` to refer to the external stylesheet `Test2.css`, as follows:

```
<LINK REL=STYLESHEET TYPE="text/css" HREF="Test2.css">
```

If we alter our style information in `Test2.css` to read as follows:

```
H1 {
   color: blue;
   text-decoration:underline;
   }

H2 {
   color: red;
   text-decoration:none;
   }
```

```
P   {
    background-color: #CCCCCC;
    color: green;
    text-decoration:underline;
    }

P.plain {
    color: blue;
    text-decoration: none;
    }

P#fancy {
    color: red;
    font-style: italic;
    }

B {
    color: red;
}
```

then we can see inheritance in action. All children of <P> elements will *inherit* the pale gray (#CCCCCC) background from the rule in item 3 of the code snippet. Text in <B> elements, with its own rule, demonstrates overriding the text color inherited from the <P> element's rule. This is illustrated below in Netscape 6.0:

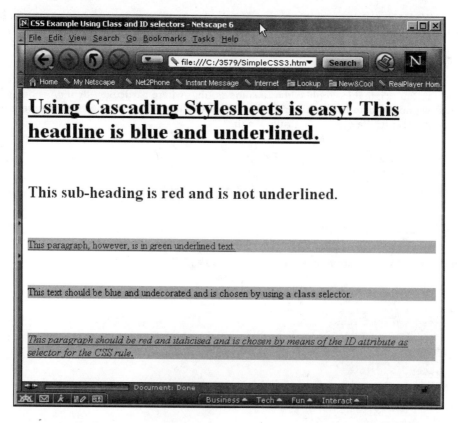

As you can see, the rendering of CSS in Netscape 6 is similar to that in Internet Explorer 5.5. However, notice that Netscape introduces significantly more extraneous whitespace than IE 5.5 for similarly sized windows. Such differences in CSS display may well have been a significant factor in stimulating the development of XSL-FO.

In the preceding example we added red color to the rule for <B> tags. We could make our rule more specific. For example, to apply the rule for red text color to <B> tags only when they occur within <P> tags, we would use this rule:

```
P B {color: red;}
```

Such CSS selectors are called **contextual selectors**, and it's important that the selectors appear in the correct order, as above. The contextual selector used in the preceding code snippet means that any <B> elements should be colored red if they are *descendants* of a <P> element. There is a more specific syntax for the narrower context of when a <B> element is a child (rather than a general descendant) of a <P> element, shown in a moment. Contextual selectors consist of two or more simple selectors separated by whitespace. Be careful to distinguish contextual selectors from grouped selectors, where the element names are separated by a comma.

We can include comments within CSS stylesheets too:

```
P B {color: red;} /* This rule applies red color to <B> elements when they occur
as descendants of <P> elements. */
```

A more specific CSS rule, which was introduced in CSS Level 2, is:

```
P > B {color: red;} /* This rule applies red color to <B> elements when they occur
only as **children** of <P> elements - not as descendants generally. */
```

which selects *children* only of the leftmost element. However, as with all CSS2 features, browser support of this syntax is far from reliable at present.

The CSS Formatting Model

The formatting model assumed by CSS is that each formatted element can be broken down into one or more boxes. An element has a core **content** area with optional surrounding **padding**, **border**, and **margin** areas.

The size of the padding, border and margin areas can be set using their given CSS properties. Technically, the `margin` and `padding` properties are not inherited but, since an element is typically contained within parent or ancestor elements, their properties do have an effect that, in practice, behaves in a manner visually similar to inheritance.

It is important to distinguish two types of element in HTML: **block-level** elements and **inline** elements. This distinction can be seen when using the `display` property in CSS and, later in the chapter, when using XSL-FO elements, which can be block, line, or inline. An important distinguishing characteristic of a block-level element in HTML is that the following element begins on a new line. In contrast, an inline element, as its name suggests, can be included within a line of its parent element.

For example, if we use <B> or <I> elements within a paragraph of text such as here:

```
<P>Extensible Markup Language, XML should really have been called <B>XMML</B>
because "XML" is actually a markup <I>meta<I> language.</P>
```

we expect it to be presented within the line of paragraph text. The fact that the <B> and <I> HTML elements are inline elements ensures the expected formatting behavior.

If we have two successive block level elements, such as HTML <P> tags as in the following file, XMML2.html:

```
<HTML>
<HEAD>
<TITLE>XMML - Extensible Markup Meta Language</TITLE>
</HEAD>
<BODY>
<P>XML, Extensible Markup Language is a misnomer.</P><P>XML is a <I>meta</I>
markup language and should be called the Extensible Markup <I>meta</I> language,
XMML.</P>
</BODY>
</HTML>
```

then we find that a new line is inserted after each block-level <P> element, as in the following screenshot, taken using Opera 5. Internet Explorer 5.5 and Netscape show the same behavior.

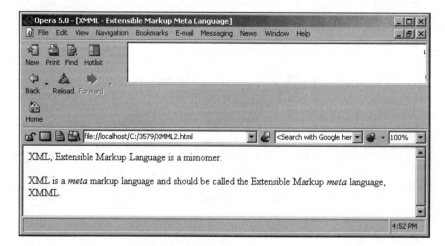

Notice that there is a vertical scroll bar in the screenshot, despite the fact that all text in the XMML2.html file is displayed. This is because of the empty line added automatically after the block-level <P> element.

CSS provides facilities for explicitly declaring whether an element is to be displayed as inline or block, using the display property. Understanding the behavior of the display property becomes particularly important when we come on to use CSS with XML in currently available browsers, since XML elements have no default block or inline behavior. Their display settings depend purely on whether the corresponding CSS display property is set to block or inline.

Applying CSS to XML

When we come to apply CSS to an XML document, we find that all the familiar HTML elements that influence presentation are absent, and we lose the implicit block or inline behaviors of familiar HTML elements. This means that for all aspects of presentation, including layout, fonts, color, etc., we are totally dependent on a formatting language, such as CSS, to define the appearance of the document.

It is possible to embed a stylesheet within an XML document, but this takes us a step backwards, away from separating content and presentation, and so won't be discussed further; instead we will normally link to an external CSS stylesheet. We don't have access to the familiar HTML <LINK> element, or the @import notation of the <STYLE> element, so how can we associate a stylesheet with an XML document?

Linking XML to a Stylesheet

To link XML to an external stylesheet, whether CSS or XSL, we use the <?xml-stylesheet?> processing instruction detailed in the "*Associating Stylesheets with XML documents Version 1.0*" Recommendation (http://www.w3.org/1999/06/REC-xml-stylesheet-19990629).

The processing instruction contained in the source XML document would look something like this:

```
<?xml-stylesheet href="stylishXML.css" type="text/css"?>
```

Note that the href attribute gives the URI that references the external CSS stylesheet. In this example, the stylesheet is named stylishXML.css and is situated in the same directory as the XML file to which it is linked. The type attribute describes the Internet media type for the CSS stylesheet. The correct type is "text/css".

To demonstrate how CSS can be used directly on an XML source document, let's take a traditional piece of verse for our source text:

```
<?xml version='1.0'?>
<?xml-stylesheet href="Psalm23.css" type="text/css"?>
<Psalm>
  <Title>Psalm 23</Title>
  <Source>Scottish Psalter</Source>
  <Date>1650</Date>

  <Verse number="1">
    <Line class="first">The LORD's my shepherd, I'll not want:</Line>
    <Line>He makes me down to lie</Line>
    <Line>In pastures green; He leadeth me</Line>
    <Line>The quiet waters by.</Line>
  </Verse>
```

```
    <Verse number="5">
     <Line class="first">Goodness and mercy all my life</Line>
     <Line>Shall surely follow me;</Line>
     <Line>And in God's house for evermore</Line>
     <Line>My dwelling place shall be.</Line>
    </Verse>
  </Psalm>
```

Notice that we have included an `<?xml-stylesheet?>` processing instruction pointing to an external CSS stylesheet.

Before we go on to discuss how this document will look after the CSS stylesheet `Psalm23.css` is applied, let's take a look at the default display options for Netscape and Microsoft browsers.

In Netscape 6, with the processing instruction omitted or commented out, we see simple, essentially unformatted, text, but with the start tags and end tags not shown. This is essentially the same as when displaying HTML – any unrecognized (XML) tags are not displayed, but their content is. Because the element names are unrecognized, the Netscape browser is unable to apply any default formatting.

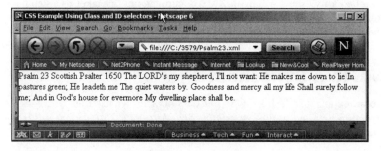

In contrast if we open the same file in Internet Explorer 5.5, with the `<?xml-stylesheet?>` processing instruction again omitted or commented out, we see a quasi-hierarchical tree structure displayed:

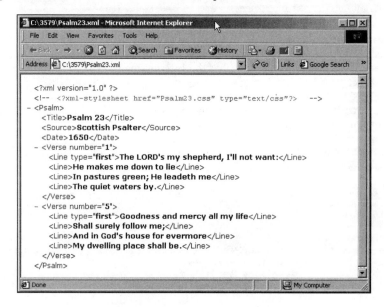

In fact, to achieve this display, Internet Explorer 5.5 applies a default stylesheet of its own. If we include or activate the `<?xml-stylesheet?>` processing instruction, then the use of the default IE 5.5 stylesheet is suppressed, even if the processing instruction points to a non-existent CSS stylesheet. In that case, the display is very similar to that shown for Netscape 6 above.

Now, let's take a step-by-step look at applying some styling to these two verses.

First, we'll create a simple CSS stylesheet where we will accentuate the title of the Psalm and its source and date, by increasing the `font-size` property. Otherwise, at this stage we will be content with displaying any other text quite simply. Our first attempt at a stylesheet, `Psalm23v1.css`, might look like this:

```css
/* Version 1 of the Psalm23.css stylesheet */

/* It attempts to highlight the <Title> element*/
Title {
  font-family: Arial;
  font-size:24pt;
  text-decoration:underline;
}

/* and add a little highlighting to the <Source> element
and the <Date> element */
Source, Date {font-family: Arial;
  font-size:16pt;
}

/* while all other elements we will display simply */
Line {font-family: TimesRoman, serif;
  font-size: 12pt;
  line-height:14pt;
  font-style:normal;
}
```

Since we want the appearance of the `<Source>` and `<Date>` elements to be the same, we make use of CSS grouping.

Let's take a look at the progress we have made so far by looking at the results of applying version 1 of the CSS stylesheet to `Psalm23.xml`:

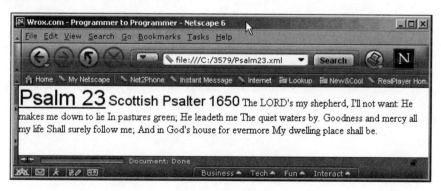

Well, we have applied the increased font size to the <Title> element and applied the slightly smaller bold text to the <Source> and <Date> elements. So far so good, but the layout leaves a lot to be desired. What we need to do is to make use of the display property, mentioned earlier, to cause elements in the source document to display as block-level elements on separate lines. We do that by setting the value for the display property of each element to block. At the same time we can make use of the class attribute on some of the <Line> elements to highlight the first line of each verse. The amended CSS stylesheet, Psalm23v2.css, now looks like this:

```
/* Version 2 of the Psalm23.css stylesheet */

/* It attempts to highlight the <Title> element*/
Title {
    font-family: Arial;
    font-size:24pt;
    font-weight:bold;
    text-decoration:underline;
    display:block;
}

/* and add a little highlighting to the <Source> element
and the <Date> element */
Source, Date {font-family: Arial;
    font-size:16pt;
    font-weight:bold;
    display:block;
}

/* while all other elements we will display simply as "blocks" which introduces a
new line at the end of each */
Line {font-family: TimesRoman;
    font-size: 12pt;
    line-height:14pt;
    font-style:normal;
    display:block;
}

/* and we will use the class="first" attribute to make the
first line of each verse bold. */
Line.first {font-family: TimesRoman;
    font-size: 12pt;
    line-height:14pt;
    font-weight:bold;
    display:block;
}
```

Now alter the <?xml-stylesheet?> processing instruction in Psalm23.xml to reference this file, and open it in your browser. In Internet Explorer 5.5 the display is considerably improved and reflects all the changes we introduced in Psalm23v2.css:

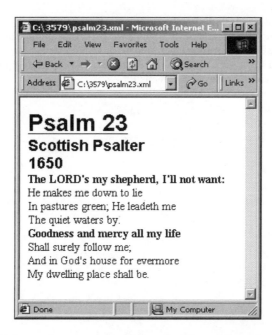

We can see that the `<Title>`, `<Source>`, `<Date>`, and `<Line>` elements are terminated by a newline, that is they are being treated correctly as block-level elements (as their `display` property is set to "`block`"). In addition, our use of the class attribute value of "`first`" in the first `<Line>` element of each verse is reflected in the bold `font-weight`.

However, even with this simple CSS stylesheet, our changes are not fully reflected in Netscape 6, as you can see in the following screenshot where Netscape 6 fails to correctly display the bold font-weight for the first line of each verse. The problem appears to relate to a failure to recognize the class selector.

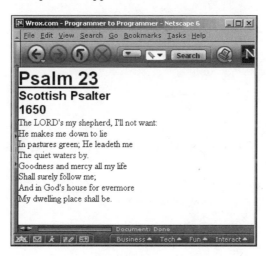

If we add a padding rule for the `<Verse>` element to our stylesheet, you might expect it to provide clear separation of the verses, but it doesn't.

Next, if we amend the CSS stylesheet `Psalm23v3.css` to make use of the `padding` property for the `<Verse>` element, setting it to a value of "10", then we get a reasonably formatted output of our XML source document. At least we do in Internet Explorer 5.5. In Netscape there seems to be a failure to implement the display of the `padding` property correctly, and it simply fails to show at all, leaving the appearance as in the previous Netscape 6 screenshot.

```
/* Version 3 of the Psalm23.css style sheet */

/* It attempts to highlight the <Title> element*/
Title {
  font-family: Arial;
  font-size:24pt;
  font-weight:bold;
  text-decoration:underline;
  display:block;
  }

/* and add a little highlighting to the <Source> element and the <Date>
element */
Source, Date {font-family: Arial;
  font-size:16pt;
  font-weight:bold;
  display:block;
  }

/* while all other elements we will display simply */

Line {font-family: TimesRoman;
  font-size: 12pt;
  line-height:14pt;
  font-style:normal;
  display:block;
  }

/* except we will use the class="first" attribute to make the first line of each
verse bold. */
Line.first {font-family: TimesRoman;
  font-size: 12pt;
  line-height:14pt;
  font-weight:bold;
  display:block;
  }

/* If we now convert the <Verse> element to block-level and add a padding
property then we improve layout. */
Verse {
  display:block;
  padding:10;
  }
```

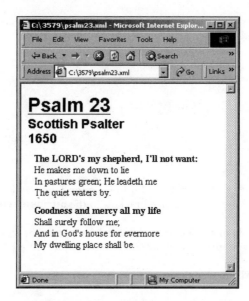

Notice that adding a `padding` property to the `<Verse>` element gives us satisfactory vertical separation of the verses, but also slightly indents each verse horizontally too (see the CSS formatting model earlier in the chapter for an illustration of why this is).

The output looks fairly respectable and is certainly much improved from the default display in either Netscape 6 or Internet Explorer 5.5 when no CSS stylesheet is applied. It resembles the typical HTML output of several years ago. It isn't pretty or sophisticated, but by applying these fairly simple CSS stylesheets to our XML source document we can achieve acceptable, if simple, display on today's desktop browsers. This approach is easy to update, for example if a third verse is added, and could be applied with little or no modification to other XML data of similar format. In addition, it is simple and our servers don't need ASP, ColdFusion, etc. to pre-format data: we simply send our data as XML with an appropriate stylesheet.

In the earlier XML source example I set the class attribute of the first `<Line>` element in each `<Verse>` in order to add bold selectively to each first line. CSS1 notation requires a class attribute for that selective display to work. However, CSS2 provides a more general notation, which can be applied to any attribute of any XML element. The problem is that, surprise surprise, implementation is not presently consistent across browsers.

If our browser reliably supports CSS2, we can use another notation to apply bold text to the first line of a `<Verse>` element. Suppose we modify our source code like this:

```
<Verse number="1">
    <Line order="first">The LORD's my shepherd, I'll not want:</Line>
    <Line order="second">He makes me down to lie</Line>
    <Line order="third">In pastures green; He leadeth me</Line>
    <Line order="fourth">The quiet waters by.</Line>
</Verse>
```

then we can apply the following CSS2 so that `<Line>` elements with an `order` attribute of `"first"` are displayed as bold underlined text:

```
Line[order="first"] {
    font-family: TimesRoman;
    font-size: 12pt;
    line-height:14pt;
    font-weight:bold;
    text-decoration:underline;
    display:block;
}
```

If you are familiar with XPath syntax or studied it in Chapter 2, you will notice some similarity to the predicate syntax of XPath in the use of square brackets in the **attribute selectors** of CSS2.

We will return to our example in a moment, but let's take a step to the side to consider how important the code I have just shown you might be, if, or when, fully implemented in browsers.

Let's suppose we had an XML source document, `Books.xml`, like this:

```
<?xml version="1.0"?>
<?xml-stylesheet href="ShowComputerCategory.css" type="text/css" ?>
<books>
<book category="Computer">Professional XSL</book>
<book category="Religious">Scottish Psalter</book>
<book category="Fiction">Alice in Wonderland</book>
<book category="Computer">Professional XML</book>
</books>
```

Suppose we wanted to display only books in the computer category. With XSLT that would be straightforward. But with CSS?

With CSS2, when it is implemented, we could filter our display using the CSS stylesheet, `ShowComputerCategory.css`:

```
book[category="Computer"] {
    font-family: serif;
    font-size:12pt;
    font-weight:bold;
    display:block;
    }

book[category="Fiction"] {
    display:none;
    }

book[category="Religious"] {
    display:none;
    }
```

I hope you can see that a syntax that superficially seems simply to duplicate the power provided by the class attribute would allows us to use CSS to filter and select our display based on the values of attributes or, using a slightly different syntax, the presence of attributes of elements in our source XML. This would give us great flexibility and control for displaying XML using CSS when browser support is widely available.

Ironically, Netscape 6, which failed to correctly handle some simpler CSS, at least in the initial release version I have been using, is successful here. The following screenshot shows the correct filtered output from the `books.xml` file "styled" with the `ShowComputerCategory.css` stylesheet. Opera 5 also implements attribute selectors. The disappointing thing is that Internet Explorer 5.5 does not, which pretty much makes this type of attribute selector impractical on the Web at present, due to IE's current position of dominance.

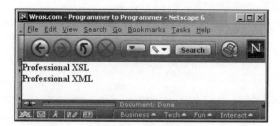

So, having taken a step aside to glimpse the future power of CSS to selectively display XML, let's return to our example.

Suppose that, for whatever reason, we want, or need, to move the content of the `<Source>` and `<Date>` elements to the end of the verses and have output that looks something like this:

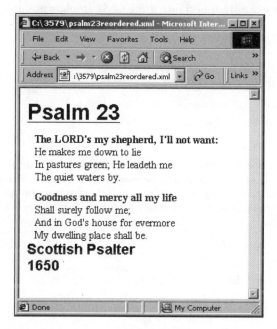

To achieve that using the same CSS stylesheet, `Psalm23v3.css`, we would have to re-order the elements in our source document, like this:

```
<?xml version='1.0'?>
<?xml-stylesheet href="Psalm23v3.css" type="text/css"?>
<Psalm>
<Title>Psalm 23</Title>
```

```
<Verse number="1">
<Line class="first">The LORD's my shepherd, I'll not want:</Line>
<Line>He makes me down to lie</Line>
<Line>In pastures green; He leadeth me</Line>
<Line>The quiet waters by.</Line>
</Verse>

<Verse number="5">
<Line class="first">Goodness and mercy all my life</Line>
<Line>Shall surely follow me;</Line>
<Line>And in God's house for evermore</Line>
<Line>My dwelling place shall be.</Line>
</Verse>

<Source>Scottish Psalter</Source>
<Date>1650</Date>
</Psalm>
```

Clearly, it is undesirable to start re-ordering source XML documents in order to achieve a specific display – we don't want to get into the situation where display needs for a particular output medium dictate the structure of our XML data.

However, we can achieve a similar appearance using CSS2 absolute positioning without reordering our source document. First we change the `<?xml-stylesheet?>` processing instruction to point to a new external CSS stylesheet, `Psalm23AbsPos.css`:

```
<?xml version='1.0'?>
<?xml-stylesheet href="Psalm23AbsPos.css" type="text/css"?>
<Psalm>
<Title>Psalm 23</Title>
<Source>Scottish Psalter</Source>
<Date>1650</Date>
```

Let's see the important parts of the new stylesheet. Notice first that in our original `Psalm23.css` we grouped the `<Source>` and `<Date>` elements, since we wanted them to share a style. However, when that style includes absolute positioning we must ungroup them, otherwise the `<Source>` and `<Date>` elements would be displayed one on top of the other, with very untidy results. The code of the amended stylesheet, `Psalm23AbsPos.css`, looks like this:

```
/* Psalm23AbsPos.css stylesheet */

/* The <Title> element is highlighted as before */
Title {
  font-family: Arial;
  font-size:24pt;
  font-weight:bold;
  text-decoration:underline;
  display:block;
}

/* The <Date> element is styled as before except it is positioned 8cm from the
   top of the screen. */
Date {font-family: Arial;
  font-size:16pt;
```

```
    font-weight:bold;
    display:block;
    position:absolute;
    top:8cm;
}

/* The only difference between the styling of the <Source> and <Date> elements
    is that the <Source> element is positioned 7cm from the top of the screen. */
Source {font-family: Arial;
    font-size:16pt;
    font-weight:bold;
    display:block;
    position:absolute;
    top:7cm;
}
```

```
/* The <Line> elements are displayed as before */
Line {font-family: TimesRoman;
    font-size: 12pt;
    line-height:14pt;
    font-style:normal;
    display:block;
}

/* As before we use the class="first" attribute to make the first line of each
    verse bold. */
Line.first {font-family: TimesRoman;
    font-size: 12pt;
    line-height:14pt;
    font-weight:bold;
    display:block;
}

/* If we now convert the <Verse> element to block-level and add a padding
    property then we improve layout. */
Verse {
    display:block;
    padding:10;
}
```

We can see the result of applying this simple absolute positioning in the following screenshot:

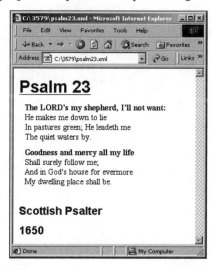

Visually, this looks very similar to the output achieved by reordering of the source XML, but the use of CSS absolute positioning allows us to display our XML source in an order that we control using CSS absolute positioning.

Detailed discussion of positioning properties in CSS2 is found in Section 9 of the CSS2 Recommendation at http://www.w3.org/TR/1998/REC-CSS2-19980512. However, don't forget that by making use of CSS2 absolute positioning, you are of course obliging your customers to use a CSS2-compliant browser.

CSS2 provides for output on many media other than web browsers. For example, CSS2 is designed to allow aural or Braille output, but again CSS2 implementation is lagging behind what is defined in the specification. Consideration of such output is unfortunately beyond the scope of this chapter.

CSS in SVG

A special case of applying CSS to XML occurs with respect to **Scalable Vector Graphics** (**SVG**). The Scalable Vector Graphics specification is currently at Candidate Recommendation, and outlines an exciting new XML-based technology intended for the display of 2D vector graphics, text, and bitmaps.

The functionality of CSS is deeply embedded in the emerging W3C SVG standard. In fact within the current November 2000 SVG Candidate Recommendation (http://www.w3.org/TR/2000/CR-SVG-20001102/) there are many references to the CSS2 Recommendation, since that is where many of the relevant parts of SVG functionality are definitively specified.

Look at the text properties in SVG; where the `font`, `font-family`, `font-size`, `font-variant`, `font-weight`, etc. have their normative definitions in the CSS Level 2 Recommendation. Within the more graphical aspects of SVG, the `fill`, `stroke`, and `visibility` properties also derive from CSS2.

Although a detailed discussion of CSS2 as it applies to Scalable Vector Graphics would be beyond the scope of this chapter, the following code illustrates some important points. The code, which displays a fairly straightforward SVG animation based on a draft DTD, contains several elements that have `style` attributes:

```
<?xml version="1.0" standalone="no"?>

<!DOCTYPE svg PUBLIC "-//W3C//DTD SVG 20000303 Stylable//EN"
"http://www.w3.org/TR/2000/03/WD-SVG-20000303/DTD/svg-20000303-stylable.dtd">

<svg width="10cm" height="10cm">
<desc>Simple case of animating 'use' on two 'rect's</desc>
<defs>
  <!-- Define a simple filled square -->
  <rect id="ARect" x="2cm" y="2cm" width="1cm" height="1cm"
    style="fill:rgb(153,102,153)"/>

  <!-- Define motion for when 1st square is clicked -->
  <animate id="move" xlink:href="#MyRect" attributeName="x"
    values="0cm; 5cm; 0cm" dur="5s"
    begin="indefinite"/>
```

```
    <!-- Define motion for when 2nd square is clicked -->
    <animate id="move2" xlink:href="#My2ndRect" attributeName="x"
      values="0cm; 5cm; 0cm" dur="5s"
      begin="indefinite"/>
  </defs>

  <!-- Set up 1st square and link to move animation -->
  <use id="MyRect" x="0cm" y="-1cm" xlink:href="#ARect" />
  <a xlink:href="#move">
    <text x="2cm" y="2.5cm" style="font-family: sans-serif;">
      Click here to move top rectangle
    </text>
  </a>

  <!-- Set up 2nd square and link to move2 animation -->
  <use id="My2ndRect" x="0cm" y="3cm" xlink:href="#ARect" />
  <a xlink:href="#move2">
    <text x="2cm" y="4cm" style="font-family: sans-serif;">
      Click here to move bottom rectangle
    </text>
  </a>
</svg>
```

The syntax of CSS used with the `style` attribute of SVG elements is essentially the same as when used with the `style` attribute of HTML/XHTML elements.

Note that to display the animation, shown in the following screenshot, in Internet Explorer 5.5, you will need the Adobe SVG Viewer plug-in (or similar SVG viewer), which can be downloaded from the Adobe SVG site at http://www.adobe.com/svg/. When either portion of text is clicked, the corresponding rectangle is animated from the left of the screen to the right and back again.

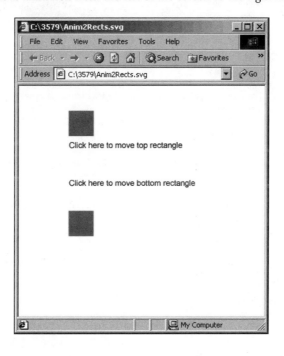

Note that the code used above corresponds to the March 2000 Working Draft, which is the relevant version for display in Version 1.0 of the Adobe SVG Viewer. Adobe are targeting Internet Explorer as their initial browser but the same plug-in can also be used with Netscape 6, although you will have to manually copy three files into the Netscape `plugins` directory. The files are, for a 32-bit Windows system, NPSVGVw.dll, SVGView.dll, and SVGViewer.zip. Copying the same files into the `Plugins` directory for Opera 5 will also work. The only difference that I have noticed is that XLinks in Opera cause a new window to be opened when clicked. If you want to visit an all-SVG web site then take a look at www.svgspider.com/default.svg.

Using CSS with XSLT

A widespread use for CSS is to combine it with HTML/XHTML results of XSLT transformations. You have seen in earlier chapters how XSLT can be used to produce HTML/XHTML or to otherwise restructure a source XML document.

So let's use our XML source document to create an XHTML 1.0 Transitional output document, to which we can apply styling from an external CSS stylesheet.

So, we again use the `Psalm23.xml` source document:

```
<?xml version='1.0'?>
<?xml-stylesheet href="Psalm23.css" type="text/css"?>
<Psalm>
<Title>Psalm 23</Title>
<Source>Scottish Psalter</Source>
<Date>1650</Date>

<Verse number="1">
<Line class="first">The LORD's my shepherd, I'll not want:</Line>
<Line>He makes me down to lie</Line>
<Line>In pastures green; He leadeth me</Line>
<Line>The quiet waters by.</Line>
</Verse>

<Verse number="5">
<Line class="first">Goodness and mercy all my life</Line>
<Line>Shall surely follow me;</Line>
<Line>And in God's house for evermore</Line>
<Line>My dwelling place shall be.</Line>
</Verse>

</Psalm>
```

We want to transform it to an XHTML file, `Psalm23XHTML.html`, that will look like this:

```
<html>
<head>
  <meta http-equiv="Content-Type" content="text/html; charset=utf-8">
  <title>Psalm 23 - The Lord's my Shepherd</title>
  <style>
    @import "Psalm23XHTML.css";
  </style>
</head>
```

```
<body>
<h1>Psalm 23</h1>
<p>The LORD's my shepherd, I'll not want:<br />
He makes me down to lie<br />
In pastures green; He leadeth me<br />
The quiet waters by.<br />
</p>

<p>Goodness and mercy all my life<br />
Shall surely follow me;<br />
And in God's house for evermore<br />
My dwelling place shall be.<br />
</p>
<br />
<h2>Scottish Psalter</h2>
<h3>1650</h3>
</body>
</html>
```

which links to the following external CSS stylesheet, `Psalm23XHTML.css`:

```
/* Psalm23XHTML.css */
/* This stylesheet is linked from Psalm23XHTML.html created by the
   Psalm23XHTML.xsl stylesheet. */

h1 {color: red;
    font-size:24pt;
    font-family:"Times New Roman", serif;
    text-decoration:underline;
    }

h2 {color: green;
    font-size:18pt;
    font-family:"Times New Roman", serif;
    text-decoration:underline;
    }

h3 {color: blue;
    font-size:14pt;
    font-family:"Times New Roman", serif;
    text-decoration:none:
    }

p   {color:#990066;
    font-size:12pt;
    font-family:"Arial", sans-serif;
    text-decoration:none;
    }
```

The output in a web browser should look something like this:

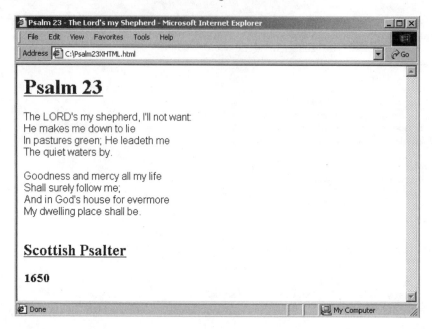

The following XSLT stylesheet, `Psalm23XHTML.xsl`, will achieve this transformation. You have covered such XSLT transformations many times in other chapters, so I will only briefly step you through some key parts of the code.

```
<?xml version='1.0'?>

<xsl:stylesheet version="1.0"
                xmlns:xsl="http://www.w3.org/1999/XSL/Transform">
<xsl:output method="html"/>
```

We set the XSLT output method to HTML:

```
<xsl:template match="/">
 <html>
 <head>
 <title>Psalm 23 - The Lord's my Shepherd</title>
 <style>
 @import "Psalm23XHTML.css";
 </style>
 </head>
 <body>
 <xsl:apply-templates select="Psalm/Title"/>
 <xsl:apply-templates select="Psalm/Verse"/>
 <br />
 <xsl:apply-templates select="Psalm/Source"/>
 <xsl:apply-templates select="Psalm/Date"/>
 </body>
 </html></xsl:template>
```

The above XSLT template, which matches the root node, does most of the work, creating the element structure for the output XHTML page. Note that, within the <style> element in the <head> of the output document, we use the @import notation mentioned earlier in the chapter to associate the external CSS stylesheet, Psalm23XHTML.css, with the generated XHTML document, Psalm23XHTML.html.

```
<xsl:template match="Psalm/Title">
 <h1><xsl:value-of select="."/></h1>
</xsl:template>

<xsl:template match="Psalm/Verse">
 <p>
 <xsl:apply-templates select="Line"/>
 </p>
</xsl:template>

<xsl:template match="Psalm/Source">
  <h2><xsl:value-of select="."/></h2>
</xsl:template>

<xsl:template match="Psalm/Date">
 <h3><xsl:value-of select="."/></h3>
</xsl:template>

<xsl:template match="Line">
 <xsl:value-of select="."/>
 <br />
</xsl:template>

</xsl:stylesheet>
```

The other five XSLT templates simply create appropriate XHTML <h1>, <h3>, and <p> elements to control display of text, as well as adding a <br /> element to the end of the content of each <Line> element in the source XML document.

The XSLT transformation produces an XHTML 1.0 Transitional file. This file includes no internal styling as this is given by CSS rules contained in the external CSS stylesheet. It is now possible to revise the appearance of the XHTML when displayed, without having to make any alterations to the XSLT transformation.

By now I hope to have given you an outline of the usage of CSS with XML and associated XSLT transformations. It is time now to move on to the newer topic of XSL-FO.

XSL-FO – XSL Formatting Objects

This section is a brief summary of XSL-FO, to give you an indication of what it is and how it is produced. XSL-FO is a complex XML vocabulary and formatting language and in the remainder of this chapter I hope to introduce you to some of its more salient features.

Most of this book has focused on the role of XSLT on the Web, especially when a selection of browsers, desktops, or mobiles might be used to view the information. As I mentioned earlier in the chapter, CSS is largely concerned with display on the Web, although CSS2 does address use of other output media, and the drafts of CSS3 that have begun to emerge will go further down this path. However, XSL-FO, was designed to display on multiple media and opens up new avenues for the "write once, display anywhere" ideal, in that XML data so described would display correctly on essentially any medium. Or, to be more precise, it will be able to do so once the XSL-FO specification is completed and a suitable range of fully functional tools becomes available. However, there are tools now emerging with very useful functionality, although not yet implementing every part of the specification.

XSL-FO Terminology

Before I continue with this discussion, I'd like to clear up a potential terminology trap. In current usage, "XSL-FO" refers to XSL Formatting Objects, "XSLT" refers to XSL Transformations and "XSL" refers to both together.

XSL was originally a single language, but was split into XSLT and XSL-FO in 1999. In parallel with that Microsoft released their flavor of "XSL" which was in fact a non-standard version of XSLT. This Microsoft type of "XSL" is now little more than a historical relic, as Microsoft has sensibly abandoned it in favor of W3C standard XSLT. However, books, articles, etc. can still be found that refer to this defunct Microsoft "XSL" without clearly stating what is being referred to.

However, it isn't only Microsoft that has introduced potential confusion in this area. The W3C Candidate Recommendation for XSL-FO is actually called "*Extensible Stylesheet Language (XSL)*" while it really describes XSL-FO alone. Also, confusingly, the URI http://www.w3.org/1999/XSL/Format is referred to in the Candidate Recommendation as the "XSL Namespace" although it again only applies to XSL-FO. Additionally, XSLT uses the indicative namespace prefix of "xsl" although that refers to just the "XSLT" namespace, http://www.w3.org/1999/XSL/Transform.

So be very careful to be clear exactly what is being referred to when you see or hear the term "XSL" in a particular context.

In passing, another terminology pitfall awaiting the unwary XSL-FO explorer stems from the terms "formatting objects" and "formatting elements" – two terms that are in fact effectively interchangeable.

Now that this potentially confusing nomenclature has been explained, let's move on to take in an overview of XSL-FO.

XSL-FO Overview

XSL-FO is an XML-based formatting vocabulary for display on a range of devices, including desktop browsers and on paper. XSL-FO is significantly more intricate than CSS.

Schematically, XSL-FO output is produced from an XML source document in two steps – an XSLT transformation to add FO markup, followed by the formatting step.

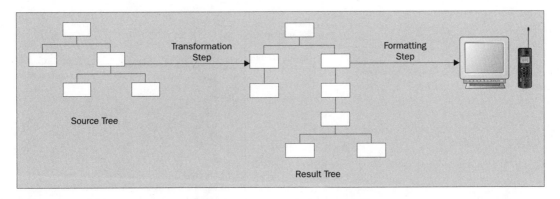

While this shows production and display of an XSL-FO document as a two-step process, an XSL-FO document is generally created by incorporating XSL-FO elements into XML source, with a suitably structured stylesheet generating the result tree in what appears to be an otherwise typical XSLT transformation. You may recognize, from XSLT examples elsewhere in the book, that including XSL-FO elements in the result tree is closely related to including HTML or XHTML elements. The latter can be displayed in a Web browser. XSL-FO is displayed in an XSL formatter/viewer or converted to PDF for display in Adobe's Acrobat Reader. With the advent of XSL formatters, such as the Antenna House XSL Formatter mentioned later in the chapter, interactive development of XSL stylesheets becomes significantly easier, although still far from a trivial task.

To express the process in other words, a suitable XML source document will be linked to an XSL stylesheet ("XSL" since it includes both XSLT and XSL-FO elements) with the output tree representing a well-formed XSL-FO document, which is then processed further by an XSL-FO formatter creating the appropriate output. If you like, you can view the creation of XSL-FO as a special case of the transformation from one type of XML to another. The output XML (XSL-FO) then provides the input for an XSL formatter that causes the XSL-FO to be visually represented on screen or on paper, saved to file, or otherwise output.

An XSL-FO Page

One of the key things to grasp when getting to grips with XSL-FO is the structure and terminology of the layout of an XSL-FO page. It is fairly complex due to two main factors.

The requirement to use XSL-FO for displaying XML-based data on paper has contributed significantly to the complexity of XSL-FO and also to the fact that development of XSL-FO has lagged significantly behind the development of XSLT. In addition, XSL-FO incorporates features to support internationalization, and is further complicated in order to allow for the display of languages that flow right-to-left or top-to-bottom, as well as left-to-right as in English.

Let's take a brief look at the areas of an XSL-FO page. It is intended to provide a comprehensive 'map' of any page and contains several subtleties, so you may find you have to come back to it more than once before the reasons behind the structure (and how it changes depending on the language displayed) have sunk in. You may also find that you need to refer back to it when I present the function of the principal XSL-FO elements later in the chapter.

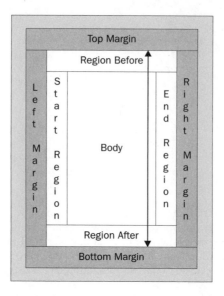

The preceding diagram shows the variously named regions of an XSL-FO page, when a left-to-right language like English is being displayed. The gray areas represent the top, bottom, left, and right margins of the page and may contain no content. The white area is divided into up to five areas – the body region (which is where normal page content goes), the region before (which appears 'before' the body content – the header), the region after (which appears 'after' the body content – the footer), the start region (at the "start" of a line) and the end region (at the "end" of a line). Any of these five may contain content but, as in many documents, not all of the five need be defined.

> *Beware! In ordinary English, "before" and "start" have similar meaning. In XSL-FO the meaning is more specific and, for an English document, the "region before" denotes the top of the page, and the "start region" is used to indicate the left side of the page. Similarly, the "region after" is at the bottom of the page, and the "end region" is at the right side of the page.*

Also note that the layout shown applies for languages written, like English, from left-to-right and top-to-bottom. For languages like Hebrew or Arabic that are written from right-to-left, the orientation of these areas is inverted: the "start region" is at the right side of the page and the "end region" is at the left side of the page. For languages written in vertical columns everything is rotated through 90 degrees.

In a common scenario, the before region, the body region, and the after region are defined for a page and contain, respectively, the page header, the page content and the page footer. Notice that, as indicated by the vertical arrows in the preceding diagram of a page, the body region extends right up to the edge of the area within the page margins. This means that it is possible to have page content overlap the header or footer, unless you are careful to also define margins for the top and bottom of the body region (not to be confused with the margins represented by the gray area above).

> *The formatting process in XSL-FO can be viewed as a multi-step process. A **formatting objects tree** is created. From that a **tree of areas** is created. Finally, that tree of areas is rendered for display on screen or on paper. The formatting process need not be linear. Discussion of its details is beyond the scope of this chapter. Detailed understanding of the tree of areas is more fully described in the W3C specification and is more relevant to implementors of XSL formatters than to users.*

In the November 2000 XSL-FO Candidate Recommendation, 56 XSL-FO elements are described. Typically a namespace prefix of "fo:" is used for XSL-FO elements. The prefix, of course, is an alias for the XSL-FO namespace, which is http://www.w3.org/1999/XSL/Format.

At first sight, the comprehensive list of these 56 XSL-FO elements can be pretty intimidating:

fo:basic-link	fo:inline	fo:multi-toggle	fo:simple-page-master
fo:bidi-override	fo:inline-container	fo:page-number	fo:single-page-master-reference
fo:block	fo:instream-foreign-object	fo:page-number-citation	fo:static-content
fo:block-container	fo:layout-master-set	fo:page-sequence	fo:table
fo:character	fo:leader	fo:page-sequence-master	fo:table-and-caption
fo:color-profile	fo:list-block	fo:region-after	fo:table-body
fo:conditional-page-master-reference	fo:list-item	fo:region-before	fo:table-caption
fo:declarations	fo:list-item-body	fo:region-body	fo:table-cell
fo:external-graphic	fo:list-item-label	fo:region-end	fo:table-column
fo:float	fo:marker	fo:region-start	fo:table-footer
fo:flow	fo:multi-case	fo:repeatable-page-master-alternatives	fo:table-header
fo:footnote	fo:multi-properties	fo:repeatable-page-master-reference	fo:table-row
fo:footnote-body	fo:multi-property-set	fo:retrieve-marker	fo:title
fo:initial-property-set	fo:multi-switch	fo:root	fo:wrapper

However, if you cast your eye more slowly over the list you will begin to pick out groups of XSL-FO elements that offer functionality similar to that provided by elements in HTML. For example, the following XSL-FO elements:

- ❑   fo:list-block
- ❑   fo:list-item
- ❑   fo:list-item-body
- ❑   fo:list-item-label

These clearly have functions related to the construction of a list. The `fo:list-item-label` provides the bullet (such as the shadowed square in the preceding list or a number for numbered lists), and the `fo:list-item-body` contains the actual content of a list item.

So, within a page you would have something like this for an XSL-FO list:

```
<fo:list-block>
  <fo:list-item>
    <fo:list-item-label>
      <!-- The character or image which is used for the bullet goes here. -->
    <fo:list-item-label>
    <fo:list-item-body>
      <!-- The actual list item text goes here. -->
    </fo:list-item-body>
  </fo:list-item>
<!-- More <fo:list-item> elements would go here. -->
</fo:list-block>
```

Similarly, the following group of XSL Formatting Objects can be expected to be applicable to the creation of tables:

❑ `fo:table`

❑ `fo:table-and-caption`

❑ `fo:table-body`

❑ `fo:table-caption`

❑ `fo:table-cell`

❑ `fo:table-column`

❑ `fo:table-footer`

❑ `fo:table-header`

❑ `fo:table-row`

In addition to the 56 elements of the Candidate Recommendation, there are well over 100 XSL-FO attributes. I will show you the use of a few of these in the remainder of the chapter.

The Structure of an XSL-FO Document

In this section I will give you an overview of how the structure of an XSL-FO document is constructed from the more commonly used XSL-FO elements. When I began to learn about XSL-FO, I found that I needed to read this type of material several times before I really grasped how the pieces fit together. You may well find the same, so be prepared to read this section more than once. XSL-FO is complex but it does have a strong underlying logic to it, which will become apparent as you begin to see how the various aspects fit together.

The following is a basic skeleton that illustrates some of the simple structure of XSL-FO documents. The listing is called XSLFOOutline.fo, and uses the standard .fo suffix for XSL-FO files:

```
<?xml version='1.0'?>
<!-- This code is for illustrative purposes only. -->
<fo:root xmlns:fo="http://www.w3.org/1999/XSL/Format">

  <fo:layout-master-set>

    <!-- Information on one or more general page layouts goes here. -->
    <fo:simple-page-master master-name="first"
               page-height="11in"
               page-width="8.5in"
               margin-top="1in"
               margin-bottom=".75in"
               margin-left="1in"
               margin-right="1in">
      <fo:region-body margin-top=".75in" />
    </fo:simple-page-master>

  </fo:layout-master-set>

  <fo:page-sequence master-name="first">
    <!-- This element defines the sequence of elements for certain pages -->
  </fo:page-sequence>

</fo:root>
```

Since a formatting objects document is an XML document, the first line of all XSL-FO documents must be the XML declaration.

Each XSL-FO document has one, and one only, root element, typically called <fo:root>, which includes a namespace declaration associating the fo prefix with the URI http://www.w3.org/1999/XSL/Format. You can, of course, use whatever prefix you desire in the namespace declaration, just as long as it is associated with the correct XSL-FO namespace URI:

```
<fo:root xmlns:ftangptang="http://www.w3.org/1999/XSL/Format">
```

If you are used to XSLT, and are in the habit of almost automatically typing the namespace URI http://www.w3.org/1999/XSL/Transform, be careful to use the correct URI. When you are using XSLT to produce XSL-FO output you will typically have both namespaces in use within your stylesheet.

The <fo:root> element encloses all other elements within an XSL-FO document.

XSL-FO is essentially a *document* description language, rather than a *page* description language. A single XSL-FO file can contain the information required to lay out lengthy documents, even documents as long as this book.

In multi-page documents there can be different layouts for individual pages, for example for a page that starts a chapter or for regular left and right pages. If you take a look at the left and right pages in front of you, you can see that the headers are not the same. XSL-FO would represent the layouts for left and right pages as individual <fo:simple-page-master> elements, with each used as appropriate throughout the document.

We see a simple example of this in the code snippet which follows.

```
<fo: layout-master-set>

    <fo:simple-page-master master-name="first"
                    page-height="11in"
                    page-width="8.5in"
                    margin-top="1in"
                    margin-bottom=".75in"
                    margin-left="1in"
                    margin-right="1in">
        <fo:region-body margin-top=".75in" />
    </fo:simple-page-master>

</fo:layout-master-set>
```

The <fo:layout-master-set> element contains nested within it one or more <fo:simple-page-master> elements.

We have given the master-name attribute of our single <fo:simple-page-master> the value of "first". The page-height and page-width attributes define sizes used for typical US letters.

Recall too that there were page margins shown with a gray background in the diagram. The margin-top, margin-bottom, margin-left, and margin-right attributes of the <fo:simple-page-master> element allow us to set those margins.

I mentioned earlier that, to prevent text in the "body region" overlapping the other four regions where text may appear, it would be necessary to set margins for the body region itself. In this <fo:simple-page-master> element we have a <fo:region-body> element whose top margin is 0.75 inches. Thus any header can extend up to 0.75 inches into the body region without infringing on the body content.

To recap, the example skeleton document has two major sections: the section which describes the <fo:layout-master-set> element:

```
<fo:layout-master-set>
    <!-- Information on one or more general page layouts goes here. -->
</fo:layout-master-set>
```

and the section that describes the <fo:page-sequence> element:

```
<fo:page-sequence master-name="first">
    <!-- This element defines the sequence of elements for certain pages -->
</fo:page-sequence>
```

Within the <fo:layout-master-set> element the layout information for the document is described, while the content for the page body and for headers and footers is contained within the <fo:page-sequence> element.

Now, I'd like us to look a little closer at how the XSL-FO elements of the `<fo:page-sequence>` element may be structured:

```
<fo:page-sequence master-name="first">

  <fo:static-content flow-name="xsl-region-before">
    <!-- The page header content would go here. -->
  </fo:static-content>

  <fo:static-content flow-name="xsl-region-after">
    <!-- The page footer content would go here. -->
  </fo:static-content>

  <fo:flow flow-name="xsl-region-body">
    <!-- The actual page content would go here. -->
  </fo:flow>

</fo:page-sequence>
```

The first thing to notice in the code above is that the `master-name` attribute of the `<fo:page-sequence>` element has the value `"first"`, which matches the value of the `master-name` attribute of the `<fo:simple-page-master>` element contained within the earlier `<fo:layout-master-set>` element. It is essential that the `master-name` matches one of the `<fo:simple-page-master>` elements, otherwise the XSL-FO formatter does not know which layout to apply to the available page content.

Next, notice that the `<fo:static-content>` element(s) must precede the `<fo:flow>` element. In other words, you must describe the content of your header and footer before going on to describe the content of your page. Notice too that the `<fo:static-content>` element has a `flow-name` attribute to differentiate the header, footer, start, and end regions. To refer to the header the `flow-name` attribute has the value `"xsl-region-before"` and to refer to the footer it has the value `"xsl-region-after"`, as shown earlier in the diagram of an XSL-FO page (in the section titled *An XSL-FO Page*).

Why call this element "static content"? Well, the content of a header and footer is typically repeated on many pages and is, in that sense at least, "static". By contrast the content in the main part of the page "flows" and so is contained in a `<fo:flow>` element.

Within a `<fo:flow>` element you can expect to find many nested XSL-FO elements, including:

- ❑ `<fo:block>`
- ❑ `<fo:block-container>`
- ❑ `<fo:table-and-caption>`
- ❑ `<fo:table>`
- ❑ `<fo:list-block>`

You will see `<fo:block>` elements used widely in the example XSL-FO documents that follow. Recall the distinction I drew earlier in the chapter between block, line, and inline elements. The `<fo:block>` element is, unsurprisingly, a block-level element. Also you won't be surprised to learn that the `<fo:table>` elements and the `<fo:list-block>` elements are used in the construction of tables and lists respectively.

Having taken a broad overview of the `<fo:layout-master-set>` elements and the `<fo:page-sequence>` elements, let's now look at the situation where the `<fo:layout-master-set>` element contains more than one `<fo:simple-page-master>` element. Note that essentially no content is present within the document: it is layout information only.

For example, in the following file, `XSLFOTemplate.fo`, we see a sample `fo:layout-master-set` for use on a multi-page document using 11 inch by 8.5 inch US letter paper:

```
<?xml version="1.0" encoding="utf-8"?>

<fo:root xmlns:fo="http://www.w3.org/1999/XSL/Format">

  <fo:layout-master-set>
    <fo:simple-page-master master-name="first"
              page-height="11in"
              page-width="8.5in"
              margin-top="1in"
              margin-bottom=".75in"
              margin-left="1in"
              margin-right="1in">
      <fo:region-body margin-top=".75in" />
    </fo:simple-page-master>

    <fo:simple-page-master master-name="others"
              page-height="11in"
              page-width="8.5in"
              margin-top="1in"
              margin-bottom=".75in"
              margin-left="1in"
              margin-right="1in">
      <fo:region-body margin-top=".75in"/>
      <fo:region-before extent=".5in"/>
      <fo:region-after extent=".75in"/>
    </fo:simple-page-master>

    <fo:page-sequence-master master-name="layout" >
      <fo:repeatable-page-master-alternatives>
        <fo:conditional-page-master-reference
                    master-name="first"
                    page-position="first" />
        <fo:conditional-page-master-reference
                    master-name="others" />
      </fo:repeatable-page-master-alternatives>
    </fo:page-sequence-master>

  </fo:layout-master-set>

  <fo:page-sequence master-name="layout">

    <!-- Header -->
    <fo:static-content flow-name="xsl-region-before">
      This is the page header
    </fo:static-content>
```

```
     <!-- Footer -->
     <fo:static-content flow-name="xsl-region-after">
       This is the page footer
     </fo:static-content>

     <!-- Page Body -->
     <fo:flow flow-name="xsl-region-body">
       This is the page body
     </fo:flow>

   </fo:page-sequence>

</fo:root>
```

The `layout-master-set` is designed to be output on US letter size paper and has different layout for those pages designated as "`first`" from for those that are "`others`".

The `<fo:static-content>` might typically contain a `<fo:block>` element with attributes that define the formatting of the page header and might, optionally include a `<fo:page-number>` element.

Creating an XSL-FO Document Using XSLT

We now have an outline of the structure of a typical XSL-FO document that will come in handy as we move on to examine the use of XSLT to transform an XML document to include XSL-FO elements for display.

In this section I will make use of the preview release of the Antenna House XSL Formatter, which is described in more detail in the next section.

We will again turn to our trusty source XML document `Psalm23.xml`:

```
<?xml version='1.0'?>
<?xml-stylesheet href="Psalm23.css" type="text/css"?>
<Psalm>
<Title>Psalm 23</Title>
<Source>Scottish Psalter</Source>
<Date>1650</Date>

<Verse number="1">
<Line class="first">The LORD's my shepherd, I'll not want:</Line>
<Line>He makes me down to lie</Line>
<Line>In pastures green; He leadeth me</Line>
<Line>The quiet waters by.</Line>
</Verse>

<Verse number="5">
<Line class="first">Goodness and mercy all my life</Line>
<Line>Shall surely follow me;</Line>
<Line>And in God's house for evermore</Line>
<Line>My dwelling place shall be.</Line>
</Verse>

</Psalm>
```

But this time, instead of using XSLT to create an XHTML file (linked to a CSS stylesheet) from this XML, the XSLT will transform it into a single XSL-FO document, such that the formatted output document looks like this:

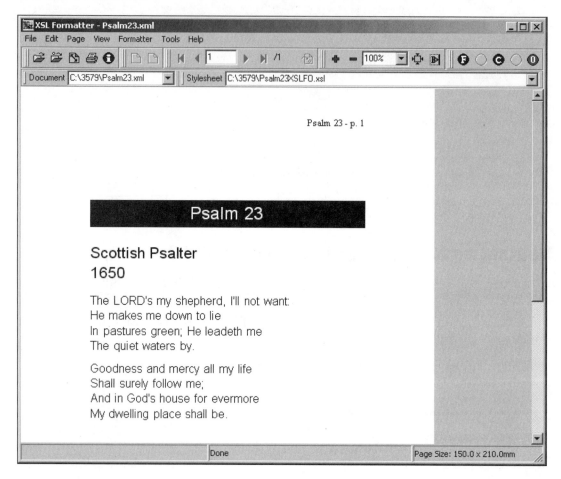

The screenshot shows our output XSL-FO document viewed using the Antenna House XSL Formatter, which also serves as an XSL-FO viewer.

To achieve this we shall create an XSLT stylesheet, Psalm23XSLFO.xsl, which follows the push model design containing many templates. In one sense this operates like any other XSLT stylesheet but the output is an XSL-FO document, rather than, say, HTML.

We start with the XML declaration and the namespace declarations for both the XSLT and XSL-FO elements that we will use within the stylesheet:

```
<?xml version='1.0'?>

<xsl:stylesheet version="1.0"
  xmlns:xsl="http://www.w3.org/1999/XSL/Transform"
  xmlns:fo="http://www.w3.org/1999/XSL/Format">
```

The first thing output by our core XSLT template is the `<fo:root>` element, which will contain the remainder of our created XSL-FO:

```
<xsl:template match="/">
  <fo:root>
```

The next section of the XSLT template generates the `<fo:layout-master-set>` element and its child `<fo:simple-page-master>` elements. The XSLT has created two `<fo:simple-page-master>` elements but, for clarity, we will only use one in the remainder of this example. However, it does demonstrate how you can format more complex documents by referring to one of these page layouts by `master-name`.

```
<fo:layout-master-set>

  <fo:simple-page-master master-name="first"
    page-height="21cm"
    page-width="15cm"
    margin-top="1cm"
    margin-bottom="2cm"
    margin-left="2.5cm"
    margin-right="2.5cm">
    <fo:region-body margin-top="3cm"/>
    <fo:region-before extent="3cm"/>
    <fo:region-after extent="1.5cm"/>
  </fo:simple-page-master>

  <fo:simple-page-master master-name="rest"
    page-height="21cm"
    page-width="15cm"
    margin-top="1cm"
    margin-bottom="2cm"
    margin-left="2.5cm"
    margin-right="2.5cm">
    <fo:region-body margin-top="2.5cm"/>
    <fo:region-before extent="2.5cm"/>
    <fo:region-after extent="1.5cm"/>
  </fo:simple-page-master>

</fo:layout-master-set>
```

Now, we create a `<fo:page-sequence>` element within which all our page content will be laid out, drawing on the appropriate `<fo:layout-master-set>` element:

```
<fo:page-sequence master-name="first">
```

The first part of the created page is the page header, given by a `<fo:static-content>` element with a `flow-name` attribute of value "xsl-region-before". Nested within the `<fo:static-content>` element is a `<fo:block>` element which, has attributes to describe the style of the contained area. Within our header we use the `<fo:page-number>` element to output the appropriate page number.

```
<fo:static-content flow-name="xsl-region-before">
  <fo:block text-align="end"
    font-size="10pt"
    font-family="serif"
    line-height="14pt" >
    <xsl:value-of select="/Psalm/Title"/> - p. <fo:page-number/>
  </fo:block>
</fo:static-content>
```

Here we add a further `<fo:static-content>` element to define the footer for our page in a similar fashion:

```
<fo:static-content flow-name="xsl-region-after">
  <fo:block text-align="end"
    font-size="10pt"
    font-family="serif"
    line-height="14pt" >
    <xsl:value-of select="/Psalm/Title"/> - p. <fo:page-number/>
  </fo:block>
</fo:static-content>
```

The `<fo:flow>` element will contain the main page content (other than the header and footer):

```
<fo:flow flow-name="xsl-region-body">
```

The first block in the page has a blue background and large white text and will show the value of the `<Title>` element of our source document:

```
<fo:block font-size="18pt"
  font-family="sans-serif"
  line-height="24pt"
  space-after.optimum="15pt"
  background-color="blue"
  color="white"
  text-align="center"
  padding-top="3pt">
  <xsl:apply-templates select="Psalm/Title"/>
</fo:block>
```

Then we add a further block, which has slightly smaller text in the default black on white. It applies templates found later in our XSLT file to display the content of the `<Source>` and `<Date>` elements found in our source XML.

```
<fo:block font-size="16pt"
  font-family="sans-serif"
  line-height="20pt"
  space-before.optimum="10pt"
  space-after.optimum="10pt"
  text-align="start"
  padding-top="3pt">
```

```
      <xsl:apply-templates select="Psalm/Source"/>
      <fo:block>
        <xsl:apply-templates select="Psalm/Date"/>
      </fo:block>
    </fo:block>
```

The end tag of the `<fo:flow>` element signals the end of the created page content. Some of it is inserted by XSLT templates from a later part of the code. We mustn't forget of course to include the end tags for the `<fo:page-sequence>`, `<fo:root>`, and `<xsl:template>` elements.

```
    <fo:block font-size="12pt"
      font-family="sans-serif"
      line-height="15pt"
      space-after.optimum="3pt"
      text-align="start">
      <xsl:apply-templates select="Psalm/Verse"/>
    </fo:block>
  </fo:flow>

  </fo:page-sequence>
  </fo:root>
</xsl:template>
```

Now come the templates applied by the above `<fo:flow>` element:

```
<xsl:template match="Psalm/Title">
  <xsl:value-of select="."/>
</xsl:template>

<xsl:template match="Psalm/Verse">
  <fo:block space-before="8pt" space-after="8pt">
    <xsl:apply-templates select="Line"/>
  </fo:block>
</xsl:template>

<xsl:template match="Psalm/Source">
  <xsl:value-of select="."/>
</xsl:template>

<xsl:template match="Psalm/Date">
  <xsl:value-of select="."/>
</xsl:template>

<xsl:template match="Line">
  <fo:block>
    <xsl:value-of select="."/>
  </fo:block>
</xsl:template>

</xsl:stylesheet>
```

The above five simple XSLT templates output the content of the various elements of our XML source document. They are called from within the main template to insert their contents in the appropriate places within the `<fo:root>` element or its descendants. We then close the XSLT stylesheet, as all required elements are now defined.

Note that significant parts of the `<fo:layout-master-set>` element are not required for the creation of a single page of output such as our two verses of Psalm 23. However, the code included in the `<fo:layout-master-set>` element provides a building block that you can develop to suit your needs during your first experimental outings with XSL-FO (I'll refrain from calling them 'hot dates'). Note also that I altered the dimensions of the layout to give reasonable on-screen presentation. For output to paper you will wish to adjust layout sizes to match the paper size you will be using.

Antenna House XSL Formatter

Earlier in this chapter I indicated that I was unaware until recently of any browser that can display XSL-FO natively. The Antenna House XSL Formatter is hardly a "browser" as such but does, in its current Preview Release incarnation, have the capability for the on screen display of a good proportion of XSL-FO. So, in one sense, it is the first XSL-FO "browser", although not what we would normally consider a browser. As its name implies, it is also a general XSL formatter too.

As you can see, the Antenna House XSL Formatter can display our output XSL-FO document using `Psalm23.xml` as the primary document and `Psalm23XSLFO.xsl` as the stylesheet (shown by the **Document** and **Stylesheet** drop-down menus in the screenshot):

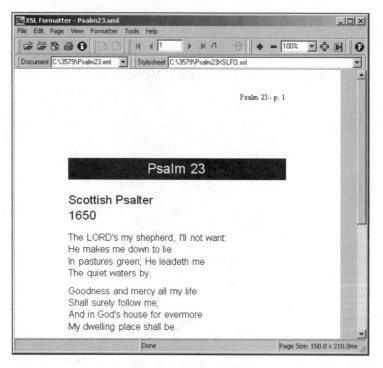

The Antenna House XSL Formatter can display multiple page documents (the area below and to the right of the **Help** menu allows navigation between the pages of a multi-page document). It can zoom in or out for suitable display (the **100%** appearing towards the top of the screen shows current scaling, and the button to the right will fit the page to the screen). The circular button with a capital "F" runs the formatter, applying the chosen XSLT stylesheet to the chosen XML source document.

Information on the Preview Release of the Antenna House XSL Formatter can be found at http://www.antennahouse.com/xslformatter.html. The version I used was 0.1.0.1227, and is designed to work with Windows 95, 98, NT 4.0, 2000, and ME. You will need to have IE 5.0 (or later) installed and also have MSXML3 and Windows Installer available. Helpful URLs are provided for any downloads necessary, should a required component not already be installed on your machine. Installation itself is straightforward and the default choices will produce a working XSL Formatter installation.

Antenna House is a Japanese company and they acknowledge that the English help files are incomplete. However, there is sufficient basic help to enable you to get started, and there is a detailed description of those formatting objects that are supported, and those that are not.

Getting started is not difficult: choose the File|Open menu option. A pop-up window will let you load an XML source file and XSL stylesheet, including options to browse appropriate directories, as in the following screenshot:

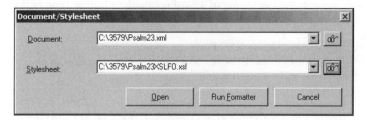

As you can see, the XML document and stylesheet shown will produce the XSL-FO output displayed in the previous section. Simply click the Run Formatter button to produce a display according to your choices for Document and Stylesheet.

Once the files are loaded you can see which document is the subject of the XSL stylesheet transformation and also the name of the stylesheet that is being used. It is possible to have multiple stylesheets that relate to a single source file, in which case alternative stylesheets can be made active simply by using the stylesheet drop-down choice.

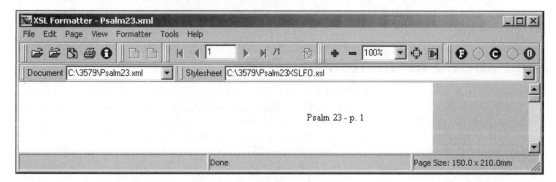

If you make mistakes in the construction of your stylesheet, the program displays reasonably helpful error messages such as this:

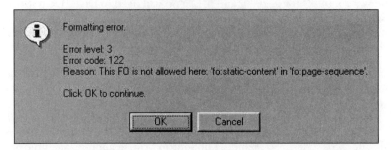

As with most XML-related code, be wary that, if your error is due to misspelling a closing tag or omitting the forward slash at the beginning of a closing tag, the place or type of the error identified by the formatter may not in fact relate the actual problem that needs to be addressed.

The availability of the Antenna House XSL Formatter opens up many new opportunities for developers to explore XSL-FO. It becomes a much more straightforward proposition to explore the effects of adding or removing code or styling information.

In my opinion this is a very exciting development for the adoption of XSL-FO. Previously, in the absence of a user-friendly XSL formatting engine/browser, the XSL-FO working drafts seemed pretty daunting. With the release of products such as XSL Formatter, exploration of the uncharted waters of XSL-FO gets a whole lot easier.

Antenna House seems to be the first truly usable XSL formatter. No doubt many other similar tools will follow once the XSL-FO Recommendation is finalized, and their availability will lead to wider awareness of XSL-FO and its capabilities, which will in turn increase the demand for developers who have useful knowledge of the subject. An XSL-FO browser is probably not too far away.

Until recently, exploration of XSL-FO has seemed, to many, to be a daunting prospect. Mastering XSL-FO is still not a trivial exercise but with the advent of further easy-to-use tools to format XSL-FO, its future looks bright.

Using XSL-FO to Create PDF: FOP

The lack of complete tools for the display of native XSL-FO means that it is still common to convert XSL-FO to Portable Document Format, PDF, for display. Additionally, PDF is a well-known format whereas XSL-FO is still not finalized at the time of writing. So, it is likely that PDF will be generated from XSL-FO for some time to come. However, once sophisticated XSL-FO tools become available and are widely used, the additional step of conversion to PDF is likely to decrease progressively.

A widely used tool, FOP, processes XSL-FO documents and converts them into Portable Document Format. FOP is a Java application that reads a formatting objects tree and turns it into a PDF document. FOP can operate on serialized XML documents (produced by an XSLT processor) or the formatting object tree can be assembled in memory as a suitable DOM document or a tree of SAX events. General information about FOP can be found at http://xml.apache.org/fop/. It is important to be aware that FOP is very much in development and does not, at the time of writing, claim to fully implement the November 2000 XSL-FO Candidate Recommendation. As such, it is a tool for exploring the capabilities of XSL-FO rather than a production-level product.

A number of options for downloading FOP are offered on the Apache site at http://xml.apache.org/dist/fop/. Among the distributions that can be downloaded is one that includes pre-compiled source code and example files. For this brief foray into XSL-FO we will use the version designed specifically for XSL-FO beginners, which can be located at http://xml.apache.org/dist/fop/fop-0_15_0-forBeginners.zip. If you wish, you may decide on another version that includes the source code and separate documentation to download.

FOP may be run from the command line or can be embedded in your own Java applications. Instructions for how to embed FOP are to be found at http://xml.apache.org/fop/embedding.html.

Installation and setup on a Windows 98 system is quite straightforward. Once the FOP zip file is downloaded, simply unzip it into an appropriately named directory. I chose c:\fop. The beginners' installation includes a number of HTML help files that can be accessed from C:\fop\docs\html-docs\index.html assuming you installed in c:\fop. This documentation is very similar to the information about FOP found on the http://xml.apache.org web site.

To run FOP you need JDK 1.1 (or higher), available from http://java.sun.com installed, and you will need to ensure that the Java Virtual Machine can find the new Java files by including their paths in the CLASSPATH environment variable. A command similar to the following in your autoexec.bat file should work for Windows 98 systems:

```
set CLASSPATH=%CLASSPATH%;c:\fop\build\fop.jar;c:\fop\lib\w3c.jar;
```

The beginner's installation of FOP includes a number of .fo files for test purposes. To test that your installation is working, run the autoexec.bat file if necessary to apply the CLASSPATH changes, and then from a command prompt change to the directory in which you installed FOP (c:\fop in my case). Then make use of the test.fo file – installed when the FOP archive was unzipped – with the following command line:

```
java org.apache.fop.apps.CommandLine test.fo test.pdf
```

If all has gone well you should see the following:

Notice, among the output on screen, the sequence of messages detailing the processing steps: building a formatting objects tree, setting up fonts, organizing the formatting objects into areas, rendering the areas into PDF, and finally writing out the PDF.

In the `c:\fop` directory a new file named `test.pdf` should have been created. Using the Adobe Acrobat PDF Reader, which may be downloaded free of charge from http://www.adobe.com, you should be able to open the `test.pdf` file that FOP has just created, and it should look like this:

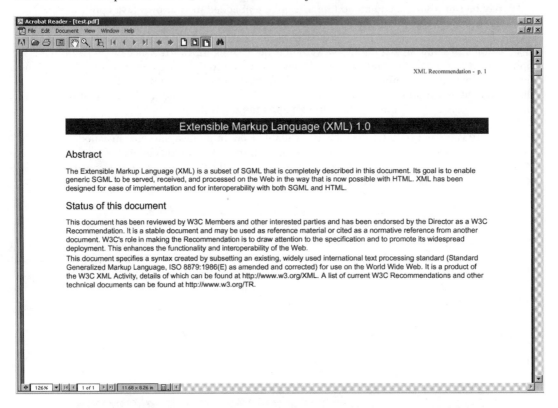

Similarly, we can just as easily create a PDF file of our extract from Psalm 23 using the following command. Be careful to ensure that you have copied the `Psalm23.fo` file to the FOP directory.

```
java org.apache.fop.apps.CommandLine Psalm23.fo Psalm23.pdf
```

So, we can view our PDF file using Acrobat. Can we view it within a web browser? If you try to view the `Psalm23.pdf` files directly from Internet Explorer 5.5, say, using either `c:\fop\Psalm23.pdf` or `file:///c:/fop/Psalm23.pdf` you will find that Acrobat opens outside of IE 5.5. If you want to display the test PDF file within a web browser you will need to copy the `Psalm23.pdf` file to a suitable server. For example, if you have Personal Web Server then you can copy `Psalm23.pdf` to the `wwwroot` directory and display the file by typing the 'URL':

```
http://127.0.0.1/Psalm23.pdf
```

Now the formatting objects file can be displayed (as a PDF file) within a web browser, whether `Psalm23.fo` or another chosen XSL-FO file in the appropriate Personal Web Server directory.

Looking Forward

I have only been able to give you a flavor of this nascent technology in this part of the chapter. For the time being you will probably find that you need turn to XSL-FO resources on the Web to expand your knowledge of the subject. For this, the World Wide Web Consortium site provides the prime source of information, http://www.w3.org/tr/XSL.

During the lifetime of this book we can expect that many new tools to process and display XSL-FO will appear. One useful online resource is the list of XSL-FO tools maintained by James Tauber at http://www.xmlsoftware.com/xslfo/. Another list of tools is maintained by the Yahoo Group located at http://www.yahoogroups.com/group/XSL-FO/. Go to the Links page of this XSL-FO mailing list, at http://www.yahoogroups.com/group/XSL-FO/links, for information on formatting objects tools.

Summary

Phew! We've covered a lot of important ground in this chapter. Both CSS and XSL-FO are broad technologies, which will become increasingly significant as browsers and other viewers improve in their capability to reliably display them.

I have shown you how to use a variety of CSS selectors to display HTML and XML, and you have seen how to link XML documents to CSS stylesheets, including how CSS stylesheets can be linked to documents created by XSLT.

Along the way you should have learned a lot of the basics of the extensive and complex XSL-FO technology, including the basic structure of an XSL-FO document, for example:

- ❑ The different layouts that may be applied to a given page of the document are defined within the `<fo:layout-master-set>` element.

- ❑ The other major element type in an XSL-FO document is the `<fo:page-sequence>` element, and is styled according to the `<fo:simple-page-master>` referred to by the `master-name` attribute.

- ❑ The `<fo:page-sequence>` element can contain one or more `<fo:static-content>` elements, where the `flow-region` attribute denotes the area of a page to which that content applies.

- ❑ Variable content in the `<fo:page-sequence>` element is contained within a `<fo:flow>` element, with the `flow-name` attribute determining the relevant area on a page.

The advent of user-friendly tools like Antenna House's XSL Formatter will make it much easier to create XSL-FO and to experiment with various techniques. We have covered how to convert XSL-FO to PDF as this is likely to remain a popular interim measure until such tools are widely available.

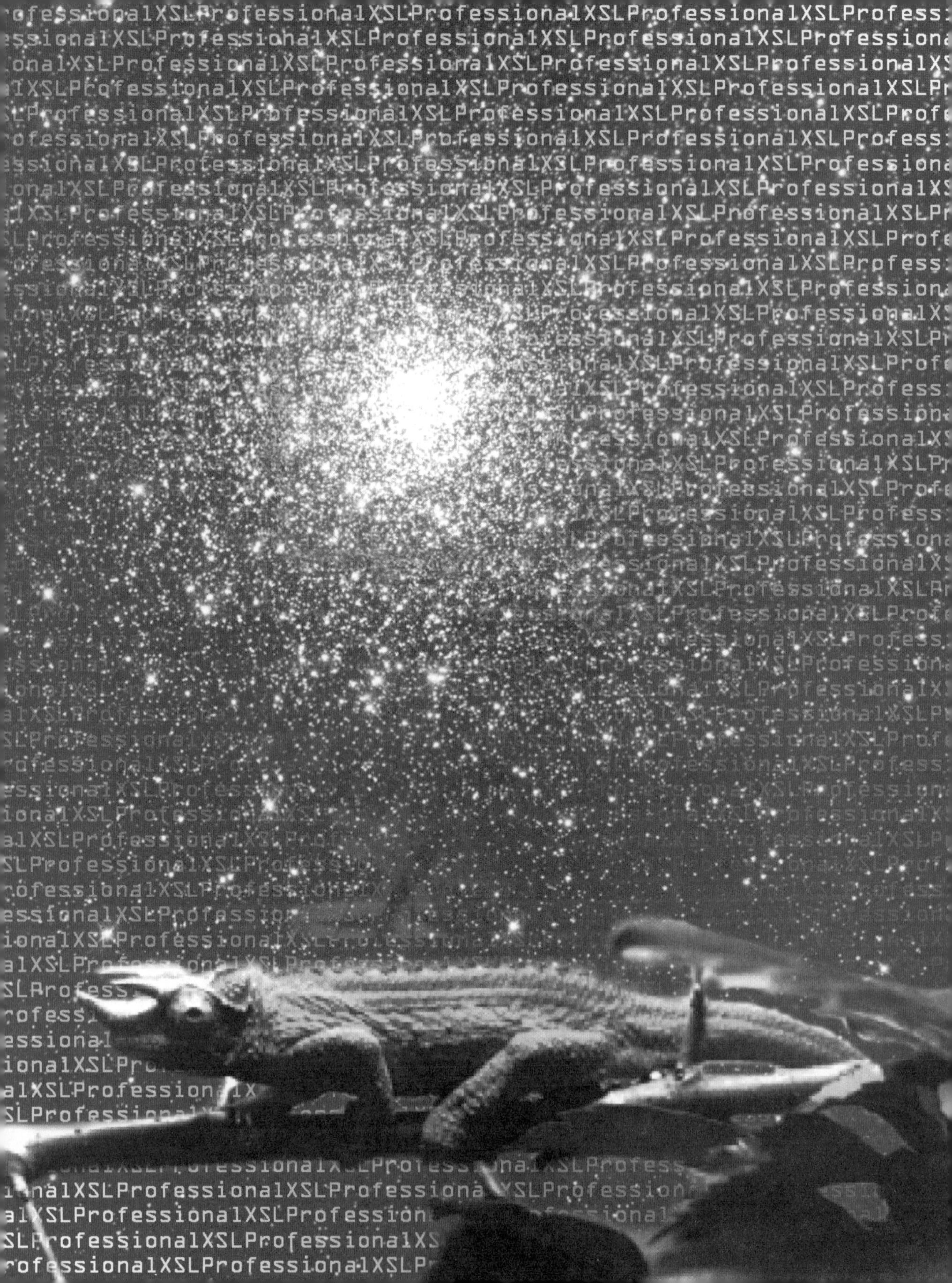

10

Common Structural Transformations

The most common use of XSL today is in transforming XML content for presentation, such as for web display. But besides the separation of content and presentation, XML offers another extremely important advantage: namely *data portability*. XML provides a platform-independent, standards-based data layer, which enables painless communication and data exchange between applications and companies using different platforms, since all parties can use parsers conforming to the same widely accepted specifications.

But, alas, the real world is far from being ideal! Different applications tend to use different XML 'dialects' that use quite different models to represent data, and therefore can't exchange data directly. Let's imagine two chefs, one speaking Russian and the other speaking Italian. Their recipes essentially contain the same kind of information (ingredients and instructions), but in different languages (and possibly different formats). No matter how willing these two chefs might be to exchange recipes, they wouldn't get far without a good knowledge of the other's language, or the services of a translator. The same applies to applications using different XML dialects to express similar data. They need some kind of translator to transform the data from one representation to another: enter XSL stage right.

In this chapter we'll focus on such *structural* transformations of XML data, using XSLT. We will begin by covering general transformations and techniques to convert between different XML formats. We'll then look at the principles behind transforming stylesheets into other stylesheets, and finally move on to look at the transformations needed when dealing with databases (in particular, Oracle).

All transformations in this chapter will be performed with the Apache Xalan Java 2 processor, a robust and highly compliant XSLT and XPath implementation that can be downloaded without charge from http://xml.apache.org. See Appendix E for further details on its setup and use.

Converting One XML Tree to Another

Converting between different XML formats to enable information exchange between companies and applications is a very common situation in the business-to-business world. In this first example I would like to demonstrate the use of XSLT to provide the translation that's all too often necessary to enable such exchange, using a couple of fictitious companies invented for the purpose. We will be looking at practical structural transformation techniques for solving some common B2B communication problems that are faced by real companies today.

One of our fictitious companies is building a system to publish an online catalog that contains information on a variety of products from many of their suppliers. Customers are able to order online, with the system sending the orders to whichever supplier is appropriate for each product. Of course, as a 21st century enterprise, they have chosen XML as the data interchange format. The company is now faced with the following problems:

- ❑ The suppliers are using different XML dialects to express their product information. The system must therefore transform the whole range of supplier formats to the native format of the product catalog.

- ❑ Purchase orders must be split into multiple orders and sent off to the relevant suppliers. This involves another range of transformations.

Now, let's explore how these problems can be solved with XSLT.

Building the Product Catalog

The product catalog format is designed to give just an overview of the products. It only contains general information, using elements that can describe all products. The XML structure of the catalog is shown below:

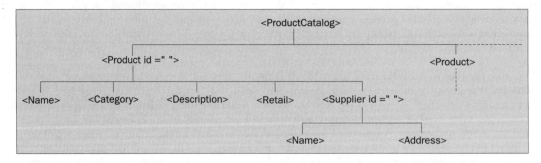

Note that in reality we would need to provide a translation between the product IDs from suppliers and the system's product IDs. This is beyond the scope of this chapter, so here we will just merge IDs from different vendors.

Unfortunately, an agreement could not be made with all suppliers for a common format to use for product data exchange. Therefore, the system needs to transform any of the possible supplier formats into the target format above. This implies a separate XSLT stylesheet for each supplier:

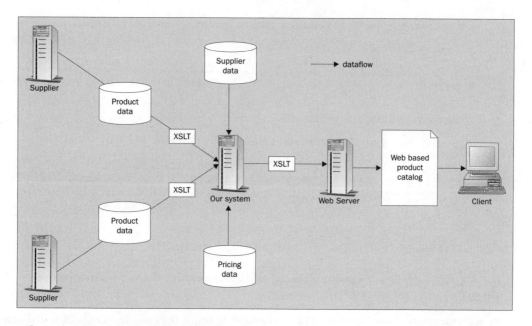

Transforming the Product Information

One of the suppliers is a book distributor, and they deliver book information (books.xml) in the following format:

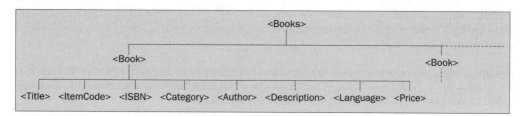

Our system then uses the following stylesheet, books-to-catalog.xsl, to transform between the book distributor's XML format and the product catalog XML format:

```
<?xml version="1.0" encoding="iso-8859-1"?>
<xsl:stylesheet version="1.0" xmlns:xsl="http://www.w3.org/1999/XSL/Transform">
  <xsl:output omit-xml-declaration="yes"/>
  <xsl:template match="/">
    <xsl:for-each select="Books/Book">

      <!-- Pour book details into variables -->
      <!-- (Chapter 4 contains full details of the variable element) -->
      <xsl:variable name="productID" select="ItemCode"/>
      <!-- Note use of nested quotes to denote string literal -->
      <xsl:variable name="supplierID" select="'14'"/>
```

```
      <!-- Create Product element on output stream using native format -->
      <Product>
        <xsl:attribute name="id">
          <xsl:value-of select="$productID"/>
        </xsl:attribute>
        <Name>
          <xsl:value-of select="Title"/>
        </Name>
        <Category>Books</Category>
        <Description>
          <xsl:value-of select="Description"/>
        </Description>
        <Retail><xsl:value-of select="Price"/></Retail>
        <xsl:copy-of select="document('suppliers.xml')/Suppliers/Supplier[@id=
          $supplierID]"/>
      </Product>

    </xsl:for-each>
  </xsl:template>
</xsl:stylesheet>
```

In reality we would of course dynamically output the ID of the supplier. But in this simple example, this supplier is our sole book supplier.

The stylesheet is pretty straightforward. Some values (for example the category) are hard coded into the stylesheet, but most of them are selected from the source document. Note that we use this element:

```
<xsl:output omit-xml-declaration="yes"/>
```

so that the output will not include the `<?xml version="1.0">` tag. We require this because the file will be included in another XML document, namely the product catalog, along with many other files corresponding to other suppliers.

For simplicity we have made the assumption that all products from a supplier fall into the same category. Even if they did not, it might be simpler to implement the system so that different categories available from one company are treated as different suppliers.

Also notice that information on the suppliers is kept in a separate file, `suppliers.xml`, which we access with the following command, described in detail in Chapter 5:

```
document('suppliers.xml')
```

This is done so that we don't have to update the stylesheet every time a supplier changes its information. The format of `suppliers.xml` looks like this:

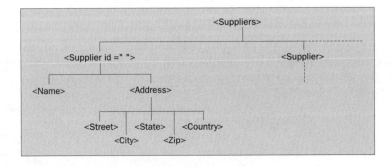

Making Improvements

The company now wishes to automatically produce the retail price by adding a markup to the price of each product, as given by the supplier. This levy is different for each product category. We could, of course, define it directly in the stylesheet, but that would mean updating all stylesheets each time we want to change its value. So, in order to facilitate easy maintenance, we keep all the levies in a separate file, `levies.xml`, an example of which is given below:

```xml
<?xml version="1.0" encoding="iso-8859-1"?>
<Levies>
   <Levy category="Books" amount="1.2"/>
   <Levy category="Videos" amount="1.1"/>
   <Levy category="Cars" amount="1.3"/>
</Levies>
```

We also have another problem: what happens when the company has a discount sale? As specific products are discounted, the price has to be changed and a comment added to the product. We, of course, want to be able to do this without editing the stylesheets. One way of implementing this would be the creation of yet another XML file, `on-sale-products.xml`, which we check against for details of products currently on sale:

```xml
<?xml version="1.0" encoding="iso-8859-1"?>
<OnSaleProducts>
   <Product id="123234">
      <Discount>0.8</Discount>
      <Comment>This product is on sale!</Comment>
   </Product>
</OnSaleProducts>
```

Now we have to incorporate the data from these files into our stylesheet. Let's look at the result:

```xml
<?xml version="1.0" encoding="iso-8859-1"?>
<xsl:stylesheet version="1.0" xmlns:xsl="http://www.w3.org/1999/XSL/Transform">

  <xsl:output omit-xml-declaration="yes"/>
  <xsl:template match="/">

    <!-- Document references -->
    <xsl:variable name="supplierDoc" select="document('suppliers.xml')"/>
    <xsl:variable name="levyDoc" select="document('levies.xml')"/>
    <xsl:variable name="onSaleDoc" select="document('on-sale-products.xml')"/>

    <xsl:for-each select="Books/Book">

    <!-- Pour book details into variables -->
    <!-- (Chapter 4 contains full details of the variable element) -->
    <xsl:variable name="productID" select="ISBN"/>
    <!-- Note use of nested quotes to denote string literal -->
    <xsl:variable name="supplierID" select="'14'"/>

    <xsl:variable name="levy" select="$levyDoc/Levies/Levy[@category='Books']/
      @amount"/>
    <xsl:variable name="discount" select="$onSaleDoc/OnSaleProducts/Product[@id=
      $productID]/Discount"/>
```

```
      <xsl:variable name="price">
        <xsl:choose>
          <xsl:when test="$discount">
            <xsl:value-of select="Price*$levy*$discount"/>
          </xsl:when>
          <xsl:otherwise>
            <xsl:value-of select="Price*$levy"/>
          </xsl:otherwise>
        </xsl:choose>
      </xsl:variable>

      <!-- Create Product element on output stream using native format -->
      <Product>
        <xsl:attribute name="id">
          <xsl:value-of select="$productID"/>
        </xsl:attribute>
        <Name>
          <xsl:value-of select="Title"/>
        </Name>
        <Category>Books</Category>
        <Description><xsl:value-of select="Description"/></Description>
        <Retail><xsl:value-of select="$price"/></Retail>
        <xsl:copy-of select="$onSaleDoc/OnSaleProducts/Product[@id=$productID]/
          Comment"/>
        <xsl:copy-of select="$supplierDoc/Suppliers/Supplier[@id=$supplierID]"/>
      </Product>

    </xsl:for-each>
  </xsl:template>
</xsl:stylesheet>
```

We've added variables to contain the documents referenced, and variables that contain the levy and discount information. Special notice needs to be taken of the price variable. We must perform a check to see whether the product is on sale, and if so the discount has to be reflected in the price calculation.

We have now finished the stylesheet for the transformation of this supplier's product information. Similar stylesheets would need to be built for each supplier, using a different format.

Creating the Catalog

Once we have the stylesheets all set up we can move on to creating the catalog itself. Since the catalog is to be displayed on the web and generated on the fly whenever requested, a perfect means for its construction would be through **Java Server Pages** (**JSP**).

JSP allows web content to be created dynamically by the server according to Java code embedded inside <% ... %> tags within the markup. In essence, when a JSP page is requested, the server fetches it, scans through and processes any code delimited by these tags before sending it off to the client. To learn more about this versatile technology, *Professional JSP*, also published by Wrox (ISBN 1-861003-62-5), provides an excellent resource on the subject.

Returning to our application, we begin by creating an XML document called supplier-settings.xml to specify the documents that are given by the suppliers concerning their products, and the stylesheets that we use to transform those documents into the same catalog format:

```
<?xml version="1.0" encoding="iso-8859-1"?>
<SupplierSettingsList>
   <SupplierSettings>
      <SupplierID>14</SupplierID>
      <CatalogSource>books.xml</CatalogSource>
      <CatalogStylesheet>books-to-catalog.xsl</CatalogStylesheet>
   </SupplierSettings>
   ...
</SupplierSettingsList>
```

This way we can easily add new suppliers to the catalog.

We'll now create a JSP that will read this file, transform the correct XML documents with the correct XSLT stylesheets, and produce the final output, `products.xml`.

The first thing we must do in the JSP is set the content type of the page appropriately:

```
<%@ page contentType="text/xml"%>
```

An XSLT processor has to be invoked from the JSP in order to transform the supplier documents, but luckily for us the `jakarta-taglibs` project at the Apache Software Foundation is very helpful here. They have developed a tag library that contains a number of tags to facilitate the processing of XML and the application of XSL transformations from within Java Server Pages. The tag library can be downloaded from http://jakarta.apache.org, and can be used by including the following line in our JSP:

```
<%@ taglib uri="http://jakarta.apache.org/taglibs/xsl-1.0" prefix="xslt"%>
```

Now the tags from the library can be used by simply prefixing the identifier with `xslt:`. For example, to include the output of applying the `books-to-catalog.xsl` stylesheet to `books.xml`, we would use:

```
<xslt:apply xml="/xsl/books.xml" xsl="/xsl/books-catalog.xsl"/>
```

Our complete JSP looks like this:

```
<%@ page contentType="text/xml"%>
<%@ page import="our.classes.CatalogCreator" %>
<%@ taglib uri="http://jakarta.apache.org/taglibs/xsl-1.0" prefix="xslt" %>
<?xml version="1.0" encoding="iso-8859-1"?>
<Products>
<%
  // Create an instance of the CatalogCreator,
  // which parses the supplier-settings.xml file:
  CatalogCreator c = new CatalogCreator("C:/Program
Files/tomcat/webapps/dataweb/xsl/supplier-settings.xml");

  // Get the names of the source files and stylesheets:
  Vector sourceFiles = c.getSourceFiles();
  Vector stylesheets = c.getStylesheets();
  String xml,xsl;
```

```
    // now, we transform each source file with the corresponding stylesheet,
    // and the output is included in the JSP
    for ( int i = 0; i < sourceFiles.size(); i++ )
    {
      xml = "/xml/" + (String)sourceFiles.elementAt(i);
      xsl = "/xsl/" + (String)stylesheets.elementAt(i);
%>
    <xslt:apply xml="<%=xml%>" xsl="<%=xsl%>"/>
<%
    }
%>
  </Products>
```

The `CatalogCreator` class (which we won't go into here – it is included with the code download) reads the `supplier-settings.xml` file. Its methods `getSourceFiles()` and `getStylesheets()` return `vectors` containing the filenames of the source files and the stylesheets. The `<xslt:apply>` tag then handles the transformation.

We now have the product catalog ready, and we can easily change the levy, add suppliers, and put products on sale – without having to change the stylesheets or our Java application code.

Delivering the Purchase Orders

The product catalog is made available on a web site, allowing customers to place orders online. The customer cannot order products before they have completed a registration process, the details of which are not pertinent to the purpose of this chapter and will be left to your imagination (details could, for example, be stored in an XML format – see below). Once they have registered the customer can log on and order whatever they wish, by browsing the catalog and adding products to their cart. When the customer selects the checkout option, the final order is constructed.

Let's assume that a customer is buying two books and a chair. The order that our system receives from the web server looks like this:

```
<?xml version="1.0" encoding="iso-8859-1"?>
<PurchaseOrder id="34817">
    <Date>2001-01-14</Date>
    <CustomerID>1667<CustomerID>
    <Product id="1234" quantity="1"/>
    <Product id="1235" quantity="1"/>
    <Product id="4567" quantity="1"/>
<PurchaseOrder>
```

Note that the order only contains the ID of the customer and products, and no supplier information is included. We keep the order as short and clear as possible – all information on customers and suppliers is stored in separate files. We have the product information in the product catalog `products.xml` that we created in the last section. All customer information is stored in the separate file `customers.xml`, which has the following format:

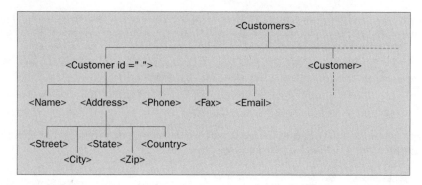

As we know each product ID, we can go to the product catalog (`products.xml`) and look up the supplier information:

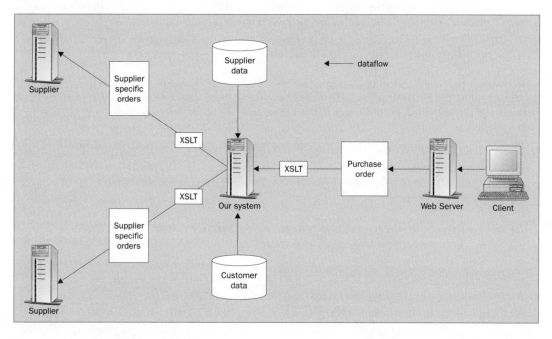

Splitting the Purchase Orders

The purchase order our system receives from the web server may contain orders needing to be fulfilled by different suppliers. Now, each supplier has specific requirements about the format in which they receive the orders, so we cannot simply transform the order using a single stylesheet that picks out the pertinent orders to send to specific suppliers. We have to split the order up into multiple documents (one for each supplier), transform those documents separately, and send the results to the correct suppliers in the correct format.

This is going to involve many stylesheets: one to split up the original order, and one for each different supplier format. But how can we use a stylesheet to split the order into multiple documents? This can be done with the help of **Xalan Java extensions**. (Also, XSLT 1.1 plans to allow multiple output documents, but this was not finalized at the time of writing.)

These Java extensions of the Xalan processor enhance the power of stylesheets greatly. They allow us to easily create instances of Java classes and call methods from within the stylesheet. To be able to use the extensions in our stylesheets, we need to add a declaration for the `java` namespace:

```
<xsl:stylesheet xmlns:xsl="http://www.w3.org/1999/XSL/Transform"
                xmlns:java="http://xml.apache.org/xslt/java"
                version="1.0">
```

We can then declare Java variables in the same way we declare other variables. For example, to create an instance of the class `java.util.Vector`, we can write:

```
<xsl:variable name="aVector" select="java:java.util.Vector.new()"/>
```

The expression `java:<fullPackageName>.new()` (where `<fullPackageName>` can be the full name of any Java class) calls the constructor for the class, and populates the variable with the newly created instance. This would be equivalent to the following Java declaration:

```
java.util.Vector aVector = new java.util.Vector();
```

(Don't forget that the class being used must be locatable by the classpath environment variable of the system running the transformation.) We can then make method calls on our instantiated class. For example, if we wanted to print the size of the vector, we would only need write:

```
<xsl:value-of select="java:size($aVector)"/>
```

> *Note that the first parameter to a method is always the object itself, that is, the variable containing the instance of the Java class.*

Now that we know how the Java extensions work, we can create our stylesheet, `order-processor.xsl`, to split up a customer's order:

```
<?xml version="1.0" encoding="iso-8859-1"?>
<xsl:stylesheet xmlns:xsl="http://www.w3.org/1999/XSL/Transform"
                xmlns:java="http://xml.apache.org/xslt/java"
                version="1.0">

  <xsl:template match="/">
    <xsl:variable name="catalogDoc" select="document('products.xml')"/>
    <xsl:variable name="settingsDoc" select="document('supplier-
     settings.xml')"/>
    <xsl:variable name="currentOrders" select=
     "java:PurchaseOrderProcessor.new()"/>
    <xsl:value-of select="java:setCustomerID($currentOrders,
     /PurchaseOrder/CustomerID)"/>
    <xsl:for-each select="PurchaseOrder/Product">
      <xsl:variable name="productID" select="string(@id)"/>
      <xsl:variable name="supplierID" select="$catalogDoc/Products/Product
       [@id=$productID]/Supplier/@id"/>
      <xsl:variable name="quantity" select="string(@quantity)"/>
      <xsl:variable name="supplierStylesheet" select="$settingsDoc/
       SupplierSettingsList/SupplierSettings[SupplierID=$supplierID]/
       OrderStylesheet"/>
```

```
        <xsl:value-of select="java:addOrder($currentOrders,$supplierID,
        $productID,$quantity,$supplierStylesheet)"/>
      </xsl:for-each>

      <xsl:value-of select="java:processOrders($currentOrders)"/>
    </xsl:template>

  </xsl:stylesheet>
```

The above stylesheet calls the constructor for the class `PurchaseOrderProcessor`, which we will look at shortly. The `setCustomerID()` method of the class is called and passes the customer ID to the class. The stylesheet then scans through the order and passes each ordered item to the class, by calling the `addOrder()` method. When all orders have been added, the `processOrders()` method is called.

The `processOrders()` method, as we will see shortly, does more than just split up the data into files for the different suppliers. It also transforms these files into the format needed by the supplier. How does it know which stylesheet to use for this transformation? We add a new element (`<OrderStylesheet>`) to our supplier configuration document (`supplier-settings.xml`):

```
<?xml version="1.0" encoding="iso-8859-1"?>
<SupplierSettingsList>
  <SupplierSettings>
    <SupplierID>14</SupplierID>
    <CatalogSource>books.xml</CatalogSource>
    <CatalogStylesheet>books-catalog.xsl</CatalogStylesheet>
    <OrderStylesheet>transform-bookorders.xsl</OrderStylesheet>
  </SupplierSettings>
</SupplierSettingsList>
```

We'll be looking at this stylesheet (`transform-bookorders.xsl`) in more detail in the next section. Again, we can easily add or modify information about the supplier-specific files without having to modify the stylesheet or the Java class.

Let's now have a look at the `PurchaseOrderProcessor` class, to see how the orders are processed:

```
// import the necessary JAXP (Java API for XML parsing) classes
import javax.xml.parsers.*;
import javax.xml.transform.*;
import javax.xml.transform.dom.*;
import javax.xml.transform.stream.*;

import org.apache.xerces.parsers.DOMParser; // a DOM parser implementation
import org.w3c.dom.*; // W3C DOM classes for traversing the document

import java.util.*; // Hashtable, Vector, and so on


public class PurchaseOrderProcessor {

  Hashtable suppliers,stylesheets;
  String customerID;
```

```
public PurchaseOrderProcessor() {
    suppliers = new Hashtable();
    stylesheets = new Hashtable();
    customerID = "";
}

/**
 * Sets the customer ID.
 *
 * @param customer ID   the ID of the customer placing these orders.
 */
public void setCustomerID( String customerID ) {
    this.customerID = customerID;
}

/**
 * Adds an order. This method is called from the stylesheet, as it loops
 * through the orders.
 *
 * @param supplierID    the ID of the supplier for the product ordered.
 * @param productID     the ID of the product ordered.
 * @param quantity      the quantity ordered.
 * @param supplierStylesheet   the stylesheet used to transform the
 * orders to the supplier-specific format.
 * @throws    Exception
 */
public void addOrder( String supplierID, String productID, String quantity,
                      String supplierStylesheet ) {

    String[] orderInfo = new String[2];
    orderInfo[0] = productID;
    orderInfo[1] = quantity;

    if ( suppliers.get(supplierID) == null ) {
        suppliers.put(supplierID, new Vector());
        stylesheets.put(supplierID, supplierStylesheet);
    }
    ((Vector)suppliers.get(supplierID)).add(orderInfo);
}

/**
 * Builds an XML document for each supplier (containing all orders for
 * that specific supplier), transform the document to the supplier
 * specific order format, and sends the document.
 *
 * @throws    Exception
 */
public void processOrders() throws Exception {

    TransformerFactory tFactory = TransformerFactory.newInstance();
    String supplierID;
    StreamResult resultDocument;
    for ( Enumeration e = suppliers.keys(); e.hasMoreElements(); ) {
```

```java
        resultDocument = new StreamResult("orders.xml");
        supplierID = (String)e.nextElement();
        Document doc = buildDocument( (Vector)suppliers.get(supplierID),
                                      supplierID );
        String supplierStylesheet = (String)stylesheets.get(supplierID);

        // transform the document
        Transformer transformer = tFactory.newTransformer( new
                                StreamSource(supplierStylesheet) );
        transformer.transform( new DOMSource(doc), resultDocument );

        // send the document
        sendToSupplier( resultDocument );
    }

}

/**
 * Builds an XML document containing all purchase orders for a specific
 * supplier.
 * @param orders    a Vector containing all the purchase orders
 *                  for this supplier.
 * @return          an XML document containing all the orders.
 * @throws          Exception
 */
private Document buildDocument( Vector orders, String supplierID )
                throws Exception {

    DocumentBuilderFactory docFactory = DocumentBuilderFactory.newInstance();
    DocumentBuilder docBuilder = docFactory.newDocumentBuilder();
    Document doc = docBuilder.newDocument();
    Element rootElement = doc.createElement("PurchaseOrder");

    rootElement.setAttribute( "customerID",customerID );
    rootElement.setAttribute( "supplierID",supplierID );

    for ( int i = 0; i < orders.size(); i++ ) {
        String[] info = (String[])orders.elementAt(i);
        Element productElement = doc.createElement("Product");
        productElement.setAttribute("id",info[0]);
        productElement.setAttribute("quantity",info[1]);
        rootElement.appendChild(productElement);
    }
    doc.appendChild( rootElement );
    return doc;
}

/**
 * Sends the document to the correct supplier. This method will not be
 * implemented here.
 */
private void sendToSupplier( StreamResult resultDocument ) {
    // not implemented
}
}
```

The class uses a `Hashtable` to store the orders for each supplier. Orders are added to the `Hashtable` by the `addOrder()` method. When all orders have been added, the `processOrders()` method is called. This method constructs XML documents containing the orders for each supplier, transforms the documents with the supplier-specific stylesheets, and calls the `sendToSupplier()` method, which takes care of sending the transformed orders to the suppliers.

Transforming the Orders

All that is left now is to build the stylesheets that transform the split purchase orders according to the suppliers' required formats. Let's say our suppliers all receive their purchase orders via a **BizTalk Framework Compliant (BFC) Server**, as covered excellently by Steven Mohr and Scott Woodgate in Wrox Press's *Professional BizTalk* (ISBN 1-861003-29-3). Our system will therefore transform any orders for the book supplier to the following BizTalk format:

```xml
<?xml version="1.0" encoding="iso-8859-1"?>
<SOAP-ENV:Envelope
            xmlns:SOAP-ENV="http://schemas.xmlsoap.org/soap/envelope/"
            xmlns:xsd="http://www.w3.org/2000/08/XMLSchema"
            xmlns:xsi="http://www.w3.org/1999/XMLSchema-instance">

    <SOAP-ENV:Header>
        <eps:endpoints SOAP-ENV:mustUnderstand="1"
                xmlns:eps="http://schemas.biztalk.org/btf-2-0/endpoints"
                xmlns:agr="http://www.trading-agreements.org/types/">
            <eps:to>
                <eps:address xsi:type="agr:organization">
                    The Book Supplier
                </eps:address>
            </eps:to>
            <eps:from>
                <eps:address xsi:type="agr:organization">
                    Our Company
                </eps:address>
            </eps:from>
        </eps:endpoints>
        <prop:properties SOAP-ENV:mustUnderstand="1"
          xmlns:prop="http://schemas.biztalk.org/btf-2-0/properties">
            <prop:identity>
                uuid:74b9f5d0-33fb-4a81-b02b-5b760641c1d6
            </prop:identity>
            <prop:sentAt>2001-01-14 03:00:00</prop:sentAt>
            <prop:expiresAt>2001-01-15 04:00:00</prop:expiresAt>
            <prop:topic>http://electrocommerce.org/purchase_order/</prop:topic>
        </prop:properties>
    </SOAP-ENV:Header>

    <SOAP-ENV:Body>
        <po:PurchaseOrder
            xmlns:po="http://electrocommerce.org/purchase_order/">
            <po:item href="#book1"/>
            <po:item href="#book2"/>
        </po:PurchaseOrder>
```

```
        <ship:shippingInfo
          xmlns:ship="http://electrocommerce.org/shippingInfo/">
            <ship:content href="#book1"/>
            <ship:content href="#book2"/>
            <ship:address>
                <ship:name>John F. Doe</ship:name>
                <ship:street>Some Street</ship:street>
                <ship:city>New York</ship:city>
                <ship:state>NY</ship:state>
                <ship:zip>10004</ship:zip>
                <ship:country>USA</ship:country>
            </ship:address>
        </ship:shippingInfo>

        <book xmlns="http://electrocommerce.org/bookInfo/"
          id="book1" SOAP-ENC:root="0">
            <ISBN>1234</ISBN>
        </book>

        <book xmlns="http://electrocommerce.org/bookInfo/"
          id="book2" SOAP-ENC:root="0">
            <ISBN>1235</ISBN>
        </book>

    </SOAP-ENV:Body>

</SOAP-ENV:Envelope>
```

We are not going to dive into the BizTalk specification here (it can be retrieved from
http://www.biztalk.org/Resources/specs.asp), but a short introduction to the above BizTalk document
is needed.

The BizTalk document is an extension of the **Simple Object Access Protocol (SOAP)** 1.1 message,
divided into header and body sections. We'll look at each of these below.

The BizTalk Document Header Entries

The BizTalk-specific SOAP header entries are concerned with document source and destination,
identification, and other properties.

The document source and destination are specified within the <endpoint> element, consisting of the
sub-elements <from> and <to>, both of which contain exactly one occurrence of an <address> sub-
element. As you have probably already guessed, the <to> element contains the destination business
entity to which the BizTalk document is to be delivered, and the <from> element specifies the source
business entity from which the BizTalk document originates.

The <address> element contains the identification of a business entity in string form. Note that the
business entity names in general reflect business-related namespaces rather than transport endpoints,
possibly because multiple transport endpoints are available for the communication (and it is possible
that they will vary over time). The delivery of the BizTalk document, once it reaches the BFC server
that is associated with the destination business, is implementation-dependent. The value of the
xsi:type attribute signifies the category of the address.

Document identification and properties are specified by the <properties> element. The <identity> tag must be a universally unique URI reference that can identify the BizTalk document for the purpose of logging, tracking, and so on during the transport process.

The <topic> element contains a URI reference that uniquely identifies the overall purpose of the BizTalk document.

The <sentAt> tag denotes the sending date of the document, and the <expiresAt> tag is used to give an expiration date, beyond which the destination business must not process the message.

The BizTalk Document Body

The <Body> element of the SOAP message that makes up a BizTalk document contains the business documents being carried. In our case, the <Body> element contains purchase orders and shipping info. Note how the information in the <book> elements is split into the <shippingInfo> and <purchaseOrder> elements. The SOAP-ENC:root="0" signals that the element is not an independent entity.

The Transformation Stylesheet

Now we are ready to build the stylesheet to transform the orders to this BizTalk format. This should be a straightforward process, but there are a few pitfalls on the way to watch out for. We will have to insert the current date and format it correctly, retrieve the supplier and customer information from separate files, and create a universally unique document identifier. Also, we have to transform each <Product> element to three different elements.

By drawing on the Xalan Java extensions, formatting the date will be easy. First we create an instance of the java.text.SimpleDateFormat (a class used to format dates) in the required format. The format string is given as a parameter to the constructor, for example a date of the format 'dd.mm.yyyy hh:mm:ss' would be '15.02.1978 21:14:39'. We then populate it with the current date and time obtained from java.util.Date (a class that represents dates) – creating an instance of this class with no parameters uses the current date.

```
<xsl:variable name="formatter" select="java:java.text.SimpleDateFormat.new
  ('yyyy-mm-dd hh:mm:ss')"/>
<xsl:variable name="currentDate" select="java:java.util.Date.new()"/>
<prop:sentAt>
  <xsl:value-of select="java:format($formatter,$currentDate)"/>
</prop:sentAt>
```

Let's look at the final stylesheet, transform-bookorders.xsl:

```
<?xml version="1.0" encoding="iso-8859-1"?>
<xsl:stylesheet xmlns:xsl="http://www.w3.org/1999/XSL/Transform"
                xmlns:java="http://xml.apache.org/xslt/java"
                version="1.0">

  <xsl:template match="/">

    <!-- variables -->
    <xsl:variable name="supplierID" select="PurchaseOrder/@supplierID"/>
    <xsl:variable name="customerID" select="PurchaseOrder/@customerID"/>
    <xsl:variable name="customer" select="document('customers.xml')/Customers
     /Customer[@id=$customerID]"/>
```

```xsl
<xsl:variable name="formatter" select="java:java.text.SimpleDateFormat
.new('yyyy-mm-dd hh:mm:ss')"/>
<xsl:variable name="currentDate" select="java:java.util.Date.new()"/>
<xsl:variable name="utilityClass" select="java:UtilityClass.new()"/>
<xsl:variable name="expirationDate" select="java:tomorrow($utilityClass)"/>
<xsl:variable name="uid" select="java:getUniqueID($utilityClass)"/>

<SOAP-ENV:Envelope
        xmlns:SOAP-ENV="http://schemas.xmlsoap.org/soap/envelope/"
        xmlns:xsd="http://www.w3.org/2000/08/XMLSchema"
        xmlns:xsi="http://www.w3.org/1999/XMLSchema-instance">

  <SOAP-ENV:Header>
    <eps:endpoints SOAP-ENV:mustUnderstand="1"
        xmlns:eps="http://schemas.biztalk.org/btf-2-0/endpoints"
        xmlns:agr="http://www.trading-agreements.org/types/">
      <eps:to>
        <eps:address xsi:type="agr:organization">
          <xsl:value-of select="document('suppliers.xml')/Suppliers
          /Supplier[@id=$supplierID]/Name"/>
        </eps:address>
      </eps:to>
      <eps:from>
        <eps:address xsi:type="agr:organization">
          Our Company
        </eps:address>
      </eps:from>
    </eps:endpoints>
    <prop:properties SOAP-ENV:mustUnderstand="1" xmlns:prop="http://
    schemas.biztalk.org/btf-2-0/properties">
      <prop:identity><xsl:value-of select="$uid"/></prop:identity>
      <prop:sentAt>
        <xsl:value-of select="java:format($formatter,$currentDate)"/>
      </prop:sentAt>
      <prop:expiresAt>
        <xsl:value-of select="java:format($formatter,$expirationDate)"/>
      </prop:expiresAt>
      <prop:topic>http://electrocommerce.org/purchase_order/</prop:topic>
    </prop:properties>
  </SOAP-ENV:Header>
  <SOAP-ENV:Body>

<po:PurchaseOrder
    xmlns:po="http://electrocommerce.org/purchase_order/">
  <xsl:for-each select="PurchaseOrder/Product">
    <po:item>
      <xsl:attribute name="href">
        <xsl:value-of select="concat('#book',position())"/>
      </xsl:attribute>
    </po:item>
  </xsl:for-each>
</po:PurchaseOrder>

<ship:shippingInfo xmlns:ship="http://electrocommerce.org/shippingInfo/">
  <xsl:for-each select="PurchaseOrder/Product">
    <ship:content>
```

```
            <xsl:attribute name="href">
              <xsl:value-of select="concat('#book',position())"/>
            </xsl:attribute>
          </ship:content>
        </xsl:for-each>
        <ship:address>
          <ship:name>
            <xsl:value-of select="$customer/Name"/>
          </ship:name>
          <ship:street>
            <xsl:value-of select="$customer/Address/Street"/>
          </ship:street>
          <ship:city>
            <xsl:value-of select="$customer/Address/City"/>
          </ship:city>
          <ship:state>
            <xsl:value-of select="$customer/Address/State"/>
          </ship:state>
          <ship:zip>
            <xsl:value-of select="$customer/Address/Zip"/>
          </ship:zip>
          <ship:country>
            <xsl:value-of select="$customer/Address/Country"/>
          </ship:country>
        </ship:address>
      </ship:shippingInfo>

      <xsl:for-each select="PurchaseOrder/Product">
        <book xmlns="http://electrocommerce.org/bookInfo/" SOAP-ENC:root="0">
          <xsl:attribute name="id">
            <xsl:value-of select="concat('book',position())"/>
          </xsl:attribute>
          <ISBN><xsl:value-of select="@id"/></ISBN>
        </book>
      </xsl:for-each>

    </SOAP-ENV:Body>
  </SOAP-ENV:Envelope>
</xsl:template>

</xsl:stylesheet>
```

Note that UtilityClass is a small Java class I wrote that is used to generate a unique ID value. I won't list this here, since it is not directly relevant to the subject in hand, but it is included with the code download.

That's all there is! We're finished.

We have now constructed a system that dynamically maintains a product catalog containing data from multiple suppliers, and has the ability to split a purchase order into multiple supplier-specific formats. Now I'd like to move on to show you some further applications for which XSLT can provide first class solutions.

Generating Stylesheets with Stylesheets

As we know, XSL stylesheets can be used to generate any type of XML document. Now, XSL stylesheets are themselves XML documents, so it follows that we can transform XML files to stylesheets using other stylesheets. We can even transform one stylesheet to another stylesheet using yet another stylesheet. This implication might sound pretty useless at first, but as a matter of fact it is not only interesting, but also very useful. Have a look at the following cases where this technique proves invaluable:

❏ **Replacing tags in stylesheets.** What if we had a large number of stylesheets using some common tags, and we wanted to change them all to use an alternative system of nomenclature? Rather than change each stylesheet separately, we could write a stylesheet to modify them all at once. For example, if we wanted to change the name of a specific element in our product catalog from the previous section, we could use a stylesheet to transform the old stylesheets (with the old element name) to new stylesheets (with the new element name), thus saving a large amount of time.

❏ **XPath parameterization.** XPath expressions cannot be constructed programmatically and executed with XSL at runtime, creating a problem when we want to define queries according to parameter values. Again, we can solve this by using a general stylesheet to generate a special stylesheet, whose structure depends on the specified parameters. The need for this arises, for example, when developing visual tools that make interactive queries and reports.

❏ **Generate stylesheets from XML schemas**. Since schemas are themselves XML documents, they can be transformed. We could use a stylesheet to transform a schema into a default stylesheet for XML documents conforming to that schema. We could also use a stylesheet to create a simple validation stylesheet from a schema (see Chapter 14 for an example on this subject).

❏ **Easy-to-use template-languages can be transformed into stylesheets.** Non-technical people can use a simplified template-language specially created to allow them to define transformations easily. These templates can then be translated into XSL stylesheets with stylesheets. An example of this will be given later in this section.

However, there is one obvious question: when generating XSLT documents, how does the XSLT processor know which `xsl` tags to process and which to leave in the output stream? The answer is simple: it doesn't! This is where the `<xsl:namespace-alias>` element comes to the rescue. This element allows a namespace used in the stylesheet to be mapped to a different namespace used in the output. We can therefore use a dummy namespace (for example, `resultXSL`) instead of the `xsl` namespace for all those elements that are not to be processed.

Although it is a dummy namespace, it still must be declared:

```
<xsl:stylesheet xmlns:xsl="http://www.w3.org/1999/XSL/Transform"
                xmlns:resultXSL="dummy-uri"
                version="1.0">
```

Then we have to add the following element as a child of the `<xsl:stylesheet>` element:

```
<xsl:namespace-alias stylesheet-prefix="resultXSL" result-prefix="xsl"/>
```

The `stylesheet-prefix` attribute specifies the dummy prefix, and the `result-prefix` specifies the prefix of the corresponding namespace to be used in the output.

To illustrate the potential power of creating stylesheets with XSLT, I now would like to take you through the process of creating a stylesheet language that can be used without having to know the nitty-gritty of full XSLT usage.

Our Own Simple Transformation Language

We are going to create a very simple transformation language that can handle some basic transformations. Our language consists of only two tags. The principal one will be the `<for-every>` element:

```
<for-every tag="">
   ...
</for-every>
```

This is kind of like a `<template>` tag, in that it specifies a transform for the element given by the `tag` attribute. It differs from a `<template>` tag in that it can contain other nested `<for-every>` tags. A `<for-every>` element can also contain the following sub-element:

```
<value-of name=""/>
```

The `<value-of>` tag checks if it can find an element with the name specified. If it is found, its value is printed. If it is not found, we check if an attribute with the name specified exists. If such an attribute is found, its value is printed. If the `name` attribute is omitted, the text value of the current element is printed.

Equipped with only these two tags, we can easily transform the following `movies.xml` data file:

```
<Movies>
  <Movie id="346" year="2000">
    <Name>Charlie's Angels</Name>
    <Genre>Action/Comedy</Genre>
    <Actors>
      <Actor>Drew Barrimore</Actor>
      <Actor>Lucy Liu</Actor>
      <Actor>Cameron Diaz</Actor>
      <Actor>Bill Murray</Actor>
    </Actors>
  </Movie>
  ...
</Movies>
```

to HTML by the following, quite straight-forward, `baby-transform.xsl` stylesheet:

```
<?xml version="1.0" encoding="iso-8859-1"?>
<ourStylesheet>
  <for-every tag="Movies">
    <HTML>
    <HEAD>
      <TITLE>Movies</TITLE>
    </HEAD>
    <BODY>
      <TABLE border="1" width="350">
      <for-every tag="Movie">
        <TR>
        <TD>
          <U>Name</U>:
          <B><value-of name="Name"/></B>
```

```
        </TD>
        <TD>
          <value-of name="year"/>
        </TD>
        </TR>
        <TR>
        <TD colspan="2">
          <U>Genre</U>: <I><value-of name="Genre"/></I>
        </TD>
        </TR>
        <TR>
        <TD colspan="2">
          <for-every tag="Actors">
            Actors:
            <UL>
            <for-every tag="Actor">
              <LI/><value-of/>
            </for-every>
            </UL>
          </for-every>
        </TD>
        </TR>
      </for-every>
      </TABLE>
    </BODY>
    </HTML>
  </for-every>
</ourStylesheet>
```

But we don't want to program our own processor to do this, and thanks to XSL we don't need to. We can code an XSL stylesheet that translates our 'baby transformation language' into 'big Daddy XSLT', which can then be applied to the data to achieve the desired HTML. Let's have a look at the stylesheet, subdialect.xsl, we will need for handling the translation:

```
<xsl:stylesheet version="1.0"
           xmlns:xsl="http://www.w3.org/1999/XSL/Transform"
           xmlns:out="TagsInThisNamespaceWillNotBeProcessed">

  <xsl:namespace-alias stylesheet-prefix="out" result-prefix="xsl"/>

  <!-- Root match -->
  <xsl:template match="/">
    <out:stylesheet version="1.0">
      <out:template match="/">
        <xsl:apply-templates/>
      </out:template>
    </out:stylesheet>
  </xsl:template>

  <!-- Replace for-every elements with xsl:for-each -->
  <xsl:template match="for-every">
    <out:for-each select="{@tag}">
      <xsl:apply-templates/>
    </out:for-each>
  </xsl:template>
```

```
<xsl:template match="value-of">
<!-- If the name attribute is omitted, -->
<!-- we output the value of the current element -->
  <xsl:choose>
    <xsl:when test="@name">
      <!-- If we find an element with the given name, we use it -->
      <!-- Else we try an attribute -->
      <out:choose>
        <out:when test="{@name}">
          <out:value-of select="{@name}"/>
        </out:when>
        <out:when test="@{@name}">
          <out:value-of select="@{@name}"/>
        </out:when>
      </out:choose>
    </xsl:when>
    <xsl:otherwise>
      <out:value-of select="current()/text()"/>
    </xsl:otherwise>
  </xsl:choose>
</xsl:template>

<!-- Copy HTML tags straight to output stream -->
<xsl:template match=" HTML | HEAD | TITLE | BODY | TABLE | TR | TD | UL |
                      LI | B | I | U | BR ">
  <xsl:copy>
    <xsl:copy-of select="@*"/>
    <xsl:apply-templates/>
  </xsl:copy>
</xsl:template>

</xsl:stylesheet>
```

Notice that we have to copy the HTML tags to the output document without transformation. Also, the output will still use the same namespace identifier for ignored XSL tags (here it's out), but this namespace now has a different declaration at the start of the file. We have now created a fully functional transformation language that is useful for simple transformations and is very easy to learn. And we have used XSL as a translator to turn our language into real XSLT. In the process, I hope I have succeeded in illustrating the power that creating stylesheets with stylesheets grants us.

Transforming Data from Relational Databases

While XML is rapidly becoming the standard format for data exchange, a substantial amount of business data resides in relational databases and probably will continue to do so for the foreseeable future. It is therefore useful to be able to transform this "traditional" data to a specific format of XML. In this section, I would like to cover how XSLT can produce dynamic XML documents from SQL queries embedded in XML documents, and the reverse: using XSLT to send data in XML files to a relational database. I have chosen to use Oracle as my database in this example, but see the end of the section for insights for other databases.

Note: the Oracle database can easily be set up using the `create-tables.sql` *script file in the code download.*

Oracle XSQL Servlet

In our demonstration we will use the Oracle XSQL (XML Structured Query Language) servlet. The XSQL servlet combines the powers of SQL, XML, and XSLT. It can easily assemble dynamic XML "data pages" based on one or more parameterized SQL queries (which may accept parameters at run time using the standard HTTP form), and transform the "data page" to produce a final result in any desired XML, HTML, or text-based format using an associated XSLT transformation. It also provides a way to insert data from XML documents (posted over HTTP) into an Oracle database.

> *Note that the Oracle XML Developer's Kit and the XML SQL Utility for Java provide all the core technology to accomplish these tasks, but the XSQL servlet automates the use of these components to enable the most common cases without programming.*

The XSQL servlet and associated utilities are available as a free download from Oracle Technology Network (http://technet.oracle.com/tech/xml/xsql_servlet). Although the Oracle XSQL servlet's intended use is as a plug-in to an existing web server, it can also be used to provide functionality to applications, using a command-line utility. It runs on any web server that includes a servlet engine, and uses a JDBC driver to connect to Oracle. The release notes cover installing and configuring XSQL with common web servers (http://technet.oracle.com/tech/xml/xsql_servlet/htdocs/relnotes.htm).

Getting the XML Out of It...

Here we will see how we can dynamically create an XML result set document from an XSQL page, and then we shall use XSLT to transform the result set document to our required XML format. The following figure gives an overview of this process:

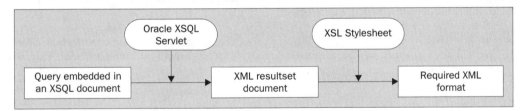

XSQL pages are easy to build, since they are themselves XML documents. To retrieve data from the database, we only need to know one tag: `<xsql:query>`. Take a look at the following, somewhat minimalist, XSQL page (`paintings.xsql`):

```
<?xml version="1.0"?>
<xsql:query xmlns:xsql="urn:oracle-xsql" connection="demo">
    SELECT artist,year,title,media FROM paintings WHERE painting_id=23
</xsql:query>
```

The `<xsql:query>` tag needs to include the namespace declaration for the `xsql` namespace. The `connection` attribute refers to a database connection specified within a configuration file correctly customized for the Oracle scenario (among other things specifying the database name). This file (`XSQLConfig.xml`) is located in the directory in which you installed the XSQL servlet:

```
<XSQLConfig>
  <connectiondefs>
    <connection name="demo">
      <username>scott</username>
      <password>tiger</password>
      <dburl>jdbc:oracle:thin:@127.0.0.1:1521:ORCL</dburl>
      <driver>oracle.jdbc.driver.OracleDriver</driver>
    </connection>
    ...
</XSQLConfig>
```

The above XSQL page dynamically generates the following output (called `resultset.xml` in the code download) by processing the embedded SQL query to the database. It contains the result set of the query, retrieved from the database:

```
<?xml version="1.0"?>
<ROWSET>
    <ROW id="1">
        <ARTIST>Jan Maspen Jeppesen</ARTIST>
        <YEAR>1969</YEAR>
        <TITLE>A View From The Balcony</TITLE>
        <MEDIA>B/W Photo</MEDIA>
    </ROW>
</ROWSET>
```

The `<ROWSET>` element contains one `<ROW>` element for each row returned by the query. The value of the `id` attribute of the `<ROW>` element is simply the order of the row within the set of rows returned. The name of the element around a specific value (for example, YEAR around the value 1969) is the name of the column from which it was selected.

However, this XML as produced by XSQL is unlikely to be of use to us in its current format. More likely, we will need to apply an XSL stylesheet to morph the document into the particular XML dialect we require, for example:

```
<Exhibit>
  <Piece>
    <Artist>Jan Maspen Jeppesen</Artist>
    <Name>A View From The Balcony</Name>
    <Date>1969</Date>
    <Media>B/W Photo</Media>
  </Piece>
</Exhibit>
```

The following stylesheet `XSQLresult-to-exhibit.xsl` accomplishes just that:

```
<?xml version="1.0" encoding="iso-8859-1"?>
<xsl:stylesheet version="1.0" xmlns:xsl="http://www.w3.org/1999/XSL/Transform">

  <xsl:template match="/">
  <Exhibit>
    <xsl:for-each select="ROWSET/ROW">
    <Piece>
```

```
        <Artist><xsl:value-of select="ARTIST"/></Artist>
        <Name><xsl:value-of select="TITLE"/></Name>
        <Date><xsl:value-of select="YEAR"/></Date>
        <Media><xsl:value-of select="MEDIA"/></Media>
      </Piece>
      </xsl:for-each>
    </Exhibit>
    </xsl:template>

  </xsl:stylesheet>
```

Associating this stylesheet with our XSQL page, by adding the following line to the top of the `paintings.xsql` file, ensures the result set document will be automatically transformed to our required format:

```
<?xml-stylesheet type="text/xsl" href="resultset-to-exhibit.xsl"?>
```

XML into Oracle Does Go

Now let's look at the reversal: decomposing XML into existing tables in our Oracle database. In order to be able to insert data automatically, the XSQL servlet requires the data in a specific XML format – in fact the same format as employed by the XSQL servlet when returning query results (see `resultset.xml` above). By writing an appropriate XSLT transform, it's not difficult to give virtually any XML document the format required by the servlet.

Let's say that we want to insert the data from our `movies.xml` file used previously into two Oracle tables called `movies` and `actors`. For this purpose we will need two XSLT transformations. The first one `movies-to-XSQL.xsl` will extract the movie details, and output them in the required row set format:

```
<?xml version="1.0" encoding="iso-8859-1"?>
<xsl:stylesheet version="1.0" xmlns:xsl="http://www.w3.org/1999/XSL/Transform">

  <xsl:template match="/">
  <ROWSET>
    <xsl:for-each select="Movies/Movie">
    <ROW>
      <ID><xsl:value-of select="@id"/></ID>
      <NAME><xsl:value-of select="Name"/></NAME>
      <YEAR><xsl:value-of select="@year"/></YEAR>
      <GENRE><xsl:value-of select="Genre"/></GENRE>
    </ROW>
    </xsl:for-each>
  </ROWSET>
  </xsl:template>

</xsl:stylesheet>
```

and the second `actors-to-XSQL.xsl` will do the same for the actors:

```
<?xml version="1.0" encoding="iso-8859-1"?>
<xsl:stylesheet version="1.0" xmlns:xsl="http://www.w3.org/1999/XSL/Transform">

  <xsl:variable name="movieID" select="'346'"/>
  <xsl:template match="/">
```

```
  <ROWSET>
    <xsl:for-each select="Movies/Movie[@id=$movieID]/Actors/Actor">
    <ROW>
      <ID><xsl:value-of select="$movieID"/></ID>
      <ACTOR><xsl:value-of select="text()"/></ACTOR>
    </ROW>
    </xsl:for-each>
  </ROWSET>
  </xsl:template>

</xsl:stylesheet>
```

We can perform the insertion into our database by one of two methods. The first makes use of `<xsql:insert-request>` to insert data into a specified file from documents sent via HTTP. For example, the following XSQL page (`insert-to-movies.xsql`) would accept information in the above movie format posted via HTTP, and insert it into the movies table:

```
<?xml version="1.0?>
<xsql:insert-request xmlns:xsql="urn:oracle-xsql"
      connection="demo"
      table="movies"
      transform="movies-to-XSQL.xsl"/>
```

We know the `connection` attribute, and the value of the `table` attribute is the name of the table to insert data into. The value of the `transform` attribute is the stylesheet that should transform the inbound document to the row set format for the `movies` table. So this document performs two steps: first it transforms the inbound document to the required row set format, and then it inserts the data in the row set format to the table specified.

The other way to insert the data into the tables is through use of the `XSQLCommandLine` utility from the DOS console:

java oracle.xml.xsql.XSQLCommandLine insert-to-movies.xsql posted-
 xml=http://www.someserver.com/movies.xml

This will use the XSQL page `insert-to-movies.xsql` to insert the XML contents retrieved from the URL.

We can also use the OracleXML class:

java OracleXML putXML –user "yourUsername/yourPasswd"
-filename actorsrowset.xml movies

This will insert the contents of `actorsrowset.xml` (the result of using `actors-to-XSQL.xsl` on movies.xml) into the table `movies`.

Note that although I've focused on Oracle in this section, it is possible to have a scenario where Oracle talks to other databases (for example MS SQL Server) using XML for data exchange between the different databases, as little effort is needed to transform the row sets with XSLT to make the data formats compatible. More and more database vendors are incorporating XML functionality into their products, for example to enable retrieval of data in an XML format which can then be transformed with XSLT. More information on the XML-related features of each database is given in *Professional XML Databases* for Wrox Press (ISBN 1-861003-58-7).

Summary

In this chapter, we've studied several scenarios where XSLT has a valuable role to play. We've:

❑ Constructed a product catalog by transforming data from suppliers into a native format

❑ Split a purchase order into multiple supplier-specific formats

❑ Generated stylesheets with other stylesheets

❑ Transformed data into XML from a relational database format and vice versa

In these processes we've used a variety of resources to assist XSL, such as JSP, Jakarta Taglibs, Xalan Java Extensions, and the Oracle XSQL Servlet.

Probably the most important feature of the XSL technology is its ability to develop transformations quickly, often with a few lines of concise code. A transformation that could be developed and tested in an hour by an experienced XSL coder might take days to write in Java. XSL is therefore extremely important in the translation between application formats, as it provides an effective means of writing high performance automated transformations, which can be developed in a relatively short time space, and with minimal effort once the principles are well understood. As with all technologies, experience is the best teacher, so I recommend you go through the samples given in this chapter, and even modify them and improve on them until you understand fully the mechanisms involved.

In the next chapter we'll look at how XSLT can be used to transform XML data into a format suitable for presentation.

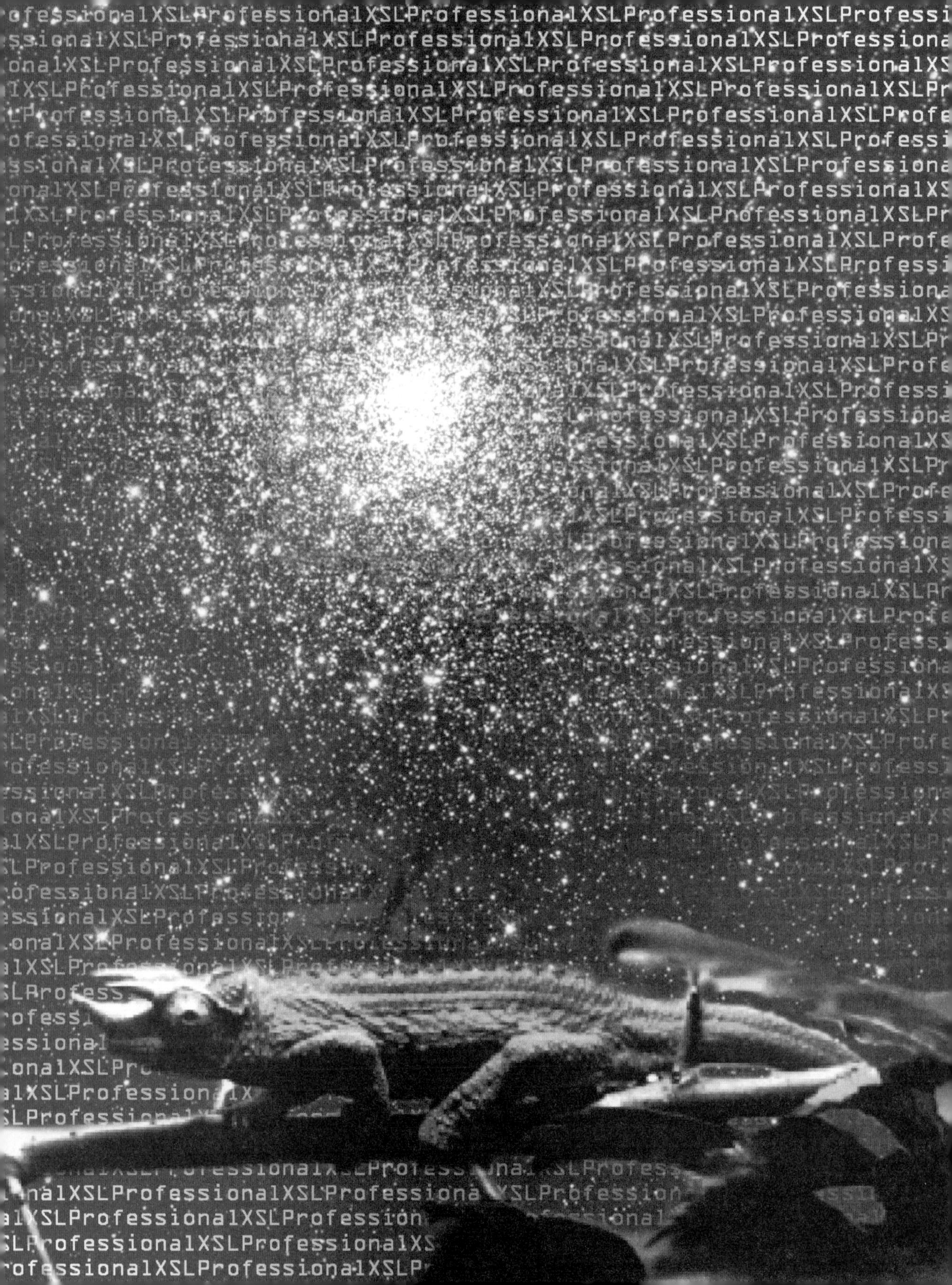
XSLProfessional

11

Adding Style with XSLT

One of the strengths of XML is that we can separate the way in which data is displayed from the data itself. In this chapter we will demonstrate this and pull together much of what we have learned, by developing an XSLT application to display the Wrox XML book catalog used earlier in this book. We will do this in several stages, adding more features and more XSLT code as we go. When we have finished, we will have:

- ❑ A version of the application running entirely on the client for IE 5 browsers with the MSXML3 XML parser

- ❑ A version running server-side using ASP for all other browser clients

- ❑ A version for WAP-enabled devices, such as mobile phones

- ❑ Means in place for detecting the client and selecting the correct version to run

On non-WAP browsers the display will be in two parts. On the left-hand side we will be able to select the book titles we see by their author, which we select from a drop-down list. We will then be able to click on one of these book titles to get more information, such as price and publishing date, in the right-hand side of the display.

For the WAP version, since the size of the display is severely limited, we will restrict the output to show only the list of titles by author.

For this application, we have a static book catalog as an XML file. However, this code would work equally well if we generated the XML dynamically from a database. We will look briefly at the implications for this at the end of the chapter.

I will be demonstrating both basic and more advanced features of XSLT. In particular I will show how to:

❑ Perform transformations on the client and server

❑ Use the mode attribute with `<xsl:template>` and `<xsl:apply-templates>` to transform the catalog in different ways for different purposes

❑ Use variables to create a list of authors, with each author included once only

❑ Use the XML DOM to modify the XSLT stylesheet before we use it

You can download the code for this application from the Wrox web site if you'd rather not type it in by hand, but to see it working, a version will be hosted at http://www.alphaxml.com/display.asp?page=catalog for some time after this book is published. Why the unusual URL? Simply that the entire site is written in XML using XSLT stylesheets to display each page via ASP. The page=catalog part of the URL is the **querystring**, and simply tells the server-side code which XML page to fetch and transform.

Application Requirements

The essential requirements for the application are very simple: we want to be able to display the catalog of our products on multiple browsers, including WAP devices. To be more specific, we wish to display the titles of the books, select titles to display according to the author, and see details for a selected book. We might also want our application to allow the user to select books by keyword, but as the mechanism required is similar to that for selecting by author, I will leave this as an exercise for the reader.

Incremental Development

I am a great believer in incremental development, that is, delivering a system in several steps with each step learning from and building on previous experience. Not only does this allow us to correct specification and design errors while things are still simple, but I have found that most people specifying systems don't really know what they want until they see something different. This might sound patronizing, but I can assure you it is not meant to be – in this case, I am acting as the customer and specifying the system, and I won't know what I want until I have developed the first prototype.

We will develop this application in six stages:

❑ Prototype 1: a simple client-side version to display the authors and book details

❑ Prototype 2: a development of this to allow us to select individual books for display

❑ Version 1: a further development to allow us to list the books for individual authors

❑ Version 2: using server-side transformations

❑ Version 3: a WAP version

❑ A means to detect the client type and select version 1, 2, or 3 as appropriate

Note that the client-side versions require IE 5 updated to incorporate Microsoft's MSXML3 parser – this combination is in fact the only web browser to currently have built-in XML and XSLT support. MSXML3 is installed as a Windows DLL and contains both an XML parser and an XSL processor. The code samples given here will not work with earlier versions of the parser as they rely on aspects of XSLT not added until the final release. The server-side versions require the server to have IIS4 or above with MSXML3 installed. These should work with any browser that has basic CSS capabilities – I have tested them with Netscape 4.07, Netscape 6 and IE 5.5.

Prototype 1: The Basic Catalog

Our first version is intended as a rapid development to get an idea of the look and feel of the application, and allow us to refine our requirements. It will look like this:

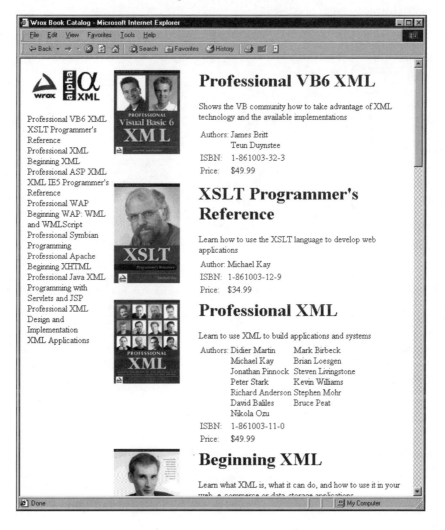

This display has been created using an XSLT stylesheet to generate XHTML. The XHTML references an external CSS stylesheet to control how individual XHTML elements (such as an <h1> heading) are displayed. One advantage of using XHTML is that, being XML, we can manipulate it using the XML DOM. Of course, the DOM also applies to HTML, but this is not well supported in IE 5. In this prototype, there is no disadvantage in terms of browser compatibility since we are targeting IE 5 only.

As a reminder of the format of the book catalog XML file (`catalog.xml`), here is one book:

```
<Book id="1861003323">
    <Title>Professional VB6 XML</Title>
    <Authors>
        <Author>James Britt</Author>
        <Author>Teun Duynstee</Author>
    </Authors>
    <Publisher>Wrox Press, Ltd.</Publisher>
    <PubDate>March 2000</PubDate>
    <Abstract>Shows the VB community how to take advantage of XML technology
              and the available implementations</Abstract>
    <Pages>725</Pages>
    <ISBN>1-861003-32-3</ISBN>
    <RecSubjCategories>
        <Category>Programming</Category>
        <Category>Visual Basic</Category>
        <Category>XML</Category>
    </RecSubjCategories>
    <Price>$49.99</Price>
    <CoverImage>3323.gif</CoverImage>
</Book>
```

To display the catalog with the stylesheet, I have added a processing instruction to the top of the XML file:

```
<?xml version="1.0" encoding="utf-8" standalone="yes"?>
<?xml-stylesheet type="text/xsl" href="catalog.xsl"?>
<!--======= The Wrox Press Book Catalog Application =======-->
```

Because we are loading this document straight into the browser and using the processing instruction to instruct IE 5 to fetch the stylesheet and perform the transformation, we need MSXML3 installed in replace mode. This involves downloading and running a file called `xmlinst.exe`. The MSXML3 Software Development Kit (SDK) provides more information about this and it is also described in Appendix E. `xmlinst.exe`, the parser, and the SDK are all available from http://msdn.microsoft.com/downloads/. If you install MSXML3 in replace mode, you will no longer be able to use "old-style" IE 5 XSL. However, it is simple to change back to the "side-by-side" configuration. This is explained in the SDK. If you don't want to go through this, you can either just move on to the next version of the catalog application, which does not have this restriction, or write a simple piece of client-side script (not included here) to load the catalog and stylesheet and perform the transformation.

Let's start by getting the CSS stylesheet, `catalog.css`, out of the way:

```
h1 {
    color:blue;
}
```

```
td {
  vertical-align: top;
}

.minorheading {
  color:blue;
}
```

This will simply be used to color the book titles on the right-hand side of the screen, color the headings for the authors, ISBN, and price, and ensure that the contents of the table cells we will be creating with XSLT are at the top. Clearly, I could have embedded this in the XSLT to output either within an XHTML `style` element or as in-line styles within each XHTML element, but I have taken this approach to facilitate maintenance should I decide to change any of these aesthetic aspects at a later date. Another advantage of this method is that someone familiar with CSS but not XSLT can change the aesthetics without having to tamper with any XSLT code.

So now let's move on to the XSLT that we'll be using to generate the XHTML pages. The following code appears in the download as `catalog.xsl`.

The structure of the display is created by the `<Catalog>` template element. This creates a table with two columns, adding logos on the left, and then applies templates for the `<Book>` elements twice – once for the list of titles on the left and once for the detail on the right.

```
<xsl:stylesheet
  version="1.0"
  xmlns:xsl="http://www.w3.org/1999/XSL/Transform"
  xmlns="http://www.w3.org/1999/xhtml">

<xsl:output method="xml" indent="yes"/>

<xsl:template match="Catalog">
  <html>
    <head>
      <title>Wrox Book Catalog</title>
      <link rel="stylesheet" type="text/css" href="catalog.css"/>
    </head>
    <body>
      <table>
        <tr>
          <td width="150">
            <table><tr>
              <td><img src="wrox.gif" alt="Wrox logo"/></td>
              <td><img src="alphaxml.gif" alt="alphaXML logo"/></td>
            </tr></table>
            <br/>
            <xsl:apply-templates select="Book" mode="toc"/>
          </td>
          <td><xsl:apply-templates select="Book" mode="display"/></td>
        </tr>
      </table>
    </body>
  </html>
</xsl:template>
```

Note the use of the mode attribute in <xsl:template> and <xsl:apply-templates>. Each time we execute the <xsl:apply-templates>, we choose one of the two templates for the <Book> element by specifying the appropriate mode. Here is the template for the table of contents:

```
<xsl:template match="Book" mode="toc">
  <div>
    <xsl:value-of select="Title"/>
  </div>
</xsl:template>
```

For the moment, this is very simple, just displaying the titles themselves. Later, we will work on this to provide *links* to select books to view.

The template for displaying the book detail is rather longer, placing information about the book into a table cell embedded in the table we created with the template for the <Catalog> element.

In the first row of the table, we show the image of the book cover, the title of the book, and the abstract, with <xsl:value-of>:

```
<xsl:template match="Book" mode="display">
  <table>
    <tr>
      <td rowspan="2" width="150" height="200">
        <img alt="Cover image">
          <xsl:attribute name="src">
            covers/<xsl:value-of select="CoverImage" />
          </xsl:attribute>
        </img>
      </td>
      <td>
        <h1><xsl:value-of select="Title"/></h1>
        <p><xsl:value-of select="Abstract"/></p>
      </td>
    </tr>
```

In this code we create <img> and <h1> elements for the cover image and book title. The <img> element uses <xsl:attribute> to create the reference to the image. Since this is in a different folder, we include the literal text covers/ to complete the relative URI.

To improve the look of the code on the printed page I have reformatted some of the text. However, you should note that in a real application it is good practice to put the following code on a single line:

```
<xsl:attribute name="src">
  covers/<xsl:value-of select="CoverImage" />
</xsl:attribute>
```

The reason for this is the handling of whitespace in XSLT. We discussed this in Chapter 3, where we saw that, if the area between one end tag and the following start tag contains a text node containing characters other than whitespace, all whitespace within this node will be preserved. In this particular case, this means that the value of the src attribute of the <img> element will have whitespace at the start, including a hard return. This will not generally cause problems, but there are circumstances where it might. For example, while IE 5.x and Netscape 4.x will ignore whitespace between the http:// and the rest of a URL, IE 4.x will not. I find that the neatest way to avoid this is to simply keep the complete <xsl:attribute> element on a single line.

In the next row we create another table for the rest of the information:

```
    <tr>
      <td>
        <table>
          <tr>
            <td class="minorheading">
              Author<xsl:if test="count(Authors/Author)>1">s</xsl:if>:
            </td>
            <xsl:choose>
              <xsl:when test="count(Authors/Author)>2">
                <td nowrap="nowrap">
                  <xsl:for-each select="Authors/Author[boolean(position() mod
                    2)]">
                    <xsl:value-of select="."/><br/>
                  </xsl:for-each></td>
                <td nowrap="nowrap">
                  <xsl:for-each select="Authors/Author[not(boolean(position()
                    mod 2))]">
                    <xsl:value-of select="."/><br/>
                  </xsl:for-each></td>
              </xsl:when>
              <xsl:otherwise>
                <td colspan="2">
                  <xsl:for-each select="Authors/Author">
                    <xsl:value-of select="."/><br/>
                  </xsl:for-each>
                </td>
              </xsl:otherwise>
            </xsl:choose>
          </tr>
          <tr>
            <td class="minorheading">ISBN:</td>
            <td colspan="2"><xsl:value-of select="ISBN"/></td>
          </tr>
          <tr>
            <td class="minorheading">Price:</td>
            <td colspan="2"><xsl:value-of select="Price"/></td>
          </tr>
        </table>
      </td>
    </tr>
  </table>
</xsl:template>
```

In the above we change the text of the heading from Author to Authors when the XPath function count() determines that there are more than one:

```
<td class="minorheading">
  Author<xsl:if test="count(Authors/Author)>1">s</xsl:if>:
</td>
```

Then, when there are more than two contributing authors, I felt that a list in a single column didn't look too good, so in these cases I have split it to use two columns, one to be used when position() returns an even number, the other for odd values:

```
<xsl:choose>
  <xsl:when test="count(Authors/Author)>2">
    <td nowrap="nowrap">
      <xsl:for-each select="Authors/Author[boolean(position() mod 2)]">
        <xsl:value-of select="."/><br/>
      </xsl:for-each></td>
    <td nowrap="nowrap">
      <xsl:for-each select="Authors/Author[not(boolean(position() mod 2))]">
        <xsl:value-of select="."/><br/>
      </xsl:for-each></td>
  </xsl:when>
  <xsl:otherwise>
    <td colspan="2">
      <xsl:for-each select="Authors/Author">
        <xsl:value-of select="."/><br/>
      </xsl:for-each>
    </td>
  </xsl:otherwise>
</xsl:choose>
```

We only split the authors into columns when there are more than two. In this case, we use the modulus function, mod, to separate the authors into two lists (in fact, two node-sets). When using a modulus of 2, the mod function effectively returns the remainder when divided by two, 0 or 1 for even or odd respectively, which we then convert to a Boolean allowing us to apply <xsl:for-each>. We could go further – perhaps when there are more than six authors we should split them into three columns. However, we need to be careful about display width, since some people might view this page on a screen with only an 800 (or even 640) pixel width.

Since we now have the possibility of an extra column, those parts of the display that have just two columns set a colspan value of 2 on the second column so as to cover the extra space.

That's about it for this stage. We have used some simple XSLT to get a reasonable display on the right-hand side of our screen. The list of titles on the left does not add much value, but this is the area we will work on next.

Project Review

This seems like a good point to hold a project review. I can assure you we are well on target for time (inside an hour) and cost, so that only leaves us to discuss how well the final product currently fulfils our brief.

It doesn't look bad to me. A little cramped between the titles and some of the book images maybe, and it is a little hard to tell where one title ends and the next one starts. We will fix these in the second prototype.

I don't believe in long meetings.

Prototype 2: Controlling the Detail Display

As a second stage, we will enhance the left-hand side of the display by allowing the user to click on a book title to display only that title. This is the effect:

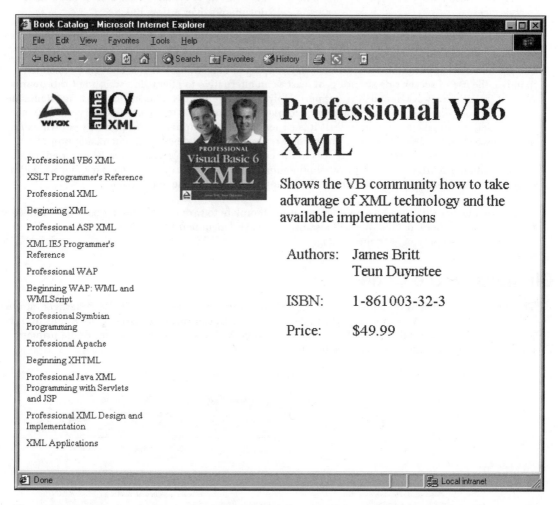

You can immediately see that we have improved the appearance of the first prototype by separating the book titles from each other and inserting space between the book titles and the cover photo. We also only display the details of a single book, as selected by clicking on a title on the left.

To make our application dynamic, we will have to make some fundamental changes to the way we have been working. To begin with, it is much easier to control the two parts of the display if we use *frames* rather than a table. However, by using a table rather than frames in the first version, I hope to have succeeded in illustrating the use of the mode attribute with templates. Now though, we need some method of scripting so that we can change the content of the right-hand frame by clicking on a book title in the left-hand one. We could do this client-side or server-side; the benefits of each are summed up below:

Benefits of client-side scripting	Benefits of server-side scripting
Reduces the load on the server	Compatible with any HTML browser
Generally faster when re-applying the same stylesheet	Faster if the alternative is to deliver large XML documents over a slow link
	Hides the code from those who might copy it

For a production application, the state of XSLT support in current browsers is enough by itself to mandate the use of server-side scripting, at least as an alternative to client-side scripting for browsers without the necessary XML and XSL support. However, there are two reasons for working client-side for this version. The first is that I would have to bias my server code to a particular server, and you, dear reader, might take exception to this! It is easier and less disruptive for a business to download a new browser than a new web server. The second reason is that by developing client-side now and server-side later, we can see the differences in the code and, in later versions, change our application to support both. As XML support improves in the future, this might become unnecessary, but we will have to accommodate browsers without native XML support for some time yet to come.

In this version, we will introduce an attribute value template to provide the linking between the title and the display of the book details. We will also use the XML Document Object Model to change the stylesheet before applying it to the catalog.

Changes to the Code

The most basic change is the move to frames. Because of this we can split the XSLT stylesheet into two – one for each frame. We can then perform two client-side transformations, writing the results into `div` elements in the appropriate frame. The frame displaying the book titles also constitutes the primary interface, giving the following structure to our code:

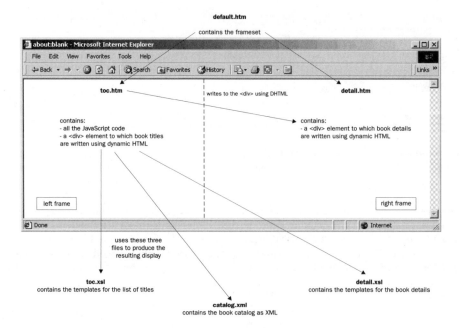

In the previous version of the code, we were building the structure of the HTML page within the stylesheet (in the template for the <Catalog> element). In this version we will be writing to <div> elements, which will already be embedded in HTML code. We will therefore no longer need to include this skeleton structure within the stylesheets.

The Frameset

There is nothing particularly clever about the code for the page default.htm. As the name indicates, it is the starting page for the application, and defines the title and set of frames to be used. It fixes the width of the left frame to 200 pixels, and then allocates all remaining screen width to the right-hand frame:

```
<html>
<head>
<title>Book Catalog</title>
</head>
<frameset cols="200,*" frameborder="0">
  <frame name="left" src="toc.htm">
  <frame name="right" src="detail.htm">
</frameset>
</html>
```

In a moment, we will look at toc.htm and detail.htm, the source files for the two frames, but first let's have a look at the changes in the stylesheets that will produce them.

The Stylesheets

Now that we have split the stylesheet from version 1 into two parts, the stylesheet toc.xsl for generating the list of titles becomes very simple:

```
<xsl:stylesheet
   version="1.0"
   xmlns:xsl="http://www.w3.org/1999/XSL/Transform">

<xsl:template match="Catalog">
  <table>
    <tr>
      <td><img src="../images/wrox.gif" alt="Wrox logo"/></td>
      <td><img src="../images/alphaxml.gif" alt="alphaXML logo"/></td>
    </tr>
  </table>
  <br/>
  <xsl:apply-templates select="Book"/>
</xsl:template>

<xsl:template match="Book">
  <div class="link" onclick="displayBook('{@id}')">
    <xsl:value-of select="Title"/>
  </div>
</xsl:template>

</xsl:stylesheet>
```

The main change here is in the second template, matching individual Book elements. For comparison, this is how the template appeared in the first prototype:

```
<xsl:template match="Book" mode="toc">
  <div>
    <xsl:value-of select="Title"/>
  </div>
</xsl:template>
```

Now that we only have a single template with a match for the <Book> element, we have dispensed with the mode attribute. However, more important is the addition of the onclick event, which invokes the client-side JavaScript function displayBook(). It does this using an attribute value template to insert the id of the book as a parameter of the function call. By now, you should be familiar with the alternative version of this code, using <xsl:attribute> in place of {@...}:

```
<xsl:template match="Book">
  <div class="link">
    <xsl:attribute name="onclick">
      displayBook('<xsl:value-of select="@id"/>')
    </xsl:attribute>
    <xsl:value-of select="Title"/>
  </div>
</xsl:template>
```

Whichever you use is a matter of individual style. I prefer the attribute value template as it is shorter and the code more closely resembles the result after transformation, making it easier to understand.

And the stylesheet for the book detail (detail.xsl)? Apart from a minor change to increase space around the book cover illustration, there is just one alteration to make:

```
<xsl:template match="Catalog">
  <xsl:apply-templates select="Book[@id='0']" mode="display"/>
</xsl:template>
```

This means that we now only display a book with a reference of zero. Looking at the references in the catalog, we will never get this, so no books will be displayed. We will see why this is important later.

The Client-side Script

There are two things our code has to do – perform the transformations and perform an action for the onclick event we created with our XSLT. In the diagram earlier, we saw that the main work is being done within toc.htm, and that detail.htm contains just a <div> element to hold the result of transforming a book from the book catalog into a detailed HTML description, as shown:

```
<html>
<head>
  <title>Book Detail</title>
  <link rel="stylesheet" type="text/css" href="catalog.css" />
</head>
<body>
  <div id="tgtDetail"></div>
</body>
</html>
```

This contains the link to the CSS stylesheet that provides styles for the individual elements and the <div> element with its id attribute. All the code, and another <div> element for the book titles, is in the toc.htm page.

Let's start with the transformations. Some of the code, all written in JavaScript, uses the standard XML DOM, but there are also several properties and methods specific to MSXML3. As we go through, I will differentiate between these.

The xmlLoad() function

```
function xmlLoad(strFile,namespaces)
{
  var dom;

  dom = new ActiveXObject("Msxml2.DOMDocument");
  dom.async = false;
  dom.setProperty("SelectionLanguage", "XPath");
  if(namespaces)
    dom.setProperty("SelectionNamespaces",namespaces);
  dom.load(strFile);
  if (dom.parseError != 0)
  {
    alert(dom.url + ": " + dom.parseError.reason +
          "\nline number: " + dom.parseError.line);
    return null;
  }
  else
    return dom;
}
```

This function loads an XML file into memory as a DOM object. Firstly, we create an ActiveX (or COM) object called dom. The W3C does not define methods for creating DOM objects, so this is the Microsoft way. In fact, all of the properties and methods used in this function are specific to the Microsoft parser, although other platforms will provide their own ways of achieving similar functionality.

Setting the async property to false stops any other processing happening while the file is loaded with the load() method. It is often useful to load a large file asynchronously so that processing can continue while it is being loaded. For example, if we had thousands of books and were starting by displaying details of only the first twenty, we could do this while the remaining <Book> elements were being loaded. However, that is not the case here, so we keep it simple by loading the document synchronously, so we know that the entire catalog is loaded when performing further instructions.

The next three lines employ Microsoft's setProperty() method, to control our use of namespaces but allow compatibility with older versions of MSXML. More detail on this will be provided later.

Once the file is loaded, we can look at the property to see if everything was OK. If, for some reason, our file is not well-formed, the test will fail. In this case, we simply call alert() to display the error for debugging, and return null so that we can detect the failure and interrupt processing. When parseError is zero, our files loaded correctly, so we return the DOM object acquired.

The onLoad() and start() functions

```
function onLoad()
{
  if(parent.right.document.readyState != "complete")
    window.setTimeout('onLoad()',200);
  else
    start();
}

function start()
{
  domCat = xmlLoad("catalog.xml");
  var domTocStyle = xmlLoad("toc.xsl");
  domDetailStyle = xmlLoad("detail.xsl",
                           "xmlns:xsl='http://www.w3.org/1999/XSL/Transform'");

  if(domCat && domTocStyle && domDetailStyle)
  {
    tgtToc.innerHTML = domCat.transformNode(domTocStyle);
    var strFirstRef = domCat.selectSingleNode("Catalog/Book[1]/@id").text;
    displayBook(strFirstRef);
  }
  else
    alert("One or more documents failed to load");
}
```

The `onLoad()` function starts by checking that the page in the other frame has loaded, since we will be writing data to it. If it has, it calls the `start()` function. Otherwise, it calls itself recursively after a short delay until loading has been completed.

We then load the three XML files we need – the XML catalog itself and the two XSLT stylesheets – using the `xmlLoad()` function described previously. If there is a problem loading these, a simple error message is displayed; in a production application, a more sophisticated error message would probably be appropriate. MSXML3 uses the `parseError` object to provide information, such as the URL of the file in error, the line number where the error was detected, and a textual description of the error.

If the documents loaded successfully, we perform the transformation and display the result. Of course, we will not display the detail of any of the books, since in the XSLT we look for a book with an `id` attribute (that is, its ISBN) of zero. So now we will make sure that the detail of the first book gets displayed, by assigning its reference to `strFirstRef` and calling `displayBook()`, which we will look at next. Take a closer look at this line:

```
    var strFirstRef = domCat.selectSingleNode("Catalog/Book[1]/@id").text;
```

Since our application is specific to IE 5, we have used the Microsoft proprietary method `selectSingleNode()` and the proprietary property `text`. The former allows us to select a node based on an XPath expression, in this case, `Catalog/Book[1]/@id`. The `text` property performs just as we would expect – it is the value of the text node that is a child of this attribute – that is the reference (ISBN) for the book.

Now we are ready to return to the `setProperty()` method that we skipped over when looking at loading an XML document.

In the function `xmlLoad()`, we have the line:

```
dom.setProperty("SelectionLanguage", "XPath");
```

If you have used versions of MSXML prior MSXML3, you may be aware that `selectSingleNode()` (and another method `selectNodes()`) originally used a pattern-matching syntax based on an early XSL draft. This has various differences from the current XPath release – in particular, when indexing a node-list, the first node was designated as index zero. By the time XPath was finalized and incorporated into XSLT, this had changed to use an index of one for the first element, but for compatibility with older applications, MSXML3 defaults to the old syntax. Setting the `SelectionLanguage` property to XPath changes this to use XPath expressions.

Now that we have our book reference to display, it's time to move on and look at the `displayBook()` function.

The displayBook() Function

```
function displayBook(ref)
{
  var xNode = domDetailStyle.selectSingleNode("//xsl:apply-
                                       templates[@mode='display']");
  xNode.setAttribute("select","Book[@id='" + ref + "']");
  parent.right.tgtDetail.innerHTML = domCat.transformNode(domDetailStyle);
}
```

When we first carry out the transformation, we use a value of zero for the `id` attribute, which cannot actually occur in our catalog. This both ensures that we do not get a whole set of book displays flashing up, and saves time that would otherwise be used transforming every book in the catalog. The main function of this code is to insert the reference to a selected book in the `<xsl:apply-templates>` in detail.xsl for selecting `<Book>` nodes to process. We want this reference to be included in the `select` XPath expression. So to display the details of Professional VB6 XML, where the following line appears:

```
<xsl:apply-templates select="Book[@id='0']" mode="display"/>
```

we want:

```
<xsl:apply-templates select="Book[@id='1861003323']" mode="display"/>
```

where `1861003323` is the reference for the book. First we set the variable `xNode` to the node in the stylesheet we are changing. We need some way of setting `xNode` to the correct `<xsl:apply-templates>` element. The method I have used is to look for a specific value of the `mode` attribute. We no longer use `mode` to select the correct template, as in the previous version of the application: it is included now purely to identify the element for `selectSingleNode()`. This method uses an attribute of the `<xsl:apply-templates>` element that is defined in XSLT. This is quick and simple, but would risk causing a conflict if we also needed the `mode` attribute for its intended purpose. In that case, we would have added our own attribute, but making sure it is in our own namespace. For example, we could have used:

```
<xsl:apply-templates
  xmlns:w="http://www.wrox.com/namespace"
  select="Book[@id='0']" w:id="target"/>
```

One other point to note is that, when finding the node, we have used the *descendant* XPath axis using the // notation:

```
var xNode = domDetailStyle.selectSingleNode("//xsl:apply-
                                         templates[@mode='display']");
```

We could instead have used the *child* axis:

```
var xNode = domDetailStyle.selectSingleNode("/xsl:template/xsl:apply-
                                         templates[@mode='display']");
```

In this case, I prefer the descendant axis as it makes our code more robust. For example, I could decide to move the <xsl:apply-templates> element in the stylesheet into a table, and the JavaScript code would still work. However, this robustness is at the expense of a slight degradation in performance since we are making the XSL processor work harder to find the element. In this case, that degradation will not be noticeable since we are only performing this operation once each time we display the details of a book. However, if this were being called recursively, we might decide to sacrifice robustness for performance and specify a less general XPath expression for selectSingleNode(). As an example, I have seen the performance of a filtering application using XSL on a large XML file improve from ten seconds to under one second just by using the child axis rather than the descendant axis.

Once we have located this <xsl:apply-templates> element, we write the revised select attribute using the standard setAttribute() method. This is an advantage of XSLT as an XML language – we can use the XML DOM to alter the stylesheet in memory before carrying out our transformation.

We can now look at the second property we set using setProperty() in the xmlLoad() method:

```
if(namespaces)
   dom.setProperty("SelectionNamespaces",namespaces);
```

This property takes a space-delimited set of namespaces as its parameter, and assigns these for use with selectSingleNode() and selectNodes(). In our source XML document, we can assign any prefix to be associated with a specific namespace. In this case, we have xsl for the XSLT namespace, but we could equally well have used another string or made it the default namespace. By setting the SelectionNamespaces property, we tell MSXML what prefix we will use for the same namespace with the selectSingleNode() and selectNodes() methods. Although I have used xsl again, there is no reason I need to do this – I could use a string that is different from that in the source XML document. This means that my JavaScript code will work on other stylesheets that use a different prefix. In many cases, it will not be necessary to set this property of the DOM object. Here, we are using selectSingleNode() on an element with a namespace, so it is necessary.

That completes our second version of the application. Our display looks better than before and, more importantly, we can select the book to view its particular details. In our next revision, we will add the ability to select book titles by author. Before doing that, here is the complete code for toc.htm:

```
<?xml version="1.0"?>
<html xmlns="http://www.w3.org/1999/xhtml">
<head>
  <title>Book Titles</title>
  <link rel="stylesheet" type="text/css" href="catalog.css" />
<script>
var domDetailStyle,domCat;
```

```
function onLoad()
{
  if(parent.right.document.readyState != "complete")
    window.setTimeout('onLoad()',200);
  else
    start();
}

function start()
{
  domCat = xmlLoad("catalog.xml");
  var domTocStyle = xmlLoad("toc.xsl");
  domDetailStyle = xmlLoad("detail.xsl");
  domDetailStyle.setProperty("SelectionNamespaces", "xmlns:xsl='
   http://www.w3.org/1999/XSL/Transform'");

  var xNode = domDetailStyle.selectSingleNode("//xsl:apply-templates[
   @mode='display']");
  var strFirstRef = domCat.selectSingleNode("Catalog/Book[1]/@id").text;
  xNode.setAttribute("select","Book[@id='" + strFirstRef + "']");

  if(domCat && domTocStyle && domDetailStyle)
  {
    tgtToc.innerHTML = domCat.transformNode(domTocStyle);

    var temp = domCat.transformNode(domDetailStyle);
    parent.right.tgtDetail.innerHTML = domCat.transformNode(domDetailStyle);
  }
  else
    alert("One or more documents failed to load");

}

function displayBook(ref)
{
  var xNode = domDetailStyle.selectSingleNode("//xsl:apply-templates[
   @mode='display']");
  xNode.setAttribute("select","Book[@id='" + ref + "']");
  parent.right.tgtDetail.innerHTML = domCat.transformNode(domDetailStyle);
}

function xmlLoad(strFile)
{
  var dom;

  dom = new ActiveXObject("Msxml2.DOMDocument");
  dom.async = false;
  dom.setProperty("SelectionLanguage", "XPath");
  dom.load(strFile);
  if (dom.parseError != 0)
  {
    alert(dom.url + ": " + dom.parseError.reason + "\nline number: " +
     dom.parseError.line);
    return null;
  }
  else
    return dom;
}
</script>
</head>
<body onload="onLoad()">
  <div id="tgtToc"></div>
</body>
</html>
```

Version 1: Selecting By Author

The basic application is now in place. Using very little code, we can display a list of book titles and select any one to get information about the book. This is fine with the number of books we have here, but if the list grew, we would find ourselves scrolling down a large list. Also, as an author, before I meet another Wrox author, I want to know what he or she has written. So the next version of the application will allow us to select book titles for a specific author. This introduces `<xsl:variable>` into our application, letting us create a variable to hold a list of unique author names.

You could just as easily search on other criteria. Since we have keywords in the catalog, we could use exactly the same technique to search by keyword, by creating a drop-down list of unique key words and limiting the titles shown to those containing the selected keyword.

The changes we are making here are very localized – adding the drop-down list (an HTML `select` element) to the XSL file for the left screen (`toc.xsl`), and adding some script to `toc.htm` that is executed when a new author is selected.

The Stylesheet Changes

The objective with `toc.xsl` is to modify it to add a `select` element that will cause the book list to be filtered to display only books by a selected author:

```xsl
<xsl:stylesheet version="1.0" xmlns:xsl="http://www.w3.org/1999/XSL/Transform">

<xsl:variable name="authors" select="//Author[not(.=preceding::Author)]"/>
<xsl:variable name="selected" select="0"/>
<xsl:template match="Catalog">
  <table>
    <tr>
      <td><img src="../images/wrox.gif" alt="Wrox logo"/></td>
      <td><img src="../images/alphaxml.gif" alt="alphaXML logo"/></td>
    </tr>
  </table>
  <br/>
  <div>Select by author:</div>
  <select id="frmAuthor" onchange="selectByAuthor(this)">
    <option value="all">all</option>
    <xsl:for-each select="$authors">
      <xsl:sort/>
      <option>
        <xsl:attribute name="value">
          <xsl:value-of select="."/>
        </xsl:attribute>
        <xsl:if test="position()=$selected">
          <xsl:attribute name="selected">selected</xsl:attribute>
        </xsl:if>
        <xsl:value-of select="."/>
      </option>
    </xsl:for-each>
  </select>
  <br/>
  <xsl:apply-templates select="Book" mode="toc"/>
</xsl:template>
```

```
<xsl:template match="Book" mode="toc">
  <div class="link" onclick="displayBook('{@id}')">
    <xsl:value-of select="Title"/>
  </div>
</xsl:template>

</xsl:stylesheet>
```

The bulk of the highlighted code contains nothing we have not seen before. We create a `select` element with an `id` attribute and an `onchange` event so we can do something when the selection is changed. We then hard-code an `option` element to include the value `all`, then a set of further `option` elements, one for each author in our list. Notice that we have not used any parameters with the `<xsl:sort>` element, therefore it will sort alphabetically on the `authors` node-set. Finally, we use a second variable to indicate which author is currently selected so that this will display in our list when we reload the frame.

As an aside, performing some operations in XSLT can seem very long-winded. For example, the equivalent of a simple function call `function(p1,p2)` might be coded as:

```
<xsl:call-template name="function">
  <xsl:with-param name="p1"><xsl:value-of select="p1"/></xsl:with-param>
  <xsl:with-param name="p2"><xsl:value-of select="p2"/></xsl:with-param>
</xsl:call-template>
```

Even the code to then access the parameters from within the template we are calling is somewhat verbose.

However, many other operations are extremely simple, and generating the list of unique author names is one of them:

```
<xsl:variable name="authors" select="//Author[not(.=preceding::Author)]"/>
```

What we are doing here is creating a node-set of author names, but avoiding duplicate entries by not including those that occur earlier in the source node-set of all author names for a book. To illustrate, the following table shows the process that occurs with a node set of the authors in the left-most column:

Input node-set	.=preceding::Author	Author[not(.preceding::Author)]
James Britt	false	James Britt
Teun Duynstee	false	Teun Duynstee
Michael Kay	false	Michael Kay
Didier Martin	false	Didier Martin
Mark Birbeck	false	Mark Birbeck
Michael Kay	true	
Brian Loesgen	false	Brian Loesgen
Jonathan Pinnock	false	Jonathan Pinnock
Steven Livingstone	false	Steven Livingstone
Peter Stark	false	Peter Stark

At the second occurrence of Michael Kay's name, the test will fail, and he will not be added again as a member of the new list.

Having created the drop-down list, all we need do now is perform an action when the selection changes, and I shall cover this next.

The Script Changes

When the selection changes, we need to do two things:

❑ restrict the display to titles of the selected author only

❑ set the `selected` attribute for the `option` element corresponding to that author

Here is the new function to add to `toc.htm`:

```
function selectByAuthor(oSelect)
{
  var strAuthor = oSelect.value;
  var xNode = domTocStyle.selectSingleNode ("//xsl:apply-templates[
                                             @mode='toc']");

  if(strAuthor == "all")
    xNode.setAttribute("select","Book");
  else
    xNode.setAttribute("select","Book[Authors/Author='" + strAuthor + "']");

  xNode = domTocStyle.selectSingleNode("//xsl:variable[@name='selected']");
  xNode.setAttribute("select",oSelect.selectedIndex);

  tgtToc.innerHTML = domCat.transformNode(domTocStyle);
}
```

The purpose of this code is to create a filter in the stylesheet to select only the books written (or co-written) by the selected author. We use DOM methods to change the `select` attribute of an `<xsl:apply-templates>` to select only the author we want, in much the same way as we selected a single book to display in our previous version.

We start by assigning the name of the author to the variable `strAuthor`, then choose the `<xsl:apply-templates>` element that needs to select the author we want. We then set the appropriate XPath pattern depending on whether we want the titles for one author or the full set. Next, we set which `option` element should be selected so that the name of the correct author is shown when the drop-down list is reloaded with the transformed data in the last line.

Now, when we access the application through `default.htm`, this is the result when I select my own name, then select the second book:

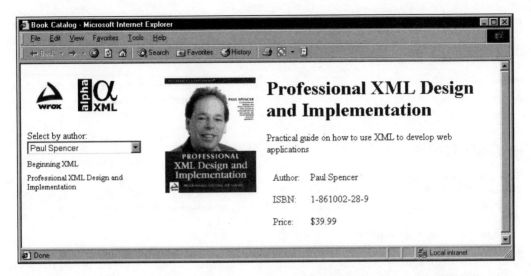

That's about it for the client-side version. We now have an application that will display a list of Wrox's XML books, allowing us to select which titles to display according to the author. We can then see detailed information about any of their books in the catalog. Of course, we can only do this if we have IE 5.x with MSXML3, so we have a rather limited audience. Now we will move our transformations to the server, granting us compatibility with a wider range of browsers.

Version 2: Moving Server-side

Earlier, we looked at the relative benefits of client-side and server-side processing, and concluded that, in most cases, we will need to process our XML and XSLT server-side until a vast majority of browsers in use provide native support for these technologies. So, having developed a client-side application mainly because it is simpler to set up and use, we need to move our application server-side before deploying it in a live environment. This does not mean that we are abandoning the client-side application. It could be used on an intranet where only the required browser type is used, and we shall use it later when we implement a means of detecting the browser type, letting us use the client-side application where possible to offload processing from the server.

The code here employs an IIS and ASP-based platform, although it should not be difficult to modify for use with Apache JSP or another web server with a suitable XML parser. Since the main purpose is to look at the changes in the stylesheets, I have kept the ASP code simple, rather than trying to optimize performance – we saw how to do that in Chapter 8.

Active Server Pages, ASP, is Microsoft's server-side programming environment. It allows us to execute some of our code on the server before sending the client a page that could itself contain script code to execute client-side. Processing on the server is often essential, for example to provide access to databases. In our case, we want our server to ensure that code sent to the client is appropriate for the browser type employed. ASP lets us code in either VBScript (a simplified form of Visual Basic) or JScript (Microsoft's version of JavaScript), or even other scripting languages, such as Perl, if appropriate third party plug-ins are available. I have chosen JScript as this makes it simple to move our code from the previous non-ASP JavaScript version. ASP substitutes any ASP script in a requested page with results derived from server-side processing before sending the page out to the client – analogous to the way that, in XSLT, the results of processing a template replace that template in the output stream.

In an ASP source file the server-side code is delimited by the angle bracket/percent sign combination:

```
<% code in here will be executed on the server %>
```

The main change we will have to make in this version of the application is in the handling of the drop-down list. Instead of managing everything on the client, we will use a form to send the selection back to the server to update the page accordingly.

The ASP Code

Now that we are working on the server, there is no need for client-side communication between frames. The code can therefore be split so that the ASP code for each frame controls that sub-page. This contrasts to the client-side version where the left frame controlled all the content.

The basic mechanism is as follows:

- ❏ The application is first called through the page `default.asp`. This loads the XML files into memory and creates the frameset.

- ❏ `toc.asp` and `detail.asp` are loaded into the left and right frames respectively. `toc.asp` uses `toc.xsl` to convert the catalog into the familiar list of titles. The stylesheet also creates a drop-down list of authors as before.

- ❏ When an author is selected by the user, the information is sent back in an HTML form element to `toc.asp`. On detecting this form element, the server-side script uses it to alter the stylesheet to present only the titles of books by the selected author. This is done using the Microsoft DOM extensions just as before, except that now this processing is carried out server-side.

- ❏ When the user clicks on the title of a book, we send the reference of the book to the `detail.asp` page as a querystring appended to the URL. For example, to view the details of the book "*Professional XML*" we will send the relative URL `detail.asp?id=1861003110`. The ASP page uses this to instruct the `detail.xsl` stylesheet which book to display.

Now that we are not processing any XML on the client, our clients will be returning to our ASP pages every time they make a change. We don't want to keep reloading the catalog and stylesheets, so we will load them once for each session. We can't give the stylesheets application scope since we are altering them before each transformation, although we could do so for the catalog if we wished. The reason I don't is that we would then need to run some code to update the catalog `Application` DOM object every time we update the catalog – perhaps not a problem in a production application, but unnecessary for small documents such as ours.

default.asp

The purpose of the initial page (`default.asp`) is to see if the catalog and stylesheets are already in memory and, if not, load them. It then either returns error messages or sets up the frameset on the client.

Here is the part that loads the XML files:

```
<%@ Language=JScript %>
<%
  var strError = "";
  try
  {
```

```
        if(!Session("domDetailStyle"))
          Session("domDetailStyle") = xmlLoad("detail.xsl","xmlns:xsl=
          'http://www.w3.org/1999/XSL/Transform'");

        if (!Session("domTocStyle"))
          Session("domTocStyle") = xmlLoad("toc.xsl","xmlns:xsl=
          'http://www.w3.org/1999/XSL/Transform'");

        if (!Session("domCat"))
          Session("domCat") = xmlLoad("catalog.xml");

        if(Session("domCat"))
          var strFirstBookRef =
          Session("domCat").selectSingleNode("Catalog/Book[1]").getAttribute("id");
      }
      catch(e)
      {
        strError = e.description;
      }
```

This uses the `try ... catch ...` error control introduced in JScript 5 to detect errors while loading the files. If an error occurs, we set a variable to the description of the error. We will use this later to display a message for the user.

We store each document in an ASP `Session` object. This produces an object that will be available throughout the user session, and so avoids the need to reload pages every time a new page is requested. For each document, we therefore check whether the document is already in memory. This test should only fail for the first access within a user session, at which time the files will be loaded.

If the catalog loaded correctly, we also get a reference to the first book in the catalog, so we can display its details in the first page displayed to the user.

The `xmlLoad()` function is very similar to our client-side version, with only slight changes for the different environment:

```
    function xmlLoad(strFile,namespaces)
    {
      var dom = Server.CreateObject("Msxml2.FreeThreadedDOMDocument");
      dom.async = false;
      dom.setProperty("SelectionLanguage", "XPath");
      if(namespaces)
        dom.setProperty("SelectionNamespaces",namespaces);
      dom.load(Server.MapPath(strFile));
      if (dom.parseError != 0)
        return null;
      else
        return dom;
    }
    %>
```

There are two main changes here. The first is that we now create a different object type – `Msxml2.FreeThreadedDOMDocument`. Now we are working on the server, we are in a multi-threaded environment, and this object type is optimized for operation in just such an environment.

The second change is that we can no longer use an `alert()` to inform the user of a problem, since this is a client-side only method. Instead, we return `null` rather than a DOM object, and allow code later to detect this and perform an appropriate action.

The code above was "pure" ASP, in that it had no client-side HTML included in it. The next part is mainly client code, and will be sent with the page to create the frameset:

```
<html>
<head>
<title>Book Catalog</title>
</head>
  <!-- if none of these return zero... -->
  <%if(Session("domDetailStyle") && Session("domTocStyle") &&
                              Session("domCat")){%>
    <frameset cols="220,*" frameborder="0">
      <frame name="left" src="toc.asp">
      <frame name="right" src="detail.asp?id=<% =strFirstBookRef %> ">
    </frameset>
  <%}
```

We check that none of the DOM objects is `null`, indicating a load failure, and proceed to create the frameset exactly as we did in previous (client-side) versions.

If, however, one or more DOM objects has not loaded properly, or we detected an error earlier denoted by a message held in `strError`, the final part of this page displays an appropriate error message:

```
  else
  {
    var strDisplay;

    if (strError != "")
      strDisplay = "<p>There was an error with the catalog application. The
                    error message was:" + strError + "</p>";
    else
    {
    if(!Session("domDetailStyle"))
      strDisplay = "<p>The stylesheet detail.xsl failed to load</p>";
    if(!Session("domTocStyle"))
      strDisplay = "<p>The stylesheet toc.xsl failed to load</p>";
    if(!Session("domCat"))
      strDisplay = "<p>The book catalog failed to load</p>";
    }
  }
  %>

<body>
  <%=strDisplay%>
</body>
</html>
```

This determines a suitable message according to the error detected and displays it. It would be possible to use the MSXML3 `parseError` object to create more sophisticated error handling when a document does not load correctly, as we did in the client-side version. I have not done this here as it obscures the structure of the code.

toc.asp

Since we are loading the DOM objects in the default page and letting each ASP page control the content of its own frame, the code for the left frame is much simpler. All it does is set the stylesheet to display only the titles for an author whose name is taken from the Form object.

```
<%@ Language=JScript %>
<html>
<head>
<link rel="stylesheet" type="text/css" href="catalog.css" />
</head>
<body>
<%
  var domTocStyle = (Session("domTocStyle"));
  var xNode = domTocStyle.selectSingleNode("//xsl:apply-templates[
                                    @mode='toc']");
  if(Request.Form.Count > 0)
    var strAuthor = Request.Form("frmAuthor").Item;
  else
    var strAuthor = "all";

  if(strAuthor == "all")
    xNode.setAttribute("select","Book");
  else
    xNode.setAttribute("select","Book[Authors/Author='" + strAuthor + "']");

  xNode = domTocStyle.selectSingleNode("//xsl:variable[@name='selected']");
  xNode.text= strAuthor;

  Response.Write(Session("domCat").transformNode(domTocStyle));
%>
</body>
</html>
```

This shows the two ways in which the page might be called. When an author is selected from the drop-down list, this is sent to the page in a form, and the variable strAuthor is set to the name of the author (or "all" if the option to display all is selected):

```
if(Request.Form.Count > 0)
  var strAuthor = Request.Form("frmAuthor").Item;
```

However, when the page is first loaded, there will be no HTML form member of the Request object, indicated by the Count property being zero, so we set strAuthor to "all":

```
else
  var strAuthor = "all";
```

The value of this variable is then used to apply the appropriate filter in toc.xsl.

detail.asp

This page also does nothing that we have not seen in the client-side application. It draws information from the `QueryString` object to select which book to display:

```
<%@ Language=JScript %>
<html>
<head>
  <title></title>
  <link rel="stylesheet" type="text/css" href="catalog.css" />
</head>
<body>
<%
  if(Request.QueryString.Count > 0)
    var strExpression = "Book[@id='" + Request.QueryString("id") + "']";
  else
    var strExpression = "Book";

  domDetailStyle = Session("domDetailStyle");
  var xNode = domDetailStyle.selectSingleNode("//xsl:apply-
                                               templates[@mode='display']");
  xNode.setAttribute("select",strExpression);
  Response.Write(Session("domCat").transformNode(domDetailStyle));
%>
</body>
</html>
```

The Stylesheets

One of the advantages of using XML and XSL in our application is that it is simple to move code between the client and the server, so we should not expect much change in the stylesheets. The stylesheet for the list of titles (`toc.xsl`) has just two main changes – one to submit the drop-down list as a form to the server and one to call the ASP page to display the book details. Since we are no longer manipulating the transformed HTML, we have also changed the value of the `<xsl:output>` method attribute to `html` to cater for older browsers. One effect of this will be to change the well-formed XHTML element `<br/>` to the more familiar `<br>` in the serialized output. The changes are highlighted below:

```
<xsl:stylesheet version="1.0" xmlns:xsl="http://www.w3.org/1999/XSL/Transform">
<xsl:output method="html" indent="yes"/>

<xsl:variable name="authors" select="//Author[not(.=preceding::Author)]"/>
<xsl:variable name="selected"/>
<xsl:template match="Catalog">
  <table>
    <tr>
      <td><img src="../images/wrox.gif" alt="Wrox logo"/></td>
      <td><img src="../images/alphaxml.gif" alt="alphaXML logo"/></td>
    </tr>
  </table>
  <br/>
  <div>Select by author:</div>
  <form name="frmForm" action="toc.asp" method="POST">
    <select name="frmAuthor" onchange="frmForm.submit();">
      <option value="all">all</option>
```

```
      <xsl:for-each select="$authors">
        <xsl:sort/>
        <option>
          <xsl:attribute name="value"><xsl:value-of select="."/></xsl:attribute>
          <xsl:if test=".=$selected">
            <xsl:attribute name="selected">selected</xsl:attribute>
          </xsl:if>
          <xsl:value-of select="."/>
        </option>
      </xsl:for-each>
    </select>
    <noscript>
      <input type="submit" value="Go"/>
    </noscript>
  </form>
  <xsl:apply-templates select="Book" mode="toc"/>
</xsl:template>

<xsl:template match="Book" mode="toc">
  <div class="link">
    <a href="detail.asp?id={@id}" class="link" target="right">
      <xsl:value-of select="Title"/>
    </a>
  </div>
</xsl:template>

</xsl:stylesheet>
```

Note the use of the onchange event in the select element and the use of the noscript element. Browsers that support script will select the new author as soon as a selection is made. Those that do not will show a submit button.

The template for the <Book> elements in the catalog now uses an attribute value template to provide a parameter to the detail.asp ASP page, which it loads in the right frame.

The detail.xsl stylesheet has even fewer changes. We just change the value of the <xsl:output> method as before and remove the reference to the default book to display, since this is now explicitly set by default.asp. The changed area is:

```
<xsl:stylesheet version="1.0" xmlns:xsl="http://www.w3.org/1999/XSL/Transform">

<xsl:output method="html" indent="yes"/>

<xsl:template match="Catalog">
  <xsl:apply-templates select="Book" mode="display"/>
</xsl:template>
```

And to show this in action, here is a similar display to the one for version 1 of the application, but using Netscape Navigator 4.07:

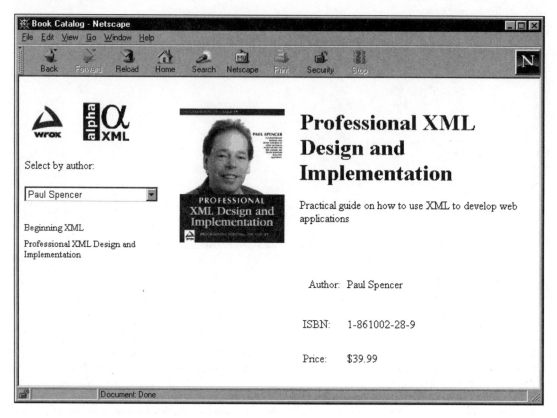

Version 3: Going Mobile

I mentioned that I would want to see what my fellow Wrox authors have written if I am going to meet them. What if I forget to look before I leave? The simplest solution for me would be if the application were available on my mobile phone, so that is what we will implement now.

Because of the limitations of the mobile phone display, we cannot show the detail display of book information, so we will just show the list of titles and allow them to be presented according to author. We have a total of 68 authors in our catalog, so we will limit each list to eight, with options to go forward to the next eight or back to the previous eight.

Here are three images of the application, using the Nokia 7110 emulator (available from http://www.nokia.com):

  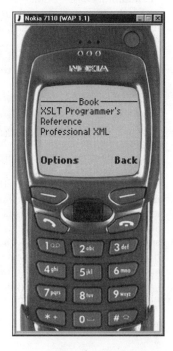

The first shows the application as it first loads. Since many WAP phones show only the first item in the select list, we have an item called **select one**. Selecting this will take us to a list containing the first eight authors (only four show at any time on the screen above, but we can scroll to see the others) and another item that allows us to select the next eight. If we select this, the next list also has an item to allow us to move back to the previous eight. In the above screenshots, I have navigated through to select Michael Kay's name. The final screenshot shows the resulting display, listing the books from Wrox by Michael. This is as far as we are going in this application – the screen is too small to show much detail of a book although we could easily extend the application to show key data such as the ISBN or price.

Obviously, we will have to process our XML and XSL server-side, and the stylesheets will be significantly different from previously. Since we have two very different types of display – the list of authors and the list of titles – we will split the previous `toc.xsl` stylesheet into two, namely `list.xsl` and `book.xsl`. Before we do this, let's have a quick look at WAP and its associated form of XML – the **Wireless Markup Language** or **WML**.

WAP and WML

If you work through this application and decide you want to know more about WAP and WML, I recommend you take a look at a book such as Wrox's *Professional WAP* (ISBN 1-861004-04-4), although I will now provide a brief overview of the topic.

No matter what the advertising departments would have us believe, WAP is *not* the "Internet on your phone"! Even when using the Internet on my desktop PC with 1600x1200 pixels, each able to display one of zillions of colors, I don't feel the excitement that they say I will get with WAP, so what hope is there with a tiny monochrome screen and a 9600 bit per second data rate? What WAP *can* do is provide limited interactive services on a small screen. This might be ideal for checking your bank balance or the value of your current share portfolio, however it is less suited to purposes such as showing a picture of your favorite film star or a map of the London Underground. Think of an application with low data volumes that you might need on the move and then you could have a perfect candidate for a WAP implementation.

To transfer this information between phone and server, WAP uses the Wireless Markup Language, a standard controlled by the WAP Forum (http://www.wapforum.org). This is a form of XML that shares many of the elements of HTML. However, there are some differences that relate to the display format, perhaps the most important of these being that WML uses the metaphor of **decks** of **cards** rather than pages to describe web content.

Each card contains information that will be displayed. Other elements in the language then control navigation between the cards in a deck. The logic behind this is that, with the slow data links currently available for mobile use, visits to the server are kept to a minimum. Sending multiple cards in a deck is analogous to our client-side processing of the catalog earlier, where downloading the entire catalog speeds up later processing. The choice between sending many cards at once or sending fewer will depend on the size of the material being sent and the likelihood of it being accessed. The aim is to strike a balance between having a long initial loading time when sending a deck of multiple cards, and having longer navigation times through the application if sending fewer and requiring access to the server for more information. In our application, we will send only a single card at a time.

Here is a simple WAP deck with a single card:

```
<?xml version="1.0"?>
<!DOCTYPE wml PUBLIC "-//WAPFORUM//DTD WML 1.1//EN"
  "http://www.wapforum.org/DTD/wml1_1.1.xml">

<wml>
   <card id="card1" title="Simple WAP">
     <p>This is a simple WAP deck</p>
   </card>
</wml>
```

Following the XML declaration, it starts with a document type declaration for the <wml> document type. This must exist in every WML file. We then have the document element, which will always be <wml>, followed by our single card. This contains a paragraph that will display the text This is a simple WAP deck.

My aim with this example is to demonstrate how XML and XSL allow us to create applications suitable for multiple clients without changing the format of the core data, in this case the catalog. We will therefore keep our application simple. We will start by looking at the stylesheets, then move on to the ASP page we use to control the application.

list.xsl

This stylesheet is significantly larger than those we have used before, although no more complex. The additional length is caused largely by the need to detect when we are at the start or near the end of the list of authors, so we know whether to add the next and prev actions. We do that by setting two parameters: start, which is the position of the author at which we are starting the list, and percard, which is the number of authors we display each time. We use the latter more as a constant than a variable, but you shouldn't be surprised that the former is set dynamically by the ASP page.

Here is the first part of the stylesheet:

```xml
<xsl:stylesheet version="1.0" xmlns:xsl="http://www.w3.org/1999/XSL/Transform">
<xsl:output method="xml"
   indent="yes"
   omit-xml-declaration="yes"
   doctype-public="-//WAPFORUM//DTD WML 1.1//EN"
   doctype-system="http://www.wapforum.org/DTD/wml1_1.1.xml" />

<xsl:variable name="authors" select="//Author[not(.=preceding::Author)]"/>
<xsl:param name="start" select="1"/>
<xsl:param name="percard" select="8"/>
```

The xsl:output element is used here to create the document type declaration we saw just now.

> *Note that we have told the XSL processor to omit the XML declaration from the output. This was because, when developing the code, I could not persuade MSXML3 to set the encoding to UTF-8 rather than UTF-16. When it was UTF-16, the Nokia WAP emulator returned an error.*

We then create the list of author names as a variable, as we have seen before, and set the start variable to the beginning of the list and the constant percard to the number of authors we want to display at any one time.

The work is done in the template for the <Catalog> element. This creates the deck structure and the list of authors, using a variable that holds the list as we did before. Since this is a fairly long template, I will take you through it bit by bit.

```xml
<xsl:template match="Catalog">
  <wml>
    <card id="main" title="Catalog">
      <p>Select by author:
        <select id="frmAuthor">
          <option>select one</option>
          <xsl:if test="$start+$percard &lt;= count($authors)">
            <option>
              <onevent type="onpick">
                <go method="get" href="wap.asp">
                  <postfield name="item" value="next"/>
                  <postfield name="current" value="{$start}"/>
                </go>
              </onevent>
              next
            </option>
          </xsl:if>
```

At the start of the template, we create the <wml> and <card> elements, just as in the very simple example of WML at the start of the section. Once we have these, we can start working on the list of authors. This uses select and option elements, much as we would in HTML. However, the option element has a set of sub-elements specific to WML. The <onevent> element with the attribute type="onpick" contains child elements to tell the WML processor what to do when the item is selected. In this case, it is a go instruction, which has an href attribute giving the URL to display. This element also has a method attribute, which can take the values post or get. Not all devices currently support the post method, so we will use the get method, which will pass parameters we provide by postfield elements after a question mark in the URL, such as wap.asp?item=next&current=1. The ampersand is added automatically as we are passing back more than one parameter.

The code above will always create an option select one, and will also create a next option if the calculation shows that there are more authors following the current list.

We now need to carry out a test to see if we should show the prev option. We only want to do this if the start variable has a value greater than 1, indicating that we are not currently showing the first page of the list:

```
<xsl:if test="$start > 1">
  <option>
    <onevent type="onpick">
      <go method="get" href="wap.asp">
        <postfield name="item" value="prev"/>
        <postfield name="current" value="{$start}"/>
      </go>
    </onevent>
    prev
  </option>
</xsl:if>
```

Finally, we create the sorted list of authors, starting from the author at the position indicated by the start parameter and stopping after the number indicated by percard or when we reach the end of the list:

```
<xsl:for-each select="$authors">
  <xsl:sort/>
  <xsl:if test="(position() >= $start) and
                (position() &lt; $start + $percard)">
    <option>
      <onevent type="onpick">
        <go href="wap.asp">
          <postfield name="item">
            <xsl:attribute name="value">
              <xsl:value-of select="."/>
            </xsl:attribute>
          </postfield>
        </go>
      </onevent>
      <xsl:value-of select="."/>
    </option>
  </xsl:if>
</xsl:for-each>
</select>
</p>
</card>
</wml>
</xsl:template>
</xsl:stylesheet>
```

Each author option will be of the form:

```
<option>
  <onevent type="onpick">
    <go href="wap.asp">
      <postfield name="item" value="Alex Homer" />
    </go>
  </onevent>
  Alex Homer
</option>
```

The action on selecting this option will be to call the page wap.asp with the relative URL wap.asp?item=Alex%20Homer. The %20, of course, is the result of the WML processor 'URL-encoding' the space character.

book.xsl

When we select an author's name, we display the titles of the books he or she has written. The stylesheet for this (book.xsl) starts as before to create the structure of the card:

```
<xsl:stylesheet version="1.0"
  xmlns:xsl="http://www.w3.org/1999/XSL/Transform">

<xsl:output method="xml"
  indent="yes"
  omit-xml-declaration="yes"
  doctype-public="-//WAPFORUM//DTD WML 1.1//EN"
  doctype-system="http://www.wapforum.org/DTD/wml1_1.1.xml" />
```

Next we create a WML template to provide a means for the user to navigate back to the previous deck, which displayed the list of authors:

```
<xsl:template match="Catalog">
  <wml>
    <!-- Note the use of the default namespace for WML template element -->
    <template>
      <do type="prev" name="Previous" label="Authors">
        <prev/>
      </do>
    </template>
```

Back in Chapter 3, we were discussing the use of namespaces in XSLT, and used the `<template>` element as an example of a name we might use in different contexts within a stylesheet. Here is an example of this, with `<template>` existing in both the XSLT and WML languages, but differentiated through the use of namespace declarations. In WML, the template is used to ensure that the same code appears in every card in the deck. Here we only have one card, but if we later added more, we would want this code to appear in them all, so it is logical to make it a WML template.

Within the card, we just apply the template for the `<Book>` elements. As before, we will be using an ASP page with XSLT to modify the XPath expression in the following `<xsl:apply-templates>` to restrict matches to books by the author chosen by the user.

425

```
      <card id="main" title="Book">
          <xsl:apply-templates select="Book"/>
      </card>
    </wml>
  </xsl:template>
```

And this template just displays the list of titles:

```
<xsl:template match="Book">
  <p>
    <xsl:value-of select="Title"/>
  </p>
</xsl:template>
</xsl:stylesheet>
```

The ASP Page

The ASP page (default.asp) consists of two principle parts – one to cause it to display the list of authors and the other to display the list of books. There is also an xmlLoad() function required, but it is identical to that used in previous ASP pages, so is not repeated here. Now follows the code to load the catalog, set the MIME type to the correct value of WML, and choose between the two types of display format:

```
<%@ Language=JScript %>
<%
  if(!Session("domCat"))
     Session("domCat") = xmlLoad("catalog.xml","");
  var strQuery = Request.QueryString.Item("item");
  Response.ContentType = "text/vnd.wap.wml";
     if(!strQuery.Count>0 || strQuery=="next" || strQuery=="prev")
        // list the authors
     else
        // list the titles
%>
```

If there is no question mark in the URL, or the value of the item in the QueryString is next or prev, we create a list of authors. Otherwise, we create a list of titles for the selected author.

Now, let's expand the blocks currently represented by the two comments at the end of this code. First, to list the authors, we need to set the variable start in the XSL to indicate where to start. If there is nothing in the QueryString object, this will be the start of list of authors. If we are moving forward, it will be eight authors further on (since the XSL variable percard is set to eight), and if we are moving back it will be eight authors further back (as long as this doesn't take us past the start of the list).

Let's insert the code to achieve that. First we load the stylesheet if this has not been done before:

```
  if(!strQuery.Count || strQuery=="next" || strQuery=="prev")
  {
    // list the authors
    if(!Session("domListStyle"))
      Session("domListStyle") =
        xmlLoad("list.xsl","xmlns:xsl='http://www.w3.org/1999/XSL/Transform'");
```

Next we find the start parameter and the value of the percard parameter that tells us how many authors to display at a time. We also get the position of the first author on the currently displayed list that is also passed back to us in the URL:

```
var xNode = Session("domListStyle").selectSingleNode("//xsl:param[@name=
'start']");
var iPercard = parseInt(Session("domListStyle").selectSingleNode("//xsl:param[
@name='percard']").getAttribute("select"));

var iCurrent = parseInt(Request.QueryString("current"));
```

Now that we have these, we can alter the value of the start parameter according to the information we have. If there were no parameters passed back in the URL, the page was being called for the first time, so we will set the value to the start of the list:

```
if (!strQuery.Count)
    xNode.setAttribute("select","1");
```

Otherwise, we jump either forwards or backwards by the value of iPerCard, ensuring that we do not go past the start of the list:

```
else
{
    if (strQuery == "next")
        xNode.setAttribute("select",iCurrent + iPercard);
    else
    {
        var iNode = iCurrent - iPercard;
        if (iNode < 1)
            iNode = 1;
        xNode.setAttribute("select",iNode);
    }
}
```

Finally, we perform the transformation and send the result to the WAP device:

```
    Response.Write(Session("domCat").transformNode(Session("domListStyle")));
}
```

When we are displaying the list of titles, we use the following code:

```
else
{
    // list the titles
    if (!Session("domBookStyle"))
        Session("domBookStyle") = xmlLoad("book.xsl","xmlns:xsl='http://www.w3.org
        /1999/XSL/Transform'");
    var xNode = Session("domBookStyle").selectSingleNode("//xsl:apply-templates[
    @select='Book']");
    xNode.setAttribute("select","Book[Authors/Author='" + strQuery + "']");
    Response.Write(Session("domCat").transformNode(Session("domBookStyle")));
}
%>
```

Here, all we are really doing is setting the XPath expression to use in the <xsl:apply-templates> of book.xsl, so as to match the author nominated in the URL as before. Then we perform the transformation and display the results.

Pulling it All Together

In five iterations, we have now created three versions of our application – one working client-side for those clients running IE 5.x with the MSXML3 parser, one working server-side for other browsers, and one for WAP. Let's pull them all together to make a single production application.

To achieve this, the main thing we need is some code to detect the client type and determine the appropriate application. We could then redirect the client to the version3 folder for the IE 5/MSXML3 client, version4 folder for other browsers, and version5 folder for WAP clients (although we will see later that this is not quite so simple). However, since some files are identical, I have decided to pull them all into a single folder (which is the root folder for this chapter's code). To do this, I have had to change some filenames where they were duplicated. This also meant minor changes in the stylesheets since the path to the cover images has changed. I have also added `default.asp` and `detect.asp` files to detect the client type.

The aim with an HTML browser is to use the client-side application where possible, or the server-side application otherwise. If the browser is a WAP phone, then the server-side WAP application will be used. What are the practical consequences for a commercial environment? With a catalog the size of this one, it is a very suitable way to operate. The XML catalog we are sending to an MSXML3 client is quite small, so will download quickly. All our manipulation after this is carried out on the client, taking load off the server and improving performance over dial-up phone lines. When this is not possible, we have lower performance from repeated return trips to the server, but at least we maintain compatibility with all browsers.

What would happen to the client-side application if we had a bigger catalog? I would envisage that in this case, we would probably want to store the catalog in a database and have more sophisticated search criteria available. We would then carry out the search on the database, create an XML file of the resulting portion of the catalog and send this to the client. The user could then browse through the subset of titles without further visits to the server except for fetching images, which will be cached locally after first use. If we wanted, we could even embed the images as `CDATA` sections within the returned XML, but the performance hit would almost certainly make this a bad idea for an Internet application.

We would also need to consider what to do if there are a large number of matches for a search. We have three choices:

❑ Send them all regardless

❑ Allow the user to specify how many to return in a single go (and also provide the means to move backwards and forwards, rather as we did in the WAP application)

❑ Switch to server-side code

My preference would generally be for the second of these, since this allows someone with a fast Internet connection to get all the information in one go, but those with slower connections can still maintain reasonable performance.

If you would like to compare the client-side and server-side applications, you can browse to http://www.alphaxml.com/catalog/start.htm and http://www.alphaxml.com/catalog /start.asp with a copy of IE 5 with MSXML3. This avoids the browser detection that you will get at http://www.alphaxml.com/catalog/ and so forces use of the client-side and server-side application respectively.

Client Detection

We know that one of the requirements for running the application client-side is the presence of MSXML3. Microsoft has not provided a means for the server to detect the version of the XML parser on the client, so a workaround is needed. What we will do is detect the browser type, and if it is IE 5, send some client-side script that will run when the page loads. By using facilities available in MSXML3, but not earlier versions of the browser, we can detect which version is in use.

This is the logic behind our detection:

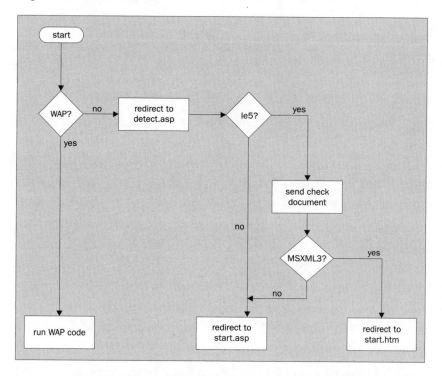

We start by checking for a WAP device. If we find one, we run the ASP code that we developed earlier, in wap.asp. Note that we include this in the same page as our checking code rather than redirect to another page. The reason is that some WAP devices do not support HTTP redirects, so the code would fail. If we do not detect a WAP device, we redirect to a page to detect which web browser we have. This is the additional code that implements the first stage of detection and the WAP code:

```
var strAccept = Request.ServerVariables("HTTP_ACCEPT").Item;
if (strAccept.search(/vnd.wap.wml/i) == -1)
    Response.Redirect("detect.asp");
```

You might be used to using the HTTP_USER_AGENT to detect the browser type (and we will use this later). We could do this, but unfortunately it does not provide a 100% reliable test for WAP devices. Although most contain the string "WAP", this is not guaranteed for all the 700 or so user agent strings used by different phones, emulators, and gateways. So instead, we will look at the MIME types accepted by the device and test for the MIME type used by all WAP devices. The Nokia 7110 emulator I am using produces the following HTTP_ACCEPT string:

```
application/vnd.wap.wmlc,
application/vnd.wap.wmlscriptc,
image/vnd.wap.wbmp,
application/vnd.wap.wtls-ca-certificate,
text/plain,
text/vnd.wap.wmlscript,
text/html,
text/vnd.wap.wml
```

If we do not detect a WAP device, we redirect to the following page detect.asp to determine the browser we are dealing with:

```
<%@ Language=JScript %>
<%
  var strOnload="";
  var strWait = "";

  var strBrowser = Request.ServerVariables("HTTP_USER_AGENT").Item;

  // Check for IE5 and parser version
  if (strBrowser.search(/MSIE 5/) > -1)
  {
    // These variables are used in the HTML at the end which will only be sent
    //  to IE5 browsers
    strOnload = "onLoad='onLoad()'";
    strWait = "Please wait while we detect your version of Microsoft's
              XML parser";
  }
  else
    // we will use server-side transforms for a browser
    Response.Redirect("start.asp");
%>
<html>
<head>
<script>

// onLoad() will be performed client-side by IE5 browsers on receiving this page
function onLoad()
{
  try
  {
    // this will fail if parser is not MSXML3
    var dom = new ActiveXObject("Msxml2.DOMDocument");
    // this will fail on beta versions of MSXML3
    dom.setProperty("SelectionLanguage", "XPath");
  }
  // Catch failure of either of the above & use server-side ASP
  catch(e)
  {
    location.href = "start.asp";
  }
  location.href = "start.htm";
}
</script>
</head>
<body <%=strOnload%>>
<p><%=strWait%></p>
</body>
</html>
```

This time, we do use the HTTP_USER_AGENT to detect the browser type.

If the test of device type shows us that we have IE 5, the function onLoad() is executed client-side, otherwise we redirect the client to the ASP version of the code. Parsers before MSXML3 will throw an error when we try to create an Msxml2.DOMDocument. However, this test is not sufficient as Microsoft released several beta versions of MSXML3, adding features each time. We are using features that were not implemented in the early betas, so we also try setting the SelectionNamespaces property, which was added at a very late stage in the development of MSXML3. If either line of code throws an error, we catch this and redirect the browser to the Active Server Page. If the code ran without error, we know we can use the client-side version.

There is another way to achieve this, but it is not so transparent. If we don't bother with this level of detection, but always direct IE 5 clients to the client-side version, we can redirect to ASP if an error is thrown. However, this approach would not display the message that we are detecting the parser version, which gives a more professional touch.

Summary

So that completes our application. We built it in six phases, the first two being experimental steps towards the three versions we finally used, and the final revision adding the ability to detect the most appropriate version to use and run it. In doing this, we have used a broad selection of the features of XSLT and seen how this approach makes it easy to tailor our application to different clients without changing the database application we might have at the back end.

In this chapter, we have seen:

❑   Practical use of much of the XSLT specification

❑   The ease with which we can move an XML/XSL application between client and server

❑   A method for detecting the version of MSXML in use

❑   Some possible avenues for scaling up the application

We can also use our code to demonstrate the performance difference between the server-side and client-side applications.

In the following chapter we'll take a look at transforming XML into SVG for graphical representation.

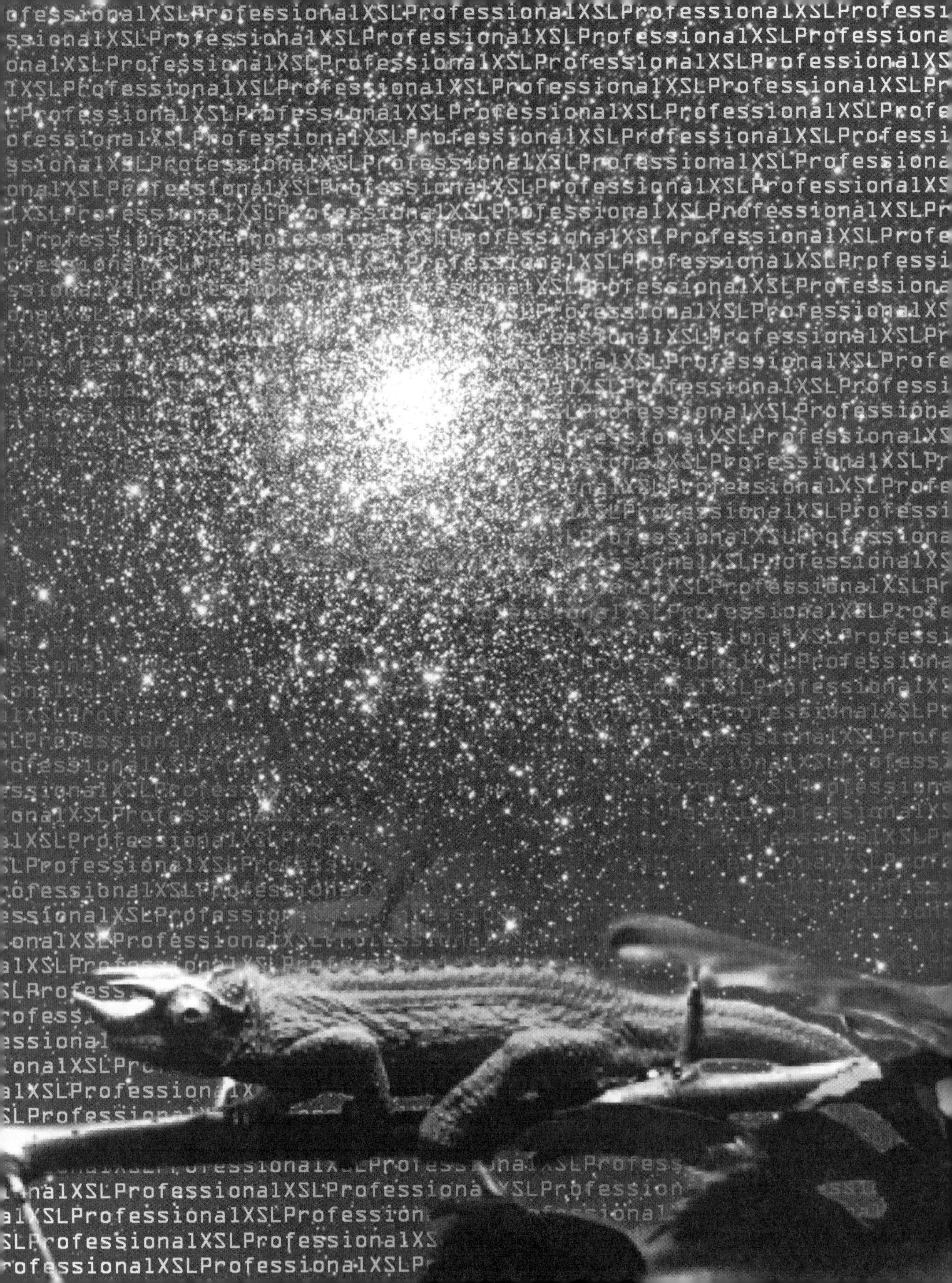

12

Transforming to SVG

In the beginning, the Web was only words. Lynx, one of the first World Wide Web browsers (when the World Wide part basically covered a few universities and research facilities in the United States and Western Europe), gave web page designers the ability to highlight text (usually by inverting foreground and background colors on a standard console CRT screen), provide underlined links, and potentially display certain text in bold.

The NCSA (National Center for Supercomputing Applications) Mosaic browser debuted in 1993, and its impact changed the world. Its designers recognized a salient fact about people – that we are fundamentally *visual* beings, and we naturally view the world in terms of images rather than words. With the innovation of being able to display inline graphics (and later of being able to change the characteristics of the background image pane), the Mosaic browser completely altered the way that people related to the Web, and fueled a period of explosive growth that is only just now, eight years later, beginning to slow down.

The problem with pictures, however, is that it takes a thousand words to describe one. More specifically, the vast majority of all pictures on the web are bitmap graphics, in which a picture consists of a grid of pixels, each pixel having its own color, with perhaps one color (or byte within a color, in the case of Portable Network Graphics or PNG) used to denote levels of transparency. There are several problems with such graphics:

❑ **Lack of Scalability.** Scaling an image requires algorithms to approximate intermediate colors in order to construct the image at a new size. The greater the scaling between the source and the final image, the more noticeable the distortion.

❑ **Contextual Irreducibility.** A bitmap image does not incorporate any contextual information about itself – it is not possible to query a bitmap image to find the components that make it up, nor is it possible to change the content of a bitmap on the fly except at pixel level.

❑ **Static.** Once an image is instantiated, it cannot be altered dynamically. It can only be replaced in its entirety by a different static image. Even the GIF variety of animations run into this problem – you cannot create an animation that reacts to external events, beyond possibly starting and stopping.

❑ **Size.** The size in bytes of an uncompressed bitmap is the height multiplied by the width in pixels, multiplied by the number of bytes per pixel. For example, a 1024x768 image at 32 bits (4 bytes) per pixel takes up more than 3.1 MB of space. Some image formats of course compress such images, sometimes dramatically, but often with a loss of quality.

❑ **Standardization.** The GIF standard – that is the Digital/Compuserve Graphic Interchange Format – has become mired in legal disputes over its ownership and use on the web. An open replacement, the PNG format, is superior in a number of respects including provision of an 8-bit alpha transparency channel, but PNG deployment is currently spotty at best.

Computer graphics have always been split into two fairly distinct camps: **bitmaps**, or **raster graphics**, which rely upon a grid of colors as described earlier, and **vector graphics**. This latter category describe an image as a composite of basic shapes, or primitives – lines, rectangles, ellipses, curves, fills, and shaped text, among others. The image is then recreated by drawing these in a specific order on the appropriate drawing surface. Vector graphics have a number of advantages over bitmap graphics:

❑ **Scalable.** Scaling a vector graphic simply involves mathematically transforming the coordinates of the component pieces, and re-rendering. This means that the graphic will contain exactly the same information at twice its original size, as it will at half.

❑ **Contextually Rich.** It is possible to label and identify specific sub-components of an image, making it possible to pull out and render just this portion without needing to display everything.

❑ **Dynamic.** Because components can be identified, it is possible to manipulate portions of a diagram in real time. Thus, for example, the text in an image can change in response to an event, without replacing the entire graphic to do so.

❑ **Compressed Size.** Up to a certain level of complexity, vector graphics typically require far fewer bytes to express information, and because the information is text, vector graphics also compress well. The drawback is the requirement for processor cycles, which could have a detrimental effect on the rendering time of a complex image.

❑ **Media Independence.** Because vector graphics consist of instructions to a processor, by changing the nature of the processor you can alter the kind of output. As a consequence, most vector graphics formats can easily handle transformations from low bandwidth, low resolution devices such as a cell phone display screen, as well as handling extremely high bandwidth, high resolution devices such as the creation of plates for a high quality color press.

❑ **Standardization.** Currently there are no limitations on the use of any vector graphics formats (though there are a number that are proprietary or semi-proprietary).

One of the earliest and most pervasive vector graphics formats was the **Postscript format** established by Adobe in the early 1980s. Postscript effectively made possible an entirely new generation of printers, and is capable of rich special effects as well as fairly standard page and illustration layout. More recently, Macromedia's **Flash format** has become the de facto standard for producing web-based illustrations and animations using vector notations. However, while vector-based graphics have several advantages over their bitmap counterparts, pure vector graphics are not ideal in all situations:

❑ **Photographs.** Photographs can have an arbitrary level of complexity in their content, complexity that is difficult to approximate using vector graphics. This means, of course, that as a significant amount of the material on the Web is photographic in nature, vector graphics will not resolve all of the graphics or bandwidth problems any time soon.

❑ **Processor Requirement.** Even with compression, most bitmaps are very easy to translate into the operating system's internal display format. However, any vector graphics format, from Postscript to SVG, requires some form of rendering engine to draw (and in some cases animate) the contents. Note also that SVG includes (limited) support for sound as well as graphics, which makes for cool SVG implementations, but also adds to the overhead on the processor.

Even given such constraints, however, vector graphics have already made significant inroads into the web sphere, with Macromedia Flash among others illustrating the capabilities offered by encoding graphics as simple elements. However, while Flash is certainly a very sophisticated animation program, it is not based on XML, instead relying on Macromedia's own proprietary format, albeit one that they have made available as open source. Because inadequate control over the graphics display of a device browsing the Internet is probably one of the major limitations that currently beleaguer in the Web, in 1998 the W3C chose to solicit ideas for a new XML-based graphics language.

PGML, VML, and SVG

The split of power in the W3C tends to result in Microsoft, Macromedia, and Hewlett Packard pulling in one direction and Sun, Adobe, and Oracle pulling in the other, and this division is no more in evidence than in the submissions for a standard for an XML-based graphics format. Adobe came up with the **Precision Graphics Markup Language** (**PGML**), that in essence took many of the more salient features of Postscript and converted them to an XML form. Meanwhile, Macromedia and Microsoft coauthored the **Vector Markup Language** (**VML**), which really attempted to render the set of Flash primitives in XML. Not surprisingly, there were some significant differences; PGML turned out to be better designed for laying out page graphics, while VML's tendency to favor the use of coordinates meant fairly sophisticated shapes could be built from some fairly complex paths, mirroring a join-the-dots children's puzzle. VML also employed a way of passing parametric information through attribute values.

Because there was no one obvious best solution, the W3C working committee chose to create a new standard that took these two proposals as the basis for a final architecture. This new standard is the **Scalable Vector Graphics** format, or **SVG**, and it addresses a number of issues that were a little skimped over by the other two languages:

❑ **Definition Templates.** You can group multiple graphic "spaces" together to create more sophisticated object definitions, then associate these object definitions with instances. This makes it fairly easy to create libraries of SVG objects.

❑ **Primitives.** SVG does define a small set of primitives – rectangles, rounded rectangles, circles, ellipses, etc. – that can be used either out of the box or as the basis for more complex shapes.

❑ **SVG Path Language.** SVG employs a notation to specify the coordinates and drawing actions of the "drawing pen" that somewhat controversially, is given by a string of tokens in an attribute. This means that any XSLT stylesheet that generates a path to describe a shape will need to create it as a space-separated list rather than by populating an XML element. Conversely, any stylesheet that reads such a path will have to be able to parse such space-delimited lists.

❑ **Cascading Style Sheets.** One of the primary motivations in producing an XML-based language was to take advantage of existing W3C standards. As a result, most of the characteristics that describe the media presentation of the graphic – its color, font characteristics, filters, and so forth – can be specified using CSS `style="xxx:yyyy;"` statements. Additionally, characteristics that are similar to those of CSS share the same CSS property names.

❑ **Text.** In SVG, the font characteristics specify paths that can then have graphic effects applied, in much the same way that other primitives are created. This makes it possible to wrap text along paths, fill text with textures and gradients, and apply special effects. The one drawback to this approach is that the SVG way of laying out text doesn't recognize HTML markup, so unlike VML you have to explicitly insert line breaks and explicitly modify text characteristics.

❑ **Animation.** In VML, animation is a function provided by the external scripting language. However, in SVG, it is possible to create animations in a declarative fashion. You can set some property to be animated – the rotation of a clock hand, the color of a banner, the transparency of a group – based upon some external event such as completion of loading, set the duration and repetitions, and even specify a final state for the transition, all using SVG XML markup alone. It is also possible to use the SVG DOM to perform animations via script, but the declarative animation feature can radically cut back the amount of scripting that one has to do.

❑ **Clip Paths.** One very common facility in graphics is to define a complex path to 'mold' an image into something other than a rectangle. SVG supports such clip paths for both text and shapes, even animated media types such as GIF or PNG.

❑ **Filters and Effects.** Adobe knows filters, so not surprisingly they lobbied hard for the filter effects capability of SVG, which makes it possible to perform passes, add noise, create drop shadows, and perform a host of other actions. Additionally it's likely that, with the mechanism in place, it will be possible to add other filter effects through URL links, adding a whole new dimension to filtered output.

❑ **Linking and Embedding.** One of the advantages of working with SVG is that it is XML. This means it's possible to embed subordinate SVG descriptions (or objects) within an SVG document via an external link either statically or dynamically, as well as provide hyperlinks to other XML or SVG documents and web pages.

❑ **SVG Document Object Model.** The purpose of a DOM is to create an interface between an object model implementation and another programming language. The SVG DOM is no different, letting users interact with SVG spaces through a language-independent mechanism, defaulting to support for Java or ECMAScript.

The SVG language is reasonably robust, and when it is universally implemented it is likely that SVG could be rendered either as inline code or as separate documents. Inline SVG is perhaps the most intriguing, because it effectively means that HTML pages could incorporate complex interactive graphics capabilities, breaking out of the simple HTML array of rectangles into a far richer user experience. Unfortunately, there are currently only a couple of SVG implementations, and they both require the use of plug-in components (arguably the best being Adobe's offering, at http://www.adobe.com/svg – this was covered in Chapter 9). Currently the Mozilla project is planning to include SVG support in its generation 6 browser, and there are some tantalizing hints that Microsoft is working on an SVG extension for Internet Explorer 6, but no formal announcements have been made in this regard. Keep an eye out at http://www.w3.org/Graphics/SVG/SVG-Implementations for updates.

From a graphics viewpoint, we are now in the 'between time', and the status of SVG may be very different six months from now. Microsoft chose to integrate their version of VML into Internet Explorer 5 in 1999, a reasonable decision given that the SVG standard was then very much in flux. However, when Internet Explorer 5.5 was released in July 2000, the decision was made not to add an SVG engine to the update, despite the fact that the SVG standard had jumped to W3C Candidate Recommendation status by then. What this has meant, as a consequence, is that VML will likely remain a viable graphics standard for the some time to come.

Both VML and SVG are relatively complex and sophisticated standards, and entire books could be written about either one of these technologies. Because of that, this chapter is not intended to teach how to use either SVG or VML. For more information about VML, take a look at http://msdn.microsoft.com/msdn-online/workshop/standards/vml/. The W3C specifications for SVG can be found at http://www.w3.org/TR/SVG, and some of the best samples and tutorials (on which some of the code in this chapter is based) can be found at Adobe's superb SVG web section, http://www.adobe.com/svg.

A Simple Graph in SVG

Perhaps the best way to illustrate the use of SVG is to start with a very simple set of data, and demonstrate how XML and XSLT can be used to transform that data into useful output. Consider, for instance, a sales report showing book sales figures by quarter, region of the country, and genre, as shown in `SalesFigures.xml` below.

```
<sales>
  <quarter title="Winter 1999">
    <region title="Northwest">
      <genre title="General Fiction">82539</genre>
      <genre title="Fantasy">94269</genre>
      <genre title="Romance">70612</genre>
      <genre title="Mystery">135969</genre>
      <genre title="Horror">52683</genre>
      <genre title="Computer">153762</genre>
      <genre title="Travel">12578</genre>
      <genre title="Art">14695</genre>
    </region>
    <region title="Southwest">
      <genre title="General Fiction">123663</genre>
      <genre title="Fantasy">131295</genre>
      <genre title="Romance">17751</genre>
      <genre title="Mystery">185587</genre>
      <genre title="Horror">18713</genre>
      <genre title="Computer">108085</genre>
      <genre title="Travel">10821</genre>
      <genre title="Art">18541</genre>
    </region>
    <region title="Midwest">
      <genre title="General Fiction">1821</genre>
      <genre title="Fantasy">16423</genre>
      <genre title="Romance">14462</genre>
      <genre title="Mystery">18652</genre>
      <genre title="Horror">19702</genre>
      <genre title="Computer">142268</genre>
```

```
      <genre title="Travel">121506</genre>
      <genre title="Art">17487</genre>
    </region>
    <region title="Southeast">
      <genre title="General Fiction">128291</genre>
      <genre title="Fantasy">144756</genre>
      <genre title="Romance">13584</genre>
      <genre title="Mystery">161513</genre>
      <genre title="Horror">109310</genre>
      <genre title="Computer">13887</genre>
      <genre title="Travel">131257</genre>
      <genre title="Art">11257</genre>
    </region>
    <region title="Northeast">
      <genre title="General Fiction">12514</genre>
      <genre title="Fantasy">165406</genre>
      <genre title="Romance">123159</genre>
      <genre title="Mystery">132536</genre>
      <genre title="Horror">1435</genre>
      <genre title="Computer">116457</genre>
      <genre title="Travel">26052</genre>
      <genre title="Art">113647</genre>
    </region>
  </quarter>
  <!-- Additional quarters -->
</sales>
```

This type of data immediately suggests a bar chart, where the figures for each genre in a given region and quarter can be compared:

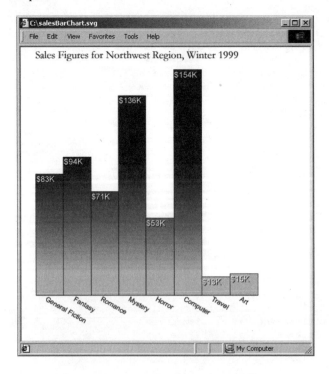

The SVG file (`salesBarChart.svg`) that contains the code to perform this is given below:

```
<?xml version="1.0" standalone="no"?>
<!DOCTYPE svg PUBLIC "-//W3C//DTD SVG 20000303 Stylable//EN"
 "http://www.w3.org/TR/2000/03/WD-SVG-20000303/DTD/svg-20000303-stylable.dtd" >
<svg width="500" height="500" viewBox="0 0 1200 1300" left="0" top="0"
enableZoomAndPanControls="true" preserveAspectRatio="xMidYMid meet"
xmlns="http://www.w3.org/2000/svg-20000303-stylable">
  <defs>
    <linearGradient id="boxGradient"
    gradientTransform="rotate(90) translate(0 -1000) scale(0.7692307692307693)">
      <stop offset="0%" style="stop-color:darkBlue"/>
      <stop offset="50%" style="stop-color:blue"/>
      <stop offset="100%" style="stop-color:lightBlue"/>
    </linearGradient>
  </defs>
  <g transform="translate(20 50)">
    <text style="font-size:48;color:black;font-family:Garamond;"
    startOffset="0">Sales Figures for Northwest Region, Winter 1999</text>
  </g>
  <g transform="translate(20 100)">
    <g transform="translate(0 464)">
      <rect width="125" height="536"
      style="fill:url(#boxGradient);stroke:black;stroke-width:2;"/>
      <text style="color: black;font-size:36;" x="5" y="37"
      startOffset="0">$83K</text>
      <text style="color: white;font-size:36;" x="2" y="34"
      startOffset="0">$83K</text>
      <g transform="translate(41.666666666666664 560)">
        <g transform="rotate(30)">
          <text style="color:black;font-size:30;" startOffset="0">
          General Fiction
          </text>
        </g>
      </g>
    </g>
    <g transform="translate(125 387)">
      <rect width="125" height="613"
      style="fill:url(#boxGradient);stroke:black;stroke-width:2;"/>
      <text style="color: black;font-size:36;" x="5" y="37"
      startOffset="0">$94K</text>
      <text style="color: white;font-size:36;" x="2" y="34"
      startOffset="0">$94K</text>
      <g transform="translate(41.666666666666664 637)">
        <g transform="rotate(30)">
          <text style="color:black;font-size:30;" startOffset="0">Fantasy</text>
        </g>
      </g>
    </g>
    <g transform="translate(250 541)">
      <rect width="125" height="459"
      style="fill:url(#boxGradient);stroke:black;stroke-width:2;"/>
      <text style="color: black;font-size:36;" x="5" y="37"
      startOffset="0">$71K</text>
      <text style="color: white;font-size:36;" x="2" y="34"
      startOffset="0">$71K</text>
```

```
      <g transform="translate(41.666666666666664 483)">
        <g transform="rotate(30)">
          <text style="color:black;font-size:30;" startOffset="0">Romance</text>
        </g>
      </g>
    </g>
  </g>
  <g transform="translate(375 116)">
    <rect width="125" height="884"
    style="fill:url(#boxGradient);stroke:black;stroke-width:2;"/>
    <text style="color: black;font-size:36;" x="5" y="37"
    startOffset="0">$136K</text>
    <text style="color: white;font-size:36;" x="2" y="34"
    startOffset="0">$136K</text>
    <g transform="translate(41.666666666666664 908)">
      <g transform="rotate(30)">
        <text style="color:black;font-size:30;" startOffset="0">Mystery</text>
      </g>
    </g>
  </g>
  <g transform="translate(500 658)">
    <rect width="125" height="342"
    style="fill:url(#boxGradient);stroke:black;stroke-width:2;"/>
    <text style="color: black;font-size:36;" x="5" y="37"
    startOffset="0">$53K</text>
    <text style="color: white;font-size:36;" x="2" y="34"
    startOffset="0">$53K</text>
    <g transform="translate(41.666666666666664 366)">
      <g transform="rotate(30)">
        <text style="color:black;font-size:30;" startOffset="0">Horror</text>
      </g>
    </g>
  </g>
  <g transform="translate(625 0)">
    <rect width="125" height="1000"
    style="fill:url(#boxGradient);stroke:black;stroke-width:2;"/>
    <text style="color: black;font-size:36;" x="5" y="37"
    startOffset="0">$154K</text>
    <text style="color: white;font-size:36;" x="2" y="34"
    startOffset="0">$154K</text>
      <g transform="translate(41.666666666666664 1024)">
        <g transform="rotate(30)">
          <text style="color:black;font-size:30;"
          startOffset="0">Computer</text>
        </g>
      </g>
  </g>
  <g transform="translate(750 919)">
    <rect width="125" height="81"
    style="fill:url(#boxGradient);stroke:black;stroke-width:2;"/>
    <text style="color: black;font-size:36;" x="5" y="37"
    startOffset="0">$13K</text>
    <text style="color: white;font-size:36;" x="2" y="34"
    startOffset="0">$13K</text>
    <g transform="translate(41.666666666666664 105)">
      <g transform="rotate(30)">
```

```
                <text style="color:black;font-size:30;" startOffset="0">Travel</text>
          </g>
        </g>
      </g>
      <g transform="translate(875 905)">
        <rect width="125" height="95"
        style="fill:url(#boxGradient);stroke:black;stroke-width:2;"/>
        <text style="color: black;font-size:36;" x="5" y="37"
        startOffset="0">$15K</text>
        <text style="color: white;font-size:36;" x="2" y="34"
        startOffset="0">$15K</text>
        <g transform="translate(41.666666666666664 119)">
          <g transform="rotate(30)">
            <text style="color:black;font-size:30;" startOffset="0">Art</text>
          </g>
        </g>
      </g>
    </g>
</svg>
```

This sample SVG document illustrates a number of basic characteristics of SVG documents in general.

The <svg> element serves as the root element, performing both the task of declaring any namespaces that may be used by the document and setting up the "viewport" by defining the coordinate system. In the example given here, the width and height are given in the default units of pixels (though they could be any valid CSS unit), creating a viewing rectangle that's 500 pixels square. After that, the viewBox attribute defines the units that will be used internally to the viewport, in essence letting developers define their own coordinate system.

```
<svg width="500" height="500" viewBox="0 0 1200 1300" left="0" top="0"
enableZoomAndPanControls="true" xmlns="http://www.w3.org/2000/svg-20000303-
stylable">
```

The attribute value viewBox="0 0 1200 1300" specifies that a relative coordinate system be set up in which 1200 user units are allocated to the horizontal dimension of the viewport, and 1300 for the vertical, starting from the origin (the bottom left), which is given as [0,0]. This is in fact one of the more useful characteristics of SVG, because you can choose whatever coordinate system best fits your needs. For example, the sales chart is set up such that the area where the bars are to be drawn will be a 1000x1000 unit square. By freeing you from depending upon pixels or explicit measurements, you can use coordinates that let you build graphics that can easily be scaled up or down if the dimensions of the viewing area are changed.

The SVG namespace http://www.w3.org/2000/svg-20000303-stylable is set as default by the <svg> header. The top-level element also includes an attribute called enableZoomAndPanControls, which tells the SVG renderer to make it possible to zoom or pan the viewport. (In the Adobe component, zoom is enabled by pressing the *Ctrl* key to zoom in or *Shift-Ctrl* to zoom out, while panning is activated by pressing the *Alt* key and moving the mouse).

In order to add a little visual punch to the illustration, a gradient was added that fades from dark blue at the top to light blue at the bottom. The gradient itself is defined as a separate object in the <svg:defs> section, which groups common objects that can be reused throughout the code. Anything that falls within the <svg:defs> section is not immediately rendered – rather, it is held in reserve until such time as a reference to the object is made.

```
<defs>
  <linearGradient id="boxGradient"
  gradientTransform="rotate(90) translate(0 -1000) scale(0.7692307692307693)">
    <stop offset="0%" style="stop-color:darkBlue"/>
    <stop offset="50%" style="stop-color:blue"/>
    <stop offset="100%" style="stop-color:lightBlue"/>
  </linearGradient>
</defs>
```

The `gradientTransform` attribute provides a set of space separated transformations that, in this order, rotate the default gradient 90° counter-clockwise, translate the resultant gradient to the bottom of the viewport, and scale it to 1000/1300 to ensure that the gradient value at the bottom of the graph corresponds to the requested stop value. This scaling factor is the ratio of the height of the active graph area (1000 user units) to the height of the graph plus labels (1300 units), or 1000/1300, which is 0.76923. Note that transformations may be non-commutative; that is, a rotation followed by a translation is not necessarily the same thing as a translation followed by a rotation.

The gradient's `<svg:stop>` elements provide key values at specific offsets and let the rendering engine evaluate intermediate values. Thus, in this case, the gradient goes from a value of dark blue at the top through regular blue at the halfway point to light blue at the end. One advantage of this approach is that you can assign `id` values to each `<svg:stop>` and change the color and offset values on the fly, making for wash effects that can shift in color and gradient dynamically.

The next section draws the text label at the top of the graph:

```
<g transform="translate(20 50)">
  <text style="font-size:48;color:black;font-family:Garamond;"
  startOffset="0">Sales Figures for Northwest Region, Winter 1999</text>
</g>
```

The format here should look familiar to HTML creators familiar with CSS, though there are a couple of minor differences that you should be aware of. The `<svg:g>` element defines a graphic context, and serves a function similar to a `<div>` tag in HTML by defining the space in which a set of graphic elements are to be drawn. In this case, the space is also transformed by moving it 20 user units to the right and 50 units down, relative to the current graphic context.

The `<svg:text>` element, as expected, defines a block of text for output. Note that SVG text does not wrap automatically, which means that you need to break up text into distinct lines, though the next section (*Breaking Up Text with XSLT*) covers this issue in some detail. You can, however, apply style elements and animations to `<svg:text>` elements, including the familiar as `font-family`, `color`, and `font-size` characteristics.

There is one thing that you must be aware of here: the `font-size` style attribute is given as `"48"` which is not the measurement in points, as the magnitude of this attribute may lead you to believe. Instead, it is a measure of the base height of the font in custom user units – that is, relative to the maximum of 1300. By using user coordinates rather than "pt" or "px" (point and pixel respectively), you ensure that if the image's base width and height change, then the font will scale itself accordingly.

The actual bar graphs themselves work by the principle of nested transformations; here there are two nested translations (motions). The outer one locates the origin one hundred units down and twenty to the right, so the title doesn't collide with the largest bar. The inner translation then shifts the origin to the top-left corner of the first bar (the height of the bar + the start position = 1000).

```
<g transform="translate(20 100)">
  <g transform="translate(0 464)">
    <rect width="125" height="536"
    style="fill:url(#boxGradient);stroke:black;stroke-width:2;"/>
    <text style="color: black;font-size:36;" x="5" y="37"
    startOffset="0">$83K</text>
    <text style="color: white;font-size:36;" x="2" y="34"
    startOffset="0">$83K</text>
    <g transform="translate(41.666666666666664 560)">
      <g transform="rotate(30)">
        <text style="color:black;font-size:30;" startOffset="0">
         General Fiction
        </text>
      </g>
    </g>
  </g>
</g>
```

The bar itself is a rectangle 125 units wide to allow eight bars to fit the display (as will be shown in the next section) and 536 units high. The boxGradient defined previously is assigned here as the default fill, along with a two unit wide black border. Within the bar, the data value associated with the bar is displayed as a percentage in white, with a black drop shadow to increase visibility. The final transform locates the label for the bar, rotating it 30 degrees so that long label names don't collide with one another.

Each bar has its own transformation to correctly position it within the primary display area (the 1000x1000 custom unit square), with eight bars in total. The way that the length of the bars is evaluated may seem a little awkward, but this is because the highest sales figure will always be represented by 1000 custom units. Thus, the heights of the other bars are essentially determined from the ratio between the highest and the current values for each bar.

Generating the Graph with XSLT

As may be fairly obvious, the SVG file wasn't written by hand. Rather, it was created using an XSLT transformation that took data from a source file and built the SVG around it. We'll look at that transformation, drawGraph.xsl, below:

```
<xsl:stylesheet xmlns:xsl="http://www.w3.org/1999/XSL/Transform"
  xmlns:msxml="urn:schemas-microsoft-com:xslt"
  xmlns="http://www.w3.org/2000/svg-20000303-stylable"
  xmlns:math="urn:schemas-cagle-com:math"
  exclude-result-prefixes="math msxml"
  version="1.0">

  <xsl:output method="xml" media-type="image/svg"
    omit-xml-declaration="yes" indent="yes"/>

  <msxml:script language="JavaScript" implements-prefix="math">
    function max(numSet)
    {
      var maxVal=0;
      for (var index=0;index != numSet.length;index++)
      {
```

```
            node=numSet[index];
            nodeVal=parseFloat(node.text);
            if (nodeVal &gt; maxVal)
            {
               maxVal=nodeVal;
            }
         }
         return maxVal;
      }
</msxml:script>

<xsl:param name="quarter" select="//quarter[1]/@title"/>
<xsl:param name="region" select="//region[1]/@title"/>
<xsl:param name="genre" select="//genre[1]/@title"/>
<xsl:param name="maxValue"
select="math:max(//quarter[@title=$quarter]/region[@title=$region]/genre)"/>
<xsl:template match="/">
   <svg width="500" height="500"  viewBox="0 0 1200 1300" left="0" top="0">
      <defs>
         <linearGradient id="boxGradient"
                         gradientTransform="rotate(90) translate(0 -1000)
                         scale({1000 div 1300})">
            <stop offset="0%" style="stop-color:darkBlue"/>
            <stop offset=".5" style="stop-color:blue;"/>
            <stop offset="100%" style="stop-color:lightBlue"/>
         </linearGradient>
      </defs>
      <g transform="translate(20 50)">
         <text style="font-size:48;color:black;font-family:Garamond;">
            <xsl:value-of select="concat('Sales Figures for ',
                               $region,' Region, ',$quarter)"/>
         </text>
      </g>
      <g transform="translate(20 100)">
         <xsl:apply-templates select="//quarter[@title=$quarter]"/>
      </g>
   </svg>
</xsl:template>

<xsl:template match="quarter">
   <xsl:apply-templates select="region[@title=$region]"/>
</xsl:template>

<xsl:template match="region">
   <xsl:apply-templates select="genre"/>
</xsl:template>

<xsl:template match="genre">
   <xsl:variable name="cx" select="floor(1000 div count(../genre))"/>
   <xsl:variable name="cy" select="floor(text() * 1000 div $maxValue )"/>
   <g transform="translate({position()*$cx - $cx} {1000-$cy})">
      <rect width="{$cx}" height="{$cy}"
      style="fill:url(#boxGradient);stroke:black;stroke-width:2;"/>
      <xsl:choose>
      <xsl:when test="$cy &lt; 50">
```

```
            <text style="color:black;font-size:40;" y="-10">
            <xsl:value-of select="format-number(. div 1000,'$###,###')"/>K</text>
        </xsl:when>
        <xsl:otherwise>
            <text style="color: black;font-size:36;" x="5" y="37">
            <xsl:value-of select="format-number(. div 1000,'$###,###')"/>K</text>
            <text style="color: white;font-size:36;" x="2" y="34">
            <xsl:value-of select="format-number(. div 1000,'$###,###')"/>K</text>
        </xsl:otherwise>
        </xsl:choose>
        <g transform="translate({$cx div 3} {$cy + 24})">
            <g transform="rotate(30)">
            <text style="color:black;font-size:30;">
                <xsl:value-of select="@title"/>
            </text>
            </g>
        </g>
        </g>
    </xsl:template>
</xsl:stylesheet>
```

This stylesheet takes the sales figures and generates a corresponding SVG document.

Look at the namespace declarations in the `<xsl:stylesheet>` element. Again I use the `"http://www.w3.org/2000/svg-20000303-stylable"` namespace as the default, named to reflect its adoption on March 3, 2000, with the suffix indicating that is designed primarily for styling documents rather than as a way of transmitting graphics data. In addition, two other helper namespace functions are defined: `msxml`, which contains both the `<msxml:script>` element and the `msxml:node-set()` function, and the custom `math` namespace, which defines the function `math:max()` to determine the largest sales figure for a given region and quarter. Because these functions aren't used by the SVG file once it's created, the `exclude-result-prefixes` attribute removes these namespace references before they get placed into the output file.

The `<xsl:output>` element is also needed to control the type of document being generated (especially when used in conjunction with the Adobe plug-in). The MIME type (also known as content type) of an SVG file is `"image/svg"`, and this should be reflected in the `media-type` attribute.

> *I have seen a number of different variants on the MIME type, such as* `text/svg`, *but according to IETF rules it should be* `image/svg`, *because the content is primarily graphical in nature.*

Some SVG parsers might not accept Unicode characters, and as a consequence you must either set the `encoding` attribute to `"UTF-8"` or omit the XML declaration outright. In these code samples, I have taken the latter option. Finally, set `indent` to `"yes"`, to ensure that the output is easier to follow and debug:

```
<xsl:output method="xml" media-type="image/svg" omit-xml-declaration="yes"
  indent="yes"/>
```

Neither XSLT nor XPath has a function for determining the largest value in a given set of nodes, but it's easy enough to write one using the `<msxml:script>` extension:

```
<msxml:script language="JavaScript" implements-prefix="math">
  function max(numSet)
  {
    var maxVal=0;
    for (var index=0;index != numSet.length;index++)
    {
      node=numSet[index];
      nodeVal=parseFloat(node.text);
      if (nodeVal &gt; maxVal)
      {
        maxVal=nodeVal;
      }
    }
    return maxVal;
  }
</msxml:script>
```

This function is invoked later to determine the largest genre sales figure in any given quarter and region, which is in turn assigned to the variable $maxValue:

```
<xsl:param name="maxValue" select="math:max(//quarter[@title=$quarter]/
  region[@title=$region]/genre)"/>
```

You could get by without this technique by setting an absolute maxValue explicitly that would override the calculated maximum value, but such a solution brings the danger of bars that exceed the maximum height, causing them to extend beyond the confines of the figure.

The root node defines the SVG outer shell, establishing the viewBox and other dimensions, and setting up any gradients. This section also displays the title of the chart, based on the <xsl:param> elements of the stylesheet:

```
<text style="font-size:48;color:black;font-family:Garamond;">
  <xsl:value-of select="concat('Sales Figures for ',$region,' Region, ',
    $quarter)"/>
</text>
```

The match templates for region and quarter pass focus down the document, with each one existing primarily to reduce the number of options down to one region containing one quarter's worth of data. The primary work is actually done at the genre match level:

```
<xsl:template match="genre">
  <xsl:variable name="cx" select="floor(1000 div count(../genre))"/>
  <xsl:variable name="cy" select="floor(text() * 1000 div $maxValue )"/>
  <g transform="translate({position() - 1) *$cx } {1000-$cy})">
    <rect width="{$cx}" height="{$cy}" style="fill:url(#boxGradient);
      stroke:black;stroke-width:2;"/>
```

The variable $cx holds the width of the bar, and is calculated by taking the width of the graph (1000) and dividing it by the number of genres in the current quarter. The variable $cy takes a similar tack, obtaining the height of the bar by scaling the sales figure for the genre relative to the maximum sales value.

Once these values are determined, the position of the graphic context is set using inline attribute evaluation with curly braces. The transformation uses the position() function to determine the relative position of the genre in the list, which in turn, when multiplied by the width of a bar, gives the offset from the previous bar. The vertical position has been normalized to 1000, which means that subtracting the value from 1000 will set the top of the bar such that the bottom rests on the 1000 mark.

It should be noted here that the XSLT serves a purpose common to any programming language – it provides a mechanism for parameterizing your documents, and with a graphics language such as SVG this implies that we should expect far more "mathematical" translations than you might find in a typical XSLT-XHTML transformation.

The next section handles the drawing of the values within the bar using an <xsl:choose> element:

```
<xsl:choose>
  <xsl:when test="$cy &lt; 50">
    <text style="color:black;font-size:40;" y="-10">
      <xsl:value-of select="format-number (. div 1000,'$###,###')"/>K</text>
  </xsl:when>
  <xsl:otherwise>
    <text style="color: black;font-size:36;" x="5" y="37">
      <xsl:value-of select="format-number(. div 1000,'$###,###')"/>K</text>
    <text style="color: white;font-size:36;" x="2" y="34">
      <xsl:value-of select="format-number(. div 1000,'$###,###')"/>K</text>
  </xsl:otherwise>
</xsl:choose>
```

Here's where a little design sense can add significantly to the value of your programming. One problem with bar charts is that if one data cell is too small compared to the others, a text value placed within the bar may overrun the bar, and potentially may even overprint both the bar and lower axis. To cover this eventuality, should the user units of the bar's height be less than 50 (1/20 of the maximum possible height) we place the text value above the bar. Otherwise, the text value is drawn within the bar in a contrasting color and drop shadow, formatted to be a currency given in 1000s such as 50K.

The final nested transformation locates the label in the x-axis (genres), and rotates it by 30 degrees to ensure that there is no overlap with other labels:

```
<g transform="translate({$cx div 3} {$cy + 24})">
  <g transform="rotate(30)">
    <text style="color:black;font-size:30;">
      <xsl:value-of select="@title"/>
    </text>
  </g>
</g>
```

One of the most exciting areas that SVG opens up is in the realm of information graphics. Typically, such graphics are data driven, and perhaps even more importantly, are dynamic – they change over time. The traditional approach of creating graphics through programs such as Excel has a number of disadvantages, not least of which being the overhead required to run instances of the whole application just to display a chart or graph. By coupling XML with XSLT to generate SVG output, the presentation of your data can be completely altered merely by switching stylesheets.

This works very well for pure data. However, how does SVG used in conjunction with XSLT stack up on the document/text-processing front?

Breaking Up Text with XSLT

The formatting that most HTML browsers perform automatically tends to make developers forget the hassles of having to break up text manually for word wrapping. Unfortunately, SVG rather forcibly reminds us of this again, as spelled out by the options that the SVG specification outlines for text display:

❑ Manually break apart a section of text and place each line in a separate `<svg:text>` element.

❑ Manually break apart a section of text and place each line in its own `<svg:tspan>` element contained within a single `<svg:text>` element (preferable when performing searches in a document – see below).

❑ Use the `<svg:foreignObject>` entity to load in an HTML DOM instance.

While the last option, the `<svg:foreignObject>`, would seem to be the most sensible choice, the major drawback is that this element is not generally supported by early SVG parsers, not surprisingly perhaps, since it would be like building an entire HTML browser into your SVG parser. Indeed, the W3C documentation itself indicates that this isn't really the ideal solution, especially as the `foreignObject` interface described by the Candidate Recommendation is still very much in flux.

Thus, breaking up a block of text into separate lines contained in `<svg:tspan>` tags is probably the best option for most cases. The distinction between `<svg:tspan>` and `<svg:text>` elements is roughly analogous to the distinction between the `<span>` and `<div>` tags of HTML where a `<span>` is typically seen as a subsection of a contiguous block of text, while a `<div>` element is generally a container of such text.

Perhaps one of the biggest distinctions between the two SVG elements has to do with selections and searches. Groups of `<svg:tspan>` elements within a `<svg:text>` block are considered part of the same block as far as text searching goes, so if you search for an expression that spans two or more `<svg:tspan>` elements, you can still select the text through the text dialog. Also, triple-clicking on a `<svg:text>` block with multiple `<svg:tspan>` elements will select all the contained `<svg:tspan>` elements, similar to the way that most word processor programs select an entire paragraph by a triple-click.

Because this is going to be a very common task when dealing with SVG, it makes sense to write a routine that, when given the maximum number of characters and the size of the font in user coordinates, turns a paragraph of text into a set of `<svg:tspan>` lines. Consider, for instance, an XML document (`paragraphs.xml`) containing a number of paragraph like so:

```
<article>
    <para>In the beginning, the Web was only words. Lynx, one of the first World
Wide Web browsers (when the World Wide part basically covered a few universities
and research facilities in the United States and Western Europe), gave web page
designers the ability to highlight text (usually by inverting foreground and
background colors on a standard console CRT screen), provide underlined links, and
potentially display certain text in bold.</para>
    <para> The NCSA (National Center for Supercomputing Applications) Mosaic
browser debuted in 1993, and its impact changed the world. Its designers
recognized a salient fact about people - that we are fundamentally visual beings,
and we naturally view the world in terms of images rather than words. With the
innovation of being able to display inline graphics (and later of being able to
change the characteristics of the background image pane), the Mosaic browser
completely altered the way that people related to the web, and fueled a period of
explosive growth that is only just now, eight years later, beginning to slow
down.</para>
```

```
    <para> The problem with pictures, however, is that it takes a thousand words
to describe one. More specifically, the vast majority of all pictures on the web
are bitmap graphics, in which a picture consists of a grid of pixels, each pixel
having its own color, with perhaps one color (or byte within a color, in the case
of Portable Network Graphics or PNG) used to denote levels of transparency. There
are several problems with such graphics:</para>
    <!-- more paragraphs -->
</article>
```

In theory, the principle behind building an XSLT transformation to wrap such text is relatively simple, though a little complicated in implementation. In essence, the word wrapper creates a buffer and adds words (where a word is an element delimited by spaces) one at a time until the number of characters in the buffer exceeds its predefined limit. Once this happens, the offending word is added back to the beginning of the source text, the contents of the buffer are sent to the output stream or in this case redirected into a variable, and the buffer is cleared, so the whole process may begin again.

Let's have a look at svgTextSplit.xsl:

```
<xsl:stylesheet xmlns:xsl="http://www.w3.org/1999/XSL/Transform"
  xmlns:msxml="urn:schemas-microsoft-com:xslt"
  xmlns:csvg="urn:schemas-cagle-com:utils"
  version="1.0">
  <xsl:output method="xml" media-type="image/svg"
    omit-xml-declaration="yes" indent="yes"/>

  <xsl:template match="/">
    <svg width="500" height="500" viewBox="0 0 1000 1000">
      <g transform="translate(0 0)">
        <xsl:call-template name="svgTextSplit">
          <xsl:with-param name="text" select="//para[1]"/>
        </xsl:call-template>
      </g>
    </svg>
  </xsl:template>

  <xsl:template name="svgTextSplit">
    <xsl:param name="text"/>
    <xsl:param name="font_size" select="36"/>
    <xsl:param name="maxCharactersPerLine" select="48"/>
    <xsl:param name="lineDiff" select="$font_size"/>
    <xsl:param name="id" select="generate-id()"/>
    <xsl:param name="style"
      select="concat('font-size:',$font_size,';font-family:Garamond;')"/>
    <text style="{$style}" id="{$id}">
      <xsl:call-template name="splitLines">
        <xsl:with-param name="text" select="$text"/>
        <xsl:with-param name="maxCharactersPerLine"
          select="$maxCharactersPerLine"/>
        <xsl:with-param name="lineDiff" select="$lineDiff"/>
      </xsl:call-template>
    </text>
  </xsl:template>
```

```
<xsl:template name="splitLines">
  <xsl:param name="text"/>
  <xsl:param name="buffer" select=" '' "/>
  <xsl:param name="maxCharactersPerLine" select="40"/>
  <xsl:param name="lineDiff" select="40"/>
  <xsl:param name="lineNum" select="1"/>
  <xsl:variable name="currentText">
    <xsl:choose>
      <xsl:when test="substring($text,string-length($text)) != ' '">
        <xsl:value-of select="$text"/><xsl:text> </xsl:text>
      </xsl:when>
      <xsl:otherwise>
        <xsl:value-of select="$text"/>
      </xsl:otherwise>
    </xsl:choose>
  </xsl:variable>

  <xsl:variable name="next_word"
    select="substring-before($currentText,' ')"/>

  <xsl:variable name="textAfter"
    select="substring-after($currentText,' ')"/>

  <xsl:choose>
    <xsl:when test="$textAfter != ''">
      <xsl:choose>
        <xsl:when test="string-length(concat($buffer,' ',$next_word)) &gt;
          $maxCharactersPerLine">
          <tspan x="0" y="{$lineDiff * $lineNum}">
            <xsl:value-of select="$buffer"/>
          </tspan>
          <xsl:variable name="new_textAfter"
            select="concat($next_word,' ',$textAfter)"/>
          <xsl:call-template name="splitLines">
            <xsl:with-param name="text" select="$new_textAfter"/>
            <xsl:with-param name="buffer" select="''"/>
            <xsl:with-param name="maxCharactersPerLine"
              select="$maxCharactersPerLine"/>
            <xsl:with-param name="lineDiff" select="$lineDiff"/>
            <xsl:with-param name="lineNum" select="$lineNum + 1"/>
          </xsl:call-template>
        </xsl:when>
        <xsl:otherwise>
          <xsl:variable name="new_buffer"
            select="concat($buffer,$next_word,' ')"/>
          <xsl:call-template name="splitLines">
            <xsl:with-param name="text" select="$textAfter"/>
            <xsl:with-param name="buffer" select="$new_buffer"/>
            <xsl:with-param name="maxCharactersPerLine"
              select="$maxCharactersPerLine"/>
            <xsl:with-param name="lineDiff" select="$lineDiff"/>
            <xsl:with-param name="lineNum" select="$lineNum"/>
          </xsl:call-template>
        </xsl:otherwise>
      </xsl:choose>
```

```
            </xsl:when>
            <xsl:otherwise>
              <tspan  x="0" y="{$lineDiff * $lineNum}">
                <xsl:value-of select="concat($buffer,' ',$next_word)"/>
              </tspan>
              <csvg:info cursorX="0" cursorY="{$lineDiff * ($lineNum + 1)}"/>
            </xsl:otherwise>
          </xsl:choose>
        </xsl:template>
    </xsl:stylesheet>
```

Note that this process does not recognize paragraph marks – the assumption here being that a paragraph would likely be specified in an XML file as a distinct marked up block, and can be handled appropriately. However, one of the problems with doing conversion of multiple paragraphs comes with deciding where the next paragraph should begin. In order to make this process somewhat easier, after the last <svg:tspan> is rendered, an additional <csvg:info> element from my own custom csvg namespace is created containing the co-ordinates for where the next line should begin.

The output for the first paragraph then looks as follows:

```
<svg width="500" height="500" viewBox="0 0 1000 1000" xmlns:csvg="urn:schemas-
cagle-com:utils">
  <g transform="translate(0 0)">
    <text style="font-size:36;font-family:Garamond;" id="IDACI1P">
      <tspan x="0" y="36">In the beginning, the web was only words. Lynx,
      </tspan>
      <tspan x="0" y="72">one of the first World Wide Web browsers (when
      </tspan>
      <tspan x="0" y="108">the World Wide part basically covered a few
      </tspan>
      <tspan x="0" y="144">universities and research facilities in the
      </tspan>
      <tspan x="0" y="180">United States and Western Europe) gave web page
      </tspan>
      <tspan x="0" y="216">designers the ability to highlight text
      </tspan>
      <tspan x="0" y="252">(usually by inverting foreground and background
      </tspan>
      <tspan x="0" y="288">colors on a standard console CRT screen),
      </tspan>
      <tspan x="0" y="324">underlining links, and potentially make some
      </tspan>
      <tspan x="0" y="360">text  bold.
      </tspan>
      <csvg:info cursorX="0" cursorY="396"/>
    </text>
  </g>
</svg>
```

The file `displayParagraphText.xsl` below imports `SVGTextSplit.xsl` to divide each paragraph into `<svg:tspan>` elements, after separating the paragraphs itself:

```
<xsl:stylesheet xmlns:xsl="http://www.w3.org/1999/XSL/Transform"
  xmlns:msxml="urn:schemas-microsoft-com:xslt"
  xmlns:csvg="urn:schemas-cagle-com:utils"
  version="1.0">
  <xsl:import href="svgTextSplit.xsl"/>
  <xsl:output method="xml" media-type="image/svg" omit-xml-declaration="yes"
    indent="yes"/>

  <xsl:template match="/">
    <xsl:variable name="paragraphs.tf">
      <xsl:apply-templates select="//para"/>
    </xsl:variable>
    <xsl:variable name="paragraphs" select="msxml:node-set($paragraphs.tf)"/>
    <svg width="1000" height="600"
      viewBox="0 0 1000 {sum($paragraphs//csvg:info/@cursorY)}">
      <xsl:for-each select="$paragraphs/*">
        <xsl:choose>
          <xsl:when test="position()=1">
            <g transform="translate(0 0)">
              <rect x="-10" y="0" width="800" height="{csvg:info/@cursorY}"
                style="fill:white;stroke:red;stroke-width:3;"/>
              <xsl:copy-of select="."/>
            </g>
          </xsl:when>
          <xsl:otherwise>
            <xsl:variable name="prevY"
              select="sum(preceding-sibling::*//csvg:info/@cursorY)"/>
            <g transform="translate(0 {$prevY})">
              <rect x="-10" y="0" width="800" height="{csvg:info/@cursorY}"
                style="fill:white;stroke:red;stroke-width:3;"/>
              <xsl:copy-of select="."/>
            </g>
          </xsl:otherwise>
        </xsl:choose>
      </xsl:for-each>
    </svg>
  </xsl:template>

  <xsl:template match="para">
    <xsl:call-template name="svgTextSplit">
      <xsl:with-param name="text" select="."/>
    </xsl:call-template>
  </xsl:template>

</xsl:stylesheet>
```

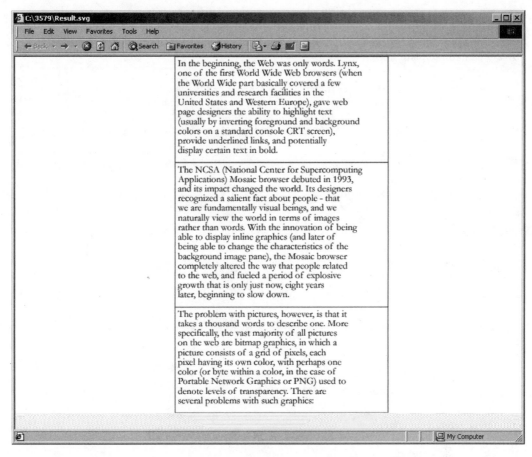

You could improve this to display long paragraphs in a scrollable form, or use animation elements to auto-scroll the text displayed. In addition, you can make use of XLink technology to replace certain paragraphs with other paragraphs when triggered by a mouse click. Unfortunately, the limited space available for this chapter means it's not possible to go into all the ways that you can present text output. The SVG specification contains more specific information on <svg:text> elements along with the techniques available to frame or move an SVG element.

A Star Is Born

SVG is a graphics description language, not a programming one. One of the major barriers to working with SVG is that, as with other vector graphics languages, determining coordinates to describe arbitrary shapes is often difficult and time-consuming to perform by hand, especially when a multiplicity of such shapes are required.

A star, as a fairly simple example, can give a powerful visual punch to a page. However, creating stars is not altogether easy. An n-pointed star can be defined by three basic parameters: the number of points n, the radius of the tips of the points, and the radius of where the points meet at the bottom. Additionally, we want to provide our star with some kind of styling (a yellow fill with a red border, for instance), including a style for any text that may appear in the star.

The following file, `drawStar.xsl`, illustrates an XSLT routine that creates a star in SVG from the parameters just described. It really doesn't matter what file is used as the XML source to use with the transformation – an XML stub will work fine – as the code to draw the star is generated in the stylesheet by the named template `star`.

```
<xsl:stylesheet xmlns:xsl="http://www.w3.org/1999/XSL/Transform"
                xmlns:msxml="urn:schemas-microsoft-com:xslt"
                xmlns:math="urn:schemas-cagle-com:math"
                xmlns:xlink="http://www.w3.org/2000/xlink/namespace/"
                version="1.0">

<xsl:output method="xml" media-type="image/svg" omit-xml-declaration="yes"/>
<xsl:param name="numPoints" select="5"/>
<xsl:param name="outerRadius" select="480"/>
<xsl:param name="innerRadius" select="184"/>
<xsl:param name="style"
  select=" 'fill:url(#gradient1);stroke:yellow;stroke-width:2' "/>
<xsl:param name="text" select=" 'WOW! ' "/>
<xsl:param name="text_style"
  select=" 'fill:black;font-size:100;font-family:Garamond' "/>
<msxml:script language="JavaScript" implements-prefix="math">
  function sin(angle)
  {
    return Math.sin(angle*3.1415927/180);
  }

  function cos(angle)
  {
  return Math.cos(angle*3.1415927/180);
  }

  function rnd()
  {
    return Math.random();
  }
</msxml:script>
<xsl:template match="/">
  <svg width="400" height="400" left="0" top="0" viewBox="0 0 1000 1000">
    <defs>
      <linearGradient id="gradient1" gradientTransform="rotate(90)
        translate(0 -1000) scale({1000 div 1300})">
        <stop offset="0%" style="stop-color:yellow"/>
        <stop offset="100%" style="stop-color:red"/>
      </linearGradient>
    </defs>
    <g>
      <g transform="translate(500 500)">
        <g transform="scale(1)">
          <xsl:call-template name="star">
            <xsl:with-param name="numPoints" select="$numPoints"/>
            <xsl:with-param name="curPoint" select="0"/>
            <xsl:with-param name="outerRadius" select="$outerRadius"/>
            <xsl:with-param name="innerRadius" select="$innerRadius"/>
            <xsl:with-param name="style" select="$style"/>
            <xsl:with-param name="text" select="$text"/>
```

```xml
              <xsl:with-param name="text_style" select="$text_style"/>
            </xsl:call-template>
          </g>
        </g>
      </g>
    </svg>
</xsl:template>

<xsl:template name="star">
  <xsl:param name="numPoints"/>
  <xsl:param name="curPoint"/>
  <xsl:param name="outerRadius"/>
  <xsl:param name="innerRadius"/>
  <xsl:param name="style"/>
  <xsl:param name="text"/>
  <xsl:variable name="lpath">
    <xsl:call-template name="outerStar">
      <xsl:with-param name="numPoints" select="$numPoints"/>
      <xsl:with-param name="curPoint" select="0"/>
      <xsl:with-param name="outerRadius" select="$outerRadius"/>
      <xsl:with-param name="innerRadius" select="$innerRadius"/>
    </xsl:call-template>
  </xsl:variable>
  <path id="star" style="{$style}"><xsl:attribute name="d">
    <xsl:value-of select="translate($lpath,'&#10;','')"/>
  </xsl:attribute></path>
  <text style="{$text_style};"
    transform="translate(-{string-length($text) * 50 div 2} 0)" >
    <xsl:value-of select="$text"/>
  </text>
</xsl:template>

<xsl:template name="outerStar">
  <xsl:param name="numPoints"/>
  <xsl:param name="curPoint"/>
  <xsl:param name="outerRadius"/>
  <xsl:param name="innerRadius"/>
  <xsl:choose>
    <xsl:when test="$curPoint = 0">M</xsl:when>
    <xsl:otherwise>L</xsl:otherwise>
  </xsl:choose>
  <xsl:value-of
    select="floor($outerRadius* math:sin($curPoint * 360 div $numPoints))"/>
  <xsl:text> </xsl:text>
  <xsl:value-of
    select="floor(-$outerRadius  * math:cos($curPoint *
            360 div $numPoints))"/>
  <xsl:text> </xsl:text>
  <xsl:call-template name="innerStar">
    <xsl:with-param name="numPoints" select="$numPoints"/>
    <xsl:with-param name="curPoint" select="$curPoint"/>
    <xsl:with-param name="outerRadius" select="$outerRadius"/>
    <xsl:with-param name="innerRadius" select="$innerRadius"/>
  </xsl:call-template>
</xsl:template>
<xsl:template name="innerStar">
  <xsl:param name="numPoints"/>
  <xsl:param name="curPoint"/>
  <xsl:param name="outerRadius"/>
  <xsl:param name="innerRadius"/>
  <xsl:variable name="outerAngle" select="360 div $numPoints"/>
  <xsl:variable name="phase" select="$outerAngle div 2"/>
```

```
      L<xsl:text> </xsl:text>
      <xsl:value-of
        select="floor($innerRadius * math:sin($curPoint *
                $outerAngle + $phase))"/>
      <xsl:text> </xsl:text>
      <xsl:value-of
        select="floor(- $innerRadius * math:cos($curPoint *
                $outerAngle + $phase))"/>
      <xsl:text> </xsl:text>
      <xsl:choose>
        <xsl:when test="$curPoint &lt; $numPoints">
          <xsl:call-template name="outerStar">
            <xsl:with-param name="numPoints" select="$numPoints"/>
            <xsl:with-param name="curPoint" select="$curPoint + 1"/>
            <xsl:with-param name="outerRadius" select="$outerRadius"/>
            <xsl:with-param name="innerRadius" select="$innerRadius"/>
          </xsl:call-template>
        </xsl:when>
        <xsl:otherwise>z</xsl:otherwise>
      </xsl:choose>
    </xsl:template>

</xsl:stylesheet>
```

The output of this stylesheet looks like this:

The recursion in `DrawStar.xsl` is a little different from that of the previous examples in this section. The primary purpose of the `star` named template is to produce the `<svg:path>` element, the SVG element for describing non-standard shapes. However, the most important part of the `<svg:path>` element is the single attribute d, which contains the actual path information. Using an attribute to define the path is somewhat controversial, because it requires yet another "standard" language that isn't terribly XML-friendly, yet the SVG design committee at the time felt that such a path notation would be faster to parse by an SVG renderer. To get an idea of what a path could look like, consider the path below that draws a five pointed star centered on an origin of (0,0) and having an outer radius of 500 custom user units:

```
<path id="star" style="fill:red;stroke:black;stroke-width:2"
d="M0 -480   L 108 -149 L456 -149 L 174 56 L282 388 L -1 183 L-283 388  L -175 56
L-457 -149  L -109 -149 L0 -480 L 108 -149 z" />
```

The d attribute comprises a string of coordinates describing how the irregular shape, our star, should be drawn. Each coordinate pair consists of a letter, 'M' or 'L', followed by a horizontal x position and a vertical y position separated by white space. The letter 'L' means a line should be drawn to the coordinates that follow, while 'M' indicates a move without drawing. It's important to note here that SVG paths can use either absolute or relative coordinates. Absolute coordinates are indicated with upper case letters, so that `"M0 -480 L 108 -149"` draws the line from {0,-480} to {108,-149}. Note that in SVG the origin is by default the upper left corner.

To use a relative coordinate system on the other hand, use lower case 'l' or 'm' followed by the new coordinates relative to the previous position of the 'pen'. Thus, `"m0 -480 l108 -149"` will jump to a point 480 units below the current point without drawing, then draw a line to a point 108 units to the right and 149 down. Assuming that the pen starts at the origin, it will end up located at {108, -629}.

The final character, z or Z, is not case sensitive and tells the SVG parsing engine that the path ends by returning to its starting point, making a closed loop. Note that in order to create a fillable polygon, the path around the polygon's circumference must have a closing z or else it's considered a one-dimensional path that consequently can't be filled, rather than a two-dimensional shape that can.

Thus, the primary function of the XSLT stylesheet is to generate a space delimited list rather than an XML structure. The `star` named template does this by invoking two additional named templates, `outerStar` and `innerStar`. The `outerStar` routine passes a counter as a parameter to keep track of which point is currently being evaluated. For instance, a five-pointed star would cycle through points 1 to 5, each point tip being drawn at an angle of 360° divided by the number of sides (72° for the five pointed default). The `outerStar` routine calls the `innerStar` routine to determine the coordinates on the inner radius where the current and next point of the star intersect. The `innerStar` routine then tests to see if the requisite number of points has been reached – if not then the `outerStar` routine is then invoked for the next point, and so on. In this way, the stylesheet oscillates between the `outerStar` and `innerStar` routines. This is still recursion; just recursion that alternates between two functions rather than working with one exclusively.

When the `innerStar` routine does reach the last point, it places a "z" into the output stream, telling the SVG parser to join the last point to the starting point, so defining an enclosed shape from the path. It is essential for successful recursion that a recursive routine of any sort must have a terminating condition that will reliably stop the routine from indefinitely calling itself. This limit can be supplied by an incremental counter of some sort that determines the "depth" of the recursion. Fortunately XSLT, unlike most procedural languages, has an extraordinarily deep stack, usually limited only by memory, so in practice, a typical system will permit somewhere in the order of a thousand recursions.

While it's conceivably possible to generate the coordinates for each point of the star using lookup tables, a general-purpose star routine really needs to resort to XSLT extensions in order to calculate the sines and cosines necessary to locate the vertices for a star. The extensions are provided using the custom math namespace to wrap the JavaScript Math.sin() and Math.cos() functions. Because it is generally simpler to work with degrees than radians when dealing with a recursive algorithm, the angles are automatically converted to radians within the sine and cosine function.

```
<msxml:script language="JavaScript" implements-prefix="math">
   function sin(angle)
   {
     return Math.sin(angle*3.1415927/180);
   }

   function cos(angle)
   {
   return Math.cos(angle*3.1415927/180);
   }
</msxml:script>
```

The star routine also places an <svg:text> element within the same graphic context as the star, making it possible to have a text label within the star itself. The simplistic routine employed is far from ideal, as it relies upon the length of the text string in characters rather than actual custom units to approximate the width of the string, but it works for many basic cases.

Having control over both the inner and outer radius means you can produce a large range of different shaped stars. You can even create any polygon with an even number of sides by setting the inner radius to the same value as the outer radius. Twice the value of numPoints then gives the number of sides for the polygon. For polygons with an odd number of vertices, you'll have to experiment by setting the inner radius slightly less than the outer radius. So then, this one routine can produce any of the following:

A 16-sided regular polygon (numPoints=8, innerRadius=500, outerRadius=500):

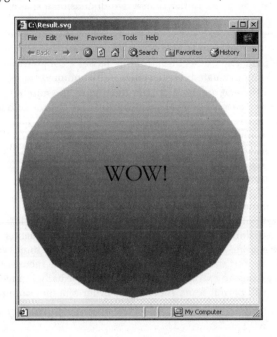

A highly concave twenty pointed star (numPoints=20, innerRadius=50, outerRadius=500):

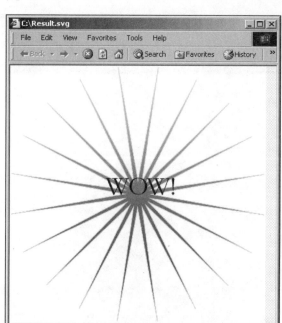

A certificate star (numPoints=100, innerRadius=470, outerRadius=500):

An intricate Moire pattern star (numPoints=200, innerRadius=250, outerRadius=500):

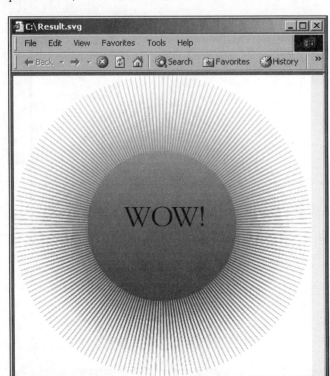

The last star illustrates how you can create very elaborate effects by taking advantage of Moire interference patterns, although these are artifacts of the medium, and when the SVG is output to print as above, the Moire effect is much less noticeable.

The Future of SVG

Back in the early 1980s, the then-new language of Postscript launched a revolution. By describing information in a resolution-independent manner, the same image could be rendered appropriately on a 96 dpi page or a 300 dpi page (as well as on the high end printers of the time that could achieve 1200 dpi). Nowadays virtually all printers natively support Postscript in some manner, yet it took a good few years of concentrated effort and evangelism by developers and graphic artists before it gained the critical recognition it deserved.

SVG promises to be a lot like that. SVG isn't just about the Web, though certainly it will play a big part on the Web. The SVG format could serve as the foundation of a graphically oriented computer interface to compete with HTML, and may even find its way into the many new kinds of hand-held device that are now emerging. What makes this a possibility is the fact that SVG is XML-based, and so can be created or modified by XSLT.

The implications here are fairly profound. Traditional approaches to user interfaces tend to look at the basic components as immutable constants. This either forces the application to accept data matching one of a very narrow set of formats or forces the developer of the application to create reams of "translation" code to ensure the data will conform to the component interfaces used.

Using XSLT, your data can be transformed in any way you like, with the result that user interfaces have the potential to dynamically accommodate data as it changes. Even HTML doesn't really have this capability, because it requires that images that change do so from one prepared picture to another. XSLT can be applied to dynamic data to create fluid varying images in SVG, making for a far more responsive interface. According to the end user's choice, a table of sales figures could become a chart or a graph or a pie chart, it could be used to generate a virtual 3D 'city' illustrating the data or even an animation showing the changes in the figures over time.

It is this last application that is perhaps the most significant – SVG is very strongly oriented toward the creation of animations that can change in response to events, in effect introducing the dimensions of time and human interaction to the two dimensional world of visual display. Because this sort of SVG can usually be generated directly from XSLT, the amount of work it takes to build such interfaces is significantly reduced, making it possible to concentrate more on the content than the structure to contain that content. While it is fair to say that HTML won't disappear any time soon, its influence is certainly waning, and there are more and more companies exploring the capabilities that SVG has to offer. This should make SVG programming, either directly or through the mechanism of XSLT, far more palatable and deployable to the masses.

Summary

This chapter has demonstrated several uses for the XML-based SVG language, generated with XSLT. These were:

❑   Displaying XML data as a bar chart.

❑   Controlling the presentation of textual content from an XML document

❑   Creating graphical images

A benefit of using XSLT to generate SVG is that when the underlying XML data or document is dynamic, the output can be regenerated with little efforts. These example have also demonstrated some of the processing power offer by XSLT.

Having looked at generating graphical output with XSLT, we're next going to see how XSLT can be used to transform XML data for non-visual display – using another XML-based language, voice XML.

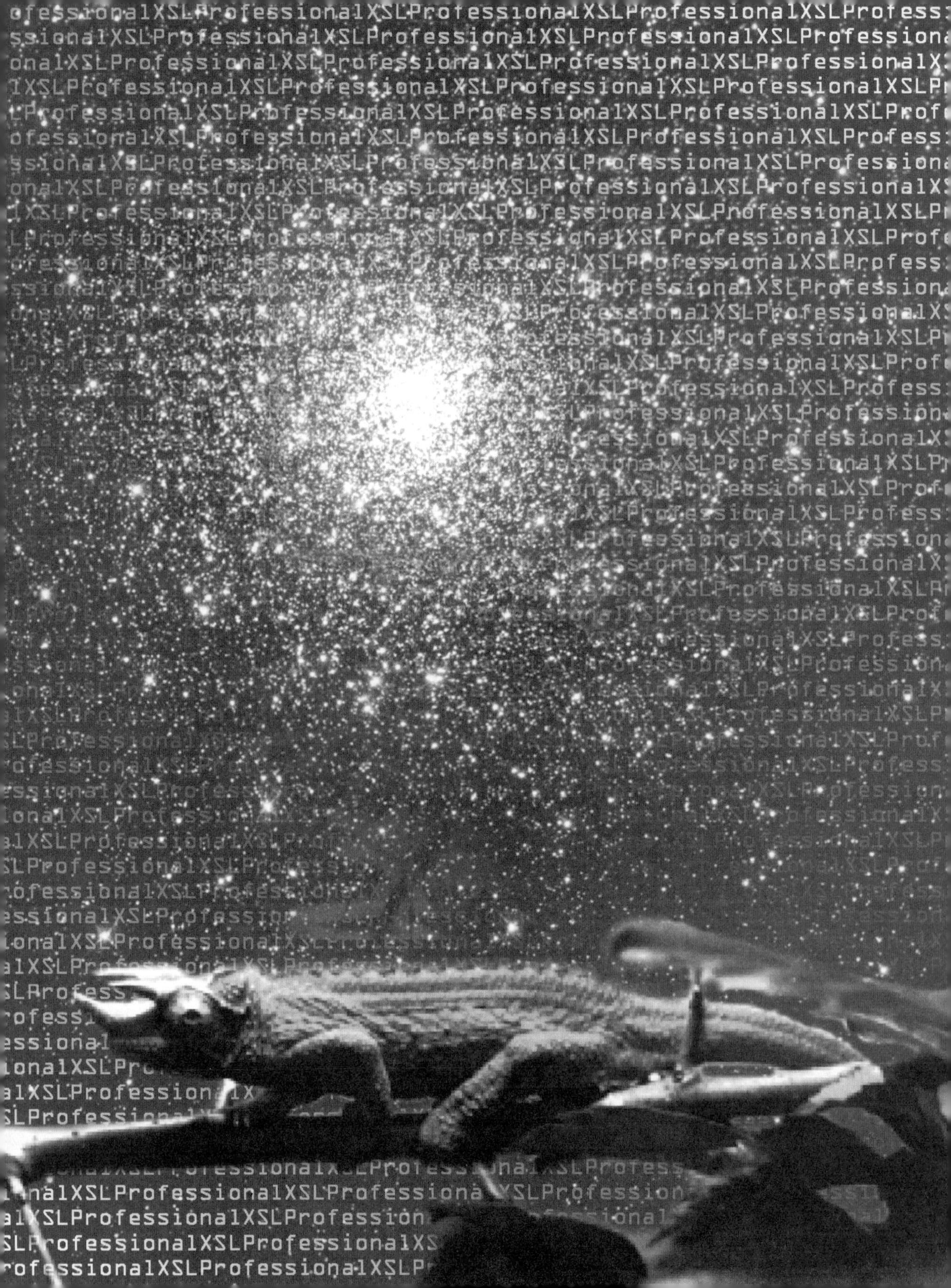
ProfessionalXSLProfessionalXSLProfessional

13

Transforming to VoiceXML

As we have seen throughout the book, XSLT is a transformation language most commonly used for transforming XML source data into other formats suitable for presentation to various end users. The target formats we've seen so far have been visual, but a technology that is becoming increasingly popular is that of audio-based applications, where users can interact with the application by listening and speaking across a phone line rather than reading and typing at a computer screen/keyboard.

Voice Extensible Markup Language (**VoiceXML**) is a relatively new XML-based language designed to enable the development of voice-activated applications that will have a broader appeal and potential user-base than mobile technologies, such as WML, can currently provide. VoiceXML is a specification created by the VoiceXML Forum's founding members, AT&T, IBM, Lucent, and Motorola. Many excellent VoiceXML related resources are available at the Forum's web site: http://www.voicexml.org.

In this chapter we'll take a look at a specific application of XSLT transformations – transforming XML data into VoiceXML documents. This can be especially useful in situations when the data to be presented aurally changes on a regular basis – an XSLT stylesheet can be run against the data whenever an updated version of the VoiceXML document is required. Before we can begin to create stylesheets to generate VoiceXML we need to understand its syntax and the development environment/tools available. So, we'll begin by briefly looking at voice-enabled application development in general, and then take a look at writing VoiceXML documents. Finally we'll demonstrate how XSLT can be used to automatically generate VoiceXML output. This will include voice enabling the book catalog application from earlier in the book. If you are already familiar with VoiceXML syntax and the development software, you might want to skip to the "*XSLT for VoiceXML*" section of this chapter.

Voice-Enabled Applications

Computer-telephony applications have been popular for many years. We are all familiar with the experience of using telephones and **Interactive Voice Response** (**IVR**) technology, which allows us to press phone keys and utter keywords in response to questions asked by an application. Examples of such technology are found when we want to check our bank account balance, flight departure and arrival information, or order status for bought goods. However, these applications generally accept only touch-tone entries or a very limited set of spoken keywords, which can be awkward when you have to navigate many layers of menus to accomplish a task. Also, the IVR user interface makes the entry of non-numeric text, such as names, difficult to handle.

On the other hand, **Automatic Speech Recognition** (**ASR**) research and development has been going on for decades, but it didn't get really practical until recently, with the massive improvements in hardware performance and the maturing of ASR technology. ASR can be **speaker dependent**, where the system gets trained by asking the user to say certain words, or **speaker independent**, where no training is required and any user can immediately start to use the system. Speaker independent systems can be **discrete**, where you have to pause between utterances, or **continuous**, where, as the term implies, no pause is required. Thanks to the advances of ASR technologies and hardware improvements, most of the current ASR applications are continuous and speaker independent, resulting in a more natural and easy-to-use interface.

There are mainly two classes of speech recognition applications. The first one is for desktop applications, for example where users can dictate and have their spoken words recognized and entered directly in applications such as Microsoft Word. The second type of speech recognition application is the over-the-phone application, which allows anyone with a telephone – no matter whether it is a home phone, office phone, mobile phone, touch-tone phone, or rotary phone – to call up the application and request information and services. Both types of applications can now use continuous speech. Desktop ASR applications are usually speaker dependent, while over-the-phone applications clearly require speaker independence. Obviously, the latter type of application should be attractive to a lot more people, and that is the topic we'll focus on in this chapter.

ASR-based voice applications have some key advantages over the traditional IVR applications:

❑ ASR voice applications can perform tasks that are difficult or even impossible with touch-tone-based IVR applications. Imagine a stock application that has a long list of symbols, or a banking application that wants to gather the user's query as quickly as possible, for example letting the user say "I'd like to transfer $5,000 from my checking to my saving account". In other words, ASR voice applications can, in some cases, provide a more natural and easy-to-navigate interface. Instead of navigating through many levels of menus typical of the traditional IVR applications, the user now can say what he/she wants in a single sentence to a well-designed voice application.

❑ Voice applications give the user a hands-free and eyes-free way to get information or perform other tasks. When you're on the move, it can be difficult to enter **DTMF** (**Dual Tone Multi-Frequency**, also called "touch tones") keypad input – using just your voice frees you from that.

❑ Voice applications don't require the user to have a touch-tone phone. Surprising as it may seem, there are many countries where touch-tone phones are still not the rule.

VoiceXML is an emerging standard for developing voice applications based on the familiar web model. The VoiceXML Forum's founding members released the **VoiceXML specification 1.0** and submitted it to the W3C in March 2000. On May 22, 2000, the W3C acknowledged this submission. The complete W3C note can be obtained at http://www.w3.org/TR/2000/NOTE-voicexml-20000505/. Although VoiceXML is still undergoing standardization within the W3C, it made tremendous strides in the year 2000. By the end of 2000, the VoiceXML Forum had more than 350 members, and the language was selected as the "Paradigm of the Year" by the Computer Telephony magazine. In a later section, *Summarizing VoiceXML*, I will present a relatively detailed introduction to VoiceXML 1.0.

VoiceXML was designed to make the content and information on the Internet accessible via phone and voice, but it is not limited to adding a voice interface to the Internet; it can be used as an open-architecture solution for building next-generation IVR voice services and voice-enabling enterprise applications where appropriate, such as the banking application discussed earlier.

In this chapter, we'll discover how to develop voice applications using VoiceXML and how to use XSLT to produce VoiceXML. By first showing you the non-VoiceXML way to develop voice applications, I hope you will appreciate the advantages that VoiceXML offers. In some cases, VoiceXML may not be the ideal solution – I'll briefly mention this and the choices available to you. However, most of the time, VoiceXML provides a convincing way to "speech up" your application development.

Developing Voice Applications: to API or Not API

Developing speech-recognition based applications to voice-enable (speech-enable, voice-activate, speech-activate) a consumer application, such as stock, weather, or news, or an enterprise application, such as e-mail or a database, would be a daunting task for most of us. Taking the traditional development route, hardware is expensive and setup is difficult and tricky – anyone who can afford the basic minimum configuration of a Dialogic 4-port telephone board with Antares support (over $6000) and who has tried to set it up could tell you that! Then of course there's the software setup with the required unique APIs, not to mention dealing with integration into existing systems.

Nuance (http://www.nuance.com) and **SpeechWorks** (http://www.SpeechWorks.com) are the two leading companies in over-the-phone speech recognition engines. Their core speech recognition engines have been used by all the leading service application vendors to provide many free voice services for consumers, as well as companies trying to voice-enable enterprise applications. Nuance and SpeechWorks both provide extensive API calls to directly integrate the engine with your applications. SpeechObjects, the major API provided by Nuance, is Java-based, while DialogModules, the API offered by SpeechWorks, is C-based.

Let's take a brief look at what would be required if you were going to develop a voice application without VoiceXML, instead using Nuance's Java API SpeechObjects. First of all, you certainly need to be familiar with Java. Then, you need to develop a deep understanding of the core SpeechObjects, which are essentially reusable IVR units, including knowledge of how to use and customize them. After that, you'll need to know how to hook them up together, how to initialize various resources such as SpeechChannel, Dialog Context, Application State, Call State, etc. You'll also need to download a copy of a Text-to-Speech (TTS) engine such as RealSpeak 2.0 (available from Nuance's web site) and then spend hours integrating it into your application in order to make use of the all-but-essential functionality of TTS for almost all voice applications.

To most people, the journey is a long and cold trek through a landscape of unwelcoming code. Wouldn't it be nice if all you needed to do was add a few new XML elements to your repertoire and, using the implied methodology of a specially tailored language, proceed straight to the heart of voice application development? This is the need that VoiceXML aims to fulfill: all the details of telephony boards, APIs, and hardware configuration are hidden behind an easy-to-learn language. Of course, by relying on someone else to take care of the underlying details, you run the risk of losing a certain amount of control. But VoiceXML has a definite role to play in helping you to assess the current status of voice technologies and the viability for your business, as it allows applications to be rapidly developed and deployed. Later on, should you find compelling reasons to really get your hands dirty, you can then go for an application built on low-level APIs.

So here we'll show you how to use currently available public voice portals (for a detailed list of the most popular ones, see the section *Setting up the Environment*) to develop your VoiceXML applications and voice-enable your current applications quickly and easily. As VoiceXML is young and still on the road to standardization, you should be aware of the incompatibilities among different vendors, and between them and the emerging standard. On the other hand, you'll be amazed, after reading this chapter and working with some real code, at how much you can already do with the simple-to-use VoiceXML language, and how much potential there is ahead.

Before I show you how to set up everything you need to get ready to develop voice applications based on VoiceXML, let's first get familiar with the VoiceXML language itself, discover what can be expressed with it, and see what is generally involved in developing a VoiceXML application.

The VoiceXML Solution

The best place to get a list of all the elements along with detailed explanations is the VoiceXML 1.0 specification. There are 47 elements or tags in total and each tag has between 1 and 13 attributes to modify the tag's behavior – for easy reference we'll duplicate the list of all the elements later. It is highly recommended that you download a copy of this specification if you need more information about the attributes and how they are used.

However, first we'll take a look at a sample VoiceXML document that has many of the commonly used elements in the VoiceXML 1.0 specification. You can test the application after you finish the next section, *Setting up the Environment*. For now, just rest assured that the example below runs well, avoiding as it does any VoiceXML that may not be fully supported by platforms that claim to comply with the draft standard. I strongly recommend you go through the specification, but always be aware that, at this stage, some elements of the emerging standard may not have been implemented by your chosen development platform.

VoiceXML Example Document

Before we present and explain the code for our first complete VoiceXML document, let's take a look at a typical user-system session based on a VoiceXML document after the user calls in and passes the login procedure:

System:	Welcome to Voice Services. Here you can check on all kinds of information easily with your phone. Please say weather, stock, news or sports.
User:	*silence as user is new to the system*
System:	Sorry I didn't hear you. Please say weather, stock, news or sports.
User:	Weather.
System:	Thank you for selecting our weather service.
	the weather service; after that, user wants to go back to the main menu
System:	Welcome to Voice Services. Here you can check on all kinds of information easily with your phone. Please say weather, stock, news or sports.
User:	Travel.
System:	Sorry I don't understand. Please say weather, stock, news or sports.
User:	Sports.
System:	Thank you for selecting our sports service.
	the sports service; after that, user wants to go back to the main menu
System:	Welcome to Voice Services. Here you can check on all kinds of information easily with your phone. Please say weather, stock, news or sports.

Now let's take a look at the code behind this application. All VoiceXML documents should start with these two lines, or a variation on them:

```
<?xml version="1.0"?>
<vxml version="1.0">
```

Two commonly used attributes of the `<vxml>` element are `version` and `application`. The `version` attribute is set to `1.0` here, corresponding to the current version of VoiceXML. The `application` attribute can be useful for applications consisting of multiple VoiceXML documents, where it specifies a VoiceXML document containing the shared variables and grammars. (We'll be looking at grammars shortly.) Even in a single-document application, this attribute may refer to a document containing elements common to all types of applications, such as `<help>`.

The `<meta>` element specifies general meta-information about the VoiceXML document in `name` and `content` attribute pairs. You can specify any `name` attribute values here, but VoiceXML 1.0 recommends `author`, `copyright`, `description`, and `maintainer`, amongst others.

```
<meta name="author"      content="Jeff Tang"/>
<meta name="application" content="Main Menu"/>
```

The `<form>` element is the key element in a VoiceXML document. There should be at least one `<form>` element in any useful VoiceXML document, and these elements should be children of the `<vxml>` element. Each `<form>` element specifies the start of a dialog that can consist of a simple utterance or a sophisticated multi-step process of collecting several relevant pieces of information before jumping to another `<form>` element or another VoiceXML document. The main components of a form are `<grammar>`, `<prompt>`, `<block>`, and `<field>` elements – we'll look at these in more detail later. The optional id attribute of the `<form>` element identifies the form; it can be used in a `<goto>` element to transfer control to this form.

```
<form id="main">
```

The `<block>` element is used for prompting the user and performing computation without gathering user input. We don't have any computation here, but later you'll see an example of using the `<if>` element inside a `<block>` and assigning different variable values depending on different test conditions.

The `<audio>` element simply plays an audio wave file or a TTS text – if the src attribute of the `<audio>` element exists and specifies a valid URL of an audio file, the audio file is played; otherwise, audio is generated from the string text of the `<audio>` element by a TTS engine. For simplicity, in this chapter we'll use TTS texts only. In real applications, it's better to minimize the use of TTS text by replacing as many as possible with pre-recorded audio clips.

```
<block>
  <audio>
    Welcome to Voice Services. Here you can check on all kinds of information
easily with your phone.
  </audio>
</block>
```

The `<field>` element is the mechanism used in VoiceXML for collecting user input. The name attribute specifies the variable name that will hold the user input, so long as that user input is recognized according to the specified grammar.

```
<field name="action">
```

The `<grammar>` element specifies the valid utterances that a user can speak. The speech recognition engine underneath your application can only recognize a word or sentence that is specified in the applicable grammar.

The VoiceXML 1.0 specification describes the use of a proposed standard for representing speech grammars, the **Java API Speech Grammar Format** (**JSGF** – see http://www.javasoft.com/products/java-media/speech/forDevelopers/JSGF), which has similar expressiveness but different syntax from the grammar format we see here. The reason we use a different format is that no online development studio yet supports JSGF. However, many of them support the format used here: the **Nuance Grammar Specification Language** (**GSL** – see Nuance Grammar Developer's Guide available at http://extranet.nuance.com). It's not important which format is used: what's important is to know which platform supports which format, and how to write effective grammar using that format for that platform. All types of grammar formats use similar ways to express valid user utterances, so the knowledge of one can be easily applied to another.

Below is a sample of an in-line grammar enclosed in a CDATA section. You can also specify a grammar using the src attribute of the `<grammar>` element to reference an external grammar file by its URI. For simplicity, we'll only use in-line grammar in this chapter.

Let's now look at our example, where the acceptable user utterances we require are "weather", "stock", "news", and "sports". I have included four DTMF strings in the grammar below to allow the user to use their touch-tone phone to enter 1, 2, 3, or 4 as alternatives to speaking out loud. The square brackets [] are the **disjunction operator**: for example, [A B C D] means that one of A or B or C or D is used. There are other operators, which we'll describe later when needed. Each `<option>` element specifies a return value for the preceding recognized word, and the return value is saved to the `<field>` element's variable, here called action.

```
<grammar>
<![CDATA[
[
[weather dtmf-1] {<option "weather">}
[stock dtmf-2] {<option "stock">}
[news dtmf-2] {<option "news">}
[sports dtmf-2] {<option "sports">}
]
]]>
</grammar>
```

Another point to note about a grammar is its **scope**: where the grammar is defined and active. There are four types of possible scope – application, document, form, and field.

❑   An application-scope grammar is defined and active in any VoiceXML documents that are part of a single application

❑   A document-scope grammar is defined and active at any point in the document

❑   A form-scope grammar is defined in a form and active when the user is in the form

❑   A field-scope grammar is defined in a field and is only active when the user is in that field

You should structure your grammars in such a way that more general grammars are defined at a higher level.

The `<prompt>` element specifies the prompt (TTS text here) that the user will hear when the system enters the field and is ready to accept user input. If you want to have an audio file played, you should use an `<audio>` element inside the `<prompt>` element.

```
<prompt>
   Please say weather, stock, news or sports.
</prompt>
```

The `<nomatch>` element specifies the handler for the nomatch event, which is fired when the user's utterance is not recognized by any of the active grammars (here we only have a field-scope grammar). After a TTS text ("Sorry I don't understand.") is played, the `<reprompt/>` element causes the system to replay whatever is defined in the `<prompt>` element inside the same `<field>` element.

```
<nomatch>
  <audio>Sorry I don't understand.</audio>
  <reprompt/>
</nomatch>
```

The <noinput> element specifies the handler for the noinput event, which is fired when the user has not responded within the timeout interval. The timeout value can be specified as the timeout attribute of the <prompt> element, but defaults for this value exist and are platform (voice portal) specific. The event handling code is similar to that of the <nomatch> element.

```
<noinput>
  <audio>Sorry I didn't hear you.</audio>
  <reprompt/>
</noinput>
```

The <help> element is for the help event, which is triggered when the user says "help" and there's an active grammar that defines the word "help". Usually, you should define the utterance "help" in an application-scope grammar, and include the <help> event handler in every <field>. This provides valuable context help to the user, so the user will never get lost.

```
<help>
  <audio>You can say what information you'd like to get.</audio>
  <reprompt/>
</help>
```

The <filled> element inside the <field> element specifies the event handler to employ when a user utterance is successfully recognized.

```
<filled>
```

The <value> element has an obligatory attribute expr containing an expression to evaluate. Here the expression is simply a variable named action, which is the <field> variable that holds the <option> value as specified in the grammar for the previously recognized user utterance.

```
<audio>Thank you for selecting our <value expr="action"/> service.</audio>
```

The <if> and <elseif> elements control the application flow. The one required attribute, cond, specifies a condition.

The <goto> element directs the application flow. Its most commonly used attribute, next, specifies either a <form> element's id attribute value from the same document, indicating the form you want to jump to, or a URI for a new VoiceXML document (or a server page that will generate a new VoiceXML document). Although the <goto> element is very useful, it has the tendency to create spaghetti code. (You may recall the famous paper *GoTo Statement Considered Harmful* by Edsger Dijkstra in 1968.) However, for a relatively simple language like VoiceXML, compared to C, you may have to live with <goto>. Here, depending on the user input, the control is transferred to different forms.

```
<if cond="action == 'weather'">
  <goto next="#weather"/>
<elseif cond="action == 'stock'"/>
  <goto next="#stock"/>
<elseif cond="action == 'news'"/>
  <goto next="#news"/>
<elseif cond="action == 'sports'"/>
  <goto next="#sports"/>
</if>
</filled>
</field>
</form>
```

According to the VoiceXML specification, if no transition is specified within a form (for example with `<goto>`), an `<exit/>` event is implied. However, some interpreters simply pass the form flow on to the next form specified in the document.

The next part of the code will define a new form for the weather service, which we'll develop later in the chapter. Notice that after we complete the processing (which here just plays a TTS message), we go back to the main form.

```
<form id="weather">
  <block>
    <!-- TODO: weather service -->
    <goto next="#main"/>
  </block>
</form>
```

Similarly we require forms for the stock, news and sports services:

```
<form id="stock">
  <block>
    <!-- TODO: stock service -->
    <goto next="#main"/>
  </block>
</form>

<form id="news">
  <block>
    <!-- TODO: news service -->
    <goto next="#main"/>
  </block>
</form>

<form id="sports">
  <block>
    <!-- TODO: sports service -->
    <goto next="#main"/>
  </block>
</form>
</vxml>
```

We'll be testing this application on an open platform at the end of the next section, but it should have given you an idea of the basic simplicity of VoiceXML.

VoiceXML Elements

To recap the elements of the VoiceXML 1.0 language we have used in the samples above, and to get a feeling of how many more are ahead of us, here's a list of all the proposed elements in VoiceXML 1.0 specification, available, again, at http://www.w3.org/TR/2000/NOTE-voicexml-20000505/. We won't use all of them in our later examples, but we'll mention all the important ones (besides those useful ones we've explained above), so you'll know what to use when developing sophisticated VoiceXML applications of your own.

Note that VoiceXML adopted a limited set of **JSML** (**Java Speech Markup Language**) elements. (See http://www.javasoft.com/products/java-media/speech/forDevelopers/JSML for details.) This language involves elements designed to express speech with the correct intonation, emphasis, pitch, speed, etc.

`<assign>`	Assign a variable a value
`<audio>`	Play an audio clip within a prompt
`<block>`	A container for (non-interactive) executable code
`<break>`	A JSML element to insert a pause in output
`<catch>`	Catch an event, such as `error`, `help`, `noinput`, or `nomatch`, thrown by the VoiceXML interpreter (Can also catch an event thrown by the `<throw>` element)
`<choice>`	Define a menu item
`<clear>`	Clear one or more form item variables
`<disconnect>`	Disconnect a session
`<div>`	A JSML element to classify a region of text as a particular type
`<dtmf>`	Specify a touch-tone key grammar
`<else>`	Used in `<if>` elements for occasions when the specified condition is not met
`<elseif>`	Used in `<if>` elements like `<else>`, but specifying another `cond` attribute to fulfil
`<emp>`	A JSML element to change the emphasis of speech output
`<enumerate>`	Shorthand for enumerating the choices in a menu
`<error>`	Catch an error event
`<exit>`	Exit a session
`<field>`	Declares an input field in a form
`<filled>`	An action executed when fields are filled
`<form>`	A dialog for presenting information and collecting data
`<goto>`	Go to another dialog in the same or different document
`<grammar>`	Specify a speech recognition grammar
`<help>`	Catch a `help` event
`<if>`	Simple conditional logic
`<initial>`	Declares initial logic upon entry into a (mixed-initiative) form
`<link>`	Specify a transition common to all dialogs in the link's scope
`<menu>`	A dialog for choosing amongst alternative destinations
`<meta>`	Define a meta data item as a name/value pair

`<noinput>`	Catch a `noinput` event
`<nomatch>`	Catch a `nomatch` event
`<object>`	Interact with a custom extension
`<option>`	Specify an option in a `<field>`
`<param>`	Parameter in `<object>` or `<subdialog>`
`<prompt>`	Queue TTS and audio output to the user
`<property>`	Control implementation platform settings
`<pros>`	A JSML element to change the prosody (speaking rate or pitch, etc) of speech output
`<record>`	Record an audio sample
`<reprompt>`	Play a field `<prompt>` when a field is re-visited after an event
`<return>`	Return from a subdialog
`<sayas>`	A JSML element to modify how a word or phrase is spoken
`<script>`	Specify a block of ECMAScript client-side scripting logic
`<subdialog>`	Invoke another dialog as a subdialog of the current one
`<submit>`	Submit values to a document server
`<throw>`	Throw a predefined or application-defined event
`<transfer>`	Transfer the caller to another destination
`<value>`	Insert the value of an expression in a prompt
`<var>`	Declare a variable
`<vxml>`	Root element in each VoiceXML document

Setting Up the Environment

To test and run a VoiceXML application, you'll need to have access to a VoiceXML interpreter or browser. Just like web browsers, voice/speech browsers can be downloaded and installed on your local machine. Alternatively (and preferably), you can make use of the tools from one of the hosting sites now available. These sites have online development environments which let you enter code and test it without the need for special software on your own machine. When the VoiceXML application is complete, whether by using the online facilities or by uploading documents created offline, these voice portals will parse and present your document in much the same way a web browser does, but using VoiceXML instead of HTML. However, web browsers run on the end-users' own machines, while voice browsers generally run server-side to create an interface independent of the caller's location and the equipment they possess. In voice interaction, the minimum required client "machine" is just a telephone handset. For development purposes, however, a voice browser running on your local machine can be more appropriate.

Just like web browsers, and following in the open source tradition, newly developed voice browsers are freely available. Speechworks' Open Source VoiceXML Interpreter, called **Open VXI**, is available at Carnegie Mellon University (CMU)'s download site http://www.speech.cs.cmu.edu/openvxi. Nuance's freely available voice browser is called **Voyager**. You can download it and its core software, which is required to run the voice browser, via their Nuance Developer Network (NDN) at http://extranet.nuance.com. You'll need to register (for free) as a member of NDN and then download Nuance 7.0.2 or 7.0.3. Besides Voyager, another cool, and free, tool Nuance provides which may be helpful during your VoiceXML application development is **V-Builder**, one of the first graphical tools for quickly building VoiceXML applications using drag-and-drop. If you are the sort of developer who likes to set up as much as possible on your own machines, the easiest way is to go to Nuance's developer site and download the software mentioned above. You may also contact SpeechWorks to request an evaluation copy of their software, including the core recognition engine and dialog building blocks, after downloading the Open VXI interpreter. We will not talk about this type of development environment in this chapter, simply because it's more difficult to set up and, of course, our focus here is VoiceXML and XSL.

There is another way which avoids the need to set up a load of software, and lets us dip our toes into the VoiceXML application development process before getting completely wet – at least for readers in the United States and Canada. There are already a few voice portal sites that offer free use of web-based development environments for you to develop and test VoiceXML applications. Even the calls are toll-free for some of them!

> *If you live outside of the United States or Canada, you may prefer the idea of downloading and setting up the Nuance development environment, as described above, because you'll probably not like the idea of paying for international long-distance calls. Another alternative is to use Dialpad (http://www.dialpad.com) to avoid the charges.*

Among the sites offering these services are:

- ❏ Tellme (http://studio.tellme.com)
- ❏ BeVocal (http://cafe.bevocal.com)
- ❏ VoiceGenie (http://developer.voicegenie.com)
- ❏ HeyAnita (http://www.heyanita.com)
- ❏ Voxeo (http://community.voxeo.com)

There are other sites, and there will certainly be more to come. Which one you choose depends on whether the site provides an easy-to-use development and deployment environment, and how compatible its VoiceXML support is. As a developer you're free to try any of the sites and choose the one that suits you. What's important is to learn how to develop pretty much standard VoiceXML applications with one platform – your experience will then easily be applied to other similar platforms. On January 31, 2001, the Computer Telephony Labs published a "Voice Portals Using VoiceXML" report with a detailed and comprehensive comparison of the VoiceXML offerings from the four leading voice portals (Tellme, BeVocal, VoiceGenie, and HeyAnita). Interested readers can find the report at http://www.commweb.com/article/COM20010129S0003.

Based on my own experience, Tellme Studio offers one of the leading platforms with regards to ease-of-use of the development environment and 1-800 toll free number (at least until January 2001), but it is missing some important pieces in its support for the VoiceXML 1.0 specification, including some key parts for developing user-friendly sophisticated voice applications. I expect this to be improved in the near future. The VoiceXML examples shown here all work on Tellme Studio at the time of writing. Some minor changes may be required, because Tellme's support of VoiceXML will almost certainly have changed and improved by the time you read this, but the examples will indicate any incompatibilities with the VoiceXML specification. I do recommend you check out their site for the latest information, although most of the code should be fine and any changes needed should be minimal.

Setting Up Tellme Studio

To set up the preview release of the Tellme Studio VoiceXML development environment, visit http://studio.tellme.com, and join Studio. You'll receive a developer ID and a PIN via e-mail. The first time you use your Studio account you'll see a default VoiceXML document that will get interpreted when you call the Tellme Studio phone number and enter your developer ID and PIN. You can edit your document, check the syntax, and debug the default VoiceXML application completely online. Or you can copy this starter VoiceXML document to your own web server and have the Studio point to your application's URL. Either way, you can see that the effort to set yourself up with an online VoiceXML development environment such as Tellme Studio really is minimal.

Now we're ready to write some real VoiceXML applications and let the real fun start. But before we move on, it's worth quickly mentioning the VoiceXML elements that Tellme Studio does not support as yet (check out their site for any changes to this list): <break>, <div>, <emp>, <enumerate>, <error>, <object>, <option>, <pros>, and <sayas>. If you do use them, they'll be simply ignored.

Note that, even for the supported elements, many attributes as specified in VoiceXML 1.0 have not been implemented. You'll need to check out the Tellme VoiceXML Reference for updates.

On the other hand, Tellme extends the VoiceXML 1.0 specification with the following elements: <debug>, <default>, <foreach>, <gosub>, <listen>, <log>, <pause>, and <result>.

Testing an Application

To test the VoiceXML application we looked at earlier in the chapter, simply login to Tellme Studio, and then type the above file, voiceservices.vxml, into your Scratchpad tab – of course it's never a bad idea to save files there to your local machine too. Or you can save the code above to your web server directory, then in the Application URL tab of the Studio, set the URL to the VoiceXML document saved in your web server. Either way, double check the syntax just to make sure everything is okay, then update the document, and call the phone number on the screen.

Note that to use the syntax checker provided by Tellme Studio, the following DOCTYPE needs to be added to the top of your VoiceXML document:

```
<!DOCTYPE vxml PUBLIC "-//Tellme Networks//Voice Markup Language 1.0//EN"
"http://resources.tellme.com/toolbox/vxml-tellme.dtd">
```

A More Advanced VoiceXML Application

In this section, we'll continue our previous example and go through the weather service option in some detail, so that you'll have a better understanding of what it takes to develop VoiceXML applications. We'll also talk about a more advanced type of VoiceXML application that can accept user input more naturally. In the second part of this chapter, we'll illustrate how to use XSLT to produce VoiceXML documents.

Before we get into the details of writing our VoiceXML applications, let's talk about the general process of developing a voice application. A voice application can be simply an application that voice-enables existing systems: in other words, an application that adds a voice/speech user interface to existing systems. The other possibility is that a voice application is a brand new application. In either case, a good understanding of the principal reasons people might like to use a voice interface to achieve their goals in any particular domain is the most important step – a full discussion of which is, however, outside the scope of this book.

After that, you need to define your **call flow** with strong emphasis on a friendly and positive user experience, especially as we're talking about voice user interfaces here. You need to carefully create grammars to cover all possible yet meaningful utterances that the user may make during the call, and create all the prompts in a professional and unambiguous way.

You also need to think about how to integrate your VoiceXML application with others, which may be web-based applications that retrieve information from the Internet, or enterprise applications that access enterprise information systems, or even transaction systems that allow the user to undertake voice-commerce. Last but not least, scalability and deployment are important topics.

To tackle all these issues would require a complete book. Let's move on and start some coding – just bear in mind that in the end, coding VoiceXML is just one piece of the whole pie.

For the weather service, let's define what a typical call interaction is like:

System:	Please say a zip code or a city and state name.
User:	New York, New York.
System:	Partly cloudy. Temperature: 17 degree. Do you want to hear the forecast?
User:	Yes.
System:	Tuesday, December 26, Partly Cloudy. Hi 35 degree, low 27 degree. Wednesday, December 27, Mostly Cloudy. Hi 36 degree, low 25 degree. Thursday, December 28, Rain and Snow. Hi 39 degree, Low 30 degree. Do you want to check the weather for another city?
User:	Yes.
System:	Please say a zip code or a city and state name.
User:	95123.
System:	San Jose, California. Sunny, Temperature: 65 degree. Do you want to hear the forecast?
User:	No.
System:	Do you want to check the weather for another city?
User:	No.
System:	Thank you for using our weather service.

To write a VoiceXML document that supports a dialog such as the one above, I'll define appropriate grammars, prompts (here we'll only use TTS text for simplicity), applications to get the information the user requests from the Internet, and a valid call flow.

Defining Grammars

Here we'll need a grammar that can recognize US city/state names and US zip codes. Fortunately, Tellme Studio provides such a grammar ready for you to use. There are about thirty intrinsic grammars in their grammar library that you can easily include in your VoiceXML document in the format below:

```
<grammar>
<![CDATA[
GrammarName
]]>
</grammar>
```

For a city/state and zip grammar, the intrinsic name is City, and the return value is City_Name@State_Name, or the zip code, for example San_Jose@California or 95123. If you develop VoiceXML documents on another platform where no such grammar is ready for you to use right away, you can write one easily – though a comprehensive list of all the cities and states may take some time and effort to code:

```
<grammar>
<![CDATA[
[
[(new york new york)] {<option "new_york@new_york">}
[(san jose california)] {<option "san_jose@california">}
...
]
]]>
</grammar>
```

With such large grammar files, you may start thinking about the performance impacts. To ease these, you could, for example, ask first for a state and then for a city, or ask for the first letter of the city and then the city name, to enable more numerous but smaller grammars to be used.

You shouldn't have to write a grammar for digits such as a zip code, as that is one of the basic grammars that tend to be available on all platforms.

The other grammar we'll need to have is the YesNo grammar, which allows the system to recognize all kinds of "yes" or "no" utterances you can say. The intrinsic grammar name for Yes/No in Tellme Studio is YES_NO.

Web-based Applications

After we have got the user's input, we'll need to go to a certain web site to obtain the content the user requests. There are many ways to develop such a web application. One is to write a Java servlet or JSP application that submits a query to a site such as http://weather.yahoo.com and then parses the result returned. We won't describe such a web application in detail here, though the getweather.jsp file we use is included with the code download for readers who are interested. For further information on this subject, try *Professional JSP*.

Call Flow

Three new things are introduced to the call flow, compared to the top-level menu example we saw previously. The first is a loop inside the form itself, for as long as the user still wants information about another city. In the previous example, we used the <goto> element to transfer the control to another form. However, in this sample I use the <clear> element, which clears (sets to undefined) the variables listed in its namelist attribute. Why does setting a variable to undefined have anything to do with looping? This is because of the way a form is interpreted: when a form is entered, each form variable, including the field name variable, is initialized to undefined, or to the default value given by the expr attribute, if there is one. Then it enters into a main loop that repeatedly selects the first form item whose variable is undefined, sets the variable to defined, and visits the item by playing prompts, collecting a user input, and handling the <filled> event. The loop continues until a transfer of control element (<goto> or <submit>) or until no form item variables are left undefined. By using the <clear> element to set a field item variable to undefined, we thus force a loop in the form.

The second new thing here is the use of JavaScript to perform some simple processing on the user input of a city/state name. We don't really have to use JavaScript here because we can pass the whole user input as a parameter to our web application and have the processing take place there. But as JavaScript support is required in VoiceXML 1.0, and as Tellme Studio fully supports this powerful scripting language within VoiceXML documents, I'll use it to extract the city name and the state name from a returned string, such as San_Jose@California, for illustrative purposes.

Finally, the third new feature is the use of the <goto> element's next attribute to refer to a web application URL. Because the control is transferred to that URL, we'll need to write a web application to dynamically generate a new VoiceXML document after gathering the Internet content based on the user request, and the call flow will continue with the new VoiceXML document.

```
<form id="weather">

<field name="cityorzip">
  <grammar>
    <![CDATA[
    City
    ]]>
  </grammar>

  <prompt>
    Please say a zip code or a city and state name.
  </prompt>

  <nomatch>
    <audio>Sorry I don't understand.  </audio>
    <reprompt/>
  </nomatch>

  <noinput>
    <audio>Sorry I didn't hear you.  </audio>
    <reprompt/>
  </noinput>

  <help>
    <audio>You can say a 5-digit zip code or a city/state name such as San
Francisco, California.  </audio>
    <reprompt/>
  </help>
```

```
    <filled>

        <script type="text/javascript">
        <![CDATA[
        vxmllog("*** cityorzip=", cityorzip);
        var userinput = vxmldata.get("cityorzip");
        var zip = "";
        var city = "";
        var state = "";
        if (userinput.indexOf('@') != -1)
        {
          var pos = userinput.indexOf('@');
          city = userinput.substring(0, pos);
          state = userinput.substring(pos + 1, userinput.length);
          vxmllog("*** pos=", pos, "city=", city, ", state=", state);
        }
        else
        {
          zip = userinput;
          vxmllog("*** zip=", zip);
        }

        vxmldata.set("city", city);
        vxmldata.set("state", state);
        vxmldata.set("zip", zip);

        vxmldata.set("url", "http://www.yourhost.com/voicexml/getweather.jsp?city="
          + city + "&state=" + state + "&zip=" + zip);
        vxmllog("url=" + url);
        ]]>
        </script>

        <goto next="{url}"/>
      </filled>
    </field>

  </form>
```

We won't show the code of the web application `getweather.jsp` used to generate the dynamic VoiceXML document, since this is not directly relevant to the topic in hand. However, the web application simply queries some weather service site such as http://weather.yahoo.com and embeds the result in the VoiceXML form below:

```
<form id="continue">

<!--the var value below is dynamically generated -->
<var forecast="Tuesday, December 26, Partly Cloudy. Hi 35 degree, low 27 degree.
Wednesday, December 27, Mostly Cloudy. Hi 36 degree, low 25 degree. Thursday,
December 28, Rain and Snow. Hi 39 degree, Low 30 degree. "/>

<field name="forecast">
<grammar>
<![CDATA[
YES_NO
]]>
</grammar>
```

```
<!--the text below is dynamically generated -->
<prompt> Partly cloudy. Temperature: 17 degree. Do you want to hear the forecast?
</prompt>

<filled>
<if cond="forecast == 'yes'">
<audio><value expr="forecast"/></audio>
</if>
</filled>
</field>

<field name="newcity">
<grammar>
<![CDATA[
YES_NO
]]>
</grammar>

<prompt>
Do you want to check the weather for another city?
</prompt>

<filled>
<if cond="newcity == 'yes'">
<goto next="#weather"/>
</if>
</filled>
</field>

</form>

<form id="weather">

<field name="cityorzip">
... <!--same code as above -->
</field>

</form>
```

Now you should have a pretty good idea of how to write similar VoiceXML documents for our stock, news, and sports services. For the stock application, you'll need to have a grammar that includes all the stock symbols and, preferably, their associated company names as well. That may sound tedious work, and indeed it is. The requirement to fully specify the accepted vocabulary is always one of the big tasks in developing useful VoiceXML applications.

Of course, we'd also need a web application that, based on the user input, retrieves stock quotes and news as requested from publicly available web sites such as http://finance.yahoo.com, http://news.yahoo.com or http://cnnfn.cnn.com. Unless you have some agreement with the companies providing the required data to respond to your query directly in XML, the query result you'll most likely get will be formatted in HTML, so you'll need to parse the response to retrieve the relevant piece of information. Don't forget that this HTML page can change without notice, potentially rendering our application useless.

The call flow could be similar to the weather application, or you can try to use a more advanced technology in VoiceXML called the **mixed-initiative form**, which aims to make the user-interaction more intelligent and natural. Using this technique, you can give the user more freedom, allowing them to initiate the conversation and speak more naturally using more words, rather than being limited to a small set of keywords, to answer questions presented by the system.

However, the dream of building human-like intelligent applications that can converse with us in true natural language is still a long way from reality: indeed whether it'll ever happen at all is a moot point. The good news though is you don't have to go too far to make your applications sound much more natural and intelligent, and mixed-initiative dialog goes some way towards achieving this. The simpler form as employed in the weather example, where the application directs the user to make an utterance, is known as **directed dialog**.

Of course, to understand any user utterance, you need grammars. The support of mixed-initiative forms in VoiceXML 1.0 comprises the ability to specify a form-level grammar along with field-level grammars, and an `<initial>` element where the application tries to collect as much information as possible from a single sentence. Then for each missing piece of information, it will enter the appropriate `<field>` element, where both the form-level grammar and the field-level grammar are active (not to mention the application-level and document-level general grammars). The application will now attempt to collect information for each incomplete field using the field-level grammar. Within any field, the form-level grammar is still referred to, enabling the application to obtain missing pieces of information for other fields.

Let's move on to looking at some real code. Note that at the time of writing, Tellme Studio doesn't support mixed-initiative forms, so we can't test the code below on their platform. But as mixed-initiative dialogs are important in developing advanced and powerful voice applications, I encourage you to be prepared for this feature of VoiceXML 1.0. By the time you're reading this, you may well find support for this in the Tellme Studio or your platforms of choice.

The following sample (`banking.vxml`) is for a banking application, which may be more interesting to enterprise application developers than the consumer services we have covered so far.

```
<form id="banking">
  <grammar>
    <![CDATA[
(transfer MONEY:m from checking to saving) { <action transfer><amount $m><from
checking><to saving> }
(transfer MONEY:m from saving to checking) { <action transfer><amount $m><from
saving><to checking> }
(check checking account balance) { <action check><account checking><what balance>
}
(check checking account activities) { <action check><account checking><what
activities> }
]]>
  </grammar>

  <initial>
    <prompt>How may I help you. </prompt>
    <nomatch>Please tell me what you want to do. </nomatch>
  </initial>
```

```
<field name="action">
  <grammar>
    <![CDATA[
      transfer { <option "transfer"> }
      check { <option "check"> }
    ]]>
  </grammar>
  <prompt>Do you want to transfer money or check balance? </prompt>
  <nomatch>Please say transfer or balance. </nomatch>
</field>

<field name="amount">
  <grammar>
    <![CDATA[
      MONEY { <option "amount"> }
    ]]>
  </grammar>
  <prompt>How much money do you want to transfer? </prompt>
  <nomatch>Please say the amount of the money you want to transfer. </nomatch>
</field>

<field name="from">
  <grammar>
    <![CDATA[
      checking  { <option "checking"> }
      saving {option "saving" }
    ]]>
  </grammar>
  <prompt>From which account? </prompt>
  <nomatch>Please say checking or saving. </nomatch>
</field>

<field name="to">
  <grammar>
    <![CDATA[
      checking  { <option "checking"> }
      saving { <option "saving"> }
    ]]>
  </grammar>
  <prompt>To which account? </prompt>
  <nomatch>Please say checking or saving. </nomatch>
</field>

<field name="account">
  <grammar>
    <![CDATA[
      checking  { <option "checking"> }
      saving { <option "saving"> }
    ]]>
  </grammar>
  <prompt>Which account? </prompt>
  <nomatch>Please say checking or saving. </nomatch>
</field>
```

```
    <field name="what">
      <grammar>
        <![CDATA[
          balance  { <option "balance"> }
          activies { <option "activities"> }
        ]]>
      </grammar>
      <prompt>What do you want to check?    </prompt>
      <nomatch>Please say balance or activities.    </nomatch>
    </field>

  </form>
```

Note that MONEY:m in the code above means that the value returned from the grammar Money is saved to the variable named m, which can be further referenced by $m. Again, for detailed coverage of Nuance GSL, see http://extranet.nuance.com.

Here we assume MONEY is a grammar defined elsewhere in the application to recognize any valid term for US dollars. In this sample, if the user says "transfer 5000 bucks from checking to saving" and the application recognizes every word, then the application can extract all the pieces of information it needs and initiate the appropriate actions. If the application only recognizes "transfer" and "from checking", however, our form-level grammar will be employed to fill in the remaining fields. In the above case then, the field with name amount will be entered first. Inside this field, the user is asked to say a money amount. Then, the next field called to will be entered and an attempt made to collect the last missing piece of information. But should the user say "5000 dollars to saving" in the amount field, then there's no need to enter any more <field> elements since all the pieces of information have now been collected.

There are a lot of details that need to be taken care of before we can make this type of banking application a reality. I hope the above example demonstrates the benefits of mixed-initiative dialogs, and you will want to explore the concept further when VoiceXML browser support is mature. In many cases, though, you will find directed dialogs to be good enough, and they can certainly lead to less complicated applications.

XSLT for VoiceXML

So far we have not mentioned XSLT at all – we've just been talking about VoiceXML and developing voice applications. There are still many elements in VoiceXML that we haven't covered, which you can explore by yourself if you wish. However, all the major elements in VoiceXML have been touched upon, and we have looked at some practical examples that should be helpful when developing your own VoiceXML applications.

Now that we have shown you how useful VoiceXML can be and you've seen the code to perform some basic and some more advanced tasks using VoiceXML, it's time to move on to learning how XSLT can help us. In the rest of this chapter, we'll be using XSLT to transform an XML document source into VoiceXML.

What source XML data might we use to produce VoiceXML documents with XSLT? Any type of structured XML data generated by an application can be used, such as weather forecasts, stock quotes, and address books. Alternatively, XML documents constructed manually, such as a Wireless Markup Language (WML) document, can also make an appropriate source.

Those readers who have developed some mobile applications with WML and now want to voice-enable their applications would find the conversion from WML to VoiceXML of particular note. Those readers who start with VoiceXML, but want to add WML to their applications – indeed, voice doesn't work in all situations, for example in quiet office environments – would find the reverse transformation useful. However, due to the scope of this chapter, we won't be able to cover these two intriguing topics. Instead, we'll be considering the more general case of conversion from XML data to VoiceXML, which will be relevant to both groups of readers. If you want to know how to use XSLT to generate WML dynamically from XML source, see *Beginning WAP: WML and WMLScript* (ISBN 1-861004-58-3) or *Professional WAP* (ISBN 1-861004-04-4) by Wrox Press.

Obviously, by using XSLT to transform our current XML documents to VoiceXML documents without having to start from scratch, we'll greatly speed up our VoiceXML application development process. I would encourage those who're interested in converting between VoiceXML and WML to explore it independently by writing some stylesheets for VoiceXML and WML documents – I'm sure you'd find it very useful. Whether it would be possible to write a pair of general XSL documents that transform any document written in WML to a VoiceXML document and vice versa is an open question.

Before we go into the details of the sample code, the following section describes how to ensure we have the right tools and development environment set up.

XSLT: Open Source Tools

To transform an XML document to a VoiceXML or WML document using XSLT, we'll need an XSLT processor. Here we will use the Apache Xalan processor – set-up instructions are included in Appendix E.

To test the processor installation, we'll use the following XML document (`sample.xml`):

```
<?xml version="1.0"?>
<CUSTOMERS>
  <CUSTOMER>
     <Name>
       Joe Smith
     </Name>
     <CompanyName>
       Voiceware, Inc.
     </CompanyName>
     <Country>
       USA
     </Country>
  </CUSTOMER>
  <CUSTOMER>
     <Name>
       Jane Lee
     </Name>
     <CompanyName>
       Wirelessware Corp
     </CompanyName>
     <Country>
       China
     </Country>
  </CUSTOMER>
</CUSTOMERS>
```

and an XSL document (`sample.xsl`):

```xml
<?xml version="1.0"?>
<xsl:stylesheet version="1.0" xmlns:xsl="http://www.w3.org/1999/XSL/Transform">

<xsl:template match="/">

<vxml version="1.0">
  <form id="start">
    <block>
    <audio>Listing Customers</audio>
    </block>
  </form>

  <xsl:for-each select="CUSTOMERS/CUSTOMER">
  <form>
    <block>
    <audio>Name is <xsl:value-of select="Name" /></audio>
    <audio>Company name is <xsl:value-of select="CompanyName" /></audio>
    <audio>Country name is <xsl:value-of select="Country" /></audio>
    </block>
  </form>
  </xsl:for-each>
</vxml>
</xsl:template>

</xsl:stylesheet>
```

After running:

java org.apache.xalan.xslt.Process -IN sample.xml -XSL sample.xsl -OUT sample.vxml

from the command prompt, you should see output similar to that shown below:

========= Parsing file:D:/voicexml/xslt/sample.xsl =========

Parse of file:D:/ voicexml/xslt/sample.xsl took 4727 milliseconds
========= Parsing file:D:/ voicexml/xslt/sample.xml =========

Parse of file:D:/ voicexml/xslt /sample.xml took 230 milliseconds
==============================
Transforming...
transform took 380 milliseconds
XSLProcessor: done

The `sample.vxml` file produced should look like this. It can be uploaded directly to your account at Tellme Studio for testing:

```xml
<?xml version="1.0" encoding="UTF-8"?>
<vxml version="1.0">
<form id="start">
<block>
<audio>Listing Customers</audio>
</block>
```

```
</form>
<form>
<block>
<audio>Name is  Joe Smith</audio>
<audio>Company name is  Voiceware, Inc.</audio>
<audio>Country name is  USA </audio>
</block>
</form>

<form>
<block>
<audio>Name is  Jane Lee</audio>
<audio>Company name is  Wirelessware Corp</audio>
<audio>Country name is  China</audio>
</block>
</form>
</vxml>
```

If you do not see something similar, you should go back to the Xalan documentation on the http://xml.apache.org site, which covers detailed steps to set up and test Xalan. Otherwise, we are ready to use XSLT to produce further VoiceXML documents.

XSLT: Producing VoiceXML Documents

In this section, we'll show you another example of producing a VoiceXML document from a general XML document. We'll use the book catalog information sample used throughout several chapters of this book as our source XML. Depending on what your goals are and how you write your XSLT stylesheets, you can generate different VoiceXML documents to serve a range of purposes. For example, one VoiceXML document can be produced that responds to queries on the source XML document, such as the price and total pages of a specific title. Another VoiceXML document can simply be a listing of all the information in the XML document, an example of which is given in the previous section. In the rest of this chapter, we'll focus on the query-type application, which is more useful in most cases.

The XML Document

Here's the sample book catalog XML document `catalog.xml` (here it is listed in a shortened form):

```
<?xml version="1.0" encoding="utf-8" standalone="yes"?>
<!--======= The Wrox Press Book Catalog Application =======-->

<Catalog>
<Book>
   <Title>Professional VB6 XML</Title>
   <Authors>
      <Author>James Britt</Author>
      <Author>Teun Duynstee</Author>
   </Authors>
   <Publisher>Wrox Press, Ltd.</Publisher>
   <PubDate>March 2000</PubDate>
   <Abstract>Shows the VB community how to take advantage of XML technology and
             the available implementations</Abstract>
   <Pages>725</Pages>
```

```
      <ISBN>1-861003-32-3</ISBN>
      <RecSubjCategories>
          <Category>Programming</Category>
          <Category>Visual Basic</Category>
          <Category>XML</Category>
      </RecSubjCategories>
      <Price>$49.99</Price>
      <CoverImage>3323.gif</CoverImage>
  </Book>
  <Book>
      <Title>XSLT Programmer's Reference</Title>
      <Authors>
          <Author>Michael Kay</Author>
      </Authors>
      <Publisher>Wrox Press, Ltd.</Publisher>
      <PubDate>April 2000</PubDate>
      <Abstract>Learn how to use the XSLT language to develop web
                applications</Abstract>
      <Pages>777</Pages>
      <ISBN>1-861003-12-9</ISBN>
      <RecSubjCategories>
          <Category>Internet</Category>
          <Category>XML</Category>
          <Category>XSL</Category>
      </RecSubjCategories>
      <Price>$34.99</Price>
      <CoverImage>3129.gif</CoverImage>
  </Book>
  ...
  </Catalog>
```

Our task is to generate a directed-form-based VoiceXML document based on it and to allow for a dialog, such as that below:

System:	Welcome to the Wrox Press Book Catalog Application. Do you want to search by title, author, or ISBN?
User:	Help.
System:	Here you can search for a book by title, author, or ISBN. Simply say the word title, author, or ISBN.
User:	Title.
System:	What's the title please?
User:	Professional VB6 XML.
System:	What do you want to know about it?
User:	Price.
System:	Price is $49.99. Do you want to know more about this book?
User:	Yes.

System:	What do you want to know about it?
User:	Total pages.
System:	Total pages are 725. Do you want to know more about this book?
User:	No.
System:	Do you want to search for another book?
User:	Yes.
System:	Do you want to search by title, author, or ISBN.
User:	By author.
System:	What's the author's name?
User:	Michael Kay.
System:	What do you want to know about it?
User:	Title.
System:	XSLT Programmer's Reference. Do you want to know more about this book?
User:	Yes.
System:	What do you want to know about it?
User:	Publish date.
System:	April 2000. Do you want to know more about this book?
User:	No.
System:	Do you want to search for another book?
User:	No.
System:	Thank you for using the book catalog service. Goodbye.

The Resultant VoiceXML

Let's start with the resultant VoiceXML document. You may wonder if we're going to create a VoiceXML document ourselves anyway, why bother to write a stylesheet to do the conversion as well? The answer is that this is one approach to developing an XSLT/VoiceXML application. We write a simple VoiceXML document first, that can handle a subset of the real XML data given. Then based on this document, we write our XSL document, which can handle the original XML document in a general way. In this way, the appropriate VoiceXML document can still be generated automatically using the same XSL file even when new data is added to the XML document.

So, the required VoiceXML document is as follows. It will be the same as the file that will be generated from the XML data using the Xalan XSLT processor and the XSL document we'll write later. The code (`catalog.vxml`) is pretty long, so I'll split it up with comments to help you better understand it.

```
<?xml version="1.0" encoding="UTF-8"?>
<vxml version="1.0">

<form id="catalog">

  <var name="key"/>

  <block name="welcome">
    <prompt>
      Welcome to the Wrox Press Book Application.
    </prompt>
  </block>
```

The above lines are the initialization part that sets a form-level variable key to hold the ISBN number of a book a user searches for. It then plays a welcome message.

```
<field name="searchby">
  <grammar>
    <![CDATA[
    [
    title {<option "title">}
    author {<option "author">}
    isbn {<option "ISBN">}
    ]
    ]]>
  </grammar>

  <prompt>
    Do you want to search by title, author, or ISBN?
  </prompt>

  <nomatch>
    <audio>Sorry I don't understand. Please say title, author, or ISBN</audio>
  </nomatch>

  <noinput>
    <audio>Sorry I didn't hear you. Please say title, author, or ISBN</audio>
  </noinput>

  <help>
    <audio>Here you can search for a book by title, author, or ISBN. Simply say
           the word title, author, or ISBN.</audio>
  </help>

</field>
```

The first field (remember that a field is the primary data collecting element of a VoiceXML document) asks the user for the search criteria, which can be title, author, or ISBN. Depending on the application, you may add more criteria. The user input is saved in the variable searchby.

Note that here we provide the <nomatch>, <noinput>, and <help> elements. These should be extended even further in real world applications by adding the count attribute as follows: <nomatch count="1">, <nomatch count="2">, and <nomatch count="3">, with different prompts placed inside each one. That way, you can make your VoiceXML application more user friendly by playing one prompt the first time the application doesn't recognize user input, playing another prompt the second time, and yet another prompt the third time. However, for the fields below, we won't add these elements so as to avoid our already lengthy example bloating further.

```
<!-- the cond attribute here means only if its value is true will the field be
entered. So this field will be active only if the user wants to search by title. -
->
<field name="title" cond="searchby == 'title'">
  <grammar>
    <![CDATA[
     [
     (professional vb6 xml) {<option "1-861003-32-3">}
     (xslt programmer's reference) {<option "1-861003-12-9">}
     ]
    ]]>
  </grammar>

  <prompt>
    What's the title please?
  </prompt>

  <filled>
    <assign name="key" expr="title"/>
  </filled>
</field>
```

The above field gets a title from the user. We use the ISBN as the index key to a book, saved in the variable key. The grammar here – the title with its associated ISBN number – should be generated automatically by our stylesheet based on the source XML document.

```
<field name="author" cond="searchby == 'author'">
  <grammar>
    <![CDATA[
     [
     (james britt) {<option "1-861003-32-3">}
     (teun duynstee) {<option "1-861003-32-3">}
     (michael kay) {<option "1-861003-12-9">}
    ]
    ]]>
  </grammar>

  <prompt>
    What's the author's name?
  </prompt>

  <filled>
    <assign name="key" expr="author"/>
  </filled>
</field>
```

```
<field name="isbn" cond="searchby == 'ISBN'">
  <grammar>
    <![CDATA[
    [
      (1-861003-32-3) {<option "1-861003-32-3">}
      (1-861003-12-9) {<option "1-861003-12-9">}
    ]
    ]]>
  </grammar>

  <prompt>
    What's the ISBN number?
  </prompt>

  <filled>
    <assign name="key" expr="isbn"/>
  </filled>
</field>
```

The two fields above are similar to the previous one. Here we're trying to get either an author name or an ISBN number to search for.

```
<field name="detail">
  <grammar>
    <![CDATA[
    [
    title {<option "title">}
    authors {<option "authors">}
    publisher {<option "publisher">}
    pubdate {<option "pubdate">}
    abstract {<option "abstract">}
    pages {<option "pages">}
    isbn {<option "isbn">}
    recsubjcategories {<option "recsubjcategories ">}
    price {<option "price">}
    coverimage {<option " coverimage">}
    ]
    ]]>
  </grammar>

  <prompt>
    What do you want to know about it?
  </prompt>

  <filled>
    <if cond="detail == 'title'">
      <if cond="key == '1-861003-32-3'">
        <prompt>The title is Professional VB6 XML</prompt>
      <elseif cond="key == '1-861003-12-9'"/>
        <prompt>The title is XSLT Programmer's Reference</prompt>
      </if>
    <elseif cond="detail == 'author'"/>
      <if cond="key == '1-861003-32-3'">
```

```
        <prompt>The authors are James Britt and Teun Duynstee</prompt>
      <elseif cond="key == '1-861003-12-9'"/>
        <prompt>The author is Michael Kay</prompt>
      </if>
    <elseif cond="detail == 'pubdate'"/>
      <if cond="key == '1-861003-32-3'">
        <prompt>The publish date is March 2000</prompt>
      <elseif cond="key == '1-861003-12-9'"/>
        <prompt>The publish date is April 2000</prompt>
      </if>
    <elseif cond="detail == 'abstract'"/>
      <if cond="key == '1-861003-32-3'">
        <prompt>The abstract is Shows the VB community how to take advantage of
                XML technology and the available implementations</prompt>
      <elseif cond="key == '1-861003-12-9'"/>
        <prompt>The abstract is Learn how to use the XSLT language to develop web
                applications</prompt>
      </if>
    <elseif cond="detail == 'pages'"/>
      <if cond="key == '1-861003-32-3'">
        <prompt>Total pages are 725</prompt>
      <elseif cond="key == '1-861003-12-9'"/>
        <prompt>Total pages are 777</prompt>
      </if>
    <elseif cond="detail == 'price'"/>
      <if cond="key == '1-861003-32-3'">
        <prompt>Price is $49.99</prompt>
      <elseif cond="key == '1-861003-12-9'"/>
        <prompt>Price is $34.99</prompt>
      </if>
    </if>
  </filled>
</field>
```

The above field is used to ask the user what type of information they want about their chosen book, and to give them that information. The grammar should again be automatically generated from our XML file by our XSL, as should all the `<if>` `<elseif>` statements.

```
<field name="moreinfo">
  <grammar>
    <![CDATA[
    YES_NO
    ]]>
  </grammar>

  <prompt>
    Do you want to know more about this book?
  </prompt>

  <filled>
    <if cond="moreinfo == 'yes'">
      <clear namelist="detail moreinfo"/>
    </if>
  </filled>
</field>
```

After we tell the user what they want to know, this code will ask if they want to know more, and if they do, start the loop again by clearing the field item variable `detail` and `moreinfo`. The form-interpretation algorithm specified in the VoiceXML specification will take care of the rest of the business.

```
<field name="moresearch" cond="moreinfo == 'no'">
  <grammar>
    <![CDATA[
    YES_NO
    ]]>
  </grammar>

  <prompt>
    Do you want to search for another book?
  </prompt>

  <filled>
    <if cond="moresearch == 'yes'">
      <clear namelist="searchby title author isbn detail moreinfo moresearch
       key"/>
    </if>
  </filled>
</field>
```

If the user wishes to know about another book, then we'll start over by clearing all the variables. Otherwise, it's time to say goodbye.

```
<block name="bye">
  <prompt>Thank you for using the book catalog service. Goodbye.</prompt>
</block>

</form>
</vxml>
```

Note that, as of February 2001, Tellme Studio, unlike some other voice portals such as BeVocal, still doesn't support the use of `cond` as an attribute of the `<field>` or `<block>` element. This is unfortunate, as `cond` is a really handy attribute for these elements. In its absence, you have to use `<if>` and `<goto>` and introduce many additional forms in your VoiceXML document to implement this logic. However, due to its importance, I expect the `cond` attribute to be fully supported by Tellme soon.

In the meantime, will the above code work on BeVocal? Yes, it will, but with one small change. BeVocal does not support the `YES_NO` grammar supported by Tellme. These `<grammar>` sections need to be replaced by:

```
<grammar>
  <![CDATA[
  [
  yes no
  ]
  ]]>
</grammar>
```

However, we will continue with the Tellme version of the code, since this is the platform we have been writing for throughout the chapter.

The XSLT Stylesheet

Now I would like to move on to consider the XSLT document, `catalog.xsl`, that can be used to transform the above XML document – to be precise, any XML document using the same DTD with as many books listed as you want – to a VoiceXML document. The following are the initial declarations:

```
<?xml version="1.0"?>
<xsl:stylesheet version="1.0"
                xmlns:xsl="http://www.w3.org/1999/XSL/Transform">

<xsl:output method="xml" cdata-section-elements="" indent="yes"/>
```

The `<xsl:template>` below is the only template we'll be using here. If you're used to writing an `<xsl:template>` for each element type in the source XML document to transform to HTML, this may sound surprising to you. But actually, what you'll see here is something similar to the pull stylesheets described in Chapter 3. Methods using multiple templates conform to the pull stylesheet model. Unlike pull model stylesheets, push model stylesheets are needed when the result document tree is dramatically different from the source tree. Instead of writing a handful of template rules and calling `<xsl:apply=templates>`, you usually use `<xsl:for-each>` to pull data from the source document.

In the first part of the following template, the code is pretty much the same as the resultant VoiceXML document. This is because what the user wants to search for (a title, an author, or an ISBN number) and other initialization code for the result VoiceXML document is not from the source document.

```
<xsl:template match="Catalog">

<vxml version="1.0">
<form id="catalog">
<var name="key"/>

<block name="welcome">
<prompt>
  Welcome to the Wrox Press Book Application.
</prompt>
</block>

<field name="searchby">

<xsl:comment>I use CDATABEGIN and CDATAEND, two labels I made up, to mark the
beginning and end of CDATA section in all grammars in the document. The two words
should be replaced later after the VoiceXML document is generated. Yes, this is
not an ideal solution, but it is the only method I can imagine at this
time.</xsl:comment>
<grammar>
<![CDATA[
CDATABEGIN
[
title {<option "title">}
author {<option "author">}
isbn {<option "ISBN">}
]
CDATAEND
]]>
</grammar>
```

```
<prompt>
Do you want to search by title, author, or ISBN?
</prompt>

<nomatch>
<audio>Sorry I don't understand. Please say title, author, or ISBN</audio>
</nomatch>

<noinput>
<audio>Sorry I didn't hear you. Please say title, author, or ISBN</audio>
</noinput>

<help>
<audio>Here you can search for a book by title, author, or ISBN. Simply say the
word title, author, or ISBN.</audio>
</help>
</field>
```

The first `<xsl:for-each>` element below is used to get a list of all the book titles in the source document and add them to the `<grammar>` section of the VoiceXML document. We use the `translate()` function to convert all the upper-case letters in a title to lower-case letters, as all words in a grammar rule need be to in lower-case.

```
<field name="title" cond="searchby == 'title'">
<grammar>
CDATABEGIN
[
<xsl:for-each select="//Book">
  <xsl:variable name="isbn" select="ISBN"/>
  (<xsl:value-of select="translate(Title, 'ABCDEFGHIJKLMNOPQRSTUVWXYZ',
   'abcdefghijklmnopqrstuvwxyz')"/>)
  <xsl:value-of
    select="concat('{', '&lt;', 'option ', '&quot;', $isbn, '&quot;', '&gt;}')"/>
</xsl:for-each>
]
CDATAEND
</grammar>

<prompt>
What's the title please?
</prompt>

<filled>
<assign name="key" expr="title"/>
</filled>
</field>
```

The next two `<xsl:for-each>` elements are similar to the one above: they extract all the authors and ISBN numbers from the source document and add them to the grammar sections. To make this code more efficient, you may consider writing a common template implementing the shared `<xsl:for-each>` functionality and call it from within the three `<field>` elements here.

```
<field name="title" cond="searchby == 'author'">
<grammar>
CDATABEGIN
[
<xsl:for-each select="//Book">
  <xsl:variable name="isbn" select="ISBN"/>
  <xsl:for-each select="Authors/Author">
    (<xsl:value-of select="translate(., 'ABCDEFGHIJKLMNOPQRSTUVWXYZ',
      'abcdefghijklmnopqrstuvwxyz')"/>)
  <xsl:value-of
  select="concat('{', '&lt;', 'option ', '&quot;', $isbn, '&quot;', '&gt;}')"/>
  </xsl:for-each>
</xsl:for-each>
]
CDATAEND
</grammar>

<prompt>
What's the author's name?
</prompt>

<filled>
<assign name="key" expr="author"/>
</filled>
</field>

<field name="isbn" cond="searchby == 'isbn'">
<grammar>
CDATABEGIN
[
<xsl:for-each select="//Book">
  <xsl:variable name="isbn" select="ISBN"/>
  (<xsl:value-of select="ISBN"/>) <xsl:value-of select="concat('{', '&lt;',
'option ', '&quot;', $isbn, '&quot;', '&gt;}')"/>
</xsl:for-each>
]
CDATAEND
</grammar>

<prompt>
What's the ISBN number?
</prompt>

<filled>
<assign name="key" expr="isbn"/>
</filled>
</field>
```

The next `<xsl:for-each>` element handles the grammar for all the child nodes of the `<book>` element in the source document, so the user can say any of the names of all the book properties to query the information about it. As Nuance GSL requires word names to be in lower-case, we use the `translate()` function to convert the upper-case letters in the book name to the lower-case letters.

```
<field name="detail" cond="key">
<grammar>
CDATABEGIN
[
<xsl:for-each select="//Book[1]">
  <xsl:for-each select="*">
    <xsl:value-of select="translate(name(), 'ABCDEFGHIJKLMNOPQRSTUVWXYZ',
      'abcdefghijklmnopqrstuvwxyz')"/>
    <xsl:value-of select="concat('{', '&lt;', 'option ', '&quot;',
      translate(name(), 'ABCDEFGHIJKLMNOPQRSTUVWXYZ',
      'abcdefghijklmnopqrstuvwxyz'), '&quot;', '&gt;}')"/>
  </xsl:for-each>
</xsl:for-each>
]
CDATAEND
</grammar>

<prompt>
What do you want to know about it?
</prompt>

<help>
You can ask for title, author, publish date, abstract, total pages, or price, etc.
</help>
```

The last three `<xsl:for-each>` elements below are the most complicated. The first one takes all the child nodes of the `<book>` element, and then for each node, outputs an `<elseif>` element testing if the field variable `detail` is equal to the node name. If yes, depending on the ISBN `key` value, we get the appropriate book's child node's value and put it in the VoiceXML `<prompt>` element, played when the user asks for that information. You may notice that this part of the code in the final VoiceXML document above is pretty lengthy. Indeed, for a source XML document with hundreds or even thousands of books listed, the resultant VoiceXML document would be extremely long, and the algorithm I'm using to handle this doesn't seem all that efficient.

One thing to be aware of is that VoiceXML is best used as a voice interface to your backend application systems. In other words, when the data gets real large, you definitely should consider shifting lots of the application functionality to the backend, creating web-based applications to access the functionality, and having the VoiceXML document call the web application interface. In that situation, your XSLT document would create calls to the web applications from the VoiceXML elements. But the example shown here should get you started in that direction when needed.

```
<filled>
<!-- The next odd-looking condition will of course never succeed, but it's used
here so we can handle the following elseifs in a consistent way. -->
<if cond="true == false">
<xsl:for-each select="//*/Book[1]">
  <xsl:for-each select="*">
  <xsl:variable name="lowername" select="translate(name(),
'ABCDEFGHIJKLMNOPQRSTUVWXYZ', 'abcdefghijklmnopqrstuvwxyz')"/>
  <xsl:variable name="originalname" select="name()"/>
  <elseif cond="detail == '{$lowername}'"/>
    <xsl:for-each select="//*/Book">
      <xsl:variable name="isbn" select="ISBN"/>
```

```
            <xsl:variable name="eleval" select="$originalname"/>
            <if cond="key == '{$isbn}'">
            <prompt>
              <xsl:value-of select="$eleval"/>
            </prompt>
            </if>
        </xsl:for-each>
      </xsl:for-each>
  <xsl:text>
  </xsl:text>
  </xsl:for-each>
  </if>
  </filled>
  </field>
```

The rest of the code in the stylesheet is simply copied from our VoiceXML document catalog.vxml listed earlier. This is because the elements here are not directly generated from the source XML document, but are more of an application interface design issue.

```
<field name="moreinfo">
<grammar>
CDATABEGIN
YES_NO
CDATAEND
</grammar>

<prompt>
Do you want to know more about this book?
</prompt>

<filled>
<if cond="moreinfo == 'yes'">
   <clear namelist="detail moreinfo"/>
</if>
</filled>
</field>

<field name="moresearch" cond="moreinfo == 'no'">
<grammar>
CDATABEGIN
YES_NO
CDATAEND
</grammar>

<prompt>
Do you want to search for another book?
</prompt>

<filled>
<if cond="moresearch == 'yes'">
   <clear namelist="searchby title author isbn detail moreinfo moresearch key"/>
</if>
</filled>
</field>
```

```
<block name="bye">
<prompt>
Thank you for using the book catalog service. Goodbye.
</prompt>
</block>

</form>
</vxml>
</xsl:template>
</xsl:stylesheet>
```

Now after you run:

java org.apache.xalan.xslt.Process -IN catalog.xml -XSL catalog.xsl -OUT catalog.out

and replace CDATABEGIN with <![CDATA[, CDATAEND with]]>, < with <, and > with > in catalog.out, you should see that catalog.out is just the same as catalog.vxml. There might be a better way to handle these grammar-related conversions. Interested readers are encouraged to explore this on their own.

One question you may have now is, if we need to copy so much of the VoiceXML code to the XSL document, why don't we skip the stylesheets and write the VoiceXML application directly? (After you get more familiar with VoiceXML, you can go straight to creating the XSL without starting by writing a typical output VoiceXML file.) Well, in the cases where all you want to do is write some VoiceXML documents starting from scratch, that makes sense. But any time you want to voice-enable existing applications, especially voice-enable application-generated XML data, you'll benefit from writing a flexible stylesheet, even though XSLT does introduce one more layer of complexity. Using XSLT in these instances can be a very powerful tool, allowing us to produce new *dynamic* VoiceXML documents on the fly based on new or updated XML source data, as long as the same DTD/Schema is followed.

Summary

In this chapter we first presented a detailed introduction to VoiceXML, to illustrate how this new specification should ease the development of voice applications. We saw how easy it can be to set up a development environment and quickly start developing voice applications with VoiceXML. We then moved on to a detailed example of using XSLT to transform XML into a VoiceXML document. This demonstrated one of the major benefits of using XSLT to produce VoiceXML (and other) documents: the automatic generation of an application document based on a dynamic XML data source.

As both VoiceXML and XSLT are relatively new technologies, you should expect to see many changes in the future. They don't work in every situation – sometimes using VoiceXML may not be the best way to develop your voice applications, and using XSLT may be overkill if you know your source data will rarely change. However, in many other cases, developing with VoiceXML and producing VoiceXML with XSLT makes a lot of sense, because together they provide a set of powerful tools to speed up your overall development time-cycle.

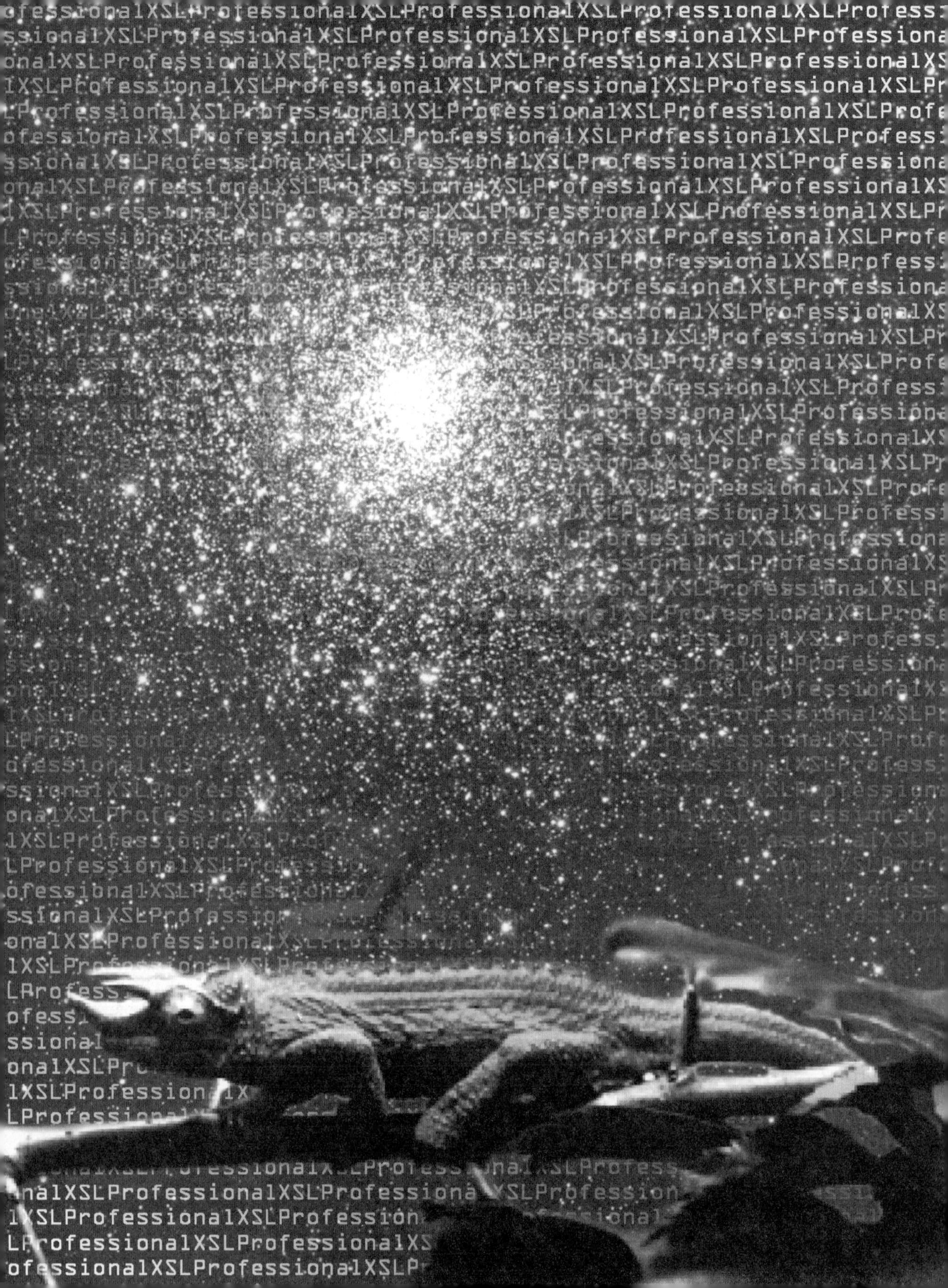

14

XSLT and XML Schemas

This chapter will focus on the use of XSL transformations with **XML Schemas**. As schemas are themselves XML documents, they can be manipulated by XSL transformations to create other XML documents. We'll look at some of the possibilities this offers. We'll also explore how XSLT can be used in conjunction with schemas to enhance their usefulness.

In this chapter we look at how to:

- ❑ Transform schemas to XML instance documents
- ❑ Create schemas from XML instance documents
- ❑ Generate XSL stylesheets for schema validation
- ❑ Use XSLT to enforce data integrity constraints

All transformations in this chapter will be performed with the Apache Xalan processor, which is a robust and highly compliant XSLT and XPath implementation. Versions of Xalan are available in both Java and C++. In this chapter I've used the Java 2 version. The Xalan processor can be downloaded for free from http://xml.apache.org. Refer to Appendix E for details.

The Xalan processor can be invoked from the command line; a feature that comes in very handy when testing your stylesheets. To transform an XML document with the command line utility, navigate to the folder containing your files and then just type:

java org.apache.xalan.xslt.Process -in inputFile.xml -xsl theStylesheet.xsl -out resultFile.xml

where the parameter following –in is the input XML document to be transformed, the parameter following –xsl is the stylesheet, and the parameter following –out is the name of the file to which the result of the transformation will be written. The –out parameter can be omitted, in which case the output of the transformation will be written to the standard output stream (usually the screen).

XML Schemas – a Very Brief Overview

As you probably know, a document type definition (DTD) establishes a set of constraints for an XML document, and defines the way an XML document should be constructed. A DTD also defines the order of nesting in tags. The DTD adds portability to a XML document, because different applications can parse and validate any XML data if they have the DTD of the document being parsed.

XML Schemas (http://www.w3.org/XML/Schema) provide a much more powerful way of constraining XML documents than DTDs. In addition to traditional constraints, XML Schemas allow **content model** constraints for generic data formats to be built. The constraints defined by a schema can be shared and referenced from other schemas by using **XLink** and **XPointer**. This object-oriented approach is much more maintainable than the DTD approach, and can save a significant amount of design time. Probably the most significant advantage of schemas is that they are themselves XML documents providing us with the very useful ability to create and instantiate schemas with XSL transformations.

Many schema languages are available, such as the official W3C XML Schema, Microsoft's XML-Data Reduced (XDR), Schematron, RELAX, and TREX, to name a few.

> **Throughout this chapter I shall concentrate on the W3C's vision of XML Schemas. At the time of writing, XML Schemas are a Candidate Recommendation from the W3C. Therefore the syntax is still subject to revision, but substantial changes to the specification are not anticipated.**

This chapter focuses on the collaboration opportunities between XSLT and schemas, rather than the schema syntax itself. First I shall quickly run through the XML Schema core syntax with the help of a very simple example.

A Simple Schema

Schemas are themselves XML documents, but use the standard .xsd file extension. If we wanted to declare an element called <Book>, we would simply write

```
<element name="Book" />
```

Also, if we wanted to declare an attribute called ISBN, we would write

```
<attribute name="ISBN" />
```

Pretty simple, huh? Now, look at the following figure showing a trivial XML format:

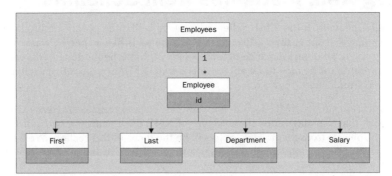

Here is the schema we might use for this simple format (employee-schema.xsd):

```
<schema xmlns="http://www.w3.org/2000/10/XMLSchema">
  <element name="Employees">
    <complexType>
      <sequence>
        <element name="Employee" type="EmployeeType" minOccurs="1"
         maxOccurs="unbounded"/>
      </sequence>
      <attribute name="id" type="string" use="required"/>
    </complexType>
  </element>

  <complexType name="EmployeeType">
    <sequence>
      <element name="First" type="string"/>
      <element name="Last" type="string"/>
      <element name="Department" type="string"/>
      <element name="Salary" type="integer"/>
    <sequence>
  </complexType>
</schema>
```

The root element of any schema must be the <schema> element. It contains the declaration of the namespace for the schema specification. The first element defined here is the <Employees> element. It contains only one element, the <Employee> element, and the id attribute. Elements with child elements, or that carry attributes, are *complex types*, defined using <complexType>. Elements that have no attributes and contain only text are *simple types*. All attributes are simple types, because they cannot contain elements or other attributes. The <sequence> element specifies that the elements within it must appear in that order. (Although this element is used within each of the <complexType> elements above, this is a coincidence – it is not mandatory.)

The schema states that the <Employee> element must occur at least once (minOccurs="1" and maxOccurs="unbounded"). The <Employee> element is defined to be of the type EmployeeType. This type is defined later in the schema , showing how we may define complex types separately thereby allowing them to be reused. The attribute id is defined to be a string, and its use is required.

From this simple example I hope I've shown that XML Schema descriptions are somewhat more logical and powerful than the corresponding DTD descriptions. Well, now that we know what schemas look like, let's get down to business!

Generating XML Instances from Schemas

Programmatically speaking, if the XML Schema language is like the programming language you use to define a class, say Java or C++, then a specific XML Schema is like a specific class. Therefore, an XML schema instance is like an object instance of a class except that schema documents cannot contain methods. Now, wouldn't it be nice to be able to instantiate XML instances from schemas just as we can instantiate objects from classes?

Now since schemas are simply XML documents, they can be freely transformed by XSLT stylesheets, and because of the way that schemas define the structure of XML documents, we can generate guaranteed-valid empty XML objects from them. This topic will be the focus of this section. We'll see three different types of XML schema design, and create a stylesheet that is able to instantiate instances from all of them.

Terminology

So, what we shall be doing is creating an instance of an XML document from a schema. But we want to be able to go one step further and create an instance not necessarily of the whole XML document, but perhaps just of a specific part of the document – that is an instance of one specific XML object defined in a schema.

Since we are going to be creating instances of XML objects from schema, we need to define the concept of an **XML object**. In this context we will define an XML object as a structured entity that has an associated **unique identifier**. That is, each object has an element or attribute that uniquely identifies it. To pick up the previous example, we could have a list of employees such that each employee is uniquely identified by their id attribute. Therefore, each employee would be an XML object.

We will also assume that more than one type of object can exist in the same XML document, that is, the root element can contain more than one type of object – it's a **variable content container**. Such a document usually comprises objects that are all **extensions** of one common type. For example we could have a vehicle catalog, containing a *ship* object, a *truck* object, and so on. All these objects would be an extension of a *vehicle* object that is defined to be in an XML schema **substitution group** of the base vehicle object.

Consequently, we assume that more than one type of object can be defined in a schema. Therefore, we can instantiate different objects from the same schema. We will determine which object type to instantiate with a parameter containing the name of the outermost element of that object.

To clarify all this, let's have a look at the following XML format:

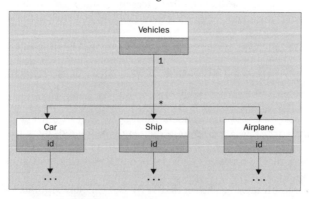

I've left out the child elements of the vehicle elements for simplicity's sake. From this XML format (where the <Vehicles> element is a variable content container) we can instantiate three different objects: a car, a ship, and an airplane.

Schema Designs

Before we dive into the code, we have to be aware of the different ways in which schemas are designed. This is necessary because it affects how we design our XSLT stylesheet. There are three different main strategies in schema design, differentiated by the way they declare elements and types (global versus local). To demonstrate, let's define a schema for the following 'Movie' object:

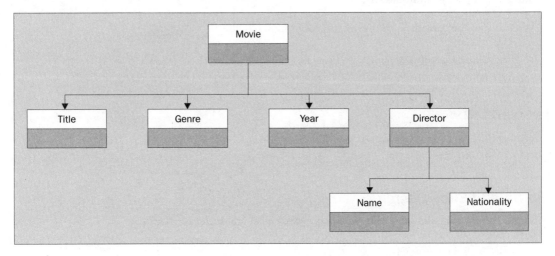

There are three different design approaches generally used for defining a schema, each one generally known by a rather evocative name.

The Russian Doll Design

With this design approach, the schema structure mirrors the object structure. That is, the inner element definitions are nested within their parent element definition, in other words all elements are defined *inline*:

```
<schema xmlns="http://www.w3.org/2000/10/XMLSchema"
        xmlns:mov="http://www.movieCatalog.org"
        elementFormDefault="unqualified">
  <element name="Movie">
    <complexType>
      <sequence>
        <element name="Title" type="string" minOccurs="1" maxOccurs="1"/>
        <element name="Genre" type="string" minOccurs="1" maxOccurs="1"/>
        <element name="Year" type="string" minOccurs="1" maxOccurs="1"/>
        <element name="Director">
          <complexType>
            <sequence>
              <element name="Name" type="string" minOccurs="1" maxOccurs="1"/>
              <element name="Nationality" type="string" minOccurs="1"
               maxOccurs="1"/>
            </sequence>
          </complexType>
        </element>
      </sequence>
    </complexType>
  </element>
</schema>
```

The outermost element definition has all other element definitions nested within it, hence the name "Russian Doll" design (A Russian Doll is a doll that when you open, contains another smaller doll inside it that itself contains an even smaller doll, and so on). This approach facilitates hiding (localizing) namespace complexities. For example, the region of the schema where <Title> and <Genre> elements declarations are applicable is localized to within the <Movie> element. Therefore, if the schema specifies elementFormDefault="unqualified" then the namespaces of these elements are hidden (localized) within the schema.

With this design, the instance document would look like this:

```
<mov:Movie xmlns:mov="http://www.movieCatalog.org">
    <Title>The Siamese Connection</Title>
    <Genre>Drama</Genre>
    <Year>1997</Year>
    <Director>
        <Name>Syrup Bionsen</Name>
        <Nationality>Danish</Nationality>
    </Director>
</mov:Movie>
```

The Salami Slice Design

In the Salami Slice design, all elements (and attributes) are declared *globally*:

```
<schema xmlns="http://www.w3.org/2000/10/XMLSchema"
    xmlns:mov="http://www.movieCatalog.org">
    <element name="Title" type="string"/>
    <element name="Genre" type="string"/>
    <element name="Year" type="string"/>
    <element name="Name" type="string"/>
    <element name="Nationality" type="string"/>
    <element name="Director">
        <complexType>
            <sequence>
                <element ref="mov:Name" minOccurs="1" maxOccurs="1"/>
                <element ref="mov:Nationality" minOccurs="1" maxOccurs="1"/>
            </sequence>
        </complexType>
    </element>
    <element name="Movie">
        <complexType>
            <sequence>
                <element ref="mov:Title" minOccurs="1" maxOccurs="1"/>
                <element ref="mov:Genre" minOccurs="1" maxOccurs="1"/>
                <element ref="mov:Year" minOccurs="1" maxOccurs="1"/>
                <element ref="mov:Director" minOccurs="1" maxOccurs="1"/>
            </sequence>
        </complexType>
    </element>
</schema>
```

Each component is defined individually, and then they are assembled together. This resembles cutting the definition of the root element into many slices, hence the name "Salami Slice" design. This approach facilitates component reuse, but namespaces of all elements will be required in instance documents.

With this design, the instance document would look like this:

```
<mov:Movie xmlns:mov="http://www.movieCatalog.org">
    <mov:Title>The Siamese Connection</mov:Title>
    <mov:Genre>Drama</mov:Genre>
    <mov:Year>1997</mov:Year>
    <mov:Director>
        <mov:Name>Syrup Bionsen</mov:Name>
        <mov:Nationality>Danish</mov:Nationality>
    </mov:Director>
</mov:Movie>
```

The Venetian Blind Design

The third design strategy both facilitates hiding namespace complexity, and achieving component reuse. The root element is disassembled into components, but instead of defining elements globally, *types* are defined globally:

```
<schema xmlns="http://www.w3.org/2000/10/XMLSchema"
    elementFormDefault="unqualified"
    xmlns:mov="http://www.movieCatalog.org">
    <simpleType name="Title">
        <restriction base="string">
            <minLength value="1"/>
        </restriction>
    </simpleType>
    <simpleType name="Genre">
        <restriction base="string">
            <minLength value="1"/>
        </restriction>
    </simpleType>
    <simpleType name="Year">
        <restriction base="year"/>
    </simpleType>
    <simpleType name="Name">
        <restriction base="string">
            <minLength value="1"/>
        </restriction>
    </simpleType>
    <simpleType name="Nationality">
        <restriction base="string">
            <minLength value="1"/>
        </restriction>
    </simpleType>

    <complexType name="Person">
        <sequence>
            <element name="Name" type="mov:Name" minOccurs="1" maxOccurs="1"/>
            <element name="Nationality" type="mov:Nationality" minOccurs="1"
             maxOccurs="1"/>
        </sequence>
    </complexType>
```

```
    <complexType name="Movie">
       <sequence>
          <element name="Title" type="mov:Title" minOccurs="1" maxOccurs="1"/>
          <element name="Genre" type="mov:Genre" minOccurs="1" maxOccurs="1"/>
          <element name="Year" type="mov:Year" minOccurs="1" maxOccurs="1"/>
          <element name="Director" type="mov:Person" minOccurs="1"
           maxOccurs="1"/>
       </sequence>
    </complexType>

    <element name="Movie" type="mov:Movie"/>
 </schema>
```

The `elementFormDefault` attribute of the `<schema>` element can be used to control namespace exposure. This approach both maximizes reuse, and nests element declarations within type definitions obviating the need to use the namespace qualifier within an element declaration.

With this design, the instance document would look like this:

```
<mov:Movie xmlns:mov="http://www.movieCatalog.org">
     <Title>The Siamese Connection</Title>
     <Genre>Drama</Genre>
     <Year>1997</Year>
     <Director>
          <Name>Syrup Bionsen</Name>
          <Nationality>Danish</Nationality>
     </Director>
</mov:Movie>
```

If we turn on namespace exposure by setting `elementFormDefault="qualified"`, then the instance document would look like this:

```
<Movie xmlns:mov="http://www.movieCatalog.org">
     <Title>The Siamese Connection</Title>
     <Genre>Drama</Genre>
     <Year>1997</Year>
     <Director>
          <Name>Syrup Bionsen</Name>
          <Nationality>Danish</Nationality>
     </Director>
</Movie>
```

Choosing Between the Different Designs

Here are the key factors to consider when choosing between these design methodologies:

❑   If you need to minimize the size of the schema, and low coupling is important, then the Russian Doll design should be used.

❑   If you need to offer to document authors the option to use synonyms/aliases for the tag names, the Salami Slice design should be used.

❑   If your schemas require the flexibility to turn namespace exposure on/off with a simple switch, and component reuse is important, the Venetian Blind design should be used.

The Transformation

Now that we've seen the basic schema design strategies, we're ready to design the stylesheet that will perform the transformation from the schema to the XML object instance. We should note, though, that our stylesheet will not follow every little detail of the schema specification here. It is a more general schema-to-instance stylesheet to illustrate the principles involved.

So, let's have a look at the schema we are going to be transforming (`catalogSchema.xsd`). To make things a little bit harder and more interesting, we have designed the schema using a mix of the three design approaches mentioned above, and added some object extensions:

```
<?xml version="1.0" encoding="UTF-8"?>
<schema xmlns="http://www.w3.org/2000/10/XMLSchema">

  <!-- Type declarations -->
  <element name="Vehicle" abstract="true" type="VehicleType"/>
  <element name="Car" substitutionGroup="Vehicle" type="CarType"/>
  <element name="SpaceShip" substitutionGroup="Vehicle" type="SpaceShipType"/>

  <element name="Catalog">
    <complexType>
      <sequence>
        <element ref="Vehicle" maxOccurs="unbounded"/>
      </sequence>
    </complexType>
  </element>

  <!-- Type definitions -->
  <complexType name="VehicleType">
    <sequence>
      <element name="Manufacturer" type="string"/>
      <element name="MaxSpeed" type="positiveInteger"/>
      <element name="Capacity" type="positiveInteger"/>
    </sequence>
  </complexType>

  <complexType name="CarType">
    <complexContent>
      <extension base="VehicleType">
        <sequence>
          <element name="Tires" type="string"/>
          <element name="Engine" type="string"/>
        </sequence>
        <attribute name="color" type="string" value="black"/>
      </extension>
    </complexContent>
  </complexType>

  <complexType name="SpaceShipType">
    <complexContent>
      <extension base="VehicleType">
        <sequence>
          <element name="WarpCore" type="string"/>
          <element name="LaserCannons" type="string"/>
        </sequence>
      </extension>
    </complexContent>
  </complexType>
</schema>
```

The <Catalog> element is a variable content container. It can only contain <Vehicle> elements, but as the <Vehicle> element is declared to be abstract, it cannot be instantiated. This is because the <Vehicle> element serves only as a guideline for the elements that implement it; that is, we always have some kind of vehicle, not just a vehicle. The <Car> and <SpaceShip> elements are declared to be in a substitution group for the <Vehicle> element, which means that they can be substituted or used in place of the <Vehicle> element. Their types are extensions of the VehicleType – that is they add their specific elements to the base abstract <Vehicle> element. We could later extend the schema by adding more vehicle extensions.

To sum up, our catalog can contain any elements that implement or extend the <Vehicle> element which here is either the <SpaceShip> or the <Car>. Therefore, its content is not constant, but variable (the objects it contains are of varying type). This is why the <Catalog> element is known as a variable content container.

Now, let's have a look at the stylesheet (schema-to-instance.xsl) which transforms the above schema into an XML instance:

```
<xsl:stylesheet xmlns:xsl="http://www.w3.org/1999/XSL/Transform"
  xmlns:xsd="http://www.w3.org/2000/10/XMLSchema"
  version="1.0"
  exclude-result-prefixes="xsd">
<xsl:output method="xml" indent="yes"/>
```

We are declaring the xsd namespace, which will be mapped onto the default namespace in the schema. Also, we set exclude-result-prefixes="xsd" to prevent the output document from using this namespace.

First, we receive the name of the outermost element of the object to be instantiated through the following parameter:

```
<xsl:param name="objectRoot" select="'Car'"/>
```

Now that we have the outermost element we can proceed. Let's have a look at the first template:

```
<xsl:template match="xsd:schema">
   <xsl:choose>
      <xsl:when test="xsd:element[@name=$objectRoot and @abstract='true']">
         Abstract elements can not be instantiated!
      </xsl:when>
      <xsl:otherwise>
         <xsl:apply-templates select="xsd:element[@name=$objectRoot]"/>
      </xsl:otherwise>
   </xsl:choose>
</xsl:template>
```

Note that we have to use the xsd namespace prefix for matching, because xsd is the default namespace of the schema. This template selects the element specified as the outermost element of the object to be instantiated by the $objectRoot parameter, and applies a template to that specific element. We first perform a check to see if it is an abstract element and print an error message if so ending the transformation, since an abstract element cannot be instantiated. If the element is not abstract, we proceed with the transformation.

We have three different templates to transform elements. The first one transforms elements that have local element declarations nested within them (Russian Doll design):

```
<xsl:template match="xsd:element[@name]">
  <xsl:if test="not(@minOccurs) or @minOccurs > 0">
  <xsl:element name="{@name}">
      <xsl:call-template name="process-attributes">
         <xsl:with-param name="parent" select="current()"/>
      </xsl:call-template>
      <xsl:apply-templates select="*"/>
  </xsl:element>
  </xsl:if>
</xsl:template>
```

This template matches every element that has a name (which is every element, but other templates overload this to handle elements that additionally have a type or reference). We will only create an instance of this element if minOccurs is greater than 0 (note that 1 is the default value, so if the attribute is not present we can continue). We then create the element with the `<xsl:element>` element, and call a named template defined later to set up the attributes.

The second template transforms elements that reference globally declared elements (Salami Slice design):

```
<xsl:template match="xsd:element[@ref]">
  <xsl:if test="not(@minOccurs) or @minOccurs > 0">
  <xsl:choose>
    <xsl:when test="/xsd:schema/ sd:element[@name=current()/@ref]/
    @abstract='true'">
        Unable to determine which element to instantiate.
    </xsl:when>
    <xsl:otherwise>
      <xsl:apply-templates select="/xsd:schema/xsd:element[@name=
      current()/@ref]"/>
    </xsl:otherwise>
  </xsl:choose>
  </xsl:if>
</xsl:template>
```

Notice that we check if the element being referenced is declared as abstract. If that is the case, we do not know which of the extending elements is to be instantiated, and therefore we print an error message and abort the transformation. In any other case, we proceed to apply templates to the element being referenced.

The third and final template matches elements that are defined to be of a specific type (Venetian Blind design):

```
<xsl:template match="xsd:element[@name and @type]">
   <xsl:if test="not(@minOccurs) or @minOccurs > 0">
   <xsl:choose>
     <xsl:when test="/xsd:schema/xsd:complexType[@name=current()/@type]">
        <xsl:element name="{@name}">
           <xsl:apply-templates
           select="/xsd:schema/xsd:complexType[@name=current()/@type]"/>
        </xsl:element>
     </xsl:when>
     <xsl:otherwise>
        <xsl:element name="{@name}"/>
     </xsl:otherwise>
   </xsl:choose>
   </xsl:if>
</xsl:template>
```

If we cannot find the type that the element is declared to be, we make an empty instance. Notice again that in the templates above we have decided that if an element's minOccurs attribute is zero, we do not create an instance of the element. Otherwise we create exactly one instance. This can, of course, be tailored to fit each application's needs.

The rest of the stylesheet is pretty straightforward:

```
<xsl:template match="xsd:complexContent">
   <xsl:apply-templates select="*"/>
</xsl:template>

<xsl:template match="xsd:complexType">
   <xsl:call-template name="process-attributes">
      <xsl:with-param name="parent" select="current()"/>
   </xsl:call-template>
   <xsl:apply-templates select="*"/>
</xsl:template>

<xsl:template match="xsd:sequence">
   <xsl:apply-templates select="*"/>
</xsl:template>

<xsl:template match="xsd:choice">
   <xsl:apply-templates select="*"/>
</xsl:template>

<xsl:template match="xsd:all">
   <xsl:apply-templates select="*"/>
</xsl:template>
```

These templates handle different schema elements, and all of them simply proceed with processing except for the template that handles the <complexType> element. It first calls a named template that handles the attributes and then proceeds with the processing. Let's take a look at the template to handle exceptions:

```
<xsl:template match="xsd:extension">
   <xsl:call-template name="process-attributes">
      <xsl:with-param name="parent" select="current()"/>
   </xsl:call-template>
   <xsl:apply-templates
    select="/xsd:schema/xsd:complexType[@name=current()/@base]"/>
   <xsl:apply-templates select="*"/>
</xsl:template>
```

Remember that the <Car> and <SpaceShip> elements extended the <Vehicle> element, so they inherit the child elements of <Vehicle> and add some elements specific to their type. First we call the named template to handle attributes, and then we simply select the global complexType that matches the value of the base attribute. The reason for using a named template for attribute handling should now be clear: we need to handle attributes in three places, and instead of duplicating the attribute handling code each time, we write a named template, which we then call. In this way, named templates facilitate maintenance tasks greatly, and the code becomes much more readable. Here is the named template process-attributes now:

```
<xsl:template name="process-attributes">
  <xsl:param name="parent"/>
  <xsl:for-each select="$parent/attribute">
    <xsl:variable name="attributeName" select="@name"/>
    <xsl:variable name="attributeValue" select="@value"/>
    <xsl:attribute name="{$attributeName}">
    <xsl:if test="$attributeValue">
      <xsl:value-of select="$attributeValue"/>
    </xsl:if>
    </xsl:attribute>
  </xsl:for-each>
</xsl:template>

</xsl:stylesheet>
```

Obviously, the stylesheet does not support global attributes, named model groups, etc., which would be relatively simple additions to the stylesheet, and as a further exercise, you may wish to further customize the stylesheet to incorporate such features.

Now to test our stylesheet, we invoke the `Process` component of the Xalan processor:

C:\MyCode> java org.apache.xalan.xslt.Process –in catalogSchema.xsd
–xsl schema-to-instance.xsl –out result.xml

The result will be written to the file `result.xml`. Don't forget that in order to make this work, the `xalan.jar` file must be included in your `CLASSPATH` environment variable.

Generating Schemas from XML Documents

A problem related to creating an XML instance document from a schema is the inverse process of building a schema from an instance document. This may seem a bit strange, but dynamically generating schemas in this way can provide a very neat solution that saves a lot of time.

The result of this transformation is not likely to be a fully finished schema, as many structural relationships cannot be deduced directly from the instance document but this technique is nonetheless useful for creating a skeleton from which a finalized schema can be produced.

Now, let's have a look at one way to accomplish this task. The following stylesheet (`instance-to-schema.xsl`) generates a schema from an instance document (don't worry if you have trouble understanding the code, it is all explained below!):

```
<xsl:stylesheet xmlns:xsl="http://www.w3.org/1999/XSL/Transform"
  version="1.0">

  <xsl:strip-space elements="*"/>
  <xsl:output method="xml" indent="yes"/>
```

```
<xsl:template match="/">
   <xsl:element name="schema">
      <xsl:attribute name="xmlns">
        <xsl:value-of select="'http://www.w3.org/2000/10/XMLSchema'"/>
      </xsl:attribute>
      <xsl:for-each select="*">
         <xsl:call-template name="process-element">
            <xsl:with-param name="theElement" select="current()"/>
            <xsl:with-param name="theElementName" select="name()"/>
         </xsl:call-template>
      </xsl:for-each>
   </xsl:element>
</xsl:template>

<xsl:template name="process-element">
   <xsl:param name="theElement"/>
   <xsl:param name="theElementName"/>
   <!-- If the element contains children, then use a sequence tag -->
   <xsl:choose>
      <xsl:when test="count($theElement/text()) = 0">
         <xsl:element name="element">
            <xsl:attribute name="name">
               <xsl:value-of select="$theElementName"/>
            </xsl:attribute>
            <xsl:element name="sequence">
               <xsl:for-each select="$theElement/*">
                  <xsl:variable name="currentName" select="name()"/>
                  <xsl:variable name="position" select="position()"/>
                  <xsl:variable name="relativePosition"
                   select="count($theElement/*[name()=$currentName
                   and position() &lt; $position]) + 1"/>
                  <xsl:variable name="lastPosition"
                   select="count($theElement/*[name()=$currentName])"/>
                  <xsl:if test="$relativePosition = $lastPosition">
                     <xsl:call-template name="process-element">
                        <xsl:with-param name="theElement"
                         select="current()"/>
                        <xsl:with-param name="theElementName"
                         select="name()"/>
                     </xsl:call-template>
                  </xsl:if>
               </xsl:for-each>
            </xsl:element>
            <xsl:call-template name="process-attributes">
               <xsl:with-param name="theElement" select="$theElement"/>
            </xsl:call-template>
         </xsl:element>
      </xsl:when>
      <xsl:otherwise>
         <xsl:element name="element">
            <xsl:attribute name="name">
               <xsl:value-of select="$theElementName"/>
            </xsl:attribute>
            <xsl:call-template name="process-attributes">
               <xsl:with-param name="theElement" select="$theElement"/>
            </xsl:call-template>
```

```
            </xsl:element>
          </xsl:otherwise>
      </xsl:choose>
    </xsl:template>

    <!-- Handle attributes -->
    <xsl:template name="process-attributes">
      <xsl:param name="theElement"/>

      <xsl:for-each select="$theElement/@*">
        <xsl:element name="attribute">
          <xsl:attribute name="name">
            <xsl:value-of select="name()"/>
          </xsl:attribute>
          <xsl:attribute name="type">string</xsl:attribute>
        </xsl:element>
      </xsl:for-each>

    </xsl:template>
  </xsl:stylesheet>
```

This stylesheet designs the schema using the Russian Doll approach of nested element declarations. Let's have a look at the first template:

```
<xsl:template match="/">
  <xsl:element name="schema">
    <xsl:attribute name="xmlns">
      <xsl:value-of select="'http://www.w3.org/2000/10/XMLSchema'"/>
    </xsl:attribute>
    <xsl:for-each select="*">
      <xsl:call-template name="process-element">
        <xsl:with-param name="theElement" select="current()"/>
        <xsl:with-param name="theElementName" select="name()"/>
      </xsl:call-template>
    </xsl:for-each>
  </xsl:element>
</xsl:template>
```

This template creates the <schema> element with the default namespace attribute, and then for each child element it calls the process-element named template, which recursively creates the element declarations. This more complex process-element template is where most of the work is done. It receives two parameters:

```
<xsl:param name="theElement"/>
<xsl:param name="theElementName"/>
```

The theElement parameter contains the element to be processed, and the parameter theElementName contains the name of that element. Now we have an <xsl:choose> element with a single <xsl:when> element to handle the case when theElement contains child elements. The simpler case of text only is handled in the <xsl:otherwise> clause reprinted now:

```
<xsl:otherwise>
   <xsl:element name="element">
      <xsl:attribute name="name">
         <xsl:value-of select="$theElementName"/>
      </xsl:attribute>
      <xsl:call-template name="process-attributes">
         <xsl:with-param name="theElement" select="$theElement"/>
      </xsl:call-template>
   </xsl:element>
</xsl:otherwise>
```

Since the element contains just text data, we simply create the element with the name attribute. We don't specify the type, since the default type of elements is string. We finally call a named template to handle the attributes. Now let's look at that tricky `<xsl:when>` clause:

```
<xsl:when test="count($theElement/text()) = 0">
   <xsl:element name="element">
      <xsl:attribute name="name">
         <xsl:value-of select="$theElementName"/>
      </xsl:attribute>
      <xsl:element name="sequence">
         <xsl:for-each select="$theElement/*">
            <xsl:variable name="currentName" select="name()"/>
            <xsl:variable name="position" select="position()"/>
            <xsl:variable name="relativePosition" select="count($theElement/*
              [name()=$currentName and position() &lt; $position]) + 1"/>
            <xsl:variable name="lastPosition" select="count($theElement/*
              [name()=$currentName])"/>
            <xsl:if test="$relativePosition = $lastPosition">
               <xsl:call-template name="process-element">
                  <xsl:with-param name="theElement" select="current()"/>
                  <xsl:with-param name="theElementName" select="name()"/>
               </xsl:call-template>
            </xsl:if>
         </xsl:for-each>
      </xsl:element>
      <xsl:call-template name="process-attributes">
         <xsl:with-param name="theElement" select="$theElement"/>
      </xsl:call-template>
   </xsl:element>
</xsl:when>
```

The test in the `<xsl:when>` clause counts the text contained within the element. If the result of the counting is zero, the element contains only child elements. The first task is to create the element, and add the name attribute with the correct value (theElementName). Then we create a `<sequence>` element, containing definitions for child elements and the order in which they must appear.

The next step is to run through all the child elements of theElement, select the last instance of each element type and apply the process-elements template recursively to that instance. Let's have a closer look. We create a number of variables that need further explaining, currentName contains the name of the element, and position contains its position among all elements at the same level. relativePosition, on the other hand, contains the relative position of the element among elements at the same level *with the same name as this element*. Finally lastPosition contains the position of the last element at the same level with the same name.

The `<xsl:if>` clause in the `<xsl:when>` block checks whether the element is the last element of its type. If so, we call the `process-element` template with that element as a parameter. This way we work our way through the elements with no danger of defining the same XML object twice. Notice that we use the last element instance of its type to create the definition, but we could have just as equally selected the first instance. The final template for us to look at is the `process-attributes` named template:

```
<xsl:template name="process-attributes">
    <xsl:param name="theElement"/>

    <xsl:for-each select="$theElement/@*">
        <xsl:element name="attribute">
            <xsl:attribute name="name">
                <xsl:value-of select="name()"/>
            </xsl:attribute>
            <xsl:attribute name="type">string</xsl:attribute>
        </xsl:element>
    </xsl:for-each>

</xsl:template>
```

It simply creates attribute elements with the correct names, defining each as `string`.

So, if we apply our stylesheet (`instance-to-schema.xsl`) to the following instance document (`sample-instance.xml`):

```
<Catalog>
    <Car id="2311" color="red">
        <Manufacturer>Mercedes</Manufacturer>
        <MaxSpeed>220 km/h</MaxSpeed>
        <Capacity>5</Capacity>
        <Tires>Michelin</Tires>
        <Engine>V8</Engine>
    </Car>
    <Car id="2312" color="black">
        <Manufacturer>Volvo</Manufacturer>
        <MaxSpeed>220 km/h</MaxSpeed>
        <Capacity>5</Capacity>
        <Tires>GoodYear</Tires>
        <Engine>V8</Engine>
    </Car>
</Catalog>
```

we create the following output:

```
<?xml version="1.0"?>
<schema xmlns="http://www.w3.org/2000/10/XMLSchema">
    <element name="Catalog">
    <sequence>
        <element name="Car">
        <sequence>
            <element name="Manufacturer"/>
            <element name="MaxSpeed"/>
            <element name="Capacity"/>
            <element name="Tires"/>
```

```
            <element name="Engine"/>
        </sequence>
        <attribute name="id" type="string"/>
        <attribute name="color" type="string"/>
        </element>
      </sequence>
      </element>
    </schema>
```

This looks fine, but our stylesheet would not be able to create a good schema for variable content containers (such as the catalog from the last section), with extensions and substitution groups. Although our transformation does not handle complex schemas, it will be useful for creating a skeleton schema very quickly from XML instance documents.

Generating Stylesheets for Schema Validation

In this section we are going to create a stylesheet that generates a **validation stylesheet** from a schema. The resulting stylesheet can then be applied at runtime to instance documents that claim to conform to that schema. The stylesheet will return an XML document containing a list of all invalid elements found.

One might wonder whether this task is not just a waste of time, since many parsers have built-in schema validation. However, there are many different schema languages available (such as XRD, Schematron, RELAX, TREX, etc.), and parsers do not support all of these languages – not yet, at least. The stylesheet-based schema validator is independent and portable – any XML environment that supports XSLT can be used to generate and run validators from XML schemas, and these validators will behave in exactly the same way regardless of parser supplier. This approach is useful for basic structural validation, although it can't provide a means of enforcing data constraints.

The following stylesheet (generate-validator.xsl) generates a schema validator:

```
<xsl:stylesheet version="1.0"
  xmlns:xsl="http://www.w3.org/1999/XSL/Transform"
  xmlns:xsd="http://www.w3.org/2000/10/XMLSchema"
  exclude-result-prefixes="xsd"
  xmlns:out="result.xsl">

  <xsl:namespace-alias stylesheet-prefix="out" result-prefix="xsl"/>

  <xsl:param name="documentRoot" select="'Movies'"/>

  <xsl:template match="/xsd:schema">
    <out:stylesheet version="1.0">
      <out:template match="/">
        <out:apply-templates select="*"/>
      </out:template>
      <out:template match="*">
        ***** Illegal element: *****
        <out:for-each select="ancestor-or-self::*">
          <out:value-of select="name()"/><out:text>/</out:text>
        </out:for-each>
        ************************
      </out:template>
```

```
      <xsl:call-template name="process-element">
        <xsl:with-param name="theElement"
         select="xsd:element[@name=$documentRoot]"/>
        <xsl:with-param name="fullPath" select="$documentRoot"/>
      </xsl:call-template>
    </out:stylesheet>
  </xsl:template>
</xsl:template>

<xsl:template name="process-element">
  <xsl:param name="theElement"/>
  <xsl:param name="fullPath"/>

  <!-- process element with nested definition within -->
  <xsl:if test="$theElement/@name">
    <out:template match="{$fullPath}">
      <out:apply-templates select="*"/>
    </out:template>
    <xsl:if test="$theElement/xsd:complexType">
      <xsl:for-each
        select="$theElement/xsd:complexType/xsd:sequence/xsd:element">
        <xsl:choose>
          <xsl:when test="@ref">
            <xsl:call-template name="process-element">
              <xsl:with-param name="theElement"
               select="/xsd:schema/xsd:element[@name=current()/@ref]"/>
              <xsl:with-param name="fullPath"
               select="concat($fullPath,'/',current()/@ref)"/>
            </xsl:call-template>
          </xsl:when>
          <xsl:otherwise>
            <xsl:call-template name="process-element">
              <xsl:with-param name="theElement" select="current()"/>
              <xsl:with-param name="fullPath"
               select="concat($fullPath,'/',@name)"/>
            </xsl:call-template>
          </xsl:otherwise>
        </xsl:choose>
      </xsl:for-each>
    </xsl:if>
  </xsl:if>

  <!-- process element of a specific type -->
  <xsl:if test="$theElement/@name and $theElement/@type">
    <xsl:if test="/xsd:schema/xsd:complexType[@name=$theElement/@type]">
      <xsl:for-each
       select="/xsd:schema/xsd:complexType[@name=$theElement/@type]
       /xsd:sequence/xsd:element">
        <xsl:choose>
          <xsl:when test="@ref">
            <xsl:call-template name="process-element">
              <xsl:with-param name="theElement"
               select="/xsd:schema/xsd:element[@name=current()/@ref]"/>
              <xsl:with-param name="fullPath"
               select="concat($fullPath,'/',current()/@ref)"/>
            </xsl:call-template>
```

519

```
          </xsl:when>
          <xsl:otherwise>
            <xsl:call-template name="process-element">
              <xsl:with-param name="theElement" select="current()"/>
              <xsl:with-param name="fullPath"
               select="concat($fullPath,'/',@name)"/>
            </xsl:call-template>
          </xsl:otherwise>
        </xsl:choose>
      </xsl:for-each>
    </xsl:if>
  </xsl:if>
</xsl:template>

</xsl:stylesheet>
```

The basic idea here is to recursively work our way down the tree, keeping the full path of the current location. Notice that since we are creating a stylesheet with a stylesheet, we use the `<xsl:namespace-alias/>` element to translate our "out" namespace to the "xsl" namespace (see Chapter 10 for more detailed information on how to generate stylesheets with stylesheets). Also the root element to use as a starting point for the validation is provided as a parameter.

Let's have a look at the first template:

```
<xsl:template match="/xsd:schema">
    <out:stylesheet version="1.0">
      <out:template match="/">
        <out:apply-templates select="*"/>
      </out:template>
      <out:template match="*">
        ***** Illegal element: *****
        <out:for-each select="ancestor-or-self::*">
          <out:value-of select="name()"/><out:text>/</out:text>
        </out:for-each>
        ************************
      </out:template>
      <xsl:call-template name="process-element">
        <xsl:with-param name="theElement"
         select="xsd:element[@name=$documentRoot]"/>
        <xsl:with-param name="fullPath" select="$documentRoot"/>
      </xsl:call-template>
    </out:stylesheet>
</xsl:template>
```

This template matches the root of the schema. It creates the basic tags for the output stylesheet, such as the `<out:stylesheet>` tag. Once again, note that the namespace URI of the out prefix will be transferred to the xsl URI in the output document. And since the URI is the crucial thing – not the prefix itself – elements preceded by the out prefix in the output document will be processed as belonging to the xsl namespace.

The idea is to create a specific template for each element type in the schema, and then a template that handles all other elements (which must be illegal elements, since they have not been defined by the schema). Therefore the template:

```
<out:template match="*">
  ***** Illegal element: *****
  <out:for-each select="ancestor-or-self::*">
    <out:value-of select="name()"/><out:text>/</out:text>
  </out:for-each>
  ************************
</out:template>
```

prints an error message for any element not handled by another template. The message includes the full path of the illegal element to facilitate tracing. We gain access to all ancestors with the XPath axis `ancestor-or-self`. Below this we call the `process-element` template, which recursively prints templates to match each element type specified by the schema.

Now, let's have a closer look at the `process-element` template. It receives two parameters: `theElement` (the element being processed) and `fullPath` (the full path to this element). The template is made up of two big `<out:if>` clauses.

The first one should handle elements that contain nested element declarations within, and elements that have no children. It first outputs the template for the element being processed, then checks whether the element is a complex type (contains children or attributes). If so, we loop through all the element declarations nested within. If an element encountered is a reference to another element, we recursively call the `process-elements` template for the element being referenced, otherwise we call the template for the element itself.

The second clause is designed to handle elements that are defined as a specific type. If we find a complex type in the schema matching the type of the current element, we loop through each element defined within that complex type. Again, if an element encountered is a reference to another element, we recursively call the `process-elements` template for the referenced element, or else we call the template with the element itself.

To understand how this works, let's see the result of transforming the following schema (`movieSchema.xsd`):

```xml
<?xml version="1.0" encoding="UTF-8"?>
<schema xmlns="http://www.w3.org/2000/10/XMLSchema">
   <element name="Movies">
      <complexType>
         <sequence>
            <element name="Movie" type="MovieType" maxOccurs="unbounded"/>
         </sequence>
      </complexType>
   </element>

   <complexType name="MovieType">
      <sequence>
         <element name="Name" type="string"/>
         <element name="Genre" type="string"/>
         <element name="Actors">
            <complexType>
            <sequence>
               <element ref="Actor"/>
            </sequence>
            </complexType>
         </element>
```

```
            </sequence>
        </complexType>

    <element name="Actor">
        <complexType>
            <sequence>
                <element name="Name" type="string"/>
                <element name="Age" type="string"/>
            </sequence>
        </complexType>
    </element>
</schema>
```

Transforming the above schema with the `generate-validator.xsd` schema would produce the following validating stylesheet:

```
<?xml version="1.0" encoding="UTF-8"?>
<out:stylesheet xmlns:out="http://www.w3.org/1999/XSL/Transform"
 version="1.0">
    <out:template match="/">
        <out:apply-templates select="*"/>
    </out:template>
    <out:template match="*">
        ***** Illegal element: *****
        <out:for-each select="ancestor-or-self::*">
            <out:value-of select="name()" /><out:text>/</out:text>
        </out:for-each>
        *************************
    </out:template>
    <out:template match="Movies">
        <out:apply-templates select="*"/>
    </out:template>
    <out:template match="Movies/Movie">
        <out:apply-templates select="*"/>
    </out:template>
    <out:template match="Movies/Movie/Name">
        <out:apply-templates select="*"/>
    </out:template>
    <out:template match="Movies/Movie/Genre">
        <out:apply-templates select="*"/>
    </out:template>
    <out:template match="Movies/Movie/Actors">
        <out:apply-templates select="*"/>
    </out:template>
    <out:template match="Movies/Movie/Actors/Actor">
        <out:apply-templates select="*"/>
    </out:template>
    <out:template match="Movies/Movie/Actors/Actor/Name">
        <out:apply-templates select="*"/>
    </out:template>
    <out:template match="Movies/Movie/Actors/Actor/Age">
        <out:apply-templates select="*"/>
    </out:template>
</out:stylesheet>
```

So, the stylesheet creates another stylesheet that contains a template for each element in the schema. When we use this validating stylesheet to transform an XML instance document conforming to the "movie" schema, all elements that don't have a special template to process them produce the "Illegal element" output due to the rules of template precedence outlined in Chapter 5. However, if no errors are found in the instance document, the validator produces an empty document.

The following is an example output with invalid elements:

```
<?xml version="1.0" encoding="UTF-8"?>

        ***** Illegal element: *****
        Movies/Movie/PhoneNumber/
        *************************

        ***** Illegal element: *****
        Movies/Movie/Actors/Editor/
        *************************

        ***** Illegal element: *****
        Movies/Movie/Actor/
        *************************
```

There are some pretty major limitations to this validator stylesheet. The validator only checks for invalid elements – it doesn't check for required attributes, and it doesn't complain if a required element is missing. It would be possible to further develop the stylesheet to meet these requirements, but this validator generator should be sufficient for performing basic structural validation. In the next section we will look at a way to provide a more comprehensive check.

Enforcing Data Integrity Constraints

In this section we will take a closer look at how we can combine XSLT with **regular expressions** to ensure that specific data (such as dates, IP numbers, etc.) is in the correct format, that is, that it conforms to the expected pattern. Here we will use a Xalan Java extension for processing regular expressions. We will start with a brief introduction to regular expressions, then see how they are used in schemas, before finally looking at an example of how they may be used with XSLT to enforce the data integrity constraints defined within a schema.

Regular Expressions – A Brief Introduction

Regular expressions (shortened to "regex" within the geek community) are pattern descriptions that enable sophisticated string matching. They are commonly associated with UNIX-based tools, such as editors, scripting languages, and shell programs. But this is not to say that regular expressions are not for the "common people". In fact, if you've ever used wildcards such as `copy *.html *.bak` from the command prompt, or entered text such as `solar array?` into a web-based search engine, you've already used a simple regular expression.

I'm not going to dive too deeply into the topic of regular expressions, but I'll list a few basic examples to help you get the idea.

Some Simple Examples

Regular Expressions are made up of a sequence of text characters, some of which have special meaning. The most common of the special characters are:

Character	Meaning
\d	Any digit (0-9)
\D	Any non-digit
\s	A whitespace character
\S	Anything that is not a whitespace character
\w	Letters, numbers, underscores
\W	Anything that does not match with \w
.	Any *one* character
^	Nothing before this character
$	Nothing after this character
+	One or more
*	Zero or more
?	Zero or one

I could go on all day with these. Now let's have a look at how they might be used:

Regular Expression	Matching Strings
A*B	B, AB, AAB, AAAB, ...
A+B	AB, AAB, AAAB, ...
A?B	B *or* AB
[DEF]B	DB, EB, *or* FB
[D-F]B	DB, EB, *or* FB
[2-4]B	2B, 3B, *or* 4B
Number\s\d	Number 1,... (not Number1 or Number R)
(A|C)B	AB *or* CB
(1a\s){2}	la la
(1a\s){1-3}	la, la la, *or* la la la

OK, I hope these examples (although simple) have given you some idea of the power of regular expressions. Now, let's explore how they can be used with schemas.

Regular Expressions in Schemas

The combination of regular expressions and XSLT makes for a powerful resource. They are very useful for searching XML documents, since they can be used to check whether individual strings conform to a specific pattern.

The `string` schema data type allows a pattern to be specified that elements of that type must match, and this pattern is described using regular expressions. Here is such a definition for an element that could be included in a schema:

```
<simpleType name="phoneNumberType">
   <restriction base="string">
      <pattern value="^\d{3}-\d{7}$"/>
   </restriction>
</simpleType>
```

This type describes a phone number. The phone numbers that this type describes are given by the regular expression `^\d{3}-\d{7}$`, meaning that they should start with three digits (the area code), followed by a hyphen (-), and finally seven digits. The "`^`" character means that nothing may come before the expression, while $ means that nothing may follow the expression. So, the number 553-1235267123 conforms to this pattern, but both 5F4-1238899123 and 555-12388888 would be invalid.

Let's say that we have an XML document that contains a list of host computers with their associated domain names and IP addresses. The following schema (`hostSchema.xsd`) describes the document:

```
<schema xmlns="http://www.w3.org/2000/10/XMLSchema">
   <element name="Hosts">
      <sequence>
         <element name="Host" type="HostType"/>
      </sequence>
   </element>

   <complexType name="HostType">
      <sequence>
         <element name="DateAdded" type="DateType"/>
         <element name="Domain" type="DomainType"/>
         <element name="IPAddress" type="IPAddressType"/>
      </sequence>
   </complexType>

   <simpleType name="DateType">
      <restriction base="string">
         <pattern value="^\d{2}\.\d{2}\.\d{4}$"/>
      </restriction>
   </simpleType>

   <simpleType name="DomainType">
      <restriction base="string">
         <pattern value="^((\w+)\.)+\w+$"/>
      </restriction>
   </simpleType>
```

```
    <simpleType name="IPAddressType">
       <restriction base="string">
          <pattern value="^((([1-9]?[0-9]|1[0-9][0-9]|2[0-4][0-9]|
             25[0-5])\.){3}([1-9]?[0-9]|1[0-9][0-9]|2[0-4][0-9]|25[0-5])$"/>
       </restriction>
    </simpleType>
</schema>
```

Now, we wish to validate the domain name and the IP address against the specified patterns, and we wish to do so from a stylesheet. For this purpose we need to use Java extensions.

Xalan Java Extensions

Here we will look at how to use Xalan Java extensions. We will begin by creating a new Java class, and then I will show how we can call its methods from a stylesheet. To process the regular expressions in our Java class we will use the regular expressions package from Jakarta (`jakarta-regexp-1.1.jar`), which can be downloaded from http://jakarta.apache.org. This `jar` file needs to be on the system classpath, as does our new class that we will write next. Now, let's look at the Java class that will be performing the pattern matching (`Validator.java`):

```java
import org.apache.regexp.*;
import java.util.Hashtable;

public class Validator {

    Hashtable regExpressions;

    /** Constructor **/
    public Validator() {
       regExpressions = new Hashtable();
    }

    /**
     * Adds a new regular expression to the Hashtable.
     */
    public void addRegExp( String name, String pattern )
            throws RESyntaxException {

        // test the expression (an RESyntaxException is thrown
        // if the pattern is invalid):
        RE r = new RE(pattern);
        regExpressions.put( name,r );
    }

    /**
     * @param    name the name of a regular expression already added
     *           with the newRegExp() method
     * @param    str some string to be validated
     * @return    true if str matches the regular expression, else false.
     */
    public boolean match( String regExpName, String str )
            throws IllegalArgumentException {
```

```
        RE r = (RE)regExpressions.get(regExpName);
        if ( r == null ) {
            throw new IllegalArgumentException(
    "No regular expression named '" + regExpName + "' has been added.");
        }
        return r.match(str);
    }
}
```

This class contains two methods. The addRegExp() method adds a new regular expression to a hashtable that stores all the expressions using the name parameter as the key. The match() method checks if the string passed to it matches the regular expression of the given name.

To be able to use Xalan Java extensions in our XSLT stylesheet, we need a namespace declaration for the java namespace:

```
<xsl:stylesheet xmlns:xsl="http://www.w3.org/1999/XSL/Transform"
                xmlns:java="http://xml.apache.org/xslt/java"
                version="1.0">
```

We can then declare Java variables the same way we would declare other variables. Now, to create an instance of our Validator class, we simply write:

```
<xsl:variable name="validator" select="java:Validator.new()"/>
```

Finally, methods from the Validator instance are called using <xsl:value-of> in the following way:

```
<xsl:value-of select="java:addRegExp($validator,'date','^\d{2}\.\d{2}\.\d{4}$'
)"/>
```

Note that the first parameter to a method is always the class instance itself. Now, let's head over to the validation stylesheet.

Validating the Schema

Now that our Validator class is ready, we can easily validate specific data in instance documents thanks to regular expressions. A stylesheet to validate the data in an instance document created from our schema, hostSchema.xsd, will look something like this (regExp-validator.xsl):

```
<?xml version="1.0"?>
<xsl:stylesheet xmlns:xsl="http://www.w3.org/1999/XSL/Transform"
        xmlns:java="http://xml.apache.org/xslt/java"
        exclude-result-prefixes="java"
        version="1.0">

    <xsl:strip-space elements="*"/>

    <!-- Instantiate the Validator class -->
    <xsl:variable name="validator" select="java:Validator.new()"/>
```

```
<xsl:template match="/Hosts">
    <!-- Create the regular expressions we are going to use -->
    <xsl:value-of select="java:addRegExp( $validator,'date',
      '^\d{2}\.\d{2}\.\d{4}$' )"/>
    <xsl:value-of select="java:addRegExp( $validator,'domainName',
      '^((\w+)\.)+\w+$' )"/>
    <xsl:value-of select="java:addRegExp( $validator,'IPAddress',
      '^(([1-9]?[0-9]|1[0-9][0-9]|2[0-4][0-9]|25[0-5])\.){3}
      ([1-9]?[0-9]|1[0-9][0-9]|2[0-4][0-9]|25[0-5])$' )"/>

    <!-- Start the validation -->
    <xsl:for-each select="Host">
        <xsl:if test="not( java:match( $validator,'date',DateAdded) )">
            Invalid date format: <xsl:value-of select="DateAdded"/>
        </xsl:if>
        <xsl:if test="not( java:match( $validator,'domainName',Domain) )">
            Invalid domain name: <xsl:value-of select="Domain"/>
        </xsl:if>
        <xsl:if test="not( java:match( $validator,'IPAddress',
          IPAddress) )">
            Invalid IP address: <xsl:value-of select="IPAddress"/>
        </xsl:if>
    </xsl:for-each>
</xsl:template>
</xsl:stylesheet>
```

We simply create the regular expressions to be used (they are then compiled within the Java class), and then we check if the date, domain name, and IP address are of the required format by calling the `match()` method with the appropriate parameters. So, for example, let's try transforming the following document (`hosts.xml`) with our `regExp-validator.xsl` stylesheet:

```
<?xml version="1.0"?>
<Hosts>
    <Host>
        <DateAdded>15.02.2001</DateAdded>
        <Domain>www.somedomain.com</Domain>
        <IPAddress>222.222.222.222</IPAddress>
    </Host>
    <Host>
        <DateAdded>16/12/2000</DateAdded>
        <Domain>www.domainname;com</Domain>
        <IPAddress>300.899.333.222</IPAddress>
    </Host>
</Hosts>
```

We would get the following output:

```
Invalid date format: 16/12/2000
Invalid domain name: www.domainname;com
Invalid IP address: 300.899.333.222
```

It's not difficult to use regular expressions in this way to enforce data integrity rules defined by a schema. This approach provides the fine-detail processing that XSLT lacks, leaving XSLT to take care of handling the complex hierarchical structure of an XML document. Therefore, regular expressions and XSLT make a perfect match!

Summary

In this chapter we've explored some of the useful collaboration opportunities that exist between XSL transformations and schemas. We've seen how to generate XML instance documents from schemas, and vice versa. We've also generated validation stylesheets from schemas, and seen how XSLT can be used with regular expressions to powerfully enforce the data integrity constraints of a schema.

As we'll see again in the next chapter, both XSLT and Schemas are vitally important to XML-related applications so an understanding of how they can be used together is very useful.

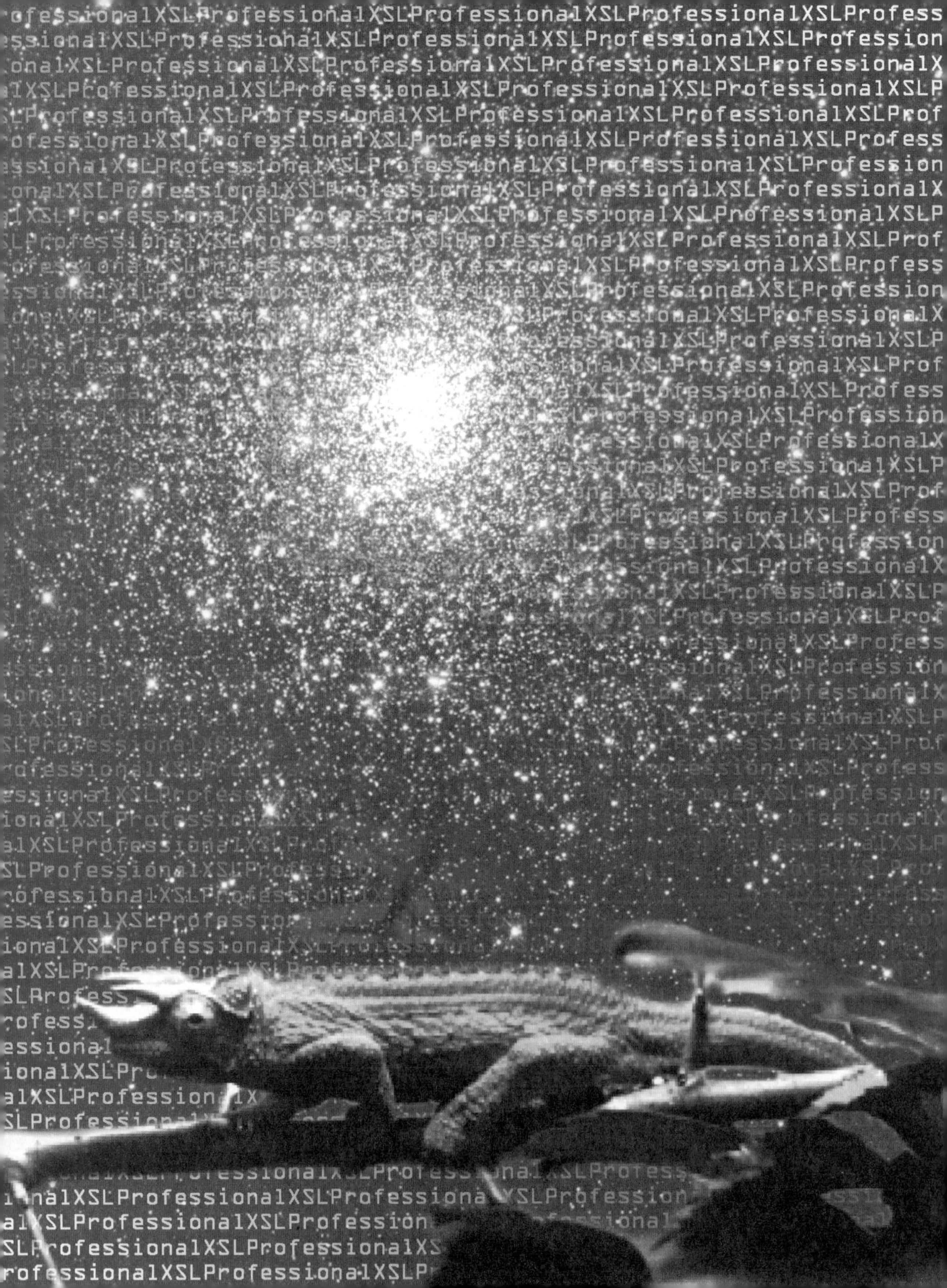

XSLT and the Future of XML

There has never been a better time to be a computer programmer. With today's technologies, not only is it possible to create exciting and powerful new applications, but you can actually be involved in the very evolution of the art of programming itself. Throughout the book you've seen how XSLT can help you to achieve the former, and in this final chapter I'll try to show you why what you've learned so far will enable you to be involved in the latter.

I would hesitate to describe the topic of this book as encompassing *XML*-based technologies, for XML, as you already know and as reiterated below, is merely a syntax, a framework for expressing information. I would prefer to characterize the book more generally, as relating to *schema*-based technologies. Schema-based technologies *are* based on XML, but go far beyond mere syntax. The word "schema" suggests structure: something that all the technologies in this book have in common in one way or another.

Whenever you create an XML file you also create a schema, even if only an implicit one resulting from your selection of element types and attribute names. Of course, you can add a formal XML Schema (itself following XML syntax) or Document Type Definition (that doesn't use XML syntax) should the need arise.

The aim of this chapter is to introduce a different way to think about programming – called **schema-based programming** (**SBP**). Everything a schema-based programmer does relates to an XML file in one way or another. SBP class files tend to have an object model that follows the structure of the corresponding XML file, and SBP source code tends to be dominated by calls to the XML parser's API (application programming interface). At the heart of some SBP applications beats one or more XSLT transforms whose declarative language means that they can be both elegant and extremely powerful. SBP is more than a collection of programming techniques and technologies: it offers a new way to think about programming problems.

This chapter is broken up into three parts. The first part contains relatively little technical detail about each of the schema-based technologies, aiming to provide an overview of the interdependency of these technologies – the absence of any one of which means that none may function.

The second part, on the other hand, is more technical, providing an example based on Petri nets (a technique for modeling processes) that involves each of the schema-based technologies covered in this book, especially XSLT.

The third part returns to a discussion of SBP by applying it to the field of Petri nets.

When you're done with this chapter I hope to have demonstrated the real difference that XSLT makes and that you will be even more excited and intrigued about the topic and technologies from the rest of the book.

Taking XSLT Out of the Box

The principle goal of this chapter is to encourage you to think 'out of the box' about XSLT. Nearly all of the current XSLT literature is built around e-business and web page construction issues. This is not surprising since these issues are the easiest to grasp and the most urgent to solve. This book concentrates on the use of XSLT for such purposes, because it is what a programmer today really needs to know. But the future of XSLT goes far beyond e-commerce and web page development. XML and XSLT are in essence technologies for describing and managing thought, and we haven't even yet scratched the surface of the use of the XML family of technologies to empower our minds.

Now relax; go brew a pot of tea, pour a cup of coffee, or make yourself a latté. Our story takes us back through the mists of time to the dawn of human civilization, and the discovery of six fundamental machines...

Six Simple Physical Machines

The enabling technologies of our civilization can perhaps all be reduced to one of six simple machines that enhance human strength in work. No other simple machines have yet been discovered; other complex machines of human invention all derive from one or more of these:

- ❑ Inclined plane
- ❑ Wedge
- ❑ Screw
- ❑ Lever
- ❑ Pulley
- ❑ Wheel and axle

The wedge and screw are both extensions of the inclined plane, and our story is mainly concerned with these three simple physical machines, for in them can be found a pattern that recurs in the enabling technologies of the information age; that is, the simple *abstract* machines that represent the topics of this book.

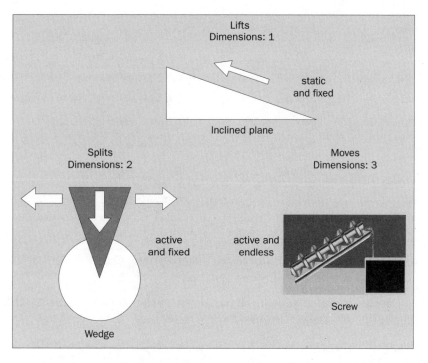

The inclined plane is the simplest of the six physical machines. It assists work by facilitating lifting. The machine was fixed, so its utility was limited by its length and position. It was static and so relied on human strength or some other force to work.

Although the inclined plane substantially reduces human effort, it is probably the least efficient of the six devices. Early humans, like good programmers, kept playing with the tools they had available. One day one bright spark said, "Hey, if we put two small inclined planes together we can get a new tool for splitting wood – even stone. I call it the 'wedge'". The wedge works in two dimensions (a downward force and orthogonal opposing vectors) and can be portable. The wedge, then, is dynamic, but its effectiveness is fixed, limited by its width.

It was someone by the name of Archimedes who took the next step. Sensing there was something more, just out of sight but within the grasp of imagination, he wondered, "What would happen if we added a third dimension of work to our toolset by wrapping an inclined plane around an axle?" And then there was the screw – perhaps the most polymorphic of the simple physical machines. The screw is everywhere, holding machines and bridges together, conveying grain and cement, propelling ships through the oceans and jets through the air.

Six Simple Abstract Machines

I like to think of the XML family as six *abstract* machines that enhance our strength of thought. Unlike their physical predecessors, these machines exist in the conceptual world of language in the mind; indeed, these simple abstract machines constitute a language in their own right, the **Extensible Markup Language**. Each simple abstract machine adds a new dimension to the language:

Specification	Contribution	URL
XML 1.0	Syntax	http://www.w3.org/TR/REC-xml
Namespaces in XML	Identity	http://www.w3.org/TR/REC-xml-names/
XML Infoset	Structure	http://www.w3.org/TR/xml-infoset/
XML Path (XPath)	Navigation	http://www.w3.org/TR/xpath
XML Schemas	Precision	http://www.w3.org/TR/xmlschema-0/
XSL	Change	http://www.w3.org/TR/XSL/

In a similar manner to how the wedge and screw derive directly from the inclined plane, XML Schemas and XSLT are languages constructed from the syntax of XML. In the same way that the wedge and screw add to the efficacy of the available toolbox, enabling humans to do things they couldn't do before, so XML Schemas and XSLT add power to what we can achieve with XML alone, and in the same order of magnitude perhaps that the screw increases the inclined plane's effectiveness.

In this analogy, XML, Namespaces, and Infoset together correspond to the inclined plane. Add XML Schemas and you have a "wedge" to split your information into well-defined types. Add XSLT to this abstract inclined plane and you have a powerful "screw".

Schemas bring specific shape to arbitrary XML, adding a second dimension to XML's functionality. XSLT brings the ability to change XML from one shape to another, the third dimension of work. Actually, it is more accurate to think of n dimensions of work, since XSLT can produce any kind of text, not just more XML, as was demonstrated throughout this book where we looked at various transformations producing HTML, SVG, WML, VoiceXML, etc. Also, where XML is "merely self-describing data", XSLT is a true programming language; XSLT can be normative as well as descriptive. With XSLT, XML not only says something, it does something.

Let's take a look at the XML specifications, grouped as four different simple abstract machines.

The First Simple Abstract Machine: XML

The first simple abstract machine is really the combination of three even simpler machines: XML, XML Namespaces, and XML Infoset. For the sake of clarity, I will refer to these first three machines as one and will simply call the first simple abstract machine "XML".

Syntax

In the broadest possible terms, the XML 1.0 specification concerns a document made up of *entities*. These entities consist of tags used by the XML processor to build a model of the data, along with the actual data itself (the parsed character data, or PCDATA). The form of the model must adhere to the following five laws, which ensure the model is well-formed and thus parseable. The first two ensure structural consistency, and the last three eliminate structural and semantic ambiguity:

1. Thou shalt have a closing tag for each opening tag or a tag shall be self-closing. There shalt be only one root element (open tag/close tag pair) in each document.

2. Thou may only close elements after all descendent elements are closed.

3. Thou shalt use the same case for all tag names, and neither tag nor attribute names may contain spaces.

4. Thou shalt enclose all attribute values in quotes.

5. Thou shalt escape any character in thy data that otherwise representeth an XML structural component, such as the less-than character <, the ampersand & (used to identify an entity reference), as well as the greater-than, apostrophe, and quote characters.

These rules are the minimal invariants required for self-describing data. This deceptively simple conception has spawned a revolution that has spread out to virtually every office, classroom, and home across the planet.

Identity

An XML document consists primarily of elements, and elements contain attributes – there are other entity types but most of these are not germane to XSLT. Both elements and attributes are identified by names that merely represent this identity; in a way they are an approximation of identity. When the same name is used to represent different things, there is a name collision, and XML can no longer unambiguously describe the data it conveys.

Attributes suffer from another problem, specific to them alone. An XML document can contain any number of, possibly nested, duplicate elements, but an attribute may only appear once in any given element. If you add the same attribute name twice to an element, XML can once again no longer unambiguously describe the data of the element, and an XML parser will not be able to proceed.

The "Namespaces in XML" specification handles these problems of identity by relying on fully qualified **Uniform Resource Identifiers** (**URIs**). URIs, in turn, can rely on the unique identity of **Uniform Resource Locators** (**URLs**) that you use every time you call up a page in your browser. The Namespaces specification also relies on **Uniform Resource Names** (**URNs**) that are locally unique (and usually not dereferenced by the browser). The URI namespace precedes an element name separated by a colon, thus allowing elements in one namespace to be uniquely differentiated from elements in any other.

Since the colon is used as a separator, the Namespaces specification restricts the use of the colon in XML. Since a URI may include a colon, we require a colon-free alias – the namespace prefix – in order to use such a URI as a namespace identifier. Though a bit awkward, this system works well, and when an XML document is both well-formed and uses namespaces correctly, the first simple abstract machine is ready for one final component.

Structure

Remember those ever curious and inventive ancients who couldn't leave well enough alone? They were the folks who combined inclined planes to create a wedge and twisted an inclined plane about an axle to create a screw. This same evolutionary compulsion is at work in the abstract world, too. Indeed, this chapter has been very selective in choosing which W3C specifications to discuss; there are currently many more in various stages of completion, and there are sure to be many more in the future. There needs to be a way to abstract an 'XML + Namespaces' document so that application programs and other components all treat the 'XML + Namespaces' constructs consistently.

This is the role of the **XML Information Set**, or the **Infoset**. The XML Infoset is similar to a program interface, class, or object model in that it encapsulates a collection of items of information with their properties.

The XML Infoset takes the well-formed XML document, along with any namespace information that disambiguates elements with the same name but different "meaning", and essentially allows that instance document to be described in abstract terms. This separation of syntax (markup and character data) from implementation (whether the XML document is rendered according to the Document Object Model (DOM) or the Simple API for XML (SAX) or a hybrid of these two, as in the new XMLNavigator class of the Microsoft .NET Framework) permits a program that processes or uses XML to continue to work even if some new implementation of XML (for example, binary XML) appears.

When you create an XML file you have some concept, perhaps even a physical thing, in mind. Your choice of XML element and attribute names is not fully arbitrary as you choose words to convey the nature of the entity. The richer this nature is, the richer will be the XML vocabulary you invent. But ultimately, your XML vocabulary is only a model of the entity, an approximation of it. The crucial thing to keep in mind is that your approximation is good enough for your purposes, and you can be confident that a reader will 'fill in the blanks' appropriately, so they know what you're talking about.

I'll return to this point a little later, but for now just remember to bind the "real thing" you approximate to your XML syntax. If your goal is communication, you cannot separate the object from its model. A question that faces the guardians of the XML Infoset specification is, "How good is good enough?" Even if you leave this question open, there is always an abstract model of XML (itself) even if you can't see it or express it.

Since creating an abstract model requires you to ask questions about everything, an XML Infoset provides a way to ask questions about the meaning of XML. This, in turn, lets you achieve things you couldn't before. For example, the XML Infoset enables the **XML MIME Transformation Protocol** (**XMTP** – http://www.openhealth.org/documents/xmtp.htm) to transform an e-mail message using XSLT to an XHTML web page without first creating an XML document. It's not difficult to envisage a similar technique to transform a Word document into a .NET web service without first converting the document to XML.

> *For the summary of a very interesting XML-DEV e-mail thread on the subject of XML Infoset, refer to Leigh Dodds' article at http://www.xml.com/pub/a/2000/08/02/deviant/infoset.html.*

To summarize, then, XML, as the first simple abstract machine, must have a well-defined syntax to render a well-formed XML document. The elements and attributes must use namespaces to ensure internal consistency between the XML and the model. XML Infoset enables any user of your XML to obtain specific, if abstract, answers to questions regarding your XML document, a trait that is important if your XML "inclined plane" is to be extended or used by someone or something else – a topic we turn to next.

The Second Simple Abstract Machine: XML Schemas

XML is simple enough for humans to read it, and precise enough for machines to understand it. If XML is a language that lets you say anything, **XML Schemas** (see http://www.w3.org/TR/xmlschema-0) helps you say it clearly and with precision.

XML Schemas has double duty. On one hand, a schema enables you to specify the nature and structure of your data, which you could only imply without a schema. For example, the data "03/31/53" can be described as a date, differentiating it from an expression meaning divide three by thirty-one and then by fifty-three.

Secondly, when data purports to be of a certain "class", that is belonging to a specified schema, XML Schemas helps you determine if the data is, in fact, what it purports to be. With an XML parser like MSXML3 you can even bind schemas to data at run time, and so schemas can be used to ascertain whether the sender is authorized to possess that data in the first place.

These two features of XML Schemas – precision in defining data and the ability to compare instance data to an existing data paradigm – are invaluable in a commercial situation.

The key to the power of schemas is that they abstract data; in a sense, they reduce complexity to its essence. For example, ADO uses a schema expressed in **XML-Data Reduced** (**XDR** – http://www.w3.org/TR/1998/NOTE-XML-data-0105/) to model all relational data. Regardless of the source or content of the data, its shape is always the same: elements represent rows, attributes represent fields. As you saw in the sample code of Chapter 8, with this deceptively simple system you can fetch the name of any arbitrary "column" of data.

The Third Simple Abstract Machine: XPath

XPath is like the axle around which our ancestors wrapped an inclined plane to produce the screw. The similarity between XPath and an axle isn't purely accidental – the axle alone is worthless, as is XPath. XPath is one of those W3C specifications that are not intended to stand alone. Its principal counterpart is XSLT, but it is also used in the XPointer specification (which was briefly covered in Chapter 2) and, for example, in the DOM implementation of Microsoft's XML parser, MSXML3.

Another point to make about XPath is that XSLT needs XPath as much as XPath needs XSLT. Just as XPath is vapid in isolation, XSLT without XPath is bored – there's nothing for it to do.

XPath is a language of trees. In order to represent data as a tree, the most important ideas are patterns and relationships; two things humans are supremely adapted to recognizing. Knowledge as a whole is a web of patterns and relationships. More precisely, information has three dimensions: names, structure, and relations. The first three simple abstract machines operate in this three-dimensional abstract space, and speak the language of XPath.

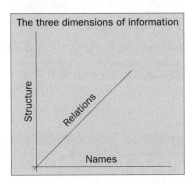

The three dimensions of information

Structure

Relations

Names

In programming terms, data must have a signature by which it can be recognized, just as a function has a signature. By signature, I mean here a pattern that can be understood by a machine to identify that data. This is the source of XML's polymorphic power; one transform can act correctly on any number of different data signatures (again, refer back to the Chapter 8 for an example). So, in a way, data signatures are similar to XML (and not merely a representation of XML).

To put this in a more direct way – XPath is related to the XML Infoset because the syntax of XPath models the logical, not the syntactic, structure of the XML. Remember that the XML Infoset has the same job as XPath; the Infoset expresses the content of a well-formed XML document, not in the syntax of XML (that's the job of the XML 1.0 specification), but as an abstraction of information items and their properties.

As you no doubt appreciate by now, the syntax of XPath makes working with XSLT an exercise in laconic efficiency. As you gain more experience with XSLT, you will find XPath expressions to be of amazing power. I recommend you create an XPath library to store the choicest examples for easy reference and reuse.

As a matter of fact, MSXML3 even treats XPath expressions like programming objects. The XML parser can "parse" an XPath expression once to resolve the path in the tree the first time it is encountered. This XPath object can then be reused without having to expend the effort to retrace the specified location path through the tree.

As was demonstrated in Chapter 8 (and you will see again in the second part of this chapter – *The First Complex Abstract Machine*), XPath expressions can specify a value for XSLT tree variables, and those tree variables can then be thought of and used as objects. In fact, the ability to deconstruct a tree into variables containing sub-trees makes XSLT programming much easier and more efficient.

The Fourth Simple Abstract Machine: XSL

All this leads us to the fourth, and arguably the most powerful of the simple abstract machines, XSL. Don't forget this is actually composed of two distinct parts, and although most of this book has discussed XSLT, the formatting capabilities of XSL-FO covered in Chapter 9 should not be overlooked.

Formatting information helps humans understand its meaning. HTML alone provides quite basic formatting. The Cascading Style Sheets specification (http://www.w3.org/TR/CSS2/) adds a great deal of flexibility to the formatting of HTML and can even be applied directly to XML. But the main difference between XSL-FO and CSS is that CSS is static, while XSL-FO data can adopt any arbitrary structure. Some of this difference is blurred when an XSLT transform creates a result tree including `class` attribute values that invoke particular CSS rules. The W3C Style Activity page (http://www.w3.org/Style/XSL/Overview.html#FAQ) has a plethora of information about XSL and CSS, which is covered in more depth in Chapter 9 along with XSL-FO. I shall focus on XSLT for the remainder of this chapter.

In a very real sense, XSLT (http://www.w3.org/TR/xslt11/), as the fourth simple abstract machine, is like time, the fourth dimension. XML alone is interesting in what it can represent, but little else. Left to its own devices XML will, literally, go nowhere. But XML with XSLT ... well, the sky is no longer the limit.

Functional Programming?

How many times have you heard the XML digerati opining, "XSLT is not a true programming language. Even if it is, it's not a true *functional* programming language!" You're probably already aware that I'm one of those guys who think otherwise. Indeed, I make a bigger deal about a fundamental feature of declarative languages than most: I believe that the absence of an assignment operator and revisable variables is a mark of programming purity.

Jonathan Marsh, program manager for XSLT at Microsoft, maintains (from an e-mail thread we shared recently):

> "...in the case of the missing [assignment] operator, you make it sound like we're the Moral Majority or something! The reason we don't have assignment is because it blows away the ability to do incremental transforms which are needed both by editing applications, and data-binding-type operations. It's too bad we don't have implementations that take full advantage of this feature yet, but I hope that we will before too long...
>
> One of the main reasons XSLT is a functional language is that DSSSL was functional (based on Schemas). So I can't take any credit here. I'm glad our desire for incremental updates also gives you all these other benefits, but I cannot say that we intended it that way..."

Moral imperatives aside, and for the benefit of those procedural (or imperative) programmers who have never heard of functional (or declarative) programming, FOLDOC (The Free Online Dictionary of Computing at http://foldoc.doc.ic.ac.uk/foldoc/index.html) defines functional programming as:

> *"A program in a functional language consists of a set of (possibly recursive) function definitions and an expression whose value is output as the program's result. Functional languages are one kind of declarative language. They are based on the typed lambda-calculus with constants. There are no side-effects to expression evaluation so an expression (e.g. a function applied to certain arguments) will always evaluate to the same value (if its evaluation terminates). Furthermore, an expression can always be replaced by its value without changing the overall result (referential transparency).*
>
> *The order of evaluation of subexpressions is determined by the language's evaluation strategy. In a strict (call-by-value) language this will specify that arguments are evaluated before applying a function whereas in a non-strict (call-by-name) language arguments are passed unevaluated.*
>
> *Programs written in a functional language are generally compact and elegant, but have tended, until recently, to run slowly and require a lot of memory.*
>
> *Examples of functional languages are Clean, FP, Haskell, Hope, LML, Miranda and SML. Many other languages such as Lisp have a subset which is purely functional but also contain non-functional constructs."*

So, is XSLT a true functional programming language? Who really cares? I use it everyday at work and home to do things with a computer I couldn't do before. I'd love XSLT one way or the other, and here's why.

Why XSLT is So Cool

The first three simple abstract machines (the well-formed XML document, the valid XML document, and XPath – the language of trees) all enable us to engineer systems of thought. The fourth simple abstract machine, XSLT, lets us leverage those systems. XSLT lets us render our XML as a presentation language such as HTML, WML, or SVG, or a presentation medium like a Microsoft Word document. *Now we can share.*

XSLT lets us weave together web pages from other XML sources, even those that don't know we exist, to produce a consistent network of knowledge where all the knowledge of our subnet is accessible from any node in the subnet. *Now we can grow.*

XSLT lets us talk to less articulate systems, including those big lugs, the relational database servers ("normalized" relational data is denormalized hierarchical XML data). Legacy files such as comma-delimited text become gold mines of facts. XSLT lets our data talk to other binary components like the new web services provided by the Microsoft .NET Framework and by extension, lets us achieve almost anything that can be rendered in text. *Now we can work.*

XSLT is the programming of shapes of data (morphological programming), driven by data; XSLT, itself, is data that can be shaped. XSLT is elegant and reliable, powerful and understated. It demands much from you and gives back more. XSLT can take you places in the mind where you may not have gone before, and it can help you think in ways you may not have thought before. *Now we can dream.*

On the Relation of XML to Other Computing Technologies

No introduction to schema-based technologies is complete without comparing them to traditional computing technologies. The two most common comparisons drawn are to the reigning technology for data, the Structured Query Language (SQL), and to the bedrock of the Internet age, HTML. For completeness, this section also compares Document Type Definition (DTD) files to XML Schema files.

XML and SQL

A key difference between data and information is that information exists in the relationships between data points. In the Relational model these relationships are *captured* (an important term, as you will see) in columns. Information arises from data in the Relational model in the JOIN statements of SQL. In XML and XSLT relations are *expressed* (another important term) in attributes. These attributes express relations descriptively and normatively. Descriptive attributes tell you something about an element (itself a surrogate of something else). Normative attributes tell you how this element here is related to that element there.

In other words, in XML and XSLT attributes tell you the facts about something *and* something about the facts. It's this duality that sets XML and XSLT apart from tabular data and SQL. If you change a relational schema, everything breaks. If you change an XML schema everything still works.

XML and HTML

Why, beginners often ask, is XML so strict while HTML is so relaxed? I don't need to enclose attributes in quotes and my browser isn't confused if I mix case in the text. And I can leave off the closing slash in <br> tags and leave out the </p> tag altogether, and for the most part, my browser still renders HTML flawlessly? Why does XML require me to be so fastidious?

One difference between XML and HTML is that XML describes data and HTML describes appearance. HTML represents a collection of basic communication constructs that humans have used for centuries, starting with a representation of documents. Documents consist of headings, paragraphs, empty lines, lists, and tables, to name just a few of the most common concepts. These basic communication constructs are self-evident and ubiquitous. It only made sense to begin the web revolution on this firm foundation. HTML's primary job, then, is to present information to humans, and browser developers are prone to making allowances for badly coded HTML rather than risk excluding their users from accessing such pages.

This leads to the second key difference between XML and HTML: ambiguity. That is, because all browser users understand the basic communication constructs, this understanding was transferred to the browser. HTML is unambiguous data to the browser. HTML is wired right into the source code that makes your browser work.

Since your browser knows what to expect, it can be more forgiving if you don't know (or care) what you're doing. It knows that if it sees two <p> tags in a row, that the text just preceding one must mark the end of the previous paragraph (for it knows that <p> means a related group of words; that is, a paragraph – even though epistemologically it hasn't the foggiest notion of what any of that really means). Your browser "knows" that <br> means you want it to print a new line (half the size of the space between paragraphs), and there's no reason to be on the look out for the closing tag; the end of the line break is sufficient.

Think of it like this: the structure of HTML is hardwired into the browser; the structure is part of the makeup of the software. And this is also what limits HTML. If HTML was all that humans had discovered, then we'd have to be satisfied with merely understanding the facts about something; we'd never be able to appreciate something about the facts. Worse, our software wouldn't even be able to know the facts themselves. HTML is sterile. XML is pregnant with meaning.

XML Schemas and DTDs

Both XML Schemas and DTDs bring order to anarchy. The DTD format is the legacy of the SGML community from which both HTML and XML spring. The DTD is a non-parseable text file that uses syntax that, as they say, only a mother could love. Actually that's not fair, I know at least one person who prefers to read DTDs over schemas: "De gustibus non disputandum est" (In matters of taste there is no argument).

Making schemas from XML was a huge improvement over the DTD. Schemas, unlike DTDs, are parseable data stores. Schemas can be queried, filtered, modified, and processed electronically. Some XML parsers (such as MSXML3) can even bind schemas to XML documents at run time. Not only can schemas validate instance documents of XML, when the schema is processed by an XSLT transform you can create empty instance valid XML documents. (See Chapter 14 for details.)

The First Complex Abstract Machine

At the beginning of this chapter you read that all complex physical machines can trace their heritage back to the dawn of time and the discovery of six simple physical machines. The first part of this chapter has been an exploration of the parallels between those simple physical machines and the newly discovered simple abstract machines, the schema-based technologies.

In this section I shall be assembling a complex abstract machine from the four simple abstract machines previously discussed. I'll be using XML files (including SVG files), XML Schemas, XSLT transforms, and some interesting XPath expressions to tie everything together.

Introducing PNML

The complex abstract machine is to be an application of **Petri Net Markup Language** (**PNML**), one of many candidate XML languages for describing Petri nets. Petri nets are graphical structures used to model systems presenting a high level of concurrency. They were first defined in 1962 by Carl Adam Petri – for more information, see, for example, http://www.daimi.au.dk/PetriNets/.

> *PNML is taken from the work of Matthias Jüngel, Ekkart Kindler, and Michael Weber, described in* "The Petri Net Markup Language" *edited by Stephan Philippi (http://www.informatik.hu-berlin.de/top/pnml/download/JKW_PNML.ps). The work originates from the proceedings of the* "Workshop Algorithmen und Werkzeuge Petrinetze" *(pages 47-52) that took place in June 2000 at the Universitat Koblenz-Landau, Germany (used by permission). Jüngel et al. based their work on* "Elements of Distributed Algorithms. Modeling and Analysis with Petri Nets" *by Wolfgang Reisig, Springer-Verlag, 1998.*

You can download the PNML file I use here, pnml.xml, (along with its schema, stNet.xsd) from http://www.informatik.hu-berlin.de/top/pnml/. The following chart provides a visual representation of the Petri net under consideration.

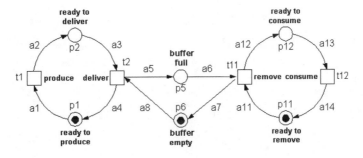

The components of the complex abstract machine are:

❑ The "place" (representing machine states). In the diagram above these are given by circles, and are labeled p1, p2, etc. Holding states (that is, states of the machine that the machine currently exists in) are marked by a black dot.

❑ The "transition" (representing events that move the machine from one state to another following a strict decision rule, see below). In the diagram above, these are given by squares, and are labeled t1, t2, etc.

❑ The "arc" (that join places and transitions and play a key role in the "firing" of transitions). In the diagram above, these are given by directed arrows, and are labeled a1, a2, etc.

The decision rule that constrains the firing of transitions is that a transition is enabled (that is, it may fire) only when all its precedent states (states connected by an arc directed towards the transition) are holding and, depending on the Petri net formalism used, when none of its antecedent states (states connected by an arc directed away from the transition) are holding. When a transition fires, all precedent states of the transition stop holding and all of it antecedent states begin holding.

So how is this represented in PNML? Well, inside nested <pnml> and <net> elements, each place, transition, and arc are represented by elements of the form:

```
<place id="p1">
  <graphics>
    <position x="-20" y="10"/>
  </graphics>
  <name>
    <value>ready to produce</value>
  </name>
  <initialMarking>
    <value>1</value>
  </initialMarking>
</place>
```

```
<transition id="t1">
  <graphics>
    <position x="-30" y="0"/>
  </graphics>
  <name>
    <value>produce</value>
  </name>
</transition>
```

```
<arc id="a1" source="p1" target="t1">
  <graphics>
    <position x="-27" y="7"/>
  </graphics>
  <inscription>
    <value>1</value>
    <graphics>
      <offset x="0" y="0"/>
    </graphics>
  </inscription>
</arc>
```

The `<initialmarking>` element and its contents within the `<place>` element, represent the fact that this state is holding.

So far our PNML application consists of a valid, well-formed XML document and an XML Schema. We will add to this an XSLT transform using XPath expressions that reflect the interesting relationships and dynamic behavior of these three components. This transform will be used to render our PNML machine for viewing using both HTML and SVG markup, and to transform the machine from one state to another.

This complex abstract machine, based on the `stNet.xsd` schema, is not only the epitome of the ideas introduced in this chapter, but the machine itself is an important prototype in a branch of schema-based programming that is exploring ways to model and analyze software designs and to automate software testing. See further remarks on this point in the final section of this chapter.

Remember, the goal of this chapter was to get you thinking about XML and XSLT outside the (usual econet/SOAP) box – now that you are familiar with XSLT and comfortable using it in your application development. Econets are where the easy money is; that is the frontier of new economic wealth. Instead I will take you into the high country of the mind. That's where the hard problems are; that is the frontier of new intellectual wealth. The complex abstract machine we turn to next is just the first settlement on that frontier.

Understand Your Schema

My first problem occurred as I attempted to create a node-list of "hot arcs", that is arcs whose `source` attribute appeared in an existing node-list of `<place>` tags with:

```
<initialMarking>
  <value> 1 </value>
</initialMarking>
```

descendants. This was a tricky assignment; and I made my share of mistakes. Fortunately, I happen to have one of the world's foremost authorities on XSLT, Jonathan Marsh, only an e-mail away, and with his help, my first problem was quickly resolved.

In retrospect, the crux of this initial problem was that I tried to write XPath expressions before I fully understood the schema I was working with. I attribute this to the "champing-at-the-bit" syndrome most self-respecting programmers experience to various degrees. I can now, quite self-righteously, suggest that if you too are susceptible to the compulsion to code before you understand your programming problem, you should resist. XSLT won't love you for it; it's too different. So if you inherit a schema, come to terms with it *before* you try to transform XML complying with it.

When I took this quandary to Jonathan, his immediate reply was the following suggestion:

```
/pnml/net/arc[@source = /pnml/net/place[initialMarking/value='1'] /@id]
```

Here's what that means in English (should be familiar to you by now): beginning at the root of the XML document, move down to the `<arc>` nodes and select those whose `source` attribute "equals" any value found in the node-set that (once again) begins at the root of the XML document, moves down to the `<place>` nodes that have a grandchild `value` element equal to 1, and selects the `id` attributes.

The Value of Variables

In the software development discipline of Cleanroom Software Engineering, there is a formal functional verification technique called "intended functions", expressed in such a way that complex processing can be given an alias and referenced in subsequent parts of the program. The technique makes formal verification of complex programs tractable if not downright straightforward.

One unexplored area in schema-based programming covers the relationship between intended functions and XSLT variables. The following example shows what is possible.

I can personally attest that trying to generate an XPath expression is not easy (unless you're Jonathan Marsh). Here's an XPath that has the same outcome as Jonathan's suggestion, but is even more laconic:

```
$arcs[@source = $holdingStates/@id]
```

This expression says, "give me any arcs node whose source attribute equals the id attribute of any holdingStates node". That's almost obvious. Of course the key was to abstract the details into aliases for arcs and holdingStates. But I didn't stop there. I partitioned the entire XML schema into variables. In a very real sense, I created a collection of objects from the schema, an API of XSL variables. Once accomplished, I could simply compose any needed variable from the variables already in existence. Here are examples of some of the variables I defined (you'll see the "hotArcs" variable at the bottom of this code snippet):

```
<xsl:variable
  name="net"
  select="/pnml/net"
/>

<xsl:variable
  name="places"
  select="$net/place"
/>

<xsl:variable
  name="arcs"
  select="$net/arc"
/>

<xsl:variable
  name="holdingStates"
  select="$places[initialMarking/value='1']"
/>

<xsl:variable
  name="hotArcs"
  select="$arcs[@source = $holdingStates/@id]"
/>
```

I also created variables to contain waitingStates, coldArcs, enabledTransitions, and disabledTransitions.

As you can see, the variables are created top-down. Each of these variables is distinguished by including element and/or attribute values, as necessary. As long as each variable works, the variables defined below it will work. This is where XSL variables and cleanroom intended functions start to look suspiciously similar (a topic that merits further research). Also, this means you can explore programming options in 'upstream' variables and know that your modified 'upstream' variable code worked if 'downstream' variables continue to work. Built in regression tests – very cool.

The next step was to see what the contents of all these defined variables were. I used an output viewer of mine (created with XSLT incidentally) to produce the following screen display of the results of the transform's analysis of the PNML data:

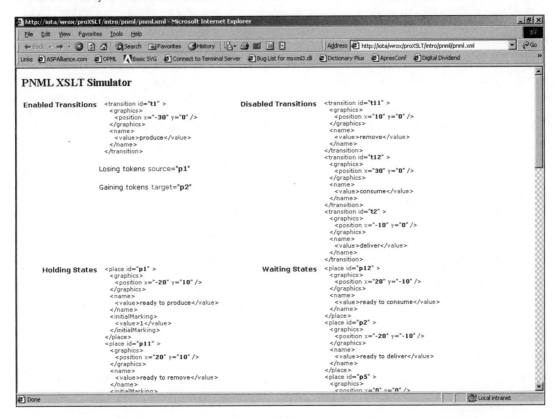

Note the lines in the **Enabled Transitions** section that list the `<place>` element representing the state that will stop holding (that is, it will 'lose token') and the `<place>` element that represents the state that will start holding (that is, it will 'gain token'). You can see by considering the PNML diagram given earlier that, indeed, the only transition that is initially enabled is t1, so p1 will lose its token and p2 will gain that token.

These two lines (**Losing Tokens** and **Gaining Tokens**) come from two more XSLT variables created from existing variables. In fact, by using the data otherwise displayed, it was trivially easy to create the two new variables. It's amazing how easy programming is when it's visual *and* abstracted, both things at which XSLT excels. Here are the two new variables:

```
<xsl:variable name="loseTokens"
  select="$hotArcs[@target = $enabledTransitions/@id]/@source" />

<xsl:variable name="gainTokens"
  select="$coldArcs[@source = $enabledTransitions/@id]/@target" />
```

Now the Hard Part

OK, at this point the system was ready for the most important phase of development. Petri nets are powerful because they can be simulated (and animated). They are also powerful because they can be morphed; that is, their structure can be topologically changed (meaning their semantic value is invariant). I note this because it points to another intriguing area of research; that is, can an XSLT transform both simulate *and* morph Petri nets? That's enough Petri net theory, though; let's get back to our transform.

The goal at this stage is to remove the `<initialMarking>` tag (the token, or holding status) from p1 and move it to p2. Once that happens, transition t2 becomes enabled. A subsequent transformation will fire t2, and both p2 and p6 will give up their tokens to p1 and p5 respectively. The PNML machine will continue in this manner as long as the PNML data is transformed (and transformable – there remains at least one enabled transition) by the XSLT.

The next templates, therefore, must move tokens. The two variables that provide the data for these new templates are, of course, `loseTokens` and `gainTokens`. These variables are like a one-dimensional array. The following templates look for any node whose id equals one of the values in these "array" variables. If found, the `<place>` node is copied through to the output tree with any necessary adjustments.

> *Note: so far this transform has not really copied any XML data to the output stream. In its development stage, this transform creates XSL variables whose data is sent to the XSLT output viewer templates (at the bottom of the transform: not shown here) that, in turn, convert the XML data into HTML for display. Once the transform displays data as I expect, I will change the transform so that only XML data is output. Ultimately, the output will be SVG so that you can view the Petri net with something like Adobe's SVG Viewer.*

Here are the new variables and templates:

```
<xsl:template match="/">
  ...
  <xsl:variable name="oldHolding">
    <xsl:for-each select="$holdingStates[@id=$loseTokens]">
      <xsl:copy>
        <xsl:apply-templates select="node()|@*" mode="moveTokens"/>
      </xsl:copy>
    </xsl:for-each>
  </xsl:variable>
  Old Holding state(s)
  <xsl:apply-templates select="msxsl:node-set($oldHolding)" mode="docs">
    <xsl:sort select="@id"/>
  </xsl:apply-templates>

  <xsl:variable name="newHolding">
    <xsl:for-each select="$waitingStates[@id=$gainTokens]">
      <xsl:copy>
        <xsl:apply-templates select="node()|@*" mode="moveTokens"/>
        <initialMarking>
          <value>1</value>
        </initialMarking>
      </xsl:copy>
    </xsl:for-each>
  </xsl:variable>
  New Holding state(s)
```

```
    <xsl:apply-templates select="msxsl:node-set($newHolding)" mode="docs">
      <xsl:sort select="@id"/>
    </xsl:apply-templates>
  </xsl:template>

  <xsl:template match="node()|@*" mode="moveTokens">
    <xsl:copy>
      <xsl:apply-templates select="node()|@*" mode="moveTokens"/>
    </xsl:copy>
  </xsl:template>

  <xsl:template match="initialMarking" mode="moveTokens"/>
```

The last empty template matches <initialMarking> nodes but does nothing with them, effectively removing them from the input tree. The result of this processing is as expected:

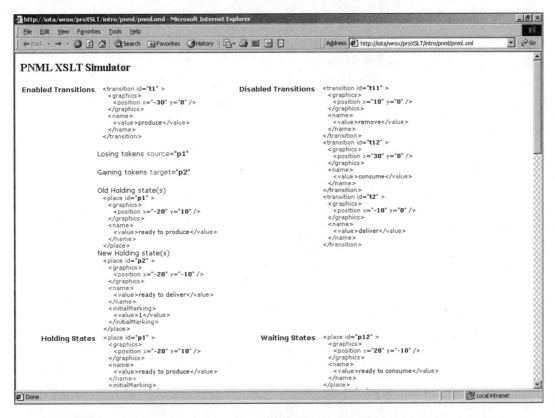

Note that under Old Holding state(s) and New Holding state(s) are displayed the new XML for the <place> elements after the transition t1 has fired.

An interesting exercise at this stage is to change the <initialMarking> element in the PNML data pnml.xml so that transition t2 is enabled. When this transition fires, p2 and p6 will lose tokens and p1 and p5 will gain tokens. Multiple entries are then shown in the Old and New Holding state(s) report, as expected.

The Last Phase of Development

Now it's time to modify the transform so that it outputs updated XML. At this next stage I need an HTML page containing JavaScript code to recycle the transformed XML. Here's part of the source code for pnml.htm (I'll describe each function in turn):

```javascript
<script language=javascript>
<!--
  window.onload=init;

  try
  {
    var xml   = new ActiveXObject("MSXML2.DOMDocument.3.0");
    xml.async = false;
    var xsl   = xml.cloneNode(false);
    var xsl2  = xml.cloneNode(false);
    try
    {
      xml.load("pnml.xml");
      xsl2.load("pnmlOutput.xslt");
      xsl.load("pnml.xslt");
    }
    catch(e)
    {
      alert(e.description);
    }
  }
  catch(e)
  {
    var url="http://msdn.microsoft.com/code/sample.asp?" _
            "url=/msdn-files/027/000/541/msdncompositedoc.xml";
    var response=prompt("You need msxml3.dll to use this page. " +
    "To continue, press enter to go download the parser.",url);
    if(response==url) location.href=url;
  }

  function init()
  {
    simulate(false);
  }

  function simulate(simulate)
  {
    if(simulate)
    {
      var xml2  = xml.cloneNode(false);
      xml.transformNodeToObject(xsl, xml2);
    }
    else
      var xml2  = xml.cloneNode(true);

    divOutput.innerHTML = xml2.transformNode(xsl2);
    xml.load(xml2);
  }
//-->
</script>
```

The "global" section of code declares the XML DOM objects I need, three of them, at least. Note: I use a technique that quickly creates new XML DOM objects – I use COM to create the first one, then I clone that XML DOM as many times as necessary, twice here and once also in the simulate() function. The XML DOM object, xml, holds the main PNML data. The two XSL XML DOM objects, xsl and xsl2, each hold their own transform. The pnml.xslt file changes the shape of the original PNML data. The pnmlOutput.xslt file then changes the shape of the transformed PNML model data so that I can render the current state of the PNML model. Note also that I included a technique to gracefully degrade when the client does not have msxml3.dll installed.

The init() function calls the simulate() function with that function's argument set to false. I send the false argument, because I don't want to transform the PNML data before I render it.

The simulate() function needs a fresh copy of the XML DOMDocument so it clones the xml object to xml2. As you just saw, when the simulate() argument is false, this unchanged XML data is sent to pnmlOutput.xslt for transformation to HTML. When the simulate() function sees an argument value of true, it first calls the pnml.xslt stylesheet in order to move the tokens into the next marking. This transformed PNML data is kept in xml2. Once the first transformation is made, the original PNML model data in xml is replaced with the transformed PNML in xml2.

Transforming XML to XML: pnml.xslt

At this point I'll show you how I split the original stylesheet you saw parts of above into two XSLT files. The original stylesheet used my XSLT viewer templates (not shown) to render the values of the XSL variables on the screen. The new stylesheet pnml.xslt below now copies the effect of the transformation to the output tree. This output tree ultimately becomes the content for the xml variable, as just described.

I've left it out of the snippet below, but the XSL variables are the same in both the pnml.xslt and pnmlOutput.xslt files as in the original stylesheet. This makes sense because the XSL variables capture the state of the PNML model data. This state is either transformed into the next marking (by pnml.xslt) or into HTML (or SVG) for viewing (by pnmlOutput.xslt).

The first template below sets the context to the document element of the PNML file, the <pnml> node. This context is copied directly to the output tree. The <xsl:copy-of> element then copies all the attributes of the <pnml> node to the output tree. Next, the template iterates over the <net> nodes, even though in this case there is only one <net> node in the PNML file. In any case, the context moves from the <pnml> node to the <net> node. Again, the <net> node and its attributes are copied directly to the output tree. Now the good stuff starts.

```
<xsl:template match="/pnml">
  <xsl:copy>
    <xsl:copy-of select="@*"/>
    <xsl:for-each select="net">
      <xsl:copy>
        <xsl:copy-of select="@*"/>

        <xsl:apply-templates select="node()|@*"/>

      </xsl:copy>
    </xsl:for-each>
  </xsl:copy>
</xsl:template>
```

The first <xsl:apply-templates> element (above) changes the context to each of the descendent nodes, and from there to an XSLT template that most closely matches the data signature of the current context.

Two of the remaining three templates will match on all elements and each element's attribute nodes. But the two element/attribute templates are called under different circumstances, circumstances not directly controlled by the data signature of the current context. That is, I, as the programmer, say when to call the second template having a mode attribute, by specifying that mode attribute within <xsl:apply-templates>. But before I show you that second template, I will drill into the first default element/attribute template.

The second template in pnml.xslt, the first element/attribute template, copies the current node to the output tree. Exactly what gets copied, and what is left behind, depends on the current context. There are three possible contexts.

Firstly, is the text value of the current context (that is, the value represented by the . in the XPath expression) found among the text values of any nodes in the holdingStates tree variable that have id attributes matching any nodes in the lostTokens tree variable? If such a text value exists, then the descendants of the current context will be passed through to the output tree *except* the <initialMarking> element and its children.

```
<xsl:template match="node()|@*">

  <xsl:copy>
    <xsl:choose>

    <xsl:when test=".=$holdingStates[@id=$loseTokens]">
      <xsl:apply-templates select="node()|@*" mode="moveTokens"/>
    </xsl:when>

    <xsl:when test=".=$waitingStates[@id=$gainTokens]">
      <xsl:apply-templates select="node()|@*" mode="moveTokens"/>
      <initialMarking>
        <value>1</value>
      </initialMarking>
    </xsl:when>

    <xsl:otherwise>
      <xsl:apply-templates select="node()|@*"/>
    </xsl:otherwise>

    </xsl:choose>
  </xsl:copy>
</xsl:template>

<xsl:template match="node()|@*" mode="moveTokens">
  <xsl:copy>
    <xsl:apply-templates select="node()|@*" mode="moveTokens"/>
  </xsl:copy>
</xsl:template>

<xsl:template match="initialMarking" mode="moveTokens"/>
```

The transform "deletes" the <initialMarking> element by calling the second element/attribute template, the one with the mode attribute equal to moveTokens, which in turn calls the fourth and final template in pnml.xslt whenever the current context is the <initialMarking> element; in that case the final template does nothing, meaning the element is not copied to the output tree.

Back in the first default attribute/element template, if the text value of the current context is found among the text values of any nodes in the waitingStates tree variable that have id attributes matching any nodes in the gainTokens tree variable, the moveTokens mode template is again called *and* an <initialMarking> element is added to the output. In this case the moveTokens mode template simply copies the current context and descendents directly through to the output tree.

So, besides capturing the state of the PNML model in XSL variables, most of the work of the pnml.xslt transform is to copy all the PNML data through to the output tree, but deleting or adding <initialMarking> elements as necessary.

Transforming XML to HTML: pnmlOutput.xslt

The second transform, pnmlOutput.xslt, takes the current state of the PNML model and transforms it structurally to HTML that uses CSS to control the actual appearance of the PNML model's data.

Indeed, the content of the pnmlOutput.xslt transform is almost identical to the original transform I used at the beginning of this section. The current state of the PNML data is captured in XSL variable objects and passed to XSL templates, my XSLT viewer templates, which convert the XML into escaped text that the browser will render as HTML source.

For example, after the PNML data has been through two transformations, the HTML output will look as below:

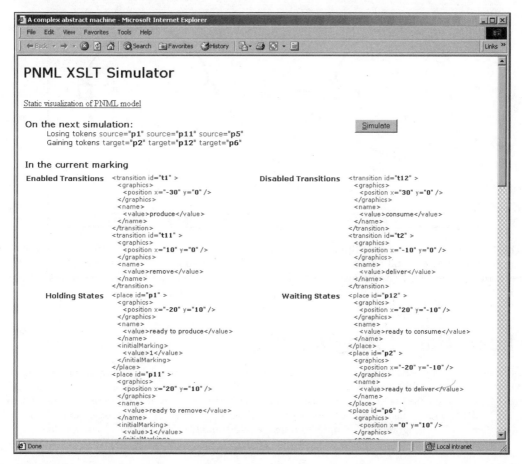

As you can see, I have improved the output of the screenshots you saw earlier, and I added a Simulate button so you can move the PNML model from one marking to the next. If you simulate the full state space of the PNML model you will note that the initial setup (where only p1 loses and p2 gains a token) is never repeated. I leave it as an exercise to the reader to explain.

By clicking the link to a Static visualization of PNML model, a diagram of the first four markings of the PNML model is given. This is just a static file – dynamic creation of each phase of the model is not implemented. If it were, SVG would be used.

Transforming to SVG

The SVG source code (and the SVG DTD file) that renders the PNML model (below) is available in the code download for this book. To view the SVG you will need the Adobe SVG Viewer Version 2.0 (not Version 1.0). At this writing, Beta 4 was available at http://www.adobe.com/svg/viewer/install/.

Notice how crisp the arcs are here. As we saw in Chapter 12, SVG is scalable; you can drill down into any part of the SVG diagram and the resolution remains as good as it is at the highest level.

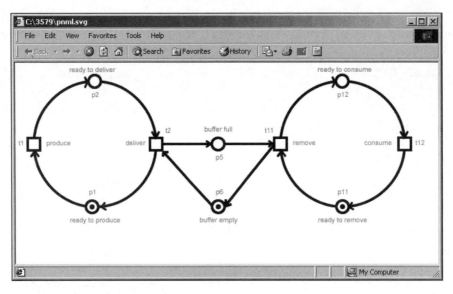

This SVG is only a prototype. Ultimately, pnmlOutput.xslt will output the SVG to browsers with the Adobe SVG Viewer installed. However, time and space don't allow me to explore the SVG file further here. In fact, I have time and space only to close this chapter. To do so I will return to where I started, with a little deeper discussion of schema-based programming (SBP).

Schema-Based Programming

I first used the term "schema-based programming" in a presentation at an XML User Group meeting on the Microsoft Redmond, Washington campus in January 2000. For the same reasons given at the beginning of this chapter, calling the use of schema-based technologies "schema-based programming" is preferable to the term "XML programming". Otherwise, Active Server Pages developers and C++ coders should call themselves "ASCII programmers" simply because their ASP and C++ files happen to be text files.

The Three Levels of Schema-Based Programming

There are three levels of SBP. The first level uses XML as a way to represent data. The second level uses XML to convey messages between applications. The third level is where the practice of programming itself is influenced by the presence of XML.

Level One

If you look around the computing world today you will see an enormous amount of work being done at the first two levels of schema-based programming. Relational database vendors like Oracle and Microsoft are busy enabling their flagship relational database servers to expose tabular data in XML hierarchies. Database updates can even be sent to the RDBMS servers as XML messages. This is wonderful for the schema-based programmer because now an SBP application need only ask for an XML file without having to first translate the request into an intermediate language like SQL. More than that, the SBP application doesn't know (and doesn't care) that the XML file is not on the file system, and that the data is dynamically fetched from a remote server somewhere.

Level Two

The second level of SBP is dominated by the work being done in the development of the **Simple Object Access Protocol** (**SOAP** – http://www.w3.org/TR/2000/NOTE-SOAP-20000508/). SOAP is a sophisticated way not only of sending messages between machines, but of conveying information to and from any source in a way more reliable than anything humans have invented before. Indeed, some companies are reinventing themselves at this second level of SBP. For example, the new Microsoft .NET initiative is built on a SOAP foundation.

Level Three

The third level of SBP is inside the program, in the way XML is changing the way programs are written, used, and tested. For instance, the `Xml.Serialization` classes of the .NET Framework promise to bring a whole new meaning to the clarion call of schema-based programmers, "The Schema is the API". With `Xml.Serialization` you build your classes from an XML Schema, you serialize to the file system as XML objects created from your class files, and you can de-serialize your objects from the file system as XML. The underlying schema provides the properties and fields for your objects.

Also, XML is what enables the new programming language, C#, to treat internal program documentation as first class objects in the language. In fact, XML is everywhere in the .NET Framework. One senior XML developer at Microsoft once quipped, "You might as well call the Common Language Runtime the XML Runtime".

Schema-Based Programming with XSLT

The most common way to get XML into your program source code is through XSLT. For example, at the Wrox 2000 conferences I demonstrated a proof-of-concept application that used XSLT in two novel ways.

First, the prototype application, "SBPNews" (http://www.aspalliance.com/mcorning/sbpNews.xml), keeps all its client-side JScript in the same XML file as that which provides the data to display in the browser. Wrapping the script in XML enables it to be an object in its own right used, for example, in the application's built-in program tutorial. Wrapping the source code in XML also enables the program's documentation to display the current (or any previous) version of the source. The XSLT transform that renders the SBPNews application lifts the JScript out of the XML and includes it in the output HTML, where most web developers would have left it in the first place.

The second use of XSLT in SBPNews is as a display object. Actually, each HTML element in the application that displays something gets that something from a small XSLT transformation called by the script. All such transformation objects, like the JScript that uses them, is inside the one XML file.

But these techniques are just the beginning. The inexorable evolution of programming, at least for the foreseeable future, seems to be centering on the schema-based technologies.

Schema-Based Programming with Petri Nets

Carl Adam Petri, as far as I'm concerned, was almost forty years ahead of his time. His discovery of Petri nets in 1962 inaugurated almost four decades of research into how those nets can model and analyze systems. But for all that time, the model and the systems they modeled were separate. Now, with XML, we can bring everything together.

Petri net researchers, as far as I can tell, are in between level one and level two of schema-based programming. They are working out XML schemas for the different kinds of Petri nets that forty years of research has produced, primarily so their legacy Petri net tools (each specialized in some aspect of Petri net theory) can share the same Petri net model data. Level three SBP would explore ways to incorporate the Petri net formalism directly into applications.

SBPNews Powered by Petri Nets

For example, the SBPNews application I mentioned above uses XML to implement its event engine. In other words, XML provides the glue between the HTML views that need data to display and the XSLT transforms that convert the application's XML data into HTML to view. Research is currently underway that is using PNML to:

❑　Provide a way to specify and simulate what a web application should do (its functional specification)

❑　Provide a mechanism to implement the event engine (and perhaps even the event handlers)

❑　Provide the software tester with a model from which tests can be developed

❑　Enable computers to execute the web application with test data (the results of the test being stored in the program's "source code")

"No way," you say. "How can this be?"

Visual Functional Specifications

It can be because we now have the graphical/mathematical formalism to model software (beyond the modeling power of a subset of Petri nets called "finite state machines") with such precision that even computers know what the software is supposed to do.

These PNML-based functional specifications are constructed visually, in a way that humans do best. These visual PNML models can even hold the source code of the application. You "Save" the model like you compile an executable.

Verification reviews in traditional software engineering are most often a manual operation comparing the functional specification (whether in a formal or a natural language) with the source code. In addition, the functional specification is manually verified for completeness and internal consistency. When the functional specification is created and expressed in PNML, it can be created graphically and verified by machine simulation. The results should be functional specifications that are more frequently created and maintained and of higher quality (making the developer's job much easier, less time-consuming, and closer to zero-defect quality).

PNML and User Interface Testing

A PNML model of any given software system uses exactly the same PNML schema. Previous research in automated user interface testing, for example, had to create and maintain a UI element-specific schema for each individual UI (and each subsequent version of each UI). PNML now provides a single schema that can be used to model any user interface.

Previous UI schemas needed a customized event model that was explicitly specified by the programmer; for example, when element type A is selected, element type B gets fresh data. With PNML, the event model is implicit, built right into the PNML schema. Events fire based on the Petri net rules of engagement: an event may fire only if it is enabled, only if all its preconditions are met, only if all its input places (and, perhaps, none of its output places) hold a token.

Indeed, a single XSLT transform can be built that will simulate and (using SVG) animate *any* user interface, now or in the future. This takes data polymorphism to a whole new level

Beyond SBPNews

It is very likely that we can repeat the same success with web-based applications when we start building application programs with the new .NET Framework from Microsoft, especially web services. A .NET utility can create a client proxy for any web service. If we bind an XSLT transform to that proxy, we can automate the testing of the web service's API just as we can automate the test of an application's user interface. Namely, an XML file holds test data that is driven by an XSLT file that uses a namespace declaration for the web service proxy. An XML message is sent to the web service by the XSLT transform and the XML returned by the web service is returned to the text XML file to be stored in the same node as the original test data. Another XSLT transform then interrogates the test XML file to report test results.

None of this power is available to us without all six of the simple abstract machines introduced in this chapter (which have been, to some degree, explored already in this book). Let's not kid ourselves. Building our complex abstract machines will not be easy, nothing worth doing ever is. But when we're done we will have machines that exaggerate our strength in thought to levels we can scarcely dream of today.

Summary

It seems that naming things is fundamental to the human experience. All knowledge begins with a name. According to Plato, all knowledge fits in a hierarchy, so knowledge has structure. But this structure is multi-dimensional. That is, the hierarchy of ideas from general to specific is one dimension of knowledge; but at any level, ideas are also related to other ideas, not "vertically" but "horizontally." Knowledge is a network of hierarchies. XML is a simple and profoundly powerful way of expressing knowledge hierarchically.

The essence of self-describing XML data is being well-formed. Well-formed data is unambiguous data. Machines can recognize well-formed data as long as that data abides by the five laws outlined earlier. This is the first simple abstract machine described in this chapter.

Sometimes, not even the accomplishment of machine understanding is sufficient. Sometimes a machine needs to know that the XML data is what it says it is. Sometimes a machine needs the data to present a passport. That XML passport is, itself, an XML file called an XML Schema. If XML can be anything you say it is, then the XML Schemas help you say it. The more complex the discourse, the more you need a schema to validate the XML data. This is the second simple abstract machine.

One way of representing the knowledge in an XML file is in the form of a tree. Following immediately on the heels of the discovery of XML was the discovery of the language of trees, the XML Path language. XPath can represent any part of an XML document, and can express that XML fragment in a non-XML syntax that lends itself to transport via URL or XML attribute value. XPath can also manipulate strings, numbers, and Booleans, thereby enhancing its knowledge management power. Finally, XPath is the driving engine in XSLT that enables XSLT to match patterns of data, data signatures, with templates that use common programming language constructs (such as `if` and `for-each`) to change the XML being processed. XPath is the third simple abstract machine.

If XPath is the power that drives XSLT, XSLT is the power that drives XML and schema-based programming. XSLT can accept any well-formed XML document and produce virtually any text result. Sounds simple, almost trivial; but the consequence of this simplicity is enough to keep you up at night.

In this chapter you saw a final example of XSLT – how it could take the model of a system represented in the Petri Net Markup Language and transform that PNML according to the rules of Petri net simulation. The result was a modeling, simulating, and analyzing engine that is immensely powerful and extremely simple (Petri nets and XML are kindred spirits). But XSLT doesn't stop there. It can transform PNML into SVG and pass that XML dialect to the Adobe SVG Viewer to be rendered graphically. Some schema-based programming researchers are extremely excited about the prospects this simple but powerful technology has on the future of computing, especially web-based development.

If you've read this chapter through, congratulations. I hope you're hooked for life. Read well and prosper...

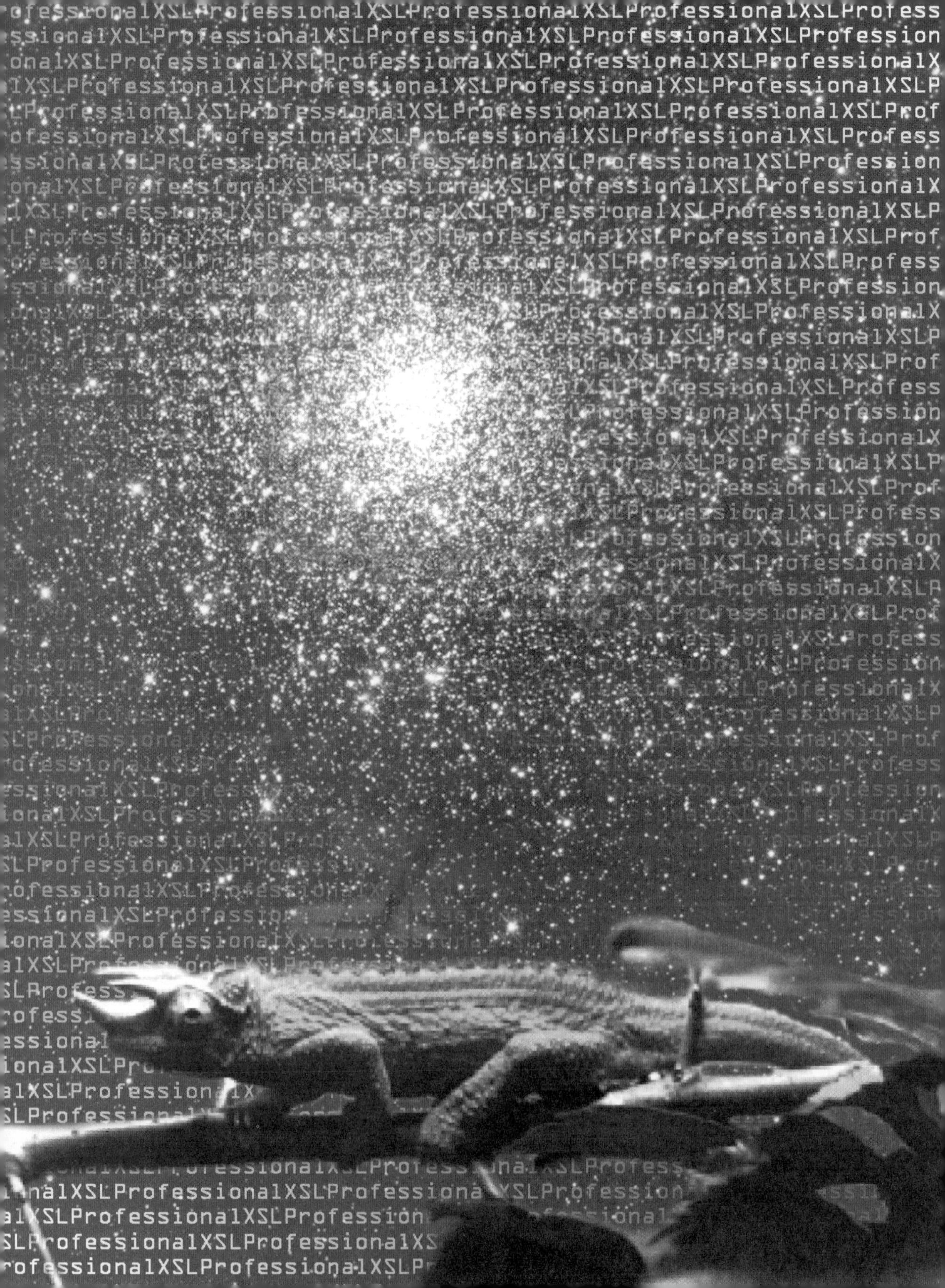

Case Study – Online Content Publication

In this case study I would like to show you a real-world use of XSLT transformations. In spite of the more advanced capabilities of XSLT, the most common use today remains the transformation of an XML source document into an HTML representation. Achieving this in an easily maintainable way that allows for code reuse is not necessarily an easy task. When you just plough into a project, primarily aiming just to get something working, the end result is often a set of XSLT files that bear a strong resemblance to the desired HTML pages. They are more like "HTML templates" than "descriptions of data transformations". Also, in this scenario you will end up coding similar logic over and over again, because for most web sites HTML pages are not all that different from one another.

What we will see in this case study is how to set up your XSLT stylesheets in such a way that you can reuse the logic in the transformation rules as much as possible, thereby keeping the total number of lines of code to a minimum. This will be of benefit later on when creating new user interfaces based on the same logic, or when making changes to the format, as it will minimize the need for changing or creating code. In the example shown in this case study we will reuse the logic inside the transformations for both:

❑ A batch transformation generating many separate static HTML pages

❑ A live transformation initiated from an ASP page, generating only the content requested

We will first present a source format that was created just for this exercise. It is designed to hold the content of an article (structured in chapters, sections, paragraphs, etc.) and some meta data, such as glossary terms and index information. After examining the source format, we will look at a very simple transformation that builds one long HTML file containing all the textual content of the article, but without the index, table of contents, glossary and such like.

Following this, we will start adding functionality to the stylesheet, bearing in mind that we want the functionality to be reusable and componentized. Therefore, along the way we will also break up the stylesheet into a number of modules that each represent a part of the overall functionality.

Our Source Format

Before we start dissecting the XSLT code, we will first have a look at the requirements of the situation: what is the format of the source code and what do we intend to transform it into? For the sake of this example, we will imagine we are a publisher of online content who owns many documents in one specific XML format. These documents should be published to the web in a fairly flexible way. This should include the possibilities of drastically changing the layout of all documents, changing platforms in the future, and publishing the content to more devices than just web browsers.

These requirements really beg for using XSLT to transform the content into HTML, setting up the transformations in a way that allows modifications (avoiding complete rebuilds) later on. Once good XSL-FO implementations are widely available, that would be a preferable way to publish the content to many output formats (check out Chapter 9 for more on XSL-FO).

Obviously, in the real world, the situation is seldom like this. Most publishers do not have their content encoded into one single XML format. Mostly they use proprietary non-XML formats, although some have been visionary enough in the past to store their content as SGML. In both cases, you'll have to transform the content to XML first or force the content deliverers to do so. This can be a hard task, but the rewards of a standardized data storage format can make it worthwhile.

The source format that we will be transforming into HTML here is a fairly straightforward hierarchical structure for describing documents. The parts of the document could be chapters, sections or paragraphs, but in the XML format they are equivalent and represented by a `<section>` element. Each `<section>` can be made up of other `<section>` elements, but can also contain its own content in the form of an HTML fragment (for reasons of well-formedness, this should be XHTML) . This inclusion of HTML in our source format means that we lose a bit of structure in the document, but it allows the authors of documents to use the rich set of layout elements that HTML offers, without us having to define a large XML based syntax. It is a bit of a trade-off.

A very small part of our example document (`sample-chapter.xml`) looks like this (the ... stands for omitted content):

```
<?xml version="1.0" encoding="iso-8859-1"?>
<document>
  <section>
    <title>XSLT in Context</title>
    <subtitle>
      First chapter from XSLT Programmers Reference by Michael Kay
    </subtitle>
    <section>
      <title>What is XSLT?</title>
      <html-content>
        <p >XSLT, which stands for
        eXtensible Stylesheet Language: Transformations,
        is a language which, according to the very first sentence in the
        ...
        success and generated so much excitement.</p>
      </html-content>
      <section>
        <title>Why Transform XML?</title>
        <html-content>
```

```
           <p >XML is a simple, standard way to interchange structured
           ...
           of formats to which we can transform XML, using XSLT.</p>
         </html-content>
         <section>
           <title>An Example: Transforming Music</title>
           <html-content>
             ...
           </html-content>
         </section>
       </section>
     </section>
   </section>
   <meta>
     <glossary>
       <entry word="glossary reference">
         Term that can be found in the glossary.
       </entry>
     </glossary>
   </meta>
 </document>
```

Let's look at the specifications of such a document, as could be specified in a DTD or a schema. These are the main things that should be noted:

- The <document> element can hold only one <section> child element (the root <section>) and one <meta> element.

- The level of nested <section> elements is unlimited.

- A <section> can hold both its own <html-content> element and nested <section> elements. The <html-content> must come before the <section> elements. The root <section> cannot hold its own HTML.

- A <section> can have a <title> child element. The root <section> can also hold a <subtitle>.

- A <section> can carry a count="off" attribute. This indicates that this section should not be counted when a chapter number is calculated (this is common for introduction chapters).

- The <html-content> element can hold any well-formed HTML code, but also some special elements (<glossary-ref> and <index-term>). In the transformations, we will have to take some special action when we encounter these within the HTML.

- The document holds no special information regarding display or formatting, other than anything that may be included within the <html-content> element.

The Transformation – Starting Simple

First, let's take a look at a very simple example of transforming our source XML into HTML. For testing our stylesheet, we took a chapter from *XSLT Programmer's Reference* (Wrox Press, ISBN 1-861003-12-9) and ported it to the format previously described. The source document is included in the source code download as `sample-chapter.xml`.

To style the document, we will attach a CSS stylesheet after processing the XML with XSLT. This stylesheet will not be the subject of this chapter, but it is included in the source code download as `style.css`. (See Chapter 9 for more details on CSS.)

The first XSLT stylesheet we will write is very simple – it will not contain much of the required functionality, but it will serve as a start. Let's have a look at the code for `simple.xsl`, explaining it as we go.

```
<?xml version="1.0"?>

<xsl:stylesheet xmlns:xsl="http://www.w3.org/1999/XSL/Transform" version="1.0" >

  <xsl:output omit-xml-declaration="yes" method="html" encoding="ISO-8859-1"/>
```

The start of the stylesheet should be fairly familiar. It starts with the XML declaration – this is not necessary, but adds to the clarity of the document (and can sometimes help the parser to recognize the encoding used). Then we start the stylesheet, declaring the `xsl` namespace and `version` attribute.

The `method` attribute of the `<output>` element indicates that our output format will be HTML and the `encoding` attribute is set to `ISO-8859-1` (ISO Latin 1). An XML declaration is not desired in the output, as it might confuse some HTML browsers, so we drop it using the `omit-xml-declaration` attribute.

The first template is the classic HTML boilerplate template. It creates the obligatory HTML elements for `<html>`, `<head>`, and `<body>`:

```
    <xsl:template match="/">
      <html>
      <head>
        <link href="style.css" rel="stylesheet" type="text/css" />
        <title>
          <xsl:value-of select="/document/section/title/text()"/>
        </title>
      </head>
      <body bgcolor="white">
        <table align="center" width="400"><tr><td>
          <h1><xsl:value-of select="/document/section/title/text()"/></h1>
          <h3><xsl:value-of select="/document/section/subtitle/text()"/></h3>
          <xsl:apply-templates select="/document/section/section"/>
        </td></tr></table>
      </body>
      </html>
    </xsl:template>
```

The value of the <title> element of the root <section> of the XML source is inserted within the <title> of the HTML document. In the HTML document <body>, we create a table of fixed width, containing only one cell. Inside the cell, we display the <title> and <subtitle> element values of the source document in <h1> and <h3> elements respectively. Then we hand over control to another template by instantiating <xsl:apply-templates>. Context is transferred to the child <section> nodes of the root <section>.

The template that matches <section> is a bit more complicated, because we want to create a different appearance for sections on different levels in the tree:

```
<xsl:template match="section">
  <xsl:element name="h{count(ancestor-or-self::section)}">
    <xsl:number level="multiple" format="1.a.A" count="section"/>
    <xsl:text> </xsl:text>
    <xsl:value-of select="title"/>
  </xsl:element>
  <xsl:apply-templates select="html-content/node()" mode="html-output"/>
  <xsl:apply-templates select="section" />
</xsl:template>
```

This template will be used for generating HTML for all levels of sections in the hierarchy. The output must consist of:

❑ The value of the <title> of the <section> – this must be in a different style for different levels of depth in the hierarchy

❑ The HTML content that is directly part of this <section>

❑ The HTML generated for underlying <section> elements

The title is created using the <xsl:element> element. The name attribute of the <xsl:element> element is an attribute value template, so we can generate a different element depending on the depth of the <section> element within the source XML. We create elements of the form <h2>, <h3>, etc. by counting the number of <section> elements on the ancestor-or-self axis. For the second level <section> (the root <section> is not processed by this template) we generate an <h2> element. This means that we cannot handle more than six levels of depth of <section> elements using HTML elements. If we would want to allow more levels, this code would have to change. We assume that six levels are enough.

The content of the heading element is created using an <xsl:number> element to generate chapter numbers, an <xsl:text> element to insert whitespace, and finally the value of the <title> element. This creates a text of the form:

```
<h3>1.a.A Why Transform XML?</h3>
```

After the title, we generate the HTML content by instantiating:

```
<xsl:apply-templates select="html/node()" mode="html-output"/>
```

We will explain the use of the special mode attribute when we look at the next template.

Passing the scope to the child <section> elements of the current <section> generates the last piece of content. It will cause this same template to be instantiated recursively. For example, this causes the subchapter "2.a" to appear directly after the HTML content of chapter "2".

The last template of the transformation is used for sending all HTML content inside the `<html-content>` element to the output.

```
<xsl:template match="node()|@*" mode="html-output">
  <xsl:copy>
    <xsl:apply-templates select="node()|@*" mode="html-output"/>
  </xsl:copy>
</xsl:template>
```

The XPath pattern `node()|@*` matches every XML node except for namespaces (`node()` matches any node except for attributes and namespaces). For each of these nodes, it creates an identical copy in the output and calls `<apply-templates>` for all child non-namespace nodes.

The special `mode` attribute value of `html-output` is employed in the sample to copy HTML to the output without interfering with other templates. The template has to be very generic, because the content that may be used within the `html-content` element can have many forms. It might, for example, contain a `<section>` element. This is not an existing HTML element, but you never know what the next version of HTML will contain. Anything `<html-content>` contains must be copied to the output, even `<section>` elements. If we did not use a special `mode` attribute, the second template (the one matching `<section>`) would also match any `<section>` element inside the HTML content. This would cause erroneous results. We will see more uses of modes in the rest of this case study.

> *Copying an entire arbitrary tree of XML to the output, as we do with the HTML content here, could also be done using `<xsl:copy-of>`. However, we do not really want everything to be copied – we want to copy everything except the elements `<index-term>` and `<glossary-ref>`. Later in this chapter, we will add functionality for doing something special whenever the processor encounters an `<index-term>` or `<glossary-ref>` element.*

The result of applying this stylesheet to the source XML will look like this (`doc.htm`):

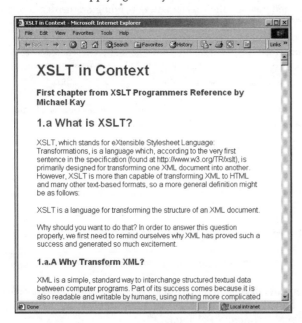

As you can see, we have a fairly decent output document already, but there are still a few flaws (the introduction chapter should not be numbered, and top-level chapters should be numbered 1, 2, 3, not 1.a, 1.b, 1.c), and some functionality is not yet available (table of contents, glossary, and index). Also, if you want to publish the documents in several formats, every format would require a new stylesheet, while the differences between each format would probably be quite small. In the rest of this chapter we will add functionality, moving some features of the stylesheet into reusable stylesheet components as we go.

Adding Functionality with Separate Stylesheets

The way to create reusable components in XSLT is by using the `<xsl:import>` and `<xsl:include>` elements (check out Chapter 5 for a full explanation). Of these, `<xsl:include>` is the most straightforward. A stylesheet referencing another file by means of this element will be treated as if the referenced document forms an actual part of the including stylesheet. Templates in the two stylesheets cannot have the same name or have the same matching expression and priority. This causes an error, just as it would when two templates with the same name are present in one stylesheet. This means that the author of the including stylesheet must have rather detailed information about the inner working of the included stylesheet – there is no isolation.

By using the `<xsl:import>` element, we can achieve (a bit) more independence for the components. When using `<xsl:import>`, the templates of the importing stylesheet always prevail over the templates in the imported stylesheet, even if they have a higher priority. The imported stylesheet elements will only be used if no matching template is available in the importing stylesheet. The result of this logic is that we can use `<xsl:import>` to create a new stylesheet by importing an existing one, and adding or overriding one or more templates of the imported document. Note that the overruled template can be called from the overruling template using `<xsl:apply-imports>`. This has some resemblance to subclassing in object-oriented programming.

In this case study we use `<xsl:import>` exclusively. In the real world, you will find that `<xsl:include>` is often easier to use and understand. However, in the long run, setting up your stylesheets using `<xsl:import>` will save you time and will result in greater flexibility, because it allows you to define a skeleton of functionality and refine parts of it by importing the skeleton and overruling one of the parts. We will see exactly how this works in the rest of this chapter.

An important thing to note about importing is that you must understand the exact working of the imported stylesheet to reuse it effectively. You can easily create unexpected behavior when you use a template name in the importing stylesheet that was already used in the imported stylesheet. Your new named template will always be used instead of the existing one (even if it has a higher priority). Always make sure that this is intentional.

Our First Import

When using reusable stylesheet components, we will often create one stylesheet per output format, importing all the reusable material and containing everything that is specific for its format. The primary transformations we are thinking of are:

❑   Batch transformation into a (potentially large) number of static HTML files

❑   Transformations that can be called from an ASP page to create a part of the document

If we now have a look at our simple stylesheet `simple.xsl`, we find two templates that might be reused for each output format: the one matching `section`, and the HTML output template. Let's copy these into a separate stylesheet (`content-output.xsl`). Just like any stylesheet document, this needs to be a valid stylesheet, with the usual `<xsl:stylesheet>` element and namespace declarations at the top:

```
<?xml version="1.0"?>

<xsl:stylesheet xmlns:xsl="http://www.w3.org/1999/XSL/Transform" version="1.0">
```

```
    <xsl:output omit-xml-declaration="yes" method="html" encoding="ISO-8859-1"/>

    <!-- This is the core template that generates the output for a section -->
    <xsl:template match="section" name="section-output">
      <!-- We use the HTML elements h1, h2, h3, etc. to control size of titles -->
      <!-- This is a limitation to the number of levels of hierarchy: if we would
      need more than six levels, we would have to change this -->
      <xsl:element name="h{count(ancestor-or-self::section)}">
        <xsl:number level="multiple" format="1.a.A" count="section"/>
        <xsl:text> </xsl:text>
        <xsl:value-of select="title"/>
      </xsl:element>
      <xsl:apply-templates select="html-content/node()" mode="html-output"/>
      <xsl:apply-templates select="section" />
    </xsl:template>

    <!-- The basic behavior for anything within the html-content element:
    copy to the output. We can later make exceptions. -->
    <xsl:template match="node()|@*" mode="html-output">
      <xsl:copy>
        <xsl:apply-templates select="node()|@*" mode="html-output"/>
      </xsl:copy>
    </xsl:template>

</xsl:stylesheet>
```

We'll remove them from the original stylesheet, replacing them with this line:

```
<xsl:import href="content-output.xsl"/>
```

Now let's fix those small problems we had with chapter numbering. First of all, it could be smart to move the generation of chapter numbers into a separate template within the imported stylesheet content-output.xsl. This can then be called from many places and be maintained in only one place (think of displaying chapter numbers after an index term in the index or when creating an entry in the table of contents). We will have to make sure that the create-number template generates numbers just the way we want them:

```
    <!-- This is the core template that generates the output for a section -->
    <xsl:template match="section" name="section-output">
      <!-- We use the HTML elements h1, h2, h3, etc. to control size of titles -->
      <!-- This is a limitation to the number of levels of hierarchy: if we would
      need more than six levels, we would have to change this -->
      <xsl:element name="h{count(ancestor-or-self::section)}">
        <xsl:call-template name="create-number"/>
        <xsl:text> </xsl:text>
        <xsl:value-of select="title"/>
      </xsl:element>
      <xsl:apply-templates select="html-content/node()" mode="html-output"/>
      <xsl:apply-templates select="section" />
    </xsl:template>

    <!-- Here we calculate the number and number-format for a section. This is
    used over and over for creating titles, references, index entries, etc... -->
    <xsl:template name="create-number">
```

```
      <xsl:param name="segment" select="current()"/>
      <xsl:if test="not($segment/@count = 'off')">
        <xsl:for-each select="$segment">
          <xsl:number level="multiple" format="1.a.A"
            count="section[not(@count = 'off')][parent::section]"/>
        </xsl:for-each>
      </xsl:if>
    </xsl:template>
```

The `create-number` template uses a parameter called `segment`. If no value is passed for this parameter, the template uses the current node. This parameter contains the node that will be counted. So, if no parameter is passed, the template will return the chapter number of the *current* chapter.

First of all, the template checks if this `<section>` should carry a number at all (if the `<section>` carries a `count="off"` attribute, no number should be displayed). If so, the template changes the current node to the one held in the `segment` parameter using `<xsl:for-each>` (this is an commonly used trick to change context). We need this context switch, because `<xsl:number>` counts the sequence number of the context node.

Finally, we changed the `count` attribute of the `<xsl:number>` element to prevent it counting `<section>` elements with `count="off"` attributes and to exclude the root `<section>`. To achieve this we added the predicates `[not(@count = 'off')]` and `[parent::section]`. The first predicate will return `true` if the `count` attribute has any other value than `off`, while the last predicate is true for all `<section>` elements except for the root `<section>`.

Creating a Table of Contents with Links to Chapters

The next step we want to take is generating a table of contents. It should allow us to show a list of links to the several parts of the document. What we need are:

❑   A template that generates the table of contents itself

❑   Templates that can be used to generate links to the `<section>` elements in the document

❑   An addition to the template that creates the `<section>` element's output to make it the target of an internal link

Enabling Linking

The last two aspects above seem to be of a more general functionality than the table of contents only, so let's build these templates into the `content-output.xsl` stylesheet. The following code shows some of the changes we make:

```
<!-- This is the core template that generates the output for a section -->
<xsl:template match="section" name="section-output">
  <a><xsl:attribute name="name">
    <xsl:call-template name="node-identifier"/>
  </xsl:attribute></a>
  <!-- We use the HTML elements h1, h2, h3, etc. to control size of titles -->
  <!-- This is a limitation to the number of levels of hierarchy: if we would
  need more than six levels, we would have to change this -->
  <xsl:element name="h{count(ancestor-or-self::section)}">
    <xsl:call-template name="create-number"/>
```

```
    <xsl:text> </xsl:text>
    <xsl:value-of select="title"/>
  </xsl:element>
  <xsl:apply-templates select="html-content/node()" mode="html-output"/>
  <xsl:apply-templates select="section" />
</xsl:template>
```

```
<!-- It is important to have a way to reference to a specific location in the
source document with a string value. This can be used to create links to
a specific location in the content and much more. XSLT provides us with
an easy function to do this. Implementing this call as a template allows
us to overrule it later. -->
<xsl:template name="node-identifier">
  <xsl:param name="id-node" select="self::*"/>
  <xsl:value-of select="generate-id($id-node)"/>
</xsl:template>
```

As you can see, we added some code to the template matching <section>. This adds an HTML anchor to the code (like: <a name="XCD45E"></a>). This allows us to refer to this place in the page from other pages. A separate template called node-identifier generates the value of the name attribute of the anchor, which will produce a unique string for each <section>. It is important that we have a uniform way to generate these unique strings, both here and when we generate the reference. In this case we used the generate-id() function from XSLT, but as you will see later, this does not always serve our goals, so we may want to override this template later on. We allow the calling code to pass a specific node that has to be identified, but if no node is passed, our template will default to the current context node (self::*).

This allows us to link to the output of any specific <section> element. Now we want to add templates to the content-output.xsl file to create the links themselves:

```
<!-- Create an HTML link to any section in the document. A link should always
be the same, both from the index or from another chapter. We locate the
logic of link-creation in this template. It relies on other templates for
determining the file location and the need for an anchor string (trailing
#blabla) -->
<xsl:template name="link-to">
  <xsl:param name="linktext" select="title/text()"/>
  <xsl:param name="target" />
  <a>
    <xsl:if test="$target">
      <xsl:attribute name="target">
        <xsl:value-of select="$target"/>
      </xsl:attribute>
    </xsl:if>
    <xsl:attribute name="href">
      <!-- first the filename -->
      <xsl:call-template name="file-of"/>
      <xsl:call-template name="anchor-of"/>
    </xsl:attribute>
    <xsl:value-of select="$linktext"/>
  </a>
</xsl:template>
```

```
<!-- For creating links, one must know the filename. Calculating the filename
is isolated in this template. In later versions, when we distribute the
content over many files, we will overrule this template with much more
interesting versions. -->
<xsl:template name="file-of">
  <xsl:text>doc.htm</xsl:text>
</xsl:template>

<!-- Here we decide if we need a trailing hash-string to identify the exact
spot in a page where we'll find a certain piece of information. For now we
have only one file, so we'll always need this extra info. -->
<xsl:template name="anchor-of">
  <xsl:text>#</xsl:text>
  <xsl:call-template name="node-identifier"/>
</xsl:template>
```

The link-to template generates an HTML link to the output of the current <section> node. The template is called with the text to describe the link and an optional target frame as parameters. The value of the href attribute is generated by calling two separate templates; one to create the filename and one to create the fragment locator part. The filename is a hard coded value (we will override it later), while the fragment locator is calculated using our node-identifier template. The hard coded filename doc.htm must be identical to the filename used on the command line in make.bat (see the code download) to indicate the output filename.

By calling the link-to template, we can now generate an HTML fragment like this:

```
<a href="doc.htm#b3ab1b9b7">Level 2: Keep Data Safe and Keep Users Calm</a>
```

Generating the Table of Contents

Now that we can generate links to parts of the document using just one line of code, let's make a new file, toc.xsl, to create a table of contents.

Note how we limit the number of levels that appear in the table using a parameter called index_maxdepth:

```
<?xml version="1.0"?>

<xsl:stylesheet xmlns:xsl="http://www.w3.org/1999/XSL/Transform" version="1.0">

  <xsl:param name="index_maxdepth">3</xsl:param>
  <xsl:output omit-xml-declaration="yes" method="html" encoding="ISO-8859-1"/>

  <!-- Jump to the root section and apply any templates with mode toc to it.
  The new mode is use to prevent interference with existing templates that
  generate the section pages and that match the same section elements. -->
  <xsl:template name="generateTOC">
    <xsl:apply-templates select="/document/section" mode="toc"/>
  </xsl:template>

  <xsl:template match="section" mode="toc">
    <div>
      <xsl:attribute name="style">
```

```
        margin-left:<xsl:value-of select="count(ancestor::section) * 5"/>pt
      </xsl:attribute>
      <xsl:call-template name="create-number"/>
      <xsl:text> </xsl:text>
      <xsl:call-template name="link-to"/>
      <br/>
    </div>
    <!-- only go on with deeper levels if the index_maxdepth parameter is
    set high enough -->
    <xsl:if test="$index_maxdepth &gt; count(ancestor::section) + 1">
      <xsl:apply-templates select="section" mode="toc"/>
    </xsl:if>
  </xsl:template>

</xsl:stylesheet>
```

Here again the `mode` attribute prevents different templates with overlapping `match` patterns from interfering with each other. The table of contents is built following the same pattern as when building the entire content. Therefore we need a template matching `<section>` elements here as well, except that here we want to generate somewhat different content: a link to the content rather than the content itself. By using `mode='toc'`, we make sure that we only instantiate templates that were written specifically for the table of contents. It also prevents us from overriding templates in other imported stylesheets.

The table of contents is created by generating a `<div>` HTML element for each `<section>` in the content document with a `style` attribute based on the nested level of the current `<section>`. The exact amount of indentation is calculated by multiplying the number of ancestors by five. Then, we display a chapter number, a space, and a link to the indicated document part.

Finally, as long as any child `<section>` elements are not above the maximum index depth, the same template will be applied recursively.

To use these new templates in the transformation, we have to update `simple.xsl` (now called `simple-with-toc.xsl`) to import the `toc.xsl` stylesheet and to call the `generateTOC` template:

```
<xsl:import href="content-output.xsl"/>
<xsl:import href="toc.xsl"/>
<xsl:output omit-xml-declaration="yes" method="html" encoding="ISO-8859-1"/>

  <xsl:template match="/">
    <html>
    <head><link href="style.css" rel="stylesheet" type="text/css" />
    <title>
      <xsl:value-of select="/document/section/title/text()"/>
    </title>
    </head>
    <body bgcolor="white">
    <table align="center" width="400"><tr><td>
     <h1><xsl:value-of select="/document/section/title/text()"/></h1>
     <h3><xsl:value-of select="/document/section/subtitle/text()"/></h3>
     <xsl:call-template name="generateTOC"/>
     <xsl:apply-templates select="/document/section/section"/>
     </td></tr>
     </table>
     </body></html>
  </xsl:template>
```

The transformation we have created so far is broken up into three parts, `content-output.xsl`, `toc.xsl`, and the primary document `simple-with-toc.xsl`. The latter is the central transformation that contains anything that does not seem reusable. The other two are separated according to the likely reusability of their constituent templates. One holds templates for outputting the content of a `<section>`, generating links to this content and generating appropriate chapter numbers, which could be of general use elsewhere. The remaining file, `toc.xsl`, has templates that, although quite specific, could be of use to a similar primary transformation.

Spreading Content Over Several Files

If documents are large it becomes less desirable to have all content together in one big file. For a user browsing our site it is more efficient if the content is split up over several files, as loading times and the need for scrolling are reduced. A user interface, such as the page below, demonstrates how we might want this to appear:

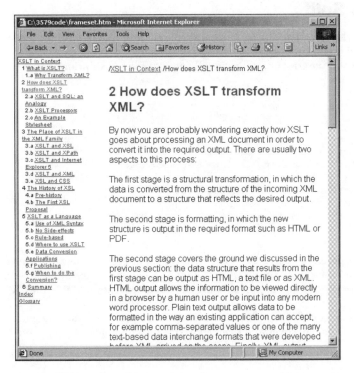

However, separating the content into multiple files poses some new problems for the developer:

❑ How can we generate multiple documents in one transformation? This is a feature that is not included in XSLT 1.0. It will be introduced in XSLT 1.1 with the element `<xsl:document>`, but currently the specification is still at 'working draft' status. However, the Saxon transformation engine offers an extension element called `<saxon:output>` (since version 6.1), and most other implementations allow this feature in one way or another. In this example we will use the Saxon syntax to allow generation of multiple files, so this code will only work with the Saxon processor.

❑ Navigation between the various files: we need a way to step easily from part of one document to part of another. The most obvious way to achieve this is by moving the table of contents into a separate file and displaying this in a frame.

❑ Keeping track of file names: when we create a link to a specific place in our content, we must indicate which file contains this content. This means we will have to change the templates that generate filenames and fragment locators.

❑ How should documents be split up? We will split up the document following the structure of the `<section>` elements. For each `<section>`, the HTML content is written to the output. Then, instead of generating the content for all child `<section>` elements, we create links for all child `<section>` elements and place their content in a new separate HTML files. We will use a global parameter to set the depth at which child `<section>` elements should still be included in their parent's document. High-level `<section>` elements have their own file; low-level `<section>` elements do not.

It's Time to Split

We will create stylesheet, specializing in creating output as multiple files. It is called `separate-output.xsl` and builds on `content-output.xsl` using `<xsl:import>`. As the importing document, any templates in `separate-output.xsl` will automatically have priority over imported ones with the same attributes.

```
<?xml version="1.0"?>

<xsl:stylesheet xmlns:xsl="http://www.w3.org/1999/XSL/Transform"
  xmlns:saxon="http://icl.com/saxon"
  version="1.0" extension-element-prefixes="saxon">

  <xsl:import href="content-output.xsl"/>

  <xsl:param name="separate_file_depth">2</xsl:param>
  <xsl:output omit-xml-declaration="yes" method="html" encoding="ISO-8859-1"/>
```

The saxon namespace is declared as an extension element prefix. This allows us to use the Saxon extension element `<saxon:output>`. Also note the global parameter `separate_file_depth` introduced here to control the level of splitting the document into multiple files.

Most HTML files that our XSLT will create will start and end with exactly identical elements. We don't want to code these elements over and over, so we create a template to wrap a piece of content inside an HTML frame:

```
<!-- Template to allow reuse of the standard start and end tags
of HTML documents. Content and title can be passed as parameters -->
<xsl:template name="pagewrapper">
  <xsl:param name="content"/>
  <xsl:param name="titlebar">
    <xsl:value-of select="/document/section/title/text()"/> - <xsl:value-of
      select="title/text()"/>
  </xsl:param>
  <html>
  <head><link href="style.css" rel="stylesheet" type="text/css" />
    <title>
```

```
          <xsl:value-of select="$titlebar"/>
      </title>
    </head>
    <body bgcolor="white">
      <table align="center" width="400"><tr><td>
        <xsl:copy-of select="$content"/>
      </td></tr></table>
    </body>
    </html>
  </xsl:template>
```

As you see, the content of the page and the page's title are passed as parameters. The `content` parameter will often hold a large tree of content that is to be placed inside the wrapper.

The first example of using the `pagewrapper` template is the new template matching `<section>`. It overrides the existing template imported from `content-output.xsl`:

```
<!-- Before generating the output for a section, we first want to decide
if this should happen within our current output document or that it
deserves a file of its own. -->
<xsl:template match="section">
  <xsl:choose>
    <xsl:when
      test="count(ancestor-or-self::section) &lt;= $separate_file_depth">
      <!-- start a new file, including headers and everything and pass it as
      content to new-file -->
      <xsl:call-template name="new-file">
        <xsl:with-param name="content">
          <xsl:call-template name="pagewrapper">
            <xsl:with-param name="content">
              <xsl:apply-imports/>
            </xsl:with-param>
          </xsl:call-template>
        </xsl:with-param>
        <xsl:with-param name="filename">
          <xsl:call-template name="file-of"/>
        </xsl:with-param>
      </xsl:call-template>
      <!-- end file -->
      <!-- now add a link to the new file -->
      <div>
        <xsl:call-template name="create-number" />
        <xsl:text> </xsl:text>
        <xsl:call-template name="link-to" />
      </div>
    </xsl:when>
    <xsl:otherwise>
      <xsl:apply-imports/>
    </xsl:otherwise>
  </xsl:choose>
</xsl:template>

<!-- this template is used to isolate the implementation specific
functionality of saxon:output in one template. -->
<xsl:template name="new-file">
```

```
      <xsl:param name="content"/>
      <xsl:param name="filename"/>

      <saxon:output file="{$filename}" omit-xml-declaration="yes" method="html"
        encoding="ISO-8859-1">
        <xsl:copy-of select="$content"/>
      </saxon:output>

  </xsl:template>
```

The template compares the depth of the current <section> with the global parameter
separate_file_depth. If no new file should be started, control is passed to the overridden template
in the imported stylesheet with <xsl:apply-imports>. If, however, the node should appear in a new
file, the new-file template is called. This template is a wrapper around the <saxon:output>
element. It is smart to use a wrapper in instances like this, because it allows us to later override only this
part of the functionality. As the <saxon:output> element is implementation-specific, it would
probably need to be replaced with different syntax if we wanted to switch to another processor. The
remainder of the logic of splitting up content would remain usable without modification.

The new-file template expects two parameters: the filename and the file content. The filename can be
generated by calling the file-of template (the current file-of template always returns 'doc.htm',
which is no longer what we want, but we will be modifying this template next). The content of the new
file can be generated by the overridden template, after being wrapped in <html> and <body> tags by
the new pagewrapper template.

The last thing we do is to generate a link to the new file in the file of the parent node. This is really easy
with the create-number and link-to templates.

How Can We Calculate the Correct Filenames?

Now we have the machinery in place to decide when to place content in a separate file. What we still
have to do is calculate the actual filenames for these files. In the previous paragraph we used the
template file-of to generate the filename for us. This is clever, because it allows us to use the same
logic for both creating files and creating links to these files. At the moment however, the file-of
template always returns a hard coded 'doc.htm'. This is not correct. There are basically three situations
for the calculation of the filename:

❑   The current node is the root node: the filename will be doc.htm

❑   The current node is not the root node, but is of a high enough level to have a separate
    filename (this depends on the value of the separate_file_depth parameter): the filename
    is doc{node-identifier}.htm (the node-identifier being a unique and reproducible
    code for any node), for example docb4a11b9.htm

❑   The current node has no file 'of its own': the filename is the filename of its parent <section>

These three factors each have a directly corresponding <xsl:when> or <xsl:otherwise> element in
the new template for file-of:

```
    <!-- We overrule the file-of template, because different sections
    can now end up in different files. -->
    <xsl:template name="file-of">
      <xsl:choose>
```

```
        <!-- the topmost node is an exception: it should point to doc.htm -->
        <xsl:when test="parent::document">
          <xsl:text>doc.htm</xsl:text>
        </xsl:when>

        <xsl:when test="count(ancestor-or-self::section) &lt;= $separate_file_depth
                        and self::section">
          <xsl:text>doc</xsl:text>
          <xsl:call-template name="node-identifier"/>
          <xsl:text>.htm</xsl:text>
        </xsl:when>

        <xsl:otherwise>
          <xsl:for-each select="ancestor::section[1]">
            <!-- this for-each is a trick to force a context switch -->
            <xsl:call-template name="file-of"/>
          </xsl:for-each>
        </xsl:otherwise>
      </xsl:choose>
    </xsl:template>
```

There are two things in this template that should be noted:

❑   When we check for the appropriate depth of the <section> element, we also demand that
     the current context has to be a <section>. This is important, because later on we want to be
     able to use the file-of template for other types of elements too (think of index terms). For
     generating a unique and reproducible code, we reuse the node-identifier template that we
     created before.

❑   Note how well the last decision rule (if you do not have a file of your own, use your parent's)
     fits in the XSLT programming model. The template just switches context using <xsl:for-
     each> and then recursively calls itself to find the parent's filename. This also makes sure that
     elements other than <section> get the filename of the <section> that holds them.

One more thing about creating links to several pages: at the moment, when we create a link to a
<section> using the link-to template, we always generate a link like this:

```
<a href="docb6ab1b7b3b1.htm#b6ab1b7b3b1">
```

Now docb6ab1b7b3b1.htm is the document containing the content of the <section> identified by
b6ab1b7b3b1. Note that the fragment locator (the part that begins with #) points to the same identifier,
which will be almost at the top of the page. Now if we follow a link like that, we will see the right page,
scrolled down to the title line of the topmost <section>. That is not what we want: when we link to a
<section> that has its own page, we want to link to the top of that page, not scroll down a few
millimeters to the title line. So we have to add a little bit more trickery to the template that will generate
the fragment locator when it is required:

```
<!--anchor-of must also be overruled, because some sections now have
their own file and need no # string appended -->
<xsl:template name="anchor-of">
  <!-- now check if a # must be appended -->
  <xsl:choose>
```

```
      <xsl:when test="count(self::section) = 0">
        <xsl:text>#</xsl:text><xsl:call-template name="node-identifier"/>
      </xsl:when>
      <xsl:when
        test="count(ancestor-or-self::section) &gt; $separate_file_depth">
        <xsl:text>#</xsl:text><xsl:call-template name="node-identifier"/>
      </xsl:when>
    </xsl:choose>
  </xsl:template>
```

Two cases are covered here:

❏   The node being linked to is not a <section>: if this is the case we always add the hash symbol and anchor to the link. We are probably linking to an index term.

❏   The current node is a <section>, but it is too deep in the tree to have its own page. Apparently, we are linking to a document part that is displayed on the page of its parent (or more remote ancestor). In this case we also want to append a # with anchor ID to the link.

If none of these apply, we do nothing, so no anchor will appear in the link. The link to the node identified by b6ab1b7b3b1 will now show up as:

```
<a href="docb6ab1b7b3b1.htm">
```

Come and Meet the Parents

For additional navigation, it would be nice if we could display at the top of every page a 'full path' of links to all ancestors of the current node. As we already have templates for creating links to other <section> elements, this task should be fairly easy:

```
<xsl:template name="full-path">
  <small>
    <xsl:for-each select="ancestor::section">
      /<xsl:call-template name="link-to"/>
    </xsl:for-each>
    /<xsl:value-of select="title/text()"/>
  </small>
  <br/>
</xsl:template>
```

```
<!-- Template to allow reuse of the standard start and end tags
     of HTML documents. Content and title can be passed as parameters -->
<xsl:template name="pagewrapper">
  <xsl:param name="content"/>
  <xsl:param name="titlebar">
    <xsl:value-of select="/document/section/title/text()"/> - <xsl:value-of
      select="title/text()"/>
  </xsl:param>
    <html>
    <head><link href="style.css" rel="stylesheet" type="text/css" />
    <title>
      <xsl:value-of select="$titlebar"/>
    </title>
    </head>
```

```
            <body bgcolor="white">
              <table align="center" width="400"><tr><td>
                <xsl:call-template name="full-path"/>
                <xsl:copy-of select="$content"/>
            </td></tr></table>
            </body>
          </html>
        </xsl:template>
```

As you can see, it is very simple to add this kind of functionality now that we have the templates in place for linking to sections. Note that the order of processing the ancestor sections is in document order; the ancestor highest in the tree comes first. The order of the ancestor axis however is 'reverse document order'; first finding the parent of the context node, then the grandparent and so on. It is important to realize that XSLT does not apply templates (including <xsl:for-each> loops) in the order of the XPath expression, but following document order (unless you specify another order using <xsl:sort>).

Minor Fixes to the Table of Contents and the Main Stylesheet

We have to adjust the way the table of contents is built for the new user interface. Most of it can stay as it appears in the old table of contents, but we have to create a separate HTML page to hold it. This is a very simple HTML page, but it cannot use the pagewrapper template, because we don't want a full path on top and a table 400 pixels wide. So we'll just create a new stylesheet called separate-toc.xsl that imports the toc.xsl stylesheet.

The generateTOC template must be wrapped by another template that generates the HTML code for the page start and end. Using an overriding template and calling the generateTOC from toc.xsl with <xsl:apply-imports> will not work in this case, because <xsl:apply-imports> works only for templates that were applied with <xsl:apply-templates>, not by <xsl:call-template>. We'll instead create a template with a new name (generateTOCFile) and call this from the main stylesheet. The generateTOCFile template will then explicitly call generateTOC.

```
    <?xml version="1.0"?>

    <xsl:stylesheet xmlns:xsl="http://www.w3.org/1999/XSL/Transform" version="1.0">

      <xsl:import href="toc.xsl"/>
      <xsl:output omit-xml-declaration="yes" method="html" encoding="ISO-8859-1"/>

      <!-- The TOC must be wrapped inside an HTML page. This is a bit
      different from the standard HTML wrapper page. It includes
      the base directive necessary for pointing from one frame to
      another and can include links for index and glossary if
      these are present. -->
      <xsl:template name="generateTOCFile">
        <html>
        <head><link href="style.css" rel="stylesheet" type="text/css" />
          <title>
            <xsl:value-of select="/document/section/title/text()"/> -
            <xsl:value-of select="/document/section/subtitle/text()"/>
          </title>
          <base target="doc-content"/>
        </head>
        <body bgcolor="white">
```

```
                <font size="1" type="Verdana, Arial, Helvetica">
                  <xsl:call-template name="generateTOC"/>
                  <xsl:if test="$index-filename">
                    <a href="{$index-filename}" target="doc-content">Index</a><br/>
                  </xsl:if>
                  <xsl:if test="$glossary-filename">
                    <a href="{$glossary-filename}" target="doc-content">Glossary</a><br/>
                  </xsl:if>
                </font>
            </body>
            </html>
        </xsl:template>

    </xsl:stylesheet>
```

Note the use of the HTML <base> element to make sure that all links in this page target the content frame. To call this new template we must make a new main stylesheet, `multi-page.xsl` as well:

```
<?xml version="1.0"?>

<xsl:stylesheet xmlns:xsl="http://www.w3.org/1999/XSL/Transform"
   xmlns:saxon="http://icl.com/saxon"  version="1.0"
   extension-element-prefixes="saxon">

    <xsl:import href="separate-output.xsl"/>
    <xsl:import href="separate-toc.xsl"/>
    <xsl:output omit-xml-declaration="yes" method="html" encoding="ISO-8859-1"/>

    <xsl:template match="/">
      <xsl:call-template name="pagewrapper">
        <xsl:with-param name="content">
          <h1><xsl:value-of select="/document/section/title/text()"/></h1>
          <h3><xsl:value-of select="/document/section/subtitle/text()"/></h3>
          <xsl:apply-templates select="/document/section/section"/>
        </xsl:with-param>
        <xsl:with-param name="titlebar">
          <xsl:value-of select="/document/section/title/text()"/>
        </xsl:with-param>
      </xsl:call-template>

      <saxon:output file="frameset.htm">
        <xsl:call-template name="generateFrameset"/>
      </saxon:output>

      <saxon:output file="toc.htm">
        <xsl:call-template name="generateTOCFile"/>
      </saxon:output>
    </xsl:template>

    <xsl:template name="generateFrameset">
      <html>
        <frameset border="1" cols="150,*" frameborder="1" >
          <frame marginwidth="0" name="ix" src="toc.htm"/>
          <frame marginwidth="10" name="doc-content" src="doc.htm"
            marginheight="10"/>
        </frameset>
      </html>
    </xsl:template>
</xsl:stylesheet>
```

The most conspicuous change is the use of the `pagewrapper` template from the main stylesheet to generate the HTML footer and header.

We also added an extra template to the main template to build the frameset document. Using the `<saxon:output>` element, we channel the output to `toc.htm` or `frameset.htm` as appropriate.

That's it: the document will now be split over multiple files. The number of separate files can be controlled using a parameter and we are still using as much functionality as possible from the original stylesheet documents, as we had created them before, enabling splitting up of the produced HTML. The only things missing now are the index and glossary.

Create a Glossary

Creating a glossary really boils down to two tasks:

❑   Creating a separate page containing all glossary entries in the document along with definitions.

❑   While creating the HTML content, we must intercept any occurrences of `<glossary-ref>` elements and make a link to the glossary in the output.

The first part is fairly easy, we just create a new stylesheet document called `glossary.xsl`. This starts with a special template that creates the page with a rather straightforward `<xsl:for-each>` loop. We use the `pagewrapper` template to do the standard HTML start and end:

```
<?xml version="1.0"?>

<xsl:stylesheet xmlns:xsl="http://www.w3.org/1999/XSL/Transform"  version="1.0">

  <xsl:output omit-xml-declaration="yes" method="html" encoding="ISO-8859-1"/>
  <!-- introduce the hardcoded filename of the glossary as a variable, so we may
  later overrule this value -->
  <xsl:variable name="glossary-filename">glossary.htm</xsl:variable>

  <xsl:template name="generateGlossary">
    <!-- Wrap the glossary in an HTML page of its own -->
    <xsl:call-template name="pagewrapper">
      <xsl:with-param name="content">
        <table align="center" width="300">
          <tr><td colspan="2">
            <h1>Glossary</h1>
          </td></tr>
          <xsl:for-each select="/document/meta/glossary/entry">
            <xsl:sort select="@word"/>
            <tr><td valign="top">
              <!-- add an anchor to each entry in the Glossary to allow
              hyperlinks to an individual word -->
              <a><xsl:attribute name="name">
                <xsl:value-of select="translate(@word, ' ,;&amp;', '____')"/>
              </xsl:attribute></a>
              <xsl:value-of select="@word"/>
            </td>
            <td valign="top">
```

```
            <xsl:value-of select="text()"/>
          </td></tr>
          <tr><td colspan="2"><hr/></td></tr>
        </xsl:for-each>
      </table>
    </xsl:with-param>
    <xsl:with-param name="titlebar">
      Glossary -
      <xsl:value-of select="/document/content/title/text()"/>
    </xsl:with-param>
  </xsl:call-template>
</xsl:template>
```

We use <xsl:for-each> for looping through all glossary entries in the document's <meta> element. They are sorted using the word attribute itself. Note how we also use the word attribute to turn the word into an anchor. This allows us to link from any page directly to this spot in the document. However, in a link like this:

```
<a href="glossary.htm#word">word</a>
```

you cannot use just any character after the #. A glossary entry with a space in it would cause an error. To prevent this, we use the XPath translate() function to turn all illegal characters (that is, the space, the comma, the ampersand and the semicolon) into underscores. The last parameter passed to translate() is a string of four underscores. If you were to pass it only one underscore, only the space would be converted to an underscore, while the comma, ampersand and semicolon would be eliminated (or rather converted to nothing).

Now we still have to create the links that actually point towards this glossary. This has to be done somewhere during the process of generating the HTML content. As you may remember, we used a special mode called 'html-output' to create the HTML code, by simply copying the source elements without interfering with other templates. In this special case however, we *want* to interfere with the process of copying HTML to the output. Only in the special case of the occurrence of a <glossary-ref> element do we want something different to happen. So we build a template that matches <glossary-ref> in the html-output mode:

```
<!-- intercept the occurrence of a glossary-ref element encountered while
sending the content of an html-content element to the output -->
<xsl:template match="glossary-ref" mode="html-output">
  <span style="background-color:#ffff66;cursor:hand;">
    <xsl:attribute name="title">
      <xsl:value-of
        select="/document/meta/glossary/entry[@word=current()/@word]/text()"/>
    </xsl:attribute>
    <xsl:attribute name="onClick">
      <xsl:text>javascript:</xsl:text>
      <xsl:text>window.open('</xsl:text>
      <xsl:value-of select="$glossary-filename"/>
      <xsl:text>#</xsl:text>
      <xsl:value-of select="translate(@word, ' ,;&amp;',' ___')"/>
      <xsl:text>', 'glossary', 'width=400,height=300,scrollbars=yes');
      return false;</xsl:text>
    </xsl:attribute>
```

```
        <!-- now go on sending the HTML code within the glossary-ref to the output
        as we were doing before this template was matched -->
        <xsl:apply-templates select="node()|@*" mode="html-output"/>
      </span>
    </xsl:template>
  </xsl:stylesheet>
```

We generate a `<span>` element with a number of attributes. First of all there is a hardcoded `style` attribute to make the background light yellow, as a visual indicator of the presence of extra information, and we specify the mouse cursor's appearance, to signal that the word can be clicked. Then a `title` attribute that holds the full text taken from the `<meta>` information, and providing the definition for the word. This `title` attribute will appear as a tool tip when the user hovers over the word (in Internet Explorer).

The `current()` function is used in the first `<xsl:value-of>` element to perform a context switch within the XPath expression, resulting in a matching operation. In this case, elements from another part of the source document are selected by matching their `word` attribute to the `word` attribute of the current context node. This is only one of the possible ways to solve this problem. Other ways would be to:

❑   Create a key using `<xsl:key>` (holding the explanations by word) and retrieve this information using the `key()` function.

❑   Store one of the two contexts in a variable using `<xsl:variable>` and use this variable in the XPath expression to make the context switch.

This last technique is more flexible and powerful, but the code can be longer and harder to read. In this case, we can create the matching operation within the XPath expression using the `current()` function. After that, we create an `onClick` attribute holding a URL of the form:

```
javascript:window.open('glossary.htm#word', 'glossary',
'width=400,height=300,scrollbars=yes');
```

which will open up a pop-up window to display the `glossary.htm` page. The name of the page (`glossary.htm`) is placed in a variable. We will use this variable in the importing stylesheet to set the name of the file to generate.

The content of the `<span>` element is generated by resuming the HTML generation process through the call to `<apply-templates>` in the `html-output` mode at the end of the `<span>`.

Create an Index

What makes up an index? As we saw before, the document's content includes occurrences of a special element called `<index-term>`. These elements indicate the presence of certain terms in the text that are interesting to the reader. These terms can be found in the index in alphabetical order, with page references to the point in the text. If the same term occurs in several places, only one entry should turn up in the index, with references to all occurrences. In a printed book (such as this one) the index entries will generally refer to page numbers. This does not really apply for a web site where we can include anchors in the text at the very spot of the occurrence and link straight to that place. We will use the chapter number as link text.

Technically, generating an index for the document is very much like generating the glossary: we have to create an extra page and make a small modification to the process of HTML generation. Therefore, it will not surprise you that the `index.xsl` stylesheet looks very similar to `glossary.xsl`:

```xml
<?xml version="1.0"?>
<xsl:stylesheet xmlns:xsl="http://www.w3.org/1999/XSL/Transform" version="1.0">

  <xsl:output omit-xml-declaration="yes" method="html" encoding="ISO-8859-1"/>
  <!-- introduce the hardcoded filename of the index as a variable, so we may
  later overrule this value -->
  <xsl:variable name="index-filename">full-index.htm</xsl:variable>

  <xsl:template name="generateIndex">
    <xsl:call-template name="pagewrapper">
      <xsl:with-param name="content">
        <h1>index</h1>
        <!-- we want to process only unique index-terms: if a term occurs twice
           in the content, we want one index entry with two page references behind
           it. We achieve this by processing only every first occurence of a term.
           In other words: only the index terms that have a title that does not
           occur in any index term preceding it. -->
        <xsl:for-each
          select="//index-term[not(@title = preceding::index-term/@title)]">
          <xsl:sort select="@title"/>
          <xsl:value-of select="@title"/>:
          <!-- Now for every unique entry, we want to generate references
           for all occurrences with that title. -->
          <xsl:for-each select="//index-term[@title = current()/@title]">
            <!-- add a comma for all but the first occurrence -->
            <xsl:if test="position() &gt; 1">
              <xsl:text>, </xsl:text>
            </xsl:if>
            <xsl:call-template name="link-to">
              <xsl:with-param name="linktext">
                <xsl:call-template name="create-number"/>
              </xsl:with-param>
            </xsl:call-template>
          </xsl:for-each>
          <br/>
        </xsl:for-each>
      </xsl:with-param>
      <xsl:with-param name="titlebar">
        Index -
        <xsl:value-of select="/document/section/title/text()"/>
      </xsl:with-param>
    </xsl:call-template>
  </xsl:template>

  <!-- intercept the occurrence of a index-term element encountered while
  sending the content of an html-content element to the output -->
  <xsl:template match="index-term" mode="html-output">
    <a>
      <xsl:attribute name="name"><xsl:call-template
        name="node-identifier"/></xsl:attribute>
      <xsl:apply-templates select="node()|@*" mode="html-output"/>
    </a>
  </xsl:template>
</xsl:stylesheet>
```

The `generateIndex` template creates an HTML page and passes this as a parameter to the `pagewrapper` template. The content is generated in an `<xsl:for-each>` loop cycling through all unique elements in the document. This uniqueness is forced by a predicate selecting only those `<index-term>` elements where no previous `<index-term>` elements (in document order) exist with the same `title` attribute. This ensures our XPath expression selects only the first occurrences of each `<index-term>`. The selection is then alphabetically sorted by the `title` attribute.

Now for each of these entries, we first write the `title` attribute itself to the HTML, followed by a colon. Then we start a new `<xsl:for-each>` loop, this time iterating through all `<index-term>` elements with the same name as the current one in the outer loop (just as when we created the glossary, we used the `current()` function to make the necessary context switch in the expression). For each of the occurrences of the `<index-term>`, we create a link. Before the link we place a comma, if it is not the first occurrence as determined by the `position()` function. We then instantiate the `link-to` template to create the link. Normally, `link-to` will generate the linking text from the context node by evaluating the XPath expression `'title/text()'`. This will not happen in this case, so we pass our own link text: the chapter number, generated by `create-number`. After the last reference we place a `<br>` element and we're done!

Now we have to include an anchor in the content at the point of the `<index-term>` element. This is a small change to the HTML generation process, so we use a template with `mode` set to `html-output` to match only `<index-term>` elements. It generates an `<a>` element with the `name` attribute set to the node identifier of the current element. Any content within the `<index-term>` element will be generated within the `<a>` element.

Changes to multi-page.xsl

The only things needed to implement the glossary and index in the main stylesheet are adding the appropriate `<xsl:import>` directives and calling the `generateIndex` and `generateGlossary` templates. The following code shows where to place the new code in the main stylesheet:

```
<xsl:import href="separate-output.xsl"/>
<xsl:import href="separate-toc.xsl"/>
<xsl:import href="index.xsl"/>
<xsl:import href="glossary.xsl"/>

<xsl:output omit-xml-declaration="yes" method="html" encoding="ISO-8859-1"/>

<xsl:template match="/">
  <xsl:call-template name="pagewrapper">
    <xsl:with-param name="content">
      <h1><xsl:value-of select="/document/section/title/text()"/></h1>
      <h3><xsl:value-of select="/document/section/subtitle/text()"/></h3>
      <xsl:apply-templates select="/document/section/section"/>
    </xsl:with-param>
    <xsl:with-param name="titlebar">
      <xsl:value-of select="/document/section/title/text()"/>
    </xsl:with-param>
  </xsl:call-template>

  <saxon:output file="frameset.htm">
    <xsl:call-template name="generateFrameset"/>
  </saxon:output>
```

```
    <saxon:output file="toc.htm">
      <xsl:call-template name="generateTOCFile"/>
    </saxon:output>

    <saxon:output file="{$index-filename}">
      <xsl:call-template name="generateIndex"/>
    </saxon:output>

    <saxon:output file="{$glossary-filename}">
      <xsl:call-template name="generateGlossary"/>
    </saxon:output>
  </xsl:template>
```

To generate the index and glossary in separate files, the main stylesheet uses the `<saxon:output>` element, but the filename is created using imported variables from the `index.xsl` and `glossary.xsl` stylesheets. This way, links to the glossary always use the same name as the element that creates the file. If the main stylesheet later needs to use another file name for the glossary, the variable could be overruled. This would also affect the use of the imported variable in the imported templates. We will see how this works in a moment when we change the transformation to be ASP compatible.

We still have to make a small change to the code that generates the table of contents: we want to include links to the index and glossary as well. It is really just a case of including links to the locations stored in the variables `glossary-filename` and `index-filename`. We want them to appear at the bottom of the table of contents in the `separate-toc.xsl` file:

```
  <xsl:call-template name="generateTOC"/>
  <xsl:if test="$index-filename">
    <a href="{$index-filename}" target="doc-content">Index</a><br/>
  </xsl:if>
  <xsl:if test="$glossary-filename">
    <a href="{$glossary-filename}" target="doc-content">Glossary</a><br/>
  </xsl:if>
```

We use a test first to only create each link if the corresponding variable exists. In a way, this modification creates a dependency between the table of contents, index and glossary stylesheets. But they can still be used separately without the need for further change, so this is acceptable.

The Family Tree

That's it: we have implemented all of the functionality required by building additions to existing code, but we always kept reusability and later additions in mind. If you take a look at the following diagram, note how the code we created for the 'document in one page' is still present in the stylesheets `content-output.xsl` and `toc.xsl`. We could still generate both the one-page version and the multi-page version using the same code for generating the chapter headers and the table of contents. If we decided that the table of contents would look better using `<ul>` and `<li>` rather than incrementing the indentation, we would have to make changes in just one place.

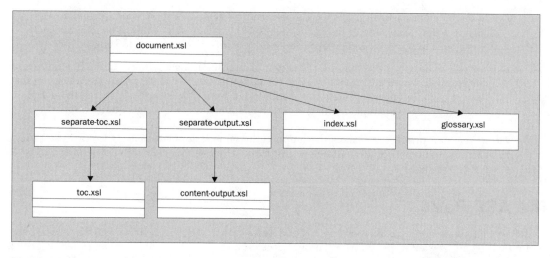

To take the reuse theme one step further, in the last part of this case study we will use our stylesheets from an ASP page to generate the HTML pages on the fly with MSXML3, as opposed to a batch process using Saxon. If we've got the design right so far, this should be possible through just replacing `multi-page.xsl` and reusing the logic in the underlying imported stylesheets with little change.

A Live Transformation Version

The transformation we have built in this case study is aimed at generating a web site from a source document. This has been done in a batch process, generating all of the available pages in one go. Often, this is just what you want: the resulting HTML files can be uploaded to any web server and the performance of serving static HTML is unsurpassed. Still, there are situations where batch processing is not suitable, for example if the source data is frequently or even continuously updated, or if you want any server side processing to occur when a page is requested. Another case would be if the form of the page varies according to user parameters in the query string (remember `separate_page_depth`?). In these sorts of situations, the obvious solution is to generate the pages on the fly (live). If the table of contents is requested, we produce only the table of contents; if chapter 2.A.1 is requested, we generate just that.

There are several techniques for generating HTML pages in response to a web client request, such as Java servlets, PHP, ColdFusion, and JSP, but in this example we will use Microsoft Active Server Pages (ASP). You could just as well use one of the other technologies: as XML and XSLT are platform-independent technologies, the issues I shall be covering will be equally applicable to all.

We will write a stylesheet and an ASP page that together create a web site with identical functionality to the one generated by batch process. There will consequently be a number of necessary changes to the transformation:

❑ The filenames will change. In the batch transformation, the filename was unique for each page; in a live transformation, any given page will be generated by a single `.asp` file where the difference between pages will be given by the CGI parameters of the query string passed to access them.

❑ The node identifier does not work for us anymore and will have to be replaced by something else. It relies on the `generate-id()` function, which is not reliable when used in several separated transformation processes.

❑ In the batch process, all pages were generated in one go. Now, we want to generate only one page at a time according to the client request. This means that we must be able to specify parameters to pass to the stylesheet depending on the page we want to generate.

❑ We will have to prevent the new-file template from doing anything. In the batch process, this template would generate a new file for nodes that were not supposed to show up in the current page. In our new situation, we still do not want to see these nodes, but there is no longer a need to generate anything until the client actually requests a node.

We will write a new primary stylesheet that imports the same stylesheets as multi-page.xsl did, but overrides templates inappropriate to the new transform. The live transformation stylesheet will be called live-transform.xsl.

The ASP Page

Before we look at live-transform.xsl, let's have a look at the ASP code we will be using. It may not be directly relevant to the transformation, but it shows us how the XSLT will be called. Especially interesting to see is how the parameters of the stylesheet are passed. The code uses the Microsoft XSLT engine in the MSXML3 DLL. This is the main code showdoc.asp:

```
Dim oStyle
Dim oDoc
Dim oTemplate
Dim oProc

Set oDoc = Server.CreateObject("MSXML2.FreeThreadedDOMDocument")
Set oStyle = Server.CreateObject("MSXML2.FreeThreadedDOMDocument")
Set oTemplate = Server.CreateObject("MSXML2.XSLTemplate")

oStyle.load Server.MapPath("live-transform.xsl")

oDoc.load Server.MapPath(CStr(Request("doc")))

Set oTemplate.stylesheet = oStyle
Set oProc = oTemplate.createProcessor

oProc.addParameter "doc", CStr(Request("doc"))
oProc.addParameter "pagetype", CStr(Request("pagetype"))
oProc.addParameter "node", CStr(Request("node"))
oProc.addParameter "separate_file_depth", "2"

oProc.input = oDoc
oProc.output = Response

oProc.transform
```

The first line in this fragment loads the live-transform.xsl stylesheet into a FreeThreadedDOMDocument object. The location of the source document is passed in the Request variable doc. This document is loaded into oDoc. Then, with an XSLTemplate object, we create our XSLTProcessor object, to which we append four parameters. Three of these parameters, pagetype, doc and node, are set to have the value of the passed CGI parameters of the same name. The separate_file_depth parameter is set to a fixed value.

The three parameters from the query string indicate which page must be created:

❑ The doc parameter indicates the location of the source document. Once we have created the ASP page, we obviously want to use it to transform many source documents. We must pass not only the intended source document as a parameter, but also its location, for the purpose of generating links.

❑ The pagetype parameter can have one of several values:

  ❑ toc: generates the table of contents.

  ❑ index: generates the index page.

  ❑ glossary: generates the glossary.

  ❑ node: generates a page for one of the <section> elements of the content, identified by the node parameter.

  ❑ In all other cases, the transformation will generate the outer frameset.

❑ node: the identifier of the <section> element that we want to appear as the content of the page.

A typical URL using this ASP page would look like this:

    http://localhost/proxsl/asp/showDoc.asp?pagetype=node&doc=sample-chapter.xml&node=36

The URL to get you to the frameset holding the document would be:

    http://localhost/proxsl/asp/showDoc.asp?doc=sample-chapter.xml

Note the use of oProc.output to specify the Response object as the output stream for the transformation. This is much more efficient than first creating a resulting document, serializing it to a string and then writing this string to the Response object.

The Stylesheet

Let's create the stylesheet now, following the list of changes presented in the introduction paragraph.

Our New Filename System

Firstly, the filenames we generate must change to reflect the new URLs, because the pages are all generated by one ASP file with variable parameters. We must make sure that all links navigating the site are changed to reflect this. Luckily, we have placed the calculation for a filename in a separate template so that it can be easily overridden by the following template which is included in the importing stylesheet:

```
<xsl:template name="file-of">
  <xsl:choose>
    <xsl:when test="count(ancestor-or-self::section) &lt;=$separate_file_depth
    and self::section">
      <xsl:text>showDoc.asp?pagetype=node&amp;doc=</xsl:text>
      <xsl:value-of select="$doc"/>
      <xsl:text>&amp;node=</xsl:text>
      <xsl:call-template name="node-identifier"/>
    </xsl:when>
```

```
      <!-- this is a trick to force a context switch to the ancestor section -->
      <xsl:otherwise>
        <xsl:for-each select="ancestor::section[1]">
          <!-- Recursively call file-of template with the new context -->
          <xsl:call-template name="file-of"/>
        </xsl:for-each>
      </xsl:otherwise>

    </xsl:choose>
  </xsl:template>
```

The template is actually simpler than the one we are overriding, containing a single <xsl:choose> with just two options:

❏   The first case holds when the current node is a <section> element that deserves its own page: we generate a URL, inserting the result of the node-identifier template as a parameter value. The parameter doc is set to the value that was passed in; the pagetype parameter is hardcoded to node.

❏   In all other cases the filename will be that produced for the closest ancestor <section> element.

This template will generate URLs for all pages that contain a part of the document. However, we have not yet accounted for links to the index from the table of contents or to the glossary from the text and table of contents. These links are generated in several places, but they always use the variables index-filename and glossary-filename. By overriding these variables in the main stylesheet, everything should be fine:

```
  <xsl:variable name="glossary-filename">
    showDoc.asp?doc=
    <xsl:value-of select="$doc"/>
    &amp;pagetype=glossary
  </xsl:variable>

  <xsl:variable name="index-filename">
    showDoc.asp?doc=
    <xsl:value-of select="$doc"/>
    &amp;pagetype=index
  </xsl:variable>
```

Secondly, we need a new node identifier. We are currently using node-identifier for generating a unique identifier to create links to nodes. The template uses the built-in function generate-id(), which has one major drawback in this scenario. The XSLT specification states that the generate-id() function must always return the same value for the same node, but a processor is not obliged to use the same identifiers in separate transformations. This is no problem in a batch transformation: the identifiers for creating links are the same identifiers for generating the filename. However, in a live transformation, each page is the result of a separate transformation and thus generate-id() cannot be relied on. Actually, both Saxon and MSXML3 seem to generate identical IDs every transformation, but if we want to use only standard XSLT, we should not rely on that. Therefore we will devise our own way to generate an identifier for elements in the content document. The most important requirement for the identifier is that it must be different for all nodes. A second requirement is that we need to be able to find a node that has a specific ID (when we get a node parameter with a certain value, we must know which node to process).

Let's use the document order number of the element, ignoring any text nodes, attributes and comments, as they are irrelevant in this case.

```
      <xsl:template name="node-identifier">
        <xsl:param name="id-node" select="self::*"/>
        <xsl:value-of select="count($id-node/preceding::*) + count($id-node/ancestor-
or-self::*)"/>
      </xsl:template>
```

To calculate the document position of an element, we calculate the number of elements on the `ancestor-or-self` and `preceding` axes. The reason to include both axes may not be immediately obvious, but the position of an element is equal to the number of elements that started (had their starting tag) before our starting tag. This includes all elements that have opened and closed (the `preceding` axis) and all elements that have started before us, but have not yet been closed (our ancestors). Finally, we must also count ourselves, so we require the `ancestor-or-self` axis.

If you need to find a node by its ID, we could then use something like:

```
/descendant::*[position() = $id]
```

The initial `/descendant::*` above implies the first descendant of the root of any type. The predicate qualifies this to read 'select the (first) element in the document whose position in document order matches the value of the `$id` variable'.

One Page At a Time

Our third requirement is to generate only one page at a time. In the batch transformation, we had a template matching the document root. In this template, the generation of all pages was started. We will create a very similar template, but instead of starting all creation processes consecutively, the template will decide which process will be started. This is implemented using `<xsl:choose>`:

```
<xsl:template match="/">
  <xsl:choose>
    <!-- Produce main content page -->
    <xsl:when test="$pagetype='node'">
      <xsl:for-each select="/descendant::*[position() = $node]">
        <!-- call the core content generation, bypassing the decision to start a
        new page -->
        <xsl:call-template name="pagewrapper">
          <xsl:with-param name="content">
            <xsl:call-template name="section-output"/>
          </xsl:with-param>
        </xsl:call-template>
      </xsl:for-each>
    </xsl:when>

    <!-- Produce index page -->
    <xsl:when test="$pagetype='index'">
      <xsl:call-template name="generateIndex"/>
    </xsl:when>

    <!-- Produce glossary page -->
    <xsl:when test="$pagetype='glossary'">
      <xsl:call-template name="generateGlossary"/>
    </xsl:when>
    <!-- Produce table of contents page -->
    <xsl:when test="$pagetype='toc'">
      <xsl:call-template name="generateTOCFile"/>
    </xsl:when>
```

```
      <!-- Produce main frameset otherwise -->
      <xsl:otherwise>
        <xsl:call-template name="generateFrameset"/>
      </xsl:otherwise>
    </xsl:choose>
  </xsl:template>
```

Which page is generated depends on the value of the `pagetype` parameter. When we have `pagetype` set to node, the `node` parameter is used as well to produce the identifier of the required node.

Note that we make a direct call to the template that matches `<section>` in `content-output.xsl`. An overriding template exists in `separate-output.xsl`, but in this special case, we do not want to instantiate this template. The template from `separate-output.xsl` will decide to start a new page for nodes that are on a high level in the document, which is what we normally require, but not at the very start of a transformation. In the batch process, this was overcome by hard coding the transformation of the root `<section>` in the root template. Now that we are doing a live transformation, any node can be the topmost node of the transformation. We can get away with calling the template in `content-output.xsl` directly instead of using `<xsl:apply-imports>`, but it seems a bit of a hack. A better solution would be to add a 'no-separation' parameter to the `section` template in `separate-output.xsl` and pass in 'yes' for the first node in a transformation.

Suppressing the New Page Template

The fourth thing we need to do is to neutralize the `new-file` template. At the moment, if the `section` template decides that a new page must be started, it calls the `new-file` template, which includes some Saxon-specific code to start a new output file. In our live transformation, we don't want to generate any other page: in fact, we want to do nothing and ignore all the information in the processed node.

```
<xsl:template name="new-file">

    <!-- override the new-file template. It should not do anything -->
    <xsl:param name="content"/>
    <xsl:param name="filename"/>

</xsl:template>
```

There are still some final details to clean up. The `generateFrameset` template must be overridden to reference the new filenames for the frames' content:

```
<xsl:template name="generateFrameset">
  <html>
    <frameset border="1" cols="150,*" frameborder="1" >
      <frame marginwidth="0" name="ix"
        src="showdoc.asp?doc={$doc}&amp;pagetype=toc"/>
      <frame marginwidth="10" name="doc-content"
        src="showdoc.asp?pagetype=node&amp;doc={$doc}&amp;node=2"
        marginheight="10"/>
    </frameset>
  </html>
</xsl:template>
```

Look at how we pass a hardcoded value of 2 for the `node` parameter in the URL of the `doc-content` frame, which refers to the second element in the document, which will always be the root `<section>`, and the `<section>` we require as the initial content of the frame.

Conclusions

It worked pretty well. We managed to reuse a lot of the batch processing templates in the live version, although the flow of events and the initialization of the transformation were changed significantly. However, we did not have to touch any of the code inside the imported stylesheets, so the batch transformation is still valid as it stands.

An important lesson I hope you've learned is never to include two different functionalities in a single template if later you might want to override one of them and not the other. Also, try to keep any platform-specific code inside a wrapper template to allow it to be overridden later.

As always, reusability has some unfortunate side effects on performance:

- ❑ Parsing a stylesheet from many different contributing stylesheets will take more time than one monolithic stylesheet. This should not be a problem if you can cache the compiled stylesheet, as MSXML3 allows you to do.

- ❑ The number of different templates in the stylesheet tends to grow with reuse. This will make matching operations more expensive.

- ❑ In the case of the new-file template, we made a template that just ignores all passed content. Still, because of the way we implemented this, the stylesheet will build all of the content below the starting node and only afterwards will some parts be copied to the result tree, and other parts discarded. This is highly inefficient. A very smart processor could spot that a passed parameter is not used at all in a template and then ignore the value of the parameter entirely. I am not aware of any processor that currently does this, although the XSLT specification has been written to allow this optimization fairly easily.

Summary

In this case study we have seen how:

- ❑ To move functionality into a separate template to encourage reuse from several locations

- ❑ To move templates into a separate stylesheet allowing reuse of their functionality in several different stylesheets

- ❑ `<xsl:import>` allows us to reuse functionality from another stylesheet, while still allowing us to tailor this functionality for the task in hand

- ❑ To create multiple interfaces to one source, not by building a transformation for each look, but by only building the parts that differentiate the new interface and the old one

- ❑ To build a template that generates a standard XML wrapper around a variable piece of XML content (the pagewrapper template)

> **In essence, when you are designing an application that includes XSLT transformations, think about which parts, and which logic, will be used again and again, maybe in many different transformations. Place this logic in a separate stylesheet and access the generic components with `<xsl:import>` and `<xsl:apply-imports>`.**

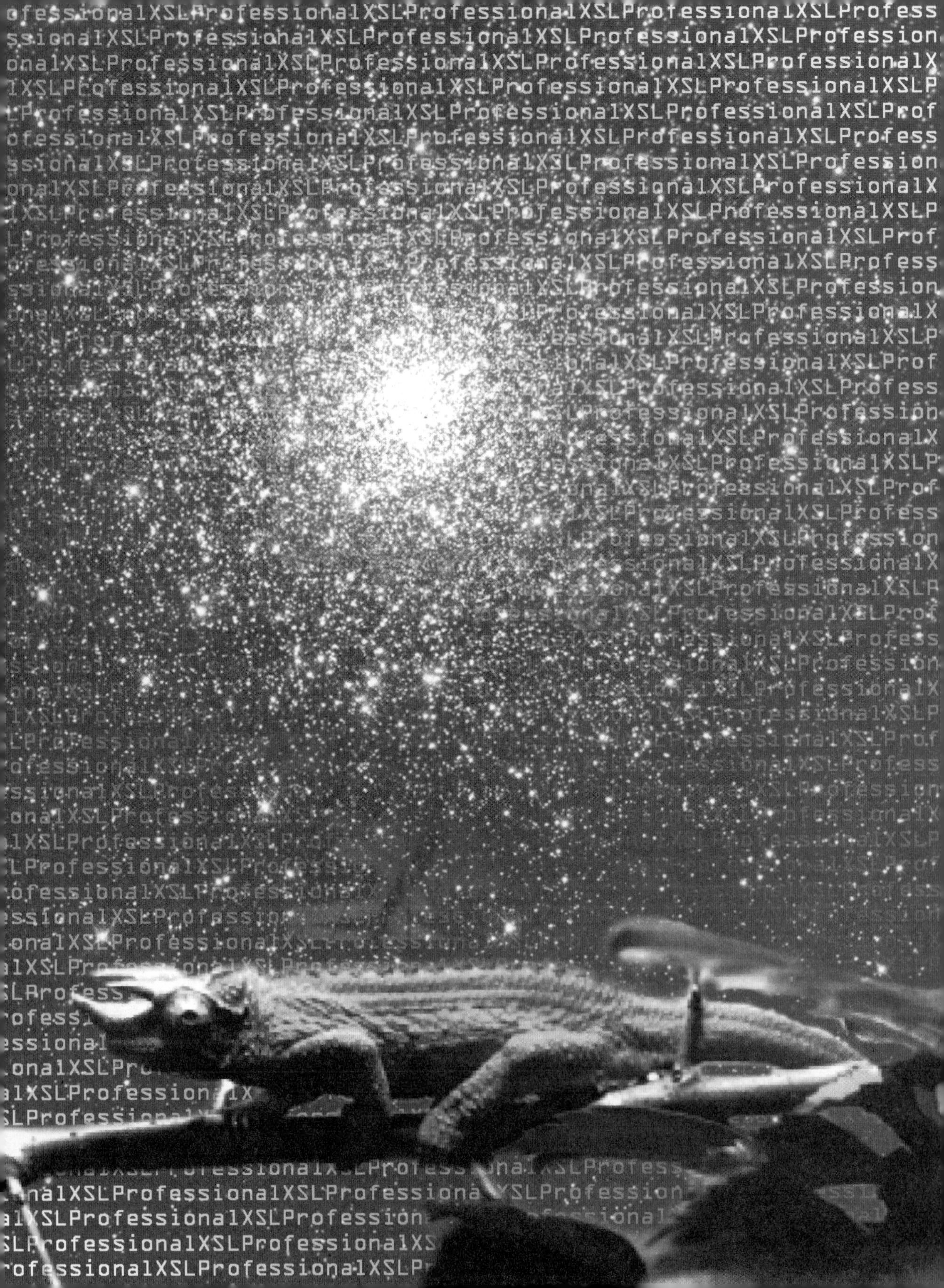

XPath Reference

XPath is a W3C Recommendation, describing a syntax for selecting a set of nodes from an XML document. Version 1.0 of XPath reached Recommendation status on 16 November 1999. The requirements document for version 2.0 was a working draft at the time of writing. XPath is an essential part of the XSLT Recommendation.

An XPath location path contains one or more "location steps", separated by forward slashes (/). Each location step has the following form:

```
axis-name::node-test[predicate]*
```

In plain English, this is an axis name, then two colons, then a node test, and finally zero or more predicates each contained in square brackets. A predicate can contain literal values (for example, 4, 'hello'), operators (+, -, =, etc.) and other XPath expressions. XPath also defines a set of functions for use in predicates.

The XPath axis defines a part of the document, from the perspective of the "context node". This node serves as the 'starting point' for selecting the result set of the XPath expression. The node test makes a selection from the nodes on the given axis. By adding predicates, it is possible to select a subset from these nodes. If the expression in the predicate returns true, the node remains in the selected set, otherwise it is removed.

In this reference we will list the XPath axes, node tests and functions. For each entry, we will list whether it is implemented in version 1.0 of the specification. Also, we will list in which versions of the Microsoft implementation the feature was implemented. Other implementations are not listed.

You can find an online version of the reference at: http://www.vbxml.com/xsl/xpathRef.asp.

We chose to list details on the several MSXML implementations, because Microsoft has chosen to ship several partial implementations of the specification. Although the latest version (MSXML 3.0) is a complete implementation, in many environments the older implementations are still in use. MSXML 2.0 is the version shipped with Internet Explorer 5, causing it to be the most widely installed XSLT implementation (and sadly one of the most incomplete as well). MSXML 2.6 is a version that was released as a preview, but was shipped with certain versions of BizTalk server. Therefore some developers are forced to work with this version.

Other implementations, such as Xalan and Saxon, are not listed here. You can more or less trust their latest versions to implement version 1.0 of the implementation and you will normally not be forced to use a specific version.

An online version of this reference can be found at: http://www.vbxml.com/xsl/XpathRef.asp.

Axes

Below, I list each axis with a description of the nodes it selects. The primary node type of an axis indicates what kind of nodes are selected by the literal node test or the * node test (see under the *literal name* node test for an example). For some axes, XPath defines a shorthand syntax. The form of this syntax and its primary node type are listed for every axis.

ancestor

Description:	Contains the context node's parent node, its parent's parent node etc., all the way up to the document root. If the context node is the root node, the ancestor node is empty.
Primary node type:	Element
Shorthand:	None
Implemented:	W3C 1.0 specification (recommendation) MSXML 2.6 (January 2000 preview) MSXML 3.0

ancestor-or-self

Description:	Identical to the ancestor axis, but including the context node itself.
Primary node type:	Element
Shorthand:	None
Implemented:	W3C 1.0 specification (recommendation) MSXML 2.6 (January 2000 preview) MSXML 3.0

attribute

Description:	Contains all attributes on the context node. The axis will be empty unless the context node is an element.
Primary node type:	Attribute
Shorthand:	@
Implemented:	W3C 1.0 specification (recommendation) MSXML 2.6 (January 2000 preview) (erroneously returns namespace declarations as well) MSXML 3.0

child

Description:	Contains all direct children of the context node (that is the children, but not any of the children's children).
Primary node type:	Element
Shorthand:	Default axis if no axis is given
Implemented:	W3C 1.0 specification (recommendation) MSXML 2.0 (IE5) (only shorthand syntax) MSXML 2.6 (January 2000 preview) MSXML 3.0

descendant

Description:	All children of the context node, including all children's children recursively.
Primary node type:	Element
Shorthand:	//
Implemented:	W3C 1.0 specification (recommendation) MSXML 2.0 (IE5) (only shorthand syntax) MSXML 2.6 (January 2000 preview) MSXML 3.0

descendant-or-self

Description:	Identical to the descendant axis, but including the context node itself.
Primary node type:	Element
Shorthand:	None
Implemented:	W3C 1.0 specification (recommendation) MSXML 2.6 (January 2000 preview) MSXML 3.0

following

Description:	Contains all nodes that come after the context node in the document order. This means that the opening tag of the node must come after the closing tag of the context node, and therefore excludes the descendants of the context node.
Primary node type:	Element
Shorthand:	None
Implemented:	W3C 1.0 specification (recommendation) MSXML 3.0

following-sibling

Description:	Contains all siblings (children of the same parent node) of the context node that come after the context node in document order.
Primary node type:	Element
Shorthand:	None
Implemented:	W3C 1.0 specification (recommendation) MSXML 3.0

namespace

Description:	Contains all namespaces available on the context node. This includes the default namespace and the xml namespace (these are automatically declared in any document). The axis will be empty unless the context node is an element.
Primary node type:	Namespace
Shorthand:	None
Implemented:	W3C 1.0 specification (recommendation) MSXML 3.0

parent

Description:	Contains the direct parent node (and only the direct parent node) of the context node, if there is one.
Primary node type:	Element
Shorthand:	..
Implemented:	W3C 1.0 specification (recommendation) MSXML 2.0 (IE5) (only shorthand syntax) MSXML 2.6 (January 2000 preview) MSXML 3.0

preceding

Description:	Contains all nodes that come before the context node in the document order. This includes only elements that are already closed (their closing tag come before the context node in the document), and therefore excludes all ancestors of the context node.
Primary node type:	Element
Shorthand:	None
Implemented:	W3C 1.0 specification (recommendation) MSXML 3.0

preceding-sibling

Description:	Contains all siblings (children of the same parent node) of the context node that come before the context node in document order.
Primary node type:	Element
Shorthand:	None
Implemented:	W3C 1.0 specification (recommendation) MSXML 3.0

self

Description:	Contains only the context node itself.
Primary node type:	Element
Shorthand:	.
Implemented:	W3C 1.0 specification (recommendation) MSXML 2.0 (IE5) (only shorthand syntax) MSXML 2.6 (January 2000 preview) MSXML 3.0

Node tests

A node test describes a test performed on each node of an axis to decide whether it should be included in the result set. Appending a predicate can later filter this result set.

*

Description:	Returns `true` for all nodes of the primary type for the axis.
Implemented:	W3C 1.0 specification (recommendation) MSXML 2.0 (IE5) MSXML 2.6 (January 2000 preview) MSXML 3.0

comment()

Description:	Returns `true` for all comment nodes.
Implemented:	W3C 1.0 specification (recommendation) MSXML 2.0 (IE5) MSXML 2.6 (January 2000 preview) MSXML 3.0

literal name

Description:	Returns `true` for all nodes of that name of the primary node type. If the node test is `'PERSON'`, it returns `true` for all nodes `<PERSON>` (if the primary node type is `Element`).
Implemented:	W3C 1.0 specification (recommendation) MSXML 2.0 (IE5) MSXML 2.6 (January 2000 preview) MSXML 3.0

node()

Description:	Returns `true` for all nodes, except attributes and namespaces.
Implemented:	W3C 1.0 specification (recommendation) MSXML 2.0 (IE5) MSXML 2.6 (January 2000 preview) MSXML 3.0

processing-instruction(name?)

Description:	Returns true for all processing instruction nodes. If a name parameter is passed (the question mark means that it is optional), it returns true only for processing instruction nodes of that name.
Implemented:	W3C 1.0 specification (recommendation) MSXML 2.0 (IE5) (called pi() in MSXML2) MSXML 2.6 (January 2000 preview) MSXML 3.0

text()

Description:	Returns true for all text nodes.
Implemented:	W3C 1.0 specification (recommendation) MSXML 2.0 (IE5) MSXML 2.6 (January 2000 preview) MSXML 3.0

Functions

To filter a subset from the result set of nodes that was selected with an axis and node test, we can append a predicate within square brackets. The expression within the brackets can use literal values (numbers, strings, etc.), XPath expressions, and a number of functions described by the XPath specification.

Each function is described below by a line of this form:

return-type **function-name** (parameters)

For each parameter, we display the type (object, string, number, node-set) and where necessary a symbol indicating if the parameter is optional (?) or can occur multiple times (+). The type object means that any type can be passed.

If an expression is passed as a parameter, it is first evaluated and (if necessary) converted to the expected type before passing it to the function.

boolean **boolean** (object)
Converts anything passed to it to a Boolean.
`boolean(attribute::name)` will return `true` if the context node has a `name` attribute.

Parameter:
object
Numbers result in `true` if they are not zero or NaN.
Strings result in `true` if their length is non-zero.
Node-sets return `true` if they are non-empty.

Implemented:
W3C 1.0 specification (recommendation)
MSXML 2.6 (January 2000 preview)
MSXML 3.0

number **ceiling** (number)
Rounds a passed number to the smallest integer that is not smaller than the passed number.
`ceiling(1.1)` returns 2

Parameter:
number
The number that must be rounded.

Implemented:
W3C 1.0 specification (recommendation)
MSXML 3.0

string **concat** (string1, string2+)
Concatenates all passed strings to one string.
`concat('con', 'c', 'a', 't')` returns `concat`

Parameters:
string1
The first string.

string2
All following strings.

Implemented:
W3C 1.0 specification (recommendation)
MSXML 2.6 (January 2000 preview)
MSXML 3.0

boolean **contains** (string1, string2)
Returns true if string1 contains string2.
contains('Teun Duynstee', 'uy') returns true.

    Parameters:
    string1
    The source string.

    string2
    The string that must be searched for.

    Implemented:
    W3C 1.0 specification (recommendation)
    MSXML 2.6 (January 2000 preview)
    MSXML 3.0

---

number **count** (node-set)
Returns the number of nodes in the passed node-set.
count(child::*[@name]) returns the number of child elements of the context node that have a name attribute.

    Parameter:
    node-set
    The node-set that is to be counted.

    Implemented:
    W3C 1.0 specification (recommendation)
    MSXML 2.6 (January 2000 preview)
    MSXML 3.0

---

boolean **false** ( )
Always returns false. This may seem useless, but XPath does not define a True and False literal value, so the function can be used to construct expressions like:
starts-with(@name, 'T') = false()

    Implemented:
    W3C 1.0 specification (recommendation)
    MSXML 2.6 (January 2000 preview)
    MSXML 3.0

---

number **floor** (number)
Rounds a passed number to the largest integer that is not larger than the passed number.
floor(2.9) returns 2
floor(-1.1) returns -2

    Parameter:
    number
    The number that must be rounded.

    Implemented:
    W3C 1.0 specification (recommendation)
    MSXML 3.0

node-set **id** (string)

Returns the element identified by the passed identifier. Note that this will only work in validated documents, because for non-validated documents the parser has no way of knowing which attributes represent ID values.

Parameter:
string
The ID value.

Implemented:
W3C 1.0 specification (recommendation)
MSXML 2.0 (IE5)
MSXML 2.6 (January 2000 preview)
MSXML 3.0

---

boolean **lang** (string)

Returns `true` if the language of the context node is the same as the passed language parameter. The language of the context node can be set using the `xml:lang` attribute on itself or any of its ancestors. This feature of XML isn't used frequently.
`lang('en')` returns `true` for English language nodes.

Parameter:
string
Language identifier.

Implemented:
W3C 1.0 specification (recommendation)
MSXML 3.0

---

number **last** ( )

Returns the index number of the last node in the current context node-set.
`child::*[position() = last()-1]` selects the penultimate child element of the context node.

Implemented:
W3C 1.0 specification (recommendation)
MSXML 2.0 (IE5) (called end() in MSXML2)
MSXML 2.6 (January 2000 preview) (does not work when used on the descendant axis)
MSXML 3.0

---

string **local-name** (node-set?)

Returns the local part of the name of the first node (in document order) in the passed node-set. For example, the local part of an `<xsl:value-of>` element is `value-of`.

Parameter:
node-set
If no node-set is specified, the current context node is used.

Implemented:
W3C 1.0 specification (recommendation)
MSXML 2.6 (January 2000 preview)
MSXML 3.0

string **name** (node-set?)
Returns the name of the passed node. This is the fully qualified name, including namespace prefix.

Parameter:
node-set
If no node-set is specified, the current context node is used.

Implemented:
W3C 1.0 specification (recommendation)
MSXML 2.6 (January 2000 preview)
MSXML 3.0

string **namespace-uri** (node-set?)
Returns the full URI that defines the namespace of the passed node.
namespace-uri(@href) in an XHTML document might return
'http://www.w3.org/Profiles/XHTML-transitional'

Parameter:
node-set
If no node-set is specified, the current context node is used.

Implemented:
W3C 1.0 specification (recommendation)
MSXML 2.6 (January 2000 preview)
MSXML 3.0

string **normalize-space** (string?)
Returns the whitespace-normalized version of the passed string. This means that all leading and trailing whitespace gets stripped and all sequences of whitespace get combined to one single space.
normalize-space('   some   text   ') would return 'some text'

Parameter:
string
If no string is passed, the current node is converted to a string.

Implemented:
W3C 1.0 specification (recommendation)
MSXML 2.6 (January 2000 preview)
MSXML 3.0

boolean **not** (boolean)
Returns the inverse of the passed value.
not(@name) returns true if there is no name attribute on the context node.

Parameter:
boolean
An expression that evaluates to a Boolean value

Implemented
W3C 1.0 specification (recommendation)
MSXML 2.6 (January 2000 preview)
MSXML 3.0

---

number **number** (object?)
Converts parameter to a number.
`number(' -3.6 ')` returns the number `-3.6`
The `number()` function does not use any localized settings, so you must only use this conversion when the format of the numeric data is language-neutral.

    Parameter:
    object
    If nothing is passed, the current context node is used.

    Implemented:
    W3C 1.0 specification (recommendation)
    MSXML 2.6 (January 2000 preview)
    MSXML 3.0

---

number **position** ( )
Returns the position of the current context node in the current context node-set.
`position()` returns 1 for the first node in the context node-set.

    Implemented:
    W3C 1.0 specification (recommendation)
    MSXML 2.6 (January 2000 preview)
    MSXML 3.0

---

number **round** (number)
Rounds a passed number to the nearest integer.
`round(1.5)` returns 2, `round(-1.7)` returns `-2`

    Parameter:
    number
    The number that must be rounded

    Implemented:
    W3C 1.0 specification (recommendation)
    MSXML 3.0

---

boolean **starts-with** (string1, string2)
Returns `true` if string1 starts with string2.
`starts-with(@name, 'T')` returns `true` if the value of the name attribute starts with a capital T

    Parameters:
    string1
    The string that must be checked.

    string2
    The substring that must be searched for.

    Implemented:
    W3C 1.0 specification (recommendation)
    MSXML 2.6 (January 2000 preview) (somehow this fails to work in the `test` attribute of an `<xsl:if>` element)
    MSXML 3.0

string **string** (object?)
Converts the passed object to a string value.

Parameter:
object
If nothing is passed, the result is an empty string.

Implemented:
W3C 1.0 specification (recommendation)
MSXML 2.6 (January 2000 preview)
MSXML 3.0

---

number **string-length** (string?)
Returns the number of characters in the passed string.
`string-length('Teun Duynstee') returns 13`

Parameter:
string
If nothing is passed, the current context is converted to a string.

Implemented:
W3C 1.0 specification (recommendation)
MSXML 2.6 (January 2000 preview)
MSXML 3.0

---

string **substring** (string, number1, number2?)
Returns the substring from the passed string starting at the number1 character, with the length of number2. If no number2 parameter is passed, the substring runs to the end of the passed string.
`substring('Teun Duynstee', 6) returns 'Duynstee'`

Parameters:
string
The string that will be used as source for the substring.

number1
Start location of the substring.

number2
Length of the substring.

Implemented:
W3C 1.0 specification (recommendation)
MSXML 2.6 (January 2000 preview)
MSXML 3.0

---

string **substring-after** (string1, string2)

Returns the substring following the first occurrence of string2 inside string1. For example, the return value of `substring-after('2000/3/22', '/')` would be `3/22`.

    Parameters:
    string1
    The string that serves as source.

    string2
    The string that is searched in the source string.

    Implemented:
    W3C 1.0 specification (recommendation)
    MSXML 2.6 (January 2000 preview)
    MSXML 3.0

---

string **substring-before** (string1, string2)

Returns the string part preceding the first occurrence of the string2 inside the string1. For example, the return value of `substring-before('2000/3/22', '/')` would be `2000`.

    Parameters:
    string1
    The string that serves as source.

    string2
    The string that is searched in the source string.

    Implemented:
    W3C 1.0 specification (recommendation)
    MSXML 2.6 (January 2000 preview)
    MSXML 3.0

---

number **sum** (node-set)

Sums the values of all nodes in the set when converted to number.

`sum(student/@age)` returns the sum of all `age` attributes on the student elements on the child axis of the context node.

    Parameter:
    node-set
    The node-set containing all values to be summed.

    Implemented:
    W3C 1.0 specification (recommendation)
    MSXML 3.0

string **translate** (string1, string2, string3)
Translates characters in string1 to other characters. Translation pairs are specified by string2 and string3. For example, `translate('A Space Odissei', 'i', 'y')` would result in A Space Odyssey, and `translate('abcdefg', 'aceg', 'ACE')` would result in AbCdEf. The final g gets translated to nothing, because the string3 has no counterpart for that position in the string2.

Parameters:
string1
String to be translated character by character.

string2
String defining which characters must be translated.

string3
String defining what the characters from the string2 should be translated to.

Implemented:
W3C 1.0 specification (recommendation)
MSXML 2.6 (January 2000 preview)
MSXML 3.0

---

boolean **true** ( )
Always returns true.
Implemented:
W3C 1.0 specification (recommendation)
MSXML 2.6 (January 2000 preview)
MSXML 3.0

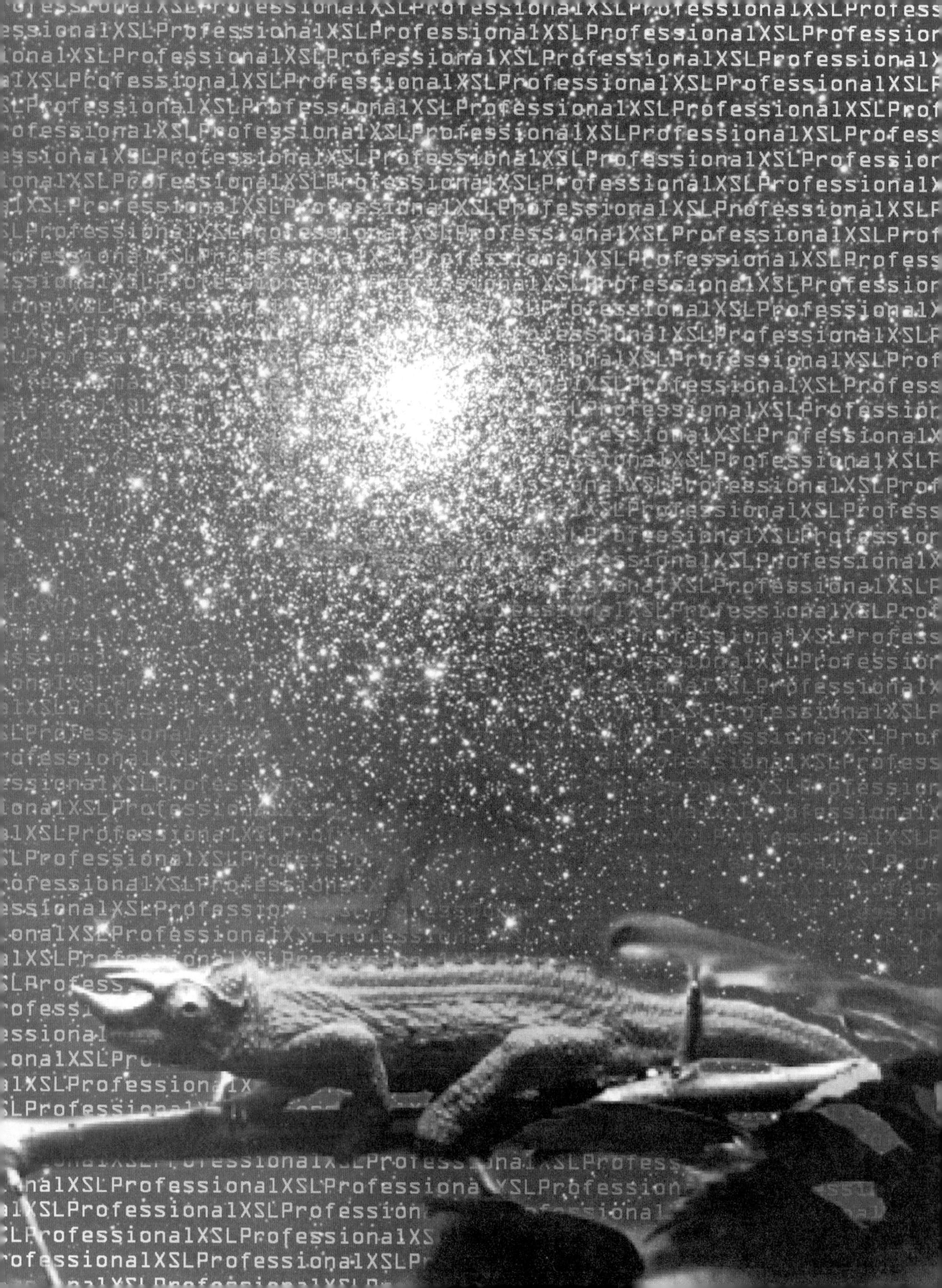
XSLProfessional

B

XSLT Reference

This reference appendix describes the elements and functions that are part of XSLT. For the XPath functions that can also be used with XSLT, see Appendix A.

The XSLT 1.0 specification became a W3C Recommendation on 16 November 1999. Version 1.1 was a Working Draft at the time of writing, as were the requirements for version 2.0. As in Appendix A, we will describe not only the functionality as described in the specifications, but also in which releases of the MSXML library the feature is implemented, since some older partial implementations of this library can still be found in many environments.

This is not done for the many other implementations, such as Xalan and Saxon. Distributions of XSLT processors will normally come with a description of the conformance to the XSLT 1.0 specification.

Both the attributes on XSLT elements and the parameters of XSLT functions can be of several types. At the end of this appendix, you will find a list of the types used in the elements and functions of XSLT.

You can find an online version of this reference at: http://www.vbxml.com/xsl/XSLTRef.asp.

Elements

The XSLT stylesheet is itself an XML document, using a number of special elements in its own namespace. This namespace is `http://www.w3.org/1999/XSL/Transform`, but in this appendix (and the rest of this book) we simply use the prefix `xsl`.

For each element we give a short description of its use, describe the attributes that can or must be used on the element, and indicate where in the stylesheet the element can occur (as a child of which other elements).

<xsl:apply-imports>

For calling a template from an imported stylesheet that was overruled in the importing stylesheet. This is normally used if you want to add functionality to a standard template that you imported using `<xsl:import>`.

Implemented:	W3C 1.0 specification (recommendation) W3C 1.1 specification (working draft) MSXML 3.0
Can contain:	No other elements
Can be contained by:	`<xsl:attribute>`, `<xsl:comment>`, `<xsl:copy>`, `<xsl:document>`, `<xsl:element>`, `<xsl:fallback>`, `<xsl:for-each>`, `<xsl:if>`, `<xsl:message>`, `<xsl:otherwise>`, `<xsl:param>`, `<xsl:processing-instruction>`, `<xsl:template>`, `<xsl:variable>`, `<xsl:when>`

<xsl:apply-templates>

Used to pass the context on to another template. The `select` attribute specifies which nodes should be transformed now; the processor decides which templates will be used.

Attributes:

`select` (optional) — Expression describing which nodes in the source document should be transformed next. Defaults to `child::*`.

Type:	node-set-expression
Attribute Value Template:	no

`mode` (optional) — By adding a `mode` attribute, the processor will transform the indicated source document nodes using only templates with this same `mode` attribute. This allows us to process the same source node in different ways.

Type:	qname
Attribute Value Template:	no

Implemented	W3C 1.0 specification (recommendation) W3C 1.1 specification (working draft) MSXML 2.0 (IE5) MSXML 2.6 (January 2000 preview) MSXML 3.0
Can contain	`<xsl:sort>`, `<xsl:with-param>`

Can be contained by	`<xsl:attribute>`, `<xsl:comment>`, `<xsl:copy>`,
	`<xsl:document>`, `<xsl:element>`, `<xsl:fallback>`,
	`<xsl:for-each>`, `<xsl:if>`, `<xsl:message>`,
	`<xsl:otherwise>`, `<xsl:param>`, `<xsl:processing-`
	`instruction>`, `<xsl:template>`, `<xsl:variable>`,
	`<xsl:when>`

`<xsl:attribute>`

Generates an attribute in the destination document. It should be used in the context of an element (either a literal, `<xsl:element>`, or some other element that generates an element in the output). It must occur before any text or element content is generated.

Attributes:

name (required)	The name of the attribute.	
	Type:	qname
	Attribute Value Template:	yes
namespace (optional)	The namespace (the default uses the namespace of the element the attribute is placed on).	
	Type:	uri-reference
	Attribute Value Template:	yes
Implemented:	W3C 1.0 specification (recommendation) W3C 1.1 specification (working draft) MSXML 2.0 (IE5) MSXML 2.6 (January 2000 preview) MSXML 3.0	

Can contain:	`<xsl:apply-imports>`, `<xsl:apply-templates>`, `<xsl:call-`
	`template>`, `<xsl:choose>`, `<xsl:copy>`, `<xsl:copy-of>`,
	`<xsl:fallback>`, `<xsl:for-each>`, `<xsl:if>`,
	`<xsl:message>`, `<xsl:number>`, `<xsl:text>`, `<xsl:value-`
	`of>`, `<xsl:variable>`	

Can be contained by:	`<xsl:attribute-set>`, `<xsl:copy>`, `<xsl:document>`, `<xsl:element>`, `<xsl:fallback>`, `<xsl:for-each>`, `<xsl:if>`, `<xsl:message>`, `<xsl:otherwise>`, `<xsl:param>`, `<xsl:template>`, `<xsl:variable, xsl:when>`	

<xsl:attribute-set>

Used to define a set of attributes that can then be added to an element as a group by specifying the `<xsl:attribute-set>` element's name attribute value in the `use-attribute-sets` attribute on the `<xsl:element>` element.

Attributes:

name (required)	Name that can be used to refer to this set of attributes.
	Type: qname
	Attribute Value Template: no
use-attribute-sets (optional)	For including an existing attribute set in this attribute set.
	Type: qnames
	Attribute Value Template: no
Implemented:	W3C 1.0 specification (recommendation) W3C 1.1 specification (working draft) MSXML 3.0
Can contain:	`<xsl:attribute>`
Can be contained by:	`<xsl:stylesheet>`, `<xsl:transform>`

<xsl:call-template>

Used to call a template by name. Causes no context switch (change of context node) as `<xsl:apply-templates>` and `<xsl:for-each>` do. The template you call by name will still be processing the same context node as your current template. This element can be used to reuse the same functionality in several templates.

Attributes:

name (required)	Name of the template you want to call.
	Type: qname
	Attribute Value Template: no
Implemented:	W3C 1.0 specification (recommendation) W3C 1.1 specification (working draft) MSXML 3.0
Can contain:	`<xsl:with-param>`
Can be contained by:	`<xsl:attribute>`, `<xsl:comment>`, `<xsl:copy>`, `<xsl:document>`, `<xsl:element>`, `<xsl:fallback>`, `<xsl:for-each>`, `<xsl:if>`, `<xsl:message>`, `<xsl:otherwise>`, `<xsl:param>`, `<xsl:processing-instruction>`, `<xsl:template>`, `<xsl:variable>`, `<xsl:when>`

<xsl:choose>

For implementing the choose/when/otherwise construct. Compare to `Case/Select` in Visual Basic or `switch` in C and Java.

Implemented:	W3C 1.0 specification (recommendation) W3C 1.1 specification (working draft) MSXML 2.0 (IE5) MSXML 2.6 (January 2000 preview) MSXML 3.0
Can contain:	`<xsl:otherwise>`, `<xsl:when>`
Can be contained by:	`<xsl:attribute>`, `<xsl:comment>`, `<xsl:copy>`, `<xsl:document>`, `<xsl:element>`, `<xsl:fallback>`, `<xsl:for-each>`, `<xsl:if>`, `<xsl:message>`, `<xsl:otherwise>`, `<xsl:param>`, `<xsl:processing-instruction>`, `<xsl:template>`, `<xsl:variable>`, `<xsl:when>`

<xsl:comment>

For generating a comment node in the destination document.

Implemented:	W3C 1.0 specification (recommendation) W3C 1.1 specification (working draft) MSXML 2.0 (IE5) MSXML 2.6 (January 2000 preview) MSXML 3.0
Can contain:	`<xsl:apply-imports>`, `<xsl:apply-templates>`, `<xsl:call-template>`, `<xsl:choose>`, `<xsl:copy>`, `<xsl:copy-of>`, `<xsl:fallback>`, `<xsl:for-each>`, `<xsl:if>`, `<xsl:message>`, `<xsl:number>`, `<xsl:text>`, `<xsl:value-of>`, `<xsl:variable>`
Can be contained by:	`<xsl:copy>`, `<xsl:document>`, `<xsl:element>`, `<xsl:fallback>`, `<xsl:for-each>`, `<xsl:if>`, `<xsl:message>`, `<xsl:otherwise>`, `<xsl:param>`, `<xsl:template>`, `<xsl:variable>`, `<xsl:when>`

<xsl:copy>

Generates a copy of the context node in the destination document. Does not copy any children or attributes.

Attributes:

use-attribute-sets (optional)	For adding a set of attributes to the copied node.

Type:	qnames
Attribute Value Template:	no

Implemented:	W3C 1.0 specification (recommendation) W3C 1.1 specification (working draft) MSXML 2.0 (IE5) MSXML 2.6 (January 2000 preview) MSXML 3.0
Can contain:	<xsl:apply-imports>, <xsl:apply-templates>, <xsl:attribute>, <xsl:call-template>, <xsl:choose>, <xsl:comment>, <xsl:copy>, <xsl:copy-of>, <xsl:document>, <xsl:element>, <xsl:fallback>, <xsl:for-each>, <xsl:if>, <xsl:message>, <xsl:number>, <xsl:processing-instruction>, <xsl:text>, <xsl:value-of>, <xsl:variable>
Can be contained by:	<xsl:attribute>, <xsl:comment>, <xsl:copy>, <xsl:document>, <xsl:element>, <xsl:fallback>, <xsl:for-each>, <xsl:if>, <xsl:message>, <xsl:otherwise>, <xsl:param>, <xsl:processing-instruction>, <xsl:template>, <xsl:variable>, <xsl:when>

<xsl:copy-of>

Copies a full tree, including attributes and children, to the destination document. If multiple nodes are matched by the select attribute, all of the sub-trees are copied. If you have an XML fragment stored in a variable, <xsl:copy-of> is the handiest element to send the variables content to the output.

Attributes:

select (required)	XPath expression leading to the nodes to be copied.

Type:	expression
Attribute Value Template:	no

Implemented:	W3C 1.0 specification (recommendation)
	W3C 1.1 specification (working draft)
	MSXML 2.6 (January 2000 preview)
	MSXML 3.0
Can contain:	No other elements
Can be contained by:	`<xsl:attribute>`, `<xsl:comment>`, `<xsl:copy>`, `<xsl:document>`, `<xsl:element>`, `<xsl:fallback>`, `<xsl:for-each>`, `<xsl:if>`, `<xsl:message>`, `<xsl:otherwise>`, `<xsl:param>`, `<xsl:processing-instruction>`, `<xsl:template>`, `<xsl:variable>`, `<xsl:when>`

`<xsl:decimal-format>`

Declares a decimal format, which controls the interpretation of a format pattern used by the `format-number()` function. This includes defining the decimal separator and the thousands separator.

Attributes:

`name` (optional)	The name of the defined format.	
	Type:	qname
	Attribute Value Template:	no
`decimal-separator` (optional)	The character that will separate the integer part from the fraction part. Default is a dot (.).	
	Type:	char
	Attribute Value Template:	no
`grouping-separator` (optional)	The character that will separate the grouped numbers in the integer part. Default is a comma (,).	
	Type:	char
	Attribute Value Template:	no
`infinity` (optional)	The string that should appear if a number equals infinity. Default is the string 'Infinity'	
	Type:	string
	Attribute Value Template:	no
`minus-sign` (optional)	The character that will be used to indicate a negative number. Default is minus (-).	
	Type:	char
	Attribute Value Template:	no

Table continued on following page

NaN (optional)	The string that should appear if a number is Not a Number. Default is the string 'NaN'.
	Type: string
	Attribute Value Template: no
percent (optional)	Character that will be used as the percent sign. Default is %.
	Type: char
	Attribute Value Template: no
per-mille (optional)	Character that will be used as the per-thousand sign. Default is the Unicode character #x2030, which looks like ‰.
	Type: char
	Attribute Value Template: no
zero-digit (optional)	The character used as the digit zero. Default is 0.
	Type: char
	Attribute Value Template: no
digit (optional)	The character used in a pattern to indicate the place where a leading zero is required. Default is 0.
	Type: char
	Attribute Value Template: no
pattern-separator (optional)	The character that is used to separate the negative and positive patterns (if they are different). Default is semicolon (;).
	Type: char
	Attribute Value Template: no
Implemented:	W3C 1.0 specification (recommendation) W3C 1.1 specification (working draft) MSXML 2.6 (January 2000 preview) MSXML 3.0
Can contain:	No other elements
Can be contained by:	`<xsl:stylesheet>`, `<xsl:transform>`

<xsl:document>

Switches the target of the result tree to another document. All output nodes instantiated within the <xsl:document> element will appear in the document indicated by the href attribute. All other attributes are identical to the attributes on <xsl:output>. Note that this element is not part of the XSLT 1.0 specification; it is an XSLT 1.1 extension.

Attributes:

method (optional)	xml is default.	
	html will create empty elements like and use HTML entities like à.	
	text will cause no output escaping to happen at all (no entity references in output).	
	Type:	xml|html|text|qname-but-not-ncname
	Attribute Value Template:	yes
version (optional)	The version number that will appear in the XML declaration of the output document.	
	Type:	token
	Attribute Value Template:	yes
encoding (optional)	The encoding of the output document.	
	Type:	string
	Attribute Value Template:	yes
omit-xml-declaration (optional)	Specifies if the resulting document should contain an XML declaration (<?xml version="1.0"?>).	
	Type:	yes|no
	Attribute Value Template:	yes
standalone (optional)	Specifies whether the XSLT processor should output a standalone document declaration.	
	Type:	yes|no
	Attribute Value Template:	yes
doctype-public (optional)	Specifies the public identifier to be used in the DTD.	
	Type:	string
	Attribute Value Template:	yes
doctype-system (optional)	Specifies the system identifier to be used in the DTD.	

Table continued on following page

	Type:	string
	Attribute Value Template:	yes
cdata-section-elements (optional)	Specifies a list of elements that should have their content escaped by using a CDATA section instead of entities.	
	Type:	qnames
	Attribute Value Template:	yes
indent (optional)	Specifies to addition of extra whitespace for readability.	
	Type:	yes|no
	Attribute Value Template:	yes
media-type (optional)	To specify a specific MIME type while writing out content.	
	Type:	string
	Attribute Value Template:	yes
Implemented:	W3C 1.1 specification (working draft)	
Can contain:	`<xsl:apply-imports>`, `<xsl:apply-templates>`, `<xsl:attribute>`, `<xsl:call-template>`, `<xsl:choose>`, `<xsl:comment>`, `<xsl:copy>`, `<xsl:copy-of>`, `<xsl:document>`, `<xsl:element>`, `<xsl:fallback>`, `<xsl:for-each>`, `<xsl:if>`, `<xsl:message>`, `<xsl:number>`, `<xsl:processing-instruction>`, `<xsl:text>`, `<xsl:value-of>`, `<xsl:variable>`	
Can be contained by:	`<xsl:copy>`, `<xsl:document>`, `<xsl:element>`, `<xsl:fallback>`, `<xsl:for-each>`, `<xsl:if>`, `<xsl:message>`, `<xsl:otherwise>`, `<xsl:param>`, `<xsl:template>`, `<xsl:variable>`, `<xsl:when>`	

`<xsl:element>`

Generates an element with the specified name in the destination document.		
Attributes:		
name (required)	Name of the element (this may include a prefix bound to a namespace in the stylesheet).	
	Type:	qname
	Attribute Value Template:	yes
namespace (optional)	To overrule the namespace that follows from the prefix in the name attribute (if any).	
	Type:	uri-reference

	Attribute Value Template:	yes
use-attribute-sets (optional)	To add a predefined set of attributes to the element.	
	Type:	qnames
	Attribute Value Template:	no
Implemented:	W3C 1.0 specification (recommendation) W3C 1.1 specification (working draft) MSXML 2.0 (IE5) MSXML 2.6 (January 2000 preview) MSXML 3.0	
Can contain:	`<xsl:apply-imports>`, `<xsl:apply-templates>`, `<xsl:attribute>`, `<xsl:call-template>`, `<xsl:choose>`, `<xsl:comment>`, `<xsl:copy>`, `<xsl:copy-of>`, `<xsl:document>`, `<xsl:element>`, `<xsl:fallback>`, `<xsl:for-each>`, `<xsl:if>`, `<xsl:message>`, `<xsl:number>`, `<xsl:processing-instruction>`, `<xsl:text>`, `<xsl:value-of>`, `<xsl:variable>`	
Can be contained by:	`<xsl:copy>`, `<xsl:document>`, `<xsl:element>`, `<xsl:fallback>`, `<xsl:for-each>`, `<xsl:if>`, `<xsl:message>`, `<xsl:otherwise>`, `<xsl:param>`, `<xsl:template>`, `<xsl:variable>`, `<xsl:when>`	

`<xsl:fallback>`

Can be used to specify actions to be executed if the action of its parent element is not supported by the processor.		
Implemented:	W3C 1.0 specification (recommendation) W3C 1.1 specification (working draft) MSXML 3.0	
Can contain:	`<xsl:apply-imports>`, `<xsl:apply-templates>`, `<xsl:attribute>`, `<xsl:call-template>`, `<xsl:choose>`, `<xsl:comment>`, `<xsl:copy>`, `<xsl:copy-of>`, `<xsl:document>`, `<xsl:element>`, `<xsl:fallback>`, `<xsl:for-each>`, `<xsl:if>`, `<xsl:message>`, `<xsl:number>`, `<xsl:processing-instruction>`, `<xsl:text>`, `<xsl:value-of>`, `<xsl:variable>`	
Can be contained by:	`<xsl:attribute>`, `<xsl:comment>`, `<xsl:copy>`, `<xsl:document>`, `<xsl:element>`, `<xsl:fallback>`, `<xsl:for-each>`, `<xsl:if>`, `<xsl:message>`, `<xsl:otherwise>`, `<xsl:param>`, `<xsl:processing-instruction>`, `<xsl:template>`, `<xsl:variable>`, `<xsl:when>`	

<xsl:for-each>

For looping through the node selected by the XPath expression in the `select` attribute. The context is shifted to the current node in the loop.

Attributes:

`select` (required)	Expression that selects the nodes to loop through.

Type:	node-set-expression
Attribute Value Template:	no

Implemented:	W3C 1.0 specification (recommendation) W3C 1.1 specification (working draft) MSXML 2.0 (IE5) MSXML 2.6 (January 2000 preview) MSXML 3.0
Can contain:	`<xsl:apply-imports>`, `<xsl:apply-templates>`, `<xsl:attribute>`, `<xsl:call-template>`, `<xsl:choose>`, `<xsl:comment>`, `<xsl:copy>`, `<xsl:copy-of>`, `<xsl:document>`, `<xsl:element>`, `<xsl:fallback>`, `<xsl:for-each>`, `<xsl:if>`, `<xsl:message>`, `<xsl:number>`, `<xsl:processing-instruction>`, `<xsl:sort>`, `<xsl:text>`, `<xsl:value-of>`, `<xsl:variable>`
Can be contained by:	`<xsl:attribute>`, `<xsl:comment>`, `<xsl:copy>`, `<xsl:document>`, `<xsl:element>`, `<xsl:fallback>`, `<xsl:for-each>`, `<xsl:if>`, `<xsl:message>`, `<xsl:otherwise>`, `<xsl:param>`, `<xsl:processing-instruction>`, `<xsl:template>`, `<xsl:variable>`, `<xsl:when>`

<xsl:if>

Executes the contained elements only if the test expression returns `true` (or a filled node-set).

Attributes:

`test` (required)	The expression that is tested. If it returns `true` or a non-empty node-set, the content of the `<xsl:if>` element is executed.

Type:	boolean-expression
Attribute Value Template:	no

Implemented:	W3C 1.0 specification (recommendation) W3C 1.1 specification (working draft) MSXML 2.0 (IE5) MSXML 2.6 (January 2000 preview) MSXML 3.0

Can contain:	`<xsl:apply-imports>`, `<xsl:apply-templates>`, `<xsl:attribute>`, `<xsl:call-template>`, `<xsl:choose>`, `<xsl:comment>`, `<xsl:copy>`, `<xsl:copy-of>`, `<xsl:document>`, `<xsl:element>`, `<xsl:fallback>`, `<xsl:for-each>`, `<xsl:if>`, `<xsl:message>`, `<xsl:number>`, `<xsl:processing-instruction>`, `<xsl:text>`, `<xsl:value-of>`, `<xsl:variable>`
Can be contained by:	`<xsl:attribute>`, `<xsl:comment>`, `<xsl:copy>`, `<xsl:document>`, `<xsl:element>`, `<xsl:fallback>`, `<xsl:for-each>`, `<xsl:if>`, `<xsl:message>`, `<xsl:otherwise>`, `<xsl:param>`, `<xsl:processing-instruction>`, `<xsl:template>`, `<xsl:variable>`, `<xsl:when>`

\<xsl:import\>

Imports the templates from an external stylesheet document into the current document. The priority of these imported templates is very low, so if a template in the importing document is implemented for the same pattern, it will always prevail over the imported template. The imported template can be called from the overriding template using `<xsl:apply-imports>`.

Attributes:

`href` (required)	Reference to the stylesheet to be imported.	
	Type:	uri-reference
	Attribute Value Template:	no
Implemented:	W3C 1.0 specification (recommendation) W3C 1.1 specification (working draft) MSXML 3.0	
Can contain:	No other elements	
Can be contained by	`<xsl:stylesheet>`, `<xsl:transform>`	

\<xsl:include\>

Includes templates from an external document as if they where part of the importing document. This means that templates from the included stylesheet have the same priority as they would have had if they were part of the including stylesheet. An error occurs if a template with the same `match` and `priority` attributes exists in both the including and included stylesheets.

Attributes:

`href` (required)	Reference to the stylesheet to be imported.	
	Type:	uri-reference

Table continued on following page

	Attribute Value Template:	no
Implemented:	W3C 1.0 specification (recommendation) W3C 1.1 specification (working draft) MSXML 2.6 (January 2000 preview) MSXML 3.0	
Can contain:	No other elements	
Can be contained by:	`<xsl:stylesheet>`, `<xsl:transform>`	

`<xsl:key>`

Can be used to create index-like structures that can be queried from the `key()` function. It is basically a way to describe name/value pairs inside the source document (like a `Dictionary` object in VB, a Hashtable in Java, or an associative array in Perl). However, in XSLT, more than one value can be found for one key and the same value can be accessed by multiple keys.

Attributes:

`name` (required)	The name that can be used to refer to this key.	
	Type:	qname
	Attribute Value Template:	no
`match` (required)	The pattern defines which nodes in the source document can be accessed using this key. In the name/value pair analogy, this would be the definition of the value.	
	Type:	pattern
	Attribute Value Template:	no
`use` (required)	This expression defines what the key for accessing each value would be. Example: if an element PERSON is matched by the `match` attribute and the `use` attribute equals "@name", the `key()` function can be used to find this specific PERSON element by passing the value of its `name` attribute.	
	Type:	expression
	Attribute Value Template:	no
Implemented:	W3C 1.0 specification (recommendation) W3C 1.1 specification (working draft) MSXML 3.0	
Can contain:	No other elements	
Can be contained by:	`<xsl:stylesheet>`, `<xsl:transform>`	

\<xsl:message\>

To issue error messages or warnings. The content of the element is the message. What the XSLT processor does with the message depends on the implementation. You could think of displaying it within a message box or logging to the error log.

Attributes:

`terminate` (optional)	If `terminate` is set to yes, the execution of the transformation is stopped after issuing the message.
	Type: yes|no
	Attribute Value Template: no
Implemented:	W3C 1.0 specification (recommendation) W3C 1.1 specification (working draft) MSXML 3.0
Can contain:	`<xsl:apply-imports>`, `<xsl:apply-templates>`, `<xsl:attribute>`, `<xsl:call-template>`, `<xsl:choose>`, `<xsl:comment>`, `<xsl:copy>`, `<xsl:copy-of>`, `<xsl:document>`, `<xsl:element>`, `<xsl:fallback>`, `<xsl:for-each>`, `<xsl:if>`, `<xsl:message>`, `<xsl:number>`, `<xsl:processing-instruction>`, `<xsl:text>`, `<xsl:value-of>`, `<xsl:variable>`
Can be contained by:	`<xsl:attribute>`, `<xsl:comment>`, `<xsl:copy>`, `<xsl:document>`, `<xsl:element>`, `<xsl:fallback>`, `<xsl:for-each>`, `<xsl:if>`, `<xsl:message>`, `<xsl:otherwise>`, `<xsl:param>`, `<xsl:processing-instruction>`, `<xsl:template>`, `<xsl:variable>`, `<xsl:when>`

\<xsl:namespace-alias\>

Used to make a certain namespace appear in the destination document without using that namespace in the stylesheet. The main use of this element is in generating new XSLT stylesheets.

Attributes:

`stylesheet-prefix` (required)	The prefix for the namespace that is used in the stylesheet
	Type: prefix|#default
	Attribute Value Template: no
`result-prefix` (required)	The prefix for the namespace that must replace the aliased namespace in the destination document.
	Type: prefix|#default
	Attribute Value Template: no

Table continued on following page

Implemented:	W3C 1.0 specification (recommendation) W3C 1.1 specification (working draft) MSXML 3.0
Can contain:	No other elements
Can be contained by:	`<xsl:stylesheet>`, `<xsl:transform>`

`<xsl:number>`

For outputting the number of a paragraph or chapter in a specified format. It has very flexible features, to allow for different numbering rules.

Attributes:

`level` (optional)	The value `single` counts the location of the nearest node matched by the `count` attribute (along the ancestor axis) relative to its preceding siblings of the same name. Typical output: chapter number.
	The value `multiple` will count the location of all the nodes matched by the `count` attribute (along the ancestor axis) relative to their preceding siblings of the same name. Typical output: paragraph number of form 4.5.3.
	The value `any` will count the location of the nearest node matched by the `count` attribute (along the ancestor axis) relative to their preceding nodes (not only siblings) of the same name. Typical output: bookmark number
	Type: single|multiple|any
	Attribute Value Template: no
`count` (optional)	Specifies the type of node that is to be counted.
	Type: pattern
	Attribute Value Template: no
`from` (optional)	Specifies the starting point for counting.
	Type: pattern
	Attribute Value Template: no
`value` (optional)	Used to specify the numeric value directly instead of using `'level'`, `'count'` and `'from'`.
	Type: number-expression
	Attribute Value Template: no
`format` (optional)	How to format the numeric value to a string (1 becomes 1, 2, 3, ...; a becomes a, b, c,).
	Type: string

	Attribute Value Template:	yes
`lang` (optional)	Language used for alphabetic numbering	
	Type:	token
	Attribute Value Template:	yes
`letter-value` (optional)	Some languages have traditional orders of letters specifically for numbering. These orders are often different from the alphabetic order.	
	Type:	alphabetic|traditional
	Attribute Value Template:	yes
`grouping-separator` (optional)	Character to be used for group separation.	
	Type:	char
	Attribute Value Template:	yes
`grouping-size` (optional)	Number of digits to be separated. `grouping-separator=";"` and `grouping-size="3"` causes: 1;000;000.	
	Type:	number
	Attribute Value Template:	yes
Implemented:	W3C 1.0 specification (recommendation) W3C 1.1 specification (working draft) MSXML 3.0	
Can contain:	No other elements	
Can be contained by:	`<xsl:attribute>`, `<xsl:comment>`, `<xsl:copy>`, `<xsl:document>`, `<xsl:element>`, `<xsl:fallback>`, `<xsl:for-each>`, `<xsl:if>`, `<xsl:message>`, `<xsl:otherwise>`, `<xsl:param>`, `<xsl:processing-instruction>`, `<xsl:template>`, `<xsl:variable>`, `<xsl:when>`	

`<xsl:otherwise>`

Content is executed if none of the `<xsl:when>` elements in an `<xsl:choose>` is matched.	
Implemented:	W3C 1.0 specification (recommendation) W3C 1.1 specification (working draft) MSXML 2.0 (IE5) MSXML 2.6 (January 2000 preview) MSXML 3.0

Table continued on following page

Can contain:	`<xsl:apply-imports>`, `<xsl:apply-templates>`, `<xsl:attribute>`, `<xsl:call-template>`, `<xsl:choose>`, `<xsl:comment>`, `<xsl:copy>`, `<xsl:copy-of>`, `<xsl:document>`, `<xsl:element>`, `<xsl:fallback>`, `<xsl:for-each>`, `<xsl:if>`, `<xsl:message>`, `<xsl:number>`, `<xsl:processing-instruction>`, `<xsl:text>`, `<xsl:value-of>`, `<xsl:variable>`
Can be contained by:	`<xsl:choose>`

`<xsl:output>`

Top level element for setting properties regarding the output style of the destination document. The `<xsl:output>` element basically describes how the translation from a created XML tree to a character array (string) happens.

Attributes:

method (optional)	xml is default
	html will create empty elements like ` ` and use HTML entities like à.
	text will cause no output escaping to happen at all (no entity references in output.)
	Type: xml|html|text|qname-but-not-ncname
	Attribute Value Template: no
version (optional)	The version number that will appear in the XML declaration of the output document.
	Type: token
	Attribute Value Template: no
encoding (optional)	The encoding of the output document.
	Type: string
	Attribute Value Template: no
omit-xml-declaration (optional)	Specifies if the resulting document should contain an XML declaration (`<?xml version="1.0"?>`)
	Type: yes|no
	Attribute Value Template: no
standalone (optional)	Specifies whether the XSLT processor should output a standalone document declaration.
	Type: yes|no

	Attribute Value Template:	no
`doctype-public` (optional)	Specifies the public identifier to be used in the DTD	
	Type:	string
	Attribute Value Template:	no
`doctype-system` (optional)	Specifies the system identifier to be used in the DTD	
	Type:	string
	Attribute Value Template:	no
`cdata-section-elements` (optional)	Specifies a list of elements that should have their content escaped by using a CDATA section instead of entities.	
	Type:	qnames
	Attribute Value Template:	no
`indent` (optional)	Specifies the addition of extra whitespace for readability	
	Type:	yes|no
	Attribute Value Template:	no
`media-type` (optional)	To specify a specific MIME type while writing out content.	
	Type:	string
	Attribute Value Template:	no
Implemented:	W3C 1.0 specification (recommendation) W3C 1.1 specification (working draft) MSXML 2.6 (January 2000 preview) (No support for methods `html` and `text`) MSXML 3.0	
Can contain:	No other elements	
Can be contained by:	`<xsl:stylesheet>`, `<xsl:transform>`	

<xsl:param>

Defines a parameter in a `<xsl:template>` or `<xsl:stylesheet>`.		
Attributes:		
`name` (required)	Name of the parameter	
	Type:	qname
	Attribute Value Template:	no

Table continued on following page

select (optional)	Specifies the default value for the parameter	
	Type:	expression
	Attribute Value Template:	no
Implemented:	W3C 1.0 specification (recommendation) W3C 1.1 specification (working draft) MSXML 2.6 (January 2000 preview) MSXML 3.0	
Can contain:	`<xsl:apply-imports>`, `<xsl:apply-templates>`, `<xsl:attribute>`, `<xsl:call-template>`, `<xsl:choose>`, `<xsl:comment>`, `<xsl:copy>`, `<xsl:copy-of>`, `<xsl:document>`, `<xsl:element>`, `<xsl:fallback>`, `<xsl:for-each>`, `<xsl:if>`, `<xsl:message>`, `<xsl:number>`, `<xsl:processing-instruction>`, `<xsl:text>`, `<xsl:value-of>`, `<xsl:variable>`	
Can be contained by:	`<xsl:stylesheet>`, `<xsl:transform>`	

<xsl:preserve-space>

Allows you to define which elements in the source document should have their whitespace content preserved. See also `<xsl:strip-space>`.		
Attributes:		
elements (required)	In this attribute you can list the elements (separated by whitespace) for which you want to preserve the whitespace content.	
	Type:	tokens
	Attribute Value Template:	no
Implemented:	W3C 1.0 specification (recommendation) W3C 1.1 specification (working draft) MSXML 3.0	
Can contain:	No other elements	
Can be contained by:	`<xsl:stylesheet>`, `<xsl:transform>`	

<xsl:processing-instruction>

Generates a processing instruction in the destination document.	
Attributes:	
name (required)	The name of the processing instruction (the part between the first question mark and the first whitespace of the processing instruction)

	Type:	ncname
	Attribute Value Template:	yes
Implemented:	W3C 1.0 specification (recommendation) W3C 1.1 specification (working draft) MSXML 2.0 (IE5) (Caution: the `<xsl:processing-instruction>` element is called `<xsl:pi>` in IE5) MSXML 2.6 (January 2000 preview) MSXML 3.0	
Can contain:	`<xsl:apply-imports>`, `<xsl:apply-templates>`, `<xsl:call-template>`, `<xsl:choose>`, `<xsl:copy>`, `<xsl:copy-of>`, `<xsl:fallback>`, `<xsl:for-each>`, `<xsl:if>`, `<xsl:message>`, `<xsl:number>`, `<xsl:text>`, `<xsl:value-of>`, `<xsl:variable>`	
Can be contained by:	`<xsl:copy>`, `<xsl:document>`, `<xsl:element>`, `<xsl:fallback>`, `<xsl:for-each>`, `<xsl:if>`, `<xsl:message>`, `<xsl:otherwise>`, `<xsl:param>`, `<xsl:template>`, `<xsl:variable>`, `<xsl:when>`	

`<xsl:sort>`

Allows specifying a sort order for `<xsl:apply-templates>` and `<xsl:for-each>` elements. Multiple `<xsl:sort>` elements can be specified for primary and secondary sorting keys.

Attributes:

select (optional)	Expression that indicates which should be used for the ordering.	
	Type:	string-expression
	Attribute Value Template:	no
lang (optional)	To set the language used while ordering (in different languages the rules for alphabetic ordering can be different).	
	Type:	token
	Attribute Value Template:	yes
data-type (optional)	To specify alphabetic or numeric ordering.	
	Type:	text|number|qname-but-not-ncname
	Attribute Value Template:	yes
order (optional)	Specifies ascending or descending ordering.	
	Type:	ascending|descending
	Attribute Value Template:	yes

Table continued on following page

case-order (optional)	Specifies if upper case characters should order before or after lower-case characters. Note that case insensitive sorting is not supported.
	Type: upper-first|lower-first
	Attribute Value Template: yes
Implemented:	W3C 1.0 specification (recommendation) W3C 1.1 specification (working draft) MSXML 2.6 (January 2000 preview) MSXML 3.0
Can contain:	No other elements
Can be contained by:	`<xsl:apply-templates>`, `<xsl:for-each>`

`<xsl:strip-space>`

Allows you to define which elements in the source document should have their whitespace content stripped. See also `<xsl:preserve-space>`.	
Attributes:	
elements (required)	Specify which elements should preserve their whitespace contents.
	Type: Tokens
	Attribute Value Template: no
Implemented:	W3C 1.0 specification (recommendation) W3C 1.1 specification (working draft) MSXML 2.6 (January 2000 preview) MSXML 3.0
Can contain:	No other elements
Can be contained by:	`<xsl:stylesheet>`, `<xsl:transform>`

`<xsl:stylesheet>`

The root element for a stylesheet. Synonym to `<xsl:transform>`.	
Attributes:	
id (optional)	A reference for the stylesheet.
	Type: Id
	Attribute Value Template: no

extension-element-prefixes (optional)	Allows you to specify which namespace prefixes are XSLT extension namespaces (like `msxml`).	
	Type:	Tokens
	Attribute Value Template:	no
exclude-result-prefixes (optional)	Namespaces that are only relevant in the stylesheet or in the source document, but not in the result document, can be removed from the output by specifying them here.	
	Type:	tokens
	Attribute Value Template:	no
version (required)	Version number	
	Type:	number
	Attribute Value Template:	no
Implemented:	W3C 1.0 specification (recommendation) W3C 1.1 specification (working draft) MSXML 2.0 (IE5) MSXML 2.6 (January 2000 preview) MSXML 3.0	
Can contain:	`<xsl:attribute-set>`, `<xsl:decimal-format>`, `<xsl:import>`, `<xsl:include>`, `<xsl:key>`, `<xsl:namespace-alias>`, `<xsl:output>`, `<xsl:param>`, `<xsl:preserve-space>`, `<xsl:strip-space>`, `<xsl:template>`, `<xsl:variable>`	
Can be contained by:	No other elements	

`<xsl:template>`

Defines a transformation rule. Some templates are built-in and don't have to be defined. Refer to Chapter 3 for more information about writing templates.

Attributes:

match (optional)	Defines the set of nodes on which the template can be applied.	
	Type:	pattern
	Attribute Value Template:	no

Table continued on following page

name (optional)	Name to identify the template when calling it using `<xsl:call-template>`.	
	Type:	qname
	Attribute Value Template:	no
`priority` (optional)	If several templates can be applied (through their `match` attributes) on a node, the `priority` attribute can be used to make a certain template prevail over others.	
	Type:	number
	Attribute Value Template:	no
mode (optional)	If a `mode` attribute is present on a template, the template will only be considered for transforming a node when the transformation was started by an `<xsl:apply-templates>` element with a `mode` attribute with the same value.	
	Type:	qname
	Attribute Value Template:	no
Implemented:	W3C 1.0 specification (recommendation) W3C 1.1 specification (working draft) MSXML 2.0 (IE5) MSXML 2.6 (January 2000 preview) (except for the `mode` attribute) MSXML 3.0	
Can contain:	`<xsl:apply-imports>`, `<xsl:apply-templates>`, `<xsl:attribute>`, `<xsl:call-template>`, `<xsl:choose>`, `<xsl:comment>`, `<xsl:copy>`, `<xsl:copy-of>`, `<xsl:document>`, `<xsl:element>`, `<xsl:fallback>`, `<xsl:for-each>`, `<xsl:if>`, `<xsl:message>`, `<xsl:number>`, `<xsl:processing-instruction>`, `<xsl:text>`, `<xsl:value-of>`, `<xsl:variable>`	
Can be contained by:	`<xsl:stylesheet>`, `<xsl:transform>`	

\<xsl:text\>

Generates a text string from its content. Whitespace is never stripped from an `<xsl:text>` element.

Attributes:

`disable-output-escaping` (optional)	If set to yes, the output will not be escaped: this means that a string `'<'` will be written to the output as `'<'` instead of `&lt;`. This means that the result document will not be a well-formed XML document anymore.

	Type:	yes|no
	Attribute Value Template:	no
Implemented	W3C 1.0 specification (recommendation) W3C 1.1 specification (working draft) MSXML 2.0 (IE5) MSXML 2.6 (January 2000 preview) MSXML 3.0	
Can contain:	No other elements	
Can be contained by:	`<xsl:attribute>`, `<xsl:comment>`, `<xsl:copy>`, `<xsl:document>`, `<xsl:element>`, `<xsl:fallback>`, `<xsl:for-each>`, `<xsl:if>`, `<xsl:message>`, `<xsl:otherwise>`, `<xsl:param>`, `<xsl:processing-instruction>`, `<xsl:template>`, `<xsl:variable>`, `<xsl:when>`	

`<xsl:transform>`

Identical to `<xsl:stylesheet>`		
Attributes:		
`id` (optional)	A reference for the stylesheet.	
	Type:	id
	Attribute Value Template:	no
`extension-element-prefixes` (optional)	Allows you to specify which namespace prefixes are XSLT extension namespaces (like `msxml`).	
	Type:	tokens
	Attribute Value Template:	no
`exclude-result-prefixes` (optional)	Namespaces that are only relevant in the stylesheet or in the source document, but not in the result document, can be removed from the output by specifying them here.	
	Type:	tokens
	Attribute Value Template:	no
`version` (required)	Version number	
	Type:	number
	Attribute Value Template:	no

Table continued on following page

Implemented:	W3C 1.0 specification (recommendation) W3C 1.1 specification (working draft) MSXML 3.0
Can contain:	`<xsl:attribute-set>`, `<xsl:decimal-format>`, `<xsl:import>`, `<xsl:include>`, `<xsl:key>`, `<xsl:namespace-alias>`, `<xsl:output>`, `<xsl:param>`, `<xsl:preserve-space>`, `<xsl:strip-space>`, `<xsl:template>`, `<xsl:variable>`
Can be contained by:	No other elements

`<xsl:value-of>`

Generates a text string with the value of the expression in the `select` attribute.

Attributes:

`select` (required)	Expression that selects the node-set that will be converted to a string	
	Type:	string-expression
	Attribute Value Template:	no
`disable-output-escaping` (optional)	You can use this to output < instead of `&lt;` to the destination document. Note that this will cause your destination to become invalid XML. Normally used to generate HTML or text files.	
	Type:	yes|no
	Attribute Value Template:	no
Implemented:	W3C 1.0 specification (recommendation) W3C 1.1 specification (working draft) MSXML 2.0 (IE5) MSXML 2.6 (January 2000 preview) MSXML 3.0	
Can contain:	No other elements	
Can be contained by:	`<xsl:attribute>`, `<xsl:comment>`, `<xsl:copy>`, `<xsl:document>`, `<xsl:element>`, `<xsl:fallback>`, `<xsl:for-each>`, `<xsl:if>`, `<xsl:message>`, `<xsl:otherwise>`, `<xsl:param>`, `<xsl:processing-instruction>`, `<xsl:template>`, `<xsl:variable>`, `<xsl:when>`	

<xsl:variable>

Defines a variable with a value. Note that in XSLT, the value of a variable cannot change – you can instantiate a variable using `<xsl:variable>`, but it cannot be changed afterwards. Refer to Chapter 4 for more information on the use of variables.

Attributes:

name (required)	Name of the variable	
	Type:	qname
	Attribute Value Template:	no
select (optional)	Value of the variable (if the `select` attribute is omitted, the content of the `<xsl:variable>` element is the value).	
	Type:	expression
	Attribute Value Template:	no

Implemented:	W3C 1.0 specification (recommendation) W3C 1.1 specification (working draft) MSXML 2.6 (January 2000 preview) MSXML 3.0
Can contain:	`<xsl:apply-imports>`, `<xsl:apply-templates>`, `<xsl:attribute>`, `<xsl:call-template>`, `<xsl:choose>`, `<xsl:comment>`, `<xsl:copy>`, `<xsl:copy-of>`, `<xsl:document>`, `<xsl:element>`, `<xsl:fallback>`, `<xsl:for-each>`, `<xsl:if>`, `<xsl:message>`, `<xsl:number>`, `<xsl:processing-instruction>`, `<xsl:text>`, `<xsl:value-of>`, `<xsl:variable>`
Can be contained by:	`<xsl:attribute>`, `<xsl:comment>`, `<xsl:copy>`, `<xsl:document>`, `<xsl:element>`, `<xsl:fallback>`, `<xsl:for-each>`, `<xsl:if>`, `<xsl:message>`, `<xsl:otherwise>`, `<xsl:param>`, `<xsl:processing-instruction>`, `<xsl:stylesheet>`, `<xsl:template>`, `<xsl:transform>`, `<xsl:variable>`, `<xsl:when>`

<xsl:when>

Represents one of the options for execution in a `<xsl:choose>` block.

Attributes:

test (required)	Expression to be tested.	
	Type:	boolean-expression
	Attribute Value Template:	no

Table continued on following page

Implemented:	W3C 1.0 specification (recommendation) W3C 1.1 specification (working draft) MSXML 2.0 (IE5) MSXML 2.6 (January 2000 preview) MSXML 3.0
Can contain:	`<xsl:apply-imports>`, `<xsl:apply-templates>`, `<xsl:attribute>`, `<xsl:call-template>`, `<xsl:choose>`, `<xsl:comment>`, `<xsl:copy>`, `<xsl:copy-of>`, `<xsl:document>`, `<xsl:element>`, `<xsl:fallback>`, `<xsl:for-each>`, `<xsl:if>`, `<xsl:message>`, `<xsl:number>`, `<xsl:processing-instruction>`, `<xsl:text>`, `<xsl:value-of>`, `<xsl:variable>`
Can be contained by::	`<xsl:choose>`

`<xsl:with-param>`

Used to pass a parameter to a template using `<xsl:apply-templates>` or `<xsl:call-template>`. The template called must have a parameter of the same name defined using `<xsl:param>`.

Attributes:

name (required)	Name of the parameter.	
	Type:	qname
	Attribute Value Template:	no
select (optional)	XPath expression selecting the passed value.	
	Type:	expression
	Attribute Value Template:	no
Implemented:	W3C 1.0 specification (recommendation) W3C 1.1 specification (working draft) MSXML 2.6 (January 2000 preview) MSXML 3.0	
Can contain:	No other elements	
Can be contained by:	`<xsl:apply-templates>`, `<xsl:call-template>`	

Functions

Within expressions in an XSLT stylesheet, you can use all the XPath functions we saw in Appendix A and also a number of special XSLT functions. These functions are described here.

Each function is described by a line of this form:

return-type **function-name** (parameters)

For each parameter, we display the type (`object`, `string`, `number`, `node-set`) and where necessary a symbol indicating if the parameter is optional (?) or can occur multiple times (+). The type `object` means that any type can be passed.

If an expression is passed as a parameter, it is first evaluated and (if necessary) converted to the expected type before passing it to the function.

---

node-set **current** ( )
Returns the current context node-set, outside the current expression. For MSXML2 you can use the `context()` function as a workaround. `context(-1)` is synonymous to `current()`

Implemented
W3C 1.0 specification (recommendation)
W3C 1.1 specification (working draft)
MSXML 2.6 (January 2000 preview)
MSXML 3.0

---

node-set **document** (object, node-set?)
To get a reference to an external source document.

Parameters:
object
If of type String, this is the URL of the document to be retrieved. If a node-set, all nodes are converted to strings and all these URLs are retrieved in a node-set.

node-set
Represents the base URL from where relative URLs are resolved.

Implemented:
W3C 1.0 specification (recommendation)
W3C 1.1 specification (working draft)
MSXML 3.0

---

boolean **element-available** (string)

To query availability of a certain extension element.

Parameters:
string
Name of the extension element.

Implemented:
W3C 1.0 specification (recommendation)
W3C 1.1 specification (working draft)
MSXML 3.0

---

string **format-number** (number, string1, string2?)

Formats a numeric value into a formatted and localized string.

Parameters:
number
The numeric value to be represented.

string1
The format string that should be used for the formatting.

string2
Reference to a `<xsl:decimal-format>` element to indicate localization parameters.

Implemented:
W3C 1.0 specification (recommendation)
W3C 1.1 specification (working draft)
MSXML 3.0

---

boolean **function-available** (string)

To query availability of a certain extension function.

Parameter:
string
Name of the extension function.

Implemented:
W3C 1.0 specification (recommendation)
W3C 1.1 specification (working draft)
MSXML 3.0

---

node-set **generate-id** (node-set?)

Generates a unique identifier for the specified node. Each node will cause a different ID, but the same node will always generate the same ID. You cannot be sure that the IDs generated for a document during multiple transformations will remain identical.

Parameter:
node-set
The first node of the passed node-set is used. If no node-set is passed, the current context is used.

Implemented:
W3C 1.0 specification (recommendation)
W3C 1.1 specification (working draft)
MSXML 3.0

---

node-set **key** (string, object)
To get a reference to a node using the specified <xsl:key>.

> Parameters:
> string
> The name of the referenced <xsl:key> .
>
> object
> If of type String, this is the index string for the key. If of type node-set, all nodes are converted to strings and all are used to get nodes back from the key.
>
> Implemented:
> W3C 1.0 specification (recommendation)
> W3C 1.1 specification (working draft)
> MSXML 3.0

object **system-property** (string)
To get certain system properties from the processor.

> Parameter:
> string
> The name of the system property. Properties that are always available are xsl:version, xsl:vendor and xsl:vendor-url.
>
> Implemented:
> W3C 1.0 specification (recommendation)
> W3C 1.1 specification (working draft)
> MSXML 3.0

node-set **unparsed-entity-url** (string)
Returns the URI of the unparsed entity with the passed name.

> Parameter:
> string
> Name of the unparsed entity.
>
> Implemented:
> W3C 1.0 specification (recommendation)
> W3C 1.1 specification (working draft)
> MSXML 3.0

Inherited XPath Functions

Check Appendix A for information on the XPath functions. They can all be used in XSLT:

boolean()	ceiling()	concat()	contains()
count()	false()	floor()	id()
lang()	last	local-name()	name()
namespace-uri()	normalize-space()	not	number()
position()	round()	starts-with()	string()
string-length()	substring()	substring-after()	substring-before()
sum()	translate()	true()	

Types

These types are used to specify the types of the attributes for the XSLT elements given in the tables above.

boolean	Can have values true and false.
char	A single character.
expression	A string value, containing an XPath expression.
id	A string value. Must be an XML name. The string value can be used only once as an id in any document.
language-name	A string containing one of the defined language identifiers. American English = EN-US.
name	A string value that conforms to the name conventions of XML. That means: no whitespace, should start with either a letter or an underscore (_).
names	Multiple name values separated by whitespace.
namespace-prefix	Any string that is defined as a prefix for a namespace.
ncname	A name value that does not contain a colon.
node	A node in an XML document. Can be of several types, including: element, attribute, comment, processing instruction, text node, etc.
node-set	A set of nodes in a specific order. Can be of any length.
node-set-expression	A string value, containing an XPath expression that returns nodes.
number	A numeric value. Can be either floating point or integer
object	Anything. Can be a string, a node, a node-set, anything
qname	Qualified name: the full name of a node. Made up of two parts: the local name and the namespace identifier.
qnames	A set of qname values, separated by whitespace.
string	A string value
token	A string value that contains no whitespace.
tokens	Multiple token values separated by whitespace.
uri-reference	Any string that conforms to the URI specification.

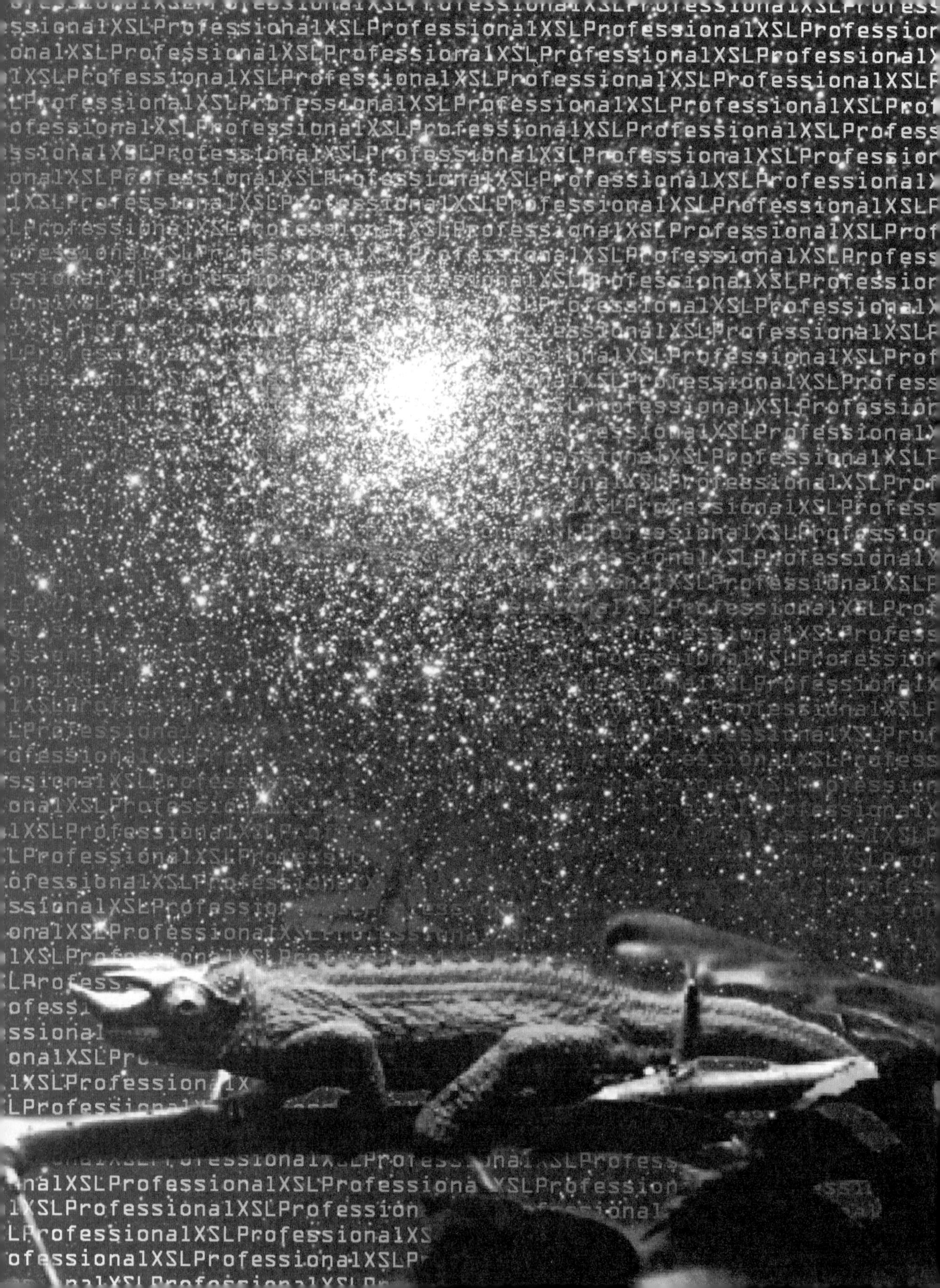
XSLProfessional

C

The XML Document Object Model

This appendix lists all of the interfaces in the DOM Level 2 Core, both the **Fundamental Interfaces** and the **Extended Interfaces**, including all of their properties and methods. Examples of how to use some of these interfaces were given in Chapter 6.

Further information on these interfaces can be found at:

http://www.w3.org/TR/1999/CR-DOM-Level-2-19991210/core.html.

Fundamental Interfaces

The DOM Fundamental Interfaces are interfaces that *all* DOM implementations must provide, even if they aren't designed to work with XML documents.

DOMException

An object implementing the DOMException interface is raised whenever an error occurs in the DOM.

Property	Description
code	An integer, representing which **exception code** this DOMException is reporting.

The code property can take the following values:

Exception Code	Integer Value	Description
INDEX_SIZE_ERR	1	The index or size is negative, or greater than the allowed value.
DOMSTRING_SIZE_ERR	2	The specified range of text does not fit into a DOMString.
HIERARCHY_REQUEST_ERR	3	The node is inserted somewhere it doesn't belong.
WRONG_DOCUMENT_ERR	4	The node is used in a different document than the one that created it, and that document doesn't support it.
INVALID_CHARACTER_ERR	5	A character has been passed which is not valid in XML.
NO_DATA_ALLOWED_ERR	6	Data has been specified for a node which does not support data.
NO_MODIFICATION_ALLOWED_ERR	7	An attempt has been made to modify an object which doesn't allow modifications.
NOT_FOUND_ERR	8	An attempt was made to reference a node which does not exist.
NOT_SUPPORTED_ERR	9	The implementation does not support the type of object requested.
INUSE_ATTRIBUTE_ERR	10	An attempt was made to add a duplicate attribute.
INVALID_STATE_ERR	11	An attempt was made to use an object which is not, or is no longer, useable.
SYNTAX_ERR	12	An invalid or illegal string was passed.
INVALID_MODIFICATION_ERR	13	An attempt was made to modify the type of the underlying object.
NAMESPACE_ERR	14	An attempt was made to create or change an object in a way which is incompatible with namespaces.
INVALID_ACCESS_ERR	15	A parameter was passed or an operation attempted which is not supported by the underlying object.

Node

The Node interface is the base interface upon which most of the DOM objects are built, and contains methods and attributes which can be used for all types of nodes. The interface also includes some helper methods and attributes which only apply to particular types of nodes.

Property	Description
nodeName	The name of the node. Will return different values, depending on the nodeType, as listed in the next table.
nodeValue	The value of the node. Will return different values, depending on the nodeType, as listed in the next table.
nodeType	The type of node. Will be one of the values from the next table.
parentNode	The node that is this node's parent.
childNodes	A NodeList containing all of this node's children. If there are no children, an empty NodeList will be returned, not NULL.
firstChild	The first child of this node. If there are no children, this returns NULL.
lastChild	The last child of this node. If there are no children, this returns NULL.
previousSibling	The node immediately preceding this node. If there is no preceding node, this returns NULL.
nextSibling	The node immediately following this node. If there is no following node, this returns NULL.
attributes	A NamedNodeMap containing the attributes of this node. If the node is not an element, this returns NULL.
ownerDocument	The document to which this node belongs.
namespaceURI	The namespace URI of this node. Returns NULL if a namespace is not specified.
prefix	The namespace prefix of this node. Returns NULL if a namespace is not specified.
localName	Returns the local part of this node's QName.

The value of the nodeName and nodeValue properties depend on the value of the nodeType property, which can return one of the following constants:

nodeType property constant	nodeName	nodeValue
ELEMENT_NODE	Tag name	NULL
ATTRIBUTE_NODE	Name of attribute	Value of attribute
TEXT_NODE	#text	Content of the text node

Table continued on following page

nodeType property constant	nodeName	nodeValue
CDATA_SECTION_NODE	#cdata-section	Content of the CDATA section
ENTITY_REFERENCE_NODE	Name of entity referenced	NULL
ENTITY_NODE	Entity name	NULL
PROCESSING_INSTRUCTION_NODE	Target	Entire content excluding the target
COMMENT_NODE	#comment	Content of the comment
DOCUMENT_NODE	#document	NULL
DOCUMENT_TYPE_NODE	Document type name	NULL
DOCUMENT_FRAGMENT_NODE	#document-fragment	NULL
NOTATION_NODE	Notation name	NULL

Method	Description
insertBefore(*newChild*, *refChild*)	Inserts the *newChild* node before the existing *refChild*. If *refChild* is NULL, inserts the node at the end of the list. Returns the inserted node.
replaceChild(*newChild*, *oldChild*)	Replaces *oldChild* with *newChild*. Returns *oldChild*.
removeChild(*oldChild*)	Removes *oldChild* from the list, and returns it.
appendChild(*newChild*)	Adds *newChild* to the end of the list, and returns it.
hasChildNodes()	Returns a Boolean; true if the node has any children, false otherwise.
cloneNode(*deep*)	Returns a duplicate of this node. If the Boolean *deep* parameter is true, this will recursively clone the sub-tree under the node, otherwise it will only clone the node itself.
normalize()	If there are multiple adjacent Text child nodes (from a previous call to Text.splitText()) this method will combine them again. It doesn't return a value.
supports(*feature*, *version*)	Indicates whether this implementation of the DOM supports the *feature* passed. Returns a Boolean, true if it supports the feature, false otherwise.

Document

An object implementing the Document interface represents the entire XML document. This object is also used to create other nodes at run time.

The Document interface extends the Node interface.

Property	Description
doctype	Returns a DocumentType object, indicating the document type associated with this document. If the document has no document type specified, returns NULL.
implementation	The DOMImplementation object used for this document.
documentElement	The root element for this document.

Method	Description
createElement(*tagName*)	Creates an element, with the name specified.
createDocumentFragment()	Creates an empty DocumentFragment object.
createTextNode(*data*)	Creates a Text node, containing the text in *data*.
createComment(*data*)	Creates a Comment node, containing the text in *data*.
createCDATASection(*data*)	Creates a CDATASection node, containing the text in *data*.
createProcessingInstruction (*target*, *data*)	Creates a ProcessingInstruction node, with the specified *target* and *data*.
createAttribute(*name*)	Creates an attribute, with the specified *name*.
createEntityReference(*name*)	Creates an entity reference, with the specified *name*.
getElementsByTagName(*tagname*)	Returns a NodeList of all elements in the document with this *tagname*. The elements are returned in document order.
importNode(*importedNode*, *deep*)	Imports a node *importedNode* from another document into this one. The original node is not removed from the old document, it is just cloned. (The Boolean *deep* parameter specifies if it is a deep or shallow clone: deep – sub-tree under node is also cloned, shallow – only node itself is cloned.) Returns the new node.

Table continued on following page

Method	Description
createElementNS(*namespaceURI*, *qualifiedName*)	Creates an element, with the specified namespace and QName.
createAttributeNS(*namespaceURI*, *qualifiedName*)	Creates an attribute, with the specified namespace and QName.
getElementsByTagNameNS(*namespaceURI*, *localName*)	Returns a NodeList of all the elements in the document which have the specified local name, and are in the namespace specified by *namespaceURI*.
getElementByID(*elementID*)	Returns the element with the ID specified in *elementID*. If there is no such element, returns NULL.

Note: all of the createXXX() methods return the node created.

DOMImplementation

The DOMImplementation interface provides methods which are not specific to any particular document, but to any document from this DOM implementation. You can get a DOMImplementation object from the implementation property of the Document interface.

Method	Description
hasFeature(*feature*, *version*)	Returns a Boolean, indicating whether this DOM implementation supports the *feature* requested. *version* is the version number of the feature to test.
createDocumentType(*qualifiedName*, *publicID*, *systemID*, *internalSubset*)	Creates a DocumentType object, with the specified attributes.
createDocument(*namespaceURI*, *qualifiedName*, *doctype*)	Creates a Document object, with the document element specified by *qualifiedName*. The *doctype* property must refer to an object of type DocumentType.

DocumentFragment

A document fragment is a temporary holding place for a group of nodes, usually with the intent of inserting them back into the document at a later point.

The DocumentFragment interface extends the Node interface, without adding any additional properties or methods.

NodeList

A NodeList contains an ordered group of nodes, accessed via an integral index.

Property	Description
length	The number of nodes contained in this list. The range of valid child node indices is 0 to length-1 inclusive.
item(*index*)	Returns the Node in the list at the indicated *index*. If *index* is the same as or greater than length, returns NULL.

Element

Provides properties and methods for working with an element.

The Element interface extends the Node interface.

Property	Description
tagName	The name of the element.

Method	Description
getAttribute(*name*)	Returns the value of the attribute with the specified *name*, or an empty string if that attribute does not have a specified or default value.
setAttribute(*name*, *value*)	Sets the value of the specified attribute to this new *value*. If no such attribute exists, a new one with this *name* is created.
removeAttribute (*name*)	Removes the specified attribute. If the attribute has a default value, it is immediately replaced with an identical attribute, containing this default value.
getAttributeNode (*name*)	Returns an Attr node, containing the named attribute. Returns NULL if there is no such attribute.
setAttributeNode (*newAttr*)	Adds a new attribute node. If an attribute with the same name already exists, it is replaced. If an Attr has been replaced, it is returned, otherwise NULL is returned.
removeAttributeNode (*oldAttr*)	Removes the specified Attr node, and returns it. If the attribute has a default value, it is immediately replaced with an identical attribute, containing this default value.
getElementsByTagName (*name*)	Returns a NodeList of all descendants with the given node *name*.

Table continued on following page

Method	Description
getAttributeNS(*namespaceURI*, *localName*)	Returns the value of the specified attribute, or an empty string if that attribute does not have a specified or default value.
setAttributeNS(*namespaceURI*, *qualifiedName*, *value*)	Sets the value of the specified attribute to this new *value*. If no such attribute exists, a new one with this namespace URI and QName is created.
removeAttributeNS(*namespaceURI*, *localName*)	Removes the specified attribute. If the attribute has a default value, it is immediately replaced with an identical attribute, containing this default value.
getAttributeNodeNS(*namespaceURI*, *localName*)	Returns an Attr node, containing the specified attribute. Returns NULL if there is no such attribute.
setAttributeNodeNS(*newAttr*)	Adds a new Attr node to the list. If an attribute with the same namespace URI and local name exists, it is replaced. If an Attr object is replaced, it is returned, otherwise NULL is returned.
getElementsByTagNameNS *namespaceURI*, *localName*)	Returns a NodeList of all of the elements matching these criteria.

NamedNodeMap

A named node map represents an unordered collection of nodes, retrieved by name.

Property	Description
length	The number of nodes in the map.

Method	Description
getNamedItem(*name*)	Returns a Node, where the nodeName is the same as the *name* specified, or NULL if no such node exists.
setNamedItem(*arg*)	The *arg* parameter is a Node object, which is added to the list. The nodeName property is used for the name of the node in this map. If a node with the same name already exists, it is replaced. If a Node is replaced it is returned, otherwise NULL is returned.
removeNamedItem(*name*)	Removes the Node specified by *name*, and returns it.
item(*index*)	Returns the Node at the specified *index*. If *index* is the same as or greater than length, returns NULL.

Method	Description
getNamedItemNS (*namespaceURI*, *localName*)	Returns a Node, matching the namespace URI and local name, or NULL if no such node exists.
setNamedItemNS(*arg*)	The *arg* parameter is a Node object, which is added to the list. If a node with the same namespace URI and local name already exists, it is replaced. If a Node is replaced it is returned, otherwise, NULL is returned.
removeNamedItemNS (*namespaceURI*, *localName*)	Removes the specified node, and returns it.

Attr

Provides properties for dealing with an attribute.

The Attr interface extends the Node interface.

Property	Description
name	The name of the attribute.
specified	A Boolean, indicating whether this attribute was specified (true), or just defaulted (false).
value	The value of the attribute.
ownerElement	An Element object, representing the element to which this attribute belongs.

CharacterData

Provides properties and methods for working with character data.

The CharacterData interface extends the Node interface.

Property	Description
data	The text in this CharacterData node.
length	The number of characters in the node.
substringData(*offset*, *count*)	Returns a portion of the string, starting at the *offset*. Will return the number of characters specified in *count*, or until the end of the string, whichever is less.
appendData(*arg*)	Appends the string in *arg* to the end of the string.
insertData(*offset*, *arg*)	Inserts the string in *arg* into the middle of the string, starting at the position indicated by *offset*.

Method	Description
deleteData(*offset*, *count*)	Deletes a portion of the string, starting at the *offset*. Will delete the number of characters specified in *count*, or until the end of the string, whichever is less.
replaceData(*offset*, *count*, *arg*)	Replaces a portion of the string, starting at the *offset*. Will replace the number of characters specified in *count*, or until the end of the string, whichever is less. The *arg* parameter is the new string to be inserted.

Text

Provides an additional method for working with text nodes.

The Text interface extends the CharacterData interface.

Method	Description
splitText(*offset*)	Separates this single Text node into two adjacent Text nodes. All of the text up to the *offset* point goes into the first Text node, and all of the text starting at the *offset* point to the end goes into the second Text node.

Comment

Encapsulates an XML comment.

The Comment interface extends the CharacterData interface, without adding any additional properties or methods.

Extended Interfaces

The DOM Extended Interfaces need only be provided by DOM implementations that will be working with XML documents.

CDATASection

Encapsulates an XML CDATA section.

The CDATASection interface extends the Text interface, without adding any additional properties or methods.

ProcessingInstruction

Provides properties for working with an XML processing instruction (PI).

The `ProcessingInstruction` interface extends the `Node` interface.

Property	Description
`target`	The PI target, in other words the name of the application to which the PI should be passed.
`data`	The content of the PI.

DocumentType

Provides properties for working with an XML document type. Can be retrieved from the `doctype` property of the `Document` interface. (If a document doesn't have a document type, `doctype` will return `NULL`.)

`DocumentType` extends the `Node` interface.

Property	Description
`name`	The name of the DTD (Document Type Definition).
`entities`	A `NamedNodeMap` containing all entities declared in the DTD (both internal and external). Parameter entities are not contained, and duplicates are discarded, according to the rules followed by validating XML parsers.
`notations`	A `NamedNodeMap` containing the notations contained in the DTD. Duplicates are discarded.
`publicID`	The public identifier of the external subset.
`systemID`	The system identifier of the external subset.
`internalSubset`	The internal subset, as a string.

Notation

Provides properties for working with an XML notation. Notations are read-only in the DOM.

The `Notation` interface extends the `Node` interface.

Property	Description
`publicID`	The public identifier of this notation. If the public identifier was not specified, returns `NULL`.
`systemID`	The system identifier of this notation. If the system identifier was not specified, returns `NULL`.

Entity

Provides properties for working with parsed and unparsed entities. `Entity` nodes are read-only.

The `Entity` interface extends the `Node` interface.

Property	Description
publicID	The public identifier associated with the entity, or NULL if none is specified.
systemID	The system identifier associated with the entity, or NULL if none is specified.
notationName	For unparsed entities, the name of the notation for the entity. NULL for parsed entities.

EntityReference

Encapsulates an XML entity reference.

The `EntityReference` extends the `Node` interface, without adding any properties or methods.

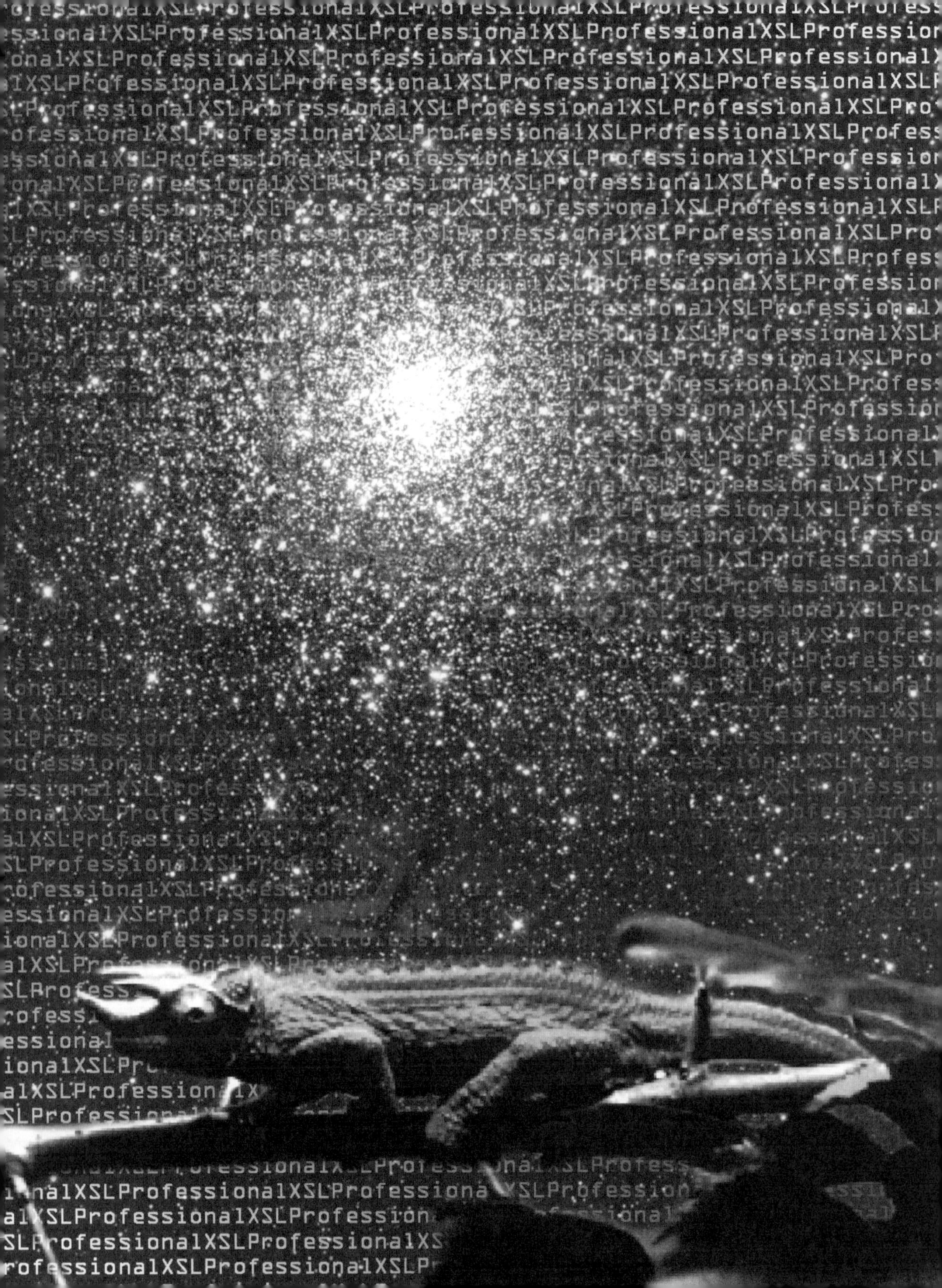

SAX 2.0: The Simple API for XML

This appendix contains the specification of the SAX interface, version 2.0, some of which is explained in Chapter 6. It is taken largely verbatim from the definitive specification to be found at http://www.megginson.com/SAX/index.html, with editorial comments added in italics.

The classes and interfaces are described in alphabetical order. Within each class, the methods are also listed alphabetically.

The SAX specification is in the public domain – see the web site quoted above for a statement of policy on copyright. Essentially the policy is: do what you like with it, copy it as you wish, but no-one accepts any liability for errors or omissions.

The SAX distribution also includes two other "helper classes":

❑ `LocatorImpl` is an implementation of the `Locator` interface

❑ `ParserFactory` is a class that enables you to load a parser identified by a parameter at run-time

The documentation of these helper classes is not included here. For this, and for SAX sample applications, see the SAX distribution available from http://www.megginson.com.

SAX2 contains complete namespace support, which is available by default from any `XMLReader` object. An XML reader can also optionally supply raw XML 1.0 names.

An XML reader is fully configurable: it is possible to attempt to query or change the current value of any feature or property. Features and properties are identified by fully-qualified URIs, and parties are free to invent their own names for new extensions.

The ContentHandler and Attributes interfaces are similar to the deprecated DocumentHandler and AttributeList interfaces, but they add support for namespace-related information. ContentHandler also adds a callback for skipped entities, and Attributes adds the ability to look up an attribute's index by name.

The following interfaces have been deprecated:

- ❑ org.xml.sax.Parser
- ❑ org.xml.sax.DocumentHandler
- ❑ org.xml.sax.AttributeList
- ❑ org.xml.sax.HandlerBase

The following interfaces and classes have been added to SAX2:

- ❑ org.xml.sax.XMLReader (replaces Parser)
- ❑ org.xml.sax.XMLFilter
- ❑ org.xml.sax.ContentHandler (replaces DocumentHandler)
- ❑ org.xml.sax.Attributes (replaces AttributeList)
- ❑ org.xml.sax.SAXNotSupportedException
- ❑ org.xml.sax.SAXNotRecognizedException

Class and Interface Hierarchies

The following diagrams show the class and interface hierarchies of SAX 2.0. We covered some of these classes in Chapter 6, although many were left out as they are outside of the scope of what you will most likely need to know. However, this appendix covers them all, and further details can be found at the SAX web site.

Class Hierarchy

```
class java.lang.Object
    class org.xml.sax.helpers.AttributeListImpl
            (implements org.xml.sax.AttributeList)
    class org.xml.sax.helpers.AttributesImpl
            (implements org.xml.sax.Attributes)
    class org.xml.sax.helpers.DefaultHandler
            (implements org.xml.sax.ContentHandler, org.xml.sax.DTDHandler,
            org.xml.sax.EntityResolver, org.xml.sax.ErrorHandler)
    class org.xml.sax.HandlerBase
            (implements org.xml.sax.DocumentHandler, org.xml.sax.DTDHandler,
            org.xml.sax.EntityResolver, org.xml.sax.ErrorHandler)
    class org.xml.sax.InputSource
    class org.xml.sax.helpers.LocatorImpl
            (implements org.xml.sax.Locator)
    class org.xml.sax.helpers.NamespaceSupport
    class org.xml.sax.helpers.ParserAdapter
            (implements org.xml.sax.DocumentHandler, org.xml.sax.XMLReader)
    class org.xml.sax.helpers.ParserFactory
    class java.lang.Throwable
            (implements java.io.Serializable)
        class java.lang.Exception
            class org.xml.sax.SAXException
                class org.xml.sax.SAXNotRecognizedException
                class org.xml.sax.SAXNotSupportedException
                class org.xml.sax.SAXParseException
    class org.xml.sax.helpers.XMLFilterImpl
            (implements org.xml.sax.ContentHandler, org.xml.sax.DTDHandler,
            org.xml.sax.EntityResolver, org.xml.sax.ErrorHandler,
        org.xml.sax.XMLFilter)
        class org.xml.sax.helpers.XMLReaderAdapter
            (implements org.xml.sax.ContentHandler, org.xml.sax.Parser)
class org.xml.sax.helpers.XMLReaderFactory
```

Interface Hierarchy

```
interface org.xml.sax.AtttributeList
interface org.xml.sax.Attributes
interface org.xml.sax.ContentHandler
interface org.xml.sax.DocumentHandler
interface org.xml.sax.DTDHandler
interface org.xml.sax.EntityResolver
interface org.xml.sax.ErrorHandler
interface org.xml.sax.Locator
interface org.xml.sax.Parser
interface org.xml.sax.XMLReader
    interface org.xml.sax.XMLFilter
```

org.xml.sax.Attributes (SAX 2 – Replaces AttributeList)

Interface for a list of XML attributes – this interface allows access to a list of attributes in three different ways:

❑   By attribute index

❑   By namespace-qualified name

❑   By qualified (prefixed) name

The list will not contain attributes that were declared `#IMPLIED` but not specified in the start tag. It will also not contain attributes used as namespace declarations (`xmlns*`) unless the `http://xml.org/sax/features/namespace-prefixes` feature is set to `true` (it is `false` by default).

If the `namespace-prefixes` feature (see above) is `false`, access by qualified name may not be available; if the `http://xml.org/sax/features/namespaces` feature is `false`, access by namespace-qualified names may not be available.

This interface replaces the now-deprecated SAX1 `AttributeList` interface, which does not contain namespace support. In addition to namespace support, it adds the `getIndex` methods (below).

The order of attributes in the list is unspecified, and will vary from implementation to implementation.

getLength	Return the number of attributes in the list.
`public int getLength()`	Once you know the number of attributes, you can iterate through the list.
	Returns:
	The number of attributes in the list.
getURI	Look up an attribute's namespace URI by index.
`public String getURI(int index)`	**Parameters**
	index – the attribute index (zero-based).
	Returns:
	The namespace URI, or the empty string if none is available, or null if the index is out of range.
getLocalName	Look up an attribute's local name by index.
`public String getLocalName(int index)`	**Parameters**
	index – the attribute index (zero-based).
	Returns:
	The local name, or the empty string if namespace processing is not being performed, or null if the index is out of range.

getQName	Look up an attribute's XML 1.0 qualified name by index.
`public String getQName(int index)`	**Parameters**
	`index` – the attribute index (zero-based).
	Returns:
	The XML 1.0 qualified name, or the empty string if none is available, or null if the index is out of range.

getType	Look up an attribute's type by index.
`public String getType(int index)`	The attribute type is one of the strings "CDATA", "ID", "IDREF", "IDREFS", "NMTOKEN", "NMTOKENS", "ENTITY", "ENTITIES", or "NOTATION" (always in upper case).
	If the parser has not read a declaration for the attribute, or if the parser does not report attribute types, then it must return the value "CDATA" as stated in the XML 1.0 Recommendation (clause 3.3.3, "Attribute-Value Normalization").
	For an enumerated attribute that is not a notation, the parser will report the type as "NMTOKEN".
	Parameters
	`index` – the attribute index (zero-based).
	Returns:
	The attribute's type as a string, or null if the index is out of range.

getValue	Look up an attribute's value by index.
`public String getValue(int index)`	If the attribute value is a list of tokens (`IDREFS`, `ENTITIES`, or `NMTOKENS`), the tokens will be concatenated into a single string with each token separated by a single space.
	Parameters
	`index` – the attribute index (zero-based).
	Returns:
	The attribute's value as a string, or null if the index is out of range.

getIndex	Look up the index of an attribute by namespace name.
`public int getIndex(String uri, String localPart)`	**Parameters**
	`uri` – the namespace URI, or the empty string if the name has no namespace URI.
	`localName` – the attribute's local name.
	Returns:
	The index of the attribute, or -1 if it does not appear in the list.

getIndex `public int getIndex( String qName)`	Look up the index of an attribute by XML 1.0 qualified name. **Parameters** qName – the qualified (prefixed) name. **Returns:** The index of the attribute, or -1 if it does not appear in the list.
getType `public String getType(String uri, String localName)`	Look up an attribute's type by namespace name. See `getType(int)` for a description of the possible types. **Parameters** uri – the namespace URI, or the empty string if the name has no namespace URI. localName – the local name of the attribute. **Returns:** The attribute type as a string, or null if the attribute is not in the list or if namespace processing is not being performed.
getType `public String getType(String qName)`	Look up an attribute's type by XML 1.0 qualified name. See `getType(int)` for a description of the possible types. **Parameters** qName – the XML 1.0 qualified name. **Returns:** The attribute type as a string, or null if the attribute is not in the list or if qualified names are not available.
getValue `public String getValue(String uri, String localName)`	Look up an attribute's value by namespace name. See `getValue(int)` for a description of the possible values. **Parameters** uri – the namespace URI, or the empty string if the name has no namespace URI. localName – the local name of the attribute. **Returns:** The attribute value as a string, or null if the attribute is not in the list.
getValue `public String getValue(String qName)`	Look up an attribute's value by XML 1.0 qualified name. See `getValue(int)` for a description of the possible values. **Parameters** qName – the XML 1.0 qualified name. **Returns:** The attribute value as a string, or null if the attribute is not in the list or if qualified names are not available.

Interface org.xml.sax.AttributeList – Deprecated

An AttributeList is a collection of attributes appearing on a particular start tag. The parser supplies the DocumentHandler with an AttributeList as part of the information available on the startElement event. The AttributeList is essentially a set of name-value pairs for the supplied attributes; if the parser has analyzed the DTD it may also provide information about the type of each attribute.

Interface for an element's attribute specifications

The SAX parser implements this interface and passes an instance to the SAX application as the second argument of each startElement event.

The instance provided will return valid results only during the scope of the startElement invocation (to save it for future use, the application must make a copy: the AttributeListImpl helper class provides a convenient constructor for doing so).

An AttributeList includes only attributes that have been specified or defaulted: #IMPLIED attributes will not be included.

There are two ways for the SAX application to obtain information from the AttributeList. First, it can iterate through the entire list:

```
public void startElement (String name, AttributeList atts) {
  for (int i = 0; i < atts.getLength(); i++) {
    String name = atts.getName(i);
    String type = atts.getType(i);
    String value = atts.getValue(i);
    [...]
  }
}
```

(Note that the result of getLength() will be zero if there are no attributes.)

As an alternative, the application can request the value or type of specific attributes:

```
public void startElement (String name, AttributeList atts) {
  String identifier = atts.getValue("id");
  String label = atts.getValue("label");
  [...]
}
```

The AttributeListImpl helper class provides a convenience implementation for use by parser or application writers.

getLength public int getLength()	Return the number of attributes in this list. The SAX parser may provide attributes in any arbitrary order, regardless of the order in which they were declared or specified. The number of attributes may be zero. **Returns:** The number of attributes in the list.

getName
 	
`public String`
`getName(int index)`
	Return the name of an attribute in this list (by position).
	
	The names must be unique: the SAX parser shall not include the same attribute twice. Attributes without values (those declared `#IMPLIED` without a value specified in the start tag) will be omitted from the list.
	
	If the attribute name has a namespace prefix, the prefix will still be attached.
	
	Parameters:
	
	`index` – the index of the attribute in the list (starting at 0).
	
	Returns:
	
	The name of the indexed attribute, or null if the index is out of range.

getType
 	
`public String`
`getType(int index)`
	Return the type of an attribute in the list (by position).
	
	The attribute type is one of the strings `"CDATA"`, `"ID"`, `"IDREF"`, `"IDREFS"`, `"NMTOKEN"`, `"NMTOKENS"`, `"ENTITY"`, `"ENTITIES"`, or `"NOTATION"` (always in upper case).
	
	If the parser has not read a declaration for the attribute, or if the parser does not report attribute types, then it must return the value `"CDATA"` as stated in the XML 1.0 Recommendation (clause 3.3.3, "Attribute-Value Normalization").
	
	For an enumerated attribute that is not a notation, the parser will report the type as `"NMTOKEN"`.
	
	Parameters:
	
	`index` – the index of the attribute in the list (starting at 0).
	
	Returns:
	
	The attribute type as a string, or null if the index is out of range.

getType
 	
`public String`
`getType(String name)`
	Return the type of an attribute in the list (by name).
	
	The return value is the same as the return value for `getType(int)`.
	
	If the attribute name has a namespace prefix in the document, the application must include the prefix here.
	
	Parameters:
	
	`name` – the name of the attribute.
	
	Returns:
	
	The attribute type as a string, or null if no such attribute exists.

getValue
 	
`public String`
`getValue(int`
`index)`
	Return the value of an attribute in the list (by position).
	
	If the attribute value is a list of tokens (`IDREFS`, `ENTITIES`, or `NMTOKENS`), the tokens will be concatenated into a single string separated by whitespace.
	
	Parameters:
	
	`index` – the index of the attribute in the list (starting at 0).
	
	Returns:
	
	The attribute value as a string, or null if the index is out of range.

getValue
 	
`public String`
`getValue(String`
`name)`
	Return the value of an attribute in the list (by name).
	
	The return value is the same as the return value for `getValue(int)`.
	
	If the attribute name has a namespace prefix in the document, the application must include the prefix here.
	
	Parameters:
	
	`name` – the name of the attribute.
	
	Returns:
	
	The attribute value as a string, or null if no such attribute exists.

Interface org.xml.sax.ContentHandler (SAX 2 – Replaces DocumentHandler)

Every SAX application is likely to include a class that implements this interface, either directly or by subclassing the supplied class `HandlerBase`.

Receive notification of general document events

Receive notification of the logical content of a document – this is the main interface that most SAX applications implement: if the application needs to be informed of basic parsing events, it implements this interface and registers an instance with the SAX parser using the `setContentHandler` method. The parser uses the instance to report basic document-related events like the start and end of elements and character data.

The order of events in this interface is very important, and mirrors the order of information in the document itself. For example, all of an element's content (character data, processing instructions, and/or subelements) will appear, in order, between the `startElement` event and the corresponding `endElement` event.

This interface is similar to the now-deprecated SAX 1.0 `DocumentHandler` interface, but it adds support for namespaces and for reporting skipped entities (in non-validating XML processors).

Implementors should note that there is also a Java class `ContentHandler` in the `java.net` package; that means that it's probably a bad idea to do the following (more like a feature than a bug anyway, as `import ... *` is a sign of bad programming):

```
import java.net.*; import org.xml.sax.*;
```

setDocumentLocator
 	
`public void`
`setDocumentLocator`
`(Locator locator)`
	Receive an object for locating the origin of SAX document events.
	
	SAX parsers are strongly encouraged (though not absolutely required) to supply a locator: if it does so, it must supply the locator to the application by invoking this method before invoking any of the other methods in the `ContentHandler` interface.
	
	The locator allows the application to determine the end position of any document-related event, even if the parser is not reporting an error. Typically, the application will use this information for reporting its own errors (such as character content that does not match an application's business rules). The information returned by the locator is probably not sufficient for use with a search engine.
	
	Note that the locator will return correct information only during the invocation of the events in this interface. The application should not attempt to use it at any other time.
	
	Parameters
	
	`locator` – an object that can return the location of any SAX document event.

startDocument
 	
`public void`
`startDocument()`
	Receive notification of the beginning of a document.
	
	The SAX parser will invoke this method only once, before any other methods in this interface or in `DTDHandler` (except for `setDocumentLocator`).
	
	Throws:
	
	`SAXException` – any SAX exception, possibly wrapping another exception.

endDocument
 	
`public void`
`endDocument()`
	Receive notification of the end of a document.
	
	The SAX parser will invoke this method only once, and it will be the last method invoked during the parse. The parser shall not invoke this method until it has either abandoned parsing (because of an unrecoverable error) or reached the end of input.
	
	Throws:
	
	`SAXException` – any SAX exception, possibly wrapping another exception.

startPrefixMapping	Begin the scope of a prefix-URI namespace mapping.

`public void`
`startPrefixMapping`
`(String prefix, String`
`uri)`
	The information from this event is not necessary for normal namespace processing: the SAX XML reader will automatically replace prefixes for element and attribute names when the `http://xml.org/sax/features/namespaces` feature is `true` (the default).

	There are cases, however, when applications need to use prefixes in character data or in attribute values, where they cannot safely be expanded automatically; the `start/endPrefixMapping` event supplies the information to the application to expand prefixes in those contexts itself, if necessary.
	Note that `start/endPrefixMapping` events are not guaranteed to be properly nested relative to each-other: all `startPrefixMapping` events will occur before the corresponding `startElement` event, and all `endPrefixMapping` events will occur after the corresponding `endElement` event, but their order is not otherwise guaranteed.
	There should never be `start/endPrefixMapping` events for the `"xml"` prefix, since it is pre-declared and immutable.
	Parameters
	`prefix` – the namespace prefix being declared.
	`uri` – the namespace URI the prefix is mapped to.
	Throws:
	`SAXException` – the client may throw an exception during processing.
endPrefixMapping	End the scope of a prefix-URI mapping.

`public void`
`endPrefixMapping`
`(String prefix)`
	See `startPrefixMapping` for details. This event will always occur after the corresponding `endElement` event, but the order of `endPrefixMapping` events is not otherwise guaranteed.

	Parameters
	`prefix` – the prefix that was being mapped.
	Throws:
	`SAXException` – the client may throw an exception during processing.

startElement	Receive notification of the beginning of an element.
`public void startElement(String namespaceURI, String localName, String qName, Attributes atts)`	The parser will invoke this method at the beginning of every element in the XML document; there will be a corresponding `endElement` event for every `startElement` event (even when the element is empty). All of the element's content will be reported, in order, before the corresponding `endElement` event.

This event allows up to three name components for each element:

❑ the namespace URI

❑ the local name

❑ the qualified (prefixed) name

Any or all of these may be provided, depending on the values of the `http://xml.org/sax/features/namespaces` and the `http://xml.org/sax/features/namespace-prefixes` properties:

❑ The namespace URI and local name are required when the namespaces property is `true` (the default), and are optional when the namespaces property is `false` (if one is specified, both must be).

❑ The qualified name is required when the namespace-prefixes property is `true`, and is optional when the namespace-prefixes property is `false` (the default).

Note that the attribute list provided will contain only attributes with explicit values (specified or defaulted): `#IMPLIED` attributes will be omitted. The attribute list will contain attributes used for namespace declarations (`xmlns*` attributes) only if the `http://xml.org/sax/features/namespace-prefixes` property is `true` (it is `false` by default, and support for a `true` value is optional).

Parameters

`uri` – the namespace URI, or the empty string if the element has no namespace URI or if namespace processing is not being performed.

`localName` – the local name (without prefix), or the empty string if namespace processing is not being performed.

`qName` – the qualified name (with prefix), or the empty string if qualified names are not available.

`atts` – the attributes attached to the element. If there are no attributes, it shall be an empty `Attributes` object.

Throws:

`SAXException` – any SAX exception, possibly wrapping another exception.

endElement

```
public void
endElement(String
namespaceURI, String
localName, String
qName)
```

Receive notification of the end of an element.

The SAX parser will invoke this method at the end of every element in the XML document; there will be a corresponding `startElement` event for every `endElement` event (even when the element is empty).

For information on the names, see `startElement`.

Parameters

`uri` – the namespace URI, or the empty string if the element has no namespace URI or if namespace processing is not being performed.

`localName` – the local name (without prefix), or the empty string if namespace processing is not being performed.

`qName` – the qualified XML 1.0 name (with prefix), or the empty string if qualified names are not available.

Throws:

`SAXException` – any SAX exception, possibly wrapping another exception.

characters

```
public void characters
(char[] ch, int start,
int length)
```

Receive notification of character data.

The parser will call this method to report each chunk of character data. SAX parsers may return all contiguous character data in a single chunk, or they may split it into several chunks; however, all of the characters in any single event must come from the same external entity so that the locator provides useful information.

The application must not attempt to read from the array outside of the specified range.

Note that some parsers will report whitespace in element content using the `ignorableWhitespace` method rather than this one (validating parsers must do so).

Parameters

`ch` – the characters from the XML document.

`start` – the start position in the array.

`length` – the number of characters to read from the array.

Throws:

`SAXException` – any SAX exception, possibly wrapping another exception.

ignorableWhitespace

Receive notification of ignorable whitespace in element content.

```
public void
ignorableWhitespace
(char[] ch, int
start, int length)
```

Validating parsers must use this method to report each chunk of whitespace in element content (see the W3C XML 1.0 Recommendation, section 2.10): non-validating parsers may also use this method if they are capable of parsing and using content models.

SAX parsers may return all contiguous whitespace in a single chunk, or they may split it into several chunks; however, all of the characters in any single event must come from the same external entity, so that the locator provides useful information.

The application must not attempt to read from the array outside of the specified range.

Parameters

ch – the characters from the XML document.

start – the start position in the array.

length – the number of characters to read from the array.

Throws:

SAXException – any SAX exception, possibly wrapping another exception.

processingInstruction

Receive notification of a processing instruction.

```
public void
processingInstruction
(String target,

String data)
```

The parser will invoke this method once for each processing instruction found: note that processing instructions may occur before or after the main document element.

A SAX parser must never report an XML declaration (XML 1.0, section 2.8) or a text declaration (XML 1.0, section 4.3.1) using this method.

Parameters

target – the processing instruction target.

data – the processing instruction data, or null if none was supplied. The data does not include any whitespace separating it from the target.

Throws:

SAXException – any SAX exception, possibly wrapping another exception.

skippedEntity	Receive notification of a skipped entity.
`public void skippedEntity (String name)`	The parser will invoke this method once for each entity skipped. Non-validating processors may skip entities if they have not seen the declarations (because, for example, the entity was declared in an external DTD subset). All processors may skip external entities, depending on the values of the `http://xml.org/sax/features/external-general-entities` and the `http://xml.org/sax/features/external-parameter-entities` properties.

Parameters

name – the name of the skipped entity. If it is a parameter entity, the name will begin with '`%`', and if it is the external DTD subset, it will be the string "`[dtd]`".

Throws:

`SAXException` – any SAX exception, possibly wrapping another exception.

Interface org.xml.sax.DocumentHandler – Deprecated

Every SAX application is likely to include a class that implements this interface, either directly or by subclassing the supplied class `HandlerBase`.

Receive notification of general document events

This is the main interface that most SAX applications implement: if the application needs to be informed of basic parsing events, it implements this interface and registers an instance with the SAX parser using the `setDocumentHandler` method. The parser uses the instance to report basic document-related events like the start and end of elements and character data.

The order of events in this interface is very important, and mirrors the order of information in the document itself. For example, all of an element's content (character data, processing instructions, and/or sub-elements) will appear, in order, between the `startElement` event and the corresponding `endElement` event.

Application writers who do not want to implement the entire interface can derive a class from `HandlerBase`, which implements the default functionality; parser writers can instantiate `HandlerBase` to obtain a default handler. The application can find the location of any document event using the locator interface supplied by the parser through the `setDocumentLocator` method.

characters `public void characters(char ch[], int start, int length) throws SAXException`	Receive notification of character data. The parser will call this method to report each chunk of character data. SAX parsers may return all contiguous character data in a single chunk, or they may split it into several chunks; however, all of the characters in any single event must come from the same external entity, so that the locator provides useful information. The application must not attempt to read from the array outside of the specified range *and must not attempt to write to the array.* Note that some parsers will report whitespace using the `ignorableWhitespace()` method rather than this one (validating parsers *must* do so). **Parameters:** `ch` – the characters from the XML document. `start` – the start position in the array. `length` – the number of characters to read from the array. **Throws:** `SAXException` – any SAX exception, possibly wrapping another exception.
endDocument `public void endDocument() throws SAXException`	Receive notification of the end of a document. The SAX parser will invoke this method only once *for each document*, and it will be the last method invoked during the parse. The parser shall not invoke this method until it has either abandoned parsing (because of an unrecoverable error) or reached the end of input. **Throws**: `SAXException` – any SAX exception, possibly wrapping another exception.
endElement `public void endElement(String name) throws SAXException`	Receive notification of the end of an element. The SAX parser will invoke this method at the end of every element in the XML document; there will be a corresponding `startElement()` event for every `endElement()` event (even when the element is empty). If the element name has a namespace prefix, the prefix will still be attached to the name. **Parameters:** `name` – the element type name. **Throws:** `SAXException` – any SAX exception, possibly wrapping another exception.

ignorableWhitespace

```
public void
ignorableWhitespace
(char ch[], int start,
int length) throws
SAXException
```

Receive notification of ignorable whitespace in element content.

Validating parsers must use this method to report each chunk of ignorable whitespace (see the W3C XML 1.0 Recommendation, section 2.10): non-validating parsers may also use this method if they are capable of parsing and using content models.

SAX parsers may return all contiguous whitespace in a single chunk, or they may split it into several chunks; however, all of the characters in any single event must come from the same external entity, so that the locator provides useful information.

The application must not attempt to read from the array outside of the specified range.

Parameters:

ch – the characters from the XML document.

start – the start position in the array.

length – the number of characters to read from the array.

Throws:

SAXException – any SAX exception, possibly wrapping another exception.

processingInstruction

```
public void
processingInstruction
(String target, String
data) throws
SAXException
```

Receive notification of a processing instruction.

The parser will invoke this method once for each processing instruction found: note that processing instructions may occur before or after the main document element.

A SAX parser should never report an XML declaration (XML 1.0, section 2.8) or a text declaration (XML 1.0, section 4.3.1) using this method.

Parameters:

target – the processing instruction target.

data – the processing instruction data, or null if none was supplied.

Throws:

SAXException – any SAX exception, possibly wrapping another exception.

setDocumentLocator
 	
`public void`
`setDocumentLocator`
`(Locator locator)`
	Receive an object for locating the origin of SAX document events.
	
	A SAX parser is strongly encouraged (though not absolutely required) to supply a locator: if it does so, it must supply the locator to the application by invoking this method before invoking any of the other methods in the `DocumentHandler` interface.
	
	The locator allows the application to determine the end position of any document-related event, even if the parser is not reporting an error. Typically, the application will use this information for reporting its own errors (such as character content that does not match an application's business rules). The information returned by the locator is probably not sufficient for use with a search engine.
	
	Note that the locator will return correct information only during the invocation of the events in this interface. The application should not attempt to use it at any other time.
	
	Parameters:
	
	`locator` – an object that can return the location of any SAX document event.

startDocument
 	
`public void`
`startDocument() throws`
`SAXException`
	Receive notification of the beginning of a document.
	
	The SAX parser will invoke this method only once *for each document,* before any other methods in this interface or in `DTDHandler` (except for `setDocumentLocator`).
	
	Throws:
	
	`SAXException` – any SAX exception, possibly wrapping another exception.

startElement
 	
`public void startElement`
`(String name,`
`AttributeList atts)`
`throws SAXException`
	Receive notification of the beginning of an element.
	
	The parser will invoke this method at the beginning of every element in the XML document; there will be a corresponding `endElement()` event for every `startElement()` event (even when the element is empty). All of the element's content will be reported, in order, before the corresponding `endElement()` event.
	
	If the element name has a namespace prefix, the prefix will still be attached. Note that the attribute list provided will contain only attributes with explicit values (specified or defaulted): `#IMPLIED` attributes will be omitted.
	
	Parameters:
	
	`name` – the element type name.
	
	`atts` – the attributes attached to the element, if any.
	
	Throws:
	
	`SAXException` – any SAX exception, possibly wrapping another exception.

Interface org.xml.sax.DTDHandler

This interface should be implemented by the application, if it wants to receive notification of events related to the DTD. SAX does not provide full details of the DTD, but this interface is available because without it, it would be impossible to access notations and unparsed entities referenced in the body of the document.

Notations and unparsed entities are rather specialized facilities in XML, so most SAX applications will not need to use this interface.

Receive notification of basic DTD-related events

If a SAX application needs information about notations and unparsed entities, then the application implements this interface and registers an instance with the SAX parser using the parser's setDTDHandler method. The parser uses the instance to report notation and unparsed entity declarations to the application.

The SAX parser may report these events in any order, regardless of the order in which the notations and unparsed entities were declared; however, all DTD events must be reported after the document handler's startDocument event, and before the first startElement event.

It is up to the application to store the information for future use (perhaps in a hash table or object tree). If the application encounters attributes of type "NOTATION", "ENTITY", or "ENTITIES", it can use the information that it obtained through this interface to find the entity and/or notation corresponding with the attribute value.

The HandlerBase class provides a default implementation of this interface, which simply ignores the events.

notationDecl public void notationDecl (String name, String publicId, String systemId) throws SAXException	Receive notification of a notation declaration event. It is up to the application to record the notation for later reference, if necessary. If a system identifier is present, and it is a URL, the SAX parser must resolve it fully before passing it to the application. **Parameters:** name – the notation name. publicId – the notation's public identifier, or null if none was given. systemId – the notation's system identifier, or null if none was given. **Throws:** SAXException – any SAX exception, possibly wrapping another exception.

unparsedEntityDecl
 	
`public void`
`unparsedEntityDecl (String`
`name, String publicId,`
`String systemId, String`
`notationName) throws`
`SAXException`
	Receive notification of an unparsed entity declaration event.
	
	Note that the notation name corresponds to a notation reported by the `notationDecl()` event. It is up to the application to record the entity for later reference, if necessary.
	
	If the system identifier is a URL, the parser must resolve it fully before passing it to the application.
	
	Parameters:
	
	`name` – the unparsed entity's name.
	
	`publicId` – the entity's public identifier, or null if none was given.
	
	`systemId` – the entity's system identifier (it must always have one).
	
	`notationName` – the name of the associated notation.
	
	Throws:
	
	`SAXException` – any SAX exception, possibly wrapping another exception.

Interface org.xml.sax.EntityResolver

When the XML document contains references to external entities, the URL will normally be analyzed automatically by the parser: the relevant file will be located and parsed where appropriate. This interface allows an application to override this behavior. This might be needed, for example, if you want to retrieve a different version of the entity from a local server, or if the entities are cached in memory or stored in a database, or if the entity is really a reference to variable information such as the current date.

When the parser needs to obtain an entity, it calls this interface, which can respond by supplying any InputSource *object.*

Basic interface for resolving entities

If a SAX application needs to implement customized handling for external entities, it must implement this interface and register an instance with the SAX parser using the parser's setEntityResolver method.

The parser will then allow the application to intercept any external entities (including the external DTD subset and external parameter entities, if any) before including them.

Many SAX applications will not need to implement this interface, but it will be especially useful for applications that build XML documents from databases or other specialized input sources, or for applications that use URI types other than URLs.

The following resolver would provide the application with a special character stream for the entity with the system identifier "http://www.myhost.com/today":

```
import org.xml.sax.EntityResolver;
import org.xml.sax.InputSource;

public class MyResolver implements EntityResolver {
  public InputSource resolveEntity (String publicId, String systemId)
  {
    if (systemId.equals("http://www.myhost.com/today")) {
                              // return a special input source
      MyReader reader = new MyReader();
      return new InputSource(reader);
    } else {
                              // use the default behaviour
      return null;
    }
  }
}
```

The application can also use this interface to redirect system identifiers to local URIs or to look up replacements in a catalog (possibly by using the public identifier).

The HandlerBase class implements the default behavior for this interface, which is simply always to return null (to request that the parser use the default system identifier).

resolveEntity

```
public InputSource
resolveEntity(String
publicId, String
systemId)throws
SAXException, IOException
```

Allow the application to resolve external entities.

The parser will call this method before opening any external entity except the top-level document entity (including the external DTD subset, external entities referenced within the DTD, and external entities referenced within the document element): the application may request that the parser resolve the entity itself, that it use an alternative URI, or that it use an entirely different input source.

Application writers can use this method to redirect external system identifiers to secure and/or local URIs, to look up public identifiers in a catalogue, or to read an entity from a database or other input source (including, for example, a dialog box).

If the system identifier is a URL, the SAX parser must resolve it fully before reporting it to the application.

Parameters:

`publicId` – the public identifier of the external entity being referenced, or null if none was supplied.

`systemId` – the system identifier of the external entity being referenced.

Returns:

An `InputSource` object describing the new input source, or null to request that the parser open a regular URI connection to the system identifier.

Throws:

`SAXException` – any SAX exception, possibly wrapping another exception.

Throws:

`IOException` – a Java-specific IO exception, possibly the result of creating a new `InputStream` or `Reader` for the `InputSource`.

Interface org.xml.sax.ErrorHandler

You may implement this interface in your application if you want to take special action to handle errors. There is a default implementation provided within the HandlerBase *class.*

Basic interface for SAX error handlers

If a SAX application needs to implement customized error handling, it must implement this interface and then register an instance with the SAX parser using the parser's setErrorHandler method. The parser will then report all errors and warnings through this interface.

The parser shall use this interface instead of throwing an exception: it is up to the application whether to throw an exception for different types of errors and warnings. Note, however, that there is no requirement that the parser continue to provide useful information after a call to fatalError (in other words, a SAX driver class could catch an exception and report a fatalError).

The HandlerBase class provides a default implementation of this interface, ignoring warnings and recoverable errors and throwing a SAXParseException for fatal errors. An application may extend that class rather than implementing the complete interface itself.

error	Receive notification of a recoverable error.
public void error(SAXParseException exception)throws SAXException	This corresponds to the definition of "error" in section 1.2 of the W3C XML 1.0 Recommendation. For example, a validating parser would use this callback to report the violation of a validity constraint. The default behavior is to take no action.
	The SAX parser must continue to provide normal parsing events after invoking this method: it should still be possible for the application to process the document through to the end. If the application cannot do so, then the parser should report a fatal error even if the XML 1.0 Recommendation does not require it to do so.
	Parameters:
	exception – the error information encapsulated in a SAX parse exception.
	Throws:
	SAXException – any SAX exception, possibly wrapping another exception.

fatalError

```
public void
fatalError(SAXParseException
exception)throws SAXException
```

Receive notification of a non-recoverable error.

This corresponds to the definition of "fatal error" in section 1.2 of the W3C XML 1.0 Recommendation. For example, a parser would use this callback to report the violation of a well-formedness constraint.

The application must assume that the document is unusable after the parser has invoked this method, and should continue (if at all) only for the sake of collecting additional error messages: in fact, SAX parsers are free to stop reporting any other events once this method has been invoked.

Parameters:

`exception` – the error information encapsulated in a SAX parse exception.

Throws:

`SAXException` – any SAX exception, possibly wrapping another exception.

warning

```
public void warning (
SAXException exception)
throws SAXException
```

Receive notification of a warning.

SAX parsers will use this method to report conditions that are not errors or fatal errors as defined by the XML 1.0 Recommendation. The default behavior is to take no action.

The SAX parser must continue to provide normal parsing events after invoking this method: it should still be possible for the application to process the document through to the end.

Parameters:

`exception` – the warning information encapsulated in a SAX parse exception.

Throws:

`SAXException` – any SAX exception, possibly wrapping another exception.

Class org.xml.sax.HandlerBase – Deprecated

This class is supplied with SAX itself: it provides default implementations of most of the methods that would otherwise need to be implemented by the application. If you write classes in your application as subclasses of HandlerBase, *you need only code those methods where you want something other than the default behavior.*

Default base class for handlers

This class implements the default behavior for four SAX interfaces: EntityResolver, DTDHandler, DocumentHandler, and ErrorHandler.

Application writers can extend this class when they need to implement only part of an interface; parser writers can instantiate this class to provide default handlers when the application has not supplied its own.

Note that the use of this class is optional.

In the description below, only the behavior of each method is described. For the parameters and return values, see the corresponding interface definition.

characters public void characters(char ch[], int start, int length) throws SAXException	By default, do nothing. Application writers may override this method to take specific actions for each chunk of character data (such as adding the data to a node or buffer, or printing it to a file).
endDocument public void endDocument() throws SAXException	Receive notification of the end of the document. By default, do nothing. Application writers may override this method in a subclass to take specific actions at the beginning of a document (such as finalizing a tree or closing an output file).
endElement public void endElement(String name) throws SAXException	By default, do nothing. Application writers may override this method in a subclass to take specific actions at the end of each element (such as finalizing a tree node or writing output to a file).
error public void error(SAXParseException e) throws SAXException	The default implementation does nothing. Application writers may override this method in a subclass to take specific actions for each error, such as inserting the message in a log file or printing it to the console.
fatalError public void fatalError(SAXParseException e) throws SAXException	The default implementation throws a SAXParseException. Application writers may override this method in a subclass if they need to take specific actions for each fatal error (such as collecting all of the errors into a single report): in any case, the application must stop all regular processing when this method is invoked, since the document is no longer reliable, and the parser may no longer report parsing events.

681

ignorableWhitespace
 	
`public void`
`ignorableWhitespace(char ch[],`
`int start, int length) throws`
`SAXException`
	By default, do nothing. Application writers may override this method to take specific actions for each chunk of ignorable whitespace (such as adding data to a node or buffer, or printing it to a file).

notationDecl
 	
`public void`
`notationDecl(String name,`
`String publicId, String`
`systemId)`
	By default, do nothing. Application writers may override this method in a subclass if they wish to keep track of the notations declared in a document.

processingInstruction
 	
`public void`
`processingInstruction(String`
`target, String data) throws`
`SAXException`
	By default, do nothing. Application writers may override this method in a subclass to take specific actions for each processing instruction, such as setting status variables or invoking other methods.

resolveEntity
 	
`public InputSource`
`resolveEntity(String publicId,`
`String systemId) throws`
`SAXException`
	Always return null, so that the parser will use the system identifier provided in the XML document.
	
	This method implements the SAX default behavior: application writers can override it in a subclass to do special translations such as catalog lookups or URI redirection.

setDocumentLocator
 	
`public void`
`setDocumentLocator(`
`Locator locator)`
	By default, do nothing. Application writers may override this method in a subclass if they wish to store the locator for use with other document events.

startDocument
 	
`public void startDocument()`
`throws SAXException`
	By default, do nothing. Application writers may override this method in a subclass to take specific actions at the beginning of a document (such as allocating the root node of a tree or creating an output file).

startElement
 	
`public void`
`startElement(String name,`
`AttributeList attributes)`
`throws SAXException`
	By default, do nothing. Application writers may override this method in a subclass to take specific actions at the start of each element (such as allocating a new tree node or writing output to a file).

unparsedEntityDecl
 	
`public void`
`unparsedEntityDecl(String`
`name, String publicId, String`
`systemId, String notationName)`
	By default, do nothing. Application writers may override this method in a subclass to keep track of the unparsed entities declared in a document.

warning
 	
`public void`
`warning(SAXParseException e)`
`throws SAXException`
	The default implementation does nothing. Application writers may override this method in a subclass to take specific actions for each warning, such as inserting the message in a log file or printing it to the console.

Class org.xml.sax.InputSource

An InputSource *object represents a container for the XML document or any of the external entities it references (technically, the main document is itself an entity). The* InputSource *class is supplied with SAX: generally the application instantiates an* InputSource *and updates it to say where the input is coming from, and the parser interrogates it to find out where to read the input from.*

The InputSource *object provides three ways of supplying input to the parser: a system identifier (or URL), a* Reader *(which delivers a stream of Unicode characters), or an* InputStream *(which delivers a stream of uninterpreted bytes).*

A single input source for an XML entity

This class allows a SAX application to encapsulate information about an input source in a single object, which may include a public identifier, a system identifier, a byte stream (possibly with a specified encoding), and/or a character stream.

There are two places that the application will deliver this input source to the parser: as the argument to the Parser.parse method, or as the return value of the EntityResolver.resolveEntity method.

The SAX parser will use the InputSource object to determine how to read XML input. If there is a character stream available, the parser will read that stream directly; if not, the parser will use a byte stream, if available; if neither a character stream nor a byte stream is available, the parser will attempt to open a URI connection to the resource identified by the system identifier.

An InputSource object belongs to the application: the SAX parser shall never modify it in any way (it may modify a copy if necessary).

If you supply input in the form of a Reader *or* InputStream, *it may be useful to supply a system identifier as well. If you do this, the URI will not be used to obtain the actual XML input, but it will be used in diagnostics, and more importantly to resolve any relative URIs within the document, for example entity references.*

InputSource `public InputSource()`	Zero-argument default constructor.
InputSource `public InputSource( String systemId)`	Create a new input source with a system identifier. Applications may use `setPublicId` to include a public identifier as well, or `setEncoding` to specify the character encoding, if known. If the system identifier is a URL, it must be fully resolved. **Parameters:** `systemId` – the system identifier (URI).

InputSource	Create a new input source with a byte stream.
`public InputSource(` `InputStream byteStream)`	Application writers may use `setSystemId` to provide a base for resolving relative URIs, `setPublicId` to include a public identifier, and/or `setEncoding` to specify the object's character encoding.
	Parameters:
	`byteStream` – the raw byte stream containing the document.
InputSource	Create a new input source with a character stream.
`public InputSource(Reader` `characterStream)`	Application writers may use `setSystemId()` to provide a base for resolving relative URIs, and `setPublicId` to include a public identifier.
	The character stream shall not include a byte order mark.
setPublicId	Set the public identifier for this input source.
`public void setPublicId` `(String publicId)`	The public identifier is always optional: if the application writer includes one, it will be provided as part of the location information.
	Parameters:
	`publicId` – the public identifier as a string.
getPublicId	Get the public identifier for this input source.
`public String getPublicId ()`	**Returns:**
	The public identifier, or null if none was supplied.
setSystemId	Set the system identifier for this input source.
`public void setSystemId (` `String systemId)`	The system identifier is optional if there is a byte stream or a character stream, but it is still useful to provide one, since the application can use it to resolve relative URIs and can include it in error messages and warnings (the parser will attempt to open a connection to the URI only if there is no byte stream or character stream specified).
	If the application knows the character encoding of the object pointed to by the system identifier, it can register the encoding using the `setEncoding` method.
	If the system ID is a URL, it must be fully resolved.
	Parameters:
	`systemId` – the system identifier as a string.

getSystemId `public String getSystemId ()`	Get the system identifier for this input source. The `getEncoding` method will return the character encoding of the object pointed to, or null if unknown. If the system ID is a URL, it will be fully resolved. **Returns:** The system identifier.
setByteStream `public void setByteStream ( InputStream byteStream)`	Set the byte stream for this input source. The SAX parser will ignore this if there is also a character stream specified, but it will use a byte stream in preference to opening a URI connection itself. If the application knows the character encoding of the byte stream, it should set it with the `setEncoding` method. **Parameters:** `byteStream` – a byte stream containing an XML document or other entity.
getByteStream `public InputStream getByteStream()`	Get the byte stream for this input source. The `getEncoding` method will return the character encoding for this byte stream, or null if unknown. **Returns:** The byte stream, or null if none was supplied.
setEncoding `public void setEncoding( String encoding)`	Set the character encoding, if known. The encoding must be a string acceptable for an XML encoding declaration (see section 4.3.3 of the XML 1.0 Recommendation). This method has no effect when the application provides a character stream. **Parameters:** `encoding` – a string describing the character encoding.
getEncoding `public String getEncoding()`	Get the character encoding for a byte stream or URI. **Returns:** The encoding, or null if none was supplied.

setCharacterStream	Set the character stream for this input source.
`public void setCharacterStream(Reader characterStream)`	If there is a character stream specified, the SAX parser will ignore any byte stream and will not attempt to open a URI connection to the system identifier.
	Parameters:
	`characterStream` – the character stream containing the XML document or other entity.
getCharacterStream	Get the character stream for this input source.
`public Reader getCharacterStream()`	**Returns:**
	The character stream, or null if none was supplied.

Interface org.xml.sax.Locator

This interface provides methods that the application can use to determine the current position in the source XML document.

Interface for associating a SAX event with a document location

If a SAX parser provides location information to the SAX application, it does so by implementing this interface and then passing an instance to the application using the document handler's `setDocumentLocator` method. The application can use the object to obtain the location of any other document handler event in the XML source document.

Note that the results returned by the object will be valid only during the scope of each document handler method: the application will receive unpredictable results if it attempts to use the locator at any other time.

SAX parsers are not required to supply a locator, but they are very strongly encouraged to do so. If the parser supplies a locator, it must do so before reporting any other document events. If no locator has been set by the time the application receives the `startDocument` event, the application should assume that a locator is not available.

getPublicId	Return the public identifier for the current document event.
`public String getPublicId()`	**Returns:**
	A string containing the public identifier, or null if none is available.
getSystemId	Return the system identifier for the current document event.
`public String getSystemId()`	If the system identifier is a URL, the parser must resolve it fully before passing it to the application.
	Returns:
	A string containing the system identifier, or null if none is available.

getLineNumber
 	
`public int`
`getLineNumber()`
	Return the line number where the current document event ends. Note that this is the line position of the first character after the text associated with the document event. In practice some parsers report the line number and column number where the event starts.
	
	Returns:
	
	The line number, or -1 if none is available.

getColumnNumber
 	
`public int`
`getColumnNumber()`
	Return the column number where the current document event ends. Note that this is the column number of the first character after the text associated with the document event. The first column in a line is position 1.
	
	Returns:
	
	The column number, or -1 if none is available.

Interface org.xml.sax.Parser – Deprecated

Every SAX 1.0 parser must implement this interface. An application parses an XML document by creating an instance of a parser (that is, a class that implements this interface) and calling one of its parse() methods.

Basic interface for SAX (Simple API for XML) parsers

All SAX parsers must implement this basic interface: it allows applications to register handlers for different types of events and to initiate a parse from a URI, or a character stream.

All SAX parsers must also implement a zero-argument constructor (though other constructors are also allowed).

SAX parsers are reusable but not re-entrant: the application may reuse a parser object (possibly with a different input source) once the first parse has completed successfully, but it may not invoke the parse() methods recursively within a parse.

parse

```
public void parse(
InputSource source) throws
SAXException, IOException
```

Parse an XML document.

The application can use this method to instruct the SAX parser to begin parsing an XML document from any valid input source (a character stream, a byte stream, or a URI).

Applications may not invoke this method while a parse is in progress (they should create a new parser instead for each additional XML document). Once a parse is complete, an application may reuse the same parser object, possibly with a different input source.

Parameters:

source – the input source for the top-level of the XML document.

Throws:

SAXException – any SAX exception, possibly wrapping another exception.

Throws:

IOException – an IO exception from the parser, possibly from a byte stream or character stream supplied by the application.

parse

```
public void parse(String
systemId) throws
SAXException, IOException
```

Parse an XML document from a system identifier (URI).

This method is a shortcut for the common case of reading a document from a system identifier. It is the exact equivalent of the following:

```
parse(new InputSource(systemId));
```

If the system identifier is a URL, it must be fully resolved by the application before it is passed to the parser.

Parameters:

systemId – the system identifier (URI).

Throws:

SAXException – any SAX exception, possibly wrapping another exception.

Throws:

IOException – an IO exception from the parser, possibly from a byte stream or character stream supplied by the application.

setDocumentHandler

```
public void
setDocumentHandler(
DocumentHandler handler)
```

Allow an application to register a document event handler.

If the application does not register a document handler, all document events reported by the SAX parser will be silently ignored (this is the default behavior implemented by `HandlerBase`).

Applications may register a new or different handler in the middle of a parse, and the SAX parser must begin using the new handler immediately.

Parameters:

`handler` – the document handler.

setDTDHandler

```
public void setDTDHandler(
DTDHandler handler)
```

Allow an application to register a DTD event handler.

If the application does not register a DTD handler, all DTD events reported by the SAX parser will be silently ignored (this is the default behavior implemented by `HandlerBase`).

Applications may register a new or different handler in the middle of a parse, and the SAX parser must begin using the new handler immediately.

Parameters:

`handler` – the DTD handler.

setEntityResolver

```
public void
setEntityResolver(
EntityResolver resolver)
```

Allow an application to register a custom entity resolver.

If the application does not register an entity resolver, the SAX parser will resolve system identifiers and open connections to entities itself (this is the default behavior implemented in `HandlerBase`).

Applications may register a new or different entity resolver in the middle of a parse, and the SAX parser must begin using the new resolver immediately.

Parameters:

`resolver` – the object for resolving entities.

setErrorHandler

```
public void setErrorHandler(
ErrorHandler handler)
```

Allow an application to register an error event handler.

If the application does not register an error event handler, all error events reported by the SAX parser will be silently ignored, except for `fatalError`, which will throw a `SAXException` (this is the default behavior implemented by `HandlerBase`).

Applications may register a new or different handler in the middle of a parse, and the SAX parser must begin using the new handler immediately.

Parameters:

`handler` – the error handler.

setLocale	Allow an application to request a locale for errors and warnings.
`public void setLocale(Locale locale) throws SAXException`	SAX parsers are not required to provide localization for errors and warnings; if they cannot support the requested locale, however, they must throw a SAX exception. Applications may not request a locale change in the middle of a parse.
	Parameters:
	`locale` – a Java `Locale` object.
	Throws:
	`SAXException` – throws an exception (using the previous or default locale) if the requested locale is not supported.

Class org.xml.sax.SAXException

This class is used to represent an error detected during processing either by the parser or by the application.

Encapsulate a general SAX error or warning

This class can contain basic error or warning information from either the XML parser or the application: a parser writer or application writer can subclass it to provide additional functionality. SAX handlers may throw this exception or any exception subclassed from it.

If the application needs to pass through other types of exceptions, it must wrap those exceptions in a SAXException or an exception derived from a SAXException.

If the parser or application needs to include information about a specific location in an XML document, it should use the SAXParseException subclass.

getMessage	Return a detailed message for this exception.
`public String getMessage()`	If there is an embedded exception, and if the SAXException has no detailed message of its own, this method will return the detailed message from the embedded exception.
	Returns:
	The error or warning message.
getException	Return the embedded exception, if any.
`public Exception getException()`	**Returns:**
	The embedded exception, or null if there is none.
toString	Convert this exception to a string.
`public String toString()`	**Returns:**
	A string version of this exception.

Class org.xml.sax.SAXParseException

Extends `SAXException`. *This exception class represents an error or warning condition detected by the parser or by the application. In addition to the basic capability of* `SAXException`, *a* `SAXParseException` *allows information to be retained about the location in the source document where the error occurred. For an application-detected error, this information might be obtained from the* `Locator` *object.*

Encapsulate an XML parse error or warning

This exception will include information for locating the error in the original XML document. Note that although the application will receive a `SAXParseException` as the argument to the handlers in the `ErrorHandler` interface, the application is not actually required to throw the exception; instead, it can simply read the information in it and take a different action.

Since this exception is a subclass of `SAXException`, it inherits the ability to wrap another exception.

SAXParseException
 	
`public`
`SAXParseException(`
`String message, Locator`
`locator)`
	Create a new `SAXParseException` from a message and a locator.
	
	This constructor is especially useful when an application is creating its own exception from within a `DocumentHandler` callback.
	
	Parameters:
	
	`message` – the error or warning message.
	
	`locator` – the locator object for the error or warning.

SAXParseException
 	
`public`
`SAXParseException(String`
`message, Locator locator,`
`Exception e)`
	Wrap an existing exception in a `SAXParseException`.
	
	This constructor is especially useful when an application is creating its own exception from within a `DocumentHandler` callback, and needs to wrap an existing exception that is not a subclass of `SAXException`.
	
	Parameters:
	
	`message` – the error or warning message, or null to use the message from the embedded exception.
	
	`locator` – the locator object for the error or warning.
	
	e - Any exception

SAXParseException

```
public
SAXParseException(String
message, String publicId,
String systemId, int
lineNumber, int
columnNumber)
```

Create a new `SAXParseException`.

This constructor is most useful for parser writers. If the system identifier is a URL, the parser must resolve it fully before creating the exception.

Parameters:

`message` – the error or warning message.

`publicId` – the public identifier of the entity that generated the error or warning.

`systemId` – the system identifier of the entity that generated the error or warning.

`lineNumber` – the line number of the end of the text that caused the error or warning.

`columnNumber` – the column number of the end of the text that caused the error or warning.

SAXParseException

```
public
SAXParseException(String
message, String publicId,
String systemId, int
lineNumber, int
columnNumber, Exception e)
```

Create a new `SAXParseException` with an embedded exception.

This constructor is most useful for parser writers who need to wrap an exception that is not a subclass of `SAXException`.

If the system identifier is a URL, the parser must resolve it fully before creating the exception.

Parameters:

`message` – the error or warning message, or null to use the message from the embedded exception.

`publicId` – the public identifier of the entity that generated the error or warning.

`systemId` – the system identifier of the entity that generated the error or warning.

`lineNumber` – the line number of the end of the text that caused the error or warning.

`columnNumber` – the column number of the end of the text that caused the error or warning.

`e` – another exception to embed in this one.

getPublicId

```
public String
getPublicId()
```

Get the public identifier of the entity where the exception occurred.

Returns:

A string containing the public identifier, or null if none is available.

getSystemId
 	
`public String`
`getSystemId()`
	Get the system identifier of the entity where the exception occurred. *Note that the term "entity" includes the top-level XML document.*
	
	If the system identifier is a URL, it will be resolved fully.
	
	Returns:
	
	A string containing the system identifier, or null if none is available.

getLineNumber
 	
`public int`
`getLineNumber()`
	The line number of the end of the text where the exception occurred.
	
	Returns:
	
	An integer representing the line number, or -1 if none is available.

getColumnNumber
 	
`public int`
`getColumnNumber()`
	The column number of the end of the text where the exception occurred. The first column in a line is position 1.
	
	Returns:
	
	An integer representing the column number, or -1 if none is available.

Class org.xml.sax.SAXNotRecognizedException (SAX 2)

Exception class for an unrecognized identifier – an XML reader will throw this exception when it finds an unrecognized feature or property identifier; SAX applications and extensions may use this class for other, similar purposes.

SAXNotRecognizedException
 	
`public`
`SAXNotRecognizedException`
`(String message)`
	Construct a new exception with the given message.
	
	Parameters
	
	`message` – the text message of the exception.

This class has also inherited a lot of methods from other classes. These are summarized below:

Methods inherited from class `org.xml.sax.SAXException`:

- ❏ `getException`
- ❏ `getMessage`
- ❏ `toString`

Methods inherited from class `java.lang.Throwable`:

- ❑ `fillInStackTrace`
- ❑ `getLocalizedMessage`
- ❑ `printStackTrace`

Methods inherited from class `java.lang.Object`:

- ❑ `equals`
- ❑ `getClass`
- ❑ `hashCode`
- ❑ `notify`
- ❑ `notifyAll`
- ❑ `wait`

Class org.xml.sax.SAXNotSupportedException (SAX 2)

Exception class for an unsupported operation – an `XMLReader` will throw this exception when it recognizes a feature or property identifier, but cannot perform the requested operation (setting a state or value). Other SAX2 applications and extensions may use this class for similar purposes.

SAXNotSupportedException	Construct a new exception with the given message.
`public SAXNotSupportedException (String message)`	**Parameters** message – the text message of the exception.

This class has also inherited a lot of methods from other classes. These are summarized below:

Methods inherited from class `org.xml.sax.SAXException`:

- ❑ `getException`
- ❑ `getMessage`
- ❑ `toString`

Methods inherited from class `java.lang.Throwable`:

- ❑ `fillInStackTrace`
- ❑ `getLocalizedMessage`
- ❑ `printStackTrace`

Methods inherited from class `java.lang.Object`:

- ❑ `equals`
- ❑ `getClass`
- ❑ `hashCode`
- ❑ `notify`
- ❑ `notifyAll`
- ❑ `wait`

Interface org.xml.sax.XMLFilter (SAX 2)

This interface is like the reader, except it is used to read documents from a source other than a document or database. It can also modify events on the way to an application (extends `XMLReader`).

Interface for an XML filter – an XML filter is like an XML reader, except that it obtains its events from another XML reader rather than a primary source like an XML document or database. Filters can modify a stream of events as they pass on to the final application.

The `XMLFilterImpl` helper class provides a convenient base for creating SAX2 filters, by passing on all `EntityResolver`, `DTDHandler`, `ContentHandler` and `ErrorHandler` events automatically.

setParent `public void setParent( XMLReader parent)`	Set the parent reader. This method allows the application to link the filter to a parent reader (which may be another filter). The argument may not be null. **Parameters** `parent` – the parent reader.
getParent `public XMLReader getParent`	Get the parent reader. This method allows the application to query the parent reader (which may be another filter). It is generally a bad idea to perform any operations on the parent reader directly: they should all pass through this filter. **Returns:** The parent filter, or null if none has been set.

Interface org.xml.sax.XMLReader
(SAX 2 – Replaces Parser)

Every SAX 2.0 parser must implement this interface for reading documents using callbacks. An application parses an XML document by creating an instance of a parser (that is, a class that implements this interface) and calling one of its parse() *methods.*

Interface for reading an XML document using callbacks. XMLReader is the interface that an XML parser's SAX2 driver must implement. This interface allows an application to set and query features and properties in the parser, to register event handlers for document processing, and to initiate a document parse.

All SAX interfaces are assumed to be synchronous: the parse methods must not return until parsing is complete, and readers must wait for an event-handler callback to return before reporting the next event. This interface replaces the (now deprecated) SAX 1.0 parser interface. The XMLReader interface contains two important enhancements over the old Parser interface:

❑   it adds a standard way to query and set features and properties

❑   it adds namespace support, which is required for many higher-level XML standards

There are adapters available to convert a SAX1 Parser to a SAX2 XMLReader and vice-versa.

getFeature	Look up the value of a feature
`public boolean getFeature(String name)`	The feature name is any fully-qualified URI. It is possible for an XMLReader to recognize a feature name but to be unable to return its value; this is especially true in the case of an adapter for a SAX1 Parser, which has no way of knowing whether the underlying parser is performing validation or expanding external entities.
	Parameters
	name – the feature name, which is a fully-qualified URI
	Returns:
	The current state of the feature (true or false)
	Throws:
	SAXNotRecognizedException
	SAXNotSupportedException
	For more on getFeature, usage, see the explanation below this table.

setFeature
 	
`public void setFeature(String name, boolean value)`
	Set the state of a feature.
	
	The feature name is any fully-qualified URI. It is possible for an `XMLReader` to recognize a feature name but to be unable to set its value; this is especially true in the case of an adapter for a SAX1 `Parser`, which has no way of affecting whether the underlying parser is validating, for example.
	
	Parameters
	
	`name` – the feature name, which is a fully-qualified URI
	
	`state` – the requested state of the feature (`true` or `false`)
	
	Throws:
	
	`SAXNotRecognizedException`
	
	`SAXNotSupportedException`

getProperty
 	
`public Object getProperty(String name)`
	Look up the value of a property.
	
	The property name is any fully-qualified URI. It is possible for an `XMLReader` to recognize a property name but to be unable to return its state; this is especially true in the case of an adapter for a SAX1 `Parser`.
	
	Parameters
	
	`name` – the feature name, which is a fully-qualified URI
	
	Returns:
	
	The current value of the property
	
	Throws:
	
	`SAXNotRecognizedException`
	
	`SAXNotSupportedException`

setProperty
 	
`public void setProperty(String name, Object value)`
	Set the value of a property.
	
	The property name is any fully-qualified URI. It is possible for an `XMLReader` to recognize a property name but to be unable to set its value; this is especially true in the case of an adapter for a SAX1 `Parser`.
	
	Parameters
	
	`name` – the feature name, which is a fully-qualified URI
	
	`state` – the requested value for the property
	
	Throws:
	
	`SAXNotRecognizedException`
	
	`SAXNotSupportedException`

setEntityResolver
 	
`public void`
`setEntityResolver(`
`EntityResolver`
`resolver)`
	Allow an application to register an entity resolver.
	
	If the application does not register an entity resolver, the `XMLReader` will perform its own default resolution.
	
	Applications may register a new or different resolver in the middle of a parse, and the SAX parser must begin using the new resolver immediately.
	
	Parameters
	
	`resolver` – the entity resolver.
	
	Throws:
	
	`java.lang.NullPointerException` – if the resolver argument is null.

getEntityResolver
 	
`public`
`getEntityResolver(`
`)`
	Return the current entity resolver.
	
	Returns:
	
	The current entity resolver, or null if none has been registered.

setDTDHandler
 	
`public void`
`setDTDHandler(`
`DTDHandler`
`handler)`
	Allow an application to register a DTD event handler.
	
	If the application does not register a DTD handler, all DTD events reported by the SAX parser will be silently ignored.
	
	Applications may register a new or different handler in the middle of a parse, and the SAX parser must begin using the new handler immediately.
	
	Parameters
	
	`handler` – the DTD handler.
	
	Throws:
	
	`java.lang.NullPointerException` – if the handler argument is null.

getDTDHandler
 	
`public`
`getDTDHandler`
	Return the current DTD handler.
	
	Returns:
	
	The current DTD handler, or null if none has been registered.

setContentHandler
 	
`public void`
`setContentHandler`
`(ContentHandler`
`handler)`
	Allow an application to register a content event handler.
	
	If the application does not register a content handler, all content events reported by the SAX parser will be silently ignored. Applications may register a new or different handler in the middle of a parse, and the SAX parser must begin using the new handler immediately.
	
	Parameters
	
	`handler` – the content handler.
	
	Throws:
	
	`java.lang.NullPointerException` – if the handler argument is null.

getContentHandler
 	
`public`
`getContentHandler`
	Return the current content handler.
	
	Returns:
	
	The current content handler, or null if none has been registered.

setErrorHandler
 	
`public void`
`setErrorHandler(`
`ErrorHandler`
`handler)`
	Allow an application to register an error event handler.
	
	If the application does not register an error handler, all error events reported by the SAX parser will be silently ignored; however, normal processing may not continue. It is highly recommended that all SAX applications implement an error handler to avoid unexpected bugs.
	
	Applications may register a new or different handler in the middle of a parse, and the SAX parser must begin using the new handler immediately.
	
	Parameters
	
	`handler` – the error handler.
	
	Throws:
	
	`java.lang.NullPointerException` – if the handler argument is null.

getErrorHandler
 	
`public`
`ErrorHandler`
`getErrorHandler`
	Return the current error handler.
	
	Returns:
	
	The current error handler, or null if none has been registered.

parse
 	
`public void parse(`
`InputSource input)`
	Parse an XML document.
	
	The application can use this method to instruct the XML reader to begin parsing an XML document from any valid input source (a character stream, a byte stream, or a URI).
	
	Applications may not invoke this method while a parse is in progress (they should create a new `XMLReader` instead for each nested XML document). Once a parse is complete, an application may reuse the same `XMLReader` object, possibly with a different input source.
	
	During the parse, the `XMLReader` will provide information about the XML document through the registered event handlers.
	
	This method is synchronous: it will not return until parsing has ended. If a client application wants to terminate parsing early, it should throw an exception.
	
	Parameters
	
	`source` – the input source for the top-level of the XML document.
	
	Throws:
	
	`SAXExeception` – any SAX exception, possibly wrapping another exception.
	
	`java.io.IOException` – an IO exception from the parser, possibly from a byte stream or character stream supplied by the application.

parse
 	
`public void parse(`
`String systemId)`
	Parse an XML document from a system identifier (URI).
	
	If the system identifier is a URL, it must be fully resolved by the application before it is passed to the parser.
	
	Parameters
	
	`systemId` – the system identifier (URI).
	
	Throws:
	
	`SAXExeception` – any SAX exception, possibly wrapping another exception.
	
	`java.io.IOException` – an IO exception from the parser, possibly from a byte stream or character stream supplied by the application.

All `XMLReaders` are required to recognize the `http://xml.org/sax/features/namespaces` and the `http://xml.org/sax/features/namespace-prefixes` feature names.

Some feature values may be available only in specific contexts, such as before, during, or after a parse.

Implementors are free (and encouraged) to invent their own features, using names built on their own URIs.

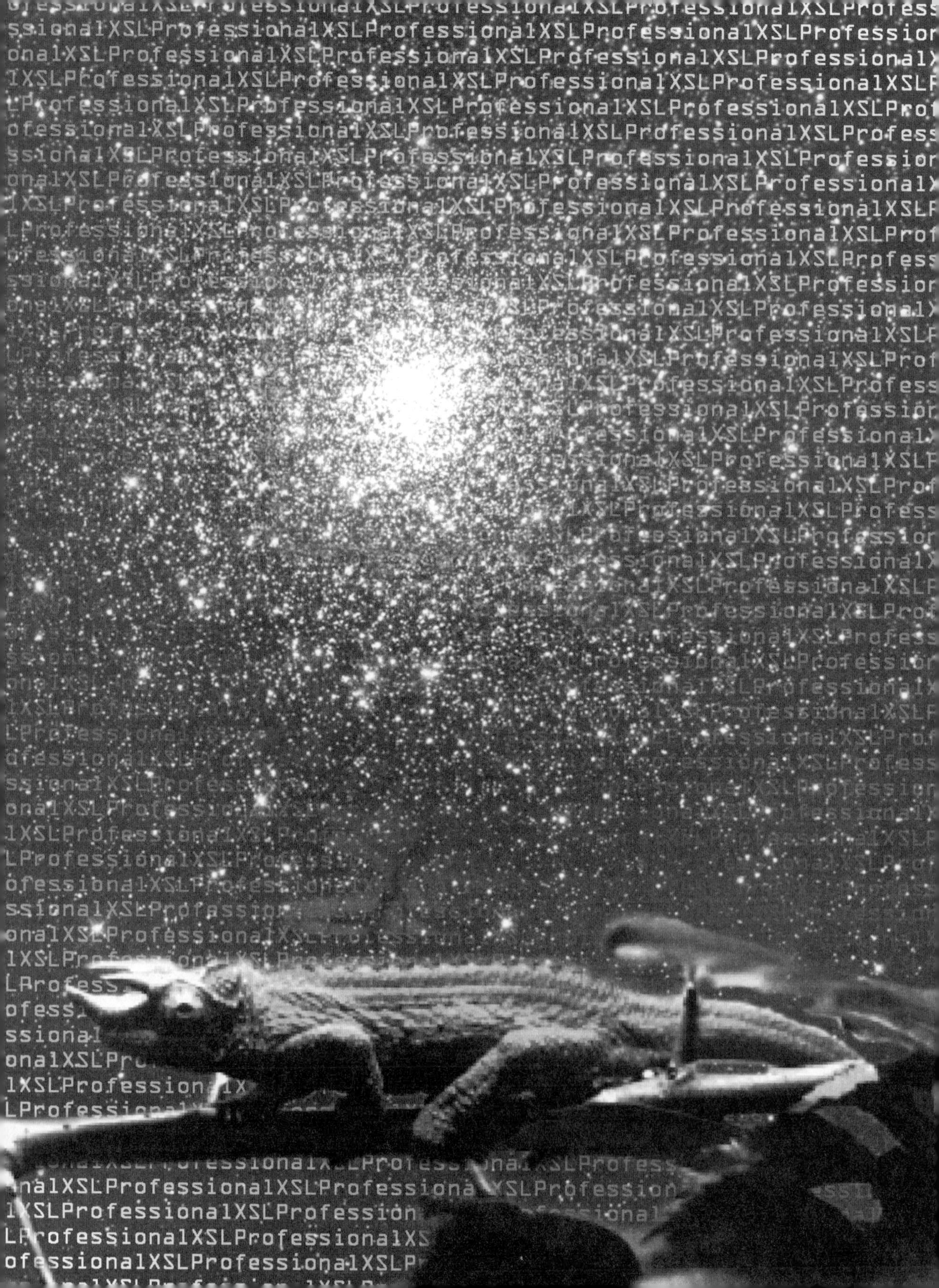

E

XSLT Processors and Tools

XSL, being an open standard, has a plethora of freely available processors and associated software that can be downloaded from the net. This appendix picks the cream of the crop, which you should find to be the most useful and widely supported when developing XSL applications. We first give a guide to the **XSLT processors** available, particularly those mentioned and used throughout the rest of the book.

Two sophisticated analytical tools, **XSLTDoc** and **XSLTracer**, are also included, along with some brief guidelines written by their developers to help you get started using these powerful applications. XSLTDoc is a browser-based tool that gives a way of examining stylesheets, with frames describing the code, the elements and XPath expressions within the code, the import tree of the application, and the various templates it contains. XSLTracer is a utility to help XSLT developers analyze their stylesheets to gain a better understanding of them, and to facilitate the debugging of complex transforms that aren't behaving quite as intended. Transformations often verge on being impenetrably opaque processes that can be very time consuming to analyze without additional tools.

XSLT Processors

There are numerous XSLT processors currently available, many of which are mature enough to have iterated through several versions. They include:

- ❑ MSXML – http://msdn.microsoft.com/xml/
- ❑ Saxon – http://users.iclway.co.uk/mhkay/saxon/index.html
- ❑ Xalan – http://xml.apache.org
- ❑ XT – http://www.jclark.com/xml/xt.html
- ❑ 4XSLT – http://4suite.org/index.epy
- ❑ iXSLT – http://www.infoteria.com
- ❑ Unicorn – http://www.unicorn-enterprises.com/

Installation instructions for the first four of these will be given within this appendix (with references, in the case of MSXML, to further information in Chapter 7).

MSXML

Full instructions on how to download and use **MSXML 3.0** are given in Chapter 7, so only a brief coverage will be given here.

MSXML 3.0 can be downloaded from http://msdn.microsoft.com/xml/, by following the link to Downloads. Once this has been done, invoking the executable will install and register the components in **side-by-side mode**.

Often you may need to use MSXML in **replace mode**: see *Installing MSXML in Replace Mode* http://msdn.microsoft.com/xml/general/replacemode.asp for details. If you need to do this, download the xmlinst file from the same site as MSXML 3.0. Double click or run the file on your computer – this will unzip two files to your system: make a note of where they are unzipped to, or change the destination folder. The two files are a readme file and xmlinst.exe. Run xmlinst.exe from the command prompt.

The easiest way to use the MSXML processor is to add the following processing instruction to the top of your source file, source.xml:

```
<?xml-stylesheet type="text/xsl" href="stylesheet.xsl" ?>
```

Opening source.xml within Internet Explorer will cause MSXML to process source.xml using stylesheet.xsl, and display the resulting result.xml.

Note that there is also an MSXML command-line utility called MSXSL. See Chapter 7 for further details.

Saxon and Instant Saxon

Saxon and **Instant Saxon** may be downloaded, without charge, from:

http://users.iclway.co.uk/mhkay/saxon/index.html

Note that there are typically several versions of Saxon available to be downloaded from this page and the exact versions available vary as Saxon is updated. Each one is briefly described on the web page – read those descriptions carefully to establish which version will best suit your needs. For example, if you do not have a Windows machine you will probably choose to download a full version of Saxon. On the other hand, Instant Saxon is a pre-packaged Windows executable suitable for easy use on the Windows platform. Also, if you are a beginner, be sure to avoid downloading any version that may be in any way "experimental".

Instant Saxon

To download the relevant version of Instant Saxon simply right-click on the download link, choose the "Save Target As" option and save to a suitable directory on your hard drive. The Instant Saxon file, which is downloaded in zipped format, is only around 340 Kb, so is a relatively quick download.

To unzip the download immediately, choose Open when it completes (I assume you have access to WinZip or a similar compression utility) and unzip to a suitably named directory. For example, in Chapter 2 we assumed you had used `c:\InstantSaxon` and that all XML source files and XSL stylesheets were also present in that directory.

Instant Saxon is run from a command line. For example, to run the stylesheet `stylesheet.xsl` against `source.xml` and store the result in `result.xml`, use the following command:

```
saxon source.xml stylesheet.xsl > result.xml
```

Saxon

The current stable version of the full Saxon processor is larger than Instant Saxon, at 2.6 MB. It contains source and object code, documentation, and sample applications, supplied in a zipped file.

The only pre-requisite for using the Saxon processor is a Java Virtual Machine. Notice that the object code for Saxon is given in a JAR file, `saxon.jar`. This needs to be included inside your `classpath` environment variable.

The following command line can be used to transform `source.xml` using `stylesheet.xsl`:

```
java com.icl.saxon.StyleSheet source.xml stylesheet.xsl >result.xml
```

Xalan

The Apache **Xalan** Java 2 processor is a robust and highly compliant XSLT and XPath implementation that can be downloaded without charge from http://xml.apache.org. It is an open source product contributed to by IBM, Lotus, Oracle, and Sun, among others.

To run this version of Xalan, you need JDK/JRE 1.1.8 or 1.2.2, and two JAR files that are included in the Xalan download: `xalan.jar` and `xerces.jar`. (`xerces.jar` represents the Xerces XML parser that Xalan uses.) Assuming you're developing under MS Windows, simply add the two JAR files to your system `classpath` environment variable.

The Xalan processor has a command-line utility, which can be very handy when testing your stylesheets. To transform an XML document with the command-line utility, just move to the folder containing your files to be tested and type:

```
java org.apache.xalan.xslt.Process –in source.xml –xsl stylesheet.xsl –out result.xml
```

where the parameter following `–in` is the XML document to be transformed, the parameter following `–xsl` is the stylesheet, and the parameter following `–out` is the name of the file to which the result of the transformation will be written. The `–out` parameter can be omitted, in which case the output of the transformation is written to the standard output (usually the screen).

XT

The **xt** processor is an open-source implementation of XSLT produced by the editor of the specification, James Clark. Note that it is an incomplete implementation of the XSLT 1.0 specification, and is not being developed any further.

Two downloads for xt are available at http://www.jclark.com/xml/xt.html. One contains the full distribution, and the other a packaged Windows executable.

XT Packaged as a Windows Executable

If you are running Windows, this version is simplicity itself to install and get working. Its only prerequisite is the Microsoft VM, which comes packaged with Internet Explorer. The downloaded zip file simply contains the `xt.exe` utility. Place this in the same directory as the documents that need testing, and use the command line:

```
xt source.xml stylesheet.xsl result.xml
```

Full Distribution

If you choose to download the full distribution, you will also need an XML parser that supports SAX, such as XP (http://www.jclark.com/xml/xp/index.html). With the full product, the typical command line is:

```
java com.jclark.xsl.sax.Driver source.xml stylesheet.xsl result.xml
```

XSLT Tools

Now that we have covered the XSLT processors that were used within the book, we'll take a look at two new XSLT tools that should help when developing applications.

XSLTDoc

XSLTDoc is an application that I, Jeni Tennison, have developed to browse XSLT stylesheets from within Microsoft Internet Explorer, and is available from my web site at http://www.jenitennison.com/xslt/utilities/, under the GNU General Public License. This means that not only is it free to use, but also that it has a lot of interesting and useful components that you can use in your own applications.

XSLTDoc has two goals:

❑ To help stylesheet authors by providing descriptions, in English, of what each XSLT element within the stylesheet does, including information about the function of any XPath expressions or patterns used in them. Where parts of an XPath expression are redundant it tells you so, and also provides hyper-links to the descriptions of the XSLT elements in the XSLT Specification.

❑ To enable you to browse an entire XSLT application, including imported and included stylesheets, from a single interface. It indicates if a template, attribute set, global variable, etc. is overridden, and gives you a link to the overriding instruction. It also provides links back to the definitions of variables whenever they're used.

System Requirements

XSLTDoc is a dynamic client-side XSLT application: it uses a set of XSLT stylesheets to process your stylesheet, producing XHTML to allow you to browse the stylesheet. As a dynamic client-side XSLT application, to run it you need to have MSXML 3.0 (final release from http://msdn.microsoft.com/xml – see Chapter 7 or earlier in this appendix for more details) or above installed in replace mode. At the time of writing, this limits XSLTDoc to Microsoft Internet Explorer 5.0 or above on Windows platforms.

Installing and Running XSLTDoc

Installing XSLTDoc involves downloading XSLTDoc.zip and unzipping it into its own directory, for example C:\XSLTDoc.

Running XSLTDoc involves the following steps:

❑ Start Microsoft Internet Explorer.

❑ Open the xslt-doc.xsl file within the directory you unzipped XSLTDoc to, for example by typing C:/XSLTDoc/xslt-doc.xsl into the address bar.

❑ You will be prompted for the name of a stylesheet to view. Enter one of:

❑ a relative path from your XSLTDoc directory

❑ an absolute filename (e.g. starting with C:/ or /)

❑ a URL (including those starting with file:///)

and click on the OK button. You can open a new stylesheet at any point by clicking on the Reload button on the toolbar or by pressing *F5*. If you haven't got a stylesheet of your own to open, you can always have a look at the stylesheets that make up XSLTDoc itself, such as notes.xsl.

Using XSLTDoc

The following screenshot shows XSLTDoc in use, browsing notes.xsl – one of the XSLT stylesheets it uses. XSLTDoc displays the following four frames to help you browse the XSLT application:

❑ **Import tree** (top left) – the hierarchy of imported and included stylesheets

❑ **Summary** (top right) – a summary of the top-level instructions in the stylesheet you're currently viewing

❑ **Source** (bottom left) – syntax-highlighted source code of the top-level instruction (and any preceding comments or processing instructions) that you're currently viewing

❑ **Notes** (bottom right) – a description and explanation of the XSLT instruction or literal result element that you're currently viewing

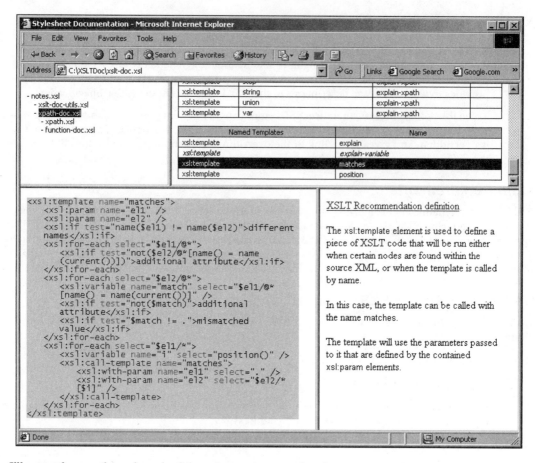

I'll now take you through each of these frames in more detail.

The Import Tree Frame

The import tree shows the stylesheet files that are used within your XSLT application. The stylesheet at the top of the tree is the one that you selected to be displayed. Stylesheets that are imported or included with `<xsl:import>` or `<xsl:include>` instructions are displayed below it; stylesheets these import or include are shown below that, and so on.

The highlighted filename indicates the stylesheet that you're currently viewing. Clicking on another filename within the tree will display details of that stylesheet.

The Summary Frame

The summary frame displays all the top-level elements in the current stylesheet in table form. The tables that can be shown are:

❑ **Imports & Includes** – the URLs referenced by any `<xsl:import>` or `<xsl:include>` instructions

❑ **Whitespace Control** – the elements affected by any `<xsl:strip-space>` or `<xsl:preserve-space>` instructions

❑ **Output Control** – the output method, and the public and system document types defined by any <xsl:output> instructions

❑ **Namespace Aliases** – the stylesheet and result prefixes defined by any <xsl:namespace-alias> instructions

❑ **Variables & Parameters** – the names and values of any global variables and parameters

❑ **Keys** – the names, match patterns, and use expressions of any keys defined in the stylesheet

❑ **Templates** – the match patterns, modes, and priorities of any standard templates in the stylesheet

❑ **Named Templates** – the names of any named templates in the stylesheet

❑ **Attribute Sets** – the names of any attribute sets in the stylesheet, along with a list of the attribute sets that they use themselves

❑ **Decimal Formats** – the names of any decimal formats defined in the stylesheet, giving the decimal and grouping separators that they use

A table will only be displayed if there are the appropriate top-level elements present in the stylesheet. Within the table, rows that are in italics indicate instructions that are overridden either later in the same stylesheet or within an importing or including stylesheet further up the hierarchy. (Note that standard unnamed matching templates that are overridden are *not* displayed in italics.)

The table rows can be sorted and the table columns rearranged by clicking on the name of the column that you want to sort by or move. When you click on a column header, a small menu will appear. The options are:

❑ **sort** – sort the table by the column

❑ **move left** – move the table column left

❑ **move right** – move the table column right

The top-level element that you're looking at in the Source frame is highlighted within the relevant summary table. Similarly, clicking on a row within a table in the Summary frame displays the relevant top-level element in the Source frame.

Source Frame

The Source frame shows the XSLT code for the top-level element that you're currently looking at. The XSLT within the Source frame is syntax highlighted; you can change the colors used by customizing XSLTDoc, as described in the next section, *Customizing XSLTDoc*.

The element that you're looking at is highlighted within the source code. Clicking on the name of an element, whether it's an XSLT instruction or a literal result element, displays a description or explanation of that element in the Notes frame.

Notes Frame

The Notes frame displays notes on the element that you're currently viewing. What kind of description is given depends on the type of element that you're looking at:

❑ Literal result elements – a link to the section on *Literal Result Elements* in the XSLT Recommendation and a brief description of the element. The description lists the attributes that are being set on the element, along with their values or a description of how their values are being decided if they are being set with an attribute value template.

❑ XSLT instructions – a link to the relevant section within the XSLT Recommendation and a brief description of what the instruction does, both in general and in this specific case.

A frequent feature of the descriptions within the Notes frame is an explanation of an XPath expression. Just as XPath expressions can be quite complicated, so can these descriptions! Within each description, any references to named instructions defined elsewhere, such as variables, templates and attribute sets, are clickable links to the relevant definition. If there's more than one definition, it shows you the one with the highest priority. This allows you to navigate through the stylesheet quickly and easily.

Customizing XSLTDoc

There are several files that you can customize to personalize your version of XSLTDoc. The first group consists of the Cascading Style Sheet (CSS) files that define the styles in each of the four frames. These CSS files are:

❑ `tree.css` – styles for the Import Tree frame

❑ `summary.css` – styles for the Summary frame

❑ `source.css` – styles for the Source frame

❑ `notes.css` – styles for the Notes frame

At the moment, most of the styles are based on your Windows Display Settings, but by changing these CSS files, you can alter the background and text colors, font styles, indents, and so on for the four frames. In particular, editing `source.css` will let you control the syntax highlighting within the Source frame.

Another customization file, `xslt-doc-prefs.xml`, is an XML file that gives you control over two things:

❑ The styles used for selected text within the Summary and Source frames

❑ The layout of the tables used within the Summary frame

The default layouts for the tables used in the Summary frame are defined within a set of `table` elements within this preferences file. Each `<table>` element contains definitions for each column in order, specifying the value to be used, the column header, and whether the column is movable within the table. You can also change the order in which the rows are sorted by default, by changing the order of the `sort` elements.

Finally, you can change the explanations that are given for the XSLT elements, by editing the `xslt-doc.xml` file. For example, you might want to add your own notes about an XSLT element or add links to other information that you find useful.

XSLTracer

XSLTracer has been developed as an educational tool under the ZVON project (http://zvon.org) of which I, Jirka Jirat, am a working member, and with generous financial support from the IDOOX B.V. company. I am glad to have the opportunity to explain the basic principles of this tool, freely available from the Downloads section of the ZVON site.

Not many people are used to thinking in terms of nodes, trees, and functional programming, and from time to time even an advanced XSLT programmer shakes his head, wondering what's causing some unexpected item in their output (or, more probably, what happened to the part they were expecting). Debugging of XSLT code is not very straightforward and the transformation itself often resembles a black-box process. XSLTracer is a free tool, completely written in XSLT with just a very small supplement of Perl code, that aims to clarify this process.

It lets us view the processing of multiple XML sources (accessed during the transformation via the `document()` function). The output file can be displayed too, as long as it is well-formed XML. The main feature of this application is the option to view the transformation process step-by-step, including dynamically highlighting the currently processed XSLT instruction and corresponding XML elements and attributes along with output tree fragments. In addition to all this, the following information is also provided during the tracing:

❑ Name and full XPath location of the currently processed XML element or attribute

❑ Values of parameters and variables

❑ All nodes of the node-set matching `select` expressions in `<xsl:apply-templates>` or `<xsl:for-each>` elements

❑ Value produced by instances of `<xsl:value-of>`

XSLTracer, together with its sister tool XSLTDoc, described above, effectively document the powerful XSLT language.

Requirements and Limitations

These software products need to be installed to use the XSLTracer:

❑ Saxon Processor Version 5.5.1. (Newer versions have abandoned some extension functions which XSLTracer requires; setup details are found later in this appendix.)

❑ Perl (available from the www.perl.com download section).

❑ A browser that supports HTML 4.0, with JavaScript and DOM (currently limited to Mozilla-based products (Netscape 6) and Internet Explorer 5.x with JavaScript/JScript enabled).

Only transformation with a single XSLT stylesheet is currently supported; that is you may not trace into imported stylesheets. The output from the examined transformation is not the last one in the transformation chain and thus must be well-formed XML only. XSLTracer is built on the top of Saxon's XSLT transformation, so the program will only be able to function for valid stylesheets because, if Saxon detects any errors, the whole process ends there and then.

Running the Program

After unzipping the XSLTracer archive, run the Perl script from the `src` subdirectory that should have been created.

```
$ cd src
$ perl run.pl <XML file> <XSL file> <outdir> [<additional_XML_file> ...]
```

This will create the output subdirectory if necessary, and place all output there. To view the results, open the `frameset.html` file in this directory from your browser.

Example

I will illustrate the use of XSLTracer for a recursive stylesheet with a parameter. While in procedural programming languages there is little need for recursion, in XSLT it is a daily task. The XSLT stylesheet, `recurse.xsl`, looks like this:

```
<xsl:stylesheet xmlns:xsl='http://www.w3.org/1999/XSL/Transform'
                xmlns:saxon="http://icl.com/saxon"
                extension-element-prefixes="saxon"
                version="1.0">

<xsl:output method="xml" indent="yes"/>

<xsl:template match = "/">
 <html>
   <body>
    <xsl:apply-templates/>
   </body>
 </html>
</xsl:template>

<xsl:template match="*">
 <xsl:param name="level">0</xsl:param>
 <xsl:text>Level: </xsl:text>
 <xsl:value-of select="$level"/>
 <br/>
 <xsl:apply-templates>
  <xsl:with-param name="level"><xsl:value-of select="$level+1"/></xsl:with-
    param>
 </xsl:apply-templates>
</xsl:template>
</xsl:stylesheet>
```

The screenshot opposite shows the result from XSLTracer for a very simple XML input file as appearing in the middle right pane. In the upper frame on the left there are buttons that enable XSLT instructions to be traced into, as shown in the center left pane – note how the active XSLT instruction is highlighted (in this example it is `<xsl:param>`). On the right-hand side of the upper frame, buttons appear that determine whether to display input or output XML files in the center right frame. When source XML is displayed, the currently processed node is highlighted (here it is the element `<CCC>`). When the output file is viewed, then the current result tree fragment is shown in a different color. Additional information is shown in the bottom frame: the name of currently processed node (CCC); the full XPath location of this node (`/AAA[1]/BBB[1]/CCC[2]`); the string-values of parameters and variables (parameter `level` has value 2); and other information that might be appropriate.

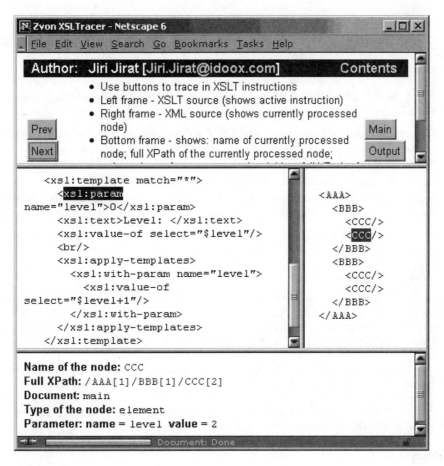

And here is the output:

```
<html>
  <body> Level: 0
    <br/> Level: 1
    <br/> Level: 2
    <br/> Level: 2
    <br/> Level: 1
    <br/> Level: 2
    <br/> Level: 2
    <br/>
  </body>
</html>
```

How It Works

This section will explain the 'backroom workings' of XSLTracer, which consists of two principal parts: the first stores information about the transformation and links it to the examined XSLT stylesheet, XML source documents, and generated output, and the second creates HTML files from JavaScript to display the process.

Principles

XSLTracer relies heavily on the creation of XSLT stylesheets using other XSLT stylesheets (see the section *Using XSL Stylesheets to Create New XSL Stylesheets* in Chapter 10). It uses multiple-step XSLT stylesheet generation. Thus the whole magic is just a tricky chain of XSLT transformations, as described below:

❑ Step 1: Inserting ID – first of all, XSLTracer copies the XML sources and the examined XSLT to new files, assigning unique IDs to each element in them using the `generate-id()` function.

❑ Step 2: Inserting trace messages – the XSLT stylesheet from Step 1 is transformed to a more verbose XSLT stylesheet, which has `<xsl:message>` elements containing trace messages inserted wherever possible.

❑ Step 3: Creating the tracer file – the stylesheet from Step 2 is used to transform the copies of the XML source documents from Step 1, at the same time writing an XML tracer file. This tracer file provides a bridge between the source XML, output XML and, XSLT stylesheet.

❑ Step 4: Formatting the files for display – each input XML file, examined XSLT stylesheet, and output file is converted to HTML documents with prettily formatted code-display.

Displaying the Inputs and Output

The interactive client-side "tracing" is based on the use of DOM interfaces and methods in JavaScript that were coded with the kind help of Jiri Znamenacek. The formatting stylesheet (Step 4) then just converts the XML files to HTML documents with many nested `<SPAN>` elements with IDs (which were assigned in Step 1). It also generates fields in JavaScript code, which contain the sequence of IDs and are used to navigate through the displayed code. Pressing the buttons marked Prev and Next then simply decreases or increases this field index accordingly. The appropriate elements can be accessed and their properties changed by the DOM method `getElementById()` (for example, to invert the colors).

The information stored in the log file is used to create JavaScript code, which provides the dynamic highlighting of the code and displays the values of parameters, variables, etc. in the bottom frame.

Tips and Tricks

Don't be scared to use your own namespaces – this helps very much! When you need to insert attributes and elements into a previously unknown XSLT stylesheet or XML document and you want to avoid confusion, this is the best choice.

Similar Software

IBM has developed a similar product, written in Java, called **XSL Trace**. It is currently available from their alphaWorks site at http://www.alphaworks.ibm.com/tech/xsltrace, for a 90-day evaluation period. It lets you see the transform side-by-side with the resulting XML or HTML output file as it is built up.

There is also **4XDebug** – a debugging tool for use with the 4XSLT processor, available from the Software section of http://4Suite.org. 4XDebug uses an interface similar to the GNU symbolic debugger (GDB), allowing users to step through 4XSLT's rendering process, setting break points and examining data along the way.

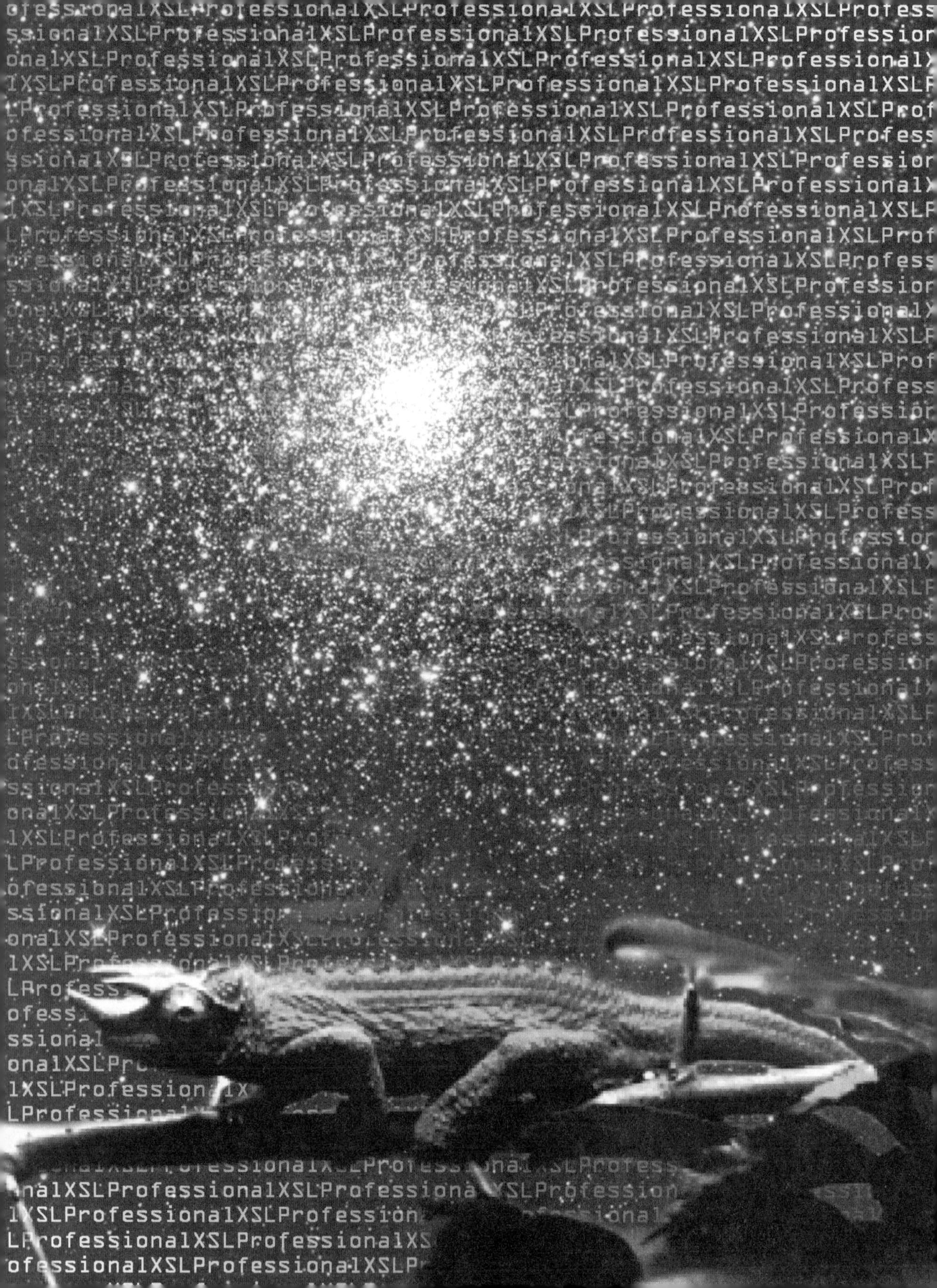

Shorthand XSLT Tools

We have seen why transforming XML is such a useful facility, and this appendix indicates some other tools that provide enhancements or alternatives to XSLT. Of these, both **XSLScript** and **XML Script** are worthy of more detailed analyses, which have been kindly provided by members of the original development teams.

XSLScript

http://www.pault.com/XSLScript/

XSLScript is a terse macro language that produces XSLT scripts for performing complex XML transformations. The scripts are either created temporarily for the duration of the transformation (using the included Saxon processor), or can be saved for later use with any XSLT processor.

XSLScript is integrated into the Hiawatha web server, but can also be used as a standalone product. It is written in Java, and the distribution includes both the compiled classes and their source code. Further details are given later in the appendix.

XML Script

http://www.xmlscript.org/

XML Script is an alternative to XSLT, and is similar in many ways. Scripts are essentially XML files that are run through an interpreter, producing XML output, hence the name. It offers additional functionality such as output of non-XML results, import of XML and non-XML data sources, and custom system connectivity. XML Script aims to provide a language that can be easily learned by programmers used to traditional programming constructs such as variables and loops. A thorough description is given in a later section of this appendix.

XSLWiz

http://www.ebprovider.com/products/xslwiz.html

XSLWiz is a visual mapping tool for creating XSLT transformations between XML formats. A drag and drop GUI is used to describe the mapping, which then generates a corresponding XSLT transformation. XSLWiz also includes a tool for converting DTDs to Schemas and for creating schemas from XML documents.

XSLbyDemo

http://www.alphaworks.ibm.com/aw.nsf/techmain/xslbydemo

XSLbyDemo is another visual tool, but users need absolutely no knowledge of XSL to use it. It produces a transform from a recording of a user editing a web page with a WYSIWYG HTML editor. The user simply clicks a "record" button before performing their edits, and a "stop" button once finished. This technique enables web designers to concentrate on the styling of their pages without worrying about XSL.

XSLbyDemo creates an XSLT stylesheet to perform the transformations, and is a plug-in module for IBM's WebSphere.

XSLScript

XSLScript, not to be confused with XML Script discussed in the latter part of this appendix, is a pre-processor, taking a script that is written in a special notation to generate a corresponding 100% conformant plain XSLT stylesheet. The program can also invoke a separate XSLT Java engine, such as SAXON, XT, or Xalan, to then perform the actual transformation of this stylesheet.

It is a tool that is intended to allow developers to write and to maintain complex server-side XSLT code. It can be used for client-side XSLT transformations, but because most client-side transformations are relatively simple, its primary use is for server-side XSLT. It is a *companion* application to XSLT rather than a *replacement* for it, and assumes that the developer is already familiar with standard XSLT coding.

The XSLScript engine can be downloaded from http://www.pault.com/XSLScript. The software, written in Java by me, Paul Tchistopolskii, is 100% free open source. However, although XSLScript is a one-man effort rather than a corporate product, it is featured on the W3C page devoted to XSL products (http://www.w3.org/Style/XSL/), an indication I hope of the professional level of the application. XSLScript is built on two years' experience of writing complex server-side code in plain XSLT.

The most important part of XSLScript that I should cover is the XSLScript notation, so we will look at this in more detail shortly. However, I'd like to briefly outline my reasoning behind the development of this alternative notation in the first place.

Why XSLScript?

You may be wondering, "What's the problem with regular XSLT? What does the XSLScript preprocessor do for me?"

One can think about XSLT as if it is yet another scripting language. For some historical reason, XSLT scripts are called "stylesheets", but in fact they are scripts. XSLT has "if", "for", and "switch" statements, functions, parameters, and variables, like almost any other well-known general-purpose language. Of course, XSLT contains some special features (for example, non-variable 'variables'), since it is not really a general-purpose programming language, but rather a specialized language for XML rendering. There is a commonly held view that XSLT should be viewed as an entirely new kettle of fish to the school of general-purpose procedural languages, because XSLT is a very special declarative language more like SQL and its ilk. However, this is misleading, as anyone who is familiar with SQL will tell you there are no "ifs, "fors", "functions", nor "switch statements" in SQL, but these constructs do exist in XSLT. When something looks like a dog and barks like a dog, maybe we should assume that it is a dog – and quickly, before it bites us!

Let me illustrate my point by considering the situation that occurs almost every day when writing code in, say, Java, C, Perl, Python, JavaScript – almost any language you could think of in fact, even assembler langauge. The situation I'm talking about is where our source code contains many similar fragments that are only slightly different – we isolate those fragments into one or more functions, which we then invoke using different parameter sets. I think this pattern is a core feature of *almost* any existing programming language – we could even call it a "fundamental" of procedural programming.

Can we do this with XSLT? Of course we can. It will look something like:

```
<xsl:template name="foo">
   <xsl:param name="bar"/>
    Hello, <xsl:value-of select="$bar"/>
</xsl:template>
```

Now let us see how we call this function in XSLT:

```
<xsl:call-template name="foo">
   <xsl:with-param name="bar">world</xsl:with-param>
</xsl:call-template>
```

Wait a minute ... just to invoke `foo("world")`, I have to type 3 lines of code? Right. If we want lots of functions in our XSLT code, the source can become quite impossible to follow, and for this reason alone a lot of tasks are simply impractical to code in XSLT.

Another problem is the lack of an 'if-then-else' construction in XSLT, missing I believe not because it is inappropriate, but because it doesn't fit naturally into an XML format. We are restricted to just `<xsl:if>` and `<xsl:choose>`, when other programming languages generally have 'if-then-else' variants at least, if not 'if-then-elseif-else'. This means that two essential procedural elements cannot be readily implemented in XSLT.

Why is it that some well-known constructions are so verbose in XSLT? Well, it has come about because the designers of XSLT have used 'special elements' to separate tokens from each other. For example, the `<xsl:call-template>` in the code above contains the name of the function to call as an attribute (in this case the function is `foo`) and we have a list of parameters separated from each other with `<xsl:with-param>` elements. When writing it as `foo("bar")`, we use special characters (such as the parentheses) to separate the tokens, instead of 'special elements', resulting in more terse code. W3C says that it is better to use 'special elements' instead of 'special characters', because it turns XSL into XML. However, within XSLT, XPath uses 'special characters' (like "/") to separate tokens, as it is not constrained by the requirement to follow XML syntax. For example, we write:

```
<xsl:value-of select="/some/path"/>
```

and not something like:

```
<xsl:value-of>
  <xsl:select>
    <xsl:path>some</xsl:path>
    <xsl:path>path</xsl:path>
  </xsl:select>
</xsl:value-of>
```

In my opinion, at some point in time the W3C was even considering using the verbose, 'special element' based notation for XPath, but they decided against it to avoid ambiguity. So in XSLT we now have two different parts. One is terse (the XPath part, using 'special symbols' to separate tokens), and another is verbose (special `xsl:` elements are used to separate tokens).

XSLScript notation turns this on its head, and is the embodiment of the idea that XSLScript should *all* be terse, in the way that XPath already is. This means that, unlike XSLT, XSLScript scripts are *not* XML files, because XSLScript notation uses 'special characters' to separate tokens instead of 'special elements'.

The 'special characters' of XSLScript are similar to those found in other programming languages: curly braces ('{' and '}'), parentheses ('(' and ')'), the exclamation mark (!), the semi-colon (;), and so on.

As a result the XSLScript notation is, I hope you'll agree, more intuitive and readable. For example, in the XSLScript notation function declaration becomes:

```
X:template foo( bar ) {
  Hello: !{$bar}
}
```

and to call the function, the following is required:

```
!foo( bar={World} )
```

XSLScript Notation: the Key Points

1: Header and Body

The general XSLT construction of an arbitrary XSLT element looks like:

```
<xsl:construction  xsl_attribute="something">
  body
</xsl:construction>
```

In XSLScript it will look like:

```
X:construction xsl_attribute="something" {
  body
}
```

2: No Need to Type the Obvious

There is no need to type match, select, test, and name XSLT attributes. For example, for
the XSLT code:

```
<xsl:if test="some condition">
   body
</xsl:if>
```

the comparable XSLScript is simply:

```
X:if "some condition" {
   body
}
```

3: A Few Handy Shortcuts Make a Big Difference

value-of

In XSLT:

```
<xsl:value-of select="/some/path"/>
```

and in XSLScript:

```
!{/some/path}
```

Function Call

The XSLT:

```
<xsl:call-template name="foo">
  <xsl:with-param name="bar">world</xsl:with-param>
</xsl:call-template>
```

is rendered in XSLScript as:

```
!foo( bar={world} )
```

apply-templates

In XSLT:

```
<xsl:apply-templates/>
```

and in XSLScript:

```
!!;
```

if-then-else

In XSLT:

```
<xsl:when>
    <xsl:choose test="$some">
        branch 1
    </xsl:choose>
    <xsl:otherwise>
        branch 2
    </xsl:otherwise>
</xsl:when>
```

and in XSLScript:

```
X:if "$some" {
    branch 1
} else {
    branch 2
}
```

Note that this shorthand is only for `if` statements followed by a single `else` statement. If you wish to use an `if-elseif-else` type construct, employ the standard XSLT `<xsl:choose>` in a similar way to how you might use switch/case in a procedural language.

These four shortcuts already make a big difference for complex XSLT stylesheets. The W3C site itself recommends XSLScript as an alternative to coding in pure XSLT, by saying "If you don't like the XSLT syntax, maybe you'll prefer XSLScript, by Paul Tchistopolskii, which allows one to write style sheets with a simplified syntax". Some people may like the XML syntax of plain XSLT, and some people won't. Check out the XSLScript web page given at the beginning of this section for some other subtleties of XSLScript notation designed to encourage terseness and readability.

XSLScript Examples

To see how XSLScript makes a difference, let's rewrite part of the example that appears in the case study earlier in the book. We won't make any logical changes to the original XSLT code, but just blindly rewrite the XSLT code using XSLScript notation.

Let's rewrite the particular component that generates the TOC (table of contents) that is located in /Case_Study/2-toc. Actually, the component consists of three XSLT modules, but for the sake of simplicity let us join all three into just one XSLScript script.

```
X:stylesheet {

  X:output omit-xml-declaration="yes" method="html" encoding="ISO-8859-1"

  <!-- CONTENT-OUTPUT.XSL -->

  X:template div-output() = "div" {

    <A>X:attribute "name" {!node-identifier()} </A>

    X:element "H{count(ancestor-or-self::div)}" {
      !create-number()X:text{ }!{title}
    }

    !! "html/node()" mode="html-output";
    !! "div";

  }


  X:template = "node()|@*" mode="html-output" {
    X:copy { !! "node()|@*" mode="html-output"; }
  }

  X:template create-number( segment="current()" ) {
    X:if "not($segment/@count = 'off')" {
      X:for-each "$segment" {
        X:number level="multiple" format="1.a.A"
                 count="div[not(@count = 'off')][parent::div]";
      }
    }
  }

  X:template node-identifier( id-node="self::*" ) {
    !{generate-id($id-node)}
  }

  X:template link-to( linktext="title/text()", target ) {
    <a>
    X:if "$target" {
      X:attribute "target" {!{$target}}
    }

    X:attribute href {!file-of()!anchor-of()}
```

```
      !{$linktext}

    </a>
  }

  X:template file-of() { X:text{doc.htm} }

  X:template anchor-of() { X:text{#}!node-identifier() }

<!-- TOC.XSL -->

  X:param index_maxdepth={3}

  X:template generateTOC() {
      !! "/document/div" mode="toc";
  }

  X:template = "div" mode="toc" {
      <div>
        X:attribute "style" {margin-left:!{count(ancestor::div) * 5}pt}
        !create-number()X:text{ }!link-to()
        <BR/>
      </div>
      X:if "$index_maxdepth &gt; count(ancestor::div) + 1" {
        !! "div" mode="toc";
      }
  }

<!-- DOCUMENT.XSL -->

  X:template = "/" {
    <HTML>
    <HEAD><LINK href="style.css" rel="STYLESHEET" type="text/css" />
    <TITLE> !{/document/div/title/text()} </TITLE>
    </HEAD>
    <BODY BGCOLOR="white">
    <TABLE align="center" WIDTH="400"><TR><TD>
     <H1> !{/document/div/title/text()} </H1>
     <H3> !{/document/div/subtitle/text()} </H3>
     !generateTOC()
     !! "/document/div/div";
     </TD></TR>
     </TABLE>
     </BODY></HTML>
  }

}
```

It should already be apparent that XSLScript notation can make hard-core XSLT stylesheets a bit more readable than they are in regular XSLT. This example does not show all the advantages of XSLScript, because the original XSLT code did not use a lot of 'functions'. Possible `<xsl:call-template>` elements were eliminated with the intensive usage of "mode". When you get used to XSLScript, you may find that there is almost no need for "mode". This is because most of what it allows can be accomplished using good old procedural techniques (passing "mode" is not that much different from passing a parameter to a function). You may find that, after switching to the procedural paradigm supported by XSLScript, your productivity in writing XML transformations increases by a factor of two.

XSLScript really shines when the stylesheet requires complex calculations that usually require recursive templates. For example:

```
X:transform {

X:template max( list ) {
    X:if "$list" {
        X:variable first="count($list[1]/LINE)"
        X:variable max-of-rest={ !max( list="$list[position()!=1]" ) }

        X:if "$first &gt; $max-of-rest"  {
            !{$first}
        } else {
            !{$max-of-rest}
        }
    } else {
        0
    }
}

 X:template ="/" {
  Longest speech is <% X:text; !max( list="//SPEECH" ) X:text; %> lines.
 }
```

The corresponding plain XSLT stylesheet is much harder to read. In fact, this is the XSLScript variant of the `longest-speech.xsl` stylesheet by Michael Kay (from his Wrox book *XSLT Programmer's Reference*). Nothing new here – just that well-known pattern of 'XSLT has no updateable variables so we should use recursion'. The stylesheet enumerates the list of speeches (<SPEECH> elements) and determines the 'longest speech' – the speech that contains more <LINE> tags than any other. Because in XSLT we can't update the variables (to find the size of longest speech when iterating over the list) this sort of thing must be done with recursion. The principle is 'Take the first element of the list; process it; call yourself with the rest of the list'.

Now try to read the original plain XSLT code. If this is easy for you – try to estimate the impact of adding one more parameters to the function. Or what might happen if you were to add one more nested `if-else` construct?

```
<xsl:transform xmlns:xsl="http://www.w3.org/1999/XSL/Transform"
                version="1.0" >
<xsl:template name="max">
<xsl:param name="list"/>
<xsl:choose>
<xsl:when test="$list">
    <xsl:variable name="first" select="count($list[1]/LINE)"/>
    <xsl:variable name="max-of-rest">
        <xsl:call-template name="max">
            <xsl:with-param name="list" select="$list[position()!=1]"/>
        </xsl:call-template>
    </xsl:variable>
    <xsl:choose>
    <xsl:when test="$first &gt; $max-of-rest">
        <xsl:value-of select="$first"/>
    </xsl:when>
```

```
        <xsl:otherwise>
            <xsl:value-of select="$max-of-rest"/>
        </xsl:otherwise>
        </xsl:choose>
    </xsl:when>
    <xsl:otherwise>0</xsl:otherwise>
    </xsl:choose>
    </xsl:template>
    <xsl:template match="/">
    Longest speech is <xsl:text/>
        <xsl:call-template name="max">
            <xsl:with-param name="list" select="//SPEECH"/>
        </xsl:call-template>
    <xsl:text/> lines.
    </xsl:template>
    </xsl:transform>
```

Using the XSLScript Engine

There are two main ways to use the XSLScript engine in practice.

1: Write in XSLScript, Deploy in XSLT

No matter what platform you're using, if you have some complex XSLT stylesheets in your framework, you may try writing the stylesheets in XSLScript, debugging them in XSLScript, and then finally generating 100% XSLT code so you can then deploy those generated XSLT stylesheets. Let's try – it should take just a couple of minutes! Create a simple stylesheet, such as `hello.xsls` below (note that the extension `.xsls` is required):

```
X:transform {

    X:template = "/" { Hello, World }

}
```

and then change to your XSLScript directory and invoke :

```
xslsdump-indent hello.xsls
```

The following output should print on your screen:

```
<?xml version="1.0" encoding="utf-8"?>
<xsl:stylesheet xmlns:xsl="http://www.w3.org/1999/XSL/Transform" version="1.0">

  <xsl:template match="/"> Hello, World</xsl:template>
</xsl:stylesheet>
```

2: Write in XSLScript, Deploy in XSLScript

The XSLScript Java engine can be plugged into any Java framework. The source code is available and the top-level XSLScript class has a fairly obvious API. It should be possible to plug the XSLScript preprocessor into different Java XSLT engines without any trouble.

Assuming that you're located in your XSLScript directory, you invoke your stylesheet to 'transform' itself:

```
xsls hello.xsls hello.xsls
```

This will print:

```
<?xml version="1.0" encoding="utf-8"?> Hello, World
```

See how XSLScript files are processed as if they are XML files. This is how the preprocessor works. In fact XSLScript is just a modified SAX / SAX2 parser, which is sensitive to the `.xsls` extension. You can transparently plug the XSLScript engine into any Java framework. The XSLScript distribution consists of the standard Saxon XSLT Engine with an XSLScript SAX2 parser plug-in.

In addition to these, there is also a free plug & play, open source web server, written in Java, supporting on-the-fly rendering of XML with XSLScript and/or plain XSLT. The server is called Hiawatha-Java and it is available for download from http://www.pault.com. Please address any difficulties or issues regarding these products to me through this site, although Hiawatha has been installed and tested by several people on various platforms from Mac OS to Windows to Solaris without problems. To install the Hiawatha web server all you need do is modify a parameter in the config file, as explained on the appropriate web page at the site.

XML Script

In early 1998, DecisionSoft, a startup company based in Oxford, England, was newly formed and struggling to make ends meet. During this time, it performed some consulting work to help pay the bills, involving systems testing of a financial trading package. It became clear that it needed a scripting language to help automate some of the testing processes, and it decided to build the utility language from XML, since everyone on the web was getting very excited about it. The requirement was to take XML documents and transform them into plain ASCII text suitable for feeding into the financial package. It also wanted to be able to take such ASCII text files and turn them back into XML.

DecisionSoft ended up with a scripting language it christened "XML Script" and an associated interpreter for the language, written in Perl, which actually performed the necessary transformations.

My Involvement with XML Script

I was an intern at DecisionSoft during my studies at the University of Oxford and in the summer of 1998, I was presented with our latest cool toy on returning to the office after a semester at college: a Perl program that ran XML Scripts. It became clear that sticking with Perl wouldn't cut the mustard with customers or investors, so we began work on a C++ version of the interpreter. We christened this **X-Tract**, and it's available from the XML Script site at http://www.xmlscript.org/download.html at no cost, although a server version called **X-Stream** may be purchased from DecisionSoft.

Since then I've moved on from the company, but continue to use XML Script, and keep up with developments of the software.

Relationship with XSLT

XML Script was developed independently of XSLT and both contain similar concepts – templates, selection strings, and so on. However, XML Script's origins as a tool developed by a single company, rather than committee-led peer review over the net, means that while it is written in XML and manipulates XML files, it's not constrained to just that field. XML Script can produce any text you like, and can input data from arbitrary text-based sources. XML Script also includes the notion of **interpolations** – text that is expanded by the processor before being output. Interpolations are similar to the `<xsl:value-of>` element in XSLT, but are considerably more powerful and less verbose. Interpolations are a prime example of the differing philosophies of the two languages: XML Script is designed to get stuff done quickly and easily, without you having to write lots of code on the way.

The remainder of this appendix attempts to give an overview of what XML Script is, how it works, and what scripts look like. We are not attempting to provide a complete reference for XML Script, but merely an appetizer. Having said that, there are sections that include all the commands and functions needed to produce intermediate-level XML Script.

A Note on Versions – 2.0 versus 1.x

Since its beginnings in 1998, the language's developers have learned a lot about how the language should work best and have taken on board a lot of feedback from users. In early 2000, we realized that the language needed a major overhaul, and so began development of version 2.0. As of the time of writing (March 2001), X-Tract 2.0 has been released as a beta.

XML Script 2.0 has been fundamentally uprated from version 1.1, including improved internal data structures, and a better end user interface. Everything that was "not quite right" about 1.1 has been addressed, working from a brand new language specification. Some work arounds for problems in the language have been removed. As a consequence, attempting to run version 2.0 syntax scripts on an XML Script 1.x processor will not work as expected, if at all.

In this chapter I'll be covering XML Script 2.0. If you have experience of version 1.1, you'll notice a few changes in the way things work, resulting in simpler, easier to understand code and you'll probably want to make the change to version 2.0. On the other hand, if you are new to XML Script, this appendix will give you a full introduction to the language.

Using X-Tract

Here I'm using X-Tract 2.0 beta for Windows, although running X-Tract on other platforms should be similar, since it's a command-line tool only. Currently, X-Tract 2.0 beta is available for Windows and Linux, with a Solaris version on the way.

Type in the following script and save it as `HelloWorld.xst`. The `.xst` extension is standard for XML Script, but in fact any extension will do.

```
<xst xmlns="http://www.xmlscript.org/2.0"
     expression-syntax="dslpath">

<output>
  Hello, world!
</output>

</xst>
```

To run this script, use the command:

xtract HelloWorld.xst

X-Tract will load the XST script, and produce output to the console that looks like this:

Note: the copyright message is output via the standard error channel stderr, *and may be removed in future. Command-line programs can output on standard output (used here for the "Hello, world!" text) or standard error. Depending on your environment, it's possible to redirect or suppress output to either of these locations. For example, to dump all the output into a file called* output.txt *from Windows, we could use the syntax* xtract HelloWorld.xst > output.txt.

The first thing to note is that an XML Script is contained within the XST element belonging to the http://www.xmlscript.org/2.0 namespace. The xmlns attribute creates a default namespace, so that we don't need to use a prefix on all our elements. All XML Script **command elements** should be in this namespace too, or they won't be recognized as commands to be run. When the script is loaded, it is placed into an XML tree called the **instruction tree**. There are two main in-memory XML trees created for an XML Script transformation: the instruction tree and the **data tree**. Elements in the instruction tree are interpreted as commands, while elements in the data tree represent information that may be referenced or modified by commands.

X-Tract traverses the instruction tree in document order, processing commands as it finds them. Briefly, "document order" means that the processor recursively examines the contents of each node as deeply as possible before examining the next node. Document order for the following XML fragment would be Mammal, Primate, Human, Gorilla, Chimpanzee, Cat, Lion, and finally Tiger.

```
<Mammal>
    <Primate>
        <Human />
        <Gorilla />
        <Chimpanzee />
    </Primate>
    <Cat>
        <Lion />
        <Tiger />
    </Cat>
</Mammal>
```

Each command produces a **result fragment**, and possibly some other side-effects that will be mentioned later. In our Hello World example, there is just one command: output. The output command evaluates its contents, collating the result fragments of any sub-elements, and copies this to a third XML tree, the **output tree**. The text node containing "Hello, world!" is the only result fragment collated by the output command in the above example, so is copied to the output tree. The result fragment for the output command is empty. Once the script has been evaluated, X-Tract serializes the output tree to produce the "Hello, world!" text. We'll talk in more detail about commands and result fragments later.

Let's move on to a slightly less trivial example. We can use the data command to populate the data tree, and then use that tree to generate output. Save the following script as DataHello.xst:

```
<xs:xst xmlns:xs="http://www.xmlscript.org/2.0"
        expression-syntax="dslpath">

<xs:data>
  <Person>Harry</Person>
  <Person>Ron</Person>
  <Person>Hermione</Person>
</xs:data>

<xs:foreach node="\xs:dd\Person">
  <xs:output>
    Hello, # . #
  </xs:output>
</xs:foreach>

</xs:XST>
```

The first thing to notice here is that we're using the XML Script namespace explicitly. By doing this, the unqualified Person elements will be copied to the data tree without being taken to belong to the XML Script namespace. This makes it easier to access them once they are in the data tree. We're going to ignore namespaces as much as we can during this appendix, although all XML Script commands and functions are namespace-aware. The data element evaluates its contents such that in this case the result fragments from evaluating each Person element are collated, and copied to the data tree. Since the Person elements are not in the xs namespace, the processor won't interpret them as commands. Instead, it simply copies the elements into the result fragment, then searches their children for any further commands, and we end up with a data tree containing three Person elements, each with different text content.

Next, we use the foreach command to iterate over the data tree and perform an output command for each node encountered. To access the data tree, we first select the special element "dd" and then select from its children. The dd element is the top level element of the data tree stored in memory, and as it belongs to the XML Script namespace we need to use xs:dd to select it. Inside the output element, we have some special text enclosed in hash characters (# . #). This instructs X-Tract to replace the XML Script expression inside the hashes with its result (more about expressions in a later section). The expression " . " evaluates the current node in the data tree, which here is each Person element in turn. This replacement is called interpolation, and will do textual substitution only. Since each node selected is an element, when the interpolation is processed the text content of the element will be returned instead, and so we get "Harry", "Ron", and "Hermione" in turn.

Each piece of output is added to the output tree, with the following result:

Hello, Harry

Hello, Ron

Hello, Hermione

It's important to note that output commands count whitespace as significant, which is why the Hellos are indented and separated by blank lines.

While we are trying to avoid namespace issues, note that above we had to explicitly select the dd element from the xs namespace. It is possible to set a default namespace for selection strings, using the exprns attribute of the top-level xst element. If we wish everything including the data to be in the XML Script namespace, we can omit explicit namespace selection as in the following example called DataHello2.xst:

```
<xst xmlns="http://www.xmlscript.org/2.0"
     expression-syntax="dslpath"
     exprns="http://www.xmlscript.org/2.0">

<data>
  <Person>Harry</Person>
  <Person>Ron</Person>
  <Person>Hermione</Person>
</data>

<foreach node="\dd\Person">
  <output>
    Hello, # . #
  </output>
</foreach>

</xst>
```

X-Tract can load external XML files into the data tree if this is specified on the command line, so we don't have to include it in the script. In this illustration, if we save the following as People.xml:

```
<?xml version="1.0"?>
<People>
  <Person>Harry</Person>
  <Person>Ron</Person>
  <Person>Hermione</Person>
</People>
```

and the following script as DataHello3.xst:

```
<xs:xst xmlns:xs="http://www.xmlscript.org/2.0"
        expression-syntax="dslpath">

<xs:foreach node="\xs:dd\People\Person">
  <xs:output>
    Hello, # . #
  </xs:output>
</xs:foreach>

</xs:xst>
```

then running:

xtract DataHello2.xst People.xml

will run the script first loading the XML into memory, giving the same output as the original
`DataHello.xst` script. Note that if we're using an external file for loading XML, it must be well
formed, so the `People` element must contain `Person` elements. If we're copying data from the
instruction tree to the data tree within a `data` element, there is no such restriction.

Node Selection Mechanisms

We have already seen an example of selecting nodes from the data tree. Inside a `foreach` command,
the `node` attribute tells the interpreter which nodes to iterate over. Our above example selected
`\dd\People\Person`, which is **DSLPath** syntax for "all `Person` child elements of all `People` child
elements of the root element of the data tree". Phew. Clearly the equivalent for XPath would be
`/People/Person`. "DSLPath" is the term used to differentiate between the selection mechanism
developed by DecisionSoft Ltd (hence *DSL*Path) and W3C's XPath, which wasn't available when
DSLPath was developed.

X-Tract 2.0 beta currently supports DSLPath only for selecting nodes, but the final release will include
full XPath support. Since other chapters in this book have dealt with XPath you will likely wish to use
that, but we'll include a brief discussion of DSLPath here. All the examples in this appendix will use
DSLPath as the selection mechanism. XPath is the default selection mechanism; to use `DSLPath` a script
needs to have the `expression-syntax` attribute of the top-level `xst` element set to "dslpath".

Let's start with some XML data that we shall load into the data tree to practice on. Here's an XML
description (`Timetable.xml`) of a student's timetable, but we've only done Monday and Tuesday so far:

```xml
<?xml version="1.0"?>
<Timetable>xmlns="http://www.xmlscript.org/2.0"
  <Monday>
    <Lesson start="0900" end="1030">
      <Subject>Divination</Subject>
      <Teacher>Professor Trelawney</Teacher>
      <Location>North Tower</Location>
    </Lesson>
    <Lesson start="1045" end="1215">
      <Subject>Potions</Subject>
      <Teacher>Professor Snape</Teacher>
      <Location>Dungeon IV</Location>
    </Lesson>
    <Lesson start="1330" end="1500">
      <Subject>Care of Magical Creatures</Subject>
      <Teacher>Mister Hagrid</Teacher>
      <Location>School Paddock</Location>
    </Lesson>
  </Monday>
  <Tuesday>
    <Lesson start="0900" end="1030">
      <Subject>Defense Against the Dark Arts</Subject>
      <Teacher>Professor Lupin</Teacher>
      <Location>Classroom VII</Location>
    </Lesson>
```

```
      <Lesson start="1045" end="1215">
        <Subject>Transfiguration</Subject>
        <Teacher>Professor McGonagall</Teacher>
        <Location>Classroom VII</Location>
      </Lesson>
      <Lesson start="1330" end="1500">
        <Subject>Herbology</Subject>
        <Teacher>Professor Sprout</Teacher>
        <Location>Greenhouse V</Location>
      </Lesson>
    </Tuesday>
  </Timetable>
```

First of all, we could obtain a list of every subject on the timetable. We need to select all the `Lesson` elements that are grandchildren of the `Timetable` root element. Using * as a wildcard to match any element, we come up with the following DSLPath:

```
\dd\Timetable\*\Lesson
```

To show this in action, save the following as `Timetable.xst`:

```
<xst xmlns="http://www.xmlscript.org/2.0"
     exprns="http://www.xmlscript.org/2.0"
     expression-syntax="dslpath">

<foreach node="\dd\Timetable\*\Lesson">
  <output>
    # Subject #
  </output>
</foreach>

</xst>
```

and run the command:

xtract Timetable.xst Timetable.xml

We can see that for each element selected in our `foreach` loop, the `output` command is executed with the current location in the data tree set to the element we're looping over. So the interpolation # `Subject` # is processed for each `Lesson` element in the data tree, causing the following to be printed:

We could also use the operator **, equivalent to XPath's // (descendant-or-self) operator, and write \dd**\Lesson instead.

We can select attributes instead of elements by using a dot followed by the attribute name (wildcards are allowed). An example could be selecting the start time for all of Monday's lessons, with the selection string \dd\Timetable\Monday\Lesson.start.

We can select indexes by using square brackets, so \dd**\Lesson[2] will select the Potions lesson with Professor Snape.

A more powerful feature of DSLPath is called **sub-content stipulation**. At any point in a DSLPath selector, we can use braces to denote an expression that will be evaluated for all nodes collected up to that point. Any nodes where the expression does not evaluate to true (more on expressions later) are removed from the selected node set at that point, and selection continues. In this way, sub-content stipulation is similar to XPath predicates. This is quite complicated, so an example is in order.

Suppose we wanted to know the start time of lessons taught in Classroom VII. We need to select only Lesson elements that have a child element Location containing the text "Classroom VII", and then select the start attribute from these. Try the following script (Timetable2.xst):

```
<xst xmlns="http://www.xmlscript.org/2.0"
     exprns="http://www.xmlscript.org/2.0"
     expression-syntax="dslpath">

<foreach node="\dd\Timetable\*\Lesson{ Location == 'Classroom VII'}.start">
  <output>
    Start time is # . #
  </output>
</foreach>

</xst>
```

From our earlier examples, we know that \dd\Timetable*\Lesson selects all the Lesson elements in the Timetable. If we then incorporate the sub-content stipulation { Location == 'Classroom VII' } we can prune away the lessons for which that expression is not true. This leaves us with just two nodes in the candidate list, from which we select the start attribute. It might have been more sensible to select the lesson itself, because in our output we could have put something more useful like:

```
# Subject # starts at # .start # and is taught by # Teacher #
```

The revised script Timetable3.xst looks like this:

```
<xst xmlns="http://www.xmlscript.org/2.0"
     exprns="http://www.xmlscript.org/2.0"
     expression-syntax="dslpath">

<foreach node="\dd\Timetable\*\Lesson{ Location == 'Classroom VII'}">
  <output>
    # Subject # starts at # .start # and is taught by # Teacher #
  </output>
</foreach>

</xst>
```

At this stage we should note that the text inside curly braces in a DSLPath expression and the text inside hashes treated as an interpolation are both examples of **expressions**.

Further documentation for DSLPath is available from the XML Script web site, at http://www.xmlscript.org/docs/V2/xtract-v2-dslpath.html.

Expressions and Interpolation

As we saw earlier, XML Script **expressions** can contain at least two things: node selections and operators. We have seen examples of node selections such as "." and "Subject" and examples of operators such as "==". Expressions can also contain function calls, constants, and variables.

Node selections can be specified in XPath or DSLPath syntax. As we said earlier, X-Tract 2.0 beta only supports DSLPath, so we will continue to use it for our examples although the final release version will support XPath expressions. Node selections allow us to use lists of nodes in expressions, and, for example, apply functions to them.

Operators include the usual arithmetic operators (+, -, *, /) with all calculations performed using double-precision floating point where necessary. XML Script uses an intelligent internal type system – if a result can be expressed as an integer it is stored as an integer, otherwise it will be stored as a floating-point number.

Functions in XML Script expressions look like they would in a traditional programming language, namely the function name followed by the function arguments enclosed in parentheses. XML Script functions include the following particularly useful ones:

Function and parameter	Description
abs(dataItem)	Calculates the absolute value of its argument interpreted as a number
and(data1, data2)	Calculates the logical AND of the two values
exists(nodeList)	Returns true if the node list has some nodes in it, false otherwise
concat(s1, s2, ...)	Concatenates string values passed to it (accepts any number of arguments)
count(nodeList)	Returns the number of nodes in the node list
not(dataItem)	Returns logical negation of the data item interpreted as a Boolean
gt(data1, data2)	Returns true if data1 > data2
gte(data1, data2)	Returns true if data1 >= data2
lt(data1, data2)	Returns true if data1 < data2
lte(data1, data2)	Returns true if data1 <= data2
or(data1, data2)	Calculates logical OR of the two values

There are many more, and you can find the full list on the XML Script web site at http://www.xmlscript.org/docs/V2/xtract-v2-functions.html.

Constants can be strings or numbers. If you're using a string constant, either " or ' can be used to delimit the string. Take care when within an XML attribute, however, because if you use the same character to enclose your attribute, your script won't be well formed XML.

Variables are accessed using the $$myVariable syntax. Variables can be created explicitly using the setvar command, or as a side effect of various looping commands.

An interpolation is a piece of text enclosed in hash characters. When the processor is evaluating the contents of a command and adding it to a result fragment, it examines text and attribute nodes for interpolations. When one is found, it is expanded and replaced by the result of the expression. The result of the expression might be empty, for example if the expression contains a function call with only tree-manipulation side effects and no direct output, such as delete().

As an example of some XML Script expressions, run the following script (Interpolation.xst) and see if the output matches what you expect:

```
<xst xmlns="http://www.xmlscript.org/2.0"
     exprns="http://www.xmlscript.org/2.0"
     expression-syntax="dslpath">

<data src="Timetable.xml" />

<foreach node="\dd\Timetable\*">
  <output>
    The current element is # tag(.) #.
    It has # count(*) # child elements,
    and # count(.*) # attributes.
  </output>
</foreach>

</xst>
```

```
 mgm@gate.mortlake: /home/mgm/wrox                    _ □ X

[mgm@gate wrox]$ xtract Interpolation.xst
X-Tract 2.0 Beta build #1. 2001-02-21,17:07:24,+0000
(c)2000 DecisionSoft Limited.
User documentation and license at http://www.xmlscript.org


    The current element is Monday.
    It has 3 child elements,
    and 0 attributes.

    The current element is Tuesday.
    It has 3 child elements,
    and 0 attributes.


[mgm@gate wrox]$ █
```

Templates

When a standard XML Script command is processed, the following steps occur:

❑ The processor moves the current instruction tree location to that of the node being executed.

❑ The processor executes the code corresponding to this element (written in a programming language such as C++ or Java), allowing it access to the current location in the instruction tree, the data tree, and the output tree.

❑ The code returns a result fragment (possibly empty) upon termination. Some method elements, such as output, have side effects like modifying the output tree.

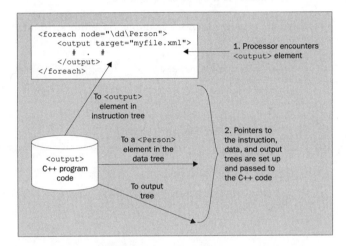

When the processor comes across an element that it does not recognize as a command, it invokes the default method on it. This default method leaves the element as is, but attempts to run methods for all of its children, and to perform any interpolations it finds. This is why when we choose to output the contents of the data tree, we get the tree without any changes. Nothing in the tree is recognized as an XML Script command, and the default method therefore runs recursively on all the elements in the tree.

Remember that interpolations can only return text content, so the following script produces different output from the interpolation and the process command. Both produce the same intermediate result, but it's only the output from the process command that maintains its XML structure. The following script is Process.xst:

```
<xst xmlns="http://www.xmlscript.org/2.0"
     exprns="http://www.xmlscript.org/2.0"
     expression-syntax="dslpath">

<data src="Timetable.xml" />

<output>
Data tree is:
# \dd\Timetable #
Processed data tree is:
<process node="\dd\Timetable" />
</output>

</xst>
```

If we run the above code, the first thing we get is the contents of the timetable with all the tags removed. This is the output from the # \dd\Timetable # interpolation. What is happening is that the expression inside the interpolation denotes a node list headed by the Timetable element in the data tree. This node list is then interpreted as text by the interpolation, removing all the tags and leaving just text content. After this, our output shows the Timetable element and descendants, this time with tags and attributes intact. This is the output that the process command has generated.

It is possible to override this default method using **templates**, in a similar manner to XSLT. A template is a named block of XML Script commands inside an <xs:template> command element. Then, we associate XML elements of a particular name with the template by using the <xs:method> command. When elements by that name are encountered, they are submitted to the template instead of the default method. The output from the template is used as the result fragment.

To demonstrate, let's modify our DataHello.xst example. Save this script as TemplateHello.xst:

```
<xst xmlns="http://www.xmlscript.org/2.0"
     exprns="http://www.xmlscript.org/2.0"
     expression-syntax="dslpath">

<data>
  <Person>Harry</Person>
  <Person>Ron</Person>
  <Person>Hermione</Person>
</data>

<template name="sayHello">
  Hello, # . #
</template>

<method name="Person" template="sayHello" />

<output>
  <process node="\dd\Person" />
</output>

</xst>
```

The process command tells the processor to run methods on the selected nodes at that point in the script. In this case, we have overridden the default behavior with our own method – the processor doesn't simply copy each of the Person elements as it knows they require special treatment. This is similar to the XSLT <xsl:template> command, but split into two stages. First we define the code to execute using <xs:template>, then associate that code with XML elements using <xs:method>.

The result fragment from the process command is the collation of the result fragments generated by applying the sayHello template to each <Person> element in turn. This result fragment is copied to the output tree by the output command, and we see the same result as in the original Hello example:

Hello, Harry

Hello, Ron

Hello, Hermione

Data Processing Commands

These commands import data into the data tree, and then cause it to be processed by X-Tract in a number of different ways.

data

```
<xs:data
  parse="xml"
  src="file://Timetable.xml"
>
```

The data command is used to import data into the data tree. The optional src attribute is interpreted as a literal URI resource to be retrieved and appended to the data tree. The content of the data element (if any) is appended after this resource.

The optional parse attribute, which defaults to xml, specifies how to interpret the resource referred to by the src attribute, in the same way as the parse attribute is used in the XInclude specification. However, X-Tract currently only supports the value xml to import data from XML sources although values that may be supported in future include "csv" for parsing comma separated value files.

The following fragment of code retrieves the current Slashdot (www.slashdot.org) news headlines, and imports them into the data tree:

```
<xs:data
    src="http://www.slashdot.org/slashdot.xml"
    parse="xml"
/>
```

foreach

```
<xs:foreach
  node="\Person"
  template="sayHello"
  index="myIndex"
>
```

The foreach command first evaluates its node attribute to form a node list. For each node in the list, the content of the foreach element is evaluated, with the current position in the data tree set to each node in turn. The result of this command is an empty list.

The optional template attribute specifies the name of a template to execute for each node in the node list before evaluation of the content of the foreach command. If the template attribute is unspecified, no template is applied. The optional index attribute gives the name of the loop variable to be created, defaulting to index. Initially set to 0, it is incremented by one for each node in the node list.

As an example, if we have the Slashdot headlines loaded into the data tree, we can number and print them using the following script:

```
<xs:foreach node="\xs:dd\backslash\story"
            index="storynum">
  <xs:output>
    Story # $$storynum # is about # title #
  </xs:output>
</xs:foreach>
```

with

```
<xs:with
   node="\Person"
>
```

The with command is similar to foreach, except that it doesn't throw away its result fragments. It collates them and returns them as the result of the command.

If we wish to use with instead of foreach to print the Slashdot headlines, we can use the following script. Note that the output command is used to print the result of the with command, which itself is the collation of several text nodes containing "Story is about..."

```
<xs:output>
   <xs:with node="\xs:dd\backslash\story">
     Story is about # title #
   </xs:with>
</xs:output>
```

process

```
<xs:process
   node="\Person"
>
```

The process command first evaluates its node attribute to produce a node list. Each of the nodes in the list is then processed as though it had been found in the instruction tree at that point. Methods are run and interpolations are evaluated as appropriate. The result of the command is the node list after evaluation.

As an example, let's use a template to print each of the Slashdot headlines. Once we have defined the template and associated it with story elements, we use the process command to explicitly instruct the XML Script processor to process those elements.

```
<xs:template name="print_story">
   I found a story about # title #
</xs:template>

<xs:method name="story" template="print_story" />

<xs:output>
   <xs:process node="\xs:dd\backslash\story" />
</xs:output>
```

At this point it is worth noting that XML Script supports both an imperative style – do this, then do this – and a declarative style – when you see this, do this. Which you choose to use is entirely down to personal preference, since both should allow a given task to be accomplished. Personally, I tend to use a declarative style for performing relatively passive transformations, such as converting XML into HTML or WML, and an imperative style for important sections of logic and general program flow.

Program Flow Commands

These commands alter the logical flow of a script, allowing loops and decisions to be taken in a manner similar to a traditional programming language.

for

```
<xs:for
  from="1"
  to="10"
  index="myIndex"
>
```

The `for` command first evaluates its required `from` attribute as an integer, and uses this as the initial value for its loop counter. If it is NaN, or positive or negative infinity, no further processing takes place, otherwise the optional `index` attribute specifies the variable name to use for the loop index. The value NaN or "Not a Number" occurs when an attempt to convert a value such as text into a number fails. Certain mathematical functions can also result in NaN.

The loop index is increased by one and the contents of the `for` command are evaluated and added to the result fragment for every cycle through the loop until the loop index equals the required `to` attribute. The command returns the data fragment generated.

As an example, we could print the squares of the numbers from one to ten:

```
<xs:output>
  <xs:for from="1" to="10" index="num">
    # $$num * $$num #
  </xs:for>
</xs:output>
```

while

```
<xs:while
  test="myTestExpression"
  index="myIndex"
>
```

The `while` command is only executed when the required Boolean `test` attribute is `true`, and loops until the test becomes `false`. The `while` command always returns an empty result fragment. Again, the optional `index` attribute specifies the loop counter, which starts at 1 and is incremented by one for each iteration through the loop.

This example searches our Slashdot headlines for one with more than 200 comments on it:

```
<xs:setvar name="story_num">1</xs:setvar>

<xs:while
    test="less_than(\xs:dd\backslash\story[$$story_num]\comments, 200)">
  <xs:output>
    Story # $$story_num # isn't very popular!
  </xs:output>
  <xs:setvar name="story_num"># $$story_num + 1#</xs:setvar>
</xs:while>
```

if, elseif, else

```
<xs:if
  test="testExpr"
>
  <xs:then> ... </xs:then>
  <xs:elseif test="testExpr2"> ... </xs:elseif>
  <xs:elseif test="testExpr3"> ... </xs:elseif>
  <xs:else> ... </xs:else>
</xs:if>
```

When the required `test` attribute evaluates as `true`, the content of the `then` element is evaluated. Otherwise, each `elseif` element (if any) is examined in document order until one is found whose required `test` attribute evaluates to `true`. Otherwise, the content of the `else` element (if any) is evaluated. An empty result fragment is returned in all cases.

switch

```
<xs:switch
  item="targetVal"
>
  <xs:case item="candidateVal1"> ... </xs:case>
  <xs:case item="candidateVal2"> ... </xs:case>
  <xs:default> ... </xs:default>
</xs:switch>
```

The `switch` command behaves as you might expect. The required `item` attribute produces a data item to match against the attribute of each `case` element in turn. If it finds such a `case` element, the contents of that element are evaluated, otherwise the contents of the optional `default` element are evaluated. The resulting fragment is returned in either case.

Tree Manipulation Commands

These commands modify the XML trees maintained by the XML Script processor and can even be applied to the instruction tree to create self-modifying code. This however is beyond the scope of this appendix.

copy

```
<xs:copy
  node="nodeList"
  into="targetPath"
  before="targetChild"
/>
```

The `copy` command copies the nodes specified in its required `node` attribute into the location in the tree specified by the required `into` attribute. The nodes will be copied to the destination at the end of its contents, unless the optional `before` attribute specifies a valid child of the node.

Suppose we have a description of items of furniture in various rooms of the house. We'll put this description in the data tree, and print the tree to see how it looks:

```
<xs:data>
  <Kitchen>
    <Table type="wooden" />
    <Cooker type="gas" />
    <Chair colour="red" />
    <Chair colour="blue" />
    <Chair colour="green" />
  </Kitchen>
  <Lounge>
    <Sofa type="leather" />
    <Armchair type="leather" />
    <Armchair type="leather" />
    <Television type="Sony" />
  </Lounge>
</xs:data>

<xs:output>
  Before copy:
  <xs:process node="\xs:*"/>
</xs:output>
```

Now suppose that we buy a new leather sofa and want to put it in the kitchen, just before the blue chair. We would do this with the following `copy` command:

```
<xs:copy node="\xs:dd\Lounge\Sofa"
         into="\xs:dd\Kitchen"
         before="\xs:dd\Kitchen\Chair{.colour == 'blue'}"
/>
```

delete

```
<xs:delete
  node="victimNodeList"
/>
```

The `delete` command deletes all nodes in the node list matching the required `node` attribute. All descendant nodes are also removed.

Suppose we had to sell our Sony TV in order to keep up the repayments on the expensive leather sofas we've been buying. We could remove the TV using the following script fragment:

```
<xs:delete node="\xs:dd\Lounge\Television" />
```

move

```
<xs:move
  node="nodeList"
  into="targetPath"
  before="targetChild"
/>
```

The move command moves the nodes specified in the required node attribute to the location given by the required into attribute. If present, the optional before attribute must specify a node that is a child of the node specified in the into attribute, or else the nodes will be moved to the destination at the end of its contents.

Back to our home-contents example, suppose the repo-men have taken away our leather sofa and armchairs because we've been unable to keep up repayments on them. We'll have to move the chairs from the kitchen into the lounge so we have something to sit on while staring at the blank wall where the TV used to be:

```
<xs:move node="\xs:dd\Kitchen\Chair"
         into="\xs:dd\Lounge" />
```

Variable Manipulation Commands

Here we will discuss simple variable usage – for more sophisticated examples navigate to the URL http://www.xmlscript.org/docs/V2/xtract-v2-simpleVariables.html. Note that any variable's value can be found using the $$variableName syntax.

setvar

```
<xs:setvar scope="local" name="myVariable">
  content
</xs:setvar>
```

The setvar command creates a new XML Script variable, scoped by the optional scope attribute and local by default. Specify global to make the variable available throughout the entire script. The content of the command is evaluated to determine the variable's value.

delvar

```
<xs:delvar scope="local"
           name="myVariable"
/>
```

The delvar command removes an XML Script variable from either the local or global scope according to the optional scope attribute.

Running the following script will produce the message "Hello, world!", followed by a warning when we attempt to use the variable $$simpleVariable after having deleted it:

```
<xs:xst xmlns:xs="http://www.xmlscript.org/2.0"
        expression-syntax="dslpath">

<xs:setvar scope="global"
           name="simpleVariable">
  Hello, world!
</xs:setvar>

<xs:output>
  The simple variable says # $$simpleVariable #
</xs:output>

<xs:delvar scope="global"
           name="simpleVariable"
/>

<xs:output>
  The simple variable now says # $$simpleVariable#
</xs:output>

</xs:xst>
```

System Access Commands

X-Tract 1.1 has a complete range of commands for accessing system resources, spawning shell commands, and interacting with network services such as SMTP mail, CGI, and custom sockets communications. These have not yet been implemented in X-Tract 2.0 beta, so I shall not discuss them here. One command we can discuss, however, is output.

```
<xs:output
   target="myFile.xml"
   mode="replace"
>
```

The output command sends its content to an XML output tree. In the absence of the target attribute, X-Tract serializes the output tree to standard output, otherwise sends output to the location given although only local files are currently supported. The optional mode attribute defaults to replace and instructs the processor to replace an existing file, or append to it if append is specified instead.

The Thank You Letter Writer

It's about time we put everything together and produced a complete example of what an XML Script application looks like. It's just after Christmas as I write this, and for a change I'd like to send decent thank you letters to people who sent me presents. We can use an XML description of the gifts I received, together with a skeleton-style letter to send to them, and produce a set of HTML documents that we can load into a browser and print. It's not quite as flashy as generating PDFs, but will demonstrate a slightly more real application.

First off, let's put the XML together. Here's an attempt at getting the information into XML (ThankYouList.xml), and while it might not be entirely the best representation, that's not what we're worried about – we want to understand how we get from this to a set of thank you letters.

```xml
<?xml version="1.0"?>
<ThankYouList xmlns="http://www.xmlscript.org/2.0">

  <Person id="mgm">
    <FirstName>Mike</FirstName>
    <LastName>Mason</LastName>
    <Address>
      <Line>6 Mortlake Drive</Line>
      <Line>Mitcham</Line>
      <County>Surrey</County>
      <PostCode>CR4 3RQ</PostCode>
    </Address>
  </Person>

  <Person id="stevie">
    <FirstName>Steve</FirstName>
    <LastName>Wells</LastName>
    <Address>
      <Line>314 Mortlake Drive</Line>
      <Line>Mitcham</Line>
      <County>Surrey</County>
      <PostCode>CR4 3RQ</PostCode>
    </Address>
  </Person>

  <Person id="mum">
    <FirstName>Lesley</FirstName>
    <LastName>Mason</LastName>
    <Address>
      <Line>987 Blackpatch Grove</Line>
      <Line>Shoreham by Sea</Line>
      <County>Sussex</County>
    </Address>
  </Person>

  <Person id="dad">
    <FirstName>Richard</FirstName>
    <LastName>Mason</LastName>
    <Address>
      <Line>123 Beaconsfield Villas</Line>
      <Line>Brighton</Line>
      <County>Sussex</County>
    </Address>
  </Person>

  <Gift from="stevie">'Excession' sci-fi novel</Gift>
  <Gift from="mum">indoor fountain</Gift>
  <Gift from="dad">Harry Potter books</Gift>
```

```
    <Letter from="mgm">
      <Greeting>Dear <Name/>,<br/></Greeting>
      <Thankyou>Thank you ever so much for the <Gift/>.
        It really made my day!
      </Thankyou>
      <Body>
        <p>Thanks, yadda yadda.</p>
        <p>So long, and thanks for all the fish.</p>
        <p>Mike.</p>
      </Body>
    </Letter>
  </ThankYouList>
```

We can see that the first thing we do is to set up a number of Person elements describing people involved in the gift giving and letter writing. Each of them has an id attribute, which we use to refer to them later. Note that this is just a plain XML file without a DTD or a schema to validate it – the id values will be checked programmatically by XML Script, not during validation of the XML when it is loaded.

Next we have a list of gifts received this Christmas. I did get more than just the three gifts, but I think we have enough to get an idea of how things work! Each gift has a from attribute which should point to the id of the person who gave the gift.

Finally, we have Letter element containing the letter outline to send to each gift giver. We use the from attribute of the letter to mark which of the people is actually sending the letter. The letter is split, fairly arbitrarily, into a greeting, a thank you sentence, and a body. We could have done this all in one section, but we did it this way to make selecting bits of it more interesting. Inside each of these elements is a fragment of HTML to use for rendering it, but also two specific tags that we will replace for each letter we write. The Name tag will be replaced by the gift sender's name, and the Gift tag will be replaced with the description of the gift.

During the letter writing process, we'll be using mostly an imperative style to get the work done, with the innermost sections – rendering the Letter element itself and the recipient's address – using a declarative template matching style.

In order to maintain track of which gift we're processing, we'll use two global variables to store the name of the gift and the name of the sender. We set these at the top of the script, making them global and available anywhere else:

```
<xs:setvar name="GiftFrom">"Nobody"</xs:setvar>
<xs:setvar name="GiftDetails">"No details here"</xs:setvar>
```

When we're rendering the letter we will need to replace any Gift elements we come across with the contents of the GiftDetails variable, and any Name elements with the contents of the GiftFrom variable. The following two templates accomplish this:

```
<xs:template name="name_replacer"># $$GiftFrom #</xs:template>
<xs:template name="gift_replacer"># $$GiftDetails #</xs:template>
<xs:method element="Name" template="name_replacer" />
<xs:method element="Gift" template="gift_replacer" />
```

We will kick off processing by telling X-Tract to look at the `ThankYouList` element on the data tree. This command is the last thing we'll write in our script, as it needs all the templates to be set up before it's run. This will become a familiar sight when you've written lots of XML Script – looking to the bottom of the file to find out where everything starts. The following command tells the processor to use the `list_to_html` template code to process the `ThankYouList` node. Here we are using the template as a subroutine, really.

```
<xs:foreach node="\xs:dd\ThankYouList" template="list_to_html" />
```

Inside the `list_to_html` template we again delegate processing of each gift to another template. We could do this all in one step, but it's nice to see how it can be broken down. Since the code is more modular, adding extra functionality should be easier this way too.

```
<xs:template name="list_to_html">
  <xs:foreach node="Gift" template="gift_to_html" />
</xs:template>
```

Finally we get to some real work. For each `gift` element, we need to check that the gift is from someone with an `id` that we know about, so we can send them the letter. We also need to check that there *is* a letter to write and that the letter is from someone we know about. The following tests check this for us:

```
<xs:template name="gift_to_html">

<xs:template name="gift_to_html">

    <!-- First check if we have a person this is from -->
    <xs:if test="not(exists(\xs:dd\ThankYouList\Person{.id == ^.from}))">
      <xs:then><xs:abort/></xs:then>
    </xs:if>

    <!-- Then check we have a letter to write -->
    <xs:if test="not(exists(\xs:dd\ThankYouList\Letter))">
      <xs:then><xs:abort/></xs:then>
    </xs:if>

    <!-- Check the letter is from a person we have -->
    <xs:if test="not(exists(\xs:dd\ThankYouList\Person{.id ==
\xs:dd\ThankYouList\Letter.from}))">
      <xs:then><xs:abort/></xs:then>
    </xs:if>
```

If these pass, we need to record the details about *who* this gift is from in our global variables. Even though we're inside a template, we can access and update the global variables, which are available in the small `name_replacer` and `gift_replacer` templates.

```
<xs:setvar name="GiftFrom"
           item="\xs:dd\ThankYouList\Person{.id == ^.from}\FirstName" />
<xs:setvar name="GiftDetails" item="." />
```

After we've done all this preparatory work, we can start on the output. We're still going to defer rendering of the recipient's address and the letter, though, to keep the code in nice small chunks.

```
<!-- We need to output to an HTML file -->
<xs:output target="# .from #.html" mode="replace">
<html>
<body bgcolor="ffffff">

  <xs:with node="\xs:dd\ThankYouList\Person{.id == ^.from}\Address">
    <xs:process node="."/>
  </xs:with>
  <xs:with node="\xs:dd\ThankYouList\Letter">
    <xs:process node="."/>
  </xs:with>

</body>
</html>
</xs:output>
</xs:template>
```

The `address_to_html` code is fairly simple, and converts the address into an HTML paragraph:

```
<xs:template name="address_to_html">

  <p align="right">
    <xs:with node="Line"># . #<br/>
    </xs:with>
    <xs:if test="exists(County)">
      <xs:then># County #<br/></xs:then>
    </xs:if>
    <xs:if test="exists(PostCode)">
      <xs:then># PostCode #<br/></xs:then>
    </xs:if>
  </p>

</xs:template>
```

The `letter_to_html` code is also very simple, since we've already set up templates to expand the Name and Gift elements. One important point to note is that we select all of the child nodes from the Greeting, Thankyou, and Body elements, not just their child elements. We have to do this since they may well contain text content as well as elements. This is done using the DSLPath `nodes()` function.

```
<xs:template name="letter_to_html">
  <p><xs:process node="Greeting\nodes()" /></p>
  <p><xs:process node="Thankyou\nodes()" /></p>
  <p><xs:process node="Body\nodes()" /></p>
</xs:template>
```

Putting the whole lot together we get the XML Script file ThankYou.xst which you can find in the code download. Running:

xtract ThankYou.xst ThankYouList.xml

will produce three disk files, called `stevie.html`, `mum.html`, and `dad.html`, with a personalized addressed letter in each.

```
<xs:xst xmlns:xs="http://www.xmlscript.org/2.0"
        expression-syntax="dslpath">

    <!-- We're going to grab info about who each
         gift is from and what the gift was into
         a couple of global variables.
    -->

    <xs:setvar name="GiftFrom" item="'Nobody'" />
    <xs:setvar name="GiftDetails" item="'No details here'" />

    <xs:template name="letter_to_html">
      <p><xs:process node="Greeting\nodes()" /></p>
      <p><xs:process node="Thankyou\nodes()" /></p>
      <p><xs:process node="Body\nodes()" /></p>
    </xs:template>

    <xs:template name="address_to_html">

      <p align="right">
        <xs:with node="Line"># . #<br/>
        </xs:with>
        <xs:if test="exists(County)">
          <xs:then># County #<br/></xs:then>
        </xs:if>
        <xs:if test="exists(PostCode)">
          <xs:then># PostCode #<br/></xs:then>
        </xs:if>
      </p>

    </xs:template>

    <xs:method name="Address" template="address_to_html"  />
    <xs:method name="Letter" template="letter_to_html" />

    <!-- Turn a ThankYouList into a series of HTML pages -->
    <xs:template name="list_to_html">
      <xs:foreach node="Gift" template="gift_to_html" />
    </xs:template>

    <!-- Output a thankyou letter for this gift -->
    <xs:template name="gift_to_html">

      <!-- First check if we have a person this is from -->
      <xs:if test="not(exists(\xs:dd\ThankYouList\Person{.id == ^.from}))">
        <xs:then><xs:abort/></xs:then>
      </xs:if>

      <!-- Then check we have a letter to write -->
      <xs:if test="not(exists(\xs:dd\ThankYouList\Letter))">
        <xs:then><xs:abort/></xs:then>
      </xs:if>
```

```
      <!-- Check the letter is from a person we have -->
      <xs:if test="not(exists(\xs:dd\ThankYouList\Person{.id ==
                          \xs:dd\ThankYouList\Letter.from}))">
        <xs:then><xs:abort/></xs:then>
      </xs:if>

      <!-- Record the gift details for our letter writing -->
      <xs:setvar name="GiftFrom"
                item="\xs:dd\ThankYouList\Person{.id == ^.from}\FirstName" />
      <xs:setvar name="GiftDetails" item="." />

      <!-- We need to output to an HTML file -->
      <xs:output target="# .from #.html" mode="replace">
      <html>
      <body bgcolor="ffffff">

        <xs:with node="\xs:dd\ThankYouList\Person{.id == ^.from}\Address">
          <xs:process node="."/>
        </xs:with>
        <xs:with node="\xs:dd\ThankYouList\Letter">
          <xs:process node="."/>
        </xs:with>

      </body>
      </html>
      </xs:output>
    </xs:template>

    <xs:template name="name_replacer"># $$GiftFrom #</xs:template>
    <xs:template name="gift_replacer"># $$GiftDetails #</xs:template>

    <xs:method name="Name" template="name_replacer" />
    <xs:method name="Gift" template="gift_replacer" />

    <xs:foreach node="\xs:dd\ThankYouList" template="list_to_html" />

  </xs:xst>
```

We can now view the output in a browser, and print letters to each recipient. The page layout is basic, but could easily be made more complicated. Here's how the HTML displays in Internet Explorer 5:

XML Script Summary

We have examined the history of XML Script in order to understand where it fits with other XML tools, and XSLT in particular. We have explored the language, and included a description of how an XML Script processor executes a script. The individual language components – commands, functions, and interpolation – have been described, including examples of the use of each one. Finally, we developed a sample application to perform the relatively simple task of writing HTML "thank you" letters.

If you have read this section, you should be equipped to write intermediate-level XML Script code. For more information, and all the latest news, it's definitely worth checking out the official web site at http://www.xmlscript.org/

There's also an XML Script discussion mailing list, which you can join by sending an e-mail to maillist@xmlscript.org with the subject "subscribe xmlscript-general".

For more information on the philosophy behind XML Script 2.0, Richard Lanyon has written an article for the XML Journal. Richard is the principal designer for XML Script 2, and it makes interesting reading:

http://www.sys-con.com/xml/archives/0107/lanyon/index.html

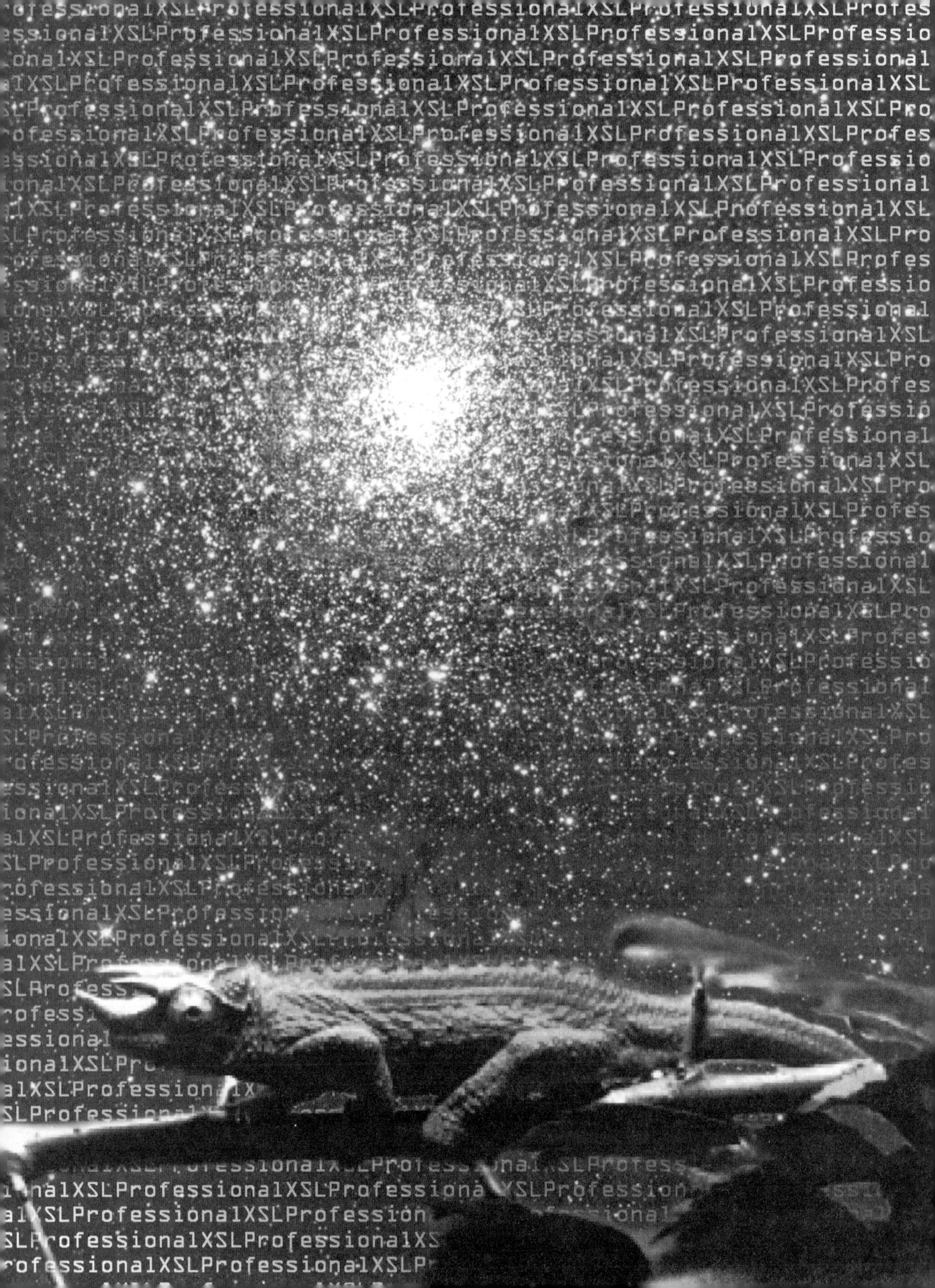
XSLProfessional

G

Resources

Wrox Resources

Web Sites

http://www.wrox.com

http://p2p.wrox.com

Books

Beginning XML, ISBN 1-861003-41-2

Professional XML, ISBN 1-861003-11-0

Beginning XHTML, ISBN 1-861003-43-9

XSLT Programmer's Reference 2nd edition, ISBN 1-861005-06-7

Beginning WAP, WML and WMLScript, ISBN 1-861004-58-3

Professional WAP, ISBN 1-861004-04-4

Professional JSP, ISBN 1-861003-62-5

Professional BizTalk, ISBN 1-861003-29-3

Professional XML Databases, ISBN 1-861003-58-7

Beginning ATL 3.0 COM Programming, ISBN 1-861001-20-7

XSL-Related Technologies

XSL-FO

W3C Extensible Stylesheet Language (XSL) Candidate Recommendation Version 1.0, 21 Nov 2000:
http://www.w3.org/TR/2000/CR-xsl-20001121/

Dave Pawson's XSL-FO FAQ:
http://www.dpawson.co.uk/xsl/sect3.html

Links to general XSL-FO information and resources:
http://www.yahoogroups.com/group/XSL-FO/links

XSLT

W3C XSL Transformations (XSLT) Version 1.0 Recommendation, 16 Nov 1999:
http://www.w3.org/TR/1999/REC-xslt-19991116

W3C XSL Transformations (XSLT) Version 1.1 Working Draft, 12 Dec 2000:
http://www.w3.org/TR/xslt11

Requirements for XSLT 2.0:
http://www.w3.org/TR/xslt20req

Teun Duynstee's XSLT Online Reference:
http://www.vbxml.com/xsl/XSLTRef.asp

XPath

W3C XML Path Language (XPath) Version 1.0 Recommendation, 16 Nov 1999:
http://www.w3.org/TR/1999/REC-xpath-19991116

Requirements for XPath 2.0:
http://www.w3.org/TR/xpath20req

Teun Duynstee's XPath Online Reference:
http://www.vbxml.com/xsl/XPathRef.asp

XSL Processors

Xerces

Xerces XML Parsers from the Apache Project, along with Java and C++ Source:
http://xml.apache.org

XSLT Processors

Saxon

Saxon XSLT Command line processors:
http://users.iclway.co.uk/mhkay/saxon/index.html

XT

XT XSLT Command line processor:
http://www.jclark.com/xml/xt.html

Xalan

Apache Xalan XSLT Processors, with documentation and Source code:
http://xml.apache.org

MSXML3

Microsoft XML Parser Version 3 (MSXML3) and Software Development Kit (SDK):
http://msdn.microsoft.com/xml/general/xmlparser.asp

Installing MSXML3 in Replace Mode with `xmlinst.exe`:
http://msdn.microsoft.com/xml/general/replacemode.asp

Microsoft XSL ISAPI Filter:
http://msdn.microsoft.com/xml/general/xslisapifilter.asp

XSL-FO Processors

James Tauber's List of XSL-FO Tools:
http://www.xmlsoftware.com/xslfo/

Antenna House Formatter

Preview Release of the Antenna House XSL Formatter:
http://www.antennahouse.com/xslformatter.html

FOP

General Information about FOP:
http://xml.apache.org/fop/

Instructions on how to embed FOP:
http://xml.apache.org/fop/embedding.html

RenderX

XEP PDF and PostScript Rendering Engine:
http://www.renderx.com/FO2PDF.html

Other Related Tools

Adobe Acrobat PDF Reader:
http://www.adobe.com/products/acrobat/readstep.html

XSLT Doc:
http://www.jenitennison.com/xslt/utilities/

XSLTracer:
http://www.zvon.org/

XSL Trace:
http://www.alphaworks.ibm.com/tech/xsltrace

4XSLT and 4XDebug:
http://www.4suite.org

XML Script:
http://www.xmlscript.org

XSLScript:
http://www.pault.com/xslscript

XSLWiz:
http://www.ebprovider.com/products/xslwiz.html

XSLByDemo:
http://www.alphaworks.ibm.com/aw.nsf/techmain/xslbydemo

Other XML-Related Technologies

XML

W3C Extensible Markup Language (XML) 1.0 (Second Edition) Recommendation, 6 Oct 2000:
http://www.w3.org/TR/2000/REC-xml-20001006

XML Infoset

W3C XML Information Set Working Draft, 2nd Feb 2001:
http://www.w3.org/TR/2001/WD-xml-infoset-20010202

Leigh Dodds' Summary of an XML-DEV e-mail thread on the subject of XML Infoset:
http://www.xml.com/pub/a/2000/08/02/deviant/infoset.html

DOM

Information on W3C XML DOM Specification:
http://www.w3.org/DOM

SAX

David Megginson's site for Information on the SAX 2.0 Specification:
http://www.megginson.com/SAX/index.htm

OASIS (current hosts of the XML-DEV Mailing List):
http://www.oasis-open.org/

Namespaces in XML

W3C Namespaces in XML Recommendation, 14 Jan 1999:
http://www.w3.org/TR/1999/REC-xml-names-19990114/

URIs

IETF Uniform Resource Identifiers (URI) general syntax memo:
http://www.ietf.org/rfc/rfc2396.txt

XPointer

W3C XML Pointer Language (XPointer) Version 1.0 Last Call Working Draft, 8 Jan 2001:
http://www.w3.org/TR/2001/WD-xptr-20010108

XPointer Information, including implementations:
http://www.w3.org/XML/Linking

XLink

W3C XML Linking Language (XLink) Version 1.0 Proposed Recommendation, 20 Dec 2000:
http://www.w3.org/TR/2000/PR-xlink-20001220/

XQuery

W3C XQuery XML Query Language Working Draft, 15 Feb 2001:
http://www.w3.org/TR/2001/WD-xquery-20010215

XML Query Data Model:
http://www.w3.org/TR/query-datamodel

XML Query Algebra:
http://www.w3.org/TR/query-algebra

XML Query Requirements:
http://www.w3.org/TR/xmlquery-req

XML Query Use Cases:
http://www.w3.org/TR/xmlquery-use-cases

DTDs

Information on DTDs:
http://www.w3.org/XML/1998/06/xmlspec-report.htm

XML Schemas

W3C XML Schemas Candidate Recommendation, 24 Oct 2000:
Part 0 Primer
http://www.w3.org/TR/xmlschema-0/
Part 1 Schemas
http://www.w3.org/TR/xmlschema-1/
Part 2 Datatypes
http://www.w3.org/TR/xmlschema-2/

XML-Data Reduced

W3C XML-Data Reduced (XDR) Note, 5 Jan 1998:
http://www.w3.org/TR/1998/NOTE-XML-data-0105/

Cascading Style Sheets

W3C CSS Level 2 Recommendation, 12 May 1998:
http://www.w3.org/TR/1998/REC-CSS2-19980512

Associating Stylesheets with XML Documents, Version 1.0, W3C Recommendation, 29 June 1999:
http://www.w3.org/1999/06/REC-xml-stylesheet-19990629

DSSSL

DSSSL:
http://www.w3.org/TR/1998/NOTE-spice-19980123.html

SVG

W3C Scalable Vector Graphics (SVG) 1.0 Candidate Recommendation, 2 Nov 2000:
http://www.w3.org/TR/2000/CR-SVG-20001102/

SVG Tools and Implementations:
http://www.w3.org/Graphics/SVG/SVG-Implementations

Adobe's SVG Viewer, plus some SVG Samples and Tutorials:
http://www.adobe.com/svg

VML

Vector Markup Language Overview:
http://msdn.microsoft.com/msdn-online/workshop/standards/vml/

VoiceXML

VoiceXML Organization Homepage:
http://www.voicexml.org

Voice Extensible Markup Language (VoiceXML) Version 1.0, W3C Note, 5 May 2000:
http://www.w3.org/TR/2000/NOTE-voicexml-20000505/

Java Speech Grammar Format Specification:
http://www.javasoft.com/products/java-media/speech/forDevelopers/JSGF

Java Speech Markup Language Specification:
http://www.javasoft.com/products/java-media/speech/forDevelopers/JSML

WAP

Wireless Application Protocol (WAP) Forum:
http://www.wapforum.org

XMTP

XML MIME Transformation Protocol (XMTP):
http://www.openhealth.org/documents/xmtp.htm

SOAP

W3C Simple Object Access Protocol (SOAP) 1.1 Note, 8 May 2000:
http://www.w3.org/TR/2000/NOTE-SOAP-20000508/

Unicode

Unicode Character Set:
http://www.unicode.org

Other Tools

Java

Java Development Kit, Version 1.1:
http://java.sun.com/products/jdk/1.1

Java 2 Platform, Standard Edition, Version 1.3:
http://java.sun.com/j2se/1.3

`jakarta-regexp-1.1.jar` Regular Expressions package:
http://jakarta.apache.org

Windows Script

Windows Script, Version 5.5:
http://www.microsoft.com/msdownload/vbscript/scripting.asp

Browsers

Amaya:
http://www.w3.org/Amaya

Microsoft Internet Explorer:
http://www.microsoft.com/windows/ie

Netscape:
http://home.netscape.com/download/index.html

Opera:
http://www.opera.com

Perlscript

An ActiveX Engine allowing any ActiveX Scripting Host to run Perl Scripts:
http://www.activestate.com/Products/ActivePerl/Download.html

JSP

Java Server Pages:
http://java.sun.com/products/jsp/

Tomcat JSP Web Server:
http://jakarta.apache.org/tomcat/

XSQL

Oracle Technology Network for the XSQL Servlet and associated utilities:
http://technet.oracle.com/tech/xml/xsql_servlet

Mobile Platform Development

Nokia 7110 Emulator:
http://www.nokia.com/corporate/wap/sdk.html

Nuance:
http://www.nuance.com

Nuance Developer Network:
http://extranet.nuance.com

SpeechWorks:
http://www.SpeechWorks.com

Speechworks' Open Source VoiceXML Interpreter, Open VXI:
http://www.speech.cs.cmu.edu/openvxi

Voice Portals

Tellme Web-based Development Environment for VoiceXML:
http://studio.tellme.com

BeVocal Web-based Development Environment for VoiceXML:
http://cafe.bevocal.com

VoiceGenie Web-based Development Environment for VoiceXML:
http://developer.voicegenie.com

HeyAnita Web-based Development Environment for VoiceXML:
http://www.heyanita.com

Voxeo Web-based Development Environment for VoiceXML:
http://community.voxeo.com

Computer Telephony Labs "*Voice Portals Using VoiceXML*" Report, Jan 31 2001:
http://www.commweb.com/article/COM20010129S0003

Free Telephone Calls to US from Overseas:
http://www.dialpad.com

Other Resources

Online Code Examples for Chapters 4, 5, and 12:
http://www.kurtcagle.com

Zvon Training Materials:
http://www.zvon.org

Jon Bosak's XML Versions of all the Shakespearean Plays; index:
http://www.andrew.cmu.edu/user/akj/shakespeare

Jon Bosak's XML Versions of all the Shakespearean Plays; zip file for download:
http://metalab.unc.edu/bosak/xml/eg/shaks200.zip

IETF Tags for the Identification of Languages memo:
http://www.cis.ohio-state.edu/htbin/rfc/rfc1766.html

BizTalk, from the Microsoft Corp:
http://www.biztalk.org

"Enhancing XSL" Article by Kurt Cagle:
http://msdn.microsoft.com/xml/articles/enhancingxsl.asp

Further Information on Petri Nets:
http://www.daimi.au.dk/PetriNets/

Downloadable Version of "*The Petri Net Markup Language*" Article by Matthias Jüngel, Ekkart Kindler, and Michael Weber, Edited by Stephan Philippi:
http://www.informatik.hu-berlin.de/top/pnml/download/JKW_PNML.ps

> **Note: the links given in this appendix were correct at the time of writing, but we are unable however to offer any guarantee of future validity.**

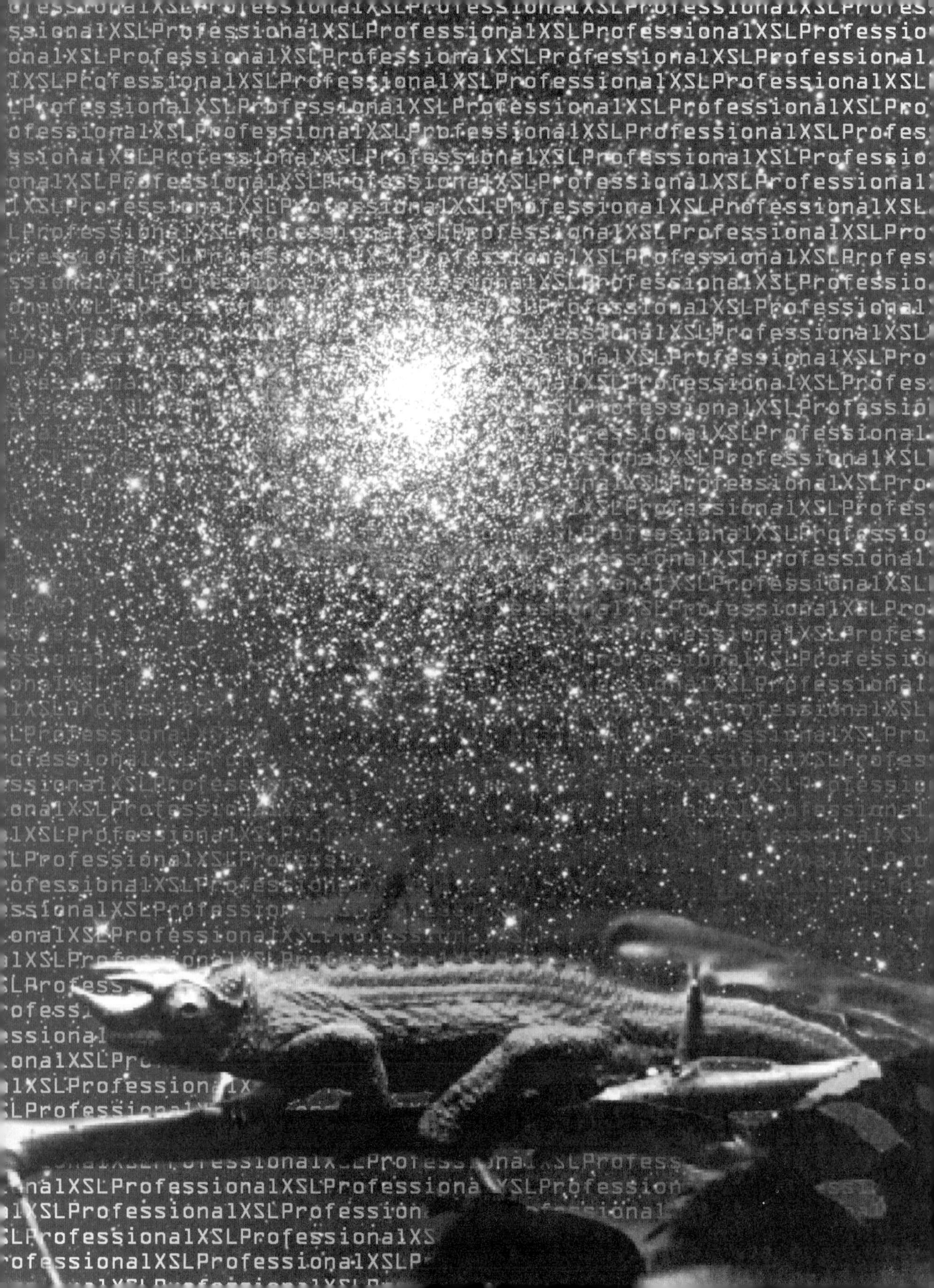
ProfessionalXSL

Index

A Guide to the Index

This index covers all numbered chapters, the Case Study and the Appendices. It is arranged alphabetically, word-by-word. Symbols and Numbers precede the letter A, except that angle-bracket element delimiters are ignored so, for example, the <xsl:apply-templates> element will be found under X, not under Symbols.

Where a main heading has both page references and subheadings, the unmodified page references include any major treatments of the topic, while the sub headings indicate pages where specific aspects only are mentioned.

Acronyms, rather than their expansions, have been preferred as main entries, on the grounds that unfamiliar acronyms are easier to construct than to expand.

S

Z

p2p.wrox.com
The programmer's resource centre

A unique free service from Wrox Press
with the aim of helping programmers to help each other

Wrox Press aims to provide timely and practical information to today's programmer. P2P is a list server offering a host of targeted mailing lists where you can share knowledge with your fellow programmers and find solutions to your problems. Whatever the level of your programming knowledge, and whatever technology you use, P2P can provide you with the information you need.

ASP — Support for beginners and professionals, including a resource page with hundreds of links, and a popular ASP+ mailing list.

DATABASES — For database programmers, offering support on SQL Server, mySQL, and Oracle.

MOBILE — Software development for the mobile market is growing rapidly. We provide lists for the several current standards, including WAP, WindowsCE, and Symbian.

JAVA — A complete set of Java lists, covering beginners, professionals,and server-side programmers (including JSP, servlets and EJBs)

.NET — Microsoft's new OS platform, covering topics such as ASP+, C#, and general .Net discussion.

VISUAL BASIC — Covers all aspects of VB programming, from programming Office macros to creating components for the .Net platform.

WEB DESIGN — As web page requirements become more complex, programmer sare taking a more important role in creating web sites. For these programmers, we offer lists covering technologies such as Flash, Coldfusion, and JavaScript.

XML — Covering all aspects of XML, including XSLT and schemas.

OPEN SOURCE — Many Open Source topics covered including PHP, Apache, Perl, Linux, Python and more.

FOREIGN LANGUAGE — Several lists dedicated to Spanish and German speaking programmers categories include .Net, Java, XML, PHP and XML.

How To Subscribe

Simply visit the P2P site, at **http://p2p.wrox.com/**

Select the 'FAQ' option on the side menu bar for more information about the subscription process and our service.

wrox
PROGRAMMER TO PROGRAMMER™

Wrox writes books for you. Any suggestions, or ideas about how you want
information given in your ideal book will be studied by our team.
Your comments are always valued at Wrox.

Free phone in USA 800-USE-WROX
Fax (312) 893 8001

UK Tel. (0121) 687 4100   Fax (0121) 687 4101

Professional XSL - Registration Card

Name _____

Address _____

_____

_____

_____

City_____ State/Region _____

Country_____ Postcode/Zip _____

E-mail _____

Occupation _____

How did you hear about this book? _____

☐ Book review (name) _____

☐ Advertisement (name) _____

☐ Recommendation _____

☐ Catalog _____

☐ Other _____

Where did you buy this book? _____

☐ Bookstore (name)_____ City _____

☐ Computer Store (name)_____

☐ Mail Order _____

☐ Other _____

What influenced you in the
purchase of this book?

☐ Cover Design

☐ Contents

☐ Other (please specify) _____

How did you rate the overall
contents of this book?

☐ Excellent   ☐ Good

☐ Average   ☐ Poor

What did you find most useful about this book? _____

_____

What did you find least useful about this book? _____

Please add any additional comments. _____

_____

What other subjects will you buy a computer

book on soon? _____

What is the best computer book you have used this year?

_____

*Note: This information will only be used to keep you updated
about new Wrox Press titles and will not be used for any other
purpose or passed to any other third party.*

Check here if you DO NOT want to receive support for this book ☐

wrox
PROGRAMMER TO PROGRAMMER™

NB. If you post the bounce back card below in the UK, please send it to:

Wrox Press Ltd., Arden House, 1102 Warwick Road,
Acocks Green, Birmingham B27 6BH. UK.

Computer Book Publishers

BUSINESS REPLY MAIL
FIRST CLASS MAIL   PERMIT#64   CHICAGO, IL

POSTAGE WILL BE PAID BY ADDRESSEE

WROX PRESS INC.
29 S. LA SALLE ST.
SUITE 520
CHICAGO IL 60603-USA